Basic Production Management

BASIC
PRODUCTION
MANAGEMENT

Second Edition
Elwood S. Buffa

John Wiley & Sons, Inc.

New York   London   Sydney   Toronto

Library of Congress Cataloging in Publication Data

Buffa, Elwood Spencer, 1923–
  Basic production management.

  Includes bibliographies and index.
  1. Production management. I. Title.
TS155.B7226 1975   658.5   74–28396
ISBN 0–471–11801–X

Printed in the United States of America
10–9 8 7 6 5 4 3 2 1

PREFACE

Basic Production Management bears a close relationship to my previous book, *Modern Production Management*, now in its fourth edition, Wiley, 1973. The present volume has been prepared in response to an expressed need in many undergraduate colleges for a book with the basic orientation of *Modern Production Management*, but abridged in both length and complexity of materials. The production management course in many such situations must take account of the fact that statistical and mathematical materials are covered elsewhere in the curriculum and that the production course is normally limited to one semester or quarter. Thus, the need for a more compact volume focused on the application of the most up-to-date concepts.

Achieving the Objective of a More Compact Volume

Substantial portions of *Modern Production Management* have been eliminated entirely for various reasons. The first priority was to subject every chapter and major section to scrutiny in terms of essential need in a basic text. The chapter on maintenance fell to the ax since it was felt to be a highly specialized topic, though clearly a common problem for production managers. The chapter on wages and labor costs met a similar fate, though for a different reason, the topic is commonly covered in other courses central to industrial relations, though from a different viewpoint. In addition materials in every other chapter were eliminated if they could not stand these kinds of tests.

Achieving the Objective of Less Complex Materials

The second priority was to reconsider the need for coverage in the production management course of the more detailed mathematical materials such as linear programming and waiting lines. It was decided that the concepts were crucial to a present day understanding of production management, but that the details of these methods were normally covered in other courses. Thus, the emphasis has been placed on the managerial use of these important models and on the results of these kinds of analyses. In maintaining the focus on concepts rather than embellishment, changes were effected in many places in the manuscript. For example, Chapter 4 in this volume on Analytical Methods in Production and

Operations Management deals with the general concepts of mathematical techniques like linear programming, waiting line analysis, and simulation, and on the ability and use of these methods in the analysis of production systems. But, the more detailed development of the supporting mathematical techniques themselves are not covered. Throughout the balance of the book references to the applicability and use of these kinds of methods are also retained. Similarly our coverage of exponential smoothing in Chapter 14 on Forecasting and Inventories has been altered to minimize the more complex models. We present the single exponential smoothing model and explain its workings, showing how the simpler model applies when trend and seasonal effects are included, since the basic principles of the single exponential model can be applied directly to the more complex situations.

Study Materials

Basic Production Management is not only a product of the abridgement of its mother volume. Substantial additions to the manuscript have been made to help the student to master each chapter more easily and effectively. An outline has been placed at the opening of each chapter to help orient the reader to what will be covered. At the end of each chapter there are lists of the main terms used, review questions, self-test true-false questions, (all with page references), and problems. The page references are meant to turn the student back into the chapter materials to help him see the point in context if he is uncertain. Answers to the true-false questions are listed in Appendix C. The chapter end problems have always seemed to help students clarify their understanding of some of the concepts covered. In this volume we have favored problems which involve fairly direct illustration of concepts rather than more complex problems.

Organization and Purpose of the Book

The development of knowledge in the production management field has been extremely rapid. It is important that the reading material available to college survey courses reflect the new conceptual framework and the increased depth of subject matter which represents current thinking. In preparing this book, I have adopted a general outline which I believe makes possible the inclusion of much of the new material in a way that is comprehensible without placing heavy emphasis on quantitative skills. The four-part outline (Introduction, Analytical Methods in Production Management, Design of the Production System, and Operation and Control of Production Systems) introduces an orientation to appropriate analytical methods early in the book, so that the broad problem areas of system design, operation, and control can be based on the analytical methods. In this framework, I believe that it has been possible for me to write the sections of the book which deal with the problem areas of production without great distortion or oversimplification of the new material that comes to us from management science, industrial engineering, and operations research.

In the introductory sections of the book I recognize a broader definition of production than has been applied in comparable books in the past, although, throughout the remainder of the book the factory model is predominant. I believe that this broader definition, which recognizes that production concepts are pervasive, is of considerable importance for the future. Our society has developed significant production systems in many kinds of activities, for example, hospitals, supermarkets, retail stores, and offices. Production really deals with the "operations" phase of any activity regardless of its setting. The development of courses in this general field is now reflecting, and perhaps should reflect even more, that the general principles of production are applicable in all of these situations.

The field of production management continues to shift in the direction of a more analytical approach based on the continued development of management science in general. The problems with which we deal are found in many settings other than manufacturing, as we have noted, and activities outside manufacturing interact with the manufacturing function. For example, inventories in warehouse and distribution systems have a bearing on problems of programming production upstream. The recognition of this fact is forcing the adoption of the broader "systems" point of view discussed in this book.

Finally, this book concentrates on the economics of production. In so doing it takes into account the fact that the student has probably already had a course in Introduction to Business, or a course in General Management or Supervision. Instead of attempting to cover a wide variety of topics from the viewpoint of the production manager we have recognized the existence of other important specialized areas, such as organization and general management, personnel, human relations, and industrial relations. The production course can recognize these topic fields best by assuming their coverage elsewhere in the curriculum, thus allowing a more adequate coverage of the truly "hard-core" production concepts.

Elwood S. Buffa

Pacific Palisades, California
January 1975

FOREWORD TO STUDENTS

The materials in *Basic Production Management* have been drawn from a combination of both theoretical concepts as well as a wealth of practical examples from business and industrial experience. Thus, it is hoped that the student who has not yet had the opportunity of practical experience will be able to see a transfer of the theoretical concepts to something more meaningful in practice. Similarly, the individual who has already had empirical practice may be able to find theoretical bases and roots for the training to which he has been exposed.

Basic Production Management was prepared especially with a study pattern in mind for students. Though one cannot expect all individuals to follow a prescribed pattern, it seems, nevertheless, that students might like a preview of my intentions.

Chapter Materials and the Learning Process

In most chapters you will find the following sequence of materials: chapter outline, text material, summary, a short list of "key concepts" introduced in the chapter, a list of "important terms," review questions, self-test true-false questions, problems, and finally references. Thus, while text material takes up the largest proportion of the space in each chapter, there are additional study materials designed to help the student test and review himself and participate actively in the learning process. As students, you may have already found that teaching and learning may be somewhat different processes. In the end, you learn for yourself and my hope is that the materials I have provided will facilitate this process. We as teachers can help by providing an environment which facilitates learning, by helping to motivate, by focusing attention on the most important and difficult concepts, by providing supplementary and illustrative materials, by answering questions, and so on. But, you learn and in a sense we do not teach but help you learn.

A Guide for Study

My suggestion for study is to read the chapter outline first in order to obtain a frame of reference concerning the chapter. What is the focus of the chapter?

What are the topics? What is the sequence of topics? Next, read the text material fairly rapidly so that the overall flow and meaning of ideas does not become lost in an attempt to master a more complex or difficult detail, perhaps noting the things you will want to come back to for a more careful examination. Then, when the overall picture seems clear reread for depth.

The chapter-end study materials should now become the focus. Review the key concepts. They are few in number but ordinarily have more general significance and may be used in the following chapters. Next, scan the list of important terms. If there is any question in your mind about the meaning of any of the terms, go to the page references given for each term and reread the pertinent material. I have given page references rather than definitions to go with each term because I want to turn you back into the text material to establish the meaning of the term in the context of the chapter.

The review questions raise more general topics for your consideration. If you can discuss these questions meaningfully with another student it probably means that you have a fairly good grasp of the main ideas of the chapter. If you can correctly answer the self-test true-false questions it probably means that you have retained some of the detailed points. (Answers to these true-false questions are in Appendix C.)

Finally, the real test to show that you have a fundamental understanding of the topic or concept is to work the problems. First, if you can organize a set of data into a useful pattern, determining which items of data are useful and whether or not some data is only garbage, you must really understand. Second, if you can carry through to a defensible solution you not only understand but gain a wonderful feeling of self-satisfaction and confidence.

The list of references at the ends of chapters is for the student who wants to go a bit further. Some of the references are articles which often deal with a specific topic giving somewhat greater penetration. Other references are books which deal with some of the chapter topics in great detail. Finally, some of the references may be landmark studies which may have been particularly important in the development of the topic area.

Elwood S. Buffa

CONTENTS

PART FIVE   SYNTHESIS   649

PART SIX   APPENDIX   663

INDEX   671

Basic Production Management

PART 1
INTRODUCTION

CONTENTS

CHAPTER 1

PRODUCTION AND OPERATIONS MANAGEMENT, A PERSPECTIVE

Some say that the postindustrial society has already been attained in the United States. The economy has the capability to produce everything needed by everyone and is indeed sometimes referred to as a surplus economy. They say that the physical production of goods and services in adequate quantities can be assumed, and therefore we must concentrate our attention on the problems of ecology, social justice, and education, as well as the problems of using leisure time effectively so that we will not be bored with the good life available for all. If the previous statements are true, then why be concerned with production management? The answer is that, if we are going to allocate a substantial fraction of our national effort toward the goals alluded to above, we must either make the production machine work smoothly, effectively, and even more abundantly, or in fact we must give up some of our physical product in order to meet the objectives of some of the new goals. However, the two objectives are intertwined because an attack on social and ecological problems necessarily depends in some measure on the capabilities of the economic system. Also, some of the methods of analysis used in production and operations management and operations research are valid mechanisms to study and solve the other problems.

Most national planners seem to be assuming that we can have both a high standard of life for all as well as allocate an increasing fraction of our effort toward the solution of our social and ecological problems. Their faith is perhaps justified by the extraordinary progress and performance made in the analysis, design, and operations of productive systems in the past fifteen to twenty years. It has become clear that many phases of productive systems can be automated, that many important areas of decision can be reduced to automatic rules, and that computers can become process controllers. Yet, we cannot assume that the production machine will automatically do its job. Someone must design the productive systems as well as the information and control systems needed to operate them.

PRODUCTIVE SYSTEMS— A CRUCIAL ROLE IN MODERN SOCIETY

It would be difficult to overemphasize the crucial role effective productive systems play in modern society and in our life style. Indeed, the stamp *developed economy* carries with it the image of large, highly organized, specialized, mechanized, efficient productive systems. On the other hand, the term *underdeveloped economy* includes the image of small, handicraft, inefficient productive systems powered mainly by the muscles of men and beasts. This contrast of images is, of course, too simple an explanation for the difference between developed and underdeveloped economies. Transforming the nature of productive systems in an underdeveloped economy would not by itself create a developed one. Nevertheless, a modern society with all of its attributes of material wealth is not possible without its characteristic productive systems.

As a matter of fact, it is unfortunate that we make the association between large output per man hour and a thrifty, industrious, hardworking people with the reverse personal characteristics assigned to low output per man hour situations. Individuals in an economy typified by low output per man hour may actually work harder in a physical sense because of the absence of mechanization to accomplish the heaviest tasks.

Production Economics—A Problem of Cost Balance

It is also true that the high output per man hour economy is thought of as being efficient while its opposite is thought of as being inefficient. But production efficiency is a relative term meaning, essentially, "how effectively we employ the appropriate available resources (input) for a given unit of output." Thus, in developed economies costs of machinery and equipment are relatively low and labor costs are relatively high reflecting the generally high output per man hour of workers in that economy. In underdeveloped economies the reverse relative costs are generally true. (The cost of raw materials may be high or low in either situation depending on a complex of factors.) Therefore, an efficient productive system in the developed economy is one which uses mechanization to a great extent and relatively little labor to yield a minimum combined cost of capital, labor, and raw material per unit of output.

For the identical product produced in an underdeveloped economy, an efficient production system would reverse the relative amounts of capital and labor inputs in order to yield a minimum combined cost of capital, labor, and raw materials. Both systems could be efficient if they minimized the resource inputs per unit of output. This is an important point to understand about the effective design and operation of productive systems. We are not always attempting to employ the most sophisticated mechanized or automated technique known. Rather, we are attempting to employ the best balance of resources in each situation. Thus, even in the United States economy, a system designed for a relatively small output will ordinarily emphasize the use of labor as an input compared to capital. Throughout this book we retain this general viewpoint, but it is most evident in Chapters 5 and 6 where we deal with costs for managerial decisions, Chapters 7 and 8 on production design of products and process planning, Chapter 9 on plant location, Chapter 10 on layout of physical facilities, and Chapter 11 on job design and man-machine systems.

Operating a Production System—A Problem of Information and Decision Analysis

In a given production system, successful management depends on plans, an information system concerning what is actually happening, and how we react (make decisions) to changes in demand, inventory position, schedules, quality level, and product and equipment innovation. In forming plans for the operation or management of a productive system, we are attempting to allocate the available resources in the most effective way for a given forecast of demand. The resources are units of productive capacity such as number of man hours available at regular time and overtime, inventories available, subcontracting, as well as a negative capacity which occurs when shortages or back orders take place. In constructing production plans, each of these capacities is provided at a cost, and the best plan is one which minimizes the sum of all costs over some future time span.

In attempting to meet the objectives of a plan, certain realities interfere, such as equipment failure, human error, discrepancies in the timing of order flow, quality variation, and so on. Therefore, systems for scheduling maintenance, quality control, and cost control are invented to help retain order where otherwise the system would naturally tend toward chaos.

Productive Systems—Conversion to Useful Products or Conversion to Pollution?

Productive systems have been commonly thought of as mechanisms for converting some sort of raw material to something useful. In the process, of course, there are normally wastes but in the past very little attention has been paid to them. The emphasis was on the useful product and wastes were disposed of in the cheapest possible way—dumped into rivers and streams or into the atmosphere. Only recently have we begun to realize that we may be fouling our own nests.

Today, socially conscious managers realize that the production function must include the processing of wastes to the point that they are benign or in themselves useful, rather than hazardous or even lethal. Waste conversion is a part of the production process and must be included in our conceptual framework.

A HISTORICAL BRIEF

The first recognized attention to production economics was paid by the great Scottish economist Adam Smith at the time the factory system was emerging. In 1776 he wrote *The Wealth of the Nations* in which he observed three basic economic advantages resulting from the division of labor. These were the development of a skill or a dexterity when a single task was performed repetitively, a saving of the time normally lost in changing from one activity to the next, and the invention of machines or tools that seemed normally to follow when men specialized their efforts on tasks of restricted scope. Smith did not deduce these ideas in a theoretical way. Instead, under the factory system, division of labor was developing as a common-sense method of production when a relatively large group of workers was brought together to produce in large quantity. Under these conditions, a cooperative approach made good sense. Smith observed this practice, noted the three advantages, and wrote about them in his book. The book was a milestone in the development of production economics, not only because Smith's observations probably accelerated the division of labor, but also because a great scholar had recognized that there existed a rationale for production. The actual development of the rationale was to take a long, long time. As we shall note, we are *now* at last in the true rapid developmental stage, where production management as a discipline is emerging from a purely descriptive phase to take on the characteristics of an applied science.

After Adam Smith, an Englishman, Charles Babbage, augmented Smith's observations and raised a number of provocative questions about production organization and economics. Basically a mathematician who became interested in manufacturing, Babbage's inquiring mind and scientific orientation led him to question many existing practices. His thoughts were summarized in the book, *On the Economy of Machinery and Manufactures* (1832). Concerning the economic advantages resulting from the division of labor, Babbage agreed with Smith, but he observed that Smith had overlooked a most important advantage. For an example, Babbage used a study of pin manufacturing (the common straight pin) as it existed at that time. The level of specialization resulted in seven basic operations for making pins.

1. *Drawing wire.* This operation consisted of drawing wire through a die to reduce it to the desired diameter.
2. *Straightening the wire.*
3. *Pointing.*
4. *Twisting and cutting heads.*
5. *Heading.*
6. *Tinning or whitening.* This operation was comparable to a modern plating process to prevent rusting of the steel wire.
7. *Papering.* This consisted of placing the completed pins in papers or cards by piercing the paper, that is, the packaging of the pins.

Babbage noted the pay scale for these different specialties in shillings and pence (s.d.) (see Table I). He then pointed out that if the shop were reorganized so that each man performed the entire sequence of operations, the wage paid to these men would be dictated by the most difficult or rarest skill required by the entire sequence. Thus the enterprise would pay for the tinning skill, even when the workman was straightening, heading, or papering. With division of labor, however, just the amount of skill needed could be purchased. Therefore, in addition to the productivity advantages cited by Adam Smith, Babbage recognized the principle of limiting skills as a basis for pay.

In the years after Adam Smith's and Charles Babbage's observations, the division of labor continued and then accelerated during the first half of the twentieth century. Our great production lines represent the the principle of division of labor carried to its greatest extreme. In fact, it has been carried so far that some people are questioning the present level of application. Cost reductions, based on broadening the scope of jobs, are being reported in the literature. A name has even been coined

TABLE I.   Analysis of Processes and Manufacturing Costs in Pin Making
English Manufacture [(178.) Pins, *"Elevens,"* 5,546 weigh one pound; *"one dozen,"* 6,932 pins weigh twenty ounces, and require six ounces of paper.]

Name of the Process	Work-men	Time of Making 1 lb of Pins, *hours*	Cost of Making 1 lb of Pins, *pence*	Work-man Earns per Day, *s.*	*d.*	Price of Making Each Part of a Single Pin, in Millionths of a Penny
1. Drawing wire (§ 170.)	Man	.3636	1.2500	3	3	225
2. Straightening the wire (§ 171.)	Woman	.3000	.2840	1	0	51
	Girl	.3000	.1420	0	6	26
3. Pointing (§ 172.)	Man	.3000	1.7750	5	3	319
4. Twisting and cutting the heads (§ 173.)	Boy	.0400	.0147	0	4½	3
	Man	.0400	.2103	5	4½	38
5. Heading (§ 174.)	Woman	4.0000	5.0000	1	3	901
6. Tinning, or whitening (§ 175.)	Man	.1071	.6666	6	0	121
	Woman	.1071	.3333	3	0	60
7. Papering (§ 176.)	Woman	2.1314	3.1973	1	6	576
		7.6892	12.8732			2320

Number of persons employed: men, 4; women, 4; children, 2; total, 10.
Reproduced from *The Economy of Machinery and Manufactures,* 1832.

for this new trend, "job enlargement." Perhaps the optimal level has been passed in some industries.

Frederick W. Taylor was undoubtedly the outstanding historical figure in the development of the production management field. Smith and Babbage were observers and writers, but Taylor was both a thinker and a doer. He was also an authoritarian with an indomitable will, a fact that caused him to be greatly criticized but, at the same time, may have been the source of his great contributions. The practice of the day was to allow the workmen themselves to decide the means by which production would be achieved. They determined how to produce a part, according to their skills and past experience, and the time and cost of production were guided by traditional methods. "Boondoggling" and spreading of the work were common.

Taylor was familiar with these practices because he entered the industrial system as a worker, in which capacity he refused to go along with the other workers and instead produced as much as he could. He advanced rapidly and was later in a position to experiment with some of his ideas. To comprehend the extent of Taylor's accomplishments, we must understand that he was an innovator in a managerial environment of general apathy, where strong traditions existed, giving the workmen a free rein to determine manufacturing methods and the right to hold their knowledge as trade secrets. In this static environment, Taylor set in motion a tidal wave of change in managerial philosophy which shook many organizations from top to bottom.

Essentially, Taylor's new philosophy stated that the scientific method could and should be applied to all managerial problems, and that the methods by which work was accomplished should be determined by management through scientific investigation. He listed four new duties of management which may be summarized as follows [4]*:

1. The development of a science for each element of a man's work to replace old rule-of-thumb methods.

2. The scientific selection, training, and development of workers, instead of the old practice of allowing the workman to choose his own tasks and to train himself as best as he could.

3. The development of a spirit of hearty cooperation between the workman and management to ensure that the work would be carried out in accordance with the scientifically devised procedures.

---

*Numbers in brackets indicate corresponding references at the end of each chapter.

4. The division of work between the workers and the management in almost equal shares, each group taking over the work for which it was best fitted, instead of the former condition in which most work and responsibility fell on the workmen.

These four ideas, which led to much new thinking about managerial organization, are so much a part of present-day organizational practice that it is hard to believe that the situation was ever any different. Taylor's work, under the general heading of Number 1, developed into the field of methods engineering and work measurement. In more recent years, this area has expanded greatly with the help of experimental psychological and physiological researchers; now the field known as "human engineering" has general application in production management. From Numbers 2 and 3 has developed the field of personnel, with its techniques of personnel selection and placement, together with the organizational function of industrial relations. Number 4, the division of work between the workman and management, has had far-reaching implications. The basic managerial functions of planning and control now cover much of the work formerly done by workmen, leaving the first-line foreman and the workmen free to concentrate on the execution of carefully laid plans.

Taylor is also known for some pioneering experiments that he performed. These were in various areas including basic production organization, wage payment theory, and the development of fundamental procedures for tasks such as metal machining, pig iron handling, and shoveling which were common in the steel industry at that time. Through his metal-cutting experiments, Taylor expended thousands of pounds of metal over a period of ten years; these experiments resulted in specifications for the feeds and speeds that could be used for different metals and tool materials. Also in connection with these experiments, he discovered high-speed steel in collaboration with Maunsel White, a discovery that made him wealthy and allowed him to spend the bulk of his later life furthering his philosophy. Taylor believed that his important contributions were his general philosophy and approach to managerial problems rather than any specific discoveries. The latter were merely applications of "scientific management" to individual situations.

Taylor's uncompromising attitude in developing and installing his ideas caused much controversy, and he was strongly opposed in many quarters. In the environment in which Taylor worked, perhaps it was necessary to have a man of his hard-driving personality to change an industrial way of life.

His followers were numerous. Carl Barth, Henry L. Gantt, Harrington Emerson, Frank and Lillian Gilbreth, and others worked within Taylor's general framework and philosophy. There were others who donned his cloak without his knowledge and competence, and for a fast dollar they passed themselves off as consultants who could install the "Taylor system." Taylor disclaimed these "jackals," but they did much harm. By the bad name they gave "scientific management," they probably slowed the development of good practice in the field. Little change occurred in Taylor's basic ideas. The literature was filled with gimmicks and variants of the manifest products of Taylor's thinking, such as the wage payment plans, time study methods, and charts and mechanical control boards. But the science of production management, in the spirit Taylor envisioned it, was very slow to evolve.

There were perhaps many reasons for this slow development. Appropriate knowledge and tools were not yet available, and the misapplications of the post-Taylor period had to be lived down. Measurements in production systems commonly display great variation. For example, how much output can we expect from an operation? Output depends on the man on the job and the job conditions. But even for a given man on the job, we can expect great variation from hour to hour, day to day, week to week, etc. To describe such a system we need probability concepts and a knowledge of statistical methods. For years men tried to approach such problems by representing the output of a man or a man-machine system by a single number, as was common in most engineering problems; this method simply did not fit the situation. In fields such as mechanical engineering, electrical engineering, and chemical engineering, variability of measurements was small and the deterministic models yielded fairly good results. In production problems, however, variability was characteristic. Today, with the general knowledge of statistics and probability concepts, and with their application to production problems increasing, our models of production systems are closer to reality than ever before.

Another great difficulty that beset serious investigators in the period after Taylor was the complexity of the large-scale problems that appeared. It seemed that all variables of any problem were completely interdependent. It was obvious that mathematical techniques were needed, but none was available to give the kinds of solutions required. Even if they had been available, the time required to develop solutions manually would have been measured in man-lifetimes. Modern high-speed digital computers were needed, but these were not to become available, even for the biggest and strongest companies, until the 1950s. An attempt at mathematical analysis was made in 1915 by F. W. Harris, who developed the first economic lot-size model for a simple situation. This was further developed by F. E. Raymond and others, but applications of the idea in industry were not general. We attempt to place these historical events in perspective in Figure 1.

THE CURRENT ERA

The present upsurge of activity in the general field of production was preceded by two developments in the 1930s which helped lay the groundwork and point the way for the future. These were the development and introduction to industry of statistical quality control by Walter Shewhart in 1931 and the development in 1934 of work sampling theory (a sampling procedure to determine standards for delays, work-time, etc.) by L. H. C. Tippett, working in England. Statistical quality

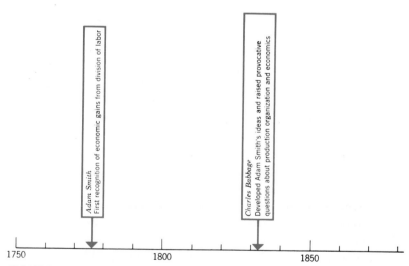

FIGURE 1.   Progression of developments in production management.

control concepts grew rapidly and application of these probability concepts to the control of product quality became fairly general, especially with the onset of World War II. The acceptance of the basic concepts of sampling, control charts, etc., by workmen, foremen, and management was an important preliminary development for what was to come in the postwar period. Tippett's work-sampling procedure, however, was to lie almost completely dormant for twenty years and then finally to be dusted off by some progressive companies and put to work in the 1950s. Today it is used extensively and will very likely continue to grow in practical usefulness.

The current rate of development of production management concept, theory, and technique began shortly after World War II. Research in war operations by the armed forces produced new mathematical and computational techniques and also brought about an awareness of how to apply old techniques to war operation problems. The latter seemed to parallel problems of production operations, so the approaches to war problems began to trickle into industrial use. One significant development was the introduction of linear programming. Here at last was a basic mathematical tool capable of handling many of the large-scale, complex problems of scheduling and allocating the limited

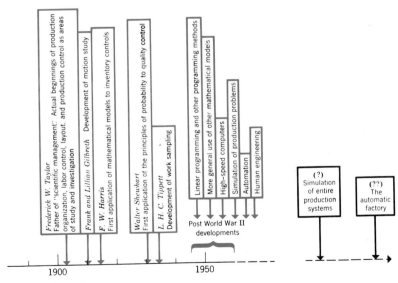

FIGURE 1.   (continued)

resources of a production system. But more important, the development of the high-speed computer made possible the solution of the large-scale linear programming problems. Linear programming without computers would have had a small field of application.

Other mathematical approaches were evolved. Waiting-line theory, which had been used for some time in the telephone industry to analyze telephone systems, found applications in production lines, toll booths, machine maintenance, etc. There developed new and more realistic inventory models that included variability and uncertainty of demand and other conditions. Models of replacement, maintenance, and competitive bidding all added to the general trend of formalizing production problems.

The computer appeared as a powerful tool in its own right, not merely as a device to perform the tedious labor of computation. With it, production systems could be simulated, modeled after fairly realistic conditions. If a complex system were simulated on a computer, the effect of alternative proposals could be determined quickly without the cost and time of actually trying the proposals in practice. On a broader scale, simulation has been done in the business decision games developed by AMA, UCLA, and others. Attempts are now being made to simulate through computer-based corporate models the actual operation of entire firms. As we shall see in Chapter 3 this is now being accomplished; in the not too distant future, progressive companies will have their operations simulated so that the probable effect of major alternative decisions can be determined before action is taken.

The computer has also contributed to the new field of automation. Here the computer is programmed to control machine tools through their entire cycle, completed parts resulting without the aid of the human hand. These developments have great future significance, both socially and economically. As technology grows in this field, computers will program systems of numerically controlled machine tools according to computer-determined schedules. An ultimate result will be the much talked of automatic factory. In some industries we are already closer to this than most people realize. For example, in the continuous chemical-processing industries, such as soap and petroleum, automatic control of processes is common and most of the labor is of an indirect or vigilance nature.

One final outgrowth of the war should be commented on, that is the attention given to human factors. This resulted from the problems that arose because of the heavy demands placed on man by radar and sonar systems, supersonic flight, high-altitude flying, etc. Research psychologists and physiologists were employed during and after the war to help design systems that more nearly matched human capabilities of sight, hearing, feeling, smell, and motor skill, as well as human tolerance of such environmental factors as heat, light, radiation, and noise. Large volumes of data were gathered. Although the human stress factors in business and industry are usually less severe than many of those experienced in war, conceptually the problems are the same, that is, to design production tasks and systems that recognize the limitations of the human operator and take advantage of man's capabilities.

The field now called human engineering, human factors, or biotechnology furnishes the basic data for job design. Standard machine tool design does not as yet take full advantage of what is known, but improvements have been made. In the factory, special machine designs reflect increasingly the fact that it is not machines that produce but man-machine systems. Human engineering is the outgrowth of motion study originally developed by the Gilbreths. It is broader in concept than motion study and accepts a broader set of criteria, such as frequency of error and psychological and physiological costs, as well as the older criteria of economy of motion and labor cost.

WHERE WE STAND TODAY

Almost two centuries have passed since Adam Smith. What have we learned about production management in that time? Where does our knowledge stand today? In assessing the past, we can say that the results speak for themselves. Productivity and total productive capacity have expanded tremendously. Life for the average man in our Western civilization has been transformed from mere existence to a scale of living undreamed of by Smith. During this period, production management has been developing largely as an *empirical* applied science. During these two hundred years, we have responded to the expanding market and to the growth of increasingly large business units by division of labor and by progressive mechanization in order to take advantage of the economies of large-scale production.

Through the years we have learned to design better work places, better material-handling equipment, and better buildings to house productive activities. We have created production lines and even automatic machines. We have learned basic principles of production economics and, thereby, have learned to employ labor, materials, and machines in a delicate balance to match the changing relative values of these basic components of production. We have learned to control the production systems that we have designed so that products or services meet quality standards and are available when needed and at a cost that may be fairly well predicted. Most of this development has been evolutionary; we improved existing systems through a process of trial and error.

Only in the last twenty years have we begun to evolve principles that make it possible to design facilities and control systems with some degree of predictability as to their performance; here is a true measure of our knowledge about production management. Today we are beginning to develop answers to problems of limited scope, knowing that the result is the best possible. That is, the result is optimal, not simply better than the previous solution. This is real progress and indicates that the applied science envisioned by Taylor is developing.

Where we stand today then, in terms of production management as an applied science, is at the threshold of the rapid developmental phase. Increased knowledge about some particular field is often related to a growth and saturation curve, where initial developments are slow and difficult. As bits of knowledge fall into place, the rate of growth accelerates to the rapid developmental phase and finally levels off as it approaches a saturation level. We have diagrammed this growth curve in Figure 2. In the years to come the scope of the problems for which we can find provable optimal solutions will increase. The theory of production systems will be pervasive and will embrace integrated systems as a whole, not just segments of a system; our ability to design facilities and control systems with predictable characteristics will increase. The use of computers to simulate systems will become common, as will numerically controlled (computer controlled) production processes of various types.

In the past the best in production management theory was represented by its actual practice in business and industry; teaching in universities was paced by this practice. Today, theory is beginning to lead the best practice, a state of affairs that will probably continue for some time to come.

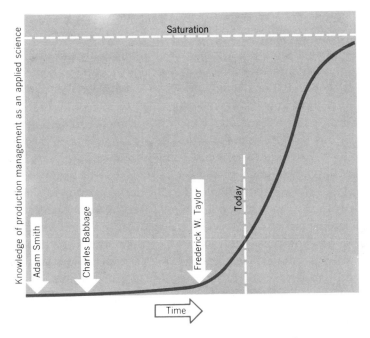

FIGURE 2.   Growth curve of knowledge of production management
as an applied science.

THE BIG COMPANY VERSUS
THE SMALL COMPANY

The following comment is often made: "All of this talk about the new
look in production management is fine for the big company—what
about the small company?" The basic principles of production economics
and facility design and control are as applicable to the small organization
as to the large. Implementation of these principles, however, must
change with the size and financial strength of the organization. A large
organization may use a high-speed computer to help generate a schedule
that meets requirements with minimum inventory. The small organization may be compelled to approximate a similar solution to their schedule
problems, using hand methods and graphical aids. Both organizations
may be attempting to apply the same principles of scheduling. The
techniques are different, but the principles are general.

We can see that production management is not a set of techniques. On the contrary, it is a set of general principles for production economics, facility design, job design, schedule design, quality control, inventory control, work measurement, and cost and budgetary control. Do we then turn our backs on technique? No. Rather, with the power of advanced technique, we evolve and refine principle. An advanced technique, such as computer simulation, may be used to develop and test various rules for scheduling to meet organization objectives. The resulting rules become principles by which we can schedule. They may be applicable in small companies as well as large ones. A mathematical technique may be used to develop decision rules for the economic amount of materials that should be purchased at one time. The resulting rules become principles by which we make certain purchasing decisions. As long as conditions are comparable, either the large or small company can use these principles. Therefore, when we study advanced analytical methods and techniques, we are not necessarily studying big company management. We are dealing with concepts and ideas that can be demonstrated by advanced methods where less powerful tools fail. The resulting concepts and ideas ordinarily have general application.

CAREERS IN THE MANAGEMENT OF PRODUCTION

It is logical to raise the question concerning the practice and application of the material presented in this book. How is the material relevant to careers? First, most enterprises, both profit-making and nonprofit, have an operations or productive phase where something is being processed. This processing might concern itself with the changing of the shape or form of materials, chemical processes, assembly, transport, clerical processes, and so on. Processing is most obvious in manufacturing enterprises and perhaps least obvious in service organizations where the "production" is not tangible in nature. Nevertheless, the operations phases of these productive systems have a large number of problems in common whether they are factories, banks, or supermarkets. They all have facilities, equipment, and personnel organized in some combination to be productive. The facilities and the jobs need to be designed in a manner which results in an effective system. Forecasting the level of operations, planning production and manpower schedules, planning inventory levels, controlling quality and costs, are all common problems though the emphasis of some of these problem areas will change with the particular system. Since there is an operations phase of any enterprise then the knowledge of production management is an important part of the background of supervisors and managers. In addition, however, the challenging nature of the problems of production management has created the need for consultants and staff specialists in job design, plant location and layout, production planning and control, industrial engineering, quality control, cost analysis, and so on. In a growing economy with an increasing technological base the need for highly trained personnel has been increasing and will probably continue to do so.

IMPORTANT TERMS

Numbers in parentheses indicate page numbers.

1. Automation (14)
2. Biotechnology (15)
3. Division of labor (6)
4. Economic lot size (12)
5. Human engineering (15)
6. Human factors (15)
7. Linear programming (13)
8. Methods engineering (10)
9. Simulation (14)
10. Statistical quality control (12)
11. Waiting line theory (14)
12. Work measurement (10)
13. Work sampling (12)

REVIEW QUESTIONS

Numbers in parentheses indicate page numbers.

1. What is the role of production management in a situation where society has decided to reallocate its resources in order to attack social and ecological problems? (3)
2. Rationalize the statement that production efficiency is a relative term meaning, essentially, how effectively we employ the appropriate available resources (input) for a given unit of output. (5)
3. Why is it that even in the United States economy, a system designed for a relatively small output will ordinarily emphasize the use of labor as an input compared to capital? (5)
4. What is the relationship of pollution control to production management? (6)

5. Discuss the role of Adam Smith in the origin of the formal study of production systems. (6, 7)
6. Discuss the contribution of Charles Babbage and the relationship of his work to that of Adam Smith. (7)
7. What were the "four new duties of management" which were the center of Frederick Taylor's philosophy of scientific management? Relate those four new duties (or principles) to current fields of management. (9, 10)
8. Who was F. W. Harris and what was his contribution to the historical development of production management? (12)
9. Relate the milestone contributions of the pioneers of production management to a time scale and appraise the current position of the field. (12–17)
10. Contrast production management technique applied in large companies versus small companies. (17)

SELF-TEST TRUE-FALSE QUESTIONS

Numbers in parentheses indicate page numbers.

1. One of Adam Smith's great contributions to production was the development of our present day concept of production lines. (6)
2. The three economic advantages of division of labor cited by Smith were: (1) a development of skill or dexterity, (2) a saving in changeover time from one activity to the next, (3) the invention of machines or tools. (6)
3. Charles Babbage disagreed with Adam Smith on the advantages of division of labor, pointing out that the only advantage resulting was in purchasing just the amount of skill needed. (7)
4. Production efficiency refers solely to high output per man hour and is not a relative term. (5)
5. Frederick W. Taylor took issue with Smith and Babbage regarding the benefits of division of labor. (9)
6. Some of the new duties which Taylor specified for management really represent a further development of the ideas of division of labor. (10)
7. Taylor felt that the workmen should develop their own methods of performing the work because it gave them a sense of participation in management's objectives. (10)
8. One of the reasons for the slow development of the ideas of scientific management as proposed by Taylor was the lack of appreciation of probability and statistical concepts by people working in the production field. (11)
9. The first attempt at mathematical analysis of a production type problem was made in 1915 by F. W. Harris, who developed the first economic lot-size model for a simple situation. (12)

10. Walter Shewhart was responsible for the development and introduction to industry of statistical quality control. (12)
11. F. E. Raymond was responsible for the development of work sampling. (12)
12. Linear programming is a basic mathematical tool capable of handling many of the large-scale, complex problems of scheduling and allocating the limited resources of a production system. (13)
13. The techniques of operations research used during World War II were direct applications of the methodology developed by Taylor and his followers in industry. (13)
14. The waiting line theory was originally developed to analyze telephone systems. (14)
15. The well-known business decision games are actually based upon a simulation of the economic characteristics of a business. (14)
16. An outgrowth of the research activities of World War II has been a field now called human engineering, human factors, or biotechnology. (15)
17. In the continuous chemical processing industries, such as soap and petroleum, automatic control of processes is common and most of the labor is of an indirect or vigilance nature. (14)
18. Human engineering is an outgrowth of motion study originally developed by the Gilbreths. (15)
19. Automation is a field in itself having nothing to do with the concepts of the modern computer. (14)
20. The computer has developed as a powerful tool in its own right, not merely as a device to perform the tedious labor of computation. (14)
21. The common criteria for measuring the human operator in the field of human engineering is economy of motion or labor cost. (15)
22. During the period from the time of Adam Smith to the present, production management has been developing largely as an empirical applied science. (15)
23. The applied science of production management is nearly fully developed today. (16)
24. Currently, the theory of production systems leads the best practice in business and industry. (16)
25. The basic principles of production economics, and facilities design and control are applicable mainly to large-scale production. (17)

REFERENCES

[1] Babbage, C. *On the Economy of Machinery and Manufactures.* Knight, London, 1832.
[2] Buffa, E. S. *Operations Management: Problems and Models* (3rd ed.). John Wiley, New York, 1972.

[3] Scanlan, B. K. *Principles of Management and Organizational Behavior.* John Wiley, New York, 1973.

[4] Taylor, F. W. *Principles of Scientific Management.* Harper & Bros., New York, 1919; reprinted in *Scientific Management.* Harper & Bros., New York, 1947.

[5] Thierauf, R. J., and R. C. Klekamp. *Decision Making Through Operations Research.* John Wiley (2nd ed.), New York, 1975.

CONTENTS

CHAPTER 2

DECISION MAKING AND THE PRODUCTION FUNCTION

Management's primary function is to make decisions that determine the future course of action for the organization over the short and the long term. These decisions may be directed in every conceivable physical and organizational area; they may deal with financial planning, marketing, and personnel, as well as with the operating or production phase. More often than not, decisions cut across these functional lines.

Decision theory is directed toward determining how rational decisions ought to be made. It attempts to establish a logical framework for decisions that is firmly rooted in science and mathematics as well as in the real world; in this scheme, which correlates the two areas of science and the real world for various alternative action paths, risks are assessed so that the decision maker, by his knowledge of the probable results, can decide what to do. These decisions are concerned with every factor in the organization. For day-to-day operating or repetitive decisions, a set of decision rules makes possible continuity and smooth operation as for example, with industrial quality control. Large-scale decisions, such as the design capacity of a new plant, employ the same general concepts of decision theory but occur only once in a while.

THE NATURE OF DECISION MAKING

The obvious implication of a decision is that alternatives exist; the process of decision making selects from these alternatives the course of action to be carried out. The simplest way to make decisions is, of course, to flip a coin or let some other chance system determine the choice. Such a system is as simple-minded as it is simple, unless the outcomes of the decisions are all equally desirable. Judging desirability immediately points up the need for: (1) a purpose and (2) criteria for measuring or comparing the desirability of the alternatives in relation to the purpose. This is certainly simple enough. We have alternatives and a purpose to achieve, and we need criteria for comparison. However, the process becomes more difficult when we realize that invariably we are talking about future values and that unfortunately these future values often conflict. Each alternative may have both desirable and undesirable aspects; these conflicting values must be reconciled. Since the results expected are future results, how sure can we be of obtaining those results? What is the probability of attaining the results for each alternative? Or, turning it around, what is the risk of not attaining the forecasted result?

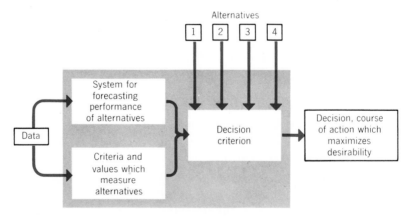

FIGURE 1.   Structure of decision making.

Actually, the final desirability of alternatives is the product of the relative benefit obtainable and the probability of attainment. Thus a "long shot" at the track that would pay $200 on a $2 ticket might have a 1 per cent chance of winning, resulting in a probability weighted payoff of $200 \times 0.01 = \$2.00$. A "favorite" paying only $2.80 but with an 80 per cent chance of winning is more desirable because the probability-weighted value of the result is greater, $2.24 versus $2.00. To be sure, *if* one wins on the "long shot," he wins much more. But the probability of winning is so small that the weighted desirability of the two alternatives makes a rational decision maker select the "favorite" in this case. Figure 1 diagrams the structure of our decision-making situation with alternatives, data from the real world, and criteria and values representing inputs to the decision maker. Inside the decision-making system are computed the predicted relative values of the alternatives based on the criteria and values. Finally, the relative desirability of the alternatives is determined by weighting the values by the probability of attainment. *The course of action that maximizes this final desirability is the rational decision.*

The sophistication of decision making for a given area depends on the level of knowledge within the area and the complexity of the decisions to be made. Sometimes we shall find that criteria and values are clear and straightforward, data are readily obtainable, future values are quite predictable, and risks are fairly clear. In these instances, decision making seems scientific, mathematical, almost automatic. In many other cases, criteria and values are vague and often take several forms whose comparability is difficult to establish. Prediction of risk and future performance may be even more difficult. Then judgment is the device by which we balance off conflicting values, assess risk, and finally select a course of action. At all times, however, decision making is the attempt to choose those courses of action that have the greatest net desirability; in this attempt we hope to use scientific methodology to the maximum and judgment to the minimum.

KINDS OF DECISIONS

There are many ways to classify decision problems. For example, one might classify the nature of the practical problems faced by the manager, the methodologies which might be used to analyze decision problems, or classify based on the amount of information available concerning the probability of occurrence of basic alternatives. The common basis for classification used in decision theory involves the latter. There are four main classes of decision problems in this context: decision making under certainty, under risk, under uncertainty, and under conflict.

When we know with certainty what will occur, given an alternative (state of nature) we have the conditions for *decision making under certainty*. In this kind of situation one need consider only one relevant payoff for each of the possible alternatives or strategies. *Decision making under risk* refers to the condition where there are a number of possible alternatives (states of nature) and the decision maker knows the probability of occurrence of each. In problems of production and operations management the probabilities of the various alternatives may be estimated based upon past experience. When the probabilities of occurrence of the various alternatives or states of nature are not known we have *decision making under uncertainty*. Such problems occur when there is no basis in past experience for estimating the probabilities of occurrence, for example, when estimating the market demand for a new untried product. Finally, *decision making under conflict* occurs when the decision maker must take account of the actions of a competitor or opponent.

Decision making in the field of production and operations management is dominated by the first two, that is, decision making under certainty and under risk. We will comment further on these two classes, giving examples.

Decision Making under Certainty.   The meaning of the term certainty is that for each alternative there is one and only one value of the payoff. Given the alternative, the probability of the occurrence of the stated payoff is presumed to be 1.0. All we need do then is to find the alternative which has the best payoff and this is the alternative which should be selected. Referring to Figure 1, then, the decision criterion is simply to select the alternative with the best payoff.

Suppose, for example, that we are constructing alternate production plans to meet forecasted requirements, given a seasonal product. Several alternate schedules for meeting sales requirements could be calculated, each involving a hypothesis about the most effective way to meet requirements, using normal capacity, overtime capacity, subcontracting, and seasonal inventories. Suppose that three plans were constructed involving the use of these four sources for meeting requirements. Plan 1, level production, has no extra labor turnover cost, overtime premium, or subcontracting cost, however, the cost of carrying seasonal inventory to meet the high peak of sales is very large. Plan 2 involves some fluctuation in production level, but not so much that plant capacity with overtime work is exceeded. The result is a somewhat smaller seasonal inventory cost than for Plan 1, no subcontracting costs, and a substantial overtime premium cost. Plan 3 tends to follow the sales requirements curve quite closely, involving considerable hiring and laying off of labor. However, because of the limitations of plant capacity it is necessary to resort to maximum use of overtime as well as subcontracting. The total cost of normal and overtime labor, sub-contracting, and carrying seasonal inventories for the three plans is:

Plan 1	$318,000
Plan 2	$298,000
Plan 3	$253,000

Given the payoff table it is easy to select Plan 3 as having the lowest cost. It is decision making under certainty because given the stated plan the payoff can be calculated with certainty. One should not con-clude, however, that decision making under certainty is always simple. In many problems of production and operations management the models required to generate the alternatives may be very complex, involving possibly thousands of alternatives. Linear programming is a decision model of this type where the possible alternative strategies may be so numerous that it would be impossible to enumerate and compute the payoffs within the time of a human life. With the linear programming model, however, it may be possible to determine the best possible strategy within a few seconds of computer time.

Decision Making under Risk.   As we noted previously, the decision maker knows the probability of occurrence of each of the possible alternatives when faced with a decision problem under risk. Normally, he depends on past experience to provide guides for the probabilities. For example, the decision to determine the optimum inventory of a replacement part to be maintained represents a decision under risk when the nature of the demand distribution is known.

Since the outcomes are associated with probabilities the decision maker will wish to make his decision in such a way that his *expected* payoff, or probability-weighted payoff, will be maximized. Again, referring to Figure 1, the decision criterion used in decision problems under risk is the expected or probability-weighted payoff.

MODELS

Models of one sort or another have been with us from childhood. The dolls, model airplanes, and toy cars we played with probably helped us learn something of value about their real world counterparts. Models are of vital importance in any intellectual attack on a problem, and we use them perhaps more frequently than we think. How often in discussion, for example, do we use analogies to explain or make a point? The professor in the classroom uses analogy and physical, graphical, and abstract models. In fact, clear thinking requires an understanding of the nature and role of models.

A model is always an abstraction to some degree of the real life thing or process for which we want to predict performance. For example, the aerodynamicist uses models and a wind tunnel to study his design. By no means does the model attempt to duplicate all characteristics of the design. Although factors of shape, weight, strength of parts, temperature, and so on are all important in determining how well the plane design may perform, the engineer is studying aerodynamic performance wherein shape is the main characteristic. Therefore, his model accurately duplicates shape and ignores other factors. The model that is used allows ease of measurement, the manipulation of variables at will, etc., and all at fairly low cost. To attempt similar studies with real planes would not only be costly and hazardous, it probably would not yield as much information. By abstracting from the real life situation, the aerodynamicist can focus his attention on something simpler and not lose much by the fact that many details have been ignored.

But the person who uses models is likely to make horrible mistakes if he stops with the model. An "armchair" model may *seem* to fit comfortably, but a model that does not accurately portray what goes on in the real world is just another model. Models must be validated—sometimes over and over again. What is needed is a model that successfully predicts what goes on in the real world situation. Certainly the first wind tunnel experiments did not do this perfectly, but by correlating results of wind tunnel tests with results of actual flight tests, the aerodynamicist has been able to improve his models so that his predictions are good. Even then, in the march of progress, new situations develop where the old models no longer can do the job as in the case of supersonic flight. Then new models must be constructed. Figure 2 shows the successive steps of forward progress in the world of models and in the real world, with intermediate evaluations used to validate a model.

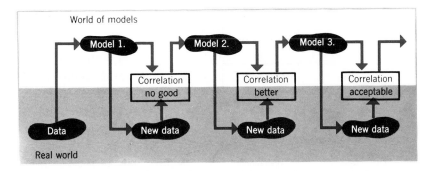

FIGURE 2.   Steps toward the development of an acceptable model.

Kinds of Models.   The aerodynamicist's model, which we have been discussing, is a physical model. Other physical models that many of us have seen include the astronomer's planetarium, the physicist's models of molecular structure, and the architect's model of his building design. In each case the physical model represents physically some aspect of the general problem. But there are other kinds of models, each of which abstracts further from the physical situation in order to permit study of some particular aspect of a problem. For example, *a graphic model* usually represents variables by lengths of lines in two- or three-dimensional space. For example, a graph showing how traffic density varies over the day for westbound traffic on the George Washington Bridge is a graphic model. A decision whether to drive, take a taxi, use public transportation, or stay home might be based partially on this model of traffic density.

Pictorial models often help transmit ideas and influence decisions by giving a visual picture of relationships. For example, a safety cartoon may be a pictorial model of what results from unsafe manufacturing practices. Management hopes that workers will take into account this model of the forecasted effect of unsafe practices and make decisions accordingly. *Schematic models* are commonly used to show things such as information flow and current flow where the physical relationship is of lesser importance. An electrician's wiring diagram or an organization chart is a schematic model. Figure 3 is an organization chart. It is a schematic model of authority relationships within the company.

In the *mathematical model*, which represents the greatest abstraction from the real world situation, symbolism is used to depict factors in a real world situation. The symbols, rather than physical objects, can then be manipulated. Mathematical models are extremely useful in

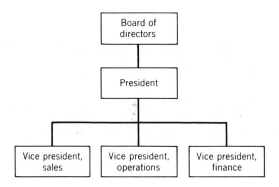

FIGURE 3.   Schematic model of an organization.

studying interrelationships of a situation. For example, the simple statement of Newton's second law of motion, $F = ma$, states a relationship between three factors: force, mass, and acceleration. Mathematical models are most common in the physical sciences and only recently have they invaded the business world. Their great advantage is that symbolic manipulation often can uncover the exact nature of interrelationships between factors that would not be obvious by other techniques.

When the complexity of the situation being studied requires mathematics that are beyond known techniques, or where the mathematics would be too complicated and time consuming to be helpful, *simulation models* can be developed and an approximation of the real life situation carried out by means of a high-speed computer. A simulation model may represent the mathematical equations that are pertinent in a way similar to the mathematical model. But instead of attempting to solve the equations for optimum answers, a series of trials is computed, thus simulating the behavior of the model under different conditions. With high-speed computers it may be possible to simulate a wide variety of conditions and simply select the decisions that perform best. There is no guarantee, of course, that the very best values or decisions have been found.

In all cases, the objective of model building is to predict some facet of performance of the system under study. That is why models are so important to decision making. Rational decision making requires forecasted performance. Models provide this link.

Models in Production Management.   Production management has made use of all of the different kinds of models discussed. Physical models have been used in plant layout studies for some time. Where projects warrant their use, very detailed three-dimensional models are made so that factors of material flow, head room, access, etc., can be studied in careful detail before a new layout is actually installed. Graphic and schematic models have been common for the study of schedules, the analysis of man-machine relationships, and other aspects of the work situation. More recently, mathematical and simulation models have been developed that involve the allocation of productive resources, production programming, optimum lot sizes, and the analysis of random processes. The entire group of chapters comprising Part 2 of this book, "Analytical Methods," deals with models of various production situations that have proved useful as analytical tools.

Advantages and Disadvantages of Models.   Why are models used? The most direct answer is that no better approach to forecasting performance ever has been developed. As systems for prediction, models come to us from science and represent scientific method. To build a model, whether it be physical, graphic, or mathematical, careful consideration is required of what needs to be abstracted from the real situation. When building a model, we are immediately struck by the degree of our ignorance on the subject with which we are working. What information is available? Where are the gaps in information? In its final application, a model gives insight into the problem we are solving.

The dangers of model building lie in the fact of its abstraction from the real world problem. If we keep the model in workable form, it may be oversimplified. If we attempt to be true to the real problem and not indulge in idealization, the model may be too cumbersome and expensive to construct and use. The final guide to the validity of a model is, of course, its test in the real problem situation. If it predicts performance accurately, it is a good model. If it does not, its only value is in possibly giving insight into the development of newer, improved models.

Models and Decision Making.   Why so much emphasis on models? Can we not make decisions without them? Certainly we can. However, without predictive models, our confidence in decisions must decline. We again would be in the position of flipping a coin to decide which alternatives to follow. Gambling based entirely on luck is foolish. A professional gambler studies the odds so that he can place his bets in the most advantageous way. What he is doing is determining models for the games he plays so that he can predict performance. Should a manager be any less shrewd in making his decisions?

THE PRODUCTION FUNCTION

Production is the process by which goods and services are created. We find production processes in factories, offices, hospitals, and supermarkets. Production management deals with decision making related to production processes, so that the resulting good or service is produced according to the specifications, in the amounts and by the schedule demanded, and at minimum cost. In accomplishing these objectives, production management is associated with two broad areas of activity: the design and the control of production systems.

For many reasons, production management is probably most often associated with factory management rather than with the broader definition just given. As a field of knowledge, production management developed largely in the factory, and logically so, because the significant problems of production first occurred in the factory. Before the factory system came into existence, the large number of one-man shops that produced goods presented an insignificant problem of production management. With the factory system, however, the situation was reversed. The question of how to organize, lay out facilities, control quality, and meet schedules had to be answered somehow. As answers were provided and became generalized, the field of production management began to develop.

The early steps concentrated on controlling factory labor costs, which was logical, because, in Taylor's time the bulk of the product cost was likely to be labor. With the continuing trend toward mechanization and automation, the situation has changed drastically. In the factory, indirect labor costs have increased tremendously in relation to direct labor costs. Given the present structure of the industrial economy, a concern finds it uneconomical to fabricate, itself, many of the components of its products, so material costs often dominate. Therefore, in the factory, production management has had to develop in the areas of equipment design and selection, indirect labor cost control, production and inventory control and quality control.

But other changes have taken place since Taylor's era. While attention has been focused on the factory, the number of office workers has multiplied rapidly. Today white collar workers outnumber blue collar workers by a margin of several million. Other activities, where production management problems might have been insignificant twenty or thirty years ago, have developed into large-scale units where the operations activities cannot be ignored. For example, the corner grocery store has all but vanished, and in its place we have the high-volume supermarket. Here, the facility design is of great importance. Location, layout, and inventory control take on new significance. We all know that hospital costs have skyrocketed. Hospital administrators are recognizing operations or production problems more than ever before. Basic questions of layout, division of labor, job design, and control of errors (quality control) cannot be ignored.

This book recognizes the breadth of productive activity. Nevertheless, in the material that follows, we shall use the factory as a general model and then try to indicate how the concepts discussed apply in other situations. This method is used because practically all of the pioneering work has been done in the factory. Therefore, the most numerous examples available still come from the factory. In the coming years, this situation should change as the general principles find application in other productive activities.

A GENERALIZED DESCRIPTIVE MODEL OF PRODUCTION

In line with the thinking we have just expressed, let us construct a model of what we mean by production. According to our definition, the factory, the office, the supermarket, the hospital, etc., all represent special cases which have special characteristics. Our production system has inputs which represent the material, parts, paperwork forms, and the customers or patients, as the case may be. The inputs are processed in some way by a series of operations whose sequence and number are specified for each input. The operations may vary from one only to any number and may take on any desired characteristics; they may be mechanical, chemical, assembly, inspection and control, dispatching to the next operation, receiving, shipping, personal contact such as an interview, and paperwork operations.

The outputs of our system are completed parts, products, chemicals, service to customers or patients, completed paperwork, etc. There is provision for storage in our system after the receipt of the input and between each operation in the system. The time in storage may vary from zero to any finite value. Inputs are transported between all operations in the system. Any means of transportation may be supplied, including self-transportation in the case of clients and customers. Our model also has an information system and a decision maker. The information system interconnects all physical activities and provides a basis for management decision. These functions provide the equivalent of a "nervous system" for the model. Figure 4 represents our production system.

Systems may occur in series. For example, when completed products are shipped from the factory to a warehouse, they are leaving the factory system only to arrive at a second productive system called a warehouse. In this way, the two systems may be considered as part of one large system. Systems also may occur in parallel, such as when a number of factories produce similar products to supply several market areas. For solving some types of problems, these factories may be considered one large production system.

Now let us consider what would happen to an input to the system. After being received, the input goes into storage to take its turn in the processing. By some set of priority rules, it is drawn from storage to begin processing. These rules might be: first in—first out, time or date required for completion or delivery, urgency, or some other system of priority rules. It is then processed according to a predetermined sequence. Let us assume the sequence b, d, c, n. From initial storage it goes to operation b and is placed in temporary storage to await processing there. We assume that operation b has already some assigned work or load and, therefore, our input takes its place in line (in storage) and will be processed at b according to the priority decision rules established. After being processed at b, it is transported to d, placed in storage, drawn out according to priority rules, processed, etc. One operation may be an inspection. The operation just preceding shipment may be a packaging operation, preparing the item for shipment.

If we are speaking of a high-volume, standardized, fabricated part, the operations may be placed in sequence and interconnected by conveying equipment. The storages would take place on the conveyors themselves, and the decision rules are first in—first out. If we are speaking of the hospital, the storages may take place in waiting rooms or in hospital beds. The priority rules may be first in—first out, with urgency exceptions. Many tasks are mobile in the instance of the hospital, such as when nurses give shots or medication.

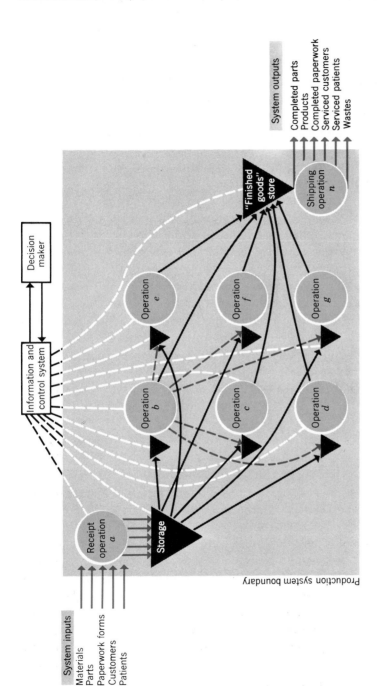

FIGURE 4.   Diagram of a generalized production system. Inputs may be processed in any specified sequence of operations and are transported between operations. The number of operations may vary from one to any finite number. Storage occurs between all operations, and the time in storage may vary from essentially zero to any finite amount. *Note:* There are interconnections between all combinations of operations *b* through *f,* although only those originating at *b* are shown. The information system interconnects all activities and provides the basis for management decision.

In a supermarket, products are received and stored on display shelves. Customer receiving is practically nonexistent as an operation. The customer picks the desired items from shelves, transports them, and takes his place in line for the single operation of check-out.

In soap manufacturing by the continuous process, materials are received and stored. Then they are taken from storage in large quantity, dissolved, and pumped through a series of chemical operations, so that transportation and storage between operations occur in the pipes. The material is chemically processed while it moves, and it emerges as soap. It is then packaged and shipped.

The job-shop manufacturing situation, where custom products are fabricated and assembled, is undoubtedly the most complex type of production system. Take a missile, for example. Thousands of individual parts must be fabricated and assembled into subassemblies and, thence, into final assemblies. This activity must be dovetailed to fit into a complex schedule, so that operation time is available when it is needed to provide parts for subassemblies and final assemblies. The pattern or flow for the multitude of parts from operation to operation is so complex that it can only be visualized by some abstract means of representation. Many parts require operation time on the same machines, but the operations occur at different times in the overall manufacturing cycle. The problem of loading the operations in such a way that the machines can be utilized effectively is obviously a difficult one.

CONTINUOUS VERSUS INTERMITTENT MODELS

Continuous flow production situations are those where the facilities are standardized as to routings and flow, since inputs are standardized. Therefore, a standard set of processes and sequence of processes can be adopted. Continuous models are represented in practice by production and assembly lines, large-scale office operations processing forms by a standard procedure, continuous flow chemical operations, etc. Intermittent production situations are those where the facilities must be flexible enough to handle a wide variety of products and sizes, or where the basic nature of the activity imposes change of important characteristics of the input (change in product design). In instances such as these, no single sequence pattern of operations is appropriate, so the relative location of the operations must be a compromise that is best for all inputs considered together.

Transportation facilities between operations also must be flexible to accommodate a wide variety of input characteristics as well as the wide variety of routes that the inputs may require. These conditions commonly define an intermittent production situation. It is intermittent because the flow is intermittent. Considerable storage between operations is required in order that individual operations can be carried on somewhat independently, resulting in ease of scheduling and in fuller utilization of men and machines. In practice, intermittent production is represented by custom or job order-type machine shops, hospitals, general offices, batch-type chemical operations, etc.

As we have shown, our generalized descriptive model in Figure 4 can be made to fit both the intermittent and continuous flow situations by the specification of some detailed characteristics. We have assumed intermittent flow in our model and defined it in general enough terms that the specification of a fixed-operation sequence, the specification of continuous flow-type transportation facilities, the assumption of low storage times between operations, and a first in—first out set of priority decision rules would all determine continuous flow conditions. The continuous flow situation is common enough today, however, that we tend to think in terms of the dichotomy of continuous and intermittent flow models.

PROBLEMS OF PRODUCTION MANAGEMENT

Using our generalized model as a background, let us outline the nature of problems generated in a production system. These problems require two major types of decisions, one that relates to the design of the system and one that relates to the operation and control of the system (that is, both long-run and short-run decisions). The relative balance of the emphasis on such factors as cost, service, and reliability of both functional and time performance depends on the basic purposes of the total enterprise and on the general nature of the good or service being produced. Thus, in general, economic enterprises will probably emphasize cost, consistent with quality and delivery commitments. Hospitals may emphasize reliability and service, consistent with cost objectives, etc.

Long-run decisions related to the design of the production system are:

1. *Selection and design of products.* There are strong interactions between product selections and design with productive capability, and vice versa.

2. *Selection of equipment and processes.* Usually alternative equipment and processes are available for a given need. Production management must make decisions that commit capital of the enterprise and its basic approach to production in the facility design.

3. *Production design of items processed.* Production cost interacts strongly with the design of parts, products, paper work forms, etc. Design decisions often set the limiting characteristics of cost and processing for the system.

4. *Job design.* Job design is an integral part of the total system design, involving the basic organization of work as well as the integration of human engineering data to produce optimally designed jobs.

5. *Location of the system.* Location decisions can, in some cases, be important if the balance of cost factors determined by nearness to markets and material supply is critical.

6. *Facility layout.* Decisions related to design capacity, basic modes of production, shifts, use of overtime, and subcontracting must be made. In addition, operations and equipment must be located in relation to each other in a pattern that minimizes overall material-handling cost or meets the requirements of some more complex criterion. The latter requirement is most difficult for the complex intermittent model where routes vary. Many detailed problems are associated with each other in order to specify adequately the layout of a production system. These include heating, lighting, and other utility requirements; the allocation of storage space, aisle space, etc.; and the design of the building to house the layout.

Short-run decisions related to the design of operation and control systems are:

1. *Inventory and production control.* Decisions must be made concerning how to allocate productive capacity consistent with demand and inventory policy. Feasible schedules must be worked out, and the load on men and machines and the flow of production must be controlled.

2. *Maintenance and reliability of the system.* Decisions must be made regarding maintenance effort, recognition of the random nature of equipment breakdown, and recognition that machine down-time may itself be associated with important costs or loss of sales.

3. *Quality control.* Decisions must be made to set the permissible levels of risk that bad parts are produced and shipped or that errors are made, as well as the risk that good parts are scrapped. Inspection costs must be balanced against probable losses due to passing defective material or services.

4. *Labor control.* Labor is still the major cost element in most products and services. Production planning requires an appraisal of the labor component; thus, much effort has gone into developing work measurement and wage payment systems.

5. *Cost control and improvement.* Production supervisors must make day-to-day decisions which involve the balance of labor, material, and some overhead costs.

The relative importance of these problems of production management varies considerably, depending on the nature of individual production systems. Nevertheless, every system has these problems in some degree. For example, equipment policy may occupy a dominant position in production systems where the capital investment per worker is very large, as in the petroleum industry. On the other hand, equipment policy may occupy a minor role in a production system that is represented by a large labor component or a large material component. Part of the art of production management involves the sensing of the relative importance of these various problems in a given situation.

The chapters that follow are organized into three broad sections. Part 2 deals with general analytical methods which are of particular value in production management. These methods serve as general models for decision making which may be altered to fit specific situations. Parts 3 and 4 deal with the general problems that are faced in production.

KEY CONCEPTS

Models.   The concept of a model and its use in managerial decision-making is of key importance to the entire book. We construct models (physical, mathematical, simulation, etc.) as a means of forecasting the performance of a system, or at least some aspect of performance. Then, the variables which define the system can be manipulated in order to determine their effects on the system performance. Alternately one could take an empirical point of view and experiment with the system itself, however, this approach is commonly more expensive and disruptive of the system.

Decision Criteria.   As an important part of the philosophy of formalized decision-making, one must express in the clearest and most concise terms the objective to be attained—this is called the decision criterion. If we know precisely the nature of the objective to be attained (for example, minimum cost or maximum contribution to profit), then we can choose from among the alternatives generated by the model the one which maximizes the desirable characteristics defined in the decision criterion.

A System.   The concept of a system is crucial for the study of most managerial problems today. A system involves a complex of interacting components, and in focussing on the system rather than simply studying the components we gain insight into what really makes the overall enterprise tick. At this stage of development, Figure 4 is a general representation of an operational system showing the general interconnections between a miltiplicity of functions and six different kinds of flows.

IMPORTANT TERMS

Numbers in parentheses indicate page numbers.

1. Continuous system (38)
2. Control system (34, 37)
3. Facility layout (40)
4. Graphic model (31)
5. Information system (36, 37)
6. Inputs (36, 37)
7. Intermittent system (38)
8. Job design (40)
9. Outputs (35, 37)
10. Production control (40)
11. Production design (40)
12. Quality control (40)
13. Reliability of system (40)
14. Schematic model (31)
15. Simulation model (32)

REVIEW QUESTIONS

Numbers in parentheses indicate page numbers.

1. Discuss the role of decision making in the management of an enterprise. (26–27)
2. Under what conditions might it be acceptable to let decisions be determined by some chance event such as the flip of a coin? (26–27)
3. Discuss the structure of decision making shown in Figure 1. What is the importance of: (a) a forecasting system, (b) criteria and values, (c) alternatives, and (d) a decision criterion? (26–27)
4. Discuss the four kinds of decision making and the kinds of decision problems to which each is applicable. Which approaches to decision making are most commonly used in production management? (27–29)
5. How does the probability of attainment of alternatives influence their net relative desirability? (27)

6.   What is the function of models in decision making? (32–33)
7.   What kinds of models are used? (31–32)
8.   How do we know when we have a useful model? (30)
9.   What are the advantages and pitfalls of models? (33)
10. What kinds of models are useful in production management? (32)
11. Define the term *production*. (34)
12. Why is the term *production* most often associated with the factory? (34)
13. What necessitates a broader definition of production today, than was called for in Taylor's time? (35)
14. Show that the generalized descriptive model of production discussed in this chapter is applicable to the "operations" side of various activities. (35–39)
15. Differentiate between intermittent and continuous models of production. (38)
16. What are the short- and long-run problems of production management? (39)

SELF-TEST TRUE-FALSE QUESTIONS

Numbers in parentheses indicate page numbers.

1.   Most managerial decisions do not cut across the functional lines of finance, marketing, and production. (25)
2.   Decision theory is directed toward determining how decisions are actually made rather than how rational decisions ought to be made. (25)
3.   In a decision making system, we are seeking the course of action that maximizes net desirability rather than simply maximizing possible gains. (27)
4.   A "long shot" at the race track paying two hundred dollars on a two-dollar ticket with a one per cent chance of winning is more desirable than a "favorite" paying only two dollars eight cents on a two-dollar ticket, but with an eighty per cent chance of winning. (27)
5.   A decision-making system need not consider criteria and values since a decision may involve criteria and values which are in conflict. (26–27)
6.   A rational decision-making system uses scientific methodology, not judgment. (27)
7.   Models should not abstract from the real-life system or process for which we want to predict performance because they will lose their value if they do not accurately duplicate all characteristics of the situation. (30)
8.   The development of a successful model involves a correlation of data from the real world with the predictions made by models. (30)
9.   An organization chart is a schematic model. (31)
10. A physical model involves no abstraction from the real-world situation

because it duplicates accurately all physical relationships involved. (30–31)

11. Mathematical models represent the greatest abstraction from the real-world situation. (31)

12. A simulation model is really nothing but a mathematical model where solutions are developed on high speed computers. (32)

13. In production management, physical models have commonly been used as a device to allocate productive resources and to program production. (33)

14. In production management, graphic and schematic models have been in common use to study schedules, and the analysis of man-machine relationships. (33)

15. Models are used because no better approach to forecasting performance has ever been developed. (33)

16. The final guide to the validity of a model is its test in the real-problem situation. (33)

17. Production is defined as the production of physical goods. (34)

18. Production processes are found in factories, offices, hospitals, and supermarkets. (34)

19. In the early development of production management, attention was concentrated on controlling factory labor costs. (34)

20. Today, white collar workers outnumber blue collar workers. (35)

21. A generalized model of production need not include an information system and decision maker, since these are management functions. (35–36)

22. Production systems may occur in series as well as in parallel. (36)

23. The job-shop manufacturing situation, where custom products are fabricated and assembled is undoubtedly the most complex type of production system. (38)

24. A continuous-flow production system is simply a special case of production as we conceive it. (38)

25. Continuous-flow production systems are represented by factories that work continuously on a three-shift basis. (38)

26. Intermittent production situations are those where the facilities must be flexible enough to handle a wide variety of products and sizes. (38)

27. In continuous production systems, considerable storage between operations is required in order that individual operations can be carried on somewhat independently. (39)

28. In intermittent production systems we normally find a fixed operation sequence. (38)

29. The problems of production management may be classified as those pertaining to design of the system and those pertaining to the operation and control of the system. (39)

30. Production management has very little to do with the design of the items being processed in the system, since these designs are taken as given. (39)

PROBLEMS

1. A hospital is attempting to determine ordering policies for supplies that it uses in quantity. The manager has taken one item as an example to show that there will be a policy that will minimize his out-of-pocket costs. He identifies his out-of-pocket costs as being made up of two components, the cost of holding the item in inventory and the costs required to reorder the item each time. If he buys large lots his annual inventory costs will increase; however, since he will have to order less often, his annual reordering costs will be lower. He has computed the two costs for each of four different lot sizes to meet the annual forecasted requirements of 12,000 units. The data are shown in Table I. What lot size should he use to minimize the sum of the two costs? (*Hint.* Plot the two costs and fit curves to them.) Why does the analysis represent decision making under certainty?

TABLE I.   Inventory and reordering costs for four lot sizes for a medical supply item.

Annual costs	$250	$350	$450	$550
Inventory costs	$18.75	$26.25	$33.75	$41.25
Reordering costs	48.00	34.29	26.67	21.82

2. The FREEZO Company is a frozen food operator, and it must decide on which crops to plant in an available tract. There are three possibilities: peas, green beans, and asparagus. Records of yields for the three crops exist that are classified according to weather conditions. The probability of excellent weather is .25, of variable weather is .45, and of poor weather is .30. The dollar yields under the three weather conditions are shown in Table II. Which strategy should be selected to maximize expected yield? Why is this decision making under risk?

TABLE II.   Yields for three crops under three weather conditions.

	Excellent Weather	Variable Weather	Poor Weather
Peas	$25,000	$15,000	$10,000
Green beans	50,000	30,000	20,000
Asparagus	55,000	20,000	15,000

3. Select some activity that may be familiar to you and classify it according to the intermittent-continuous classification discussed in the chapter. Identify the item being processed. Develop the structure of the network of flow of the thing being processed in the general format of a diagram similar to Figure 4.

4. For the operational system developed in problem 3, develop what you feel are the *dominant* problems of production for this particular system. Use the lists of "Production Management Problems" discussed at the end of the chapter. Discuss why these particular problems are the dominant ones for your system.

REFERENCES

[1] Albers, H. H. *Principles of Management: A Modern Approach* (4th ed.). John Wiley, New York, 1974.
[2] Alcalay, J. A., and E. S. Buffa. "A Proposal for a General Model of a Production System." *International Journal of Production Research*, Mar. 1963.
[3] Boulden, J. B., and E. S. Buffa. "Corporate Models: On-Line, Real-Time Systems." *Harvard Business Review*, July-August 1970, pp. 65–85.
[4] Boulden, J. B., and E. S. Buffa. "The Strategies of Interdependent Decisions." *California Management Review*, 1 (4), 94–100, 1959.
[5] Forrester, J. *Industrial Dynamics*. MIT Press, Cambridge, Mass., 1961.
[6] Miller, D. W., and M. K. Starr. *Executive Decisions and Operations Research* (2nd ed.). Prentice-Hall, Englewood Cliffs, N.J., 1969.
[7] Reisman, A., and E. S. Buffa. "A General Model for Production and Operations Systems." *Management Science*, Sept. 1964.
[8] Schoderbek, P. P. *Management Systems* (2nd ed.). John Wiley, New York, 1971.
[9] Starr, M. K. "Evolving Concepts in Production Management." In: *Evolving Concepts in Management*. E. Flippo, editor. Academy of Management Proceedings, 24th Annual Meeting, Dec. 1964. Also reprinted as Chapter 2 in: *Readings in Production and Operations Management*. E. S. Buffa, editor. John Wiley, New York, 1966.

CONTENTS

CHAPTER 3
THE SYSTEMS CONCEPT

An emerging basis for unifying and relating the complexities of managerial problems is the systems concept and methodology. These concepts have been applied more to the analysis of productive systems than to other fields, but it is clear that the value of the concept in management is pervasive.

The word itself has become so commonplace in the general literature of management that one often wants to scream, for its common use almost depreciates its value. Yet the word itself is so descriptive of the general interacting nature of the myriad of elements that enter managerial problems that we can no longer talk of complex problems without using the term *systems*. Indeed, throughout this book we use the term liberally. We must learn to distinguish the general use of the term and its specific use as a mode of structuring and analyzing problems.

One of the great values of the systems concept is that it helps us to take a very complex situation and lend order and structure to it. A major contribution of the concept is the reduction of complexity in managerial problems to a block diagram

49

showing the relationship and interacting effects of the various elements which affect the problem at hand. At its present state of development and application, the systems concept is most useful in helping us gain insight into problems. At a second and very powerful level of contribution, however, systems analysis is gaining prominence as a basis for generating solutions to problems and evaluating their effects, and for designing alternate systems.

"SYSTEMS" DEFINED

But, we have been using the term *systems* without defining it. Though nearly everyone may have a general understanding of the term it may be useful to be more precise. Webster defines a system as "a regularly interacting or interdependent group of items forming a unified whole." Thus a system may have many components and objects, but they are united in the pursuit of some common goal. They are in some sense unified, organized, or coordinated. The components of a system contribute to the production of a set of outputs from given inputs which may or may not be optimal or best with respect to some appropriate measure of effectiveness. Systems are often complex although the definition does not specify that they need to be.

It is probably correct to say that some of the most interesting systems for study are complex and that a change in one variable within the system will affect many other variables of the system. Thus, in productive systems a change in production rate may affect inventories, hours worked per week, overtime hours, facility layout, and so on. Understanding and predicting these complex interactions between variables is one of our main objectives in this book.

One of the elusive aspects of the systems concept is in the definition of a specific system. The fact that we can define the system which we wish to consider and draw boundaries around it is important. We can then look inside the defined system to see what happens, but it is just as important to see how the system is affected by its environment. Thus, invariably, every system can be thought of as a part of an even larger system. One of the dangers of defining systems which are too narrow in scope is that we may fail to see broader implications. On the other hand, a broad definition of systems runs the risk of leaving out important details involved in the functioning of the system. Obviously, there is a large element of "art" in the application of systems concepts.

OPEN AND FEEDBACK SYSTEMS

A crucial part of understanding the systems concept is in seeing clearly the modules on which it is built. Forrester [4] has described open and feedback systems as follows:

> An open system is one characterized by outputs that respond to inputs but where the outputs are isolated from and have no influence on the inputs. An open system is not aware of its own performance. In an open system, past action does not control future action. An open system does not observe and react to its own performance. An automobile is an open system which by itself is not governed by where it has gone in the past nor does it have a goal of where to go in the future. A watch, taken by itself, does not observe its own inaccuracy and adjust itself—it is an open system.
>
> A feedback system, which is sometimes called a "closed" system, is influenced by its own past behavior. A feedback system has a closed loop structure that brings results from past action of the system back to control future action. One class of feedback systems—negative feedback— seeks a goal and responds as a consequence of failure to achieve the goal. A second class of feedback systems—positive feedback—generates growth processes wherein action builds a result that generates still greater action.

Both open and feedback systems have interactions with their environment so this is not the crucial distinction. An open production system, for example, might be one where the quantity and quality of the output were determined in a way which completely ignored the user environment. Such a system would continue to produce at the output rates set, regardless of finished goods inventory position and the actual demand in the marketplace. Alternately, such an open production system might continue to produce preset quality levels regardless of the marketplace acceptance of the output. As we know, however, while such systems may not observe and react directly to their own performance there is a broader level second order feedback involved which puts such enterprises out of business ultimately because they were attempting to behave like open systems where a closed system, responsive to the environment, was really appropriate. Most of the feedback systems in managerial problems are of the negative feedback type where the objective is to control a process.

Elements of Feedback Control.   The elements of a basic feedback control loop are shown in Figure 1. In Figure 1, assume that the production system itself has inputs which it processes to produce outputs of

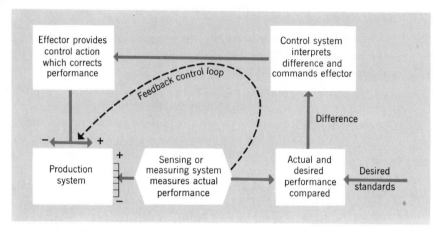

FIGURE 1.   Elements of simple feedback control loop.

goods or services. In order to control the performance of the system, measurements are made on aspects of the output, perhaps in both quantity and quality terms. These measurements are compared with the desired performance and the control system interprets the difference, commanding the effector to correct performance. Thus a control system always involves some kind of measurement of what is actually happening. This information is fed into some kind of data processing system where the measurements are compared with standards which have been derived. These standards are based on managerial policies directly or indirectly.

For example, there may be a policy in a bank which states that we want to offer customer service at the windows such that the average waiting time is only one minute. If the waiting time exceeds the one minute standard by perhaps more than 10 per cent, then additional tellers' windows are opened. Alternately, one might consider a physical measurement such as a quality control on the dimension of a part or the chemical composition, or the rate of output might be the measurement to be controlled. In some instances feedback controls may require high technology and be virtually automatic and in other instances the control may require managerial intervention. Whether automatic or not, however, the same basic principles of feedback control are being used.

Combinations of Simple Feedback Systems.   In Figure 2a we represent the simple subsystem module of an input-output transformation process involving information feedback to provide control of the process. These simple modules may be combined in series and in parallel

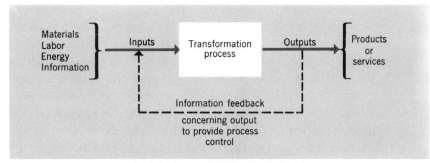

(a) Subsytem module of an input–output
transformation process

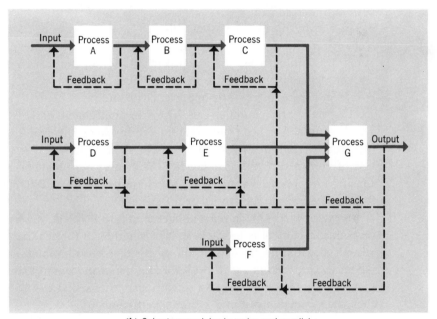

(b) Subsytem modules in series and parallel

FIGURE 2.   Input-output concept of systems and subsystems with information feedback to provide the basis for control.

as shown in Figure 2*b*. In Figure 2*b* we see that each process has its own feedback loop for control; however, the final output of the system of processes also provides feedback for control purposes to the critical processes upstream. These elements of managerial control might be in terms of the quality of output, the quantity of output, or some other aspect of performance.

Feedback-Time Lag Effects.   How a system under control by information feedback responds depends on a number of factors. Referring back to Figure 1, if the difference between actual and desired performance is fed back with no time lag, the effector commands the system to change settings immediately by the observed difference, and the system responds immediately, then the system would be completely responsive and presumably exhibit perfect control since any deviation is corrected immediately. Even in completely automatic, high technology, process control systems, however, this ideal is not attained. How the system responds to control depends on time lags in the feedback response system, and in the transformation process itself, on how much control action is called forth, and on the sensitivity of the system under control.

The sensitivity of the system refers to the response in the output to a change in the input. For example, in the steering mechanisms of most autos the ratio between the amount of rotation of the front wheels and a given degree of turn of the steering wheel is modest, so one does not oversteer (overcontrol). The opposite situation has been experienced by most of us in the "bumper car" autos in amusement parks where the steering ratio has been deliberately set to cause the front wheels to turn considerably for a small turn of the steering wheel. The result is a loss of control as well as some fun. Thus a system may be relatively sensitive or insensitive to control. How much control action is called for is related to the sensitivity of the system.

Another extremely important factor in the way the system output responds to control is in the time lags inherent in the feedback control system and in the process itself. If it takes substantial time for the feedback control system to respond and command an adjustment, and if the process itself is sluggish in response to changed control settings, then the system output may exhibit oscillation.

For example, if you were attempting to drive an auto with the only vision being to the rear (through the rearview mirror) the information feedback that you needed to turn would occur after you had passed the curve. To adjust you might then turn the steering wheel. But suppose it was in fact a winding road and having turned you now see that the road has subsequently turned the other way. It would require a very wide road to drive under these conditions and stay on the road, and in any case you would be oscillating back and forth over the smooth line you would drive if you could see out the windshield.

Feedback and Managerial Systems.   Managerial control systems suffer from all of the unfortunate effects: time lags, sensitivity, and amount of control action. In general, long time lags and low sensitivity are the big culprits; however, there are situations where supersensitivity is difficult to deal with.

Consider the operations manager attempting to control the employment, production, and inventory levels of his operations based on month-old information feedback on the progress of retail sales. If he reacts to an increase in retail sales recorded one month ago he might increase employment and production levels at a time when sales in the field were actually decreasing. Also, retail sales might exhibit random fluctuations so that if the manager were to respond to the retail sales increase (whether the time lag was long or short) he might respond by small increases in employment and production level, taking a wait-and-see attitude, i.e., to see if the increase is permanent or only a random change in sales level.

THE OPERATIONS FUNCTION IN CONTEXT

As we commented earlier, every system can be regarded as a part of a larger system and this is the case with the production or operations function of an enterprise. Let us now consider the operations function, with all of its internal complexities, to be one block in the much larger enterprise system. The operations function itself might be internally represented by a complex network of processes such as Figure 2b, however, we will represent it by a single block with its own inputs and outputs. Figure 4 of Chapter 2 is also descriptive of activities going on inside the operations function.

Figure 3 is a basic schematic diagram which places the broad operations function in context. The diagram is highly aggregated both in terms of flows and in terms of functions performed. Yet it shows the nature of flow paths and the major places where transformations of one sort or another take place. Note that we have drawn certain boundaries to the system which establish pools outside the system for labor, materials and energy, equipment, external services, and financial resources. These functions are a part of the environment of the system, and there are flows between these functions external to the system and the system itself.

The flows, as indicated on the schematic diagram, are of six distinct types. The dashed line with circles represents the flow of orders. It can be seen that the orders originate in the surroundings of the system studied. They may originate in the environment as inputs to the system or they may be responses to information originating in and emanating from the system as might be the case where a sales organization actively solicits orders. Orders enter the system through the professional and/or service function. This is the intelligence arm of the model. Based on decisions made in this function, the incoming orders may be either routed to a sink, that is, "filed," or, after certain transformations, be sent on to the operations function, the inventory, or the proposals and/or sales function.

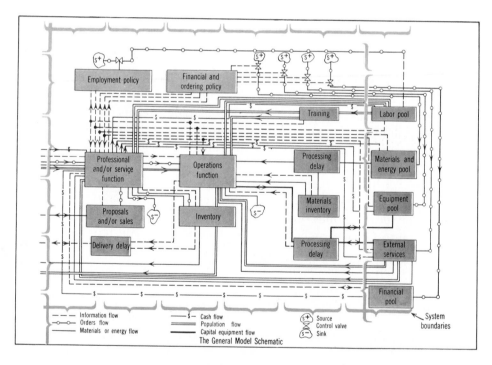

FIGURE 3.   General model for operational systems—basic schematic diagram. (From Reisman and Buffa. "A General Model for Production and Operations Systems." *Management Science*, Vol. II, No. 1, Sept. 1964; all rights reserved.

If the order is for proposals, it is routed to the proposals and/or sales group from which a proposal in the form of information (dashed line) is sent out. On the other hand, if the order is for goods, services, or energy which cannot be filled from inventory, the operations function fills the orders through production. If, however, the decision is made to fill the order from inventory, it is routed to that function. Where orders are sent to operations, the intelligence arm or professional and/or service function must satisfy operations with the necessary labor, materials, energy, equipment, and external services, all at the correct time and of the right kind. (Labor as referred to here may be highly professional, as in hospitals or universities.) Thus information must be sent through the employment policy and the financial and ordering policy functions so that orders may go out to the various pools.

On receipt of an order, the labor pool routes people into the system (double solid line). The population flows enter through the training function where they are processed and sent on to either operations or, perhaps, the professional function itself. Similarly, the material and energy pool routes its resources to the system through the processing delay from where they may be sent on to either the material inventory or to the operations function directly. The equipment pool sends capital equipment (solid wide line) into its processing delay and on to operations. The external services pool performs as the name implies, that is, services which cannot be performed internally within the system, owing to lack of capability, capacity limitations, and so on.

The financial pool represents the banks or the investment sector of the economy. This is the originator for all external financing. It provides the necessary capital for the system, while at the same time, being the place where surplus cash is stored (dashed lines with dollar signs). Of course, cash also enters the system from the general environment in payment for the goods produced or services rendered, and, for similar reasons, leaves the system to various pools. Notice that there is no flow of cash between segments of the internal system. The reason is, of course, that manufacturing does not pay in cash or even by check for materials coming from in-plant materials inventory since these transactions are covered by intraplant flows of information.

Information flows (dashed line) may be of several types. They may be in the form of reports or memoranda or they may be verbal; they may be requests for further information or they may be commands or instructions. In addition, information flows may contain the routine data from operations, inventory, delivery, or processing delays. Information flows may exhibit all of the characteristics of physical flows; that is, information may be generated, stored, transformed, and dissipated, and its flow may exhibit inertia.

Goods or energy may enter the professional and/or service function first. Here intelligence operations are performed and they are routed to either operations or inventory, depending on need.

Operations Function—Materials and Information Flow. The highly aggregated function blocks, of Figure 3, as well as the flows, may be broken down to any level of aggregation desired for each type of flow through schematic diagrams such as Figure 4. Figure 4 diagrams the materials and information flow for the operations function in relation to other pertinent functions. Within the operations function boundary,

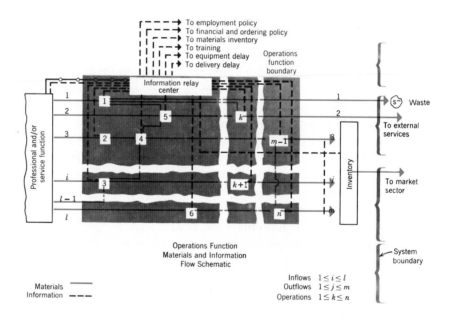

FIGURE 4.   Operations function—materials flow schematic diagram. (From Reisman and Buffa [8].)

each small block represents either a transformation (physical, chemical, or other) or a flow element such as transportation or storage. In addition, these small blocks represent the nodes or junctions of the flow system and are the focus of much of the analysis which can be performed on the system. Note that the nodes are numbered from one to **n**. The interconnection of all pertinent flow diagrams such as Figure 4, according to the overall structure of Figure 3, represents the entire system for the six kinds of flow diagrams.

The value of constructing models patterned after the general form of Figures 3 and 4 for specific real systems is that we may now be subjected to rigorous analysis. Such analysis may be either mathematical in form, since we may now write equations which describe the nature of the various flows taking place, or we may simulate the operation of such a system by means of large-scale computers. The general mathematical analysis is described in [8].

CONTROL SUBSYSTEMS

Systems concepts can be useful in understanding how the broad control subsystems function in relation to the production system itself. Figure 5 is a block diagram showing the production system in relation to control subsystems which fall within the boundaries of the dashed line. For day-to-day control of the production system we see that there is a control loop which involves measurements made on the system which are fed into data processing for interpretation and comparison with desired performance, with action taken by the day-to-day control functions. With the present capability of automatic measurement, data processing, and effector mechanisms, it is conceivable that day-to-day control can be completely automatic as it is in most petroleum refining situations.

While the day-to-day control process is going on, there is a broader control system which seeks optimum operation. The optimum control system is taking as inputs information from the day-to-day control system (short range), forecasting and planning, and policy information to create a broader range (perhaps broader horizon) criterion of performance. Such a control system might involve the alteration or correction of standards of performance. There is another type of function for the optimum control system, however, where optimum operations

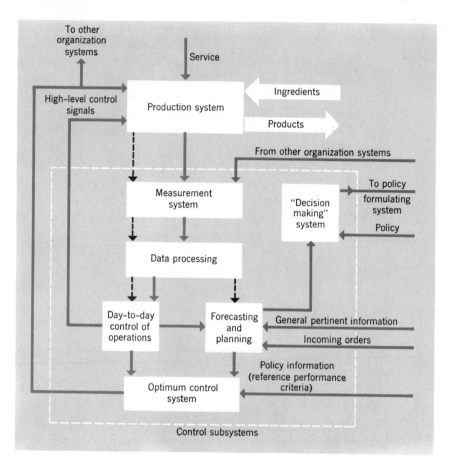

FIGURE 5.   Production system in relation to control subsystems. (From Alcalay and   Buffa   [1].)

might not be defined on a day-to-day basis. Production scheduling is an example where a broader time horizon and broader criterion function are required to develop an optimum control system for production programs. These programs may involve complex models which balance the costs of inventories and the costs of changing production levels in anticipation of forecasted sales. The day-to-day schedule in itself may be far from optimum, but the longer range production programs may approach optimality.

EXAMPLES OF LARGE-SCALE SYSTEMS

The availability of high-speed computers has fostered the development and use of large-scale systems which have most often been used to simulate operations. These simulations provide the basis for evaluating the impact of alternate policies and plans. Since the interacting effects are so complex in such systems the analyses can provide a basis for important decisions. We shall look briefly at two such large systems: Potlatch Forests, Inc., and Inland Steel Company.

Potlatch Forests, Inc. [2, 3]. This organization is a large forest products company having annual sales in the range of about $335 million, and employing over 12,000 individuals in 44 plants and 36 sales offices spread over the entire country. The company developed 22 interlinked computer-based models to describe various operations, groups, and subsidiary companies. The gross structure of the input-output relationships of the various divisions, groups, and subsidiaries is shown in Figure 6. Each major block in Figure 6 represents in itself a system of substantial size. Prior to the existence of the corporate system models, management's assessment of the financial effects of the interactions of interplant buying and selling and changing product mixes involved long time lags. The interactive computer system, however, greatly reduced the effort needed to evaluate alternate plans because the logic of the 22 models takes into account the complex financial flows between divisions and groups.

Inland Steel [2, 3]. While the Potlatch Forests example emphasizes the successive aggregation and consolidation of financial flows, the Inland Steel Company's example shown in Figure 7 focuses first on the basic production processes and finally consolidates the financial effects in terms of standard financial statements. Given the system models, Inland Steel Management can easily raise questions such as the following:

1. How much raw material is required to meet production forecasts?
2. What are the cost effects of various hot metal-to-scrap ratios and the resulting yields under various assumptions of raw material costs?
3. What are the capacity requirements for proposed levels of operation?

The management of Inland Steel used the system models in preparing contingency plans for 1971 when the company faced unusual uncertainties involving the possibility of a major automotive industry strike. The system models have also been used as a basis for its annual five-year planning cycle and for evaluating the profit sensitivity of a wide variety of input factors.

IMPLICATIONS OF THE SYSTEMS CONCEPT FOR THE MANAGER

A manager who puts the systems concept to work is rewarded initially by the development of a deeper understanding of the system he manages. By developing the structure of the interacting effects of system components and the various feedback control loops in the system he can see better which "handles" to twist in order to keep himself in control of the system he manages. Indeed, with a knowledge of the system structure, he can see how he might restructure the system in order to create the most effective feedback control mechanisms.

With the availability of large-scale system models such as Potlatch Forests and Inland Steel, a manager is better able to assess the effects of changes in one division component on another and on the organization as a whole. Furthermore, the manager of any one of the productive operations is better able to see how his unit fits into the whole and to understand the kinds of tradeoffs which are often made by higher level management which sometimes seemingly affects his unit adversely.

The basic systems concepts which we have discussed are applied again and again throughout the balance of the book. For example, feedback control processes are central in our discussion of automation in Chapter 7, man-machine systems in Chapter 11, the forecasting and inventory control systems of Chapter 14, the aggregate planning methods of Chapter 15 and the quality control concepts of Chapter 19. Input-output transformation processes are the basis for the entire set of chapters in Part 3 on the design of productive systems, and, in general, the kinds of tradeoffs which are required in the various decision problems throughout the book are a reflection of the systems concept.

Perhaps one of the most important contributions of systems thinking is the concept of suboptimization. Suboptimization often occurs when one views a problem narrowly. For example, one can construct mathematical formulas to determine the minimum cost (optimum) quantity of products or parts to manufacture at one time, which results in a supposedly optimum inventory level. If one broadens the definition of the system under study, however, and includes not just the inventory and reorder subsystem but the production and warehousing subsystems as well, he may find that the inventory connected costs are a measure of only part of the problem. If the product exhibits seasonal sales, the costs of changing production levels may be significant enough to warrant carrying extra inventories to smooth production and employment. In such a situation the minimum cost inventory model would be a suboptimal policy.

Organizational suboptimization often occurs when the production and distribution functions of an enterprise are operated as essentially two different businesses. The factory manager will try to minimize his costs independently as will the sales-distribution manager. The factory manager will be faced with minimizing production cost while the sales-distribution manager will be faced mainly with an inventory management, shipping, and customer service problem. Each suborganization attempting to optimize separately will likely result in a combined cost somewhat larger than if the attempt were made to optimize the combined system. The reasons are fairly obvious, since in minimizing the costs of inventories the sales function transmits directly to the factory most of the effects of sales fluctuations instead of absorbing these fluctuations through buffer inventories. Suboptimization is the result. By coordinating their efforts, however, it may be possible to achieve some balance between inventory costs and the costs of production fluctuation.

SUMMARY

Systems concepts and methods have great significance for the analysis and management of productive systems because of the complex interacting effects of the many elements in such systems. The mere fact that the word "system" is used to describe the nature of production situations is indicative.

Feedback systems are of greatest interest because they react to their own past behavior. Negative feedback systems are of particular interest in all managerial situations, since such systems provide the basis for managerial controls. The simplest subsystem module shown in Figure 2a provides the basis for constructing more complex networks.

One of the difficulties that arises in all managerial systems is that information feedback usually occurs with a time lag so that conditions may actually have changed by, the time the manager is aware of the problem. Also, the sensitivity of the system to control is important for the manager.

Very large-scale planning systems such as those illustrated for Potlatch Forests and Inland Steel provide a basis for planning and control that would be difficult or impossible to achieve without the power of systems concepts and computing.

KEY CONCEPTS

Feedback System.   The concept of a system that can be influenced by its own past behavior is extremely important for it forms the basis for constructing a system that is automatically adaptive to new and changing conditions. Depending on whether the feedback is positive or negative, the system is either unstable and grows or is stabilized and seeks a goal such as in control systems.

Time Lag Effects.   Invariably information feedback occurs with some time lag and the effect of the time lag is to make the system oscillate. The implications of this fact for the manager are significant, since by the time he receives information the actual situation could have changed. For example, if he reacts to an increase in retail sales recorded one month ago, he might increase employment and production levels at a time when sales in the field were actually decreasing.

Feedback Control.   The concepts of managerial control are based on the elements of a simple feedback control loop. In all such systems there is some sensing or measurement system that observes actual performance, and this performance is compared with desired standards. Some one or a control system interprets the difference and commands an effector to correct performance.

Suboptimization.   Suboptimization often occurs when one views a problem narrowly. In such circumstances possible interacting effects are discounted or ignored. One of the most important contributions of systems thinking leads to minimizing the possibility of suboptimization by broadening problem definition and taking into account the effects of all possible influences.

IMPORTANT TERMS

Numbers in parentheses indicate page numbers.

1. Control subsystems (59–60)
2. Delivery delay (56–58)
3. Effector (52)
4. Equipment pool (56, 57)

5. Feedback control (51–52)
6. Feedback system (51)
7. Feedback-time lag effects (53–55)
8. Labor pool (56, 57)
9. Large-scale system (61)
10. Materials and energy pool (56, 57)
11. Negative feedback (51)
12. Open system (51)
13. Operations function (55–57)
14. Positive feedback (51)
15. Processing delay (56, 57)
16. Sensing system (52)
17. Suboptimization (62–63)
18. System (50)

REVIEW QUESTIONS

Numbers in parentheses indicate page numbers.

1. What is a system? (50)
2. On observing an exhibit containing an automobile, a bus, a helicopter, a train, a motorcycle, and a bicycle, a systems analyst remarked, "It's an interesting collection of ways to get around, but it's no system!" What characteristic would have had to be present to describe the exhibit as a system? (50)
3. What are the values of the systems concept in operations management problems? (55)
4. If every system is a part of an even larger system, how can the concept be made useful and brought to bear on specific problems? (50, 55)
5. How do we separate and understand the difference between the system under study and the environment in which it operates? (51)
6. What is an open system? a closed or feedback system? What is the crucial distinction between the two kinds of systems? (51)
7. Distinguish between a negative and a positive feedback system. (51)
8. What are the elements which are a part of any feedback control loop? Describe these elements in a simple thermostatic control system for a home heating plant. (51–52)
9. Describe the dynamic effects of feedback control systems. What is the effect of the introduction of time lags into feedback control systems? (53–54)
10. Take some specific productive system such as a bank, supermarket, hospital, or manufacturing concern, and describe the nature of the operations function. Then place the operations function into context within the overall enterprise system such as was done in Figure 3 in the text. What general kinds of flows are of particular importance in the system you have defined? Is there waste in the system? How is the waste processed? Justify the system boundary which you have drawn in relation to the environment in which the system operates. Describe the broad feedback control loops that exist in enterprises for the control of the production aspect of the enterprise. Differentiate between day-to-day control of operations and optimum system control. (55–60)

11. How can the large8scale systems such as those described for Potlatch Forests and Inland Steel be of day-to-day value to managers? Of longer-range value? (61–62)

12. What is the meaning of suboptimization? How is it related to the systems concept? (62–63)

SELF-TEST TRUE-FALSE QUESTIONS

Numbers in parentheses indicate page numbers.

1. At its present state of development and application, the systems concept is most useful in helping us to gain insight into problems. (50)

2. Unfortunately, systems analysis is not useful for generating solutions to problems or evaluating their effects. (50)

3. A system is any collection of components or objects. (50)

4. When a set of components are organized into a system they produce a set of optimal outputs from given inputs. (50)

5. Invariably, every system can be thought of as a part of an even larger system. (50)

6. An open system observes and reacts to its own performance. (51)

7. A feedback system may be regarded as an open system when it involves positive feedback. (51)

8. Both open and feedback systems have interactions with their environment. (51)

9. Most of the feedback systems in managerial problems are of the negative feedback type where the object is to control a process. (51)

10. One of the amazing facts about a thermostatic control system is that it achieves its control without the usual elements in a feedback control loop. (51–52)

11. If the difference between actual and desired performance is fed back with no time lag, the effector commands the system to change settings immediately by the observed difference, and the system responds immediately, then the system would be completely responsive and presumably exhibit perfect control since any deviation is corrected immediately. (53–54)

12. The sensitivity of feedback control systems refers to the response in the output to a change in the input. (54)

13. If it takes substantial time for the feedback control system to respond and command an adjustment, and if the process itself is sluggish in response to changed control settings, then the output may exhibit oscillation. (54)

14. With the present capability of automatic measurement, data processing, and effector mechanisms, it is conceivable that day-to-day control can be completely automatic. (59)

15. It is conceivable that day-to-day production schedules might, in themselves, be far from optimum, but the longer range production programs might approach optimality. (59–60)
16. Suboptimization occurs when one is attempting to view the problem as a whole instead of taking a carefully defined, narrow definition of the problem. (62)
17. Organizational suboptimization often occurs when the production and distribution functions of an enterprise are operated as essentially two different businesses. (63)

REFERENCES

[1] Alcalay, J. A., and E. S. Buffa. "A Proposal for a General Model of a Production System." *International Journal of Production Research*, Mar. 1963.

[2] Buffa, E. S. *Operations Management: Problems and Models* (3rd ed.). John Wiley, New York, 1972. . .

[3] Boulden, J. B., and E. S. Buffa. "Corporate Models: On-Line, Real-Time Systems." *Harvard Business Review*, July-Aug. 1970.

[4] Forrester, J. *Principles of Systems*. Wright-Allen Press, Inc., Cambridge, Mass., 1968.

[5] Hare, V. C., Jr. *Systems Analysis: A Diagnostic Approach*. Harcourt, Brace, and World, Inc. New York, 1967.

[6] Johnson, R. A., F. E. Kast, and J. E. Rosenzweig. *The Theory and Management of Systems* (2nd ed.). McGraw-Hill Book Co., New York, 1967.

[7] McMillan, C., Jr., and R. F. Gonzalez. *Systems Analysis: A Computer Approach to Decision Models* (Rev. ed.). Richard D. Irwin, Homewood, Ill., 1968.

[8] Reisman, A., and E. S. Buffa. "A General Model for Production and Operations Systems." *Management Science*, 11 (1), Sept. 1964.

[9] Schoderbek, P. P. *Management Systems* (2nd ed.). John Wiley, New York, 1971.

PART 2
ANALYTICAL METHODS

CONTENTS

CHAPTER 4

ANALYTICAL METHODS IN PRODUCTION AND OPERATIONS MANAGEMENT

Perhaps the thing that distinguishes the production and operations management field at its present stage of development is the degree to which analytical methods have been applied. These analytical methods have been used both to establish a conceptual framework and to solve practical problems. Early methods of analysis represented graphic and schematic models of various aspects of a production system. Since World War II, however, there has been an increased use of more sophisticated techniques such as mathematical, statistical, and simulation models as well as the emphasis on systems and the systemic point of view, discussed in Chapter 3. This increased use of analytic and systemic techniques is the most important indication that production and operations management is well on the road to becoming an applied science.

Analytical methodology in production and operations management essentially follows the basic framework of scientific method and is based on the use of various kinds of models which represent some part of the system or subsystem under study. Our general discussion of models and their place in decision making in Chapter 2 is pertinent in this regard.

A FRAMEWORK FOR ANALYSIS

This book leans heavily on the analytical approach to production and operations management and focuses at various points on both new and traditional methods of analysis. Whether new or traditional, however, the basic framework for analysis follows a pattern. The important aspect of analysis is not whether the technique used is new or traditional but whether it is the best mode of analysis available for the nature of the problem and for the practical situation surrounding the problem. It is often true that the traditional technique may be the appropriate one for a particular situation even though new and more powerful approaches exist. This might be the case where the management of the organization is just emerging into an analytical frame of mind and wishes to proceed cautiously, or where the cost of applying the newer, more sophisticated technique is not warranted. As we shall see, it is also true that some traditional approaches to analysis have not been superseded and are therefore still dominant in certain types of problems. The following outline summarizes the process of analysis for production and operations management.

Define the System under Study. This step is perhaps the most important one in the analysis of any problem in any field because it sets the horizons for analysis. If the problem is defined narrowly, the final solution is likely to be limited in application and probably wrong under certain circumstances. Recall that this is referred to as a *suboptimum* solution. Suboptimization occurs, for example, if in attempting to determine a program for the production of a seasonal product, we establish the scope of the problem as being one of minimizing labor costs. Consider a program for production to be the number of units produced in each period during a planning span of time such as a year. The program resulting in such a situation could be one of level production throughout the year even though sales vary seasonally. The reason is that to change production levels as sales vary requires the hiring and layoff of part of the labor force so that additional costs result as compared to level production.

Figure 1 shows a production program where a seasonal sales requirement is to be met by a level production plan. A broader definition of the problem reveals, of course, that other costs may be involved such as the cost of carrying inventories to absorb fluctuations in sales level. The level production program is a suboptimum solution in this instance; a solution that considers both labor and inventory costs will specify a balance between these costs rather than minimizing either of them by ignoring the other. One guide to help define the problem is then to determine what factors or variables may have an influence on the behavior of the system under study.

In general, the broader the definition or scope of the problem, the less likely is it that suboptimization will occur. This broad definition is often referred to as the "system" viewpoint; that is, we attempt to view the problem in the context of the overall system rather than narrowly. In reference to the production programming problem just discussed, the system view of the problem would suggest that we include as part of the system under study the procurement of raw materials prior to actual production as well as the distribution of finished goods to the market, since

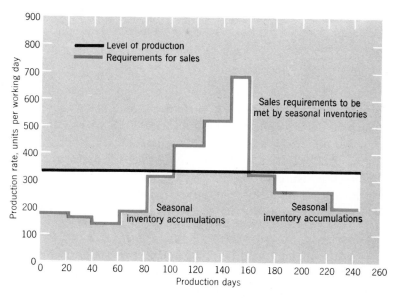

FIGURE 1.   Level production program for a product having seasonal sales requirements.

the nature of the production program can affect procurement and distribution costs. Also, we should consider other ways of absorbing fluctuations in sales level such as subcontracting part of the peak requirements. The broader system view changes the nature of the apparent best solution.

It often happens, however, that the ideal of the system viewpoint cannot be achieved, either because of time and effort limitations for a practical solution or because we are as yet incapable of handling the larger problems. This inevitably results when the scope of the problem is defined as being very large. Some of the new tools of analysis which we shall discuss, such as linear programming and large-scale system simulation, have helped to improve our capability to view problems broadly. Also, rapid data processing has made the solution of some kinds of large system problems feasible, although we could not even consider them as being practical problems only a decade ago.

In defining the system to be studied, it is often of value to develop graphic, schematic, and pictorial models of the system which may help in visualizing the problem. For complex systems, the development of block diagrams that represent flow, functions, interconnections, and interactions are often helpful in this regard. Figures 3 and 4 in Chapter 3, which diagram the flow aspects of generalized systems of production, are representative of schematic models.

Define a Measure of Effectiveness. In other words, establish criteria which measure the effectiveness of alternate courses of action. Some measures might be profits, contribution, total costs, incremental costs, machine down time, machine utilization, labor costs, labor utilization, number of units processed, and flow time. Measures of effectiveness for analysis of operational systems are commonly related to some direct or indirect measure of profit, cost, quality, service or delivery time. Ordinarily then, measures of effectiveness define what it is we wish to maximize or minimize.

Construct a Model Where E, the Effect, Can Be Expressed as a Function of the Variables That Define the System. Recall from our discussion in Chapter 2 that models are the means by which we forecast the performance of alternatives for the system under study. As we pointed out there, the validity of the model is determined by the accuracy with which it is capable of forecasting performance. In developing the model, we attempt to identify the controllable factors or variables, X_i, and those which are uncontrollable, Y_j, and attempt to formulate relationships between the measure of effectiveness E and the variables of the general form:

$$E = f(X_i, Y_j)$$

This expression merely says E, the measure of effectiveness, is a function of the controllable variables X_i and the uncontrollable variables Y_j. The specific relationships would have to be developed.

Controllable variables are those that may be manipulated pretty much at the will of management. In the production programming problem discussed previously, an example of a controllable variable is the program itself, that is, the number of units to be produced in each period. Uncontrollable variables are those that management cannot control, at least not within the limitations of the problem.

In the programming problem, consumer demand, wage rates, and inventory carrying costs are examples of uncontrollable variables. We might argue that management can influence these variables by advertising, labor negotiations, and so on. Nevertheless, management cannot change demand, wages, and carrying costs at will. In general, changes in all of these uncontrollable factors would be reflected in E, and management would respond by adjusting the production program to minimize E again. The new program would then be the best one, given the new values of the uncontrollable factors.

Generate Alternatives Based on Analysis.   Evaluate these alternatives through the model, using E as a measure of effectiveness. The objective of analysis is to form a basis for problem solution; however, we should beware of becoming enthralled with "the solution." Ordinarily there are good alternate courses of action, many of which may be nearly equivalent in terms of their effectiveness as measured by E. The model constructed should make it possible to generate alternative solutions which may be appraised by the criterion E as well as other nonquantifiable factors.

At this stage, various *hypotheses* for the best solution can be stated. The model forms a basis for measuring the effect of each of these and comparing results. Of course, the informal or formal statements of logical hypotheses to be tested may have been developed prior to this step and such hypotheses may well have been the basis for undertaking the study in the first place. As a matter of fact, a large fraction of problems leading to the use of analytical methods are recognized in this way. That is, someone suggests alternate policies or procedures, and these essentially become hypotheses that must stand the tests of analytical methodology.

For the example of the production program, several alternate schedules for meeting sales requirements could be calculated, as shown in Figure 2. Each of the three alternate plans shown involves a hypothesis about the most effective way to meet requirements, using normal and overtime capacity, subcontracting, and seasonal inventories. The effects on incremental costs of the three plans is rather startling as is shown in Table I. Plan 1, level production, has no extra labor turnover cost, overtime premium, or subcontracting cost; however, the cost of carrying seasonal inventory to meet the high peak of sales in the summer is very large. Plan 2 involves some fluctuation in production level, but not so much that plant capacity with overtime work is exceeded. The result is a somewhat smaller seasonal inventory cost than for Plan 1 and a total incremental cost which is $20,000 per year less than Plan 1. Plan 3 tends to follow the sales requirement curve more closely and this involves considerable hiring and laying off of labor. Also, because of limitations of plant capacity, even with the use of overtime capacity, it is necessary to resort to subcontracting to meet the peak requirements. Nevertheless, the tremendous reduction in inventory cost makes Plan 3

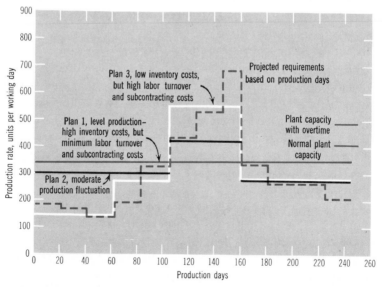

FIGURE 2.   Comparison of three production programs that meet requirements.

TABLE I. Comparative Incremental Costs for Three Production Programs

	Plan 1	Plan 2	Plan 3
Inventory Requirements, units	8,000	6,885	3,691
Peak capacity required: (Plan 1 = 100)	100	126	165
Incremental costs:			
Seasonal stock cost*	$318,000	$239,000	$ 47,300
Labor turnover cost†	0	48,000	104,000
Overtime premium‡	0	11,000	44,000
Subcontracting cost**	0	0	57,750
	$318,000	$298,000	$253,050

*Inventory carrying cost computed at $60 per unit per year.
†A change in production rate at 20 units per day requires the employment or separation of 40 men at a cost of hiring and training an employee of $200.
‡Units produced at overtime labor rates cost $10 per unit extra.
**Units produced by subcontractors cost $15 per unit extra.

the cheapest of the three plans. There are obviously other possible programs for which the total incremental costs could have been computed. For example, using a computer search programming model, we could determine a program that would approximate the minimum possible or optimum cost for the items of cost considered.

Weigh and Decide. Weight and decide what course of action to take based on a balancing of quantitative analysis and the nonquantitative factors in the situation. It might seem on the surface that the model should make this step unnecessary. After all, the measure of effectiveness is supposed to measure the effect of alternate courses of action. But does it do this completely? Usually, measures of effectiveness are not capable of reflecting all aspects of performance. There will be nonquantitative factors which must be given weight.

In the production programming example, one factor which might be given heavy weight in today's economy would be the amount of hiring and laying off to be tolerated. The organization has a social responsibility and also feels the pressure of labor, public, and community reactions. The decision maker must balance off the $65,000 per year advantage of Plan 3 over Plan 1 against the disadvantage of the labor turnover induced by Plan 3. Compared to Plan 2, which involves more moderate swings in production level, Plan 3 has an economic advantage of $45,000 per year. In addition, Plan 3 involves considerable subcontracting to meet peak sales requirements. Can quality levels be held if we work through a subcontractor? Is it worth the difference to use either Plan 1 or 2 in order to maintain closer in-house control over quality?

The generation and evaluation of alternatives are of extreme importance in the overall process because they give flexibility to the decision maker. Quite often, alternate solutions may have differences in effectiveness as measured by E which are not large, but one alternative may deal with a nonquantitative factor in a more satisfactory way. One great trap in quantitative analysis is the siren song of the "optimal solution." People are often drawn to mathematically provable optimal solutions, but we must remember that such solutions face the often severe limitations of the definition of the measure of effectiveness. If E is really all inclusive for a given situation, then judgment may not need to enter, but this is seldom the case. In the really large-scale systems with which we may deal, it is often impractical to think in terms of optimality because the system is so complex. In these situations we must think in terms of improving existing conditions rather than in terms of optimizing the overall system.

The overall framework for analysis is roughly parallel to the steps shown in Figure 3, regardless of the nature of the problem or the exact kind of analytical model used. The steps are not necessarily independent of each other in the actual solution of problems.

In Parts 3 and 4 of this book, which deal with some of the major problems that occur within the production and operations management field, we shall call attention to applications of various analytical techniques discussed generally here. These applications occur both for the analysis of problems as well as for synthesis, that is, the design of overall systems.

KINDS OF ANALYTICAL METHODS

The various kinds of models which have been shown to have applicability in one or more kinds of typical problems arising in production or operational systems are shown in Figure 3. This figure shows the overall framework for the analysis we have been discussing. They are not simply standardized models which can be "plugged" in to obtain answers; rather they are fairly general models which, when adapted to

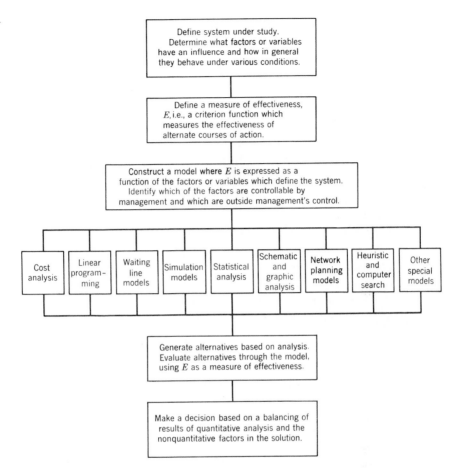

FIGURE 3.   Framework for the analysis of operational systems.

local conditions, fit a surprisingly large number of cases. We shall discuss the general characteristics and usefulness of each later in this section.

Cost Analysis

Cost analysis is still perhaps the most common of analysis methods. It takes many forms and is based on a knowledge of the behavior of cost factors. It is not simply a drawing together of cost information from accounting data because many of the accounting data have a significance only within the accounting system. Our interest is in the actual behavior of pertinent costs under the alternatives considered. *Breakeven analysis* makes use of the differences in behavior of certain costs as volume of operation varies. Breakeven analysis is useful in helping to establish a proper volume of operation, to diagnose problems, and to evaluate the appropriateness of a production process.

One of the most valuable simple techniques of analysis, *incremental cost analysis*, deals with only those costs affected by the alternate policies or actions considered. The problem of alternate production programs discussed previously in this section is an example of incremental cost analysis. Recall that we did not atempt to evaluate the alternative costs by calculating total operating costs with alternate plans. This approach would have been tedious and time consuming. Instead, we determined the levels of just those costs affected by the alternate programs, that is, inventory costs, labor turnover costs, overtime premium, and extra subcontracting costs. Incremental cost concepts are useful in virtually all areas of analysis of operational systems and occur commonly in the formal mathematical models of analysis such as linear programming and waiting line analysis as well. Both breakeven analysis and incremental cost analysis are discussed in greater detail in Chapter 5.

Another kind of cost problem occurs when capital assets are considered in the alternatives generated. The nature of cost behavior is somewhat different under these circumstances and requires special treatment. The question of when to replace a capital asset is a related problem. Since almost all production systems depend heavily on the use of capital equipment, this important topic is covered in Chapter 6.

Linear Programming

Linear programming is representative of the new methodologies that come to us from mathematics and economics. The field of application of this relatively new and very important general model is in dealing with the problems of allocating the scarce resources of an organization.

Distribution Methods.   Suppose, for example, that we face a distribution problem where production of a product takes place in four factories located one each in the East, West, South, and Midwest. The market is nationwide and there are ten distribution points scattered throughout the country from which the product is shipped to the local market. Looking at just the network from factories to distribution warehouses, what is the most economical distribution system? That is, which factories should ship to which distribution warehouses and what quantities in order to minimize shipping costs? The solution is not a simple or obvious one because it is not just a matter of finding the cheapest shipping routes. The reason is that output at each of the factories is limited and the demand at each of the ten distribution warehouses is set by the market. The problem is therefore to find the most economical combination of shipments; the number of possible combinations is tremendous.

To illustrate the nature of the problem, let us take a slightly simpler but parallel situation to the distribution problem just discussed. Suppose that we have three factories located at Atlanta, Chicago, and Detroit, and that there are five distribution warehouses at Buffalo, Cincinnati, Des Moines, Milwaukee, and New York City. Figure 4 shows the general geographic relationships. Let us suppose that the capacity of each factory and the district demand at each warehouse are as shown in the far-right column

FIGURE 4.   Geographical locations of factories and distribution points.

TABLE II. Distribution Matrix for Three Factories and Five Distribution Warehouses						
To From	Buffalo	Cincinnati	Des Moines	Milwaukee	New York City	Factory capacity (cases) ↓
Atlanta	50	42	49	51	55	200
Chicago	45	44	45	37	53	150
Detroit	42	43	47	42	51	180
Warehouse demand (cases) →	70	90	120	50	200	530

and bottom row, respectively, of Table II. Also, the numbers in the small boxes show the shipping cost in dollars between all combinations of factories and warehouses. The shipping cost must be directly proportional to the number of units shipped or, in mathematical language,

TABLE III. Optimum Allocation of Capacity to Demand						
To From	Buffalo	Cincinnati	Des Moines	Milwaukee	New York City	Factory capacity (cases)
Atlanta		42 90	49 20	51	55 90	200
Chicago	45	44 100	45	37 50	53	150
Detroit	42 70	43	47	42	51 110	180
Warehouse demand (cases)	70	90	120	50	200	530

Total shipping cost:

Detroit–Buffalo, 70 × 42 = $2,940
Atlanta–Cincinnati, 90 × 42 =   3,780
Atlanta–Des Moines, 20 × 49 =   980
Chicago–Des Moines, 100 × 45 =   4,500
Chicago–Milwaukee, 50 × 37 =   1,850
Atlanta–New York City, 90 × 55 =   4,950
Detroit–New York City, 110 × 51 =   5,610
$24,610

be expressible by linear equations. Table II is called a distribution matrix.

The best possible pattern of shipments is that shown in Table III where the circled numbers indicate the number of units shipped. The solution was established by distribution methods of linear programming. There are some interesting things about the solution. First, note that all conditions of supply and demand can be satisfied with just seven shipments—one less than the sum of the number of origins (factories) plus destinations (warehouses). This is always true; a solution can always be determined which has no more than this number of shipments. Sometimes a solution can be obtained with fewer shipments. Second, note in Table III that the best solution does not necessarily involve only the lowest cost routes. For example, almost half of the shipments to New York City come by way of the most expensive shipment route in the entire matrix, yet there is no other combination of shipments which reduces the total shipping cost below the minimum cost of $24,610.

The example is, of course, a very simple problem, and we could establish a fairly good solution without the use of linear programming. By simply using common sense, we could assign shipments to the lower cost routes as far as possible, using other routes to balance off the supply and demand constraints. This is not so simply done with a problem of practical size, however. If the matrix size is increased to only 5 × 10, the problem becomes baffling. Without linear programming, we then do not know whether the solution we have developed is optimum or not, or whether it is even very good at all. With linear programming the best solution can be obtained directly, and we can prove that it is the best possible. Since there are literally thousands of possible solutions, linear programming has really accomplished something worthwhile.

Simplex Methods.   While some allocation problems can be handled in the format of the distribution methods just discussed, others require the more general simplex model. Problems to determine the optimal mix of products to produce are often approached by simplex methods of linear programming, and we shall use such a problem as an example. Suppose that an electrical equipment manufacturer makes two models of an item of test equipment and is attempting to decide how many units of each model to make for next month. The market is not the limiting factor; thus the manufacturers can sell any quantity of either model that they can produce within the limits of their capacity. Therefore, they wish to plan a mix of the two products which will maximize the total profit from the two. The profit contribution of Model 1 is $50 per unit and is $45 per unit for Model 2.

The two units are manufactured with the same facilities involving three departments: Main Frame, Electrical Wiring, and Assembly. Assuming that the entire department capacities were used for Model 1, the capacity limits would be:

	Capacity for Model 1, Units per Month
Main Frame	400
Electrical Wiring	500
Assembly	600

On the other hand, if all capacity were turned over to Model 2, the capacity limits would be:

	Capacity for Model 2, Units per Month
Main Frame	533
Electrical Wiring	400
Assembly	800

We can visualize these capacity limits best by plotting them on a graph such as Figure 5. The axes of the graph are the numbers of units produced of the two different models. First, let us look at the limiting capacity of the Main Frame Department for the two models. If all capacity is turned over to Model 1, 400 Model 1 units can be produced (point *a* in Figure 5), and if all capacity is turned over to Model 2, 533 Model 2 units can be produced (point *b* in Figure 5), as noted before. The straight line which connects points *a* and *b* represents Main Frame Department capacities for combinations of the two models. Combinations on or below the line are all feasible, but any point falling above the line exceeds Main Frame Department capacity. Points below the line are feasible but do not use all available capacity.

Similarly, the limiting capacities of the Electrical Wiring Department for the two products are represented by points *c* and *d* and the connecting straight line represents Electrical Wiring Department capacity for

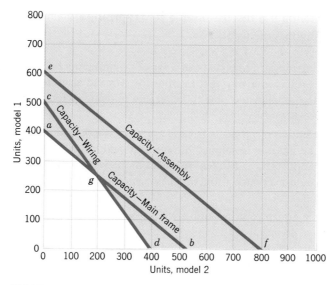

FIGURE 5.   Capacities of three departments to produce two models of test equipment.

combinations of the two models. Finally, the line *ef* represents the Assembly Department capacity in a similar way. Note that the line for Assembly Department capacity is entirely in the shaded portion of the graph and so places no limits on the production of the two models. The Main Frame and Wiring Departments, however, place limits on the production program which can be achieved and the maximum profit contribution occurs at a production program represented by point *g*. Point *g* represents a production program of 250 units of Model 1 and 200 units of Model 2, or a profit contribution of $50 \times 250 + 45 \times 200 = \$21,500$. There is no production program within the limits of the problem which will exceed the contribution given by this allocation of capacity to the two products. Simplex methods of linear programming can yield optimum product mix programs of this general type for extremely complex problems where the answer is not at all obvious.

With a little thought and projection, we can see that there are a large number of practical problems which are special cases of the general allocation problem. Some may be solved by distribution methods in the general format of the distribution problem discussed previously. Others require the use of the simplex method of solution and still others require other kinds of mathematical programming methods.

The following is a discussion of a few typical problems where linear programming may be useful:

1. Distribution of products from a set of origin points to a number of destinations in a way that satisfies the demand at each destination and the supplies available at the origins, minimizing total transportation costs.

2. Distribution of products from factories to warehouses, similar to 1, but minimizing combined production and distribution costs. If the products have different revenues in the various marketing areas, we could maximize a function of revenue minus production-distribution costs.

3. Multiple-plant location studies where common products are produced with a decentralized complex of plants. Here we wish to evaluate various alternate locations for the construction of a new plant. Each different location considered produces a different allocation matrix of product from the factories to the distribution points because of differing production-distribution costs. The best new location is the one that minimizes total production-distribution costs for the entire system; this, of course, is not necessarily the location that seems to have the lowest production costs.

4. Locational dynamics for multiple plants. Here the problem is somewhat similar to 3 but the question is which plants to operate at what levels for a given total demand. Since additional capacity at each location can normally be obtained through overtime, and since certain overhead costs can be saved by shutting down a plant, there are conditions when total costs are minimized by shutting down a plant and supplying the total demand from the other plants, even though overtime costs are incurred. The plant to be shut down is not necessarily the high production cost plant—this depends on the relative importance of production and distribution costs.

5. Redistribution of empty freight cars from their existing locations to points where they are needed in a way that minimizes transportation costs.

6. Allocation of limited raw materials used in a variety of products so that total profit is maximized, meeting market demands insofar as is possible.

7. Allocation of production facilities when alternate routings are available. Given the unit machine time for the alternate machine routes, total hours available on the different machine classes, requirements for the number of each product, and unit revenue for each product, linear programming can give a solution that maximizes some profit

function, minimizes incremental costs, or meets some other management objective.

8. Blending problems. For example, a paint manufacturer may need to prepare paint vehicles that are a blend of several constituents. The constituents, such as oil and thinner, are available in limited quantity and in commercial blends of fixed proportions. Costs per gallon of the various possible raw materials are known. The problem is to determine the amount of each raw material so that required amounts for the new blends are obtained at minimum cost. Another similar problem is the blending of animal feed to provide certain minimum nutrient values at minimum cost.

9. Maximizing material utilization. Many times different stock sizes must be stamped or cut from standard raw material sizes. The problem is to determine the combination of cuts that will meet requirements for the amounts of different sizes with a minimum trim loss.

10. Developing a program for production when demand is seasonal. Here we are attempting to allocate available capacity to various production periods for the products to be produced in such a way that requirements for all products are met, and combined incremental inventory and production costs are minimized. The incremental production costs may include overtime premium, turnover costs, and extra subcontracting costs.

11. Product mix problems. Here we have a general class of problems of considerable interest. If we have production facilities that can be used to produce several different items which may have different costs, revenues, and market demands, we wish to know how best to allocate the available capacity to various products within the limitations of market demand.

12. Long-range planning. The general capacity planning problem has been treated as being met by ownership, leases, or short-term contracts. A model cast in a linear programming framework may help in answering questions such as: (a) the effect of a given demand forecast on capacity plans, (b) the effect of changes in ownership cost, (c) the effect of changes in the costs of leased capacity, and (d) the sensitivity to forecast error of various decisions and costs.

Waiting Line or Queuing Models

Many production problems are related in some way to the build-up of waiting lines. In these types of problems, we have men, parts, or machines that need some sort of service at random time intervals. The activity required to service them may take a variable amount of time. Under certain conditions of arrival rates and servicing rates, a waiting line builds up. Waiting line theory provides a means of forecasting the *probable length* of the waiting line and the *probable delay or waiting time*, as well as other important data. Knowledge of these facts makes possible more intelligent decisions for questions of the following types.

1.　How many men are needed to service a tool crib? The tool crib attendant checks out special tools to machinists and other workmen. If the number of attendants is small, they will be very busy, but a waiting line of high-paid machinists will build up. If the number of attendants is large, they will be idle much of the time, but the average waiting line will be small. A measure of effectiveness, E, is then the combined cost of waiting time for the attendants and the machinists. A solution indicates the number of attendants required for minimum total waiting time cost. Waiting line theory can provide the critical data required for a solution.

2.　How long should a conveyor be between two stations on an assembly line? If we assume that items are not rigidly fixed to the conveyor, the length depends on the probable maximum bank that will build up between the two stations. The first station determines the arrival rate of parts. The second station determines the rate at which parts are processed and passed on. Waiting line theory can determine the probable maximum bank which, in turn, determines the length of conveyor needed to accommodate the maximum expected in-process inventory at that point.

3.　How many automatic machines should one man operate? Where the machines need service, such as setup, loading, and adjusting, at random intervals, as is true with automatic looms, the optimal assignment depends on a balance between the loss of productive time from the machines and the idle time of the operator when no machines need service.

An Example

Let us take as an example the situation of the tool crib where mechanics come to obtain special tools. The attendant checks out the tool to the mechanic in exchange for a "tool check" with the mechanic's name or number on it. We assume that the mechanics arrive at random times at an average rate of 12 per hour or 1 each 5 minutes. The attendant can service the mechanics in 3 minutes and initially we shall assume that this service time is constant for all mechanics. Table IV shows a record of the servicing of 15 mechanics. The average interval between arrivals is slightly less than 5 minutes for this sample. We see that the attendant had 32 minutes of idle time and the various mechanics waited a total of 39 minutes.

Let us see what happens if the service time is increased from 3 to 4 minutes. We assume the same schedule of arrivals and Table V results. The result is predictable. The attendant is busier now, as evidenced by the smaller idle time, but the waiting time of the mechanics is almost twice as large as before. We see immediately that the waiting time and the length of the waiting line can increase dramatically by such a change. When the average rate of arrival equals the rate at which the mechanics can be served, theoretically the length of the waiting line will increase and become infinitely long.

Now let us introduce random service times, using the same arrival schedule of the mechanics. This makes the problem a fairly realistic one, since the time required to service a mechanic should vary depending on the number of tools the mechanic needs and the size, weight, and location of the tool or tools. Table VI is a record of such a situation where the mechanics arrive at random

TABLE IV.   Random Arrival Time of Mechanics, Service Time Constant at 3 Minutes

Arrival Time of Mechanics	Service Begins at	Service Ends at	Idle Time of Attendant*	Wating Time of Mechanics†	Length of Line, Excluding Mechanic Being Serviced
10:00	10:00	10:03	0	0	0
10:09	10:09	10:12	6	0	0
10:13	10:13	10:16	1	0	0
10:19	10:19	10:22	3	0	0
10:34	10:34	10:37	12	0	0
10:36	10:37	10:40	0	1	1
10:37	10:40	10:43	0	3	1
10:38	10:43	10:46	0	5	2
10:39	10:46	10:49	0	7	3
10:42	10:49	10:52	0	7	3
11:02	11:02	11:05	10	0	0
11:03	11:05	11:08	0	2	1
11:05	11:08	11:11	0	3	1
11:05	11:11	11:14	0	6	2
11:09	11:14	11:17	0	5	2

*Attendants' idle time = 32 minutes.
†Mechanics' waiting time = 39 minutes.

TABLE V.   Random Arrival Time of Mechanics, Service Time Constant at 4 Minutes

Arrival Time of Mechanics	Service Begins at	Service Ends at	Idle Time of Attendant*	Wating Time of Mechanics†	Length of Line, Exclud- ing Mechanic Being Serviced
10:00	10:00	10:04	0	0	0
10:09	10:09	10:13	5	0	0
10:13	10:13	10:17	0	0	0
10:19	10:19	10:23	2	0	0
10:34	10:34	10:38	11	0	0
10:36	10:38	10:42	0	2	1
10:37	10:42	10:46	0	5	2
10:38	10:46	10:50	0	8	2
10:39	10:50	10:54	0	11	3
10:42	10:54	10:58	0	12	3
11:02	11:02	11:06	4	0	0
11:03	11:06	11:10	0	3	1
11:05	11:10	11:14	0	5	2
11:05	11:14	11:18	0	9	3
11:09	11:18	11:22	0	9	2

*Attendants' idle time = 22 minutes.
†Mechanics' waiting time = 64 minutes.

times and the service times vary randomly, averaging 3.07 minutes for the sample given. For a particular sample, the attendant's idle time and the mechanics' waiting time will depend on how well the arrivals of the mechanics match up with the longer and shorter service times. If several mechanics arrive almost simultaneously with requests requiring long service times, their waiting time will be relatively long while the attendant is continuously busy. If the long service time requests are distributed in a particular sample, their effect on the mechanics' waiting time will be smaller. Waiting line theory can forecast the *probable* waiting time and the *probable* length of the line, so management can decide what is the optimum allocation of personnel and equipment to minimize incremental costs. To do this, we must know the nature of the distributions of arrivals and of service times.

From Table VI, let us make some typical calculations, recognizing that the sample is probably too small for decision-making purposes. If the attendant is paid $2.00 per hour, then the cost of the attendant's idle time is

$$\tfrac{26}{60} \times \$2.00 = \$0.87$$

for the sample of 72 minutes, or

$$\tfrac{480}{72} \times \$0.87 = \$5.80$$

per day. If the mechanics' wages average \$3.50 per hour, the cost of their idle time is

$$\tfrac{56}{60} \times 3.50 = \$3.27$$

for the sample, or

$$\tfrac{480}{72} \times 3.27 = \$21.80$$

per day. The total cost of idle and waiting time is \$5.80 + \$21.80 = \$27.60 per day.

The question now is: Would it be economical to add a second attendant? If the second attendant were added, mechanics' waiting time would be reduced, but the total attendant's idle time would be increased. If the net effect on the cost of the combined idle plus waiting time is negative, the second attendant would be justified.

TABLE VI.   Random Arrival Time of Mechanics and Random Service Times

Arrival Time of Mechanics	Service Begins at	Service Ends at	Idle Time of Attendant*	Waiting Time of Mechanics†	Length of Line, Excluding Mechanic Being Serviced
10:00	10:00	10:01	0	0	0
10:09	10:09	10:14	8	0	0
10:13	10:14	10:15	0	1	1
10:19	10:19	10:22	4	0	0
10:34	10:34	10:40	12	0	0
10:36	10:40	10:44	0	4	1
10:37	10:44	10:51	0	7	2
10:38	10:51	10:53	0	13	3
10:39	10:53	10:57	0	14	4
10:42	10:57	11:02	0	15	4
11:02	11:02	11:03	0	0	0
11:03	11:03	11:04	0	0	0
11:05	11:05	11:07	1	0	0
11:05	11:07	11:08	0	2	1
11:09	11:09	11:12	1	0	0

*Attendants' idle time = 26 minutes.
†Mechanics' waiting time = 56 minutes.

Analytical Solutions for Waiting Line Problems.   In Tables IV, V, and VI, we have simulated simple waiting line problems. In cases where the distributions of arrivals and of service times fit certain standard mathematical distributions, equations have been developed which give directly the items of data in which we are interested such as the average length of the waiting line, average waiting time, and average number of units in the system. The important restrictions are the distributions. If the actual distributions of arrivals and service times fit the standard mathematical distributions fairly well, very little work is required to determine a solution. On the other hand, if the fit is not good, a great amount of work could be needed to develop a mathematical solution. In such instances, simulation methods can be used to develop a solution, regardless of the nature of the actual distributions. These methods are discussed later in the chapter.

Poisson Arrivals.   The mathematical function known as the Poisson distribution is commonly used to describe arrival rates. Figure 6 shows a Poisson distribution for arrival rates averaging 12 per hour. The simulated examples which we have been using had arrival rates that were based on this distribution. If the average arrival rate were 12 per hour and the service rate were constant at 20 per hour (3 minutes per mechanic served), as in our first simulated example (Table IV), mathematical solutions would give directly:

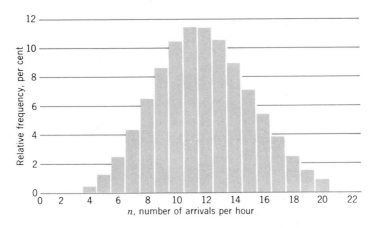

FIGURE 6.   Poisson distribution of arrival rates averaging 12 per hour.

Average length of waiting line = 0.45 men in line excluding mechanic
being served

Average waiting time   = 0.0375 hour/man or 2.25 minutes/man
(See Appendix B, Equations 1 and 2.)

Our limited sample gave an average line length of 0.50 men and an average waiting time of $\frac{39}{15}$ = 2.6 minutes per man. Had our sample been larger in the simulated example, we would have approached the answers given by the formulas more closely.

We mentioned earlier that, theoretically, when the mean arrival and service rates were equal, the waiting line length and, therefore, the waiting time became infinitely long. We say that this is true only theoretically, because in a practical situation several things may happen to prevent it. If people are the units involved in the waiting line, new arrivals are apt to be discouraged by an excessively long line and leave. Also, where people are involved, working hours limit the line length since it falls to zero when the work day is over. Finally, the people performing the services tend to react to the build-up of a waiting line by speeding up the rate of service. Where the units requiring service are parts or perhaps machines, some of these compensating effects may not take place.

Poisson Arrival Rates and Service Rates. The most common analytical model used assumes that both arrival rates and service rates are approximated by the Poisson distribution. These distributions seem to be good approximations for some situations, as in maintenance problems. Where these assumptions apply, the formulas are available for use. The data in Table VI were drawn from Poisson distributions in which the average arrival rate was 12 per hour and the average service rate was 20 per hour. The figures for line length, etc., based on the analytical solutions, would be:

Average length of waiting line   = 0.9 men

Average number in line, including
   the one being serviced   = 1.5 men

Average waiting time of an arrival = 0.075 hour
                                                        = 4.5 minutes

Average time which an arrival
   spends in the system   =0.125 hour
                                                  =7.5 minutes

(See Appendix B, Equations 3, 4, 5, and 6.)

The data computed from the small sample approximate these figures, and would approach them more closely for a larger sample.

Simulation Models

Simulation of production management problems is a rapidly growing technique. Although the fundamental ideas behind simulation can stand alone, its rapid growth actually has been paced by the high-speed electronic computer, because the arithmetic work required for practical problems is ordinarily too great for hand computation. This approach to problems sets up a simulated experiment and then carries through the experiment completely on paper (or in a computer) to see the effect of the variables of interest on the measure of effectiveness, E, which has been chosen. Simulation models follow a conceptual structure similar to that discussed under "A Framework for Analysis," except that the model may be empirical. Also, the simulation model does not produce an optimum answer as with some mathematical models. Comparisons between alternatives can be made by means of the simulation model, but the analyst must set up the alternatives himself. It is a systematic trial-and-error method for solving complex problems.

Where is simulation useful? Examples might be: (a) waiting line problems where standard distributions do not approximate actual distributions for arrival and processing rates or (b) complex waiting line problems with each station having several channels, or with stations in tandem, such as on a production line. On a large scale, this technique may be used to simulate the entire production operation. Here lies the great future of simulation.

Imagine the power of such a tool for the decision maker faced constantly with a legion of alternatives regarding work scheduling, equipment, layout, methods, inventory policies, changes of work load, etc. His basic objectives are clear. He wishes to make decisions that will maximize return on investment or minimize costs—if only he could see clearly and quickly the effect of the various alternatives he faces without waiting to see how they will work out in practice. For the decision maker, the ideal situation is to be able to try out an idea without first risking or committing company funds; with a simulation model and a computer, he can try out dozens of alternatives. Also, he can learn a great deal about the interdependence of the variables in the complex system. For example, he may observe the effect of a change in inventory policy on plant capacity and labor cost. In this way he can learn to make many decisions jointly instead of separately and thereby avoid costly mistakes of suboptimization. Simulation, with the aid of high-speed computers, ultimately makes available an experimental laboratory to production management personnel.

Simulated Sampling.   The sampling method, known generally as Monte Carlo, is a simulation procedure of considerable value. In the last section under waiting line theory, we spoke of distributions that did not fit the standard ones for which the theory had been worked out, and of complex waiting line situations where the mathematical complexity becomes very great. The required data can be built up through simulation of the conditions of the problem.

Let us assume that a product is being assembled by a two-station assembly line. There is one operator at each of the two stations. Operation A is the first of the two operations. The operator completes approximately the first half of the assembly and then sets the half-completed assembly on a section of conveyor where it rolls down to operation B. It takes a constant time of 0.10 minute for the part to roll down the conveyor section and be available to operator B. Operator B then completes the assembly. The average time for operation A is 0.52 minute per assembly and the average time for operation B is 0.48 minute per assembly. The simple setup is shown in Figure 7. We wish to determine the average inventory of assemblies that we may expect (average length of the waiting line of assemblies) and the average output of the assembly line. This may be done by simulated sampling as follows:

1. The distributions of assembly time for operations A and B must be known or procured. For example, these are represented by Figures 8 and 9. A study was taken for both operations and the two frequency

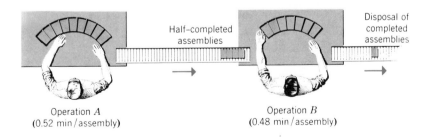

Operation A
(0.52 min/assembly)

Operation B
(0.48 min/assembly)

FIGURE 7.   Layout of two-station assembly line.

distributions resulted. For Figure 8 the value 0.25 minute occurred three times, 0.30 occurred twice, etc. The two distributions do not necessarily fit standard mathematical distributions but this is not important.

2. Convert the frequency distributions to cumulative probability distributions. This is done in Figures 10 and 11. It is done by summing the frequencies that are less than or equal to each performance time and plotting them. The cumulative frequencies are then converted to percents by assigning the number 100 to the maximum value. As an example, let us take Figure 8 and convert it to the cumulative distribution of Figure 10. Beginning at the lowest value for performance time, 0.25 minute, there were 3 observations. Three is plotted on the cumulative chart for the time 0.25 minute. For the performance time, 0.30 minute, there were 2 observations, but there were 5 observations that measured 0.30 minute or less, so the value (5) is plotted for 0.30 minute. For the performance time, 0.35 minute, there were 10 observations recorded, but there were 15 observations that measured 0.35 minute or less. Figure 10 was constructed from Figure 8 by proceeding in this way. When the cumulative frequency distribution was completed, a cumulative per cent scale was constructed on the right of Figure 10 by assigning the number 100 to the maximum value, 167, and dividing the resulting scale into equal parts. This results in a cumulative probability distribution. From Figure 10 we can say

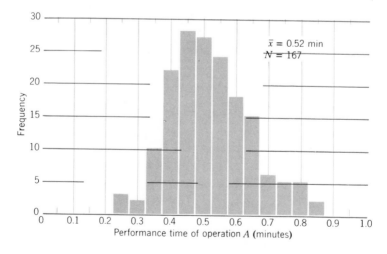

FIGURE 8. Distribution of performance times for operation A.

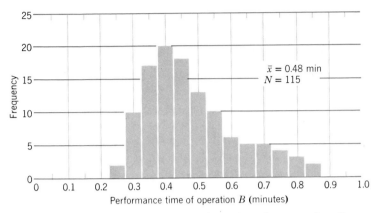

FIGURE 9.   Distribution of performance times for operation *B*.

that 100 per cent of the time values were 0.85 minute or less, 55.1 per cent were 0.50 minute or less, etc.

3. Sample at random from the cumulative distributions to determine specific performance times to use in simulating the operation of the assembly line. We do this by selecting numbers between 0 and 100 at

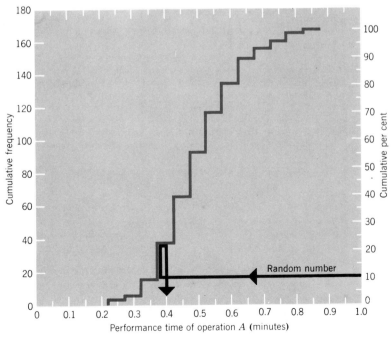

FIGURE 10.   Cumulative distribution of performance times for operation *A*.

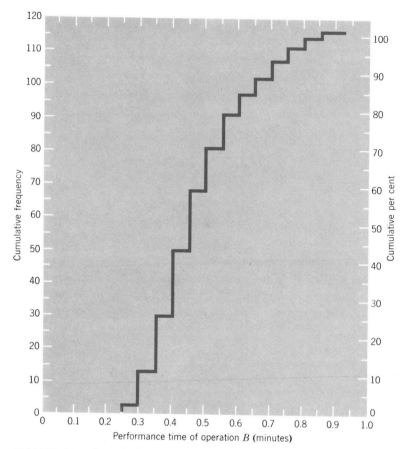

FIGURE 11. Cumulative distribution of performance times for operation *B*.

random (representing probabilities or per cents). The random numbers could be selected by any random process, such as drawing numbered chips from a box. The easiest way is to use a table of random numbers such as the one in Appendix A, Table IV.

The random numbers are used to enter the cumulative distributions in order to obtain time values. In the example shown in Figure 10, the random number 10 is used. A horizontal line is projected until it intersects the distribution curve; a vertical line projected to the horizontal axis gives the midpoint time value associated with the intersected point on the distribution curve, which happens to be 0.40 minute for the random number 10. Now we can see the purpose behind the conversion of the original distribution to a cumulative distribution. Only one time value can now be associated with a given random number. In the original distribution, two values would result because of the bell shape of the curve.

Sampling from the cumulative distribution in this way gives time values in random order which will occur in proportion to the original distribution, just as if assemblies were actually being produced. Table VII gives a sample of 20 time values determined in this way from the two distributions.

4. Simulate the actual operation of the assembly line. This is done in Table VIII which, of course, is very similar to the examples of waiting

TABLE VII.   Simulated Sample of 20 Performance Time Values for Operations *A* and *B*

	Operation *A*		Operation *B*
Random Number	Performance Time from Figure 10	Random Number	Performance Time from Figure 11
10	0.40	79	0.60
22	0.40	69	0.50
24	0.45	33	0.40
42	0.50	52	0.45
37	0.45	13	0.35
77	0.60	16	0.35
99	0.85	19	0.35
96	0.75	4	0.30
89	0.65	14	0.35
85	0.65	6	0.30
28	0.45	30	0.40
63	0.55	25	0.35
9	0.40	38	0.40
10	0.40	0	0.25
7	0.35	92	0.70
51	0.50	82	0.60
2	0.30	20	0.35
1	0.25	40	0.40
52	0.50	44	0.45
7	0.35	25	0.35
Totals	9.75		8.20

TABLE VIII.   Simulated Operation of the Two-Station Assembly Line When Operation *A* Precedes Operation *B*

Assemblies Available for Operation *B* at	Operation *B* Begins at	Operation *B* Ends at	Idle Time in Operation *B*	Waiting Time of Assemblies	Number of Parts in Line, Excluding Assembly Being Processed in Operation *B*
0.00	0.00	0.60	0	0	0
0.40	0.60	1.10	0	0.20	1
0.85	1.10	1.50	0	0.25	1
1.35	1.50	1.95	0	0.15	1
1.80	1.95	2.30	0	0.15	1
2.40	2.40	2.75	0.10	0	0
3.25	3.25	3.60	0.50	0	0
4.00	4.00	4.30	0.40	0	0
4.65	4.65	5.00	0.35	0	0
5.30	5.30	5.60	0.30	0	0
5.75	5.75	6.15	0.15	0	0
6.30	6.30	6.65	0.15	0	0
6.70	6.70	7.10	0.05	0	0
7.10	7.10	7.35	0	0	0
7.45	7.45	8.15	0.10	0	0
7.95	8.15	8.75	0	0.20	1
8.25	8.75	9.10	0	0.50	1
8.50	9.10	9.50	0	0.60	2
9.00	9.50	9.95	0	0.50	2
9.35	9.95	10.30	0	0.60	2

Idle time in operation *B*   = 2.10 minutes
Waiting time of parts   = 3.15 minutes
Average inventory of assemblies between *A* and *B* = 3.15/9.35
                                                                                      = 0.34 assemblies

Average production rate of *A* $= \dfrac{20 \times 60}{9.75} = 123$ pieces/hour

Average production rate of *B* (while working) $= \dfrac{20 \times 60}{8.20} = 146$ pieces/hour

Average production rate of *A* and *B* together $= \dfrac{20 \times 60}{10.30} = 116.5$ pieces/hour

Note: In the above computations, 20 is the total number of completed assemblies; 9.75 is the total work time of operation *A* for 20 assemblies from Table VII; 8.20 is the total work time, exclusive of idle time, for operation *B* for 20 assemblies from Table VII.

line problems we used earlier. The time values for operation A (Table VII) are first used to determine when the half-completed assemblies would be available to operation B. The first assembly is completed by operator A in 0.40 minute. It takes 0.10 minute to roll down to operator B, so this point in time is selected as zero. The next assembly is available 0.40 minute later, and so on. For the first assembly, operation B begins at time zero. From the simulated sample, the first assembly requires 0.60 minute for B. At this point, there is no idle time for B and no inventory. At time 0.40 the second assembly becomes available, but B is still working on the first so the assembly must wait 0.20 minute. Operator B begins work on it at 0.60. From Table VII the second assembly requires 0.50 minute for B. We continue the simulated operation of the line in this way.

The sixth assembly becomes available to B at time 2.40, but B was ready for it at time 2.30. He therefore was forced to remain idle for 0.10 minute because of lack of work. The completed sample of 20 assemblies is progressively worked out.

The summary at the bottom of Table VIII shows the result in terms of the idle time in operation B, the waiting time of the parts, the average inventory between the two operations, and the resulting production rates. From the average times given by the original distributions, we would have guessed that A would limit the output of the line since it was the slower of the two operations. Actually, however, the line production rate is less than that dictated by A (116.5 pieces per hour compared to 123 pieces per hour for A as an individual operation.). The reason is that the interplay of performance times for A and B do not always match up very well, and sometimes B has to wait for work. B's enforced idle time plus his total work time actually determines the maximum production rate of the line.

A little thought should convince us that, if possible, it would have been better to redistribute the assembly work so that A is the faster of the two operations. Then the probability that B will run out of work is reduced. This is demonstrated by Table IX which assumes a simple reversal of the sequence of A and B. The same sample times have been used and the simulated operation of the line has been developed as before. With the faster of the two operations being first in the sequence, the output rate of the line increases and approaches the rate of the limiting operation, and the average inventory between the two operations increases. With the higher average inventory there, the second operation in the sequence is almost never idle owing to lack of work. Actually, this conclusion is a fairly general one with regard to the balance of assembly lines; that is, the best labor balance will be achieved when each succeeding operation

TABLE IX.   Simulated Operation of the Two-Station Assembly Line When Operation B Precedes Operation A

Assemblies Available for Operation A at	Operation A Begins at	Operation A Ends at	Idle Time in Operation A	Waiting Time of Assemblies	Number of Parts in Line, Excluding Assembly Being Processed in Operation A
0.00	0.00	0.40	0	0	0
0.50	0.50	0.90	0.10	0	0
0.90	0.90	1.35	0	0	0
1.35	1.35	1.85	0	0	0
1.70	1.85	2.30	0	0.15	1
2.05	2.30	2.90	0	0.25	1
2.40	2.90	3.75	0	0.40	1
2.70	3.75	4.50	0	1.05	2
3.05	4.50	5.15	0	1.45	2
3.35	5.15	5.80	0	1.80	3
3.75	5.80	6.25	0	2.05	3
4.10	6.25	6.80	0	2.15	4
4.50	6.80	7.20	0	2.30	4
4.75	7.20	7.60	0	2.45	5
5.45	7.60	7.95	0	2.15	5
6.05	7.95	8.45	0	1.90	5
6.40	8.45	8.75	0	2.05	5
6.80	8.75	9.00	0	1.95	6
7.25	9.00	9.50	0	1.75	5
7.60	9.50	9.85	0	1.90	6

Idle time in operation A   = 0.10 minute
Waiting time of parts   = 25.75 minutes
Average inventory of assemblies between A and B = 25.75/7.60
                                                                         = 3.4 assemblies

Average production rate of A (while working) $= \dfrac{20 \times 60}{9.75} = 123$ pieces/hour

Average production rate of B $= \dfrac{20 \times 60}{8.20} = 146$ pieces/hour

Average production rate of A and B together $= \dfrac{20 \times 60}{9.85} = 122$ pieces/hour

in the sequence is slightly slower than the one before it. This minimizes the idle time created when the operators run out of work because of the variable performance times of the various operations. In practical situations it is common to find safety banks of assemblies between operations in order to absorb these fluctuations in performance.

We may have wanted to build a more sophisticated model of the assembly line. Our simple model assumed that the performance times were independent of other events in the process. Perhaps in the actual situation, the second operation in the sequence would tend to speed up when the inventory began to build up. This effect could have been included if we had knowledge of how inventory affected performance time.

If we have followed this simulation example through carefully, we may be convinced that it would work but that it would be very tedious for problems of practical size. Even for our limited example, we would probably wish to have a larger run on which to base conclusions, and there would probably be other alternatives to test. For example, there may be several alternative ways to distribute the total assembly task between the two stations, or more than two stations could be considered. Which of the several alternatives would yield the smallest incremental cost of labor, inventory costs, etc.? To cope with the problem of tedium and excessive man-hours to develop a solution, the computer may be used. If a computer were programmed to simulate the operation of the assembly line, we would place the two cumulative distributions in the memory unit of the computer. Through the program, the computer would select a performance time value at random from the cumulative distribution for A in much the same fashion as we did by hand. Then it would select at random a time value from the cumulative distribution for B, make the necessary computations, and hold the data in memory. The cycle would repeat, selecting new time values at random, adding and subtracting to obtain the record that we produced by hand. A large run could be made easily and with no more effort than a small run. Various alternatives could be evaluated quickly and easily in the same manner.

Statistical Analysis

A knowledge of statistics and probability provides a framework for the rigorous handling of data in such a way that we can not only draw conclusions based on the predictive model constructed but also assess the risk that the forecasts or predictions may be in error. Thus a correlation study of two factors, such as paint viscosity and paint defects, may indicate that the two factors do move together but that the probable error may be very large if we attempt to forecast the number of paint defects expected from the viscosity measured. Similarly, a statistical control chart of errors in a clerical operation, or of labor turnover, may indicate that we are experiencing an abnormal situation, either above or below accepted limits of variation. In addition, however, we know that the chance that we are in error in assuming that the process is out of control is only 0.27 per cent if the usual probability control limits have been assigned.

One great contribution of modern statistics to production analysis is in the general field called statistical inference. Here we find the development of a methodology for the formal testing of hypotheses. This field in statistics is of such great value because it allows us to deal with problems that exhibit great variation in the measured values of the factors or variables that may define the system. Yet we can draw conclusions about the system, and these conclusions may be quite precise. Thus it may be possible to test the hypothesis that a new method for a clerical operation is faster or produces fewer errors. Or we may test a somewhat more complex hypothesis that of several factors which may contribute to poor quality, only one is significant.

Suppose, for example, that there are four machines used to perform an operation in the production of a part and we are experiencing difficulty with the quality of output. The foreman maintains that his four machines are not equally reliable. The plant superintendent accuses the machine operators on the theory that one simply cannot obtain qualified help these days. The workers say that the raw material is sometimes faulty, especially when it comes from a certain supplier. When the quality reports are examined, it is not at all obvious whether the machines, workers, or suppliers are at fault. It is possible, however, by resorting to a statistical inference technique, *analysis of variance*, to perform a simple experiment which will tell us with a preassigned level of confidence the contributions toward poor quality from each of the three sources.

Statistical analysis in production and operations management has a large field of application of its own. For example, techniques such as *work sampling* and *statistical quality control*, both of which are described in somewhat greater detail in Chapters 12 and 19, respectively, are based on statistical models. As a general tool of analysis, however, statistical concepts often provide help in the application of some other kinds of analytical techniques already described. For example, in attempting to determine what factors or variables are of significance in a simulation model of flow through a production system, we may test the hypothesis that the time required for flow through the system is dependent on the number of operations to be performed. Or, in studying the nature of an existing wage structure, we may wish to determine the regression line of a measure of job difficulty versus wages paid. In neither of these instances is statistical analysis the central model used; however, it contributes to the overall analysis.

Network Planning Models

The post-World War II importance of research and development and other large-scale one-time projects in our economy have called forth special planning techniques. These techniques, commonly known by the name PERT, represent the work required to be done as a network of activities which takes account of the interdependencies of timing and phasing of operations. From the basic network model, schedule statistics can be computed which make it possible to determine which activities must be done on time (are critical) and which have schedule slack. This results in a concept known as the critical path schedule. The network of activities and the schedule statistics then become a basis for plans for the deployment of resources to the project.

We shall discuss network planning methods in Chapter 18 on planning, scheduling and control for large scale projects.

Heuristic Models

It is interesting that one of the current emphases in operations management research finds considerable value in the old, perhaps arbitrary, "rules of thumb" for which management was originally criticized by management scientists. Heuristic methods, models, and programs have recently found a respectable place in analytic methodology. The term "heuristic" originally meant aiding in or guiding discovery. But in its common managerial meaning, it refers to a rigorous set of rules or guides to decision which, though not necessarily optimal, are applied consistently, are efficient, and avoid a lot of complicated problem solving. Wiest [8] gives the following simple example of a heuristic rule:

> When the sky is cloudy, take an umbrella to work.
> The problem at hand is how to defend oneself from the potential discomforts of the weather. This simple heuristic avoids more complicated problem-solving procedures such as reading the weather reports, calling the weather bureau, analyzing barometer readings, and so forth. For

many problems of this kind, we lack the time or inclination to employ more thorough problem-solving procedures. A simple (if not infallible) rule serves us best.

The difficulty in many managerial problems with using some other kinds of analysis is that the problem itself is so complex that it may be difficult or impossible to approach it mathematically. Still answers must be developed; rules of thumb which have some basis of logic may be the best methods to use. As we shall see, however, this does not mean just any rule for generating decisions but rather a logical and consistent set of rules. Within a large heuristic program, some of the individual heuristic rules used may come from the results of mathe-

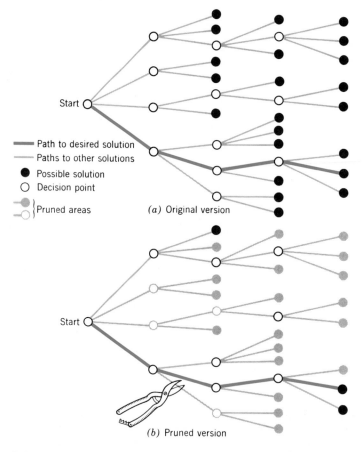

FIGURE 12. A tree diagram representation of a problem. (From Wiest [8].)

matical analysis or other research on smaller, more manageable problems.

With many problems in production and operations management, there is an extremely large number of decision points in a sequence; thus the number of possible combinations of decisions is enormous. This is illustrated by the "tree diagram" of Figure 12a. Each node represents a decision point and the lines connecting them indicate a path or sequence of decisions which lead to some particular solution. Of course, one way to find the best solution is to evaluate the end result for every combination of decision points. This we call enumeration, and it is practical only when the number of possible paths is relatively small. But the kinds of problems to which we are referring cannot be approached in this way, even with the aid of high-speed computers. The heuristic approach is to examine the tree diagram and to prune branches of the tree, as shown in Figure 12. Of course it is entirely possible that the pruning process may eliminate branches which could lead to excellent solutions, but this is the trade-off involved in heuristic methods. Search effort is reduced through heuristic methods at the price of possibly throwing away the very best solution.

A simplified version of a heuristic program developed by Wiest [8] as a basis for scheduling the activities in large-scale one-time projects is shown in Figure 13. The heuristic program is based largely on three heuristic rules.

1. Allocate resources serially in time. That is, start on the first day and schedule all activities possible; then do the same for the second day, and so on.

2. When several jobs compete for the same resources, give preference to the jobs with the least slack.

3. Reschedule noncritical jobs, if possible, in order to free resources for scheduling critical (nonslack) jobs.

Heuristic methods in operations management have been applied successfully in such problem areas as assembly line balancing, facilities layout, job shop scheduling, warehouse location, inventory control, and the scheduling of large-scale one-time projects.

Computer Search Methods

Another relatively new approach for obtaining excellent solutions to some very complex problems is through use of computer search methods. In the past the complexity of many operations management kinds of problems has been so serious that the model builder has had to restrict

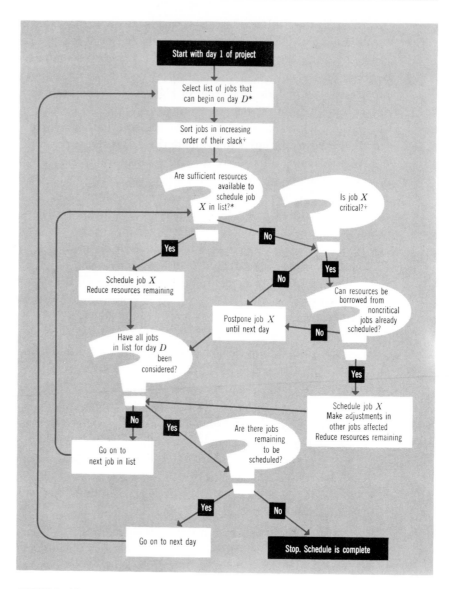

FIGURE 13.   Simplified heuristic program flow chart for large project scheduling. (From Weist [8].)

*Day *D* is day under consideration; job *X* is job under consideration.
†*Slack* is a measure of the number of days a job may be delayed without delaying the project as a whole. A job is *critical* if it has no slack.

his attentions to simple models that could be solved by analytic techniques or resort to simulation or possibly heuristic methods. Today, however, the computer has made possible new quasi-analytic and heuristic search techniques. These techniques have significantly increased the probability of finding the global optimum of complex models. One such optimum seeking technique is known as a direct computer search procedure. "Direct search" methods consist of a sequential examination of a finite set of feasible trial solutions of a criterion function. A single trial evaluation is produced by specifying values for each independent variable, evaluating the criterion function, and recording the result. Each trial value is compared to the best previous value; if an improvement is observed the trial value is accepted and the previous best value rejected. The procedure continues in this way until no further improvements can be found, when a predetermined number of trial evaluations has been made, or when the computer time limit is exceeded. At this point the computer program prints out the best combination of independent variables which has been found.

The advantage of using direct search methods is in building the model of the criterion function. There are no constraints of mathematical form imposed, such as linearity. Also, to date, problems have been solved with as many as 200 independent variables, using modest computer time, and it appears that the possible number of independent variables in such programs can be expanded even more. In operations management, direct search methods have been applied to the aggregate planning and scheduling problem which we shall discuss in Chapter 15, and to the network scheduling problem with limited resources which we shall discuss in Chapter 18.

Schematic and Graphic Analysis

The traditional modes of analysis used in production systems have been schematic and graphic methods supplemented by incremental cost analyses. The most prominent analytical tools of this type are in the form of flow charts that show the sequence and/or timing of activities. For example, Figure 14 shows a procedure flow chart for a stores requisition. It shows the step-by-step activities involved in handling the four copies of the requisition by means of a system of standard symbols. The chart is in fact a schematic model of the overall system for handling stores requisitions. The flow chart can be analyzed for overlapping or

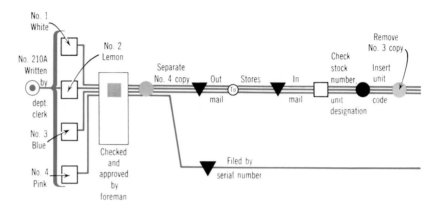

FIGURE 14.   Procedure flow chart for stores requisition. (From Close [2].)

duplicate functions, control, logic of flow patterns, and so on. Basically similar flow charts may follow the physical flow of material being processed through a sequence of operations as illustrated by Figure 15. Here we see a schematic diagram of the processing required by a potentiometer shaft. Here again, the flow diagram can be analyzed for the logic of flow, duplication of effort, or overlapping functions.

There are many other kinds of graphic and schematic diagrams used in the analysis of various phases of a production system, particularly in the analysis of labor utilization, production scheduling and control, and facility layout. We shall discuss these tools of analysis when we discuss the problems for which they are applicable. They are integrated as a part of our discussion of job design in Chapter 11, facility layout in Chapter 10, and scheduling and control in Chapter 17.

SUMMARY

In this chapter we have attempted to lay out a general framework for the analysis of production systems and to discuss the nature and application of some prominent modes of analysis used. In most instances the discussion of specific methods of analysis has been meant to be introductory to other sections or chapters in the book. These following sections either focus directly on an analytical methodology, such as is the case

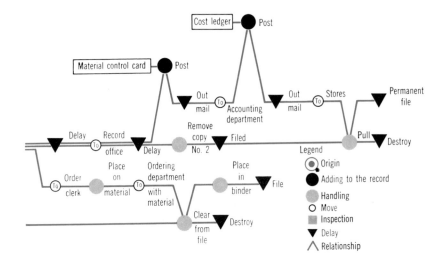

FIGURE 14.   (*continued*)

with incremental and capital cost analysis, statistical analysis, and linear programming, or are introductory to a discussion of the problems encountered in production systems. In the latter instance, the analytic techniques are discussed in relation to the problems to which they are applicable. This has been the case for waiting line models, simulation models, and schematic and graphic methods. With waiting line and simulation models, illustrations of applications are discussed at various points throughout the book. For schematic and graphic methods, most of the detailed techniques used are explained in connection with the applications.

There are some additional special analytical methods used which we have not attempted to discuss here. For example, inventory models are of great importance and are discussed within the chapter dealing with inventory control. Also, there is a wide variety of other models which have been constructed as special applications. They are discussed by other authors in many of the references given in this book.

KEY CONCEPTS

Scientific Method.   What we have termed, "a framework for analysis," is in fact an outline of the scientific method adapted for our purposes. The major elements:

Define the system under study,
Define a measure of effectiveness, E,

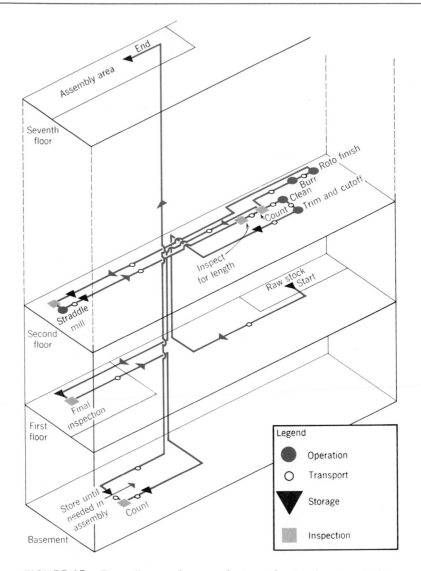

FIGURE 15.　Flow diagram for manufacture of potentiometer shafts.

Construct a model where, the effect, can be expressed as a function of the
　variables that define the system,
General alternatives based on analysis, weight and decide,

are steps which are involved in the attack on any problem.

Optimum Solution.   The concept of optimum solutions is one which runs throughout the analyses of production systems. In its most rigorous sense, it refers to the mathematically provable best possible solution to a problem given a carefully defined criterion function. For example, if the criterion function was represented by the sum of the operating costs of the system under study, then the optimum solution would be that course of action which was associated with the minimum cost of operation.

Suboptimization.   If a problem is too narrowly defined in the first place, the final solution is likely to be suboptimum. In general, the broader the definition or scope of the problem, the less likely it is that suboptimization will occur. If the system is defined broadly, then the best way of operating one component of the system might be somewhat different than if one looked only to that component. For example, viewed locally a certain production department should seemingly carry no finished goods inventories. However, from the point of view of the effective operation of the entire system, total costs might be minimized if that department did carry extra inventories in order to facilitate the operation of other units. To understand the meaning of the concept of suboptimization is to understand the need for a system point of view. Economic trade-offs must be made to avoid suboptimization.

Mathematical Model Building.   A formal mathematical model building approach to managerial problems, normally focussed on the development of optimum solutions to problems of limited scope. Therefore, the solutions are often suboptimizations in reference to the broad systemic problems of production management.

Simulation.   An empirical approach to the definition and solution of managerial problems, normally with the aid of a high speed computer. Because the conceptual framework of simulation does not depend on the limitations imposed by mathematical form, it is possible to represent large-scale interacting systems somewhat more effectively than with mathematical analysis. Simulation has been referred to as "management's laboratory," because one can perform experiments on the simulated system.

Heuristics.   The concept of a heuristic rule is rapidly gaining prominence and acceptance. Because of the great complexity of large-scale systems, it is often impossible to specify rules of action which are anything but systematic and in many instances generally logical. While in a sense, the heuristic method is the oldest of managerial modes of thinking, its present-day usage is more rigorous in concept.

IMPORTANT TERMS

Numbers in parentheses indicate page numbers.

1.	Arrival rate (93)	15.	Poisson arrivals (92)
2.	Breakeven analysis (79–80)	16.	Poisson service rates (93)
3.	Cost analysis (80)	17.	Procedure flow chart (109–110)
4.	Cumulative distribution (96–97)	18.	Queuing model (87–88)
5.	Flow diagram (112)	19.	Schematic model (110–111)
6.	Graphic model (110)	20.	Seasonal inventory (76)
7.	Heuristic (105)	21.	Service rate (93)
8.	Hypothesis testing (104)	22.	Simulated sampling (95)
9.	Incremental cost analysis (80)	23.	Statistical inference (104)
10.	Locational dynamics (86)	24.	Statistical quality control (104)
11.	Measure of effectiveness (74)	25.	Tree diagram (106)
12.	Monte Carlo (95)	26.	Waiting line (87–88)
13.	Network planning (105)	27.	Work sampling (104)
14.	Optimum seeking methods (109)		

REVIEW QUESTIONS

Numbers in parentheses indicate page numbers.

1. Outline a framework for analysis of production and operations management problems. (72–78)
2. What is meant by a suboptimum solution? (72)
3. What is the meaning of the term "measure of effectiveness" as it applies to managerial problems? Name some typical measures of effectiveness which might be used in production problems. (74)
4. What are controllable and uncontrollable variables? (75)
5. What is the nature of the general linear programming model? Name three situations where it might prove useful as a model of system behavior. (80–87)
6. In a waiting line model, why is it necessary that the service rate exceed the arrival rate? (87–93)
7. How is a simulation model different from a mathematical model? (94)
8. In simulated sampling, why are frequency distributions cumulated? (98–99)
9. Discuss the application of statistical methods and statistical analysis in the general field of production and operations management. (103–105)
10. What are graphic and schematic methods of analysis? For what kinds of problems are they of value in the analysis of production problems? (110)

SELF-TEST TRUE-FALSE QUESTIONS

Numbers in parentheses indicate page numbers.

1. Suboptimization might occur if in attempting to determine a program for the production of a seasonal product we establish the scope of the program as being one of minimizing labor costs. (72)
2. In applying the system point of view one constructs a model where E, the effect, can be expressed as a function of the variables which define the system. (75)
3. Wage rates, or inventory carrying costs, are examples of controllable variables which may be manipulated pretty much at the will of management. (75)
4. Linear programming represents a formal model for the general allocation problem. (80)
5. When random distributions are introduced, a linear programming model is useful for the analysis of waiting line or queuing situations. (80, 87)
6. Waiting line models often make it possible to analyze the relative importance of idle time. (88)
7. Poisson arrivals are often compensated for by exponential service times. (92–94)
8. The difference between simulation models and mathematical models is that one cannot express the measure of effectiveness as a function of the variables of the system in a simulation model. (94)
9. When a simulation involves Monte Carlo methods, optimum answers can be generated. (94–95)
10. Monte Carlo methods are often also called simulated sampling. (95)
11. Analysis of variance is a simulation technique of considerable value in operations analysis. (104)
12. A flow chart may be regarded as a quasi-mathematical model represented in schematic fashion. (110)
13. Waiting-line theory can provide answers to problems dealing with the allocation of limited resources to competing demands. (80, 88)
14. The formulas for waiting-line situations which assume Poisson arrival rates and processing rates may be used in any situation where the arrivals and processing times are random. (93)
15. When the service rate exceeds the arrival rate, the waiting-line length becomes infinitely long. (90, 93)
16. Simulation models follow a conceptual structure similar to that of mathematical models, except that the model may be empirical instead of mathematical. (94)
17. The sampling method known as Monte Carlo, is a simulation procedure. (95)

18. In simulated sampling, frequency distributions are commonly converted to cumulative distributions so that only one value can be associated with a given random number. (96–98)
19. In the example showing the simulation of a two-station assembly line, the conclusion was that the first operation in the sequence should be the slower of the two. (101–103)

PROBLEMS

1. Table III in the text gives the optimal distribution pattern for the particular conditions stated. Suppose you vary from the optimal solution and ship 20 of Cincinnati's requirement from Chicago in order to take advantage of a special shipment going to Cincinnati anyway, thus giving a carload rate of $41 per case. How does this change the total shipping cost of $24,610 stated for the optimal solution?

2. A distributor of pharmaceutical products has four large warehouses in major cities spread geographically around the country. From the four warehouses he ships to 20 independent distributors each two weeks. How many separate shipments must he normally make each two weeks to supply all of the individual distributors?

3. The WASH-N-DRY Manufacturing Company produces a line of washing machines and dryers. The major manufacturing departments are the stamping department, the motor and transmission department, and final assembly lines for each product. The stamping department fabricates a large number of the the metal parts for both the washer and the drier. The motor and transmission department produces the drive units for both product lines. Monthly department capacities are as follows:

Department Name	Capacity for Washers	Capacity for Dryers
Stamping department	10,000 or	10,000
Motor and transmission department	16,000 or	7,000
Washer assembly line	12,000	—
Dryer assembly line	—	5,000

Plot the restrictions on a graph similar to Figure 5 in the text. Which department capacities are likely to limit the output of the plant as a whole? What is likely to be the best number of washers and dryers to produce, assuming that the market is not restricting? Why?

4. Trucks arrive at a dock in a manner described by the Poisson distribution at the rate of eight per hour. The time to unload trucks is closely approximated

by the negative exponential distribution. The average unloading time is 5 minutes. Calculate the following, using Equations 3, 4, 5, 6, and 7 in Appendix B:

(a) The mean number in the waiting line.

(b) The mean number in the system.

(c) The mean waiting time.

(d) The mean time in the system.

(e) The probability of six units being in the system.

5.   People arrive at a theater ticket booth in a Poisson distributed arrival rate of 25 per hour. Service time is constant at 2 minutes. Calculate the following using Equations 1 and 2 in Appendix B:

(a) The mean number in the waiting line.

(b) The mean waiting time.

6.   The Caribbean Tea Company is a nationwide chain of supermarkets with headquarters in Chicago, Illinois. The vice-president in charge of western operations is located in Los Angeles and controls all areas west of the Rocky Mountains. The largest portion of the western operations is centered in the greater Los Angeles metropolitan area.

Although the Los Angeles population is increasing at a rapid rate, total company sales have been leveling off. The vice-president believes that the primary cause of this condition is increased competition. Recent association publications report that the number of supermarkets is growing at a faster rate than the population.

To meet this impending crisis, the vice-president believes that the only answer lies in becoming more competitive. In pursuit of this objective, he has formed a task force to deal with the following problem areas:

(1) Product line.
(2) Pricing
(3) Labor-saving   equipment.
(4) Advertising.
(5) Improved customer service.

As part of this effort, the vice-president calls you in and says: "I want you to investigate customer service at the check-out stands and make recommendations. I don't want to influence your judgment, but it seems strange to me that when I go into a store, I frequently see long lines and about one-half of the check-out stands not being used. I think we need to do some hard thinking about how many checkers we should have. I want you to prepare a preliminary proposal of how you intend to investigate customer service at the check-out stands and submit it at the next task force meeting."

(a) Translate the vice-president's instructions into a meaningful statement of the problem as you see it.

(b) Outline a proposal to solve the problem that you have stated in question

(a) Prepare your proposal in sufficient detail so that a third party could implement it with no further instructions from you.

7.   You are studying a two-station assembly line with each operator doing approximately half of the work. The distributions of assembly times are as follows:

Cycle Time (minutes)	Frequency of Cycle Times for	
	Operation A	Operation B
0.20	4	2
0.30	9	5
0.40	28	17
0.50	22	10
0.60	15	8
0.70	10	2
0.80	8	3
0.90	4	3
	100	50

(a) Construct a cumulative probability distribution which could be used in the simulation of the two-station assembly line.
(b) Simulate the assembly of 10 parts.
(c) What is the average length of the waiting line of the half-completed assemblies ahead of station B?
(d) What is the average output per hour of the assembly line?

8.   A sample of 100 customer arrivals at a check-out station of a small store is represented in the following distribution:

Time between Arrivals (minutes)	Frequency
0.5	2
1.0	6
1.5	10
2.0	25
2.5	20
3.0	14
3.5	10
4.0	7
4.5	4
5.0	2
	100

A study of the time required to service the customers by adding up the bill, receiving payment, making change, placing packages in bags, etc., yields the following distribution:

Service Time (minutes)	Frequency
0.5	12
1.0	21
1.5	36
2.0	19
2.5	7
3.0	5
	100

Set up the foregoing data in a form useful for simulation. Determine a simulation procedure which will use this revised data to furnish an estimate of the mean number of customers serviced per minute. Develop a flow chart that completely specifies the decision rules used for the simulation.

REFERENCES

[1] Buffa, E. S. *Operations Management: Problems and Models* (3rd ed.). John Wiley, New York, 1972.
[2] Close, G. *Work Improvement*. John Wiley, New York, 1960.
[3] Dixon, W. J., and F. J. Massey, Jr. *Introduction to Statistical Analysis* (3rd ed.). McGraw-Hill, New York, 1969.
[4] Hoel, P. G., and R. J. Jessen. *Basic Statistics for Business and Economics*. John Wiley, New York, 1971.
[5] Nadler, G. *Work Design: A Systems Concept* (Rev. ed.). Richard D. Irwin, Homewood, Ill., 1970.
[6] Taubert, W. H. "A Computer Search Solution of the Aggregate Scheduling Problem." *Management Science*, 14 (6), Feb. 1968.
[7] Thierauf, R. J., and R. C. Klekamp. *Decision Making Through Operations Research* (2nd ed.). John Wiley, New York, 1975.
[8] Wiest, J. D. "Heuristic Programs for Decision Making." *Harvard Business Review*, Sept–Oct. 1966.

CONTENTS

CHAPTER 5
COST DATA FOR DECISIONS

Is there anything significant about the term *cost data for decisions?* Why not simply talk about *cost data?* Between the two terms there are important differences; the objective of cost data resulting from the accounting function is different from the objective of cost data constructed for decision making. In general, accounting systems meet the needs of federal and state tax laws, as well as the needs of certain phases of financial management of an organization. When the end use of cost data is for decision making, however, we must be careful that average costs and allocations of fixed overhead cost items do not make the actual behavior of costs. We shall be interested in the *net effect* on costs of each alternative being considered. As we shall see, the implications of this "net effect" criterion shift somewhat with the nature of the problem.

As a point of departure, let us recall that expense classification for a manufacturing firm follows the general structure of Figure 1. The labor and material costs

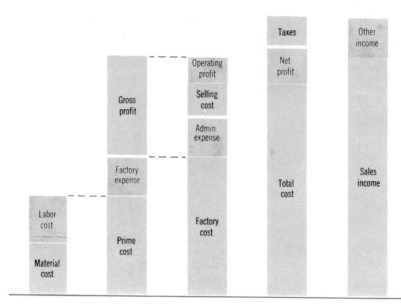

FIGURE 1.   Elements of cost of manufacture. Typical items of factory ex-
expense are: indirect labor, utilities, factory supplies, maintenance and repair,
depreciation on plant and equipment, insurance, and property taxes. Typical
items of administrative expense are: salaries, office supplies, depreciation of
office property, insurance, taxes on office property, corporate income taxes,
and legal expenses. Typical items of selling expense are: sales salaries, advertising, travel, bad debts, telephone and telegraph, and office supplies.

at the left are considered direct since ordinarily they can be attributed to
a product. Factory expense or factory overhead items are ordinarily indirect because it is often difficult to attribute them to a specific product
without an arbitrary allocation. Administrative and selling expenses are
general overhead costs that are even more indirect in their nature. Sometimes the costs we want to consider do not even appear in the chart of
accounts, yet our decisions may be drastically affected by them. Sunk
costs and opportunity costs are in this category. In this chapter we want
to examine the general nature and behavior of certain kinds of costs so
that we may draw on these ideas in later chapters that deal with decision
problems in specific areas.

FIXED AND VARIABLE COSTS

It is often worthwhile to consider how costs vary with the volume
produced. We think of cost items such as property taxes, indirect labor,
and building depreciation as being nonvariable, or fixed, and of items

such as direct labor, materials, and certain supplies used in the production process as being variable with volume. This dichotomy of thought is often dangerous, however, because "fixed" costs may in some instances be thought of as varying with volume, and costs commonly thought to be variable may behave as fixed costs. Many cost items may be fixed only over short ranges of volume. Indirect labor is commonly in this class. One material handler may be adequate to a certain volume level above which we must have two handlers. To be sure, our handler is not fully utilized until we approach the critical volume, and when we add the second, both men will probably be underutilized. The semivariable nature of such cost elements can be important in certain decision problems.

BREAKEVEN ANALYSIS

Breakeven analysis makes use of the fixed and variable nature of costs to indicate the range of volume necessary for profitable operation. If we could divide all costs into those that vary with volume and those that do not, we could compute an average total cost per unit for a given volume. Semivariable costs can be reduced to a fixed component and a variable component. This concept of average unit cost is correct only at the one volume of computation, however, since the fixed costs per unit would change as we averaged them over different volumes. Conceptually, then, it would be helpful to consider the fixed costs as a total pool of costs which must be covered by net revenue, over and above variable costs, before any profit whatever is made. This point or volume of sales where total net revenue after variable costs just equals the total pool of fixed costs is called the breakeven point. It is precisely that because it is the point in the progress of sales where the total revenue just covers the total cost, variable and fixed. Below this volume a loss is recorded; above it a profit is recorded.

Figure 2 is a diagram of the structure of a simple breakeven chart. Units of volume are plotted on the horizontal scale and dollars of sales or cost on the vertical scale. The sales line begins at the origin and is a straight line, since dollar sales are assumed to be proportional to units sold. The total cost line intersects the vertical axis at a value equal to the fixed costs and increases in proportion to the number of units sold. Above the breakeven point the ratio of profits to sales increases with each unit sold. This is because of the broadened base for the absorption of fixed costs. Contribution is at a fixed ratio, however.

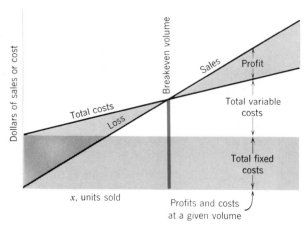

FIGURE 2.   A simple breakeven chart.

Contribution. What is contribution and how can it be used? Contribution is the difference between sales and variable costs or the contribution to fixed costs and profit; that is,

$$C = S - V \tag{1}$$

and

$$S = F + V + P \tag{2}$$

where

$$C = \text{contribution} \qquad F = \text{fixed costs}$$
$$S = \text{sales} \qquad\qquad P = \text{profit}$$
$$V = \text{variable costs}$$

Since both S and V vary with volume, C varies with volume also. C can then be calculated easily by knowing the percentage of the sales dollar that is V. Suppose, for example, that variable costs are 60 per cent of the sales dollar and fixed costs are $3,000,000. Then, from equation (1), C is 40 per cent. The only costs which have not yet been deducted are the fixed costs, so:

$$C = F + P \tag{3}$$

or

$$P = C - F$$

Now we can compute profit at any level of sales. If total sales are $10,000,000, then C is 40 per cent or $4,000,000 and

$$P = C - F = \$4,000,000 - \$3,000,000 = \$1,000,000$$

If total sales are \$8,000,000, C is 40 per cent or \$3,200,000 and

$$P = C - F = \$3,200,000 - \$3,000,000 = \$200,000$$

The contribution concept has allowed us to compute total profit at various levels of sales rather easily. Contribution is often called a "profit pickup."

Construction of Breakeven Charts. Although the theory behind breakeven charts is simple, it is not so simple to obtain good data from which to develop the chart because the line between fixed and variable costs is not definite. We may not be safe in taking armchair classifications as valid. We deduce that certain direct labor costs ought to be variable, but are they so actually? There may be a fixed element in them. The point is this: to construct an accurate breakeven chart from cost elements, a great deal of prior work is required in order to establish the actual behavior of cost elements in relation to volume. Good breakeven charts require excellent cost accounting systems.

Another way to approach the problem is by means of the scatter diagram of costs. Data on total costs are plotted for several years and an average line drawn in. The presumption is that the different years will represent different volumes; a total cost line in relation to volume then can be inferred. The point at which the line crosses the vertical axis is an estimate of the fixed costs. Let us take the following data and plot them in Figure 3.

Year	Total Costs (dollars)	Sales (dollars)	Year	Total Costs (dollars)	Sales (dollars)
1968	1.45 million	1.75 million	1970	2.20 million	3.10 million
1969	1.70 million	2.20 million	1971	2.30 million	3.50 million

The result looks good and is easy to obtain. We must question, however, whether the relation of costs to volume is perhaps more representative of inflationary tendencies during the period than it is of the way costs vary with volume. If this is a possibility, the data may be deflated to remove the effect of rising costs and prices.

It is also important that the data for the several years be fairly representative of a single set of conditions of technology, product mix, and

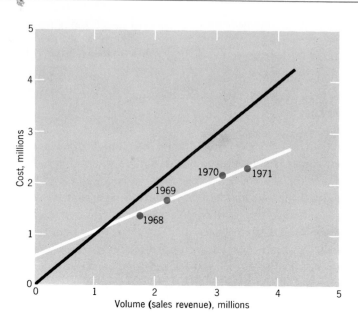

FIGURE 3. Scatter plot of total costs versus sales volume.

cost performance. If major technological changes occurred during the period, we would not expect the several years to yield consistent data on which to base the construction of a breakeven chart.

Why Breakeven Points and Profits Change. Following is a list of some items that may affect profits or both breakeven points and profits:

1. Change in volume. This has a direct effect on profits; breakeven point and contribution ratio does not change.

2. Change in product mix. Profits, breakeven point, and contribution ratio can all change. This suggests the development of breakeven charts on a product basis.

3. Performance changes of labor or of material utilization. Profits, breakeven point, and contribution ratio all change.

4. Change in fixed costs. This affects profits and breakeven point, but contribution ratio remains constant.

5. Change in selling prices. Profits, breakeven point, and contribution ratio all change.

Effect of Managerial Decisions on the Breakeven Point. The following is a sample list of some important typical decisions:

1. Replacement of obsolete plant and equipment. Usually fixed costs will go up even though existing assets are disposed of. The most common reason for obsolescence is probably the development of new equipment that has lower variable costs. The net effect on the breakeven point is then likely to be either neutral or a decrease with resulting increased profits; this is due to the lowered variable costs (lower slope of total cost line) or to a combination of lower variable costs and lower breakeven point. Other reasons for obsolescence, such as changes of product design, would cause other patterns of change.

2. Manufacture of components previously bought. If unused capacity can be put to work, as is often the case, the net effect is on variable costs which have a direct effect on the breakeven point. If new equipment must be purchased, fixed costs go up. Then the net effect on breakeven point and gross profit will depend on the direction and magnitude of the change in variable costs.

3. Purchase of components previously manufactured. Effect depends on the actual magnitude of the costs that can be disposed of. Most fixed costs will remain, but disposal of some assets may be possible. Variable costs could change in either direction; the net effect on factory breakeven points and gross profits may be either positive or negative, depending upon the relative magnitudes of the disposals and increased variable costs.

4. Decision to retain certain labor skills at the bottom of a seasonal swing. Some variable cost has been converted to fixed. The factory breakeven point may go up.

5. Decision to utilize overtime to increase capacity. Variable costs increase, breakeven point goes up. Presumably, volume has increased and the net effect on profit will depend upon the relationships of the beginning and ending slopes of the total cost line and the magnitude of the actual volume gain.

Usefulness of Breakeven Analysis.   The breakeven concept is an important one for analysis of many production and companywide problems. It is well to realize, however, that our best estimate of the breakeven "point" for a company is actually a good-sized "blob" on the chart, and the point itself lies within the blob. This is true because of the inherent difficulties of getting exact data on the ratio of fixed and variable costs and because day-to-day managerial decisions are constantly changing the breakeven point. In multiproduct, integrated organizations the meaning of the figures becomes gross and vague. The resulting gross figures for variable cost, fixed cost, and volume mask important details, so the picture that emerges of overall company operations may seem acceptable, even though serious problems exist. To measure volume for General Motors Corporation, automobiles, refrigerators, huge diesels, trucks, washing machines, spark plugs, and many other items must be included. Excellent performance in one product or department covers up poor performance in others. The use of different breakeven charts for each product makes some sense, but we must beware here. It is often very difficult to allocate many costs properly, especially if the product mix is subject to change. The most clear-cut situations are those where a fairly homogenous product is produced and volume can be measured fairly well in physical units, that is, pieces or units, tons, gallons, barrels, etc.

In spite of these difficulties, breakeven analysis is important in forming a conceptual framework for budgetary controls, profit planning, and process selection. It shows management what will happen to the breakeven point and to profits as a result of volume changes or proposed courses of action.

INCREMENTAL COSTS

Incremental costs are costs that vary with the alternative courses of action considered. They are the "net effects" that result. (The terms *incremental costs, marginal costs, out-of-pocket costs,* and *differential costs* are used somewhat interchangeably.)

We should recognize that decision making in an on-going business must always take account of the status quo. Existing conditions may favor one alternative. An example of this is the common "make-versus-buy" decision. If we are currently purchasing an item and are considering the possibility of making it instead, it will be important to note if we have capacity to do so. If we do, the incremental costs of making the item will be only the direct costs of labor and materials, plus any actual net additions to other costs such as power and supplies. The machinery, building, and supervisory and executive staffs already exist; the cost of these does not change in manufacturing the item. Therefore, we dare not use the accountant's concept of average manufacturing cost as a basis for making the decision. Only the net incremental costs need be considered. If available capacity does not exist, the net incremental costs will have to include the costs of providing the needed capacity. Conversely, if we are currently making an item which we propose to buy instead, we shall not rid ourselves of the average manufacturing cost of the item. The building, supervisory and executive staff, etc., still remain. Incremental costs that are eliminated will ordinarily be far less than the average manufacturing cost.

The concept of incremental cost often reveals a shifting line between fixed and variable costs. For example, consider the direct labor costs on a continuous production line. The sum of all labor costs for the entire line can be fairly well visualized as being variable with the number of units produced, assuming that if the line is stopped, workers are either sent home or assigned other jobs. On the other hand, if we view individual operations on the line, we find that their labor costs, in general, are not subject to managerial control. It may appear that one of these operations could be improved by the use of a better tool, better motion patterns, etc. If improvements are installed, we shall probably find that labor costs per unit on that operation do not go down (are fixed) because that operation is paced by the line. The only individual operation on the line that can have variable direct labor costs is the "bottleneck" or limiting operation. If that operation can be improved, then direct labor costs for the entire line will decrease in proportion to the improvement, but not beyond the limits imposed by the next most limiting operation.

There may be as many cost patterns within an organization as there are alternative plans. The important point to keep in mind is that incremental costs are associated with whole plans or alternatives, so average costs are almost never good estimates of the net cost effects of a decision. Following is a series of examples which illustrate incremental cost behavior in some types of problems.

Example 1

A company selling about $100,000 annually has three factory employees. The company specializes in plating operations on a jobbing basis. Current conditions in the labor market make employment of part-time help difficult, and work load variations would make it undesirable anyway. One man, who is the foreman, has the essential knowledge and skill required for the various plating operations. He is paid $200 per week. The other two men are general laborers, each paid $160 per week. The three men work 40 hours per week. Production could rise considerably before a fourth man would be necessary and also must fall considerably before it would be possible to get along with only the foreman and one laborer.

For a certain special plating process, it has been the practice to route the work to an outside plater for a particular operation that demands special equipment. The company is now considering purchasing the special equipment so that the operation could be performed in the home plant. Cost figures are:

Cost of outside processing per piece	$0.50
Expected volume of work on special equipment next year	10,000 pieces
Estimated hours per piece spent by:	
Foreman	0.04 hour
Laborers	0.075 hour
Value of power used by new equipment per piece	$0.02
Average value of materials used	$0.02
Burden rate per hour of labor	100%

There is extra room in which to locate the new equipment, which would cost $2,000 installed. What should the company do?

In this situation, labor is a fixed cost and can be ignored. The conventional burden rate is irrelevant. The only new overhead costs are the power and the cost of the equipment itself. The only pertinent direct cost is the material. The total incremental cost of the two alternative plans for next year is:

Outside processing	$5000
In-plant processing $2000 + 400 =	$2400

Here the economics of the situation are obviously in favor of in-plant processing. However, note that this is not the proper way to handle the equipment cost item, for we have ignored opportunity cost of alternative investments and the fact that the equipment has a probable life greater than a year. We shall discuss these capital costs later in Chapter 6.

Example 2

A job-order tool and die shop is operating at essentially full capacity. The usual estimating procedure for new work involves an analysis of the customer's drawings and specifications to determine the materials required and the sequence and type of machining operations needed. Standard time data for the machine operations are then referred to in order to obtain estimates of the number of labor hours required. The resulting estimate of labor hours is then multiplied by $6, the total material costs are added, and finally 15 per cent is added for profit. The $6 labor rate is actually composed of an average hourly pay rate to workers of $4 per hour plus burden at 50 per cent of direct labor hours. The burden rate is commonly adjusted each six months to reflect current conditions. It includes the usual items of overhead: depreciation, supplies, *overtime premium*, administrative and selling expense, etc.

A new order is currently being considered. The estimating procedure yields $1000 for material and 1750 labor hours. The total bid including profit is then $13,225. Should the company take the order if the customer agrees to the price and delivery?

The usual accounting practice of putting overtime premium in as overhead works very well for the computation of profit and loss and for computing average costs. For evaluating this contract, however, incremental costs are needed. Since the plant is operating at full capacity, we can probably assume operation beyond the breakeven point; therefore, all fixed costs have already been covered. On the other hand, overtime labor would be required to do the job. Total out-of-pocket costs would be material plus labor plus variable overhead. Therefore, the incremental income would be $13,225 − 1000 − 1750 × 4.00 × 1.5 − variable overhead, or $1725 − variable overhead.

Example 3

A chemical company regularly uses a certain chemical in several end products. Some of the end products are standard items and others are made in batches on special customer order. The chemical is used at an average rate of 1000 pounds per month. The supplier is nearby and is reliable about delivery, so the company normally purchases 1000 pounds at a time and reorders when the supply dwindles to 500 pounds. With normal rates of usage and delivery time, the new order is received before the inventory falls below 200 pounds, which is considered a safe minimum.

The supplying company has now announced a change of price policy. Formerly the price was $10 per 100 pounds. The new policy includes a quantity discount schedule as follows:

0–499 pounds	$12.00 per 100 pounds
500–999 pounds	11.00 per 100 pounds
1000–1999 pounds	9.50 per 100 pounds
More than 2000 pounds	9.00 per 100 pounds

Should the chemical company change its ordering policy in view of the discount schedule?

This is a complex question and cannot be answered on the basis of data already given. Other incremental costs are involved which must be considered. For example, larger orders would increase the average inventory level and the variable costs associated with inventory such as insurance, interest on working capital, and space. On the other hand, larger orders mean that fewer orders are placed in a year to satisfy needs, thereby decreasing incremental costs associated with the placing of an order, such as the labor to write up the order and the order materials themselves. The purchase plan that has the lowest total cost for all of the pertinent cost factors will be one that strikes a balance between the increasing costs of carrying inventory and the decreasing costs of preparing orders which occur as the quantity per order increases. The "price breaks," or discount schedules, tend to complicate the problem. We shall study this problem more carefully in Chapter 14, where a mathematical model of "economic lot sizes" is discussed and where the question of price breaks is considered.

Example 4

A machine shop occupies the lower floor of a two-story industrial building which is leased for three years at $1000 per month. Each floor has approximately 10,000 square feet of floor space. The shop has followed the practice of sending much of its grinding work to a production grinding shop. It is now considering whether to perform the grinding operations itself and, if so, how best to incorporate the operation. It is estimated that two additional surface grinders and one cylindrical grinder could do almost all of the work that the shop now sends out. These can be purchased for $18,000. The remaining problem is where to locate the new grinders on the floors. At present there is no open space, but the foreman says that about 300 square feet could be opened up and the grinders squeezed in at the north end of the shop if two machines are moved and some space is taken from the tool crib. The latter step will cramp the tool crib operation as well as the operation of machines in the area; nevertheless, the foreman thinks that he can manage.

There is another alternative. The lease for the company occupying the second story is about to expire, and that company is planning to move. The lessor has offered the space to the machine shop on a two-year basis, to expire at the same time as the first-floor lease, at $800 per month. This alternative provides ample room for the grinders. Which items of cost would you compare for purposes of decision making for the three alternatives?

1. Continue to send grinding out. There are the billings from the grinding company plus possible transportation costs and incremental paper work costs to do business with the grinding company.

2. Squeeze three machines into existing space. Immediate increased costs are caused by greater congestion in other departments plus relayout costs, plus costs of operating the grinders, plus costs of owning the grinders. The space, or proportional part of the rent, is irrelevant. It is actually a sunk cost for the total lease obligation. The congestion costs are difficult to measure; they are incremental material-handling

costs, the additional idle time in other departments caused by inter-ference and waiting for materials, and increased carrying charges on larger in-process inventory caused by slower progress of materials.

3. Use second floor for grinding operations. Total incremental lease cost of $19,200 would be sunk, plus operating costs of the grinders, plus costs of owning the grinders, plus additional material handling between floors.

SUMMARY

Our viewpoint must always be: "What costs are affected by alternate action paths?" This requires that we recognize the "going concern" realities which may favor one alternative over another, for example, when idle capacity exists in a make-versus-buy comparison. The incremental cost viewpoint must be retained in reading the rest of this book. As emphasized in the next chapter, concepts of sunk costs and opportunity costs are important when evaluating alternatives that involve capital assets.

Cost data for decision-making purposes have a somewhat different function than the usual accounting reports. Accounting systems meet the needs of tax laws and are of great value in certain phases of the financial management of an organization. From the viewpoint of mana-gerial decision making, it is of great importance to know the structure of an accounting system in order to judge whether these data will mask the true effects which we may wish to measure for a given decision-making problem.

Breakeven analysis takes advantage of a two-part classification of costs into fixed and variable components. Although the breakeven point is not easy to determine accurately, the concept is an extremely valuable one in assessing the advantageous and disadvantageous effects of many typical managerial decisions relating to plant capacity, equip-ment replacement, make-versus-buy decisions, and so on. As we shall see in Chapter 8, a marginal breakeven concept is of considerable value in the selection of processes. Also, we can conceive of variations of the concept of breakeven charts where revenue or cost curves or both are not linear in the operating range. We might experience de-creased revenue per unit when price decreases are used to expand volume. When operating near capacity limitations, cost per unit may increase due to congestion or the use of less efficient methods or equipment. In these situations it is possible for more than one breakeven point to appear.

In the examples given under "incremental costs," we can see in every instance how we might have been misled by accepting "unit cost" figures based on ordinary cost accounting concepts. This is not to damn the accountant, because the unit cost figures that he shows are not designed particularly to help management select from the types of alternatives we have discussed. Probably the most common area of difficulty is in the burden, or burden rate, which represents an *allocation* of fixed and indirect expenses, often on an arbitrary basis. Since our thinking seems to have been structured in terms of labor, material, and overhead costs, there is a temptation to use this burden rate in all situations in order that "each product bears its fair share of these costs." Yet this view can mask important differences in alternatives. If we adopt the view of the alternative plan as a basic cost unit, instead of unit costs, it often becomes unnecessary to worry about how costs are allocated because we are concerned with the incremental costs associated with the plan.

Finally, we should recognize that an incremental cost analysis can take the form of a general model applicable to a class of problems. Part of the purpose of Example 3 was to point out this fact; in developing a policy for purchase quantities, we find that the pertinent incremental costs vary in a predictable way with changes in the quantity purchased, and that there is one purchase quantity which minimizes the sum of these incremental costs. The problem of how many parts to manufacture at one time can be approached in the same general way.

KEY CONCEPTS

Breakeven.   The concept of breakeven is important not only because it indicates the point at which all costs have been covered and the enterprise begins to make a profit. The concept is probably most important because it involves an understanding of the relationship and interaction between fixed and variable costs, and revenue.

Incremental Costs. Though basically simple, the concept of incremental costs seems to be a difficult one to comprehend fully. This may be true because the costs which might be termed "incremental" vary with the nature of the problem being analyzed. Understanding the concept of incremental costs is crucial to the construction of rational criterion functions for all kinds of mathematical and simulation models.

IMPORTANT TERMS

Numbers in parentheses indicate page numbers.

1. Contribution (124)
2. Differential costs (128)
3. Fixed cost (124–125)
4. Make versus buy decision (128)
5. Marginal breakeven analysis (133–134)

6. Marginal costs (128)
7. Out-of-pocket costs (128)
8. Price breaks (131–132)
9. Variable cost (124)

REVIEW QUESTIONS

Numbers in parentheses indicate page numbers.

1. Discuss the differences between fixed, variable, and semivariable costs. (122–123)
2. Define breakeven point and contribution. (123–124)
3. How can we obtain data to construct breakeven charts? Appraise these methods. (125–126)
4. Discuss the effect of the following on breakeven points and profits: change in volume, change in product mix, labor performance changes, increase in fixed costs, increase in selling prices. (126)
5. What is the effect on the breakeven point of the following typical managerial decisions: increase in plant capacity, replacement of obsolete equipment, manufacturing components previously bought, decision to retain certain labor skills at the bottom of a seasonal swing, decision to utilize overtime to increase capacity? (126–127)
6. Appraise the usefulness of breakeven analysis for a multiproduct organization. (127–128)
7. Define the term *incremental costs*. (128)
8. What is the effect of idle capacity on the incremental costs to manufacture an item instead of purchasing it? (128–129)

9. Give examples of the following: direct labor cost is a fixed expense; material is a sunk cost; investment in plant and equipment is a variable cost. (128–129)

SELF-TEST TRUE-FALSE QUESTIONS

Numbers in parentheses indicate page numbers.

1. When the end use of cost data is for decision making, we must be careful that average costs and allocations of fixed overhead cost items do not mask the actual behavior of costs. (121)
2. Sunk costs do not appear as such on the chart of accounts. (122)
3. If a cost is fixed, this means that it can be ignored for all decision-making problems. (123)
4. Many cost items, such as some indirect labor, may be fixed only over short ranges of volume. (123)
5. Semivariable costs can be reduced to a fixed component and a variable component. (123)
6. The breakeven point is the volume of sales where total net revenue just equals the total pool of fixed costs. (123–124)
7. Contribution is proportional to sales; however, profit is not (124)
8. Contribution is equal to sales minus fixed costs. (124)
9. Contribution is equal to fixed costs plus profit. (124)
10. The contribution concept makes it possible to calculate total profit at any level of operation, given the total pool of fixed costs. (124–125)
11. One of the great values of breakeven charts is that they may be constructed easily since fixed and variable costs are readily available from accounting records. (125)
12. Breakeven charts constructed from historical data on total costs for several years may be invalid if technology, product mix, or cost performance have changed. (125–126)
13. A change in volume has a direct effect on profits, but the breakeven point does not change. (126)
14. If the product mix were to change, profits and the breakeven point would change, but the contribution ratio would remain constant. (126)
15. If changes in the performance of labor or of material utilization were to take place, profits and the breakeven point would change, but the contribution ratio would remain constant. (126)
16. If total fixed costs were to change, profits and the breakeven point would change, but the contribution ratio would remain constant. (126)

17. If selling prices were to change, profits, the breakeven point and the contribution ratio would all change. (126)
18. Breakeven analysis is of greatest usefulness to multiproduct, integrated organizations. (127–128)
19. The breakeven point for an organization can be estimated within rather close limits. (127)
20. Breakeven charts are most meaningful where a fairly homogeneous product is produced and volume can be measured in physical units. (128)
21. Incremental costs are costs that vary with the alternative courses of action considered. (128)
22. The terms incremental costs, marginal costs, out-of-pocket costs, and differential costs are used somewhat interchangeably. (128)
23. The concept of incremental cost is identical with the accountant's definition of variable costs. (129)
24. Direct labor costs on a conveyorized production line may, in general, be conceived as fixed costs. (129)

PROBLEMS

1. A nursing home operator bases his income and costs on the number of rooms he has filled. Each room has an income earning potential of $350 per month. Variable costs are food, materials, and supplies, plus nursing care. Food, materials, and supplies average $150 per month per patient, and nursing care averages $4 per day per patient. By using a corps of permanent nurses plus nurses on monthly call, the manager can keep nursing costs quite variable. The pool of fixed costs is $5000 per month. The home has 100 rooms and currently 75 of them are occupied.

What is the monthly contribution to profit and overhead? At what occupancy level does the manager break even? What would his profit be at 90 per cent occupancy?

2. For the nursing home in problem 1, what would be the price per room per month at which the operator could break even with a 75 per cent occupancy?

3. A machine shop operator has three kinds of machines, all of which do "turning" operations, but the machines have different degrees of mechanization and, with special tools, the productivity of the three machines is quite different for the same job. The out-of-pocket fixed costs to set up each machine plus the cost of special tools, as well as variable costs are as follows:

Machine	Fixed Costs, Set up Labor plus Special Tooling	Variable Costs, Labor, Supplies, Power, etc., per Unit
A	$ 5.00	$00.19
B	30.00	00.10
C	70.00	00.06

What are the breakeven volumes between machines A and B, B and C?

4.   A university operates its own printing plant in conjunction with a variety of printed materials such as catalogs, announcements, special pamphlets, academic journals, etc. There is also a university press that publishes hardbound and softbound books, and these books are printed by the university printing department. The university administration is considering the printing of department and school announcements and catalogs with outside printers in order to reduce the long lead times associated with the internal printing department. As a typical example, the catalog of the Graduate School of Management is put out to bid and the bid is compared with the internal cost break down. The lowest outside bidder quotes $2000 for 10,000 copies with delivery guaranteed in three weeks. The cost analysis for internal printing with delivery in three months is as follows:

Paper	$ 150	
Composition labor	1000	
Press labor	200	
Direct costs		$1350
Press room overhead, 200 per cent of direct labor	2400	
Total press room costs		$3750
General and administrative overhead, 25 per cent of total press room costs		937.50
Total costs		$4687.50

The university president is astounded by the difference between the outside and inside bids. Should the outside bid be accepted? Why?

5.   The Stamped Metal Products Company (StaMCo) is considering the manufacture of a special item for the Air Force. After considerable analysis, the company has identified the following costs:

Material	$0.5 per unit
Tooling	20 hours
Unit direct labor	0.4 hour
Labor rate	$2 per hour
Factory burden	115% of labor
General and administrative burden	20% of factory cost
Target profit	10% of total cost

Construct a breakeven chart on a 10,000 unit basis with a unit sales price of $3.

6. A foreman in an automatic screw machine department uses screw machines of essentially two sizes for all work done. One size is for small parts and the other for larger parts, the dimensions of the part dictating when it must be run on the large machines. In general, the large machine costs more originally, uses more power, and operates more slowly than the small one. These differences are summarized below for a typical order.

	Small Screw Machine	Large Screw Machine
Original cost	$18,000	$23,000
Setup time	6 hours	6 hours
Total run time (lot of 10,000 parts)	50 hours	65 hours
Value of energy	$10	$13

Labor is paid at $3.25 per hour and the departmental burden rate is 100 per cent of labor cost.

The foreman finds that he is operating to capacity with the small machines but has additional small parts to run. These parts can also be run on the large machines but, as noted before, at higher cost. He also can schedule overtime on the small machines to accomplish the work. Assume the job in question is the typical one for which data are given. Which machine should the foreman use? Why?

REFERENCES

[1] Anthony, R. N. *Management Accounting Principles* (Rev. ed.), Richard D. Irwin, Homewood, Ill., 1970.
[2] Grant, E. L., and W. G. Ireson. *Principles of Engineering Economy* (5th ed.). Ronald Press, New York, 1970.
[3] Keller, I. W., and W. L. Ferrara. *Management Accounting for Profit Control.* McGraw-Hill, New York, 1966.
[4] Stanbus, G. J. *Activity Costing and Input-Output Accounting.* Richard D. Irwin, Homewood, Ill., 1971.

CONTENTS

CHAPTER 6
CAPITAL COSTS AND INVESTMENT CRITERIA

Capital costs affect decision problems in production management whenever a physical asset or expenditure is involved that provides a continuing benefit or return. From an accounting point of view, the original capital expenditure must be recovered through the mechanism of depreciation and must be deducted from income as an expense of doing business. The number of years over which the asset is depreciated and the allocation of the total amount to each of these years (i.e., whether straight-line or some accelerated rate of depreciation) represent alternate strategies directed toward tax policy. We must remember that all these depreciation terms and allocations are arbitrary and are not designed from the point of view of cost data for decision making relative to operations. Our interest will be in capital cost data, which will aid us in deciding between alternative courses of action involving different systems of production, different degrees of mechanization, the replacement of existing assets, etc.

Let us begin our analysis with a very simple example which we shall treat in an unsophisticated way. We have just installed a piece of equipment which performs a highly specialized operation for us. The installation was a custom job which fit into our particular situation. Because of the specialized nature of the equipment and the custom installation, the equipment is of no value to anyone else; its salvage value is zero. As with many kinds of productive equipment, its useful physical life can be prolonged almost indefinitely by maintenance and repair, so it is difficult to say as yet what the life of the equipment will be. Since the equipment has no salvage value, we must face the fact that the entire $10,000 seems to go down some sort of economic sink the minute the equipment becomes ours. We say that the $10,000 is a *sunk cost*, meaning simply that it is gone forever, regardless of what we may list as the "book value" of the equipment. Since the $10,000 is "sunk," it is completely irrelevant to any future decisions because no future decision can affect it.

The cost of owning the equipment (as distinct from the costs of operating and maintaining it) is simply $10,000. We hope to spread this total over a period of time so that the *average* annual cost of ownership will not be too great. In five years the average cost of owning the equipment is only $10,000/5 = $2000 per year. In ten years the average annual cost is down to $1000 per year. This decreasing average annual cost of owning the machine is diagrammed in Figure 1. Regardless of how long we keep the equipment, this cost of owning is irrelevant because it is a past cost. The only future costs that we shall incur for this equipment are the costs of operating and maintaining it. Once the machine is installed, these are the only costs subject to managerial control by future decisions.

Let us assume that two men are required to operate the equipment at $4000 per year per man. Maintenance costs are expected to be $2000 the first year, thereafter increasing $200 per year. Figure 2 shows the total of these costs diagrammed in relation to time. We assume that there are no other pertinent costs. Since the original cost of the equipment is sunk and the only future costs are the operating and maintenance costs, we are in a position to see under what conditions we would consider this setup to be obsolete and would replace it. We would want to replace it at any time that we could find a functionally equivalent setup that could offer a total average annual cost of owning plus operation and maintenance that fell below the cost curve of Figure 2. Let us assume that during the fourth year of operation of this setup (which we shall now call the present setup), a new equipment design is developed.

This *new equipment design* has an important advantage over the old

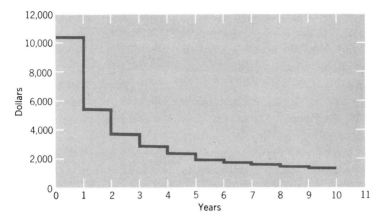

FIGURE 1.   Decreasing annual average cost of owning a machine that cost $10,000 originally and has no salvage value at any time.

one. Because it is more automatic, it can be operated by one man. The more automatic features require an additional $1000 maintenance effort, however; therefore the first-year operating and maintenance cost is expected to be $4000 operating labor plus $3000 maintenance. This total

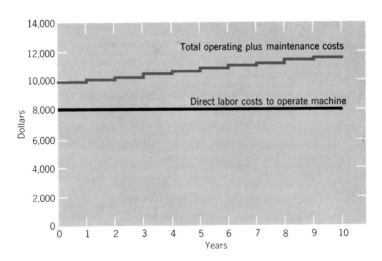

FIGURE 2.   Operating and maintenance costs, showing rising costs of maintenance.

of $7000 is expected to increase by $200 per year as before because of mounting maintenance charges. The improved design costs $12,000 installed. Now we want to see if the average annual total of the costs of owning plus operating and maintaining the improved equipment design is less than the $10,600 current annual expense (fourth year) for the present setup. First, let us note that while we ignore the original sunk cost of the present setup, this is not true for the installed cost of the improved design. It is still a future cost. We have not bought it yet, so the installed cost must be considered.

To see the picture clearly, let us plot, on the same chart, the average annual cost of owning (capital cost) and the annual operating and maintenance costs for the improved equipment design. These costs are shown in Figure 3, where we also show the total of the two costs year by year. The total cost curve is developed simply by adding the cost of owning to the operating and maintenance costs for each year. Note that the total cost is very high during the first two years, reaches a minimum during the eighth year, and then begins to rise again. It is high in the early years because the annual average costs of owning the equipment are very high during those years. It begins to rise again, but slowly, after the eighth year because of the influence of rising maintenance costs. Now let us examine the significance of the total cost curve for this simplified example. For the present setup the total incremental cost for this year is $10,600, as we have already noted, a sum that we expect will become larger in future years. However, the total average annual cost for the proposed setup will be less than $10,600 after the fourth year. It seems clear that a decision to replace the present setup is needed.

The situation we have assumed is quite clear cut. However, we may raise the question: "What criteria for comparison are we using here?" The answer is that we are looking at the best possible future cost performance for both the present and proposed setups. The best cost performance possible for the present design is $10,600, which is this year's operating and maintenance cost. The best cost performance possible for the proposed design is achieved if it is held in service for eight years; its total cost would average only $9900 per year for the entire eight-year span. As long as the best performance of the proposed design (represented by the minimum of the total cost curve) is less than the best performance of the present design, it would be economical to make the switch. Of course, this statement must be tempered with a

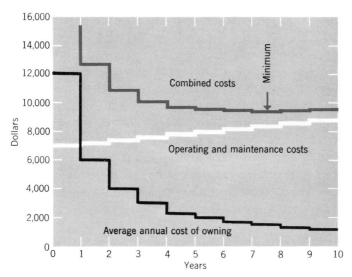

FIGURE 3.   Year-by-year average costs for a proposed replacement machine costing $12,000 initially and having no
salvage value at any time.

recognition of important intangible values and the accuracy of the
cost estimates.

Opportunity Costs

We have been assuming a fairly simple situation where we have chosen
to ignore certain factors. Let us introduce some additional ideas. Suppose
that we are discussing an asset that is used for more general purposes,
such as an over-the-road semitrailer truck. Let us assume that we own
such a truck and the first question before us is: "How much will it
cost us to *own* this truck for one more year?" These costs of owning,
or capital costs, cannot be derived from the ordinary accounting records
of the organization. The cost of owning it for one more year depends on
its current value. If the truck can be sold on the second-hand market for
$5000, this is a measure of its economic value. Since it has value, we have
two basic alternatives: we can sell it for $5000 or we can retain it. If
we sell, the $5000 can earn interest or a return on an alternative invest-
ment. If we keep the truck, we forego the return, which then becomes
an *opportunity cost* of holding the truck one more year. Similarly, if
we keep the truck, it will be worth less a year from now, so there is a

second opportunity cost measured by the fall in salvage value during the year.

The loss of opportunity to earn a return and the loss of salvage value during the year are the costs of continued ownership. They are opportunity costs rather than costs paid out; nevertheless, they can be of real importance in comparing alternatives that require different amounts of investment. There is one more possible component of capital cost for the next year if the truck is retained—the cost of possible renewals or "capital additions" necessary to keep the truck operating. We are not thinking of ordinary maintenance here, but major overhauls such as a new engine or an engine overhaul that extend the physical life for some time. In summary, the capital costs or costs of owning the truck for one more year are:

1. Opportunity costs:
   a. Interest on opening salvage value.
   b. Loss in salvage value during the year.
2. Capital additions or renewals required to keep the truck running for at least an additional year.

By assuming a schedule of salvage values, we can compute the year-by-year capital costs for an asset. This is done in Table I for a truck that cost

TABLE I.   Year-by-Year Capital Costs for a Semitrailer Truck, Given a Salvage Schedule (interest at 10%)

Year	Year-End Salvage Value	Fall in Salvage Value during Year	Interest on Opening Salvage Value	Capital Cost, Sum of Fall in Value, and Interest
New	$10,000	—	—	—
1	8,300	$1,700	$1,000	$2,700
2	6,900	1,400	830	2,230
3	5,700	1,200	690	1,890
4	4,700	1,000	570	1,570
5	3,900	800	470	1,270
6	3,200	700	390	1,090
7	2,700	500	320	820
8	2,300	400	270	670
9	1,950	350	230	580
10	1,650	300	195	495

$10,000 initially and has the salvage schedule indicated. The final result is the projected capital cost incurred for each year. If we determine the way operating and maintenance costs increase as the truck ages, we can plot a set of curves of yearly costs. The combined capital plus operating and maintenance cost curve will have a minimum point as before. This minimum of the combined cost curve defines the best cost-performance year in the life of the equipment. Beyond that year, the effect of rising maintenance costs more than counterbalances the declining capital costs. Note that such a plot is different from Figure 3 where we were plotting annual average costs instead of yearly costs.

Obsolescence and Economic Life

What is the effect of obsolescence on the cost of owning and operating a machine? By definition, when a machine is obsolete there exists an alternative machine or system that is more economical to own and operate. Clearly, the existence of the new machine does not cause any increase in the cost of operating and maintaining the present machine. Those costs are already determined by the design, installation, and condition of the present machine. However, the existence of the new machine causes the salvage value of the present setup to fall and, therefore, induces an increased capital cost. Thus, for assets in technologically dynamic classifications, the salvage value schedule falls rapidly in anticipation of typical obsolescence rates. Economic lives are very short. On the other hand, where the rate of innovation is relatively slow, salvage values hold up fairly well.

Table II compares year-by-year capital costs for two machines which cost $10,000 initially but have different salvage schedules. The value of machine 1 holds the best, machine 2 having more severe obsolescence reflected in its salvage schedule. The result is that capital costs in the initial years are greater for machine 2 than for machine 1. The average capital costs for the first five years are:

Machine 1	$1913
Machine 2	$2198

Therefore, if the schedules of operating expenses for the two machines were identical, machine 1 would seem more desirable. However, since the timing of the capital costs is different for the two machines, it would be better, for comparative purposes if we could adjust all figures to their equivalent present values.

TABLE II. Comparison of Capital Costs for Two Machines Costing $10,000 Initially but with Different Salvage Schedules (interest at 10%)

Machine 1				Machine 2			
Year-End Salvage Value	Fall in Value During Year	Interest at 10% on Opening Value	Capital Cost	Year-End Salvage Value	Fall in Value During Year	Interest at 10% on Opening Value	Capital Cost
$10,000	—	—	—	$10,000	—	—	—
8,330	$1,670	$1,000	$2,670	7,150	$2,850	$1,000	$3,850
6,940	1,390	833	2,223	5,100	2,050	715	2,765
5,780	1,160	694	1,854	3,640	1,460	510	1,970
4,820	960	578	1,538	2,600	1,040	364	1,404
4,020	800	482	1,282	1,860	740	260	1,000
3,350	670	402	1,072	1,330	530	186	716
2,790	560	335	895	950	380	133	513
2,320	470	279	749	680	270	95	365
1,930	390	232	622	485	195	68	263
1,610	320	193	513	345	140	49	189

Present Values

Since money has a time value, future expenditures and opportunity costs will have different present or current values to us. What do we mean by the time value of money? Since money can earn interest, $1000 in hand now is equivalent to $1100 a year from now if the present sum can earn interest at 10 per cent. Similarly, if we must wait a year to receive $1000 due now, we should expect not $1000 a year hence but $1100. When the time spans involved are extended, the appropriate interest is compounded and its effect becomes much larger. The timing of payments and receipts can make an important difference in the value of various alternatives.

Let us illustrate this point briefly and more precisely before returning to the example of the two machines. We know that if a principal sum P is invested at interest rate i, it will yield a future total sum S in n years hence if all of the earnings are retained and compounded. Therefore, P in the present is entirely equivalent to S in the future by virtue of the compound amount factor. That is,

$$S = P(1 + i)^n$$

where $(1 + i)^n$ = the compound amount factor for interest rate i and n years.

Similarly, we can solve for P to determine the present worth of a sum to be paid n years hence. That is,

$$P = \frac{S}{(1 + i)^n} = S \times PV_{sp}$$

where PV_{sp} = the present value of a single payment S to be made n years hence with interest rate i. Therefore, if we were to receive a payment of \$10,000 in ten years, we should be willing to accept a smaller but equivalent sum now. If interest at 10 per cent were considered fair and adequate, that smaller but equivalent sum would be:

$$P = 10,000 \times 0.3855 = \$3,855$$

since

$$\frac{1}{(1 + 0.10)^{10}} = PV_{sp} = 0.3855$$

Now let us return to the example of the two machines. The capital costs for each machine occur by different schedules because of different salvage values. If all future values were adjusted to the present as a common base time, we could compare the totals to see which investment alternative was advantageous. This we have done in Table III, where we have assumed an operating cost schedule in column (2), determined combined operating and capital costs in columns (5) and (6), and listed present values in columns (8) and (9). The present value of the entire stream of expenditures and opportunity costs is \$32,398 for machine 1. The net difference in present values for the two machines is shown at the bottom of Table III. Since the operating cost schedule was identical for both machines, the difference reflects differences in the present worth of capital costs. Obviously, the method allows for different operating cost schedules as well.

There are some difficulties with the methods just described. First, we have assumed that the schedule of salvage values is known, which, more often than not, is not true. Second, at some point in the life of the machines it becomes economical to replace them with identical models. Therefore, a chain of identical machines should be considered for comparative purposes; the machine is replaced in the year in which operating and capital costs are just equal to the interest on the present worth of all future costs. The essence of this latter statement is that we are seeking a balance between this year's costs (operating and capital costs) and opportunity income from disposal (interest on the present worth of all future costs). When the opportunity income from disposal is

TABLE III. Present Value of Capital and Operating Costs for the Two Machines from Table II; Schedule of Operating Costs Is the Same for Both Machines (interest at 10%)

Year (1)	Operating Cost (2)	Capital Costs (from Table II)		Combined Operating and Capital Costs		Present Worth Factor for Year Indicated** (7)	Present Worth of Combined Costs for Year Indicated	
		Machine 1 (3)	Machine 2 (4)	Machine 1 (5)	Machine 2 (6)		Machine 1 (8)	Machine 2 (9)
1	$3,000	$2,670	$3,850	$5,670	$6,850	0.909	$5,154	$6,227
2	3,200	2,223	2,765	5,423	5,765	0.826	4,479	4,762
3	3,400	1,854	1,970	5,254	5,370	0.751	3,946	4,033
4	3,600	1,538	1,404	5,138	5,004	0.683	3,509	3,418
5	3,800	1,282	1,000	5,082	4,800	0.621	3,160	2,981
6	4,000	1,072	716	5,072	4,716	0.565	2,866	2,665
7	4,200	895	513	5,095	4,713	0.513	2,614	2,418
8	4,400	749	365	5,149	4,765	0.467	2,405	2,225
9	4,600	622	273	5,222	4,873	0.424	2,214	2,066
10	4,800	513	189	5,313	4,989	0.386	2,051	1,926
Totals							$32,398	$32,721

Machine 1, present worth of all future values is total of column (8) less present worth of tenth-year salvage value, i.e., $32,398 − 1610* × 0.386 = 32,398 − 621 = $31,777.

Machine 2, $32,721 − 345* × 0.386 = 32,721 − 133 = $32,588.

*Tenth-year salvage values from Table II.

**From Table I (Appendix A).

the greater of the two, replacement with the identical machine is called for. Most common criteria for comparing alternative capital investments attempt to circumvent these problems by: (a) assuming an economic life and (b) assuming some standard schedule for the decline in value of the asset. We shall now consider some of these criteria.

COMMON CRITERIA FOR COMPARING ECONOMIC ALTERNATIVES

Some of the common criteria used for evaluating proposals for capital expenditures and for comparing alternatives involving capital assets are: (a) present values, (b) average investment, (c) rate of return, and (d) payoff period.

Present Value Criterion

Present value methods for comparing alternatives take the sum of present values of all future out-of-pocket expenditures and credits over the economic life of the asset. This figure is compared for each alternative. If differences in revenue are also involved, their present values must also be accounted for. Table I in Appendix A gives the present values for single future payments or credits; Table II in Appendix A gives present values for annuities for various years and interest rates. An annuity is a sum that is received or paid annually. The factors in Table II convert the entire series of annual sums to a single sum in the present for various interest rates and years. We shall use the notation PV_a for the present value factor of an annuity.

An Example

Suppose we are considering a machine that costs $15,000 installed. We estimate that the economic life of the machine is eight years, at which time its salvage value is expected to be about $3000. For simplicity, we take the average operating and maintenance costs to be $5000 per year. At 10 per cent interest, the present value of the expenditures and credits is:

Initial investment	$15,000 \times PV_{sp} = 15,000 \times 1.000 =$	15,000
Annual operating and maintenance costs	$5,000\ PV_a = 5,000 \times 5.335 =$	26,675
		41,675

Less credit of present
value of salvage to be
received in eight years $3,000 \times PV_{sp} = 3,000 \times 0.467 =$ 1,401
                                                                        $$\overline{\$40,274}$$

The net total of $40,274 is the present value of the expenditures and credits over the eight-year expected life of the machine. The initial investment is already at present value; that is, the present value factor is 1.000. The annual costs of operation and maintenance are an eight-year annuity, so the entire stream of annual costs can be adjusted to present value by the multiplication of PV_a from Table II (Appendix A). Finally, the present value of the salvage is deducted. This total could be compared with comparable figures for other alternatives over the same eight-year period. If another alternative machine is estimated to have a different economic life, perhaps four years, then to make the present value totals comparable, two cycles of the four-year machine would be compared with one cycle of the eight-year machine. If the operating and maintenance costs increased as the machine aged, the present value of the expenditure in each year would be determined separately by PV_{sp}.

Average Investment Criterion

Average investment methods estimate an average annual cost of owning plus operating and maintaining an asset. The average annual capital costs are approximated by average salvage loss plus interest on the average investment, assuming the decline in value of the asset is on a uniform or straight-line basis. Figure 4 shows the assumed structure for the decline in value of an asset and the calculation of average investment. Thus, if a machine cost $10,000 and was estimated to have a ten-year life with a salvage value at the end of that time of $1000, the capital costs are approximated by:

$$\text{Average annual salvage loss,} \quad \frac{10,000 - 1,000}{10} = \$900$$

Annual interest on average investment, at 10%
$$\frac{(10,000 + 1,000)0.10}{2} = 5,500 \times 0.10 = \$550$$

Average annual capital cost $= \$900 + \$550 = \$1,450$

If operating and maintenance costs were estimated to average $12,500 per year over the ten-year machine life, the total average annual cost for comparison would be $1,450 + 12,500 = \$13,950$. Differences in annual revenue between alternatives can be accounted for in the operating costs. Comparable calculations for alternative machines would form the basis for comparison. For a strictly economic comparison, the alternative presenting the lowest average annual cost would be selected.

Rate of Return Criterion

One common method of evaluating new projects or comparing alternative courses of action is to calculate a rate of return which is then judged for adequacy. Usually no attempt is made to take account of interest costs, so the resulting figure is referred to as the "unadjusted" rate of return, that is, unadjusted for interest values. It is computed as follows:

Unadjusted rate of return

$$= \frac{100 \,(\text{net monetary operating advantage} - \text{amortization})}{\text{average investment}}$$

The net monetary advantage reflects the algebraic sum of incremental costs of operation and maintenance and possible differences in revenue. If the rate computed is a "before-tax" rate, then the amortization

$$\left(\frac{\text{Incremental investment}}{\text{Economic life}}\right)$$

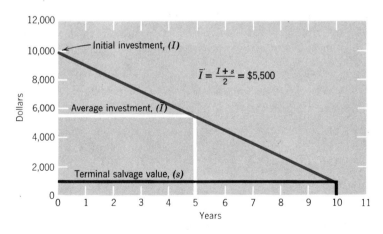

FIGURE 4.   Relationship of initial investment, terminal salvage value, and average investment for "average investment methods."

is subtracted and the result is divided by average investment and multiplied by 100 to obtain a percentage return. If an "after-tax" rate is sought, the net increase in income taxes due to the project is subtracted from the net monetary advantage and the balance of the calculation is as it was before. Obviously, the adequacy of a given rate of return changes drastically if it is being judged as an after-tax return.

An Example

Let us carry through a simple example. We assume that new methods have been proposed for the line assembly of a product which had been assembled in a central area, each assembly being completed by one individual. The new methods require the purchase and installation of conveyors and fixtures that cost $50,000 installed including the costs of relayout. The new line assembly methods require five fewer assemblers. After the increased maintenance and power costs are added in, the net monetary operating advantage is estimated as $20,000 per year. Economic life is estimated at five years. The unadjusted before-tax return is:

$$\frac{20,000 - \dfrac{50,000}{5}}{\dfrac{50,000}{2}} \times 100 = 40\%$$

The after-tax return requires that incremental taxes be deducted. Incremental taxable income will be the operating advantage less increased allowable tax depreciation. Assuming straight-line depreciation and an allowed depreciation term of eight years, incremental taxable income is $20,000 less $50,000/8, or $20,000 - $6,250 = $13,750. Assuming an income tax rate of 50 per cent, the incremental tax due to the project is $6875. The after-tax return is therefore:

$$\frac{20,000 - 6,875 - 10,000}{25,000} \times 100 = \frac{3,125 \times 100}{25,000} = 12.5\%$$

Whether or not either the before- or after-tax rates calculated in this example are adequate is a matter to be judged in relation to the risk involved in the particular venture and the returns possible through alternate uses of the capital.

Payoff Periods

The payoff period is the time required for an investment to "pay for itself" through the net operating advantage that would result from its installation. It is calculated as follows:

$$\text{Payoff period in years} = \frac{\text{Net investment}}{\text{Net annual operating advantage after taxes}}$$

The payoff period for the conveyor installation which we discussed previously is

$$\frac{\$50,000}{\$13,125} = 3.8 \text{ years}$$

It is the period of time for the net after-tax advantage to just equal the net total amount invested. Presumably, after that period, "it is all gravy"; the $13,125 per year is profit since the invested amount has been recovered. The question might be raised: "If the economic life of the equipment is five years and 15 percent is regarded as an appropriate rate of after-tax return for the project, what *should* the payoff period be?" Obviously, the period for both capital recovery and return is the five-year economic life. The period that recovers capital only, but that also allows enough time left in the economic life to provide the return, will be somewhat shorter and will depend on the required rate of return. Let us note now that the payoff period is another interpretation that can be given to the present value factors for annuities, PV_a, given in Table II (Appendix A). As an example, for an economic life of five years and a return rate of 15 percent, $PV_a = 3.352$ from Table II (Appendix A). This indicates that capital recovery takes place in 3.352 years. The equivalent of 15 percent compound interest takes place in $5.000 - 3.352 = 1.648$ years. Therefore, any of the PV_a values in Table II (Appendix A) for a given economic life in years and a given return rate indicate the shorter period in years required to return the investment. Or, more simply, they give directly the payoff period.

The proper procedure would be to estimate economic life and determine the applicable return rate. From the present value tables, determine the payoff period associated with these conditions. Then compute the actual payoff period of the project in question and compare it to the standard period from the tables. If the computed period is less than, or equal to, the standard period, the project meets the payoff and risk requirements imposed. If the computed value is greater than the table value, the project would earn less than the required rate.

SUMMARY

In this chapter we have attempted to survey the cost concepts that bear on investment decisions, such as sunk costs and opportunity costs, as well as to describe the most common investment criteria used by business and industry today. All these methods represent some approximation and idealization of the general investment problem. For example, all require an assumption of an economic life and of some standard schedule for the decline in value of the assets being analyzed. In addition, there are many less obvious conceptual ideas for which they do not account.

The various criteria are not all equivalent or interchangeable. The present value methods are the most flexible and involve the least assumptions. They can be tailored to meet specific situations involving wide variations in salvage schedules, projected cost patterns, and future periodic capital additions. The average investment criterion is basically an approximation to a variant of present value methods which expresses the data in terms of an equivalent average annual cost adjusted for interest values. The average investment criterion computes an average annual cost which assumes a uniform decline in salvage value of the assets and ignores the timing of expenditures by computing interest on average investment. The average investment, rate of return, and payoff criteria all approximate future operating costs by an average period. For simple machines, this may be a reasonable assumption; but for complex equipment and for buildings, future costs may have a pattern in relation to time which is not well represented by an average figure.

In terms of the preference of using one criterion over another, there are some reasonable guides. If the project involves long projected lives with complex patterns of future expenditures, interest values may tip the balance in favor of one alternative, and the present value criterion should be used. When future operating costs are reasonably well represented by an average figure, the choice between average investment, rate of return, and payoff period may rest on the preference for a particular way of expressing answers; that is, in terms of return on investment, annual costs, or time to pay off.

KEY CONCEPTS

Capital Costs.   Most production systems involve a fairly heavy investment in plant and equipment. The term, "capital cost" relates these capital outlays to a time dimension. Thus, in a given year the capital costs are represented by the shrinkage in market value of the assets plus interest on the market value.

Opportunity Costs.   Though opportunity costs are never recorded in the chart of accounts of an enterprise, they have considerable significance in certain kinds of managerial decisions. The capital costs referred to previously were in fact opportunity costs. If the assets in question have a certain market value at the beginning of the year, and are projected to have a somewhat smaller value at the end of the year, the difference is an opportunity cost since by retaining the asset we have foregone the opportunity to prevent the loss. Similarly, the interest cost is an opportunity cost since by retaining the asset instead of selling it, we forego the opportunity to invest the proceeds to earn interest income.

Sunk Cost.   The concept of a sunk cost is important to the understanding of capital costs and investment decisions. The accounting concept of "book value" confuses the understanding of sunk costs for many individuals for it conveys the notion that managerial decisions can somehow affect these costs through capital investment decisions. When a cost is "sunk" it is completely irrelevant to any future decisions because no future decision can affect it.

Economic Life.   The understanding of production economics cannot be complete without an understanding of the concept of economic life of physical assets. Economic life has nothing to do with the quality characteristics of a machine or the excellence of its original conception and design. Rather, it has to do with the excellence in concept and design of its successors which become its competitors. A machine is obsolete when there exists an alternate machine or system that is more economical to own and operate. Thus, we have a ruthless competition among machines.

Present Value.   The concept of present value has considerable significance in models where cost values extend over a long time period into the future. Where futures are involved with large cash flows, the opportunity costs become significant and all costs must be placed on a basis which takes into account the time value of money.

IMPORTANT TERMS

Numbers in parentheses indicate page numbers.

1.   Annuity (151)
2.   Average investment criterion (152)
3.   Capital addition (146)
4.   Cost of operating (143)
5.   Cost of owning (142, 145)
6.   Economic life (147)
7.   Obsolescence (147)
8.   Payoff period (154)
9.   Present value criterion (151)
10.   Rate of return criterion (153)
11.   Salvage loss (146)
12.   Salvage value (146)

REVIEW QUESTIONS

Numbers in parentheses indicate page numbers.

1. Why is a sunk cost irrelevant in models for investment? (142)
2. How are book values of equipment handled in investment analysis? (142)
3. What is an opportunity cost? (145)
4. What are capital costs? (146)
5. What is the structure of capital costs incurred by retaining ownership of an asset one more year? (145–146)
6. What is the meaning of the term, "economic life"? Physical life? (145–147)
7. How is obsolescence reflected in the actual costs of owning and operating an asset? (147)
8. What is the compound amount factor? How is it computed? (148–149)
9. What is the meaning of the reciprocal of the compound amount factor? (149)
10. What is an annuity? (151)
11. Define the factor PV_a. (151)
12. Why is it that most common criteria for comparing alternate capital investments assume an economic life and some standard schedule for the decline in value of the asset? (149)
13. Outline the methodology for comparing alternative investments by the present value criterion. (151–152)
14. How are the capital costs approximated in the average investment criterion? (152)
15. Compare the calculations required for the before- and after-tax rate of return (153–154)
16. Outline the payoff period criterion methodology. With what standard payoff period should the computed value be compared to determine if the investment is justified? How is the standard payoff period determined? (154–155)
17. Compare and evaluate the four criteria for investment analysis discussed. Under what conditions might we use each of them? (154–155)

SELF-TEST TRUE-FALSE QUESTIONS

Numbers in parentheses indicate page numbers.

1. Depreciation policy is commonly determined in such a way as to aid us in deciding between alternative courses of action involving different systems of production, different degrees of mechanization, the replacing of existing assets, etc. (141)
2. Depreciation on equipment is commonly classified as a sunk cost. (142)

3.   When operating costs tend to rise as a piece of capital equipment ages, the curve of the average annual cost of owning the equipment plus operating and maintaining it will have a minimum point in it. (145)

4.   The capital costs, or costs of owning an asset for one more year, are made up of opportunity costs and possible capital additions or renewals. (146)

5.   The opportunity costs of owning a piece of equipment for one more year are made up of interest costs and fall in salvage value during the year. (146)

6.   An obsolescence cost for capital equipment tends to show up in terms of increased operating and maintenance charges. (147)

7.   Present value methods in equipment analysis reduce all revenues and expenditures at an appropriate interest rate to their value at the time of replacement. (151)

8.   In the average investment criterion for comparing economic alternatives, average annual salvage loss is approximated by straight line depreciation. (152)

9.   When using the rate of return criterion for comparing economic alternatives, the rate of return yielded by a proposed new asset must exceed 10 percent or the project is eliminated from consideration. (153–154)

10.   The "payoff period" is the time required for an investment to "pay for itself" through the net operating advantage which would result from its installation. (154)

11.   The proper "payoff period" for any situation may be obtained from standard present value tables. (155)

PROBLEMS

1.   A trucking firm owns a five-year-old truck that it is considering replacing. The truck can be sold for $5000, and blue book values indicate that this salvage value would be $4000 one year hence. It also appears that the trucker would need to spend $500 on a transmission overhaul if he were to keep the truck. What are the trucker's projected capital costs for next year? Interest is at 10 percent.

2.   What is the present value of the salvage of a machine that can be sold 10 years hence for $2500? Interest is at 10 percent.

3.   What is the future value in 25 years of a bond that earns interest at 10 per cent and has a present value of $10,000?

4.   At what interest rate would a $10,000 bond have to earn to be worth $50,000 in 10 years?

5.   At 8 percent interest, money will double itself in how many years?

6.   What is the present value of an income stream of $1500 for 15 years at 10 percent interest?

7.   What is the value of an annuity of $2000 per year for 10 years at the end of its life? Interest is at 10 percent.

8.   The proud owner of a new automobile states that he intends to hold his car only two years in order to minimize repair costs which he feels should be near zero during the initial period. He paid $4,000 for the car new and blue book value schedules suggest that it will be worth only $2,000 two years hence. He normally drives 10,000 miles per year and he estimates that his cost of operation is $0.10 per mile. What are his projected capital costs for the first two years, if interest of 6 percent represents a reasonable alternate investment for him?

9.   Suppose we are considering the installation of a small computer to accomplish internal tasks of payroll computation, invoicing, and other routine accounting. The purchase price is quoted as $300,000 and salvage value five years later is expected to be $100,000. The operating costs are expected to be $100,000 per year, mainly for personnel to program, operate, and maintain the computer. What is the present value of the costs to own and operate the computer over its five-year economic life? The value of money in the organization is 15 percent.

10.   Using the average investment criterion as a basis for comparison, at what annual lease cost would we break even for the data on the computer in Problem 9? If the machine is leased, maintenance is furnished, reducing annual operating costs to $70,000.

11.   An aggressive marketer of a new office copier has made its machine available for sale as well as lease. The idea of buying a copying machine seems revolutionary, but less so when we examine our present costs which come to $6,500 per year for lease plus per copy charges. If we own a machine the costs of paper and maintenance is projected to be $1,500 per year. The new copier costs $10,000 installed and is assumed to have an economic life of five years and a salvage value of $2,000.
    (a) What is the projected unadjusted rate of return if we install the copier?
    (b) If incremental taxes for the project are $1,000, what is the adjusted rate of return?

12.   What is the actual payoff period for the office copier project discussed in Problem 11? If interest is 10 percent what should the minimum payoff period be to make the investment economically sound? Does the office copier project meet the payoff standard?

13.   A concern is considering the purchase of two alternate machines to perform an important operation in their manufacturing process. The first machine is a standard one. The second is more expensive but has a higher degree of automation incorporated in it. Both meet capacity needs. Comparative data are as follows:

	Machine 1	Machine 2
Installed cost	$20,000	$30,000
Estimated economic life	10 years	10 years
Salvage value	$5,000	$7,000
Labor cost/year	$12,000	$6,000
Maintenance cost, first year	$1,000*	$2,000†

The value of money within the organization for investments of this kind is 10 percent. Which machine is preferable, using the present value criterion?

14.   A trucking firm is in the shorthaul local trucking business, servicing industrial plants which require the transfer of a wide variety of parts, materials, and packages. One large local firm has established a new plant 100 miles (6-hour round trip) away and has called for bids to truck 50 tons per day of an important subassembly unit one way to the new plant (assume 20 working days per month) and would permit transfer either during the day or during the night. The contract to be let is for a year with an option for the industrial firm to renew if performance is satisfactory. The trucking firm currently owns two 10-ton trucks which service the local shorthaul business during regular daytime working hours, but they are available for service at night. Truck drivers earn $24 for an 8-hour day with 8 hours work guaranteed.
    To take the contract the trucking firm would need to enlarge its capacity. It has narrowed the field to two types of 10-ton trucks, one of which is available on a lease basis and the other for purchase. The cost characteristics of the two trucks are as follows:

Leased diesel truck:
Lessors pays all taxes, insurance and license fees as well as maintenance. Operating costs to be absorbed by the leasee are:

*Increases $100 per year after first year.
†Increases $200 per year after first year.

Lease charges	$800 per month per truck
Fuel, oil, and tires	5¢ per mile

Purchased gasoline truck:

Purchase price is $20,000 with terminal salvage value of $4000 at the end of 6 years. Other costs are:

Fuel, oil, and tires	8¢ per mile
Maintenance	2¢ per mile
Taxes, insurance and license	$100 per month per truck

Determine the number of additional trucks required, assuming that no truck can be operated more than 16 hours per day. Using the *average* investment criterion, determine which alternative is the cheaper of the two. (Interest rate = 15 percent.) What action do you recommend?

15.   A new office duplicating machine costing $5600 will enable a company to save $0.03 per sheet. The present usage rate is approximately 9000 sheets per month. Calculate the after-tax rate of return.

Economic life	8 years
Depreciation term	10 years
Depreciation method	Straight-line
Incremental tax rate	50 percent
Interest rate	10 percent

16.   You have been offered the popcorn concession at the Stamped Metal Products Company (StaMCo) for five years at a cost of $2000 including equipment. A preliminary analysis indicates that annual operating costs would be $4000 and mean annual sales would be $5000. You would like a 12 percent return on your investment. (Ignore taxes; use $500 salvage value.)

(a) Determine the acceptance or rejection of this investment on the basis of the payoff period criterion.

(b) Determine the acceptance or rejection on the basis of present value criteria.

(c) If the equipment costs $1500 and will be worth $500 at the end of five years, what is the annual straight-line depreciation?

(d) What is the yearly investment in equipment?

17.   A new machine costing $108,000 will give a $64,000 per year net operating advantage before taxes. Calculate the after tax rate of return.

Depreciation term	6 years
Depreciation method	Straight-line
Economic life	4 years

Tax rate   50 percent
Interest rate   10 percent

REFERENCES

[1] Grant, E. L., and W. G. Ireson. *Principles of Engineering Economy* (5th ed.). Ronald Press, New York, 1970.

[2] Reisman, A. *Managerial and Engineering Economics*. Allyn and Bacon, Boston, 1971.

[3] Reisman, A. and E. S. Buffa. "A General Model for Investment Policy." *Management Science*, 8 (3), Apr. 1962.

[4] Terborgh, G. *Business Investment Policy*. Machinery and Allied Products Institute, Washington,D.C., 1958.

[5] Thuesen, H. G., W. J. Fabrycky, and G. J. Thuesen. *Engineering Economy* (4th ed.). Prentice-Hall, Englewood Cliffs, N.J., 1971.

PART 3
DESIGN OF PRODUCTIVE SYSTEMS

CONTENTS

CHAPTER 7
PRODUCTION DESIGN AND PROCESSES

The minimum possible cost of producing a part or product is established originally by the designer. The most clever production engineer cannot change this
situation, he can only minimize the production cost within the limitations of the
design. Therefore, the obvious time to start thinking about basic modes of production for parts and products is while they are still in the design stage. This conscious effort to design for low manufacturing cost is referred to as *production
design,* as distinct from functional design. To be sure, the designer's first responsibility is to create something that functionally meets requirements, but once this
is accomplished, ordinarily there are alternatives of design, all of which meet
functional requirements. Which of these alternatives will minimize production
cost? A well-conceived design has already narrowed the available alternatives
and specified, for example, a sand-casting, if that is appropriate in view of both
function and cost considerations.

Given the design, *process planning* for manufacture must be carried out to

167

specify, in careful detail, the processes required and their sequence. Production design first sets the minimum possible cost that can be achieved through the specification of materials, tolerances, basic configurations, methods of joining parts, etc. Final process planning then attempts to achieve that minimum through the specification of processes and their sequence which meet the exacting requirements of the design specifications. Here, the process planner may work under the limitations of available equipment in small lot manufacture (see Chapter 17 on production scheduling). But if the volume is great or the design stable or both, he may be able to consider special-purpose equipment and special-purpose layout (see Chapter 10 on layout). In performing his functions, the process planner is setting the basic design of the production system.

PRODUCTION DESIGN

The strong relation between product design and production cost has long been recognized by industry; various attempts to cope with the problem have been made. In general, engineers who design products are trained in the technical aspects of their specialties, such as mechanical design, electronics, and thermodynamics, and not in manufacturing methods and costs. On the other hand, production men often simply ignore the functional requirements of a part and meet the exact specifications while they curse the designer. This lack of mutual understanding is expressed by the following little poem, credited to Mr. Kenneth Lane, a design engineer at the General Electric Company [6].

As Some Men See Us

The Designer bent across his board
Wonderful things in his head were stored
And he said as he rubbed his throbbing bean
"How can I make this thing tough to machine?
If this part here were only straight
I'm sure the thing would work first rate,
But 'twould be so easy to turn and bore
It never would make the machinists sore.
I better put in a right angle there
Then watch those babies tear their hair
Now I'll put the holes that hold the cap
Way down in here where they're hard to tap.

Now this piece won't work, I'll bet a buck
For it can't be held in a shoe or chuck
It can't be drilled or it can't be ground
In fact the design is exceedingly sound."
He looked again and cried—"At last—
Success is mine, it can't even be cast."

To combat the problem, some companies have tried to train their designers concerning basic manufacturing processes and costs. Others have had production engineers consult with designers at the time of critical decisions; still others have turned over functional designs to an entirely different group whose responsibility is production design. Lockheed Aircraft Corporation [8] has a cost analysis group within their engineering division which is used primarily in making comparative cost analyses of design proposals. A monthly control graph is kept which shows the effect of design decisions on projected manufacturing cost in relation to the limits of the possible high and low, indicated by alternative designs that meet functional requirements.

The thesis of a production design philosophy is that nearly always alternatives of design exist that still meet functional requirements. For the projected volume of the part or product, then, what differences in cost would result? Here we must broaden our thinking because the possible areas of cost which can be affected by design are likely to be more pervasive than we imagine. There are the obvious cost components of direct labor and materials, but perhaps not so obvious are the effects on equipment costs, tooling costs, indirect labor costs, and the non-manufacturing costs of engineering. Indirect costs tend to be hidden, but suppose one design required 30 different parts whereas another required only 15. There are differences in indirect costs due to the greater paperwork and the cost of ordering, storing, and controlling 30 parts instead of 15 for each completed item. Figure 1 shows a comparison for just such a situation involving alternate designs of a typical aircraft control surface. The indirect cost for each design is composed of those items necessary to process parts through the paperwork system and includes items such as planning; tool ordering; material purchasing; shop and assembly order writing; storage of material; dispatching of material, tools, and parts; order control; accounting; transportation; inspection; etc.

A typical cost breakdown showing how design affects various com-

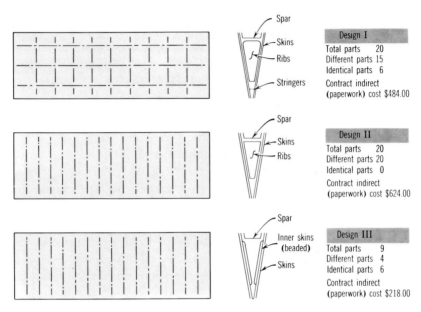

FIGURE 1.   Effect of alternative designs on indirect labor costs. (From [8].)

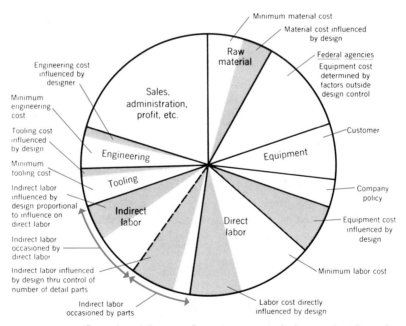

FIGURE 2.   Cost breakdown of a transport airplane, showing the effect of design alternatives on various major components of cost. (From [8].)

ponents is shown in Figure 2. The shaded areas of Figure 2 indicate the relative amount of the cost category under the direct control of the design engineer. The shaded areas were determined by studies at Lockheed of detailed cost estimates over a period of years. Hundreds of designs were analyzed "by taking the difference in cost between two or more designs which were functionally acceptable, the difference in cost between the least and most expensive indicating the effect the Design Engineer had in determining the cost of the product [8]."

PROCESSES

The scope of production processes covers the entire spectrum from the completely manual task, through man-machine systems, to auto-mated processes where labor is either indirect or of a vigilance nature. Manual tasks, usually in combination with mechanical aids, still account for a large share of productive activity. The design of these manual tasks and the manual or vigilance phases of machine operations are considered separately in Chapters 11 and 12. Manual operations, or man-machine operations that have a strong manual component, are typical of assembly work, offices, supermarkets, hospitals, and so on.

Some production processes have a considerable technological base. The metal-working industries, wood-working industries, plastics, and chemicals are representative of these.

Processes Involve Transformation

The basic nature of processing is one of transformation, that is, some-thing is happening which in some way transforms the thing being worked on. In general, these transformations may effect a chemical change, alter the basic shape or form, add or subtract parts as in assembly, change the location of the thing being processed as in transportation operations, provide or alter information systems as in clerical operations, or check on the accuracy of any other process as in inspection operations.

Chemical Processes.   Chemical processes are common in industries such as petroleum, plastics, steel-making, and aluminum. It is, of course, impossible to generalize in a short time the nature and range of chemical processing. Industrially, these processes occur both as batch processes and continuous processes. Illustrative of batch processes is the operation of a blast furnace in the steel industry. Figure 3 is a diagram of the basic flows involved. In the operation of a blast furnace, pig

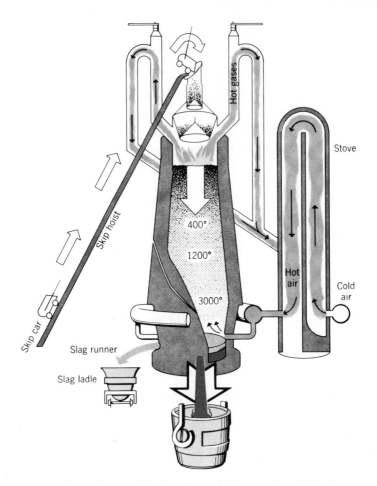

FIGURE 3.   Diagram of a blast furnace for making pig iron.

iron is produced from iron ore, coke, and limestone. Skip cars running up an inclined track charge iron ore, coke, and limestone into the top hopper in alternate layers. Blasts of hot air are injected at the bottom of the furnace which serves to support the combustion of the coke. As the coke burns, the oxygen in the iron ore is absorbed. The charge gradually moves downward in the furnace into progressively higher temperature zones until the iron becomes molten and forms a pool at the bottom of the furnace. The limestone absorbs certain impurities. Periodically a batch of molten iron is drawn off into the ladle and is later poured into ingots. Continuous chemical processes might be typified by petroleum processes. Here the material being processed moves continuously through a series of heating, pressurizing, mixing, etc.—processes of great complexity.

Processes to Change, Shape, or Form.   The most common processes of this general type are found in the metal-forming and machining industries, the wood-working industry, and in plastic molding and forming. In the metal industries, some of the primary forming operations may take place at the mill, such as the rolling of basic shapes in steel, aluminum, or other metals. The result of these processes are bars, sheets, billets, I-beams, and many other shapes which are standard and can be used to advantage for further processing. Alternately, some products would require beginning with some molding process such as sand-casting or die-casting to establish the basic shape or form which may or may not require further processing. Figure 4 shows four important steps in the die-casting process. Other basic forming processes are powder metallurgy, drop-forging, and stamping. Table I shows a comparison of various forming processes together with conditions for their appropriate use.

Metal machining is accomplished through basic machine tool processes which involve the generation of cylindrical surfaces, flat surfaces, complex curves, and holes. This classification seems simple enough, but the number of different types of machine tools to accomplish these tasks is multiplied by different sizes and shapes of parts to be machined, the quality of finish required, accuracy demands, and differences in output rate demanded in various manufacturing situations. Thus a shaper and a planer are both used to generate flat surfaces. For the planer, however, the work reciprocates instead of the tool, and its reciprocating table accommodates large pieces better than does the shaper. Similarly, a grinder can produce cylindrical surfaces as does the lathe, or flat surfaces like the mill, but the big difference in application is in resulting accuracy and finish. The grinder, therefore, is largely a finishing tool, used only after other machine tools have made the rough cuts that produce the basic dimensions.

A lathe produces cylindrical surfaces, holes, threads, plain surfaces on the face of the work, and so on. But different types of lathes are adapted to different production rates. The engine lathe might be used if one or a few parts are to be produced. But if several thousand parts are to be produced, some type of automatic lathe would probably be considered. In this proliferation of machine types, we are not including special-purpose machines. The automatic lathe would still be considered

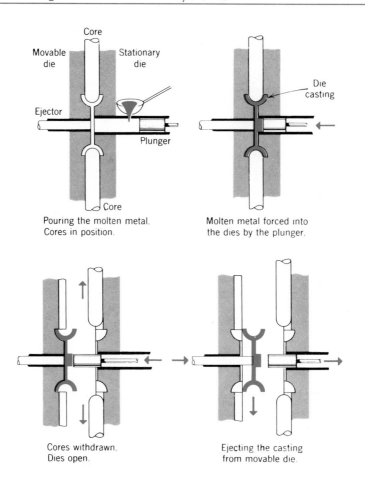

Core
Movable die
Stationary die
Die casting
Ejector
Plunger
Core
Pouring the molten metal. Cores in position.
Molten metal forced into the dies by the plunger.
Cores withdrawn. Dies open.
Ejecting the casting from movable die.

FIGURE 4.   The die-casting of brass, aluminum, or magnesium in horizontal plunger cold-chamber machine. (Courtesy Reed-Prentice Corporation.)

a general-purpose machine, since it can be set up to run various kinds of materials and parts in its general capability class. In all of these machining operations, metal is removed from the part in small chips by the cutting action of a tool. The cutting action is accomplished by either a rotating or reciprocating action of the tool relative to the part. In combination with this motion, either the tool or the work must "feed" to produce a continuous cutting action over an entire surface. Figure 5 shows a summary of tool and work piece motion for the main machine tools. Many machine tool processes have been automated through a process which combines computer instructions with the

TABLE I. Comparison of Forming Processes

Forming Processes	Tolerances Held	Setup or Tools	Run or Process Time	Finishing Required	Appropriate Volume	Other Comments
Sand-casting	Loose, 1½%/inch	Pattern, core	Long	Relatively large amount of metal to be removed	Low	Great flexibility
Die-casting	Very good, no finish machining required in many cases	Dies expensive: $1000–$10,000	Short	None to relatively small	High	In general, limited to low melting-point alloys
Powder metallurgy	Very good, ±.05%/inch	Dies, $2000 and more	Mold and sintering (intermediate)	Usually none	>5000	Very hard parts can only be made this way
Drop forge	Good	Dies, expensive	Intermediate	Relatively small	Intermediate to high	Great strength
Stamping	Good	Dies, expensive	Short	Small	High	

machine. These automated processes, known as numerically controlled processes, are discussed in greater detail later in this chapter.

Assembly Processes.   Some processes used to assemble parts and materials are welding, soldering, riveting, screw-fastening, and stapling and adhesive joining. Assembly processes are common in the automotive industry, the electronics industry, the appliance industry, and many others. Indeed, they are extremely common in all mechanical-electrical industries. The usual situation prevailing for assembly operations involves a considerable proportion of manual work, usually

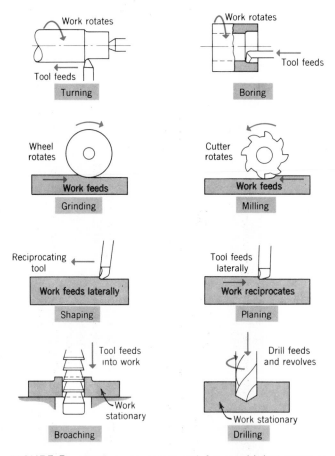

FIGURE 5.   Basic processes used for machining parts to planned dimensions. (From [2].)

supplemented by mechanical aids. In general, automation has not touched most assembly operations with the exception of high-volume electronics assembly. With the development of printed circuitry, the electronics industry has designed automatic equipment to assemble component parts, such as resistors and condensers, to the printed circuit boards. Much of the analysis of assembly types of operations depends on the analysis of hand motions and the relationships between the operator and his tools.

Transport Processes.   The transformation taking place in a transport process is the transformation of place. The economist would state that by means of a transport process we have given a part or product "place utility." Whatever the rationale, transport processes are of extreme importance in most production systems. In some phases of operations management, such as distribution, the transport operation is the one of central interest. In manufacturing, internal material handling represents one of the most costly kinds of operations performed. In Chapter 10 we focus on the nature of material-handling activities for functional and line production.

Clerical Processes and Information Systems.   Whereas mechanical kinds of processes tend to change shape or form, clerical processes transform information. The volume of clerical activity has grown rapidly to the point where the number of clerical workers in the United States is greater than the number of blue-collar workers. The equivalent of clerical activity is accomplished with a broad spectrum of techniques extending from the purely manual through all degrees of mechanization to the epitomy of automation, the integrated data processing system.

The design of the item being processed in information systems is dependent on the nature of the system itself and the degree of mechanization involved. Manual clerical operations exert a relatively small influence on the design of the item being processed. On the other hand a punched card system, or a computer based system virtually dictates the use of punched cards, magnetic tape, or perforated paper tape as the bases for information storage and input to the system. One punched card has 80 columns or a capacity for 80 characters (letters or numbers). A little over eight inches of perforated paper tape and about three-eighths inch of magnetic tape can contain the same number of characters. Magnetic tape input also has the advantage of speed. Data can be read at rates up to 170,000 characters per second, while cards are typically read at the rate of 250 to 300 characters per second and perforated tape is read at about 400 characters per second. By contrast, good human reading speeds are in the range of 300 to 500 words per minute of text with reading of numbers being very much slower. Perforated paper tape systems have been integrated with present methods of developing and transcribing records by incorporating tape writing units with typewriters and adding machines, etc. Modular systems are now available in which data entry is by a typewriter-like device, and all information is stored in files on-line to the computer. All of the usual activities associated with punched cards are eliminated. Figure 6 shows a typical application.

Figure 7 shows an overview of a total management information system for the Able Manufacturing Company, a hypothetical company manufacturing styled goods with manufacturing plants in various parts of the country and nationwide sale and distribution facilities. The concept of the system as a whole is based on a central information processing unit with a broad, up-to-date data base pertinent to sales, planning, control, finance, procurement, production, warehousing, and distribution. Current information from the various functional areas of the enterprise flows into the central processor as inputs. By a variety of models and/or programs, the various outputs are generated in the form of regular and special reports. With such an integrated system, different kinds of reports for different purposes and for different levels of management are relatively easy to generate. For example, a sales forecast by sales regions in gross dollars of sales may be of value to the sales function and to general management. But in that form it is useless to the production function which needs the information translated into products, assemblies, parts, and the equivalent demand on various classes of equipment in order to procure materials and schedule production.

General- versus Special-Purpose Machines.   General-purpose machines have general use capability in their field. For example, a typewriter is a general-purpose machine. It can be used for various kinds of copy: letters, manuscripts, some kinds of charts, and figures. On the other hand, a typewriter can be made special purpose by adapting it to the special uses of accounting. The accounting machines do the accounting tasks very well, but perform poorly on many tasks demanded of a general typewriter. In the machine shop we find the general-purpose lathe, drill press, milling machine, and planers which are capable of performing their functions by generating cylindrical surfaces,

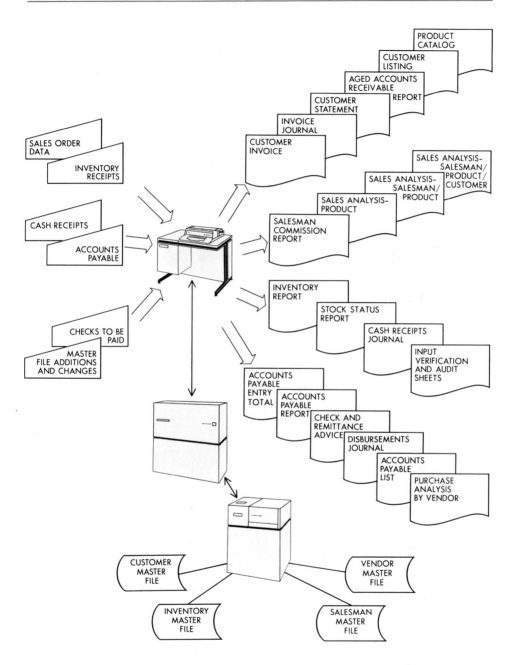

FIGURE 6.   The Singer SYSTEM TEN in which typewriter-like input updates files stored on-line to the computer. (Courtesy Singer Business Machines.)

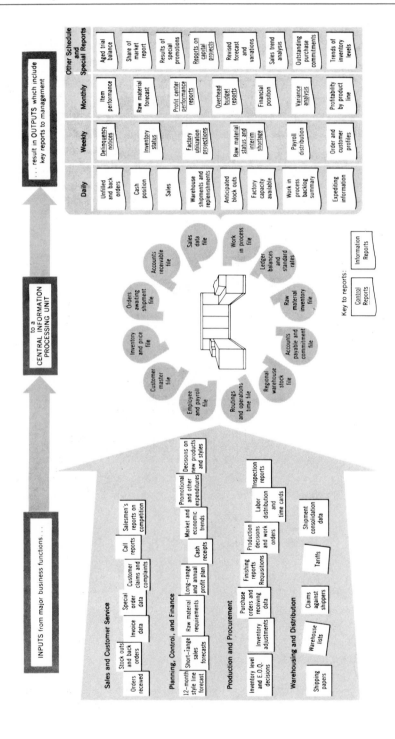

FIGURE 7. Overview of Able Manufacturing Company's integrated management information system. (From J. W. Konvalinka and H. G. Trentin, "Management Information Systems," *Management Services*, Sept.–Oct. 1965.)

holes, and flat surfaces on a wide variety of parts and materials. Yet, where the situation warrants it, we find special designs of these types of machines which are meant to produce some one part or group of parts very efficiently.

An example might be a special lathe to produce proper outside diameters for an automotive piston. It has special quick-clamping devices and special cutters, is of the right size, and runs at the proper spindle speed to machine the outside diameter surface in minimum time, yet its capability would be restricted in the machining of other parts. Since the volume of pistons is so great, this specialization of equipment design is warranted.

General-purpose machines find their field of application in an atmosphere of low volume and instability of part or product design, or of market; that is, where conditions demand flexibility. They are of fairly standard design and, therefore, first cost and obsolescence costs are likely to be lower than for an equivalent special-purpose machine. Special-purpose machines commonly have evolved from their general purpose counterparts as the volume of a particular part or product increased. By specializing designs, higher production rates can be achieved. The special design might include special fixtures, more automatic devices, and better integration of the machine design with the special conditions of the task.

Thus, incoming work might be fed automatically to the machine, instead of requiring the operator to procure a part and place it in the machine. Sometimes the special design incorporates additional machine operations which also serve to increase productivity. The more costly special-purpose design may result in lower unit production cost because of considerably lower labor costs. The economic methods of analysis of Chapters 5 and 6 may be used as a basis for decision making between general- and special-purpose machines for specific instances. The use of economic analysis, of course, assumes conditions of market stability and stability of part or product design, so that machine obsolescence is not likely to occur immediately from these sources.

AUTOMATION

No discussion of processes is complete today without reference to automation. Although automation is new in the sense that principles have only recently been applied to the mechanical and assembly types of processes, the basic ideas are not new. Such processes as the thermostatic control of room temperature have been known and used for some time. The common float valve used in toilets automatically fills the tank to a given level and then shuts off. The process industries have used the principals of automation for some time to control chemical processes.

The economics of industrial mechanization logically began with the tasks where mechanization could be justified and where machines could perform tasks that could not be accomplished manually. In the march of economic events, labor has become more expensive relative to machines and a continuous process of substitution has taken place. It is logical that the most difficult technological developments should not be the first ones applied. Even if known one hundred years ago, these ideas would not have been justified economically. Therefore, the substitution of machines to perform the *control* functions of the human operator had to wait until the present when labor rates are very high. The ultimate development in this trend is a completely integrated automatic sequence beginning with the input of raw material and ending with a final product, without human labor or control other than to design and build the original equipment and process and to maintain the system once installed.

Actually, automation has two main branches. The first is concerned with the control of processes as we have discussed, and involves the *feedback* of information to maintain control of a variable such as temperature, pressure, dimension, or chemical composition within certain predetermined limits. Here we find the field of process control and the digital or numerical control of machine tools. The second branch may or may not involve feedback of information, but it is essentially the automatic handling of parts between operations in such a way that the part is indexed and placed in the exact position to be processed by the subsequent operation or machine. The whole sequence is coordinated carefully so that the several operations in the sequence go through their cycles at just the right instant when all parts have been indexed in position. What we have then is one giant machine where the individual operations are components of the machine, coordinated to work as a unit.

The possible types of operations that can be included in such a sequence are limited only by economics and the imagination of the engineers. Most types of metal machining, gaging, and inspection processes have been incorporated as well as some assembly or joining operations. These developments are typical of large-volume, standard-ized product designs such as automobiles. The first type which employs feedback control is termed a *closed loop*. The second type, which we might characterize as progressive mechanization, is termed *open loop*. Both are automation since the result is automatic production. First, let us examine the nature of feedback so we can see the difference between open and closed loops.

Feedback.   We can demonstrate the nature of feedback and feedback control by contrasting a simple processing situation with and without feedback. In Figure 8 we have diagrammed one station of what could be considered a series of operations. Parts are fixed to the transfer device which moves them past cutting tools such as the one shown in Figure 8. Other cuts might be sidecuts, slots, induction hardening, grinding, lapping, or gaging. All of the tools, as well as the one illustrated, are preset to yield the desired dimensions on the output. Once set, the operations proceed automatically. Direct labor would be required only to load parts into the line series of operations, unload at the far end, and to start and stop the entire process. Depending on the part design and the relative economic advantage, the loading and unloading operations could be mechanized also. At each operation, including the one shown, established standards must be met. These standards must be related to the dimensions produced, the surface quality, hardness, etc. For the

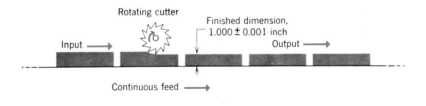

FIGURE 8.   Open-loop setup for milling a part to the standard dimen-sion, 1.000 ± 0.001 inch. Once set, the cutter should continue to produce parts that are in control unless something in the system changes, such as tool wear or movement from the original setting. When out-of-control dimensions are noted, the operator must determine the cause and reset the cutter. The system presumably will produce parts in control for another period of time. The system is an open loop because there are no direct means of ensuring that the finish dimension continuously will meet control standards.

operation shown in Figure 8, the standard to be controlled is the dimension 1.000 ± 0.001 inch.

Through quality control procedures at the end of the sequence of operations or through intermediate checkpoints, we gain information about the state of control of the process. If part dimensions go out of control, the machine will be stopped, the cause determined, cutters reground, reset, or changed, and the machine started up again. Once the cutters are reset, we can assume that parts will be produced automatically again for some time until future changes or adjustments are required. This is *automation*, but we term it *open-loop* automation because there is no direct automatic means for insuring that the output of the system will meet the desired standards. How do we close the loop?

Figure 9 shows schematically what is required to close the loop. Closing the loop is called *feedback*. In a feedback loop we need a *sensing unit* to measure the output (in our example, a dimension) and a *means of comparison* of the actual output with the desired output. The difference, which may be either positive or negative, is then fed to a *decision maker* which interprets the error information and commands

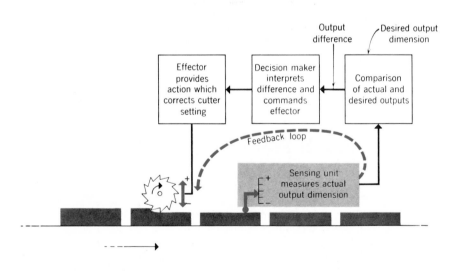

FIGURE 9.   Schematic representation of closed-loop setup for milling a part. Loop is closed because a measure of output is now fed back to provide direct and automatic means for correcting cutter setting.

the *effector* to make a correction in the proper magnitude and direction so that the output will meet standards. In our example, this feedback loop could compensate for expected tool wear and other deviations from normal operation.

A Computer-Controlled Production Line. As mentioned earlier, the ultimate in the development of the automation trend is a completely integrated automatic sequence beginning with the input of raw material

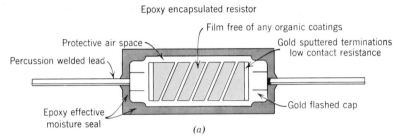

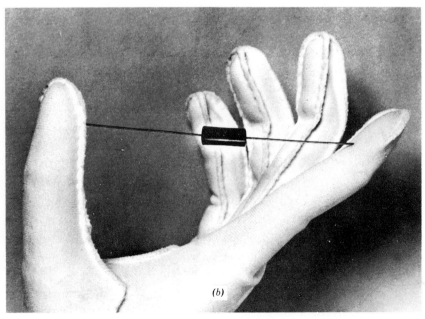

FIGURE 10.   Typical resistor for which computer-controlled production line was developed. (*a*) Basic design and components of resistor. (*b*) Relative size of carbon resistors. (Courtesy Western Electric Company.)

and ending with a final product, without human labor and control. This concept, applied to the manufacturing and control of carbon resistors, has been carried through by the Western Electric Company. These resistors are shown in Figure 10 and are used in immense quantities in a variety of electronic equipment. The resistors must work under extreme conditions of cold, heat, humidity, vibration, and shock. In certain defense equipment, a failure rate of no more than one per 200 million hours (23,000 years) of operation is permissible. This very high reliability requirement triggered the design and development of the automated system. In the past, individual precision components of this type have been made by manual or semiautomatic processes which invited contamination from handling and related difficulties stemming from human control.

The 110-foot long machine shown in Figure 11 has eleven machine stations on the line as well as the computer and control cabinets. In addition to controlling step by step details of manufacture, the computer which controls the entire process can accept a production schedule for a month's output and thereafter automatically issue detailed instructions to the fabricating machines to make and package any or all of

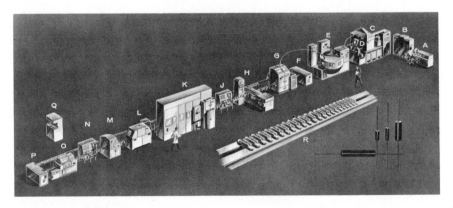

FIGURE 11.   Machine stations in the automated production line for manufacturing deposited carbon resistors: A, computer; B, input-output control station; C, coating station; D, first inspection station; E, terminating station; F, conveyor control equipment; G, capping station; H, helixing station; J, second inspection station; K, encapsulating station; L, leak detector station; M, marking station; N, third inspection station; O, packing station; P, conveyor control equipment; Q, cap-lead welding machine; R, detail of conveyor line. (Courtesy Western Electric Company.)

four basic physical sizes of resistors in whatever quantities and resistance values desired. Feedback of processed data from three key points along the line permits rapid closed-loop operation. The process begins with the deposition of carbon on a tiny ceramic core. This core goes successively through inspection, termination, capping, establishment of resistance value, second inspection, molding of a protective case, electrical leakage inspection, final inspection, and packing. Throughout the entire sequence, the resistor is untouched by human hands.

The heart of the control equipment is a digital computer with a magnetic drum memory. Basically, the computer performs in three areas:

1. It programs production. A month's requirement can be fed into the computer at random. The computer then completely schedules and programs the work, arranging it according to the four resistor power sizes and an almost infinite number of possible resistance values.
2. Using the methods of statistical quality control, it analyzes control data plotted at three critical points in the automated process and applies statistical tests to determine if a trend in quality characteristics is developing.
3. It formulates quality control information to detect any drift away from the accepted manufacturing tolerances. No control action takes place while this analysis indicates normal statistical distributions around desired mean values. When a trend away from normality develops, however, the computer uses stored data to calculate new set-up information for the station that has gone out of control.

Numerically Controlled Processes

When positions and paths of cutter tools are under the control of a digital computer, we have numerical control. The feedback paths or circuits in this case do not emanate from a measurement taken on the workpiece itself, but from the basic positioning controls of the tools or tables which determine the position of cutters relative to the work. The feedback loops continually compare actual position with programmed position and applied correction when necessary.

Position Control.   Position control is the simplest to achieve and is perhaps best illustrated by the drilling of holes that must be positioned accurately to meet standards. The drill tool can be moved in two dimensions to accomplish the desired position after which the tool advances

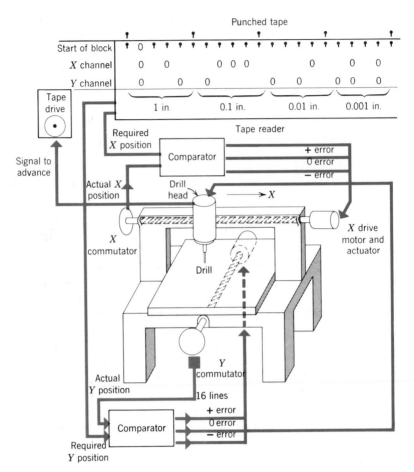

FIGURE 12.   Position-controlled drill press. (From [5].)

into the work to produce the hole. Figure 12 shows a diagram of a position-controlled drill press. The system uses a punched paper tape for instructions. The instructions are coded to indicate the beginning of a new block of data concerning the position reading for the x dimension and the y dimension. For both the x and y dimensions, the tape reads four numbers so the positions may be specified to the nearest 0.001 inch for the system diagrammed.

Let us use the x dimension as an example. If the actual reading is greater than that specified, the comparator registers a plus error which drives the x drive motor to rotate in the proper direction to correct the error. A negative error would cause the drive motor to rotate in the opposite direction. When the difference is zero, the drive motor stops. When differences for x and y dimensions are zero, the drillhead is signaled. It then drills the holes, retracts, and signals the tape unit to read in the next drill position data.

Contour Control.   Contour control takes the ideas just stated one step further. Three dimensions must be controlled instead of two; in addition, it is not only position that must be specified, but the actual *path* that the cutter must take. This involves a much more complicated programming problem since complex curves and surfaces must often be specified. Such a system has great inherent flexibility in terms of part shapes that can be produced as well as in changeover from job to job. One of the system's major advantages is that the machine tool is not tied up for long periods during setup, since practically all preparation time is in programming. Thus, its big field of applicability is for parts that are produced in low volumes.

Programming Systems.   Programming for numerically controlled systems has been carried to the point where the computer itself can do much of the detailed programming. It is given instructions in a special programming language similar to FORTRAN. One such programming language, called APT—Automatic Programming for Tools, includes over 300,000 instructions to a computer and is particularly pointed toward the continuous path or contour control problem. In this system the programmer works from design specifications; he gives instructions to the computer in terms of geometrical definitions of the part to be made and appropriate cutting routines. Each instruction calls forth an entire series of computer machine language instructions. The result is that an experienced part programmer using the APT language can program a complex part with relatively few instructions. Figure 13 shows an example of the instructions required to machine a "saddle surface."

The overall process is shown in Figure 14. The programming instructions prepared from the blueprint specifications are commonly called a "manuscript," as shown at (2) in Figure 14. This information is punched into control cards at (3) and read by a high-speed reader (4) into the central processing unit (5). Within the central processor the data are interpreted and processed according to the internally stored program. These results are translated into numerical control codes and simul-

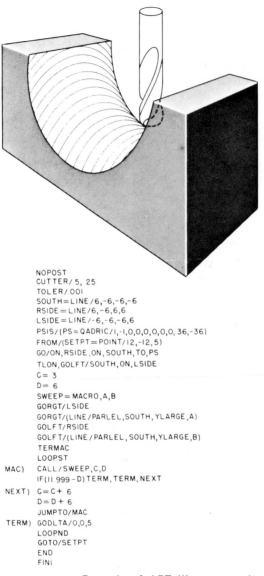

```
        NOPOST
        CUTTER/5, 25
        TOLER/.00I
        SOUTH=LINE/6,-6,-6,-6
        RSIDE=LINE/6,-6,6,6
        LSIDE=LINE/-6,-6,-6,6
        PSIS/(PS=QADRIC/I,-I,0,0,0,0,0,0, 36,-36)
        FROM/(SETPT=POINT/I2,-I2,5)
        GO/ON,RSIDE,ON,SOUTH,TO,PS
        TLON,GOLFT/SOUTH,ON,LSIDE
        C=3
        D=6
        SWEEP=MACRO,A,B
        GORGT/LSIDE
        GORGT/(LINE/PARLEL,SOUTH,YLARGE,A)
        GOLFT/RSIDE
        GOLFT/(LINE/PARLEL,SOUTH,YLARGE,B)
        TERMAC
        LOOPST
MAC)    CALL/SWEEP,C,D
        IF(II.999-D)TERM,TERM,NEXT
NEXT)   C=C+.6
        D=D+6
        JUMPTO/MAC
TERM)   GODLTA/0,0,5
        LOOPND
        GOTO/SETPT
        END
        FINI
```

FIGURE 13.   Example of APT III programming
instructions required for a "saddle surface."
(Courtesy Dr. Gastone Chingari, Remington Rand
Univac Division of Sperry Rand Corporation.)

taneously printed on a high-speed printer which produces a listing (6)
of the part program instructions; control cards are printed out by a

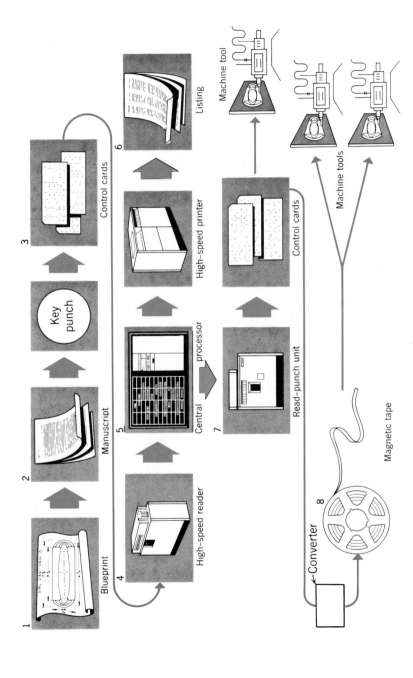

FIGURE 14. Overall programming system and information flow for a numerical control program system. (Courtesy Dr. Gastone Chingari, Remington-Rand Univac Division of Sperry Rand Corporation.)

repunch unit (7). These output cards contain all of the control data necessary to guide the tool through the complete manufacture of the part in question. For tools that are guided by magnetic tape, the cards are converted. The resulting tape (8) controls the machine tool through the complete manufacturing cycle.

Basic Design Alternatives

Much of the designers latitude lies in the selection of materials and, often, the basic kind of processes. The real point is that each material and process is appropriate under certain combinations of conditions of functional requirements and manufacturing cost. Manufacturing cost is drastically affected by the contemplated volume. Therefore, in general, sand-casting is economical for low volumes and the other methods for intermediate and high volumes. But we can give no definite number of parts that represents a breakeven volume between any pair of the materials and processes because the breakeven volume depends on the particular part.

Thus, a mere 1000 parts could justify a die-casting in preference to a sand-casting if the part were fairly simple and the resulting surfaces were of adequate finish and tolerance, since the machining and finishing costs would be somewhat less than those for sand-casting. On the other hand, a very high die cost for a more complex part might shoot the breakeven volume to 10,000. The important point is that for each design situation the functional alternatives must be compared on an incremental cost basis according to the principles discussed under economic analysis (Chapters 5 and 6). The following examples of contrasting designs and costs illustrate the kinds of cost factors that can be affected by the differences in the basic part design.

Processes and Materials.   Figure 15 shows a design contrast of a bracket for a Westinghouse electric motor. Originally it was machined from a casting. Analysis of functional and economic considerations revealed that it could be made in three pieces, as shown, and be stronger, lighter, and more economical to manufacture. The body and hub were designed to be drawn to shape from sheet steel, and the flange was designed to be formed in a press. The volume required of such brackets justified the expenditure of forming dies and resulted in a superior functional design as well.

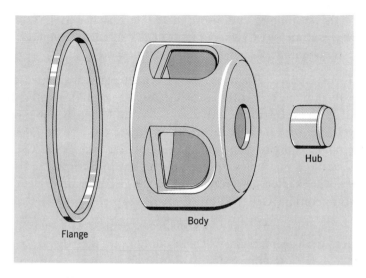

FIGURE 15.   Motor bracket designed to be formed in presses instead of from a casting resulted in a stronger, lighter design which was more economical to manufacture. (Courtesy Westing-house Electric Corporation.)

Figure 16 shows two designs of a cam switch assembly. The design on the right involved a brass casting with the other parts assembled to it. The design on the left is from an extrusion and was functionally equivalent to the assembled design. The extruded design eliminated

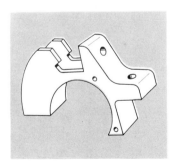

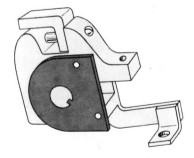

FIGURE 16.   The extruded design on the left cost only 55 per cent of the cast and assembled design. (Courtesy Westinghouse Electric Corporation.)

most of the machining and also cost less in raw material. The net difference was dramatic. To manufacture the extruded design cost 55 per cent of the amount needed for the assembled design.

Joining of Parts.   The methods by which parts are joined together can result in important differences in cost. Figure 17 shows contrasting designs of a resistor tube. The design on the left makes it possible to spot weld the bracket at a substantially lower cost. Figure 18 makes a similar point, showing contrasting designs of a tank liner. The riveted design required that holes be made in the liners to admit the rivets and washers. The stapled design eliminated the need for the holes, and the stapling operation itself was much faster than riveting.

Tolerances.   Design engineers are always accused of specifying closer tolerances than are necessary. This undoubtedly happens. It is obvious that to achieve a tolerance of ± 0.0001 inch is more expensive than to hold to only ± 0.0010 inch because of greater skill requirements, because of better equipment requirements, because of more scrap, and because such operations as grinding may need to be added. But sometimes a closer tolerance will save adjusting and fitting time when parts are assembled. Figure 19 shows just such a case. The requirements for the assembly shown there are that the holes at the ends of the three contact arms be in line within ± 0.005 inch. These arms are mounted

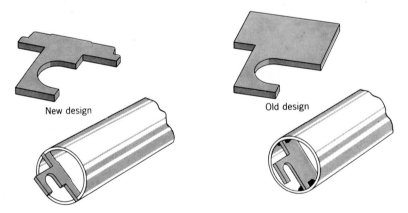

New design   Old design

FIGURE 17.   The design of this resistor was functionally acceptable as either an arc-welded joint (right) or a spot-welded joint (left). However, spot welding was substantially more economical. (Courtesy Westinghouse Electric Corporation.)

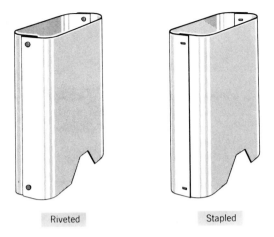

Riveted   Stapled

FIGURE 18. Either riveted or stapled tank liners meet functional requirements, but stapling eliminates the need for holes to be made, rivets and washers to be positioned, and rivets to be upset. On balance, the stapled design is much more economical. (Courtesy Westinghouse Electric Corporation.)

on a micarta bar with a steel center and are held in place by a part called a staple. The square bar could not be held to a tolerance closer than 0.012 inch and, as a result, the arms often fit too loosely or too tightly,

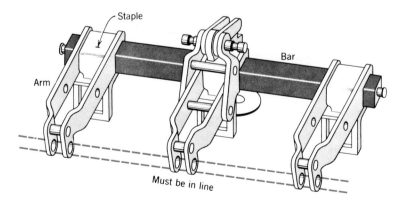

FIGURE 19. Specification of closer tolerances reduced overall production costs on this assembly by eliminating costly adjusting operations. (Courtesy Westinghouse Electric Corporation.)

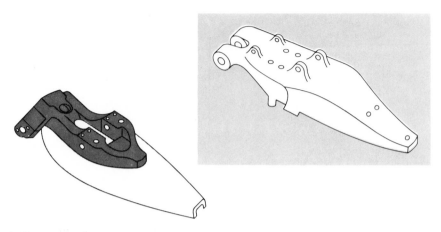

FIGURE 20.   The simplified design on the right involves a precision casting which requires only 74 per cent as much machining time, 50 per cent as much assembly time, and a substantial decrease in material cost compared to the design on the left. (Courtesy Westinghouse Electric Corporation.)

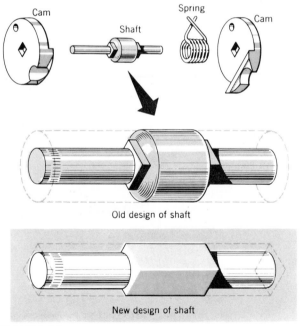

Cam

Spring

Shaft

Cam

Old design of shaft

New design of shaft

FIGURE 21.   New and old designs for a cam sub-assembly of a limit switch. (Courtesy Westinghouse Electric Corporation.)

with adjusting operations required. A closer tolerance specification of ± 0.002 inch for the bar eliminates the adjusting. The bar is molded oversized and broached to the closer tolerance. A special assembly fixture permits the broaching to be accomplished as a part of the assembly operation.

Simplified Designs.   When two or more parts are finally assembled rigidly together, it raises the question of whether or not the assembled unit could be designed as one piece. This is often feasible when a single material will meet service requirements for all surfaces and cross sections of the part. Figure 20 shows such an example for a contact arm of a circuit breaker. The design on the left is made of two parts, a casting and a punching. The parts are machined separately and then joined together with two screws. The one-piece design shown on the right involves a precision casting which eliminates all but the very close machining. The one-piece design requires 74 per cent as much machining time, 50 per cent as much assembly time, and a substantial decrease in material cost. Because of very high volume, the one-piece design is $50,000 cheaper over a two and one-half year period.

Reduced Machining.   Figure 21 shows a contrasting design for a cam subassembly of a limit switch, the difference being based on a substitution of raw materials. In the original design the shaft was machined from a solid bar. The large-diameter middle section of the shaft centered the spring and separated the two cams. A square was milled on each side to key with the square holes of the cams. The new design used square raw stock, with the size of the raw stock matching that of the square that was formerly milled. A sleeve was provided as a spacer for the cams which slipped over the square of the shaft. The milling operation was eliminated and the amount of material to be removed was greatly reduced; the savings more than offset the cost of manufacturing the new sleeve.

SUMMARY

In effect, the product designer establishes the constraints within which the production system designer must function. A broad knowledge of processes and their capabilities provides the basis for the rational consideration of basic alternatives available. These processes involve all types of transformations including physical, chemical, place, information content, etc. Processes also involves a complete range of the mode of execution from purely manual to completely automatic.

KEY CONCEPTS

Process.   Processes involve some kind of transformation and the concept is fundamental to production management. While we may tend to think in restricted terms of those processes that change, shape, or form, such as occurs in metals machining or chemical changes, the concept is, in fact, somewhat broader. A process can change location of the item being processed, provide or alter information as in clerical or information processing operations, or check the accuracy of any other process such as in inspection.

Production Design.   The limiting minimum production cost of an item is determined by its design. If the product design and process planning for producing the item go on independently the likelihood of the occurrence of a joint optimum for both is considerably lessened. When a conscious effort is made to bring these two processes together, we have what is referred to as production design. The concept of designing the item from the point of view of its producability as well as its function is crucial for the attainment of minimum cost operations.

Feedback.   The concept of feedback is crucial not only to automation, but also to management control systems in the general sense. To complete a feedback loop, we need a sensing unit to measure the output of whatever it is we wish to control and a means of comparing this measurement with a desired output. The difference is then fed back to a decision maker, which interprets the error information and commands a correction in the proper magnitude and direction so that the output measure will again meet standards.

Position Control.   A concept fundamental to automation and involving an application of feedback concepts in controlling machine tools. Control of the cutting tool is maintained in two dimensions to position the tool at any point in time and through a sequence of operations.

Contour Control.   Like position control, contour control is fundamental to automation and employs feedback concepts. It is more complex in that not only position must be specified, but the actual path that the cutting tool must take. The programming required is somewhat more complex since curves and surfaces must often be specified.

IMPORTANT TERMS

Numbers in parentheses indicate page numbers.

1. APT (189)
2. Automation (181–183)
3. Closed loop (183, 184)
4. Effector (185)
5. General purpose machine (178)
6. Management information system (178, 180)
7. Numerical control (187)
8. Open loop (183)
9. Process control (182, 184)
10. Product design (168)
11. Production design (167)
12. Sensing unit (184)
13. Special purpose machine (181)

REVIEW QUESTIONS

Numbers in parentheses indicate page numbers.

1. Discuss the relationship of functional design and production design in determining a product design that meets functional requirements, cost considerations, and the limitations of available processes. (167–169)
2. Discuss the nature of costs that can be affected by alternate designs. (168–171)
3. What are the areas of applicability of molded plastics, sand-castings, die-castings, drop-forgings, stamped and formed parts, and machined parts? What kinds of considerations affect the choice? (173–175)
4. Contrast the conceptual differences between mechanization and automation. (181–182)
5. What are the elements of feedback control? (182–183)
6. Describe automation with and without feedback control. (182–183)
7. What is unique and different about the feedback control loops used with numerically controlled machine tools and the feedback control illustrated by Figure 9? (184, 187)
8. What is position control? Contour control? (187, 189)
9. Select a consumer or industrial product and critically analyze its design in terms of:
   (a) production design and producibility
   (b) its use by the consumer
   (c) its maintainability (168)
10. Discuss the statement, "close tolerances in part manufacture result in high costs." (194)
11. Select some nonmanufacturing activity and survey the nature of transformation operations which you find in the operations phase. Classify these operations in terms of the classification given in the text, for example,

chemical, processes to change, shape or form, assembly, transport, and clerical. Classify the equipment used in the operations activity in terms of its general or special-purpose nature. (171, 173, 176–181)

12.   Discuss the level and sophistication of automated activity in offices, banks, hospitals, warehousing, supermarkets, and department stores. (181–185)

SELF-TEST TRUE-FALSE QUESTIONS

Numbers in parentheses indicate page numbers.

1.   The conscious effort to design for low manufacturing cost is referred to as production design, as distinct from functional design. (167)

2.   Given the product design, process planning for manufacture must be carried out to specify in careful detail the processes required and their sequence. (167–168)

3.   The thesis of a production design philosophy is that alternatives of design nearly always exist that still meet functional requirements. (169)

4.   In operations management the term "process" is restricted to mean the change of shape or form of a part or product as in metals forming and the machining industries. (171)

5.   In general, a sand casting process is appropriate for low volume of manufacture. (192)

6.   Whereas mechanical kinds of processes tend to change shape or form, clerical processes transform information. (177)

7.   General purpose machines find their field of application in an atmosphere of low volume and instability of part or product design, or of market. (181)

8.   We can characterize automation based on closed loop feedback control as progressive mechanism. (183)

9.   Closed-loop automation involves the following functions in a closed loop: sensing; comparison of actual and desired outputs; a decision maker, which interprets differences; and, an effector for proficing corrective action. (184–185)

10.   Digital control of machine tools is an application of open-loop systems. (187)

11.   In position control the actual path of cutters must be programmed. (187–189)

12.   Contour control poses a more complicated programming problem since complex curves and surfaces must often be specified. (189)

13.   The most important field of application of numerically controlled machine tools is for mass production (189)

14.   One of the major advantages of numerically controlled machine tool processes is that the machine tool itself is not tied up for long periods during setup. (189)

PROBLEMS

The Precision Aerospace Manufacturing Company (PAMCo) is considering the installation of its first numerically controlled machine tool. The machine being considered is a highly flexible numerically controlled (N/C) milling machine capable of handling a wide variety of machining tasks. The machine could be purchased for $150,000. Since the machine would be PAMCo's first N/C machine, the manufacturing engineer held that it was justified as *manufacturing research* and need not meet the same rigid justification requirements normally established for conventional equipment. This view found small support when presented to the manufacturing manager. The frustrated engineer, now determined to make his point, decided to dig deeply to show the far-reaching effects that numerical control methods could have on manufacturing costs. He felt that the direct cost reductions were relatively obvious, but that the indirect cost reductions were not properly understood and were perhaps more important than the direct cost reduction for N/C. To make the contrast a specific one, the engineer selected one particular part which he felt was typical (see Figure 22) and based all calculations on that part.

Direct Cost Reductions

The engineer obtained actual data for the manufacture of the part by conventional means and supplemented these data with estimates for part programming and the expected production cycle for the N/C machine. Table II is a summary of the time requirements for the two contrasting technologies. The engineer then projected his figures to an annual basis by assuming two-shift operation (4000 hours per year) for the N/C machine and the equivalent man-machine hours required by conventional methods, $\frac{0.895}{0.405} \times (4000) =$ 8840 hours. The reduction in man-hours by use of the N/C machine was then 4840 hours per year. He then took the average hourly machine shop wage of $2.75 per hour. To this he added 30 per cent for fringe benefits to cover retirement, vacations and holidays, social security, insurance, and so on. In addition, the factory overhead was computed at the rate of 25 per cent of direct labor cost so the resulting effective hourly labor cost was $4.26 per hour. The computed direct labor cost reduction was then $4840 \times \$4.26 = \$20,618$ per year.

Indirect Cost Reductions

Some of the indirect effects the enginer found were in the category of tooling costs, inventories, intraplant material handling, and inspection.

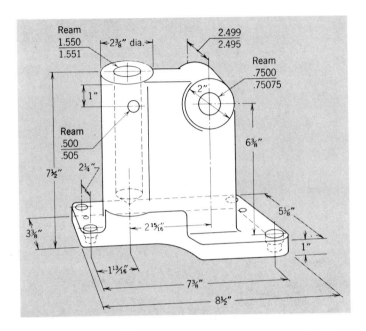

FIGURE 22.   Casting to be machined by N/C methods at
PAMCo.

Tooling Costs.   On investigation the engineer found two kinds of tooling
cost reductions. The first was a one-time savings which would occur initially
as new jobs were tooled up for the N/C machine to the point where the machine
was operating at full load. He felt that these were not annual savings in tooling
costs but a reduction in investment required; therefore, this savings should
be deducted from the investment required for the N/C machine. The average
tooling cost per job by conventional machining had been $1300; $600 was
projected for the average N/C job. The engineer figured that 50 new jobs would
load the new machine so an additional investment in tools of $35,000 was
prevented in his view. The net installed cost of the N/C machine was then
$115,000. In addition, he figured that there was an annual tool cost reduction
which stemmed from two sources: the annual turnover of jobs for the machine,
each new job requiring the smaller tool cost typical of N/C methods, and the
annual reduction in the costs of storing, transporting, and repairing conventional tools. He found from company records that about 25 per cent of the
jobs turned over each year, which would result in an annual tool cost reduction of $8750. On investigating the tool repair and carrying costs, the engineer
found them to be 20 per cent of the value of tooling. He felt that legitimate cost
reductions to include were the inventory carrying and repair costs on the

TABLE II.   Estimated Time Requirements, Conventional versus N/C Machining Methods

Conventional Machining				N/C Machining			
	Hours per 20-Part Lot				Hours per 20-Part Lot		
Operation	Setup	Run	Total	Operation	Part Programming and Setup	Run	Total
Mill boss	0.70	0.80	1.50	All operations	1.70	6.40	8.10
Drill, ream, and center bore boss hole	1.70	4.20	5.90				
Straddle mill 2 bosses	0.90	0.75	1.65				
Drill, bore, and ream 1½″ hole	1.20	4.00	5.20				
Drill, bore, and ream ½″ hole	1.05	2.60	3.65				
Totals	5.55	12.35	17.90	Totals	1.70	6.40	8.10
Total time per part, hours, 0.895				Total time per part, hours, 0.405			

one-time tool cost saving of $35,000, or an additional annual cost reduction of $7000.

Inventory Cost Reductions.   The engineer reasoned that the combination of many operations into one, as indicated in Table II, eliminates the dead time between operations for handling and storage. This results in a shorter overall time that the job spends in process. In addition, the typically smaller setup time (cost) leads to shorter, more frequent runs which result in smaller finished goods inventories. Another factor leading to smaller finished goods inventories was the short lead time for N/C processes which would make possible a smaller safety or "buffer" stock requirement. Finally, typical inventory losses due to obsolescence should result from the shorter turn around or lead times. Because of the short lead times, parts formerly made to stock could be made to order, thus reducing substantially the risk of obsolescence.

On checking with the production control department, the engineer found that a typical job was in process for 3 months. Experience in plants where N/C had been tried seemed to average 2 months. In addition, the value of in-process inventory would be smaller because of the smaller direct costs indicated in Table II. Thus the amount of in-process inventory would be 33 per cent less and the value of an item in inventory would be 24 per cent less, assuming that valuation for inventory purposes would be average material cost of $5 per piece plus value added by manufacture. Thus the total value of in-process inventory should be reduced by 51 per cent. Calculating present equivalent in-process inventory levels, the engineer came up with a figure of $11,800 based on the average number of parts in process and their average value. The reduction of in-process inventory was therefore .51 × 11,800 = $6018. Previous studies had shown that the cost of carrying in-process inventory was 25 per cent, so the cost reduction was therefore $1505. The engineer did not attempt to appraise the cost reductions due to effects on finished goods inventories and risk of obsolescence.

Intraplant Material-Handling Cost Reductions.   The combining of operations due to N/C methods completely eliminates the usual material-handling activities normally required between operations. Previous studies in the Industrial Engineering Department indicated that the average material-handling trip cost $0.75. If we assume the part under study to be the typical one, five operations are combined into one. There will be about 500 lots per year, so 4 × 500 = 2000 trips per year saved. The annual cost reduction which results is 0.75 × 2000 = $1500. For some of the parts manufactured there was the possibility of considerable damage in transit; in some instances, special handling and packaging were used to avoid damage. A reduction in handling would, of course, also reflect itself in a reduction in these costs but no records existed to help estimate the magnitude of the saving. Besides, the engineer felt that he must be getting close to the needed total cost reduction to justify the new N/C machine. Before stopping, however, he investigated one more possibly fruitful area: inspection.

Inspection Cost Reduction.   The engineer reasoned that fewer inspections would be required if operations were combined, that less frequent inspection would be necessary, and that necessary inspection would often be less detailed. Since there is less human error involved in the operation of N/C machines, the inspector is in effect checking the correctness of the part program by checking carefully the first part produced. The result is that good control often can be maintained by first piece inspection only. Since in programming a part, all dimensions are in reference to some point, the inspection of the spacing of a series of holes may be accomplished by inspecting the first and last holes only. If these two holes are correctly positioned, those in between will be too. Not being sure how to estimate these savings, the engineer surveyed the N/C literature and found that a rule of thumb being used placed N/C inspection costs at one-half those for conventional machining. He estimated that approximately

TABLE III.   Summary of Direct and Indirect Cost Reductions for an N/C Milling Machine Costing $150,000 Installed

Direct cost reduction:	
Labor	$20,618
Indirect cost reduction:	
Tool cost (annual turnover of jobs)	8,750
Carrying charges on one-time tool cost reduction	7,000
Inventory	1,505
Material handling	1,500
Inspection	1,750
Total annual cost reduction	$41,123
One-time reduction in tooling investment	$35,000

$3500 per year were being spent for inspection labor on a volume of parts approximately equivalent to what the N/C machine could handle. He, therefore, set the cost reduction due to inspection at $1750.

Summary of Cost Figures

On completing his survey the engineer summarized his cost study as shown in Table III. He completed a new report summarizing the advantages of N/C machines, together with his recommendation that the machine be purchased immediately. Then he presented it to the manufacturing manager.
(a) Evaluate the engineer's cost study.
(b) Should the manufacturing manager approve the recommendation?

REFERENCES

[1] Amber, G. H., and P. S. Amber. *Anatomy of Automation*. Prentice-Hall, Englewood Cliffs, N.J., 1962.
[2] Begeman, M. L., and B. H. Amstead. *Manufacturing Processes* (6th ed.). John Wiley, New York, 1969.
[3] Culliton, J. W. *Make or Buy*. Harvard University Graduate School of Business Administration, Soldiers Field, Boston, Mass., 1942.
[4] Eary, D. F., and G. E. Johnson. *Process Engineering for Manufacturing*. Prentice-Hall, Englewood Cliffs, N.J., 1962.

[5] Grabbe, E. M., editor. *Automation in Business and Industry*. John Wiley, New York, 1957.

[6] Hahir, J. P. "A Case Study on the Relationship Between Design Engineering and Production Engineering." *Proceedings, Fifth Annual Industrial Engineering Institute*, University of California, Berkeley–Los Angeles, 1953.

[7] Moore, H. D., and D. R. Kibbey. *Manufacturing Materials and Processes*. Richard D. Irwin, Homewood, Ill., 1965.

[8] Papen, G. W. "Minimizing Manufacturing Costs Through Effective Design." *Proceedings, Sixth Annual Industrial Engineering Institute*, University of California, Berkeley–Los Angeles, 1954.

[9] Wilson, F. W., editor-in-chief. *Numerical Control in Manufacturing*. McGraw-Hill, New York, 1963.

CONTENTS

CHAPTER 8
PROCESS PLANNING

Where does production design end and process planning begin? We have said that the basic process planning must begin during the product design stages where selections of materials and initial forms, such as casting, forgings, and die-castings, take place. The accepted end point for production design is manifested by the drawing release, which summarizes the exact specifications of what is to be made. Process planning takes over from this point and develops the broad plan of manufacture for the part or product. Thus we are using the term *process planning* in its organizational sense. In its functional sense, it includes the basic selection of processes necessitated in the design stage.

Another important distinction that must be drawn is the relation of process planning to layout and facilities planning. Process planning necessarily blends with the layout of physical facilities. Some process planning takes place during the layout phases of the design of a production system. To accommodate physical and sequential limitations, to take advantage of available space, or to improve methods or sequence, modifications of the original process plans may be made. The division between process planning and layout is manifested by documents such as *route sheets* and *operation sheets* (which summarize the operations required, the preferred sequence of operations, auxiliary tools required, estimated operation times, etc.). We may regard the process plans as inputs to the development of a layout. Figure 1 shows the overall conceptual framework of process planning in diagrammatic form.

Process planning takes as its inputs the drawings or other specifications which indicate *what* is to be made, and also the forecasts, orders, or contracts which indicate *how many* are to be made. The drawings are then analyzed to determine the overall scope of the project. If it is a complex assembled product, considerable effort may go into "exploding" the product into its components of parts and subassemblies. This overall planning may take the form of special drawings that show the relationship of parts, cutaway models, and assembly diagrams. Preliminary decisions about subassembly groupings to determine which parts to make and which to buy, as well as to determine the general level of tooling expenditure, may be made at this point. Then, for each part, a detailed routing is developed. Here technical knowledge of processes, machines and their capabilities is required, but of almost equal importance is a knowledge of production economics, as discussed in Chapters 5 and 6. Ordinarily the range of processing alternatives is considerable. The selection should be influenced strongly by the overall volume and projected stability of design. The concepts of breakeven volumes between basic alternatives come into play.

Product Analysis

Consider the problem of the initial setting up to manufacture the 12-part capacitor shown in Figure 2. It is an assembled product, although not complicated as assembled products go.

Assembly or "Gozinto" Charts.   Of what use are schematic models here? Particularly when the product is a complex one, they can help to visualize the flow of material and the relationships of parts: where they flow into the assembly process, which parts make up subassemblies, and where the purchased parts are used in the assembly sequence. Using the capacitor of Figure 2 as an example, a first step might be the preparation of an "assembly chart" or, as it is often called, a "Gozinto"

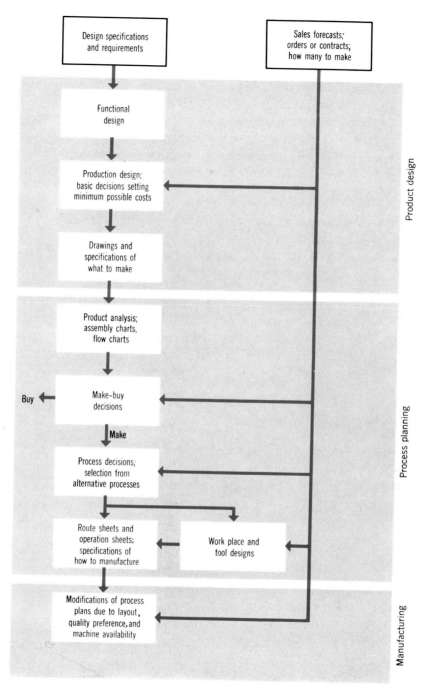

FIGURE 1. Diagram of the overall development of processing plans.

chart (from the words "goes into"). Figure 3 is an assembly chart for the capacitor. Notice how clearly the chart shows the relationship of the parts, the sequence of assembly, and which groups of parts make up subassemblies. It is, in essence, a schematic model of the entire manufacturing process at one level of information and detail. Actually, the capacitor is simple enough so that the assembly chart could be eliminated; the operation process chart which follows also shows these relationships as well as additional information. However, for a really complex

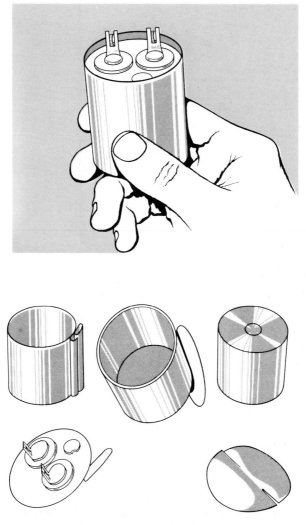

FIGURE 2.   A capacitor, showing its several parts.

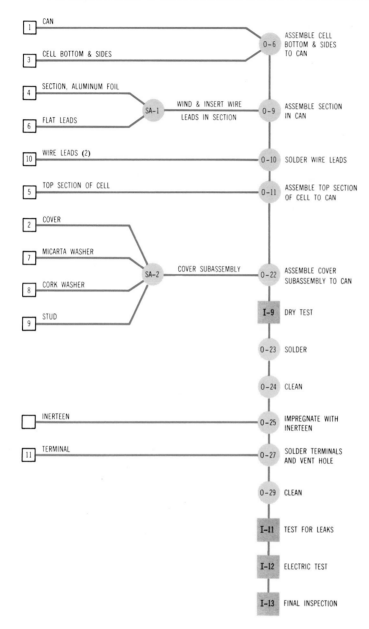

FIGURE 3.   Assembly or "Gozinto" chart for capacitor of
Figure 2.

product such as an airplane or a missile, it would be difficult to comprehend the grand plan for manufacture without an assembly chart.

The assembly chart can be useful in making preliminary plans regarding probable subassemblies (alternatives usually exist; for instance, the cover subassembly could be assembled separately) and approprirate general methods of manufacture. For example, where do production lines fit in and where does process or functional layout seem appropriate? Final decisions depend on many factors. (See Chapter 10 on layout of physical facilities.)

Operation Process Charts.   Assuming that the product is already engineered, we have complete drawings and specifications of the parts and their dimensions, tolerances, and materials to be used. From the specifications and of "how many to manufacture" (contracts or sales forecasts), we can develop a plan of "how to manufacture." Decisions have to be made as to which parts to purchase and which to manufacture in our plant. The engineering drawings specify the locations, sizes, and tolerances for holes to be drilled, surfaces to be finished, etc., for each part. With this information and knowledge of the quantity to be produced and of manufacturing processes, the most economical equipment, processes, and sequences of processes can be specified.

The result of this work is a partial specification of "how to manufacture," usually summarized on a "route sheet" or "operation sheet," which specifies for each manufactured part the operations required in the preferred sequence, equipment to be used, special tools, fixtures, and gages. Estimates of the required setup time and run time are often added. All of this information can be summarized in the form of an operation process chart. Such a chart for the capacitor is shown in Figure 4. It is essentially a summary of all required operations and inspections for the capacitor. Symbols have been adopted: a large circle for an operation and a square for an inspection. This is all cast

Operation

Inspection

in the basic framework of the assembly chart so that now we have a schematic diagram of the basic flow of the parts from machine to machine, as well as the structure of how parts are related in the subassembly and assembly processes.

The operation process chart is of great value in the development of a layout plan. It shows clearly the operations to be performed, their sequence, and the equipment to be used. In the development of a layout, basic questions can be raised regarding the necessity of certain operations and possibilities for combining and rearranging the sequence of operations to improve physical flow.

Analysis of Existing Operations.   We have been discussing the operation process chart in terms of the development of a plan for manufacturing a new product and developing new facilities, but it is equally applicable to the analysis of existing operations. As time passes, changes creep into manufacturing plans because of redesign, the addition or elimination of products, and advances in manufacturing technology.

Sometimes operations are added to meet a temporary emergency; they then become permanent because no one takes action to delete them when the need passes. Reviews of existing operations are often very fruitful for eliminating duplication and illogical flow. The breakdown of the overall manufacturing process into its operations, and examination of the logical structure of the operation process chart form the basis for questioning the existence of every activity as well as the relationship of the activities.

Product Flow Process Charts.   The flow process chart is similar in concept to the operation process chart, except that it adds more detail and has a slightly different field of application. The flow process chart adds transportation and storage activity to the information already recorded on an operation process chart. Thus, whereas the latter focuses only on the productive activity, the flow process chart focuses on the nonproductive activity as well.

The nonproductive activities of moving the material from place to place and storing it (while it waits for men and equipment to become available) actually represent by far the major amount of the total time spent in the manufacturing cycle for the common "job-shop" conditions which prevail in industry. These nonproductive activities require labor and equipment for transportation, loading, and unloading; capital investment for the plant storage space; and carrying charges on the inventory. Naturally, industrial management is strongly motivated to focus attention on these activities so that their expenditures can be minimized within the framework of minimum overall production cost. It is obvious that decreasing in-process inventories by reducing lot sizes to an extremely low level might result in much higher material-handling costs and idle direct labor at machines. In general, the operation process chart would be used at the broadest level dealing with entire complex products, and the flow process chart would be used with a smaller segment of the product. There is overlap, however, in the areas of their actual cost.

The flow process chart requires additional symbols in order to include nonproductive activities. There is some variation in the number and character of the symbols used, but it is of minor importance. For example, some analysts divide storage into temporary and permanent storage, using two different symbols; also, the symbol for transportation varies considerably. These are some of the symbols used:

For purposes of illustration, we shall use the symbols shown in Figure 5.

As an example, let us take the machining of the main frame for an

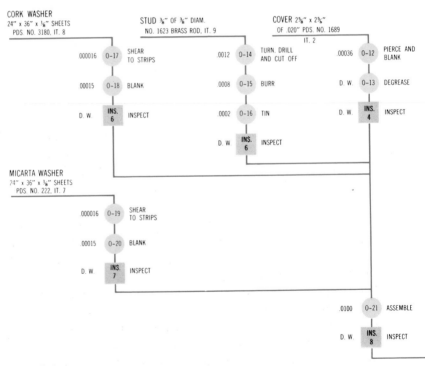

FIGURE 4. Operation process chart for the capacitor of Figure 2. (Courtesy Westinghouse Electric Corporation.)

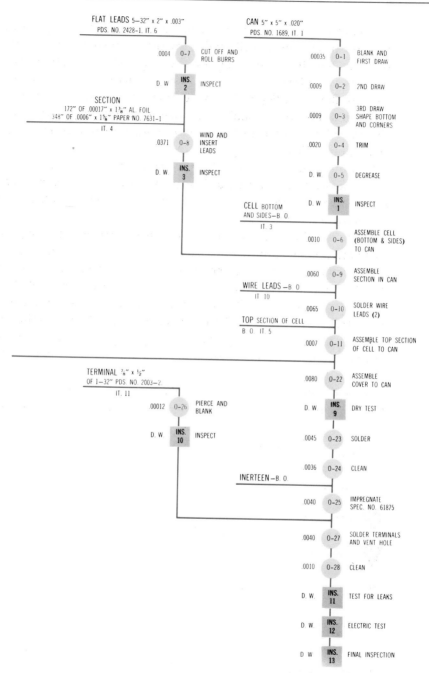

FLAT LEADS 5–32″ x 2″ x .003″
PDS. NO. 2428-1. IT. 6

.0004 0-7 CUT OFF AND ROLL BURRS

D. W INS. 2 INSPECT

SECTION
172″ OF .00017″ x 1⅜″ AL. FOIL
348″ OF .0006″ x 1⅝″ PAPER NO. 7631-1
IT. 4

.0371 0-8 WIND AND INSERT LEADS

D. W INS. 3 INSPECT

CAN 5″ x 5″ x .020″
PDS. NO. 1689, IT. 1

.00035 0-1 BLANK AND FIRST DRAW

.0009 0-2 2ND DRAW

.0009 0-3 3RD DRAW SHAPE BOTTOM AND CORNERS

.0020 0-4 TRIM

D. W 0-5 DEGREASE

D. W INS. 1 INSPECT

CELL BOTTOM AND SIDES—B. O.
IT. 3

.0010 0-6 ASSEMBLE CELL (BOTTOM & SIDES) TO CAN

.0060 0-9 ASSEMBLE SECTION IN CAN

WIRE LEADS—B. O.
IT 10

.0065 0-10 SOLDER WIRE LEADS (2)

TOP SECTION OF CELL
B. O. IT 5

.0007 0-11 ASSEMBLE TOP SECTION OF CELL TO CAN

TERMINAL ⅞″ x ½″
OF 1–32″ PDS. NO. 2003–2.
IT. 11

.00012 0-26 PIERCE AND BLANK

D. W INS. 10 INSPECT

.0080 0-22 ASSEMBLE COVER TO CAN

D. W INS. 9 DRY TEST

.0045 0-23 SOLDER

.0036 0-24 CLEAN

INERTEEN—B. O.

.0040 0-25 IMPREGNATE SPEC. NO. 61875

.0040 0-27 SOLDER TERMINALS AND VENT HOLE

.0010 0-28 CLEAN

D. W. INS. 11 TEST FOR LEAKS

D. W. INS. 12 ELECTRIC TEST

D. W INS. 13 FINAL INSPECTION

FIGURE 4.   (*continued*)

air breaker, as shown in Figure 6. The completed flow process chart was constructed by actually following the progress of the parts through the machine shop and gathering the required information. Armchair analysis is seldom accurate for these schematic charts. The resulting chart is shown in Figure 7. Notice how clearly each inverted triangle highlights the storages and each circle highlights the operations. Note the other information that the chart contains: distance moved in feet and required times.

It is often helpful to supplement the flow process chart by superimposing the flow chart on a floor plan of the work area in order that spatial relationships can be better visualized. The result is called a *flow diagram.*

Every detail of the process is questioned, first with the objective of completely eliminating steps that cannot be justified and then with the objective of combining operations. Let us see what sorts of questions might be raised about the air breaker flow process chart of Figure 7.

First, note that O-1 calls for "straighten" (and grind). See Figure 8a. This straightening should be investigated to see if the reinforcing rib can be cast in such a way that warping is prevented. If the casting technique could be improved, the straightening operation could be eliminated.

Second, note in Figure 8b that our attention is focused on the fact that the casting is washed at O-8 in preparation for the painting opera-

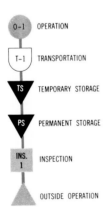

FIGURE 5.   Flow process chart symbols.

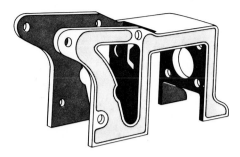

FIGURE 6.   Main frame for a DA-50 air
breaker. (Courtesy Westinghouse Electric
Corporation.)

tions. This is followed by O-9, which is a grinding and polishing operation. Does not O-9 produce some grinding dust and dirt on the casting
and, therefore, is it not better to wash after grinding?

Third, in Figure 8c we see that considerable time is spent in baking,
after the application of filler and also after the black enamel spray.
Filler and paint materials should be investigated. Perhaps there is a
filler available that does not require baking. Would an "air dry" enamel
be satisfactory?

Fourth, in Figure 8d we see that the casting goes to the milling section
three times. This raises the question: Is it feasible to change sequence
and perform all of the milling operations while the casting is in the
department and thus eliminate backtracking?

Other questions could be raised, for example, the fact that holes
are produced in three places. Can these operations be done at one time,
perhaps on a radial drill? Finally, note that grinding is performed in
O-1 and O-9 on the same surface, once as a rough grind and finally to
produce a finished surface. Can the first grinding be postponed and the
entire job be done in O-9? If it can, a transportation and a storage can
be eliminated.

These questions and others were raised by Westinghouse industrial
engineers in analyzing the manufacture of air breakers. We do not
mean to imply that all milling should always be done at one time, that
air dry enamels should always be used, etc. But there should be good
sound reasons for not doing these things, because manufacturing costs
are drastically affected by the differences between the actual and
proposed methods.

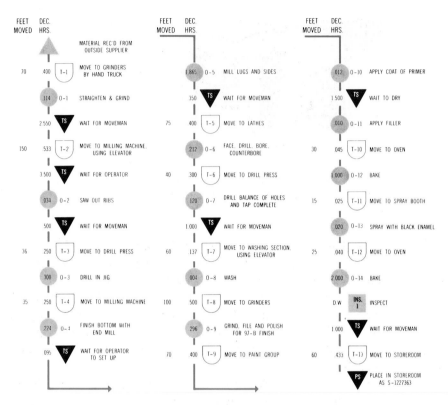

FIGURE 7. Flow process chart of main frame for a DA-50 air breaker. (Courtesy Westinghouse Electric Corporation.)

When all unnecessary operations have been eliminated and all possible gains from combinations of operations and from sequence changes have been effected, the final question remains. Are necessary operations, transportations, and storages being accomplished in the best known way?

We then move to the next level of analysis which considers the individual operation as a unit. Here the definition of an operation does not necessarily coincide with that used by the operation and flow process charts, but includes any activity where a man is involved. It could be the activity of transporting materials or of placing them in storage, or any indirect labor that is ancillary to the direct flow of the product, or any of the direct labor operations defined as "operations" in the foregoing process charts. We refer to the types of analysis used to aid in the design or improvement of "jobs" as "man or man-machine analysis."

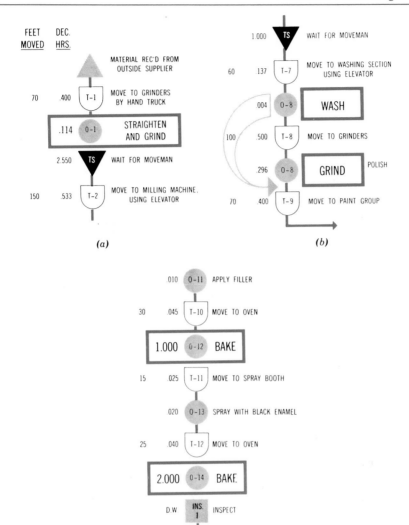

FEET   DEC.
MOVED HRS.

MATERIAL REC'D FROM
OUTSIDE SUPPLIER

70   .400   T-1   MOVE TO GRINDERS
                     BY HAND TRUCK

.114   O-1   STRAIGHTEN
               AND GRIND

2.550   TS   WAIT FOR MOVEMAN

150   .533   T-2   MOVE TO MILLING MACHINE,
                      USING ELEVATOR

(a)

1.000   TS   WAIT FOR MOVEMAN

60   .137   T-7   MOVE TO WASHING SECTION
                     USING ELEVATOR

.004   O-8   WASH

100   .500   T-8   MOVE TO GRINDERS

.296   O-8   GRIND   POLISH

70   .400   T-9   MOVE TO PAINT GROUP

(b)

.010   O-11   APPLY FILLER

30   .045   T-10   MOVE TO OVEN

1.000   O-12   BAKE

15   .025   T-11   MOVE TO SPRAY BOOTH

.020   O-13   SPRAY WITH BLACK ENAMEL

25   .040   T-12   MOVE TO OVEN

2.000   O-14   BAKE

D.W   INS. 1   INSPECT

(c)

FIGURE 8.   Details of the process chart of Figure 7 are questioned
to eliminate unnecessary steps, combine operations, or improve
operation sequences.

Make or Buy

Every manufacturing concern must decide whether to use its production
skill and effort to make each of a multitude of items or whether to buy
them. The possibilities, of course, are tremendous when we consider
all of the materials, supplies, and finished products with which a

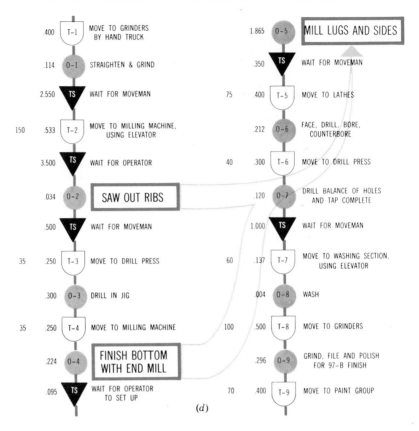

.400	T-1	MOVE TO GRINDERS BY HAND TRUCK
.114	O-1	STRAIGHTEN & GRIND
2.550	TS	WAIT FOR MOVEMAN
150 .533	T-2	MOVE TO MILLING MACHINE, USING ELEVATOR
3.500	TS	WAIT FOR OPERATOR
.034	O-2	SAW OUT RIBS
.500	TS	WAIT FOR MOVEMAN
35 .250	T-3	MOVE TO DRILL PRESS
.300	O-3	DRILL IN JIG
35 .250	T-4	MOVE TO MILLING MACHINE
.224	O-4	FINISH BOTTOM WITH END MILL
.095	TS	WAIT FOR OPERATOR TO SET UP

1.865	O-5	MILL LUGS AND SIDES
.350	TS	WAIT FOR MOVEMAN
75 .400	T-5	MOVE TO LATHES
.212	O-6	FACE, DRILL, BORE, COUNTERBORE
40 .300	T-6	MOVE TO DRILL PRESS
.120	O-7	DRILL BALANCE OF HOLES AND TAP COMPLETE
1.000	TS	WAIT FOR MOVEMAN
60 .137	T-7	MOVE TO WASHING SECTION, USING ELEVATOR
.004	O-8	WASH
100 .500	T-8	MOVE TO GRINDERS
.296	O-9	GRIND, FILE AND POLISH FOR 97-B FINISH
70 .400	T-9	MOVE TO PAINT GROUP

(d)

FIGURE 8.   (continued)

manufacturing concern deals. Fortunately, we need not consider manufacturing a very large share of these items. For such supply items as paper clips, pencils, and erasers, specialization makes their manufacture uneconomical to all concerns except those in that particular field. As a matter of fact, because of this pattern of buying many items which are out of the main line of effort, real opportunities are sometimes overlooked.

The product has been designed and its specifications are summarized on blueprints or drawings. Analysis of the product may reveal one, 10, 1000, or 10,000 parts that go into making it. A large transport aircraft is made up of over 50,000 parts. Which are to be made and which bought? What criteria are valid for making these decisions?

Economic Analysis.   Most businessmen would agree that the major criterion for decision making in the make-buy area is cost. If a part can be bought cheaper than it can be made, buy it! When it comes to the kind of cost comparison needed, however, there is often much confusion because no standard cost comparison fits each case. Every situation must be analyzed in terms of the *incremental costs* involved, and the nature of these costs varies tremendously. Recall our discussion of incremental costs in Chapter 5. Many of the examples cited there were of a make-buy nature. The only real principles of make-buy economic analysis are those of incremental cost analysis. We must ask ourselves: If we buy this part instead of making it, what costs do we *actually* shed, and are these reductions in costs greater than the costs that we assume by buying the item? If so, we should buy. Conversely, if we are presently buying instead of making, what actual *added* costs will be involved in making and are these less than the reductions we shall experience by ceasing the purchase of the item? If so, we should make.

These statements sound simple enough, but the difficulties come in the interpretation of them. For example, if we already have idle capacity in the necessary equipment classifications, the cost of making will look relatively more attractive, because we cannot justify the allocation of overhead costs for equipment, floor space, supervision, etc., to the new product. On the other hand, if it is necessary to acquire equipment, floor space, and supervision, the analysis would have to reflect these facts. Conversely, if we consider buying an item for $2.00 which we now make for an average manufacturing cost of $2.25 each, we had better look closely at the overhead items in our manufacturing cost figure. It is likely that very few of these overhead cost items will actually be reduced by purchasing the part. The supervision, floor space, and general factory overhead will probably remain as continuing cost items. If the equipment involved is general purpose, we may retain it too. The incremental cost figure for comparison with the $2.00 per piece purchase cost may begin to look more like $1.50. The sunk costs of equipment and buildings and the realistic facts of idle capacity are strong economic pressures for making instead of buying.

The types of cost factors that can enter into a make-buy decision are often surprising. For example, one company found that they had not included extra material-handling costs for the buy situation; since it was a heavy and bulky part, this turned out to be important. The simple price per unit of purchased parts does not necessarily reflect the incremental costs for comparison of the alternative plans of make or buy. Another company failed to consider that there were incremental paperwork costs for its make program. Where previously they had bought a single assembled item and placed it in storage to await assembly into their final product, now they had to purchase several component parts plus the raw material for the parts made, as well as write shop orders, control inventories for the several parts, write assembly orders, etc. It turned out that some of these costs were measurable and significantly greater than the cost of buying the part. The important thing to remember is that the cost analysis must fit the particular case, and each case will be a little different.

We have been discussing this question as though we were either making or buying an item and considering a change of policy. Now, how about the new part or product? Is this situation any different? Not really, because we are faced with similar complicating factors that prohibit the assumption of traditional manufacturing cost figures compared with purchase prices. Purchase prices alone may not reflect accurately the comparative cost of buying. Similarly, we may have available idle equipment that could do the job so that incremental make costs are mainly the direct items. Perhaps the one best guiding comment for make-buy comparisons is that we must remember we are dealing with a *going concern*. A going concern carries with it conditions that are unique to itself alone. It has buildings, equipment, technical skill, and a supervisory and executive staff. Decide to buy a part instead of make it. How has the going concern changed? Reverse your decision. Did this fact require new equipment, floor space, or supervisors? For going concern X, perhaps not; but for going concern Y, it could affect all of these factors.

Noneconomic and Intangible Factors.   Other factors often influence a company to follow a given make-buy policy. Quality, reliability, and availability of supply; control of trade secrets; patents; research and development facilities; flexibility; and alternative supply sources are some of the factors entering into a make or buy decision in the face of apparent economic disadvantage. Companies dealing with large defense contracts often have imposed on them as a contract condition the subcontracting of a certain minimum proportion of the total contract.

Make-Buy Policies.   Most concerns wish to follow a basic policy that places the economic criterion in the driver's seat; they want to vary from this policy only in situations which they regard as limiting, such as when quality considerations, supply, patents, etc., seem to dictate a certain course of action. In these situations, the limiting noneconomic factor has been consciously or unconsciously equated to the cost disadvantage. Although make-buy policies commonly assume the outside purchase of the great bulk of standard items such as nuts, bolts, switches, and valves, they are likely to vary somewhat with overall plant load. It would be common practice to make parts for which basic processes are already available; but when the plant load requires overtime work, economic analysis may change considerably. Buying of parts formerly made increases almost automatically, reflecting a recognition of the effect of overtime premiums on cost, as well as the need to increase effective capacity to meet schedules.

It is realistic to recognize that businesses often buy when they could make for none of the reasons we have discussed but to retain goodwill of an important supplier and because of reciprocity arrangements with customers. Finally, make-buy decisions are often based on a company policy of specialization and the concentration of effort and skill in some one basic line rather than responding to economic pressures to move in many directions simultaneously.

The *decision rules* for make-buy situations used by process planners are based on a variety of reasons and logic. Any one of the following, or combinations of several, depending on the company, its policies, and the nature of the specific item under consideration, may be the basis for these decision rules: economic advantage, quality considerations, reliability of supply, need for alternative sources of supply, control of trade secrets, research and development facilities of a supplier, retention of goodwill; reciprocity, desire to specialize activities, and imposed subcontracting as with some government contracts.

Estimating and Process Selection

Let us take the lathe family as an example of process selection. Assume that we have a part requiring turning operations. The operations can be performed on an engine lathe, a turret lathe, or an automatic lathe. These are the functional alternatives. The most economical selection depends on the volume that we contemplate and the relative magnitudes of the incremental costs for each alternative. To determine the most economical alternative, we must estimate the costs of setup and tooling, as well as the variable costs for the three alternatives. The estimates of labor cost might be based on standard data, reference to past costs of similar parts, or the skill of an experienced estimator.

Many organizations have developed standard data for various machine classes based on accumulated time studies. In the hands of an estimator who understands machine work, good estimates of setup and operation time can be developed. The bases and techniques for developing time standards are covered later in Chapter 12. Figure 9 shows an estimate built-up from these standard time data for the automatic lathe operations of an iron casting. It is obvious that a careful analysis of the part itself is needed in order to determine the cuts required and the sequence of the cuts. If manual operations are required which are not covered by the standard elements, time values for them can be synthesized by means of motion standard data such as MTM, Methods-Time Measurement, as discussed in Chapter 12.

By one or more of these approaches, estimates of labor cost can be made. Tooling costs, the costs of power and supplies, and other pertinent incremental costs can be estimated also. We assume illustrative figures shown in Table I for a part that can be machined equally well on an engine lathe, turret lathe, or an automatic lathe.

Figure 10 shows the range of volumes appropriate for each machine and specifies that range. Of course, the breakeven point between any two machines would change for different parts as the fixed and variable cost elements changed.

The appropriate decision rules are now obvious. If the lot quantity is less than 278, the engine lathe minimizes incremental cost; if the quantity is between 278 and 1000, the turret lathe yields minimum cost; in lots above 1000 parts, the automatic lathe yields the lowest cost. Note that this particular analysis assumes ownership of all three machines, so no capital costs enter the solution since these costs go on regardless of which of the three machines is selected. If it were necessary to purchase the automatic lathe, for example, the analysis would have to reflect this fact.

There are reasons, other than strictly economic ones, why one machine might be selected over another. Even though all alternatives meet functional requirements, a machine that holds closer tolerances might be selected for a "ticklish" job. For intermittent manufacture of custom-built parts and products, machine availability would be an overriding factor of importance. The most economical machine to use

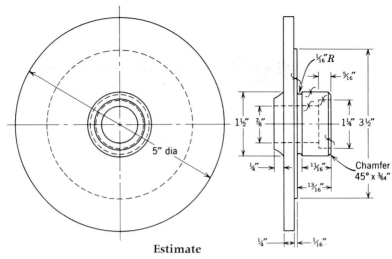

Estimate

Part. Cover plate.

Material. Cast iron.

Operation. Chuck on 5″ diameter. Face 5″ diameter to $\frac{1}{4}$″ dimension. Turn and face $3\frac{1}{2}$″ dimension. Form $\frac{1}{16}$-inch radius, 45° by $\frac{3}{64}$″ chamfer, and face end to $\frac{13}{16}$″ dimension. Bore $\frac{7}{8}$″ diameter through, and counterbore $1\frac{1}{4}$″ diameter $\frac{5}{16}$ inch deep.

		Minutes
1.	Pick up part, install casting in 3-jaw chuck. (Includes releasing of part and aside)	.200
2.	Position splash guard, adjust coolant, and start machine	.070
3.	Advance tool to work	.020
4.	Tool slide	
	(a) Back tool slide—face, counterface, form radius, and face end (500 rpm, .003 feed, 2″ length of cut)	1.334
	(b) Front tool slide—turn, bore, and counterbore	(.918)
	Note: .918 is smaller than 1.334; therefore, use 1.334 time value	
5.	Back tools from work	.015
6.	Stop coolant (automatic), stop machine (automatic), and position splash guard into clear	.040
7.	Release part and aside with part See element 1	
	Total time	1.679
8.	Allowances	
	(a) Check parts (this is done during element 4)	
	(b) Sharpen tools (10%)	.168
	(c) Personal (5%)	.084
	(d) Fatigue (10%)	.168
	Total estimate	2.099

FIGURE 9. Sample estimate for a machined part based on standard data.

TABLE I.   Fixed and Variable Incremental Costs for Machining a Part on Three Alternative Machines

Machine	Fixed Costs, Setup Labor Plus Tooling	Variable Costs, Labor, Supplies, Power, Etc., per Unit
Engine lathe	$ 5.00	$00.19
Turret lathe	30.00	00.10
Automatic lathe	70.00	00.06

might be in use or broken down, thus, rather than hold up the order for long periods, the next most economical machine would be used. Therefore, while basic managerial philosophy of machine and process selection is one of using the most economical system, factors of expediency, quality, and functional preference may modify these selections.

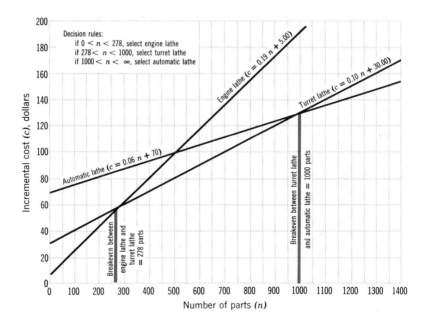

FIGURE 10.   Concept of process selection based upon marginal break-even analysis.

Route Sheets and Operation Sheets.   At each stage of its processing, every part is analyzed in order to determine the operations required and to select and specify the processes that perform the functions required. Thus, the *routing* of the part is determined. This information is commonly summarized on *route sheets*. The route sheet (a) shows the operations required and the preferred sequence of these operations, (b) specifies the machine or equipment to be used, and (c) gives the estimated setup time and run time per piece. When a part is a standard part, which is run and rerun periodically to fill needs, the standard routing sheets are maintained as the accepted manufacturing methods. More precise specifications of manufacturing methods are often developed in the form of *operation sheets*, which tell in greater detail how the operation is to be accomplished; in other words, they give a standard method.

The route sheet, together with operation sheets, specifies how the part or product is to be manufactured. These documents are basic to the manufacturing organization and take the same relative position to the design of a production system as the blueprint or drawing does to the design of a part or product. The drawing specifies *what is to be made*; the route and operation sheets specify *how to make it*.

Process Planning for Continuous Industries.   The situation that we have been discussing is generally applicable to industrial process planning; however, those familiar with high-volume, continuous types of industries may comment on the lack of route sheets in such industries. This lack is common, but originally someone performed the equivalent task of process planning and routing. Once the process planning is done and the system installed, route sheets would serve no purpose because routes are either standardized or follow mechanical paths so operation sequence is not a problem. Similarly, although operation sheets often exist, they are maintained as records of job conditions and methods; they may be referred to only when it is necessary to train new personnel in the standard procedures of the job. Alterations to the standard routing are required only periodically to incorporate product design changes or to take advantage of some advance in production technology.

Network Planning for Large Projects

In the post-World War II era, there has been a recognition of the importance to our economy of the large-scale one-time project as a managerial problem. The massive scale and complexity of missile projects and the space programs demanded special methods for project planning as well as for scheduling and control. Thus there emerged the network planning methods known as PERT (Performance Evaluation and Review Technique) and CPM (Critical Path Methods). The technological fallout of these developments has provided new and important methodology for all sorts of large project-centered activities such as in the construction industry, research and development activities, the planning and execution of new product introductions, and new plant start-up and relocation of an existing plant. We discuss these network planning methods in Chapter 18.

PROCESS PLANNING IN NONMANUFACTURING ACTIVITIES

Process planning in nonmanufacturing activities is usually not so complex as in manufacturing but nevertheless follows a parallel conceptual framework. Make-buy considerations enter some systems. For example, data processing centers process payrolls, inventory records, etc., on a time-rental basis. This represents an alternative to internal manual or semimechanized processing. A building contractor must decide which parts of a structure he will subcontract and which parts he will do with his own crew.

Also, the specification of processes or methods and their sequences can have an important bearing on costs in many nonmanufacturing activities. Systems and procedures analysts perform these functions in office systems. The sequence of operations is very important in building construction in determining the costs incurred. For example, if the rough plumbing is not done until a house is framed and roofed, it is necessary to cut holes in the rough flooring and walls and to work in awkward positions in order to make the plumbing runs. Also, once a house is partially built, it is often impossible to get grading equipment to the back of the lot. Grading is then accomplished by the alternative means of sweat and muscle. Most people who have built homes have similar tales to tell of the poor planning of work sequences. Figure 11 is illustrative of this point.

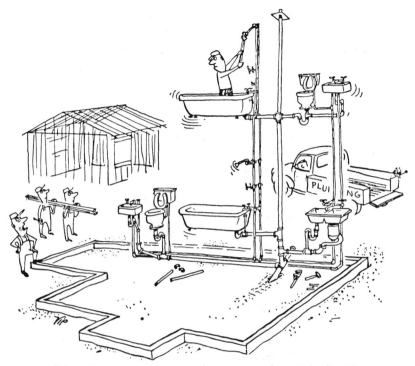

"Aren't you jumping the gun a bit, Schultz?"

FIGURE 11.   Courtesy Pomona Tile Manufacturing Company.

SUMMARY

We have begun to deal with the design of *systems* of production with the subject matter of production design and process planning. Following in Chapters 9 to 12 we deal with components of the system. In Chapter 11 we emphasize man and the design of jobs for man, and in Chapter 12 we deal with production standards and work measurement. In the present chapter we have seen the importance of the processes we use in establishing the minimum possible production cost. Process planning in the organizational sense takes the drawings and specifications for the completed part or product and then specifies the remaining details of how to manufacture it. In performing this activity, decisions whether to make or buy parts must be made. For the manufactured parts, a specification of the required operations and their sequence must be made. The specification is commonly summarized on route sheets, supplemented by operation sheets, which give, in greater detail, instructions for the performance of each operation.

KEY CONCEPTS

Flow.   The concept of flow is important to the analysis of production processes. Conceptually we can visualize the flow of the items being processed through a sequence of various types of processes (transport, storage, change of shape or form, etc.). In manufacturing we visualize this flow as the flow of discrete items rather than fluid flow. On the other hand, in continuous industries, we see that we are approaching the concepts of fluid flow and in continuous processing industries such as oil refining we are in fact dealing with fluid flow. The various charts discussed, such as assembly charts, operation charts, flow-process charts, and Gozinto charts, help one to visualize and analyze a complex flow process.

Marginal Cost Breakeven.   In selecting from among alternate processes on the basis of cost performance, the concept of marginal cost breakeven becomes important. The result of such analysis can specify the appropriate economic ranges in relation to output volume for using various competitive processes.

Going Concern Value.   In dealing with make-buy decisions particularly, we must recognize that we are dealing with a *going concern*. A going concern carries with it conditions that are unique to itself, and this must be taken into account in decision making. The going concern has a staff and existing assets. In making decisions, one must ask how the going concern has changed. Thus, in make-buy decision we may have available idle equipment that can be put to work. The result would be that only direct costs need be considered.

IMPORTANT TERMS

Numbers in parentheses indicate page numbers.

1. Assembly charts (210–211)
2. Flow process chart (215, 218)
3. Gozinto chart (210–211)
4. Network planning (229–230)
5. Operation process chart (214, 216–217)
6. Operation sheet (229)
7. Process planning (209)
8. Process selection (225–228)
9. Product analysis (210–220)
10. Route sheet (229)

REVIEW QUESTIONS

Numbers in parentheses indicate page numbers.

1. What is process planning? Relate it to product design, production design, plant layout, and production control. (209–210)
2. What is the nature of the economic analysis for a make versus buy decision? How does the "going concern" concept affect it? (223–224)
3. Discuss the nature of noneconomic and intangible factors that may bear on the make-buy decision. (224)
4. How does the breakeven concept apply in process selection? (226)
5. Are there reasons for selecting a given process that are noneconomic? (226–228)
6. What are route sheets and operation sheets? What information do they contain? (229)
7. Does process planning in continuous industries follow the same general pattern as in intermittent industries? (229)
8. Discuss production design and process planning as it applies in non-manufacturing industries. (230)

SELF-TEST TRUE-FALSE QUESTIONS

Numbers in parentheses indicate page numbers.

1. The basic process planning must begin during the product design stages. (209)
2. The accepted endpoint for production design is manifested by the route sheet which summarizes the exact specifications of what is to be made. (209)
3. Some process planning takes place during the layout phases of the design of a production system. (209)
4. Process planning takes as its inputs the drawings or other specifications which indicate what is to be made, and also the forecasts, orders, or contracts which indicate how many are to be made. (210)
5. A "gozinto" chart is a graphic means of showing the amount of direct labor which goes into a particular part or product. (210–211)
6. An assembly chart shows the parts and subassemblies which go into an assembled product. (210–214)
7. The difference between an assembly chart an an operation process chart is that the latter shows the required operations and inspections. (214)
8. The flow process chart is similar in concept to the operation process chart, except that it adds greater detail in the form of required transportations, storages, and possible outside operations. (215)
9. Make-buy analysis is one situation where conventional cost accounting is extremely helpful for decision making purposes. (223)
10. In breakeven analysis for process selection, machine depreciation is the main element of fixed cost. (225–228)

11.   An operation sheet is the summary of various classifications of operations taken from an operation process chart. (229)
12.   The route sheet shows the operations required and their preferred sequence, specifies the machine or equipment to be used, and gives the estimated setup time and run time per piece. (229)
13.   The PERT chart is nothing but a glorified route sheet. (230)

PROBLEMS

1.   Figure 12 shows a pipe valve with its various parts together with an assembled view.* Construct an assembly chart for this product.

2.   Construct an operation process chart for the pipe valve based on the following additional information concerning processing requirements. The machines are available for use on the parts indicated as well as for other parts.

Assembly Operations	Operations	Machine	Output in Parts Per Hour
	1. Final assembly	Bench	30
	2. Clean	Solvent tank	100
	3. Inspect (pressure test)	Water test stand	50
	4. Pack in boxes	Bench	500
Fabrication Operations			
Body, Part #1			
Cast bronze	1. Cast	Bench mold	40
	2. Clean	Tumble barrel	150
	3. Machine—thread and face three surfaces	Turret lathe	25
Bushing, Part #2			
	1. Cast	Bench mold	80
	2. Clean	Tumble barrel	300
	3. Machine all inside and outside diameters	Turret lathe	60
Stem, Part #3			
$\frac{3}{8}''$ bar stock	1. Machine all surfaces and cut off	Automatic screw machine	200

*The pipe valve problems are reproduced from A. L. Roberts, *Production Management Workbook*, John Wiley, New York, 1962, p. 22.

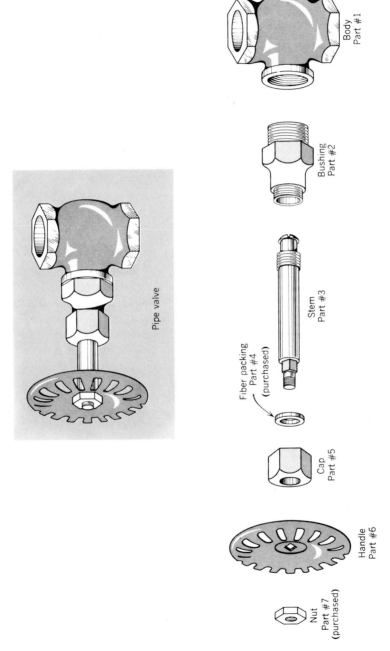

FIGURE 12.   Pipe valve, assembled and exploded views.

Fabrication Operations	Operations	Machine	Output in Parts Per Hour
Cap, Part #5			
$\frac{3}{4}''$ hex bar stock	1. Machine all surfaces	Automatic screw machine	500
Handle, Part #6			
Cast bronze	1. Cast	Bench mold	50
	2. Clean	Tumble barrel	200
	3. Machine two surfaces	Turret lathe	80
	4. Broach square hole	Broach	80

Note: 100 per cent inspection required for all fabricated parts prior to delivery to final assembly.

3.   Develop a summary of equipment requirements for the production of 200 pipe valves per hour. How are the equipment requirements affected by an increase in production rate to 350 valves per hour?

4.   The Laudenbach Beer Company has for a number of years used pasteboard cases to pack six units of six-pack cans for shipment to wholesalers and retailers in its regional marketing area in eleven western states. The total volume of beer shipped from its two plants in Los Angeles and San Francisco was 36 million cans (1 million cases) last year, and this volume is expected to be maintained and probably increased by 15 per cent over the next five years.

The Laudenbach Company has always purchased its pasteboard cases in "knocked down" form imprinted with the company name and other information. At each of the two plants the company has box-folding equipment in its production lines which set up the box blanks. This requires a gluing operation for the bottom flaps as well as the forming of the case and is done automatically except for maintaining a supply of the case blanks in the machine supply hopper, maintaining glue supply, and a general surveillance of the machine and its operation.

A new machine has come to the attention of the company's production analyst; it will perform the case-making operation, feeding case blanks to the case-forming machine. Printing requirements would be handled separately on sheets of paper to be glued to the case as a part of the case-making operation. The existence of the machine has raised the issue of whether the case blanks should be purchased or made in-plant, as well as some side issues regarding the company's general make-buy policies. The new machine costs $40,000 each, installed, and has a capacity considerably in excess of the needs at each of the two plants. Approximately 12 hours production per day from the case-making machine will satisfy two-shift requirements in the San Francisco plant.

TABLE II.   Cost Data for the Laudenbach Company

	Cost per Hundred		
	Purchase Blanks	One Case, Machine in Los Angeles Plant	One Case, Machine in Each Plant
Purchased blanks	$22.39	—	—
Glue	0.70	$ 0.70	$ 0.70
Labor	3.02	3.90	3.90
Freight, blanks to plants	0.95	—	—
Insurance	0.09	0.15	0.15
Maintenance	0.12	0.15	0.15
Pasteboard (raw material)	—	8.20	8.20
Printed labels	—	0.30	0.30
Scrap	—	0.20	0.20
Floor space	0.30	0.40	0.75
Trucking blanks to San Francisco	—	1.50	—
Totals	$24.57	$15.50	$14.35

Other data :
  Installed cost of case machines $40,000 each
  Expected economic life   8 years
  Tax depreciation term (straight-line)   10 years
  Incremental tax rate   50 per cent
  Interest rate   15 per cent
  Overhead factor at current output rates
    (25 per cent variable) $10/1000
  Cases required per year   1,000,000

The alternatives being considered are the continuance of the current practice of purchasing case blanks, the installation of one case-making machine at the Los Angeles plant with trucking of the blanks to the San Francisco plant, and the installation of a case-making machine in each of the two plants. In the Los Angeles location, space for the new machine can be found by a minor relayout of the packaging area. This relayout is estimated to cost $500 for the relocation of one machine and rerouting of a small section of conveyor. Suitable space exists in the San Francisco location. Cost data are as shown in Table II.

The Laudenbach Company has a reputation in the community as a steady employer and with its vendors as a stable customer. Suppliers commonly quote a better price to Laudenbach than they would to customers whose future business might be uncertain because of business fluctuations. On being presented with the production analyst's report, Laudenbach executives were hesitant, fearing a breakdown in relations with suppliers because rapid obsolescence of the case-making machine was anticipated. A review of the history of such machines showed that the designs had changed radically in the last few years, although there was no indication that the present machine design was not reliable in performance. A final issue discussed at length by the company officials centered on the nature of the new operation. The Laudenbach Company has been exclusively a beer company, not a paper company. "Wasn't it smarter to stay out of case making and stick to beer making? We know beer making and our reputation rests on that fact. If we go into case making, perhaps we should also consider integrating back one more step and make the pasteboard too. If we are going to consider backward integration, there are probably other possibilities more closely allied to beer making which we should consider. Let the case makers have this business of ours. They are specialists and so are we."

In the light of all factors, what analysis would you make and what action do you recommend?

5.   The manufacturing manager of a company making a line of toys for the high-volume Christmas market is considering three options for a particular toy where market testing has indicated good acceptance. The plastic and metal parts are fabricated by outside suppliers, and it is possible to have the plastics molder set up to completely assemble the item for a cost of $1 per unit. Alternatively, the toy company can set up work places at a cost of $1500 and hand assemble for an additional variable cost of $0.75. Finally, if the volume warrants it, some aspects of the assembly can benefit from mechanization and line assembly. The line-mechanization will cost $5000 to set up and install, but variable costs will be only $0.55 per unit. The market studies indicate a season's sale of 15,000 units and possibly as large as 20,000 units. Which of the three alternatives should the manufacturing manager select?

6.   Another dimension of the situation in problem 5 is the relationship between the toy company and the plastics molder. The molder is one of the best in the business and is currently operating at full capacity. He gives preferred delivery to profitable relationships. We estimate that if the toy company can assemble the item for $0.75 each with a $1500 setup cost, that the plastics molder probably has similar costs. What is the plastic molder's probable contribution to his profit and overhead? Should the toy manufacturer give the contract to the molder in order to retain good delivery schedules?

7.   A Graduate School of Management (GSM) does a surprising amount of office copying for classroom materials, research materials, and for general administrative activities. Because the number of copies run per year was increasing rapidly, the possibility of having this work done at a campus duplication center near the GSM building was being considered. The last year's increase from a total of 600,000 copies to 900,000 copies triggered the study of relative costs.

The "in-house" costs for 900,000 copies were based on the use of two machines, one of which was somewhat faster than the other. The costs were as follows:

Machine leases and related costs:

Large machine, including 22,000 copies per month	$575.00 per month
Small machine, including 5000 copies per month	$150.00 per month
Maintenance, additional copy charges, and developer	$8811.00 per year
Paper	$1839.00 per year
Toner	$1440,00 per year

The labor cost to run the machines in GSM is a difficult value to establish because it is commonly done by staff who would not be discharged if no copy work were to be done, and by faculty and students. An estimate was made that it required approximately 10 minutes per 100 sheets plus an average waiting plus travel time of 10 minutes. An average hourly rate of $2 was felt to be representative. Still, it was unclear whether or not the labor cost should be included.

There were other difficult problems of assessing whether or not this service should be bought outside. There was the matter of convenience of having the machines handy for last minute class preparations, although it was known that because the process was available, it was often used as an expedient, even though other processes such as mimeographing would have been less expensive. Also, the open nature of the service encouraged the use of the machines for personal business as well as some "walk-in" trade by students from other departments. The number of copies run for these reasons was unknown.

The comparative cost for the outside copying service was simple—a flat $.03 per copy, including labor, to run the copies. What are the comparative economics of buying the copy service versus retaining the in-house capability? What decision should be made?

REFERENCES

[1] Begeman, M. L., and B. H. Amstead. *Manufacturing Processes* (6th ed.). John Wiley, New York, 1969.

[2] Culliton, J. W. *Make or Buy.* Harvard University Graduate School of Business Administration, Soldiers Field, Boston, Mass., 1942.

[3] Eary, D. F., and G. E. Johnson. *Process Engineering for Manufacturing.* Prentice-Hall, Englewood Cliffs, N.J., 1962.

[4] Moore, H. D., and D. R. Kibbey. *Manufacturing Materials and Processes.* Richard D. Irwin, Homewood, Ill., 1965.

[5] Nordhoff, W. A. *Machine-Shop Estimating.* McGraw-Hill, New York, 1947.

CONTENTS

CHAPTER 9
PLANT LOCATION

The design of a production system is dependent on its location, because resulting physical factors influence layout and because the location partially determines operating and capital costs. In terms of the purely physical factors of plant design, location may determine whether or not power is purchased; the extent of heating and ventilating requirements; the necessary capacity for parts made, depending on the local availability of subcontractors; the amount of storage space needed to provide for raw materials, depending on reliability of supply; the types of carriers to provide for in shipping and receiving; etc. From the standpoint of operating and capital costs, ease of shipping raw materials and finished goods, costs of labor, taxes, land, construction, and fuel—all these factors and others in a complex interplay—contribute to the overall competitive position of an organization.

Location analysis for the multiplant situation is particularly interesting because of its dynamic character. The addition of a new plant is not a matter of determining a location independent of the location of existing plants. Rather, each location

241

considered involves a new allocation of capacity to market areas, so a solution from the economic viewpoint is one that minimizes combined production and distribution costs for the network of plants rather than for the additional plants alone. Also, in the multiplant situation, locational factors continually influence the extent of production in each plant to meet demand requirements and help determine which plants to operate and which to shut down if demand falls.

How Important Is a Plant's Location?   The pressures to secure advantageous locations are continuous, especially for multiplant operations. There have been, for example, wholesale movements of industries, such as the textile industry, to the South in order to secure advantages of low labor costs. The industrialization of the South in recent years has been based partly on this attraction to industry. Currently, American producers of many lines of products are considering foreign locations in order to combat competition from Japanese and European manufacturers. The formation of the Common Market in Europe binds together 200 million people in a free trade area for participating countries. Many American producers feel that the only way they can compete with the Common Market producers, both in the United States and in foreign markets, is to establish plants within the Common Market area.

Within the United States we must recognize that our present industrial decentralization within industries means that many good locations exist for each industry. There is no such thing as a unique location that is clearly superior to all others. For example, television and radio plants are found in New England, the Middle Atlantic states, various parts of the Midwest, the South, and in the far West. Plastics raw material plants are located in Massachusetts, New York, New Jersey, Pennsylvania, Ohio, Michigan, and Tennessee. Plastics molding plants are dispersed throughout industrial America. Furniture is manufactured in North Carolina, New York, Illinois, Indiana, Virginia, Pennsylvania, California, Michigan, Ohio, Massachusetts, Wisconsin, Texas, and other states. The steel industry, which we tend to picture as being centralized, has plants in eighteen states that produce pig iron, plants in twenty-seven states that produce steel ingots, and plants in twenty-eight states that produce hot-rolled products.

Dynamic Nature of Plant Locations.   We tend to think that the location problem occurs only once in a while and, as a conscious consideration by management officials, perhaps it does. We can all cite examples of companies that settled in a certain city and remained there twenty-five to fifty years and longer. This does not mean that the location problem was not considered during this period, especially if the organization expanded. The alternate choice of moving or staying put is always present, but it is emphasized when expansion is contemplated. The following alternate choices are commonly available:

1. Instead of expanding physical facilities, expand subcontracting to achieve an overall expansion.
2. Expand the existing plant if possible.
3. Retain the existing plant and locate a second one elsewhere.
4. Junk the old plant and relocate everything in a new one.

Companies that stay put over the years always have these choices and continually elect either to expand their existing plant or to extend subcontracting to meet the demands for their products.

An initially good location does not necessarily remain so over the years. The center of gravity of market areas can change drastically. Changes in industry pricing policies can render an old location obsolete, as when the steel industry shifted from the basing point pricing system to f.o.b. plant. Some companies have moved in order to get away from what they considered an undesirable labor situation.

OBJECTIVE AND SUBJECTIVE FACTORS

The businessman's aim in location analysis is to minimize the sum of all costs affected by location. He recognizes that in the comparison of alternate locations, some cost items, such as freight, may be higher in Area 1 and lower in Area 2, whereas power costs, for example, may show the reverse pattern. He is seeking the location that minimizes costs on balance; however, he is thinking not only of cost today but of long-run costs, so he will be interested in some of the intangible factors that may influence future costs. Thus, factors such as the attitude of city officials and townspeople toward a company's location in their city may be an indication of future tax assessments. Poor local transportation facilities may mean future company expenditures to counterbalance this disadvantage. A short labor supply may cause labor rates to be bid up beyond rates measured during a location survey. The type of labor available may indicate future training expenditures.

Thus, although a comparative cost analysis of various locations may point toward settling in one community, an appraisal of intangible factors may be the basis of a decision to select another.

This situation is brought out by Figure 1, which shows the results of one company's study of nine alternate locations. On the basis of cost comparisons only, City *E* is most favorable, with a difference of about

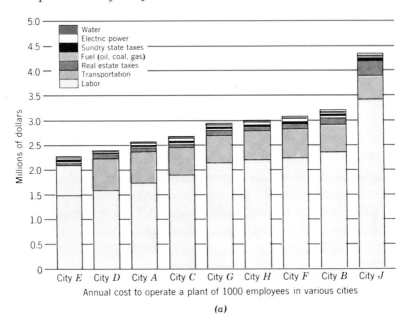

Annual cost to operate a plant of 1000 employees in various cities

(a)

COMPARISON OF OTHER FACTORS INFLUENCING CHOICE OF PLANT SITE

Factor	City E	City D	City A	City C	City G	City H	City F	City B	City J
Labor supply	adeq.	adeq.	plent.	plent.	adeq.	adeq.	plent.	plent.	plent.
Type of labor	good	good	excel.	excel.	excel.	excel.	excel.	excel.	excel.
Union activity	sign.	sign.	neg.	neg.	mod.	sign.	sign.	mod.	act.
Attitude	good	good	v.g.	v.g.	good	good	v.g.	v.g.	good
Appearance	fair	fair	good	good	excel.	fair	good	good	good
Transportation	good	good	v.g.	good	v.g.	good	v.g.	v.g.	v.g.
Recreation	good	v.g.	v.g.	v.g.	v.g.	good	v.g.	v.g.	v.g.

(b)

FIGURE 1. Summary of company *X*'s study of nine alternate locations. (Reprinted by special permission of National Industrial Conference Board, [14].)

$150,000 a year in annual operating expenses compared with City D, the next cheapest. However, in Figure 1b, seven intangible characteristics of the cities are rated. For each factor the cities are rated as excellent, plentiful, very good, good, adequate, or fair, except for the factor of union activity which carries the ratings active, significant, moderate, or negative. Both cities A and C rate higher than E on these characteristics. Does this mean that E's present cost advantage will vanish in the future? This is a question for individual management judgment. Note also in Figure 1a that the real estate taxes of City E are somewhat lower than for the other cities. This fact should raise the question: Is this condition likely to continue as an advantage?

Table I shows further general and specific information on the nine cities. Note that the bonded indebtedness of City E is over five times the per capita rate of City A and that City C has no bonded indebtedness. This may have future implications for tax loads. City E has no airport, nor does City C. Will this have any future implications in terms of both future tax load and of convenience of business transportation for company officials? The weighing of these intangible factors could be continued; however, the questions raised are typical.

SITE SELECTION

Although selecting the general area is the most important phase, the selection of the site is also important for both objective and subjective reasons. The area chosen must contain a site zoned for industrial use which meets the minimum needs of the company at reasonable development costs.

To choose a site that will meet minimum requirements, preliminary estimates of the building floor space requirements must be made. A site must then be obtained that is large enough to accommodate present floor space requirements, room for expansion, employee parking space, transportation facilities for receipt and shipment of material, extra space for trucks and rail cars waiting to be loaded or unloaded, etc. A site five times the actual contemplated plant area is considered minimum to allow for all of these things, including future expansion. If possible, open land adjacent to the site should be available to allow for future site expansion.

The site should also provide for necessary transportation facilities, utilities and sewage disposal. The soil structure must be sufficient to

TABLE I. Company X: Comparison of Proposed Plant Locations

City	Population 1940 Census	Population Est. 1949	Per Cent Colored	Bonded indebtedness Total × 1000	Bonded indebtedness Per Capita × 1000	Bank Deposits Total × 1000	Bank Deposits Per Capita	Taxes For Plant (1)	State Personal Income	General Sales Taxes	Municipal Airports	Hospitals	No. of Beds	Churches	Schools	Hotels	No. of Rooms	Electric Power Cost (2)	Water Cost (3)	Gas Rate (4)	Coal Rate (5)	Oil Rate (6)	No. of Present Industries (7)	Per Cent Unionized	Unskilled M	Unskilled F	Semiskilled M	Semiskilled F	Skilled M	Skilled F
City A	14,585	20,000	12.5	$ 277	$13.86	$18,335	$ 916.74	$75,000	Yes	None	Yes	3	118	23	9	4	295	$2,287	$419.45	35¢	$4.11	9¢	4	25%	.50/.75	.45/.60	.75/1.00	.60/.75	1.00/1.50	.75/1.00
City B	20,129	27,600	8.0	1,677	60.75	24,911	902.60	111,430	None	Yes	Yes	1	106	30	8	2	50	3,695	603.06	55¢	10.44	10.5¢	5	80%	1.00/1.15	.60/.90	1.10/1.25	.96/1.22	1.25/1.75	.80
City C	6,734	10,500	15.0	None	0.00	10,000	925.50	46,100	Yes	None	No	1	75	10	5	1	120	4,066	484.60	32¢	5.68	9¢	1	0	.60/.80	.50/.65	.90/1.00	.65/.75	1.25/1.50	.80/1.00
City D	11,729	14,852	15.0	11	0.73	17,278	1,163.50	48,000	Yes	Yes	Yes	1	100	21	22	2	200	1,800	259.86	20¢	6.00 to 7.50	—	3	67%	.60	.60	.80	.70	1.60	—
City E	7,256	9,000	17.0	690	76.66	9,296	1,032.91	440	None	Yes	No	2	85	9	5	3	190	2,542	242.20	90¢	5.63	11.4¢	3	67%	.60/1.00	.45/.75	.75/1.10	.65/.90	1.00/1.30	.75/1.00
City F	62,693	76,800	5.4	1,431	18.64	82,456	1,073.65	96,822	None	None	Yes	2	433	99	37	14	1,163	5,000	396.20	62¢	5.00	10¢	30	87%	1.05	.80	1.15	.95	1.35	1.05
City G	21,940	25,100	7.8	373	14.86	20,009	797.19	110,880	None	Yes	No	1	192	28	8	3	167	3,925	605.00	35¢	6.00	12.5¢	8	100%	.80/1.00	.73/.96	.90/1.25	.85/1.05	1.25/1.80	.95/1.15
City H	12,514	16,087	1.0	40	2.49	14,472	900.00	81,180	None	None	No	1	70	21	10	3	161	5,000	978.00	55¢	4.35	10¢	8	88%	.75/.90	.60/.70	.90/1.30	.75/.90	1.60/1.80	None
City J	109,912	125,000	4.5	5,974	44.60	164,233	1,313.86	282,186	None	None	Yes	4	611	78	47	8	4,010		676.80	75¢	7.64	7.5¢	36	89%	1.434 av.* (incentive)		1.718 av.* (incentive)		1.475 (incentive)	1.945

Reprinted by special permission of National Industrial Conference Board.

(1) Computed total tax on hypothetical plant.
(2) Per 200,000 kwh per month (1500 kw demand, 85% power factor).
(3) Cost for 3,000,000 gal (400,000 cu ft) per month.
(4) Per 1000 cu ft at lowest rate (1000 btu/cu ft).
(5) Per ton, stoker coal, delivered.
(6) Per gal. No. 2 fuel oil, delivered.
(7) Employing 100 people or more.
*Same rate for male and female.

carry the bearing loads of building foundations. All of these factors are important in determining the development cost of the site.

Industrial districts are very often an excellent solution, since they are planned solely for factory site development. The needed utilities commonly are already provided and there is no problem of zoning or hostility from nearby residents.

Obviously the selection of an area and finally a site for a plant involves a careful study if a good job is to be done. A tremendous amount of information needs to be obtained and correlated if any sense is to be made out of a complex problem.

CAPITAL EXPENDITURE—VOLUME EFFECTS

Another important variable between alternate locations is the necessary capital expenditure for land, building, and possible moving expenses. These fixed investment costs can differ considerably, depending on local construction and land costs and variations in the particular site selected, such as availability of railroad spurs into the property and adequacy of power and gas lines. Therefore, the concept of breakeven analysis could be used to contrast the objective cost factors of individual locations. Figure 2 shows such a contrast between the operating costs and assumed values of capital expenditure for the company and locations in Figure 1. Of course, such a breakeven analysis is valid only for volumes near the designed operating capacity, since large changes in volume would entail differences in capital investment, as well as possible differences in variable costs. Note that although City *J* offers attractive fixed costs, the operating costs make it the most expensive location for the volume contemplated. When viewed in this way, City *D* appears to be the most economical location.

MULTIPLANT LOCATION

As we mentioned earlier, multiplant location is influenced by existing locations as well as by the kinds of economic factors that we have already discussed. Each location considered must be placed in economic perspective with the existing plants and market areas. The objective is to select the new location that minimizes the total production-distribution cost. This aim is somewhat different from the location analysis for a single plant because each location requires a different allocation of capacity to markets from the several plants in order to

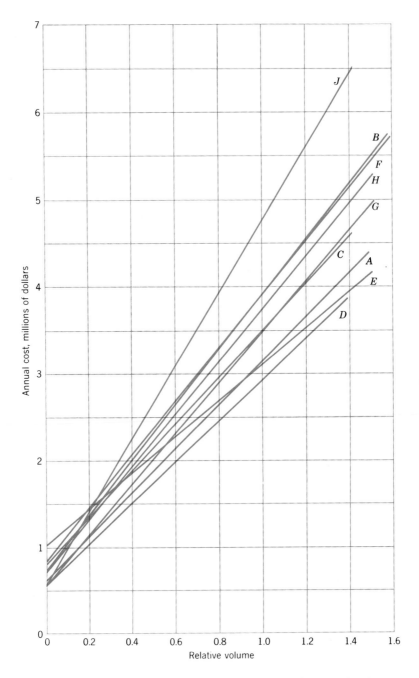

FIGURE 2.   Fixed and variable cost relationships for the nine locations of Figure 1. Breakeven costs between pairs of alternatives occur
where their cost-volume lines cross.

minimize overall costs. The formal problem can be placed in a linear programming framework and solved in a distribution matrix.

An Example

Let us examine the problem conditions of the Good-Wear Shoe Company case. The company manufactures a line of inexpensive women's shoes in two plants, Detroit and Chicago, and now distributes to five main distribution centers, Milwaukee, Cleveland, Cincinnati, Buffalo, and Atlanta, from which the shoes are shipped to retail shoe stores. The fifth center, Atlanta, has been added recently to serve the Southeast, an area in which the company has been expanding sales effort. To meet increased demand, the company has decided to

FIGURE 3.   Geographical locations of factories, distribution centers, and potential new factory locations.

TABLE II.   Production Costs, Distribution Costs, Plant Capacities, and Market Demands for the Good-Wear Shoe Company

From plants / To distribution centers	Distribution costs per pair, handling, warehousing, and freight					Forecast weekly market demand pairs
	Existing plants		Proposed plant locations			
	Detroit	Chicago	Cincinnati	Cleveland	Atlanta	
Milwaukee	$0.42	$0.32	$0.46	$0.44	$0.48	10,000
Cleveland	0.36	0.44	0.37	0.30	0.45	15,000
Cincinnati	0.41	0.42	0.30	0.37	0.43	16,000
Buffalo	0.38	0.48	0.42	0.38	0.46	19,000
Atlanta	0.50	0.49	0.43	0.45	0.27	12,000
Normal weekly plant capacity, pairs	27,000	20,000	25,000	25,000	25,000	
Unit production cost	$2.70	$2.68	$2.64	$2.69	$2.62	

build a new plant with a capacity of 25,000 pairs per week. General surveys have narrowed the choice to three locations, Cincinnati, Cleveland, and Atlanta. (See Figure 3.) The production and distribution costs, as well as the plant capacities and distribution demands, are shown in Table II. The proposed plant capacity of 25,000 pairs weekly reflects average forecast demand in the several market areas and allows for some expected growth of sales. Distribution costs include freight, handling, and warehousing costs. As expected, the production costs would be low in the Atlanta plant, but distribution costs are relatively high compared to the other two locations. The important question now is: Which location will yield the lowest cost for the enterprise in combination with the existing plants and distribution centers? To determine this, we solve three distribution matrices, one for each combination. Capacities and demands are as given, and the costs in each cell are the production-plus-distribution costs for each factory-distribution center combination. Figure 4 shows the resulting three optimum matrices with the total cost for each.

The solutions to the formal linear programming problems show the Atlanta plant to be a slightly better location in terms of variable costs. Atlanta is favored again by lower land and construction costs. Finally, if we consider future possible expansion of markets in the South, the Atlanta location seems to have an edge in terms of both present and future costs, without going into a discussion of other intangible factors. The problem solution as shown is a fairly simple one; however, other restricting conditions could have been added, such as inventory levels in the various locations as well as the location of future distribution centers.

Locational Dynamics for Multiplants. The decision to build the Atlanta plant was based on current costs, demand breakdowns, and an assessment of the future. But suppose that the balance of these factors changes. Then the allocation of capacity to markets should change also in order to yield a minimum total cost for whatever conditions exist. Thus, location analysis is continuous and necessary.

Suppose, for example, that after the Atlanta plant was built, our shoe company experienced a decline in demand because of increased competition from the low-cost Italian imports. Assume that instead of a total demand of 72,000 units per week as hoped and planned for, there is a demand of only 56,000 units divided among the market areas as follows: Milwaukee, 9,000; Cleveland, 13,000; Cincinnati, 11,000; Buffalo, 15,000; Atlanta, 8,000.

The Atlanta and Detroit plants can meet this demand without the Chicago plant by resorting to overtime work. In fact, any two of the three plants can meet the demand if overtime work is used. Therefore, we have these alternatives as well as the alternative of continuing to operate all three plants at partial capacities. Which alternative is best, and how much difference does it make? To determine the answers, we must know, in addition to the data that we have already, the cost of overtime work in each plant, the additional capacity available through overtime, and the cost reductions available by shutting down one plant. For each plant these data are as follows:

	Detroit	Chicago	Atlanta
Production cost at overtime	$ 3.37/unit	$ 3.33/unit	$ 3.27/unit
Additional overtime capacity, units	7,000/wk	5,000/wk	6,000/wk
Fixed costs:			
When operating	$12,000/wk	$9,000/wk	$13,000/wk
When shut down	5,000/wk	4,000/wk	6,000/wk

We can now set up a distribution matrix for each of the four alternatives and determine the total costs for each plan, as well as the appropriate fixed costs. This is done and the optimum distribution solution for each plan, including the appropriate fixed costs, is shown in Figure 5. Note that to keep the problem within the linear programming framework, we have regarded the overtime capacity as a separate source of

To distribution centers \ From plants	Detroit	Chicago	Cincinnati	Demand, 1000's
Milwaukee	3.12	3.00 (10)	3.10	10
Cleveland	3.06 (8)	3.12	3.01 (7)	15
Cincinnati	3.11	3.10	2.94 (16)	16
Buffalo	3.08 (19)	3.16	3.06	19
Atlanta	3.20	3.17 (10)	3.07 (2)	12
Capacity, 1000's	27	20	25	72

Production cost = $192,500
Distribution cost = 26,450
Total = $218,950

To distribution centers \ From plants	Detroit	Chicago	Cleveland	Demand, 1000's
Milwaukee	3.12	3.00 (10)	3.13	10
Cleveland	3.06	3.12	2.99 (15)	15
Cincinnati	3.11 (8)	3.10	3.06 (8)	16
Buffalo	3.08 (19)	3.16	3.07	19
Atlanta	3.20	3.17 (10)	3.14 (2)	12
Capacity, 1000's	27	20	25	72

Production cost = $193,750
Distribution cost = 26,960
Total = $220,710

To distribution centers \ From plants	Detroit	Chicago	Atlanta	Demand, 1000's
Milwaukee	3.12	3.00 (10)	3.10	10
Cleveland	3.06 (15)	3.12	3.07	15
Cincinnati	3.11	3.10 (10)	3.05 (6)	16
Buffalo	3.08 (12)	3.16	3.08 (7)	19
Atlanta	3.20	3.17	2.89 (12)	12
Capacity, 1000's	27	20	25	72

Production cost = $192,000
Distribution cost = 26,400
Total = $218,400

FIGURE 4.   Optimum production-distribution solutions for three proposed locations for the added plant.

supply. In actual shipment there would be no need to separate units produced on overtime. The results speak loudly. The most advantageous action is to shut down the Chicago plant and depend on the Detroit and Atlanta plants with 4000 units per week produced on overtime in the Atlanta plant. This alternative is $1500 per week better than the next best solution and $2250 per week better than the worst.

If the situation were even more serious, we might want to consider disposing of a plant. A similar analysis could be made to determine which plant. In such a case, all fixed costs attributed to the discarded plant would be eliminated and the capital recovered from the sale would have to be evaluated.

WAREHOUSE LOCATION

While plant location often involves the personal preferences of the owners and managers, especially if the location also dictates their residences, warehouse location more often yields to rational analysis. A number of approaches are currently being taken to the problem including linear programming, simulation, heuristic procedures, and the branch and bound technique. For example, simulation models have been developed and used by the Nestle Company [8] and H. J. Heinz [13]. Heuristic models have been developed [9] and applied at the B. F. Goodrich Company [10]. Finally, the branch and bound technique has been applied at ESSO [6, 7].

Even with a single producing plant the problem is not simple, for the entire distribution system design is involved. If the organization is committed to the site of the production plant then it can be concerned with designing a distribution system to link its plant with its markets. Some of the remaining problems for resolution are:

1. Whether or not to use field warehouses and if so, how many and where to locate them.
2. What modes of transportation to use.
3. What inventories will be required to operate the system including those at the plant, in transit, and in the warehouses.

When markets are concentrated, then warehouse locations tend to be determined at or near the major points of concentration. Boundaries between warehouse territories are theoretically determined so that the distribution cost from either warehouse would be equal at the boundary. As a practical matter natural boundaries often occur in the form of rivers, mountains, state lines, etc.

The practical problems increase substantially when multiple plants producing multiple products are servicing multiple warehouses. The products produced by the several plants may be overlapping or independent. Should each plant supply customers (or warehouses) directly or should products not made in all plants be cross-shipped among plants so that orders can be filled as a unit? What territory should be served by a given plant for products made in more than one plant? For products made in more than one plant, how should production schedules be dovetailed to serve the entire market? The real problems are plant location, production system design, inventory control, production schedule, etc.

FOREIGN LOCATIONS

As noted in the introductory section, the lure of foreign countries as potential plant locations has become increasingly strong in the post-World War II era. Part of this lure is based upon the fear by United

To distribution centers \ From plants	Detroit	Chicago	Atlanta	Demand, 1000's
Milwaukee	3.12 ⑨	3.00	3.10	9
Cleveland	3.06 ⑬	3.12	3.07	13
Cincinnati	3.11	3.10 ⑪	3.05	11
Buffalo	3.08 ⑭	3.16 ①	3.08	15
Atlanta	3.20	3.17 ⑧	2.89	8
Unused capacity	0 ⑪	0 ⑤	0	16
Capacity, 1000's	27	20	25	72

Variable cost = $169,650
Fixed cost:
Detroit, 12,000
Chicago, 9,000
Atlanta, 13,000   34,000
Total = $203,650

(a) All plants operating

To distribution centers \ From plants	Chicago	Atlanta	Chic.-O.T.	At.-O.T.	Demand, 1000's
Milwaukee	3.00 ⑨	3.10	3.65	3.75	9
Cleveland	3.12	3.07 ⑧	3.77 ⑤	3.72	13
Cincinnati	3.10 ⑪	3.05	3.75	3.70	11
Buffalo	3.16 ⑨	3.08	3.81 ⑥	3.73	15
Atlanta	3.17 ⑧	2.89	3.82	3.54	8
Capacity, 1000's	20	25	5	6	56

Variable cost = $177,730
Fixed cost:
Detroit, 5,000
Chicago, 9,000
Atlanta, 13,000   27,000
Total = $204,730

(b) Detroit plant shut down

FIGURE 5.   Optimum production-distribution solutions for four alternatives of plant operations; (b), (c), and (d) have other equally optimal solutions.

States manufacturers of the growing competitive strength of foreign producers. Almost daily, articles expressing this fear and sounding a warning appear in newspapers and magazines. For example, one newspaper article headlined, "Security Danger Seen in Foreign Competition," told the story of a large turbogenerator to be purchased by a large city water and power department. The lowest bid for the unit was made by an overseas supplier and was nearly $3 million or 38 per cent below that of the lowest United States bidder. The reason for the price difference given by the article was that the European worker is paid approximately one-third the rate of an equivalently skilled worker in the United States.

Invariably, the wage advantage is cited as the reason for foreign com-

To distribution centers \ From plants	Detroit	Atlanta	Det.–O.T.	At.–O.T.	Demand, 1000's
Milwaukee	3.12 ⑥	3.10	3.79 ③	3.75	9
Cleveland	⑬ 3.06	3.07	3.73	3.72	13
Cincinnati	3.11 ⑪	3.05	3.78	3.70	11
Buffalo	⑭ 3.08	3.08	3.75 ①	3.73	15
Atlanta	3.20 ⑧	2.89	3.87	3.54	8
Unused capacity	0	0 ⑦	0 ②	0	9
Capacity, 1000's	27	25	7	6	65

Variable cost = $173,150
Fixed cost:
Detroit, 12,000
Chicago, 4,000
Atlanta, 13,000   29,000
Total = $202,150

(c) Chicago plant shut down

To distribution centers \ From plants	Detroit	Chicago	Det.–O.T.	Chic.–O.T.	Demand, 1000's
Milwaukee	3.12 ⑨	3.00	3.79	3.65	9
Cleveland	⑨ 3.06	3.12 ④	3.73	3.77	13
Cincinnati	③ 3.11	3.10 ⑧	3.78	3.75	11
Buffalo	⑮ 3.08	3.16	3.75	3.81	15
Atlanta	3.20 ③	3.17	3.87 ⑤	3.82	8
Unused capacity	0	0 ③	0	0	3
Capacity, 1000's	27	20	7	5	59

Variable cost = $178,400
Fixed cost:
Detroit, 12,000
Chicago, 9,000
Atlanta, 6,000   27,000
Total = $205,400

(d) Atlanta plant shut down

FIGURE 5. (continued)

petitive advantage. The most common solution to the problem offered is to establish manufacturing plants in these low-wage areas. Careful location analysis, however, dares not accept either low-wage rates as the reason, or the establishment of foreign plant locations as the panacea.

For a particular manufacturer, the important question is: *Is there a net advantage to him in a foreign location?* There are several important reasons why there may not be. The great attraction in establishing foreign manufacturing operations is, apparently, low wages. But, actually, wage levels themselves are not the important parameter; rather, *labor costs* will determine the advantage or disadvantage of foreign location. Indeed, the American manufacturer perhaps knows better than others that wages can be high and simultaneously labor costs can be low. The equating factor is *productivity.* The American worker is paid much more per hour, but through the relatively large capital investment behind him, his efforts are multiplied by tools, mechanization, and automation. The wages question, then, turns on the difference in labor costs, not on hourly wages.

Can a manufacturer couple the advantage in lower wages with high productivity by using the same levels of mechanization and managerial practice abroad as he does at home? Perhaps, but we must note the difference in basic production economics here and abroad. Since labor is cheap relative to equipment abroad, he may find it wise to use relatively more labor and less expensive machinery, with resulting productivity and final labor costs more in line with that achieved by his foreign counterpart. The most economical manufacturing methods and techniques are not necessarily always those with the greatest possible mechanization, but those which for a given situation strike a balance between the costs of labor and the costs of machinery.

Can a net advantage in labor costs be offset by a net disadvantage in other costs? Assume for a moment that a particular manufacturer will have a net labor cost advantage through foreign manufacture. Will items of costs, such as materials, fuel and power, equipment, and credit, partially or completely counterbalance the labor cost advantages? The answer is undoubtedly different for different organizations and product lines. There is no one answer. The components of labor, materials, and capital in different product lines vary considerably. In the petroleum industry, labor costs are low, perhaps 5 percent, but material and capital are very important. For the turbogenerator cited in the opening paragraph of this section, the proportion of the total that was labor cost was undoubtedly very high because this kind of equipment is custom-built to specifications.

The result of this discussion of net advantage or disadvantage of all costs indicates that a company could be burned badly by rushing to low-wage areas in foreign countries unless low wages translate into *low labor costs* for *their* products, and provided that this labor cost advantage will not be erased by higher material, energy, and equipment costs. On the other hand, companies with cost distributions that fit, might be missing a real opportunity if they do not manufacture abroad.

Wage Level Comparisons.   In making wage level comparisons with foreign countries, it is important to note that the wage paid in many European countries often drastically understates the costs to the employer for an hour of work. The reason is that the so-called social charges (social security, workmen's compensation, vacations, etc.) are somewhat larger proportionately than is usual in the United States. Particularly in countries such as Western Germany, France, and Italy, the social charges are very large, 41, 42, and 64 per cent, respectively [3].

Real Labor Costs.   Good data on labor costs are very difficult to obtain for obvious reasons. Relative productivity figures, however, are available from special studies. Figure 6 shows the productivity in manufacturing for Canada, Western European countries, and the United States, all expressed as a per cent of the United States productivity figures. Figure 7 shows the comparison of the relative cost of an hour's work in the United States, Canada, and several Western European countries. Although we must still conclude that labor costs are lower in other countries in general, the differential is not as great as would be indicated by hourly wage rates. Indeed, on the average, in the case of France and Italy, labor costs may not be far different than in the United States. It would be dangerous to attach very strict interpretations to average country figures, however, because there are rather wide differences in productivity and wages paid by industry within each of these countries.

Other Manufacturing Costs.   Material is usually the other component of costs that is direct and important in the final cost of the product. The National Industrial Conference Board made a special study [12] of production costs among companies with both domestic and foreign operations.

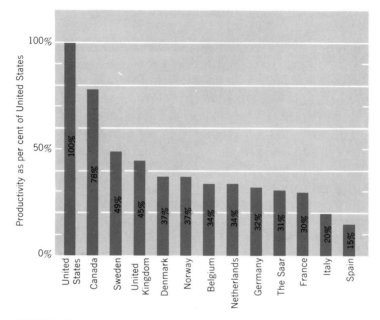

FIGURE 6.   Relative productivity in several countries. (From Dresch [5].)

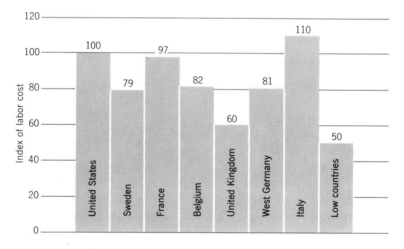

FIGURE 7.   Relative cost of an hour's labor in several countries. (Adapted from [3].)

The data were obtained by means of a questionnaire which asked for the percentage breakdown, for both domestic and foreign operations, of total unit cost between labor, material, and overhead on products that were basically similar. With these data, plus ratios of total unit costs, it was possible to tabulate relative figures on the three classifications of cost. Our interest is now in the material cost category of that study. It shows that only 29.9 per cent of the products were reported with material costs lower in foreign countries; 70.1 per cent were either equal or higher. This indicates a pattern that is somewhere the reverse of the labor cost picture. Thus, the company in an industry where the labor component is relatively large and the material component relatively small might find an advantageous balance of costs abroad. On the other hand, the reverse pattern might be true for a company in which material costs are large. Not only were material costs higher on the average in foreign countries, but, for *each* industry listed, higher material costs in foreign plants were reported with greater frequency.

In the general category of overhead costs, there is such a variety of items that generalizations are difficult. Some costs may be lower and some higher than would be typical for American plants. We would expect the labor component of overhead costs to be generally lower, in line with the generally lower wage rates. Capital costs in Europe are somewhat higher. The cost of the equipment itself may be higher or lower. Fuel and other sources of industrial energy are significant costs for some industries. Here again it appears that foreign costs are not attractive.

Overall Production Costs.   Of the products for which total unit cost ratios were given, 44.2 per cent were below United States costs, 19.3 per cent were equal to United States costs, and 36.5 per cent were greater than United States costs. When all costs are considered, there is no picture of either generally lower or generally higher costs abroad. On the other hand, what is indicated is considerable variability, with foreign costs ranging from less than 55 per cent to more than 145 per cent of domestic costs (see Figure 8). Apparently there are some products, industries, or companies that are favored by the structure of foreign costs; for others the conditions are unfavorable. Products in the industries that have relatively low labor content are predominant in the "Unit Cost Higher" column. Similarly, those industries that have the reverse pattern of labor and material costs, that is, chemicals, fabricating

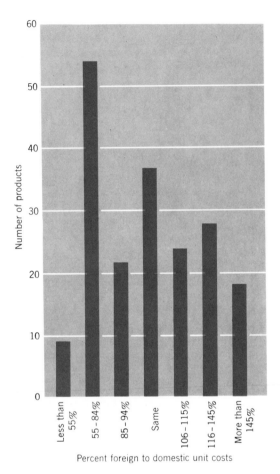

FIGURE 8.   Distribution of number of products by ratio of foreign to domestic unit costs. (Based on data from [12].)

metal, and machinery, are predominant in the "Unit Cost Lower" column.

It does not appear logical that low-wage rates in foreign countries generally threaten the United States industry. It is true that foreign companies have an advantage in certain product lines. But, on the other hand, American companies have an advantage in other product lines. The most powerful defense against the low-wage rate appears to be the great advantage of high productivity enjoyed by America. The American lead here is significant, but not equally so in all industries. While European countries are increasing their productivity, so is the

United States. Location studies in foreign countries need to take account of these differences in productivity, material, and other costs, as well as the differences in wage rates.

SUMMARY

There is a trend toward decentralization in plant location. This decentralization is taking place both on a nationwide scale and within industrial communities. Many small communities that have never had industry before have offered attractions, such as tax reductions, low-cost or even free land, and buildings, to lure industry to their communities. Within large industrial communities, decentralization has taken industry to the suburbs where land is cheaper and the more efficient one-story building is feasible. These suburban locations offer space for expansion and parking, as well as the opportunity to design plants of architectural beauty that fit into the landscape and in which employees are proud to work.

Location is of great importance because it fixes some of the physical factors of the overall plant design. In addition, location determines what investment costs must be incurred and the level of many operating costs. Although these factors are important, we must remember that there is normally a number of good locations. Although it is certainly possible to pick poor ones, careful analysis and planning ordinarily uncover good locations. The personal factor is a strong one in plant location. Owners of business often choose, or retain, plant locations because they prefer to live in those areas. This, too, speaks for the theory that many locations are acceptable, for many enterprises have survived over long periods even though location has been determined solely by the owner's personal preference.

IMPORTANT TERMS

Numbers in parentheses indicate page numbers.

1. Capital expenditure–volume effects (247)
2. Distribution costs (250, 251)
3. Fixed costs of location (249)
4. Fixed costs when operating (251)
5. Fixed costs when shut down (251)
6. Foreign locations (254–256)
7. Locational dynamics (251)
8. Multiplant location (247)
9. Productivity (256)
10. Real labor costs (257)
11. Variable costs of location (249)

REVIEW QUESTIONS

Numbers in parentheses indicate page numbers.

1. How important is a plant's location to its profitability? (242)
2. How often does the question of plant location arise? What are the location alternatives that an organization faces? (242–243)
3. What is the object of location analysis? What is the importance of subjective factors in appraising alternate choices for location? (243)
4. What kinds of data are needed to perform an analysis of alternate sites within a given general location? (245–247)
5. Can an advantage in projected operating costs be counterbalanced by capital expenditures required for a given location? What sort of analysis is called for? (247)
6. How is the problem of locating a single plant different from locating an additional plant which manufactures the same items as existing plants? What sort of analytical technique is useful? (247–250)
7. What do we mean by "locational dynamics" for multiple plants? (251)
8. On what basis can foreign labor costs be compared with those in the United States? What are the general comparisons in labor costs between the United States and various European countries? (254–261)
9. How do material costs compare between the United States and foreign countries? (257–259)
10. On balance, are foreign locations attractive for U.S. manufacturers? In which kinds of industries? (259–260)

SELF-TEST TRUE-FALSE QUESTIONS

Numbers in parentheses indicate page numbers.

1. For a given enterprise there is usually a unique location that is clearly superior to all others. (242)
2. Plastics raw material plants are concentrated in the state of Tennessee. (242)
3. Many of the intangible factors in plant location can have an effect on long-run costs. (243)
4. A site ten times the actual contemplated plant area is considered minimum to allow for room for expansion, employee parking space, incoming and outgoing transportation facilities, dock space, etc. (245)
5. Breakeven analysis makes it possible to relate site development costs and other fixed costs with the variable costs of operation for various alternate plant locations. (247)

6. In multiplant location analysis, each alternate location will require a different allocation of capacity to markets from the several plants, in order to minimize overall costs. (247–248)

7. In a multiplant situation where demand had fallen to the point where one plant could be shut down and still supply the market from the others, the optimal solution always indicates the shutdown of the plant with the highest production cost. (251–253)

8. Low wages in foreign countries translate directly into low product labor costs. (256)

9. An American manufacturer establishing a foreign plant may find it economical to adopt methods resulting in lower labor productivity in the foreign plant as compared to his American operations. (256)

10. The social charges, such as Social Security, Workmen's Compensation, etc., in countries such as Western Germany, France, and Italy are somewhat larger than they are in the United States. (257)

11. The average cost of an hour of labor in the United States, France and Italy is approximately equal. (257, 258)

12. For most industries, material costs in foreign countries are about the same as material costs in the United States. (257–259)

13. The European manufacturer must pay a somewhat higher cost for capital than his United States counterpart. (259)

14. Overall, foreign costs of manufacture are somewhat less than costs in the United States for comparable products. (259)

15. Location is of great importance because it fixes some of the physical factors of the overall plant design. (261)

PROBLEMS

1. A company with plants in Seattle, Chicago, and Louisville is considering the establishment of a manufacturing plant in a foreign location. The primary reasons are these: First and foremost is a steady decline in unit profit due to relatively higher manufacturing costs. Second is the growing popularity of the products in foreign countries. After a preliminary analysis, the list of possible locations has been narrowed down to the following countries: Japan, West Germany, and Puerto Rico.

A. In any analysis of alternative plant locations, some assumptions are necessary for the degree of political stability, attitude toward foreign investors, currency fluctuations, etc. For each proposed alternative, assign a subjective value between one and ten (ten = best) and give your rationale for the values assigned.

(a) United States
(b) Japan
(c) West Germany
(d) Puerto Rico

B.　Determine the best plant combination for the existing demand, using objective data (the comparison will basically narrow down to the alternatives of foreign locations versus overtime in existing plants). Data follows:

Present unit manufacturing costs:

	Seattle	Chicago	Louisville
Raw material	$0.02	$0.03	$0.02
Direct labor	0.04	0.03	0.05
Variable burden	0.02	0.02	0.01
Nonvariable burden	0.09	0.10	0.08
General and administrative	0.01	0.01	0.01
	$0.18	$0.19	$0.17

Annual present factory capacity; units:

	Seattle	Chicago	Louisville
(One-shift operation)	100,000	200,000	120,000

Additional production may be attained by using overtime (direct labor = 150 per cent of normal costs, all other costs constant). Maximum overtime capacity = 50 per cent of regular capacity.

Present annual demand; units:

Seattle	Chicago	Louisville	Japan	West Germany	Puerto Rico
90,000	150,000	100,000	30,000	40,000	20,000

Estimated foreign production costs:

	Japan	West Germany	Puerto Rico
Raw material	$0.018	$0.019	$0.017
Direct labor	0.037	0.040	0.022
Variable burden	0.005	0.011	0.011
Nonvariable burden	0.061	0.093	0.098
General and administrative	0.009	0.007	0.012
	$0.130	$0.170	$0.160

Estimated plant costs (50,000 annual capacity in units for one-shift operation, ignore the possibility of second-shift foreign operation):

Japan	West Germany	Puerto Rico
$10,000	$30,000	$20,000

Projected market growth per annum (not compounded):

United States	Japan	West Germany	Puerto Rico
5%	6%	7%	8%

Distribution costs, including import taxes, etc.:

To:

From:	Seattle	Chicago	Louisville	Japan	West Germany	Puerto Rico
Seattle	$0.02	$0.06	$0.08	$0.12	$0.16	$0.10
Chicago	0.06	0.04	0.05	0.15	0.15	0.09
Louisville	0.08	0.05	0.03	0.16	0.16	0.08
Japan	0.14	0.16	0.17	0.02	0.21	0.18
West Germany	0.17	0.16	0.17	0.20	0.03	0.19
Puerto Rico	0.11	0.10	0.09	0.22	0.20	0.01

C. Determine the optimal plant output combination for five years from the present. Include a 10-per-cent annual interest cost for proposed plants.
D. Based on your answers to problems A, B, and C and any other relevant information, what suggestions would you make to the company regarding foreign locations? Why?

2. The Good-Wear Shoe Company discussed as an example in the text installed the Atlanta plant discussed there. With the initial success of that producing location, and the incursion of imports in existing markets, management turned its attention to the exploration of new markets. They found ready opportunities by expanding their sales efforts westward and in the South and Southwest. They have been supplying these markets from existing distribution centers, but current volume in the new locations has raised the question of the advisability of a new warehouse location. Three possible locations are suggested because of market concentrations: Denver, Houston, and New

TABLE III.   Production Costs, Distribution Costs, Plant Capacities, and Market Demands for the Good-Wear Shoe Company

| From Plants | Distribution Costs per Pair, Handling, Warehousing, and Freight | | | | | | | | Normal Weekly Capacity Pairs | Unit Production Cost |
| | Existing Warehouses | | | | | Proposed New Warehouses | | | | |
	Atlanta	Buffalo	Cincinnati	Cleveland	Milwaukee	Denver	Houston	New Orleans		
Atlanta	$0.27	$0.46	$0.43	$0.45	$0.48	$0.65	$0.58	$0.55	25,000	$2.62
Chicago	0.49	0.48	0.42	0.44	0.32	0.50	0.54	0.60	20,000	2.68
Detroit	0.50	0.38	0.41	0.36	0.42	0.55	0.60	0.65	27,000	2.70
Forecast weekly market demand, pairs	8,000	15,000	11,000	13,000	9,000	16,000	16,000	16,000		

Orleans. Data concerning capacities, demands, and costs are given in Table III. Based on these data which warehouse location should be chosen? What additional criteria might be invoked to help make a choice? How should they decide whether or not to build the new warehouse or continue to supply from the existing warehouses?

3.   In the Good-Wear Shoe Company example discussed in the text the conclusion was that the Chicago plant should be shut down because of the decline in demand. The solution to that problem was presented in Figure 5.

  How does the recommended conclusion change if the market demands in the five market areas are Milwaukee, Cleveland, Cincinnati, and Buffalo 11,000 pairs each, and Atlanta 12,000? All other data remain the same.

4.   In the text, a set of comprehensive data are given in Figure 1 and Table I concerning nine alternate plant locations for Company X. City E has the lowest overall estimated operating cost but, as noted in the text, that location has some disadvantages relative to other locations. Analyze all of the data carefully, considering trade-offs between objective costs and other factors and write the "recommendations" section of a consultant's report that draws on the data given and justifies your recommendations for location.

REFERENCES

[1] *Basic Industrial Location Factors.* U.S. Department of Commerce, Washington, D.C., 1946.
[2] Brown, P. A., and D. F. Gibson. "A Quantified Model for Facility Site Selection—Application to a Multiplant Location Problem." *AIIE Transactions*, **4** (1), 1–10, March 1972.
[3] Buffa, E. S., and A. E. Bogardy. "When Should a Company Manufacture Abroad." *California Management Review*, **2** (2), 1960.
[4] Dillon, J. D. "The Geographical Distribution of Production in Multiple Plant Operations." *Management Science*, **2** (4), 353–365, July 1956.
[5] Dresch, F. W. *Productivity in Manufacturing.* Stanford Research Institute, Palo Alto, Ca., 1953.
[6] Effroymson, M. A., and T. L. Ray. "A Branch-Bound Algorithm for Plant Location." *Operations Research*, **14** (3), May–June 1966.
[7] Feldman, E., F. A. Lehrer, and T. L. Ray. "Warehouse Locations Under Continuous Economics of Scale." *Management Science*, **12** (5), May 1966.
[8] Gerson, M., and R. B. Maffei. "Technical Characteristics of Distribution Simulators." *Management Science*, **10**, 1968.
[9] Keuhn, A. A., and M. J. Hamburger. "A Heuristic Program for Locating Warehouses." *Management Science*, **9** (7), July 1963.

[10] Khumawala, B. M. "A Heuristic Simulation Approach to Warehouse Locations." *Proceedings of IBM's Third MS/OR Conference*, IBM Publication No. 320–2968, April 1969.

[11] Khumawala, B. M., and D. C. Whybark. "A Comparison of Some Recent Warehouse Location Techniques." *The Logistics Review,* **7** (31), 1971.

[12] "Production Costs Here and Abroad." *Studies in Business Economics,* National Industrial Conference Board, No. 61, New York, 1958.

[13] Shycon, H. N., and R. B. Maffei. "Simulation-Tool for Better Distribution." *Harvard Business Review*, Nov.–Dec. 1960.

[14] "Techniques for Plant Location." *Studies in Business Policy*, National Industrial Conference Board, No. 61, New York, 1953.

[15] Weston, F. C., Jr. "Quantitative Analysis of Plant Location." *Industrial Engineering,* **4** (4), 22–28, April 1972.

CONTENTS

CHAPTER 10
LAYOUT OF PHYSICAL FACILITIES

Plant layout is the integrating phase of the design of a production system. The basic objective of layout is to develop a production system that meets requirements of capacity and quality in the most economical way. Here the specifications of what to make (drawings and specifications), how it is to be made (route sheets and operation sheets), and how many to make (forecasts, orders, or contracts) become the basis for developing an integrated system of production. This integrated system must provide for: machines, workplaces, and storage in the capacities required so that feasible schedules can be determined for the various parts and products; a transportation system which moves the parts and products through the system; and auxiliary services for production, such as tool cribs and maintenance shops, and for personnel, such as medical facilities and cafeterias.

Because of the dynamic character of our economy, the design of this integrated production machine must retain an appropriate degree of flexibility to provide for future changes in product designs, product volumes, and mixes for advancing

271

production technology. Both the site and the building should make it possible to expand operations in a way that dovetails with existing operations. Certain financial and physical restrictions are a normal part of the layout problem. The physical restrictions may be due to the site: its size, shape, and orientation in relation to roads, railroads, and utilities. Or they may be due to local ordinances or state laws which specify building restrictions and safety codes. In redesign or relayout of facilities, the existing building imposes severe restrictions.

These general statements of the layout problem indicate something of its complexity. Almost all of the factors which enter the problem tend to interact. For example, providing flexibility affects the nature of processes and capacities, which, in turn, interact with short- and long-run costs. Material transportation methods affect not only transportation costs but also the amount of handling at machines and workplaces. The physical arrangement and relative location of work centers are important in determining transportation costs and direct labor costs. Storage locations and capacities interact with transportation costs and delay times.

We could continue for some time in describing the interdependent nature of the factors that enter into the layout problem, but our present point is that optimizing the design of such a system is largely an art. We have principles, rules, and guides which have been shown to be valuable in determining suboptimal solutions for components of the large problem. For example, queuing theory can provide a basis for optimal design capacities of service centers such as tool cribs and maintenance crews. Human engineering data can help in optimizing workplace design; operation sequence analysis can help to determine the best relative work center locations (discussed later in this chapter). And principles of production economics can aid in selecting the most economical processes, designs, handling systems, etc.

However, there is no overall general theory that makes it possible to relate the multitude of influencing factors in a composite optimal design. Rather, the development of a good plant layout is the result of a sequence of major decisions on such questions as location, design capacity, and general modes of manufacture. These decisions are followed by a multitude of less significant, but important, decisions related to the selection and placement of equipment, allocation of space, basic flow patterns, etc. Several components of plant design are discussed separately, because we have special knowledge about them and because they are important. Production processes, job and method design, production design, process planning, and plant location are examples. These, however, tend to blend with the overall activity of layout during the actual development of a plant design.

THE CAPACITY DECISION

In contemplating a new plant design or the redesign or expansion of an existing system, a high-level decision on the design capacity is required. It is not enough simply to look at annual sales of various products, because the sales pattern may reveal seasonal fluctuations. Do we design for the peak or for some average level? If we choose to follow the sales curve, we shall minimize inventory risks, but we shall have a fluctuating labor force and our plant will have idle capacity except during peak production. If we adopt some intermediate level, we shall tend to stabilize employment levels and utilize plant facilities better, but it will be necessary to build inventories to meet the sales peak. Which plan will minimize the combined cost of inventories, plant investment costs, and labor turnover costs? We have here a problem in economic analysis that is of major significance. It can be approached as a programming problem where production capacity is allocated to operating periods, minimizing the combined plant investment costs, inventory costs, and turnover costs. Investment costs would be approximated by a nonlinear function of capacity.

Future Capacity.   Then there is the question of sales forecasts. Do we build for a capacity that matches our present sales experience or do we attempt to build for some forecast level of one, five, or ten years hence? Can we afford to build for more capacity than is needed now? We must remember that successive units of capacity are not equally expensive because capacity is bought in "chunks." Moreover, it is commonly true that at any one level there will be idle capacity in certain equipment classifications. Therefore, to move to the next level does not entail the purchase of equipment items where we already have idle capacity. Where capacity is built to match some forecast of future needs, it is common to buy equipment for current needs only and provide space in the building and layout for the additional equipment when it is needed. Thus, planning is for a future capacity, but extra overhead is carried for the building space only; as the capacity is needed, machines can be integrated into the system without need for relayout.

The question then really relates to the provision for extra space to match a future forecast. Some additional space can probably be justified when we consider that space added later is more expensive per square foot because existing walls must be removed, doors cut through to the new space, etc. More important than the cost of the additional space itself are relayout costs, which would be required to integrate the new space into the production system. If the new space is not integrated into the system but becomes a "thumb" stuck on to the existing layout, we would pay extra costs daily in the form of higher material-handling costs. These extra costs of adding future space must be balanced against the incremental costs of building more space now and carrying it as added overhead until it is needed.

Subcontracting and Multiple-Shift Effects on Capacity. Another aspect of the capacity problem is the question of how we shall meet our capacity needs. The investment-capacity ratio can be altered by the amount of subcontracting and by the intensity with which we use facilities, that is, one, two, or three shifts. The economics of make versus buy are especially significant where new capital equipment is involved, as it would be with the design of a new facility, for now we have no idle capacity behind which "make" can hide. Rather, we are setting the future pattern, so overall make-buy policies need to be reviewed.

The number of shifts appropriate for a given organization is not a simple question. If we use two shifts instead of one, investment costs are not halved because, as we noted before, increments of capacity are not equally expensive. Many other costs are also involved. Wage premiums of 10 to 15 per cent are common for second shifts, and many people question whether productivity and scrap ratios are as good on multiple shifts. Multiple shifts ordinarily increase supervision costs, also. There is no single answer to the question of shift operation, since the relative importance of building and equipment investment costs and labor costs varies from industry to industry. Economic analysis is required for each situation. In general, industries with very heavy investments in buildings and equipment per worker, such as steel, chemical, and oil refining industries, find multiple shifts more economical; those with moderate and low investments per worker find that wage premiums more than counterbalance the investment savings of multiple shifts.

Translating Capacity into Workable Units.   What is the meaning of the term *capacity*? A steel man would think in terms of tons of steel per day, week, or month; an automobile manufacturer in terms of cars, etc. How about a job-shop machining company? Its products are so different that capacity in terms of the output of finished products is quite meaningless. Here capacity must be expressed in more universal terms. The units commonly used are *available hours* in various machine classifications per day, week, or month. This output potential is a good general measure of capacity for plant design because we can convert fairly easily to a physical capacity equivalent, the number of *machines* required. The number of machines required in various classifications is the data that we finally want to work with in developing a layout. We need to translate everything into physical units of capacity. In doing this, we must be careful to make allowances for two factors which reduce the utilization of equipment: the plant efficiency factor and the scrap factor.

Through the *plant efficiency factor* we recognize that because of scheduling delays, machine breakdowns, preventive maintenance, etc., a portion of the available hours cannot be used. Plant efficiency factors vary with the type of equipment and the company; they range generally from 0.50 to 0.95. Thus, if 100 outboard motors per week translated into the need for 550 milling machine-hours per week (summarized from data on route sheets, time studies, estimates, etc.), we need the equivalent of $550/0.80 = 688$ hours if our plant efficiency factor is 0.80, since we expect that about 138 machine-hours will be unavailable to us.

Through the *scrap factor* we recognize that for any real production process we shall produce some bad parts or products. When a decision was made to design a plant to build 100 outboard motors per week, we were obviously thinking of good motors, free of defective parts. But some of our milling capacity will be used up producing scrap, and so we must allow for this event too. If we expected 3 percent scrap in our milling operations, 688 hours of available machine hours must be increased to $688/0.97 = 709$ hours. Now, if we expect to work 75 hours per week on two shifts, we need $709/75 = 9.45$ machines. As we noted, physical capacity comes in "chunks," so we must provide for either 9 or 10 milling machines. If we decide on 10 machines, we shall expect to have some idle capacity. If we decide to squeeze by with 9 machines, we should expect some bottlenecks now and then, which we may try to make up by overtime work. Thus, a capacity of 100 outboard motors translates into an equivalent milling machine capacity of 9 or 10 machines.

Summarizing, the capacity question involves important decisions that will determine total plant investment and future operating costs of the plant through: the selection of production levels in relation to seasonal sales levels, the determination of how many shifts are most economical, the decision of what proportion of the total effort to subcontract, and the determination of how much excess or "growth" capacity is economical. The financial strength and ability of the organization are always present as restrictions in determining how close we may approach ideal capacity conditions at a given time. A company with limited financial resources must constantly appraise alternative uses for available funds: for advertising and promotion, for product development programs, or for capital improvement.

BASIC LAYOUT TYPES

Which type of layout is appropriate? Do we have prerequisites for a streamlined production line layout such as we find in automobile assembly? During the development of a new plant design, these fundamental decisions plague production executives, and they should, for at this time they hold in balance the opportunity of the future on one side and miserable failure on the other. A shiny new plant housing an obsolete layout or an inappropriate layout would result in increased manufacturing costs. The appropriate type of layout may set the pattern for efficient manufacture for a long time to come.

In general, layouts can be classified as either process oriented or product oriented. In a *process layout,* equipment of the same functional type is grouped together, so we would have lathes grouped together, milling machines together, inspection in one place, all assembly in one place, etc., as shown in Figure 1. Process layout follows closely our model for intermittent production systems. Figure 2 shows the typical arrangement for product or line layout, which follows our model for continuous production systems. The name *product layout* comes from the fact that the basic organization of the layout is dictated by the part or product. Equipment is arranged according to the sequence in which it is used for a given part or product, following the route sheet sequences. If similar equipment is required for both parts A and B, it would nor-

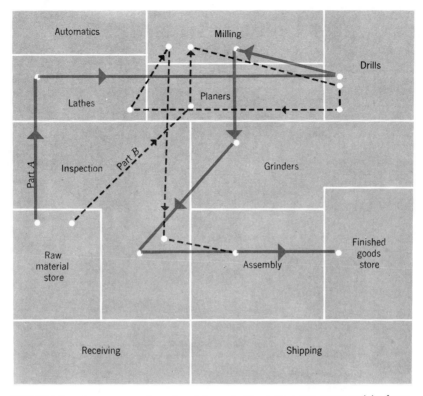

FIGURE 1.   Process or functional layout. Machines are arranged in functional groups. Parts take various routings as dictated by their design requirements. Illustrative routes for two parts, *A* and *B*, are shown. Parts are moved
from operation to operation in batches or lots and stored temporarily at
each work station to await their turn.

mally be duplicated in the two lines of Figure 2, even though the equipment is not fully utilized for either part. Flow patterns for line layout
are fixed by the nature of the layout and the type of transportation
equipment commonly used.

    Process layout is often called functional or job-lot layout. It is em-
ployed when the same facilities must be used to fabricate and assemble a
wide variety of parts or when part and product designs are not stable.
Quite often the volume of individual parts is low, and even though the
total may be very large, as with aircraft parts fabrication, no single
sequence of operations will accommodate very many parts. These are
the general conditions that dictate the use of process layout. The prime

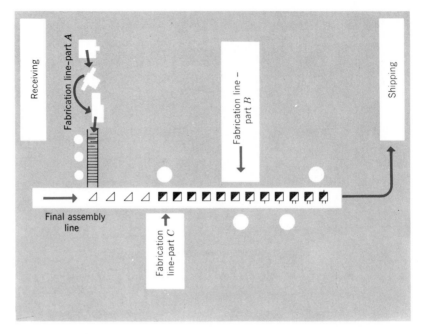

FIGURE 2.   Product or line layout. Machines and equipment are arranged according to the sequence of operations required to fabricate and assemble. Machines and workers are specialized in the performance of specific operations, and parts approach continuous movement.

requirement is flexibility: routing flexibility, part design flexibility, and volume flexibility.

In this missile age, many of us have been led to believe that process layout is used by inefficient manufacturers and line layout is used by "sharp" production men. Nothing could be further from the truth. Both types of layout can be inefficient if poorly designed, and both can be efficient. The important question is: Does the layout match the requirements imposed by the nature of the manufacturing problem? Actually, given the conditions described in the above paragraph, process layout would be more economical than line layout. This is because process layout leaves the equipment in flexible condition so it can be used on various parts. Equipment utilization is thus very good, and total investment in equipment is low. If we attempted line layout under these conditions, the specialization of equipment for specific parts would result in very low utilization and a resulting high equipment investment in order to meet capacity requirements. If a machine breaks down in process layout, only that operation is affected. On a production line, however, breakdowns affect the entire sequence of operations and this affects overall utilization factors. If product designs change, line layouts become obsolete.

When the conditions for line layout are met, the result is very low-cost manufacture. We might summarize these requirements as follows:

1. Volume adequate for reasonable equipment utilization.
2. Reasonably stable product demand.
3. Product standardization.
4. Part interchangeability.
5. Continuous supply of material.

Each of these requirements needs to be qualified. There is no one volume that we can point to as being "adequate." Rather, economic analysis would determine the breakeven volume between process and line layout for a given part or product. Reasonably good equipment utilization is associated with high volume. Stable demand is required in terms of a minimum run which would at least cover the extra costs of tooling the line. Thus, stable demand is associated with product standardization. Engineering changes in product designs can be accommodated by production lines (witness automobile manufacture), but they cannot be too frequent. We must have an "economical run" to cover the costs of retooling and relayout which design changes may require. Part interchangeability is required so that no special reworking or fitting is needed on the line. If parts are not interchangeable at assembly, the flow of work is disrupted because of imbalance. Finally, where we have the high volume standardized product situation described by the foregoing requirements, continuous supply of material is crucial. The lack of supply of a single part or item of raw material can force the entire process to be stopped.

Line layout has found its great field of application in assembly rather than in fabrication. A moment's reflection will reveal why this is true. Machine tools commonly have fixed machine cycles while the cut is being made; this factor makes it difficult to achieve balance between successive operations. The result is poor equipment utilization and relatively high manufacturing costs. In assembly operations where the work is manual, balance is much easier to obtain because the total job can be fractionated into minute elements. If operation 10 is too short and 16 too long, a part of the work of 16 can probably be transferred to 10 (perhaps the tightening of a single bolt). Since very little equipment is involved at each operation anyway, utilization of equipment may not be too important.

Attempts to establish fabrication lines are sometimes premature. The general range of breakeven volumes is much higher for fabrication than for assembly. In one situation a plant actually had been laid out in a series of fabrication lines to serve major parts. However, an analysis of the utilization of the equipment by random sampling techniques revealed a shocking 21 per cent utilization figure. It was an obvious misapplication of line layout, and immediate steps were taken to relayout the shop.

When the conditions for line layout are met, it offers significant advantages. The production cycle is speeded up since materials approach continuous movement. And since very little manual handling is required, the cost of material handling is low. Since materials are not moved in batches or lots and because of the fast manufacturing cycle, in-process inventories are lower. Since aisles are not used for material movement and since in-process storage space is minimized, the total floor space required by a line layout is commonly less than for an equivalent process layout, even though more individual pieces of equipment may be required. Finally, the control of the flow of work (production control) is greatly simplified for a line layout because routes become direct and mechanical. No detailed scheduling of work to individual workplaces and machines is required; each operation is an integral part of the line. Scheduling the line as a whole automatically schedules the component operations.

Pure process or pure line layouts are rare. We are most apt to find fabrication shops arranged by process, with fabrication lines occurring sporadically where conditions permit. Assembly today is customarily accomplished on lines, except for very low volumes or for very large, bulky, heavy items such as locomotives, aircraft, and ships. For these items, fixed position assembly is common. A unique combination-type layout is possible where a product is made in various sizes and types. Since the sequence of operations is similar, machines can be arranged together in functional groups, as in process layout, but the process groupings can be arranged in a sequence that fits the various sizes and types fairly well.

PROCESS LAYOUT

The major problem of a strictly "layout" nature in process layout is the determination of the most economical relative location of the various process areas. The best arrangement is not immediately obvious, except for trivial cases. This fact is emphasized by the realization that for only six process areas arranged in a simple grid, as in Figure 3, there are 6! (six factorial) or $6 \cdot 5 \cdot 4 \cdot 3 \cdot 2 \cdot 1 = 720$ arrangements possible. Fortunately, only 90 of them are really different in terms of their effects on idealized measures of material-handling cost. The number of combinations goes up very rapidly as we increase the number of process areas.

Let us consider first the nature of our objective. The major criterion for selecting an arrangement is material-handling cost. Thus, we want an arrangement that places the process areas in locations relative to each other such that the material-handling cost for all parts is minimized. Therefore, if we examined the required material-handling activity between Departments A and C of Figure 3 and found that it was heavy compared to AB, we would want to consider switching the locations of Departments B and C. But before jumping to the conclusion that this switch would be advantageous, we would want to see if this advantage would be wiped out by an increase in the relative material-handling activity between DB and DC. We might take as a measure of material-handling cost the product of the distance times the number of loads that must be moved in some period of time. For each combination of arrangements, then, we could simply add up the load-distance products between all combinations of departments. The combination with the

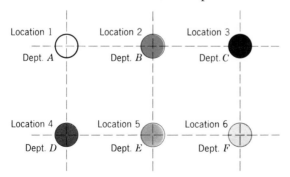

FIGURE 3.   There are 6! = 720 arrangements of the six process areas in the six locations of the grid.

smallest total is the basic arrangement that we are looking for. To formalize this statement of our objective, the measure of effectiveness, E, is:

$$E = \sum_i \sum_j A_{ij} X_{ij} = \text{minimum}$$

where

> A_{ij} = number of loads per week, month, or period required to be transported between departments i and j
>
> X_{ij} = distance between departments i and j

This measure of effectiveness closely approximates material-handling costs. Each material-handling operation requires certain fixed times associated with picking up the load, positioning it to set down, etc. These costs, mainly labor costs, would be about the same for large or small loads. The variable costs associated with a material-handling operation (mainly labor plus power) are related to distance.

Operation Sequence Analysis

The data that we need are the number of loads that must be transported between all combinations of work centers. This type of data can be sum-

TABLE I. Load Summary (Number of Loads per Month between All Combinations of Work Centers)

From		To										
Departments		Rec. 1	Stores 2	Saw 3	Eng. Lathe 4	Turret Lathe 5	Drill 6	Mill 7	Grinder 8	Ass'y 9	F.G. 10	Ship 11
Receiving	1		600									
Stores	2			400	100			100				
Saw	3				350	50						
Engine Lathe	4						100	450				
Turret Lathe	5							50				
Drill	6				100				150	100		
Mill	7						50		450	100		
Grinder	8						200			250		
Assembly	9										500	
Finished Goods	10											600
Shipping	11											

From Buffa [5].

marized from route sheets and drawings. The route sheets indicate sequences; from the drawings of the parts themselves and the production rates, we can determine the number of parts transported at one time and, therefore, the number of loads. Table I shows a summary of the number of loads per month for all combinations of work centers for a typical small production situation.

In initial design we idealize our problem by assuming a structure similar to Figure 3, with circles representing the functional groupings of equipment. We regard departments as being adjacent if they are either next to each other, as are A and B, or diagonally across from each other, as are A and E. Nonadjacent locations are those which are more than one grid unit away from each other horizontally, vertically, or diagonally, represented by AC, AF, DC, and DF in Figure 3. We can see now that for our idealized layout, the measure of effectiveness reduces to minimizing the sum of the nonadjacent loads (unit distance) × (loads). For problems of reasonable size, the minimum nonadjacent (distance) × (load) solution is fairly readily seen by graphical methods.

This graphical approach to the solution is accomplished by placing the information contained in the load summary, Table I, in an equivalent schematic diagram in which circles represent work centers (functional groups of machines), and labeled connecting lines indicate the number of loads transported between work centers. Figure 4 is a first solution obtained by merely placing the work centers on the grid, following the logic from the pattern indicated by Table I. When all connecting lines are on the diagram and labeled we have an initial solution which may be improved by inspecting the effect of changes in location. When an advantageous change is found, the diagram is altered. For example, in Figure 4 we see immediately that work center 4 has a total of 300 loads that are transported to or from work centers that are not adjacent, that is, 2 and 6. If 4 is moved to the location between 2 and 6, all loads to and from 4 become adjacent. Further inspection shows that 200 nonadjacent loads must be transported between work centers 6 and 8. Is an advantageous shift possible? Yes, by moving 9 down and placing 8 in the position vacated by 9, the number of nonadjacent loads is reduced from 200 to 100. Figure 5 shows the diagram with the changes incorporated.

Further inspection reveals no further advantageous shifts of location, so we adopt Figure 5 as our ideal schematic layout which has a 2 × 100 = 200 load-distance rating. For larger problems the grid distance becomes

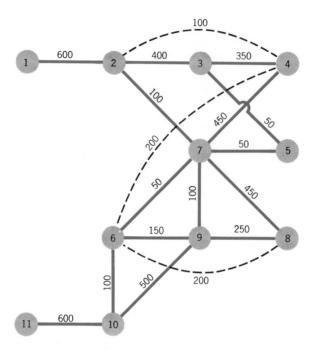

FIGURE 4. Initial graphic solution developed from load summary of Table I. It can be seen by inspection that 4 can be moved to the position between 2 and 6 to eliminate 300 nonadjacent loads. The positions of 8 and 9 are improved by replacing 9 by 8 and moving 9 to the position just below 8. (From Buffa [5].)

an important part of the measure of effectiveness, because work centers might be separated by two, three, or four grid units. Figure 5 is not a provable optimum solution in the mathematical sense, because we have no test of optimality. The ideal schematic diagram is now the basis for developing a physical layout in which the work center or department locations are specified.

The Block Diagram

Now that we know how the work centers should be located in relation to each other in our idealized layout, we can use the ideal schematic diagram as a basis for developing a block diagram in which the physical areas required by the work centers take the same relative locations. Estimates of the areas required by each work center can be developed

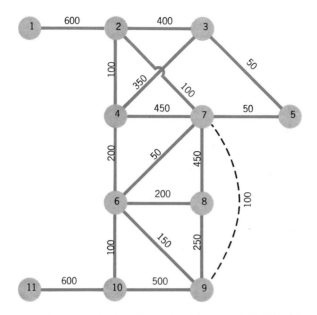

FIGURE 5.   Ideal schematic diagram incorporating changes suggested by Figure 4. Solution is not necessarily optimal but no further location changes seem to yield improvement. (Based on Buffa [5].)

from the number of machines required in each center and the floor area required by each machine. Commonly, the machine areas are multiplied by a factor of 3 or 4 to obtain an estimate, or first approximation, of the total area required, including working space for the operator, material storage, and pro rata aisle space.

The block diagram itself is developed by substituting estimated areas for the small circles in the idealized schematic layout. Initially this can be done with block templates to find an arrangement that is compatible with both the flow pattern of the ideal schematic diagram and the various size requirements for work centers. Figure 6 shows such an initial block diagram for our example. We can see that the essential character of our ideal schematic diagram is retained. However, Figure 6 obviously does not represent a practical solution as yet. Slight variation of the shapes of work areas will make it possible to fit the system into a rectangular configuration and meet possible shape and dimension restrictions that may be imposed by the site or by an existing building if we are dealing with relayout. Figure 7 shows such a block diagram.

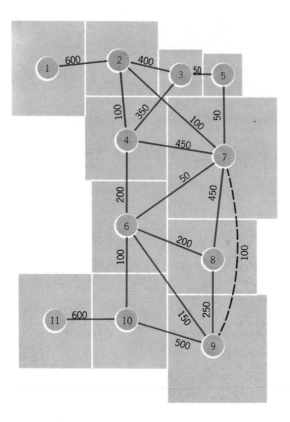

FIGURE 6.   Initial block diagram. Estimated work center areas are substituted for circles in the ideal schematic diagram of Figure 5. Block templates are used for estimated area requirements for the various work centers. (Based on Buffa, [5].)

The final block diagram represented by Figure 7 marks the end point of general, overall layout. The block diagram presents a frame of reference for the development of the details of the layout. Now we can proceed with aisle layout, machine arrangement within work centers, workplace layout, design of plant and personnel service areas, selection of specific material-handling equipment, etc., knowing that the work centers are located relative to each other in the most economical way.

When the block diagram is complete, combinations of work centers can be made for practical departmentalization. These combinations can be based on work center sizes, the numbers of workers involved,

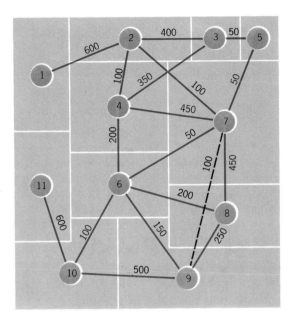

FIGURE 7.   Block diagram which takes account of rectangular building shape and other possible restrictions of shape and dimension imposed by site but still retains approximate work center area requirements and idealized flow pattern. (Based on Buffa [5].)

similarity of work, and other criteria important to the particular application.

We should comment that our example was a simple one and that the solution to actual problems usually would involve many more non-adjacent loads. Therefore, the ideal schematic would not develop so easily.

The detailed layout phase undoubtedly requires minor shifts in space allocation and shape. Here, the templates and models discussed later in this chapter become valuable aids in visualizing the developing details. Standards for minimum machine spacing, aisle widths for different uses, and column spacings for different building designs all exist in handbook form. The allowances for in-process storage space and warehousing space and the design of material-handling systems depend on the specific conditions of the problem.

Computerized Relative Allocation of Facilities

The graphical approach to the determination of the relative location of departments just discussed has obvious limitations. The technique depends on an individual analyst's insight to evolve better schematic diagrams; as the number of activity centers increases, the technique rapidly breaks down. Practical problems in facility location often involve 20 or more activity centers, and this number is already at the limit for feasible use of the operation sequence analysis technique. To overcome this limitation a Computerized Relative Allocation of Facilities Technique (CRAFT) was developed [2, 6] which easily handles up to 40 activity centers and has other important advantages. Before describing the structure and operation of the CRAFT program, let us state what were thought to be the basic requirements of such a program.

1. It must take account of wide variations in flow paths.
2. It must allow for different material-handling systems to be used for different materials or parts, each handling system possibly having different costs in proportion to distance moved.
3. It must account for different floor area requirements for activity centers or departments.
4. It must meet the possible requirement that certain activity centers need an exact and specific location and cannot be moved.
5. It must incorporate a rigorous algorithm which minimizes material-handling costs jointly for the entire set of parts or products moved through the system.

Managers also are giving increased recognition to the needs of the "small group." The location of work groups in an existing facility may have developed working relationships that contribute to the overall effectiveness of operations. Will a new layout take this human problem into account? If management places a high value on this factor, we should be able to show how much extra material-handling cost is involved to retain a close physical relationship between two or more work groups, activities, or departments. Conversely, it may be desirable to separate two or more departments because of noise, vibration, dust, fumes, or other conditions which may call for isolation. If the data indicating the material-cost differentials which result from these requirements can be provided, a rational decision can be made.

Actually since there is such a large number of layouts possible, it is probable that several are quite good. It may easily be that one of them will accommodate the requirements of human relations or other constraints and still be a really excellent layout from the point of view of material-handling costs. What is needed then is a technique that can generate and evaluate a relatively large number of alternate layouts without a tremendous expenditure in time and money.

The basic problem is not trivial. With only 20 departments to consider, there are over 608,000,000,000,000 different combinations of layouts that could be generated. This makes it impossible to consider calculating the material-handling costs for all possible combinations to find the best one, even with rapid data processing equipment. The CRAFT program, a description of which follows, is governed by a rigorous heuristic algorithm which can provide answers that are excellent solutions to the problem.

The CRAFT Program. The basic idea on which the computer program is based is similar in general concept to the method by which some programming algorithms converge on an optimal solution. The answers generated are not mathematically provable, unique optimums in the same sense as are the answers to linear programming problems, but rather represent solutions that cannot easily be improved. CRAFT takes as inputs data on interdepartmental flow and material-handling costs, together with a representation of a block layout. The block layout which is fed in may be the actual existing layout or any arbitrary starting solution if a new facility is being developed. The program calculates department centers and an estimate of total material-handling costs for the input layout. The governing heuristic algorithm then asks the following question: What change in material-handling costs would result if the locations of two departments were exchanged? Within the computer, the locations of the two departments or activity centers are exchanged and material-handling costs are recomputed. The result may be either an increase or decrease but the difference is recorded in the memory of the computer. The program then proceeds by asking the same question for other combinations of two departments, recording cost differences again. It proceeds in this way through all combinations of exchanges. When the number of departments is 20, the possible number of pair exchanges is computed as the number of combinations of 20 departments taken two at a time, or 190.

This number of computations is relatively small. When the cost differences for all such combinations have been computed, the program selects the exchange that would result in the largest reduction, makes the exchange in locations on the block diagram, and prints out the new block layout, the new total material-handling costs, the cost reduction just effected, and the departments involved in the exchange. The basic procedure is then repeated, generating a second, third, etc., improved block layout. Finally, when the procedure indicates that no exchanges in location which reduce material-handling cost can be made, the final block layout is printed out which becomes the basis for a detailed template layout of the facility.

As presently constructed, the program has the capacity for handling 40 departments or activity centers. Any departmental location can be fixed down by simply specifying in the instructions that the department or departments are not candidates for exchange. This feature is of great practical importance because existing layouts cannot be completely rearranged. Fixed locations may develop when costly heavy equipment has been installed, or the location of receiving or shipping facilities may be determined by the location of roads or railroad spurs. Finally, as mentioned previously, the locations of some work groups often make it desirable to treat them as fixed location points in the layout.

Whereas the explanation given previously indicates that the program considers the possible exchange of two departments at a time, the present construction of the program actually can consider the exchange in location of three departments simultaneously. When departments are exchanged three at a time, the number of computations required for each iteration is 1140. Whether the two- or three-way exchange is used is of small importance, however, since a trivial amount of computer time is required in either case. It turns out that the three-way exchange routine is somewhat more efficient than the two-way exchange routine, and the use of both routines together is still more efficient.

A Case Study Application.   The computer program has been used widely in industrial and architectural practical situations. The application described here uses the program at its fully developed stage with the capability just described. The company was a precision manufacturer in the aerospace industry, and the plant involved was a general machine shop with about 42,000 square feet of floor area. The majority of shop orders were for small precision parts in low quantities, so most material handling was accomplished by the machinists themselves carrying orders to and from a central holding and dispatch area (Department K) in tote pans. The current layout had grown around the central holding and dispatch department. One important question which management wished to evaluate, in addition to the layout itself, was the validity of having material flow through the central holding area. Although the use of the central holding area had certain advantages of close control for a small plant, it was obvious that the physical flow of material to and from the holding area entailed incremental material-handling costs. The alternate policy was, of course, to dispatch orders directly from department to department, utilizing an information system for control.

Another operating policy which management wished to evaluate was the use of machinists to accomplish the majority of interdepartmental material handling. Originally, when the plant was small, the machinists had been used for this purpose because distances were short and it was felt that these short walks gave machinists a break from usual routines. The plant had been enlarged as time passed, however, and it was felt that the use of specialized material handlers should be evaluated. In summary then, there were four basic conditions for which it was desirable to determine the best layout and the material-handling costs associated.

1. Current practice: material flow through Department K—machinists used for handling.
2. Material flow through Department K—using material handlers.
3. Dispatch utilizing information system—machinists used for handling.
4. Dispatch utilizing information system—using specialized material handlers.

For purposes of analysis, there were 22 plant areas designated as department centers. Table II shows the department name, the letter code used for that department, and the approximate area requirement for each department. In the balance of our discussion, we shall use the letter codes for departments. Note that Departments U and V were the only ones fixed in location by the program. Department U, the washroom, was not a candidate for exchange because it was not feasible to relocate plumbing. Department V was actually not a real area but was included as a dummy department to fill out the need of the program for a rectangular configuration.

Input Data.   As mentioned previously, three kinds of data are required for the program.

1. Interdepartmental flow per time unit—per week, per month, or some other time unit.

2. Unit load material-handling cost per unit distance such as per 100 feet of movement.

3. An initial block layout—in this application the existing plant layout.

To determine interdepartmental flow, it was necessary to analyze approximately 1600 shop orders (approximately an eight-week sample) which had indicated on them the routing required to fabricate the parts. Fortunately these data were available on punched cards so that it was relatively simple to develop a matrix which showed the number of loads flowing between all combinations of departments. This matrix

TABLE II.   List of Departments with Letter Codes and Area Requirements

Letter Code	Department Name	Area, Square Feet
A	Electrical maintenance	1200
B	Drill presses	1800
C	Degrease	500
D	Milling machines	3900
E	Turret lathes and automatic screw machines	2000
F	Jig borers	1900
G	Boring mills	800
H	Hardinge and hand screw machines	400
I	Lathes	1500
J	Slabbing mills	600
K	Central holding and dispatching	1700
L	Grinding machines	2000
M	Saws	100
N	Gear hobbing machines	1700
O	Tool room	7500
P	Numerically controlled Fosdick jig borers	1400
Q	Numerically controlled Burgmasters	600
R	Deburring	600
S	Pantograph	1400
T	Inspection	3000
U	Washrooms (fixed location)	2400
V	Vacuous area not in building (fixed location)	5000
	Total area	42,000

From Buffa, Armour, and Vollmann [6].

is similar although not identical to that shown in Table I as the load summary for the operation sequence analysis graphical technique.

A similar matrix was developed to show the material-handling cost in dollars per 100 feet of movement for combinations of departments for which flow occurred. The existing block layout for the plant was reduced for input to the computer in the form shown by Figure 8 where the scale is 10 feet per character. Since there are 15 columns and 28 rows, we have represented an area 150 × 280 feet. Looking at Department T

```
        1  2  3  4  5  6  7  8  9 10 11 12 13 14 15
 1      T  T  T  T  T  V  V  V  V  V  V  V  V  V  V
 2      T           T  V                          V
 3      T           T  V                          V
 4      T           T  V                          V
 5      T           T  V  V  V  V  V  V  V  V  V  V
 6      T  T  T  T  T  N  N  N  N  N  B  B  B  A  A
 7      S  S  S  S  S  N           N  B     B  A  A
 8      S           S  N  N  N     N  B     B  A  A
 9      S  S  S  S  P  M  L  L  N  N  B     B  A  A
10      R  R  R  P  P  L        L  L  B     B  A  A
11      R  R  R  P  P  L           L  B  B  B  A  A
12      Q  Q  P     P  L        L  L  D  D  D  C  C
13      Q  Q  P     P  L  L  L  L  K  K  D     C  C
14      Q  Q  P  P  P  K  K  K     K  D     D  C  D
15      0  0  0  0  0  0  K        K  D        D  D
16      0           0  K  K  K  K  K  D              D
17      0        0  U  U  U  U  U  U  U  D        D
18      0        0  U              U  D        D
19      0        0  U              U  D        D
20      0           0  U  U  U  U  U  U  U  D  D  D  D
21      0              0  E  E  E  E  E  E  E  E  E
22      0              0  E  E  E  E  E  E  E     E
23      0              0  I  I  I  I  I  J  J  E  E
24      0              0  I           I  J  J  J  J
25      0              0  I  I  I  I  I  F  F  F  F
26      0              0  H  H  H  H  F           F
27      0              0  G  G  G  G  F           F
28      0  0  0  0  0  0  G  G  G  G  F  F  F  F  F

TOTAL COST    3294.98    EST. COST REDUCTION       0.    MOVEA    MOVEB    MOVEC
```

FIGURE 8.   Existing block layout for a small aerospace precision manufacturer. (From [6].)

in the upper left-hand corner, for example, we can see that it has been allocated 50 × 60 feet or 3000 square feet in the existing layout, the equivalent of 30 characters. The computer output prints the outline of the area of each department for easy reading and recognition. Each department is represented in a similar way, and the total eight-week simulated material-handling cost for the existing layout with existing practices has been computed by the program as $3294.98, as shown at the bottom of Figure 8.

```
        1  2  3  4  5  6  7  8  9 10 11 12 13 14 15
   1    P  P  P  P  P  V  V  V  V  V  V  V  V  V  V
   2    P              P  V                       V
   3    T  P  P  P  P  V                          V
   4    T  T  T  T  T  V                          V
   5    T           T  V  V  V  V  V  V  V  V  V  V
   6    T           T  B  B  B  B  B  B  D  D  H  H
   7    T           T  B        B     D     D  H  H
   8    T           T  B     B  B  B  D           D  D
   9    T  T  T  T  M  B  B  K  K  K  D           D
  10    S  S  S  L  L  L  L  K     K  D           D
  11    S     S  L        L  K     K  D           D
  12    S     S  L        L  K     K  D           D
  13    S     S  L        L  K     K  D           D
  14    R  S  S  L  L  L  L  I  K  K  D  D  D  D  N
  15    R  R  R  C  I  I  I     I  I  I  N  N  N  N
  16    R  R  C  C  I  I  I  I  I  I  I  N        N
  17    Q  Q  Q  C  U  U  U  U  U  U  U  N  N     N
  18    Q  Q  Q  C  U              U  G  G  N  N  N
  19    F  F  F  F  U              U  G     G  J  J
  20    F        F  U  U  U  U  U  U  G  G  G  J  J
  21    F        F  E  E  E  E  E  E  A  A  A  J  J
  22    F        F  E              E  A        A  A
  23    F  F  F  E  E  E  E  E  E  E  E  A  A  A  A
  24    O  O  O  O  O  O  O  O  O  O  O  O  O  O  O
  25    O                                         O
  26    O                                         O
  27    O                                         O
  28    O  O  O  O  O  O  O  O  O  O  O  O  O  O  O

TOTAL COST   2645.08   EST.  COST REDUCTION      39.17   MOVEA  R   MOVEB  S   MOVEC
```

FIGURE 9.   Best block layout for alternative 1, existing policies and practices. (From [6].)

The program proceeded as described previously. It was found that the best first exchange involved Departments P and S which reduced material-handling costs by \$168.74. For the particular conditions and policies of the current situation, the program went through 14 cycles or iterations. It finally produced the block layout shown in Figure 9, which represents a best layout for the restrictions of alternative 1, that is, existing policies and practices. At the time the program printed Figure 9, it could find no further improvements in location. Note that in the last iteration the program exchanged Departments R and S, which reduced material-handling cost to its minimum of \$2645.08, as shown at the bottom of Figure 9.

Results for Four Alternatives.   The four conditions were computed, and the total material-handling costs per eight-week period were as shown in Table III, the far right column indicating the percent reduction in cost of each alternative compared to the cost of the existing layout. Each alternative required less than one minute to compute. Alternative 4, by using an information system for control and specialized material handlers, resulted in a startling 73 percent reduction. When the eight-week figures are placed on an annual basis, the cost reduction potential is approximately \$15,500. If the company demands a 10 percent return on plant investments of this kind and imposes a severe three-year payback period for capital recovery and return, it could afford to spend over \$38,000 for the plant relocations and alterations necessary for relayout. The program has made it possible to compute improvement potential without attempting detailed template layouts of any alternative. When basic decisions are made concerning the course of action to be taken, a detailed template layout can be prepared for only one block layout.

Office Layout.   The same general concepts apply to the layout of large offices with functional groupings, though the measure of effective layout may change. As an example, a layout study made in the regular face-to-face contact has been used to form the basis for effective layout.

Usefulness of CRAFT.   The CRAFT program is applicable for overall location of major activities as well as more detailed departmental locations within activities. For example, one project worked on was the relocation of major activities within a huge multibuilding complex in the aerospace industry. The complex of buildings and activities contained therein had grown and been added to piece by piece over a long period

Alternatives	Total 8-Week Material-Handling Cost	Per Cent Reduction from Existing Layout
TABLE III. Material-Handling Costs for Five Layouts		
Existing layout—current policies	$3294.98	—
Cost for best layout under following conditions:		
1. Current practice: Material flow through Department *K*—machinists used for handling	2645.08	20%
2. Material flow through Department *K*— using material handlers	2402.97	27%
3. Dispatch utilizing information system— machinists used for handling	1186.89	64%
4. Dispatch utilizing information system— using specialized material handlers	900.93	73%

From [6].

of time. The CRAFT program helped determine the best relative location of each major activity.

A similar kind of application has also been carried out to help determine the best relative location of major activities within a large integrated movie studio. Although it is not commonly thought of in this way, a movie studio can be conceived of as a very large job shop since each film sequence is a custom-made item. Material handling on the "lot" is much more expensive relatively than it would be in the average machine shop, so the relative location of major activity centers becomes a matter of extreme importance.

The CRAFT program is also applicable to a wide variety of other nonmanufacturing situations, such as hospital design and warehouse location, as well as certain equipment design problems where manufacturing costs may vary with component location.

Material Handling in Process Layouts

The prime requirement of material-handling methods used in process layouts is flexibility: flexibility of path and flexibility of size, weight, and shape of load. The types of material-handling equipment that fit this requirement are, in general, mobile trucks, tractor trains, and cranes.

Low *terminal time*, that is, the time required to set down or pick up a load, is an important characteristic of efficient material-handling equipment; therefore, quick pickup systems have developed around skids and pallets (see Figure 10). Material is loaded directly on a skid or pallet by the worker as he completes his operation on the part. Without further handling, a skid truck, pallet truck, or fork truck (Figure 10) can pick up the entire load very quickly and move it to its destination. Therefore, one important consideration in developing the details of a layout is to provide easy access to all operations by efficient material-handling equipment. The fork truck is designed specifically to stack loads so that storage floor area can be used efficiently. Pallets and skids, properly loaded, can be stacked four or five layers high. Overhead cranes

FIGURE 10. Typical methods of handling material for process layouts. (Courtesy Yale and Towne Manufacturing Company.)

are used to transport and position large, heavy pieces within a fixed area. Supplementary cranes are often required at workplaces to handle heavy pieces to and from machines.

Although it is not commonly done, material handling in process layouts can be accomplished by an overhead carrousel conveyor system when parts are small. The conveyor circulates to all work centers, so transportation between all combinations of work centers can be accomplished. Pans or boxes of parts may be placed on racks suspended from the chain conveyor with the destination work center indicated by some code. When the load arrives at its destination, the parts can be removed by assigned personnel and dispatched to the required machine, according to whatever assignment rules are in effect. If a shipment is not removed when it arrives, it merely recirculates in the system. Higher levels of mechanization could provide for automatic removal from the conveyor rather easily. Under such a material-handling system, the emphasis in the development of gross layout changes from one of minimizing the (distance) × (load) sum to one of minimizing the total length of the conveyor.

How much material-handling equipment is needed? This has always been a difficult question in process layouts because the demand for transporting capacity is on a random basis, and the material handling tasks vary in time somewhat. It is common even to find material-handling equipment idle a considerable share of the time and at the same time to hear complaints that the material can never be moved when it is wanted. The general problem situation has all of the characteristics of a waiting line model, as recognized by recent research [9]. Demand for transportation service can be analyzed and a distribution of equivalent *arrival rates*, or arrival times, can be constructed. Service time or handling time must be defined *as the interval from the moment a handling unit is assigned to move a certain load until it is available to be assigned to another load*. These service or handling times can then be formed into a distribution.

If the distribution fits a standard one for which mathematical models have been developed, as discussed in Chapter 4, direct mathematical solutions can be developed. If it does not fit the standard models, solutions can always be developed by simulation. The logic of economic analysis is to provide material-handling capacity to the extent that the combined costs of the handling capacity and incremental operating costs are minimized. These incremental operating costs are of three general types. First, if we add capacity, we add personnel to service that capacity, that is, a material handler. But, in addition, the added capacity will reduce delays and delay costs of two types: in-process inventory and idle labor at machines and workplaces. Additional capacity produces savings from reduced delay. The optimal capacity to provide is that which minimizes the combined costs that are affected. Optimal solutions will undoubtedly specify considerable idle time for material-handling equipment in order to reduce delay costs to reasonable levels. Table IV shows the relation of the delay times to truck idle time for a single truck and the indicated assumptions of distributions. To hold delays to an average of 15 minutes, the truck must be idle 50 per cent of the time.

PRODUCT OR LINE LAYOUT

Balance is the central problem in designing a production or assembly line. This is not to minimize the other problems of physical positioning of equipment, material-handling devices, design of special tools, and workplace layout, for in many instances solutions to these problems will contribute to the balance of the line. Balance refers to the equality of output of each successive operation in the sequence of a line. If they are all equal, we say that we have perfect balance and we expect smooth flow. If they are unequal, we know that the maximum possible output

TABLE IV.   Delays and Idle Time for a Single Unit with Various Loadings*

Loading, in Calls per 15 Minutes	Average Per Cent of Time Truck Is Idle	Average Delay in Hours, of Goods to Be Moved
0.1	90	0.03
0.5	50	0.25
0.8	20	1.0
0.9	10	2.25
0.95	5	4.75
0.99	1	24.75
1.00	0	Infinite!

*The assumptions underlying the table are Poisson call rates and negative exponential service times. From Fetter and Galliher [9, p. 203].

for the line as a whole will be dictated by the slowest operation in the sequence. This slow operation, often called the bottleneck operation, restricts the flow of parts in the line in much the same way that a half-closed valve restricts the flow of water, even though the pipes in the system might be capable of carrying twice as much water. Thus, where imbalance exists in a line, we have wasted capacity in all operations, except the bottleneck operation.

Balancing Techniques

First we shall consider procedures for *assembly* line balancing. Later we shall see what differences might exist if we were dealing with a fabrication line. To have the greatest ability to achieve balance, we need to know the performance times for the smallest possible whole units of activity, such as tightening a bolt or making a solder joint. We must also have a knowledge of the flexibility in the sequence of these tasks or activities. There are, of course, certain limitations on the sequence of the tasks. For example, a washer must go on before the nut, wires joined physically before they can be soldered, a hole drilled before it can be reamed and reamed before it can be tapped. On the other hand, the sequence may be irrelevant; for example, the order in which a series of nuts is put on. This sequence flexibility is important in helping us to specify the groups of elements making up operations, or stations, for the line which achieves the best balance.

Let us see the nature of the problem through an example. Figure 11 shows the cylinder subassembly for a typical small air compressor with the parts named and numbered. By examining the assembly we can readily see the sequence restrictions that we would have to observe. When assembling the cylinder head to the cylinder, the cylinder head gasket (part No. 8) would have to be positioned first. Also, when assembling the discharge valve unit, the valve itself (part No. 3) must go in first, followed by a valve spring (part No. 6) and finally by a discharge valve fitting (part No. 4). A similar procedure for the suction valve unit would be followed, but the sequence of the valve and the spring would be reversed. These are the sequences that must be observed, because the cylinder subassembly cannot be assembled correctly any other way. On the other hand, it makes no difference whether the valve units are assembled to the cylinder head before or after the cylinder head is assembled to the cylinder. Similarly, which valve unit is assembled

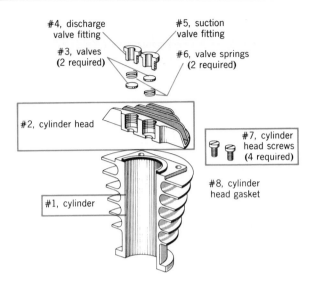

#4, discharge valve fitting

#5, suction valve fitting

#3, valves (2 required)

#6, valve springs (2 required)

#2, cylinder head

#7, cylinder head screws (4 required)

#8, cylinder head gasket

#1, cylinder

FIGURE 11.   Cylinder subassembly for a typical air compressor.

first is irrelevant. The cylinder head is joined to the cylinder by four screws. All four need not be assembled at the same time, and there is no required sequence for their assembly.

These task sequence restrictions are summarized in Table V so we can use the result to advantage. The assembly tasks listed in Table V are, in general, broken down into the smallest whole activity. Note, for example, that the screws and the valve fittings are first positioned and the threads engaged, so tightening can take place separately, perhaps as a part of the next station or some subsequent station. Also, for each task, we note in the far right-hand column the task or tasks which must precede it. Thus, tasks *a*, *e*, and *i* can take any sequence, because no tasks need precede them. However, task *b*, position cylinder head on cylinder, must be preceded by task *a*, position cylinder head gasket on cylinder. Task *c*-1 must be preceded by tasks *a* and *b*. The repetition of *a* is not absolutely necessary, since we know that *b* must be preceded by *a*. With this information, together with the task times also given in Table V, we can construct the diagram in Figure 12.

Figure 12 merely reflects in a graphical way the sequence requirements that we have determined. The performance times are indicated beside the tasks for convenience. Now we can proceed with the grouping of tasks in order to obtain balance. But, balance at what level? What

TABLE V.   List of Assembly Tasks Showing Sequence Restrictions and Performance Times for the Cylinder Subassembly of Figure 11

Task	Performance Time, Seconds	Task Description	Task Must Follow Task Listed Below
a	1.5	Position cylinder head gasket (No. 8) on cylinder (No. 1)	—
b	2.0	Position cylinder head (No. 2) on cylinder (No. 1)	a
c-1	3.2	Position cylinder head screw (No. 7) in hole and engage threads	b
c-2	3.2	Repeat	b
c-3	3.2	Repeat	b
c-4	3.2	Repeat	b
d-1	1.5	Tighten cylinder head screw	c
d-2	1.5	Repeat	c
d-3	1.5	Repeat	c
d-4	1.5	Repeat	c
e	3.7	Position valve (No. 3) in bottom of discharge hole	—
f	2.6	Position valve spring (No. 6) on top of valve in discharge hole	e
g	3.2	Position discharge valve fitting (No. 4) in hole and engage threads	f
h	2.0	Tighten discharge valve fitting	g
i	3.1	Position second valve spring (No. 6) in bottom of suction hole	—
j	3.7	Position second valve (No. 3) on top of spring in suction hole	i
k	3.2	Position suction valve fitting (No. 5) in hole and engage threads	j
l	2.0	Tighten suction valve fitting	k

is to be the capacity of our line? This is an important point and one which makes a balancing problem difficult. With no restriction on capacity, the problem would be simple; we could take the lowest common multiple approach. For example, if we had three operations that required 3.2, 2.0, and 4.0 minutes, respectively, we could provide eight workplaces of the first, five of the second, and ten of the third, so that the capacity of the line would be 150 units per hour at each of the operations, all happily in balance. But capacity has been specified by balance rather than the considerations which we discussed previously.

We must take the capacity of the line as given and develop good balance within that restriction. For illustrative purposes, let us assume that we must balance our line for a 10-second cycle. A completed unit would be produced by the line each 10 seconds; to meet this capacity requirement, no station could be assigned more than 10 seconds worth of the tasks shown on the diagram of Figure 12. Proceeding then, we could group the tasks into station assignments. The total of all task times is 45.8 seconds. Therefore, with a 10-second cycle, five stations would be the minimum possible. Any solution that required more than five stations would increase direct labor costs. Figure 13 shows one solution that yields five stations. While this is a simple example, it illustrates the conceptual problems of line balancing.

Practical Balancing Methods.   The general concepts of line balancing which we have discussed have been implemented through a number of practical methods for the large-scale problems in industry. These methods have ranged from linear programming models [3] and dynamic

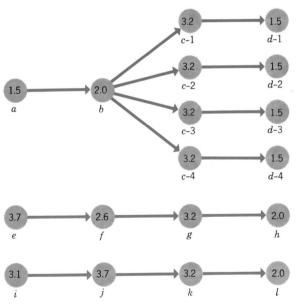

FIGURE 12.   Diagrammatic representation of the sequence requirements shown in Table IV. Numbers indicate performance times of tasks.

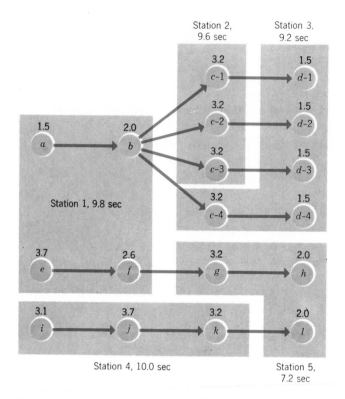

FIGURE 13. A solution to the line balancing problem which requires no more than 10 seconds per station and does not violate the task sequence requirements.

programming [10] to heuristic methods [11, 14, 24] and a computer-based biased sampling technique [1]. Perhaps of greatest interest for large-scale problems are the heuristic methods of Kilbridge and Wester [14, 30] and COMSOAL: a Computer Method for Sequencing Operations for Assembly Lines, developed by Arcus [1].

The heuristic methods involve the generation of a precedence diagram in a particular way which indicates the flexibility available for shifting tasks from column to column to achieve the desired balance. The heuristic rules are simple, but considerable individual ingenuity is required to obtain good solutions. The heuristic methods have been applied to television assembly line problems with 45 and 133 tasks and have achieved excellent results [30]. COMSOAL methodology is based on the rapid generation of feasible solutions by a computer routine.

The probability of generating either optimal, or very good, solutions is finite and dependent on the sample size of feasible solutions generated. The nature of the computer program biases the generation of feasible solutions toward the better ones in order to save computer time. COMSOAL has already been implemented at Chrysler Corporation; Arcus has used it on a hypothetical line of 200 stations with 1000 tasks, achieving the known optimal solution of 0 idle time.

Mastor [17] evaluated a large number of different line balance models in a set of experiments involving a range of problem sizes (numbers of tasks to be assigned), line lengths (number of stations in the line), and order strengths (degree of sequence restriction imposed in the precedence relationships). He found that the dynamic programming formulation model [10] was consistently the best performer, with COMSOAL [1] a close second; however, the computer time requirements for the latter were very much smaller. For large problems (70, 92, and 111 tasks), the two techniques performed almost identically when the COMSOAL program was run for 999 sequences. Even for the large sample size on the 111-task problem, COMSOAL required only 56 seconds of computer time compared to 94.3 for the dynamic programming model.

Auxiliary Balancing Techniques.   Other techniques are available to obtain balance in both the design and operation stages. If one station requires greater time than the others, a careful study of the activities, as well as the psychophysiological aspects of the tasks, may result in a reduction of time. The material discussed in Chapter 11 would be applicable. Compensations for imbalance can be accomplished by assigning fast operators to the limiting operations. When there are some very fast operations which cannot be combined into a single station, as might be true with machine operations, material banking before and after the fast operations may be required. These fast operations would be operated only a small portion of the day; the machine, the operator, or both, could be used for other purposes.

Balancing Fabrication Lines.   Conceptually, there is no difference in the balancing procedures for assembly and fabrication lines. However, the fixed machine cycles found in fabrication operations considerably limit freedom in achieving balance. It is often impractical to divide a machine operation into two or more suboperations in order to level out the time requirements at each station. This situation partially accounts for the fact that fabrication lines are generally economical only for very high volumes, since good balance is likely to be achieved only at high levels of output. Otherwise, equipment utilization is very low. If we try to use the idle capacity to machine other parts, material-handling costs increase because the equipment has been located to minimize handling costs for the line product. The process layout, which minimizes overall handling costs, is usually more economical under these conditions.

Material Handling in Line Layouts

Material-handling methods and equipment, like the layout itself, tend to be special purpose in nature for line layouts. There is often considerable confusion about the relation of conveyors and line layout. The mere existence of conveyors does not make a line layout, nor does it guarantee the efficiency of any kind of a layout. The nature of line layout does, however, require some direct means of transportation between operations. This may be accomplished in some instances by simply arranging flow so that each operator places the unit down in such a position that it can be picked up by the succeeding worker. Where the nature of the product permits it, gravity chutes can be used effectively. Finally, where these cheaper means are impractical, conveyors to fit all types of applications of size, shape, and weight of parts are available commercially. Figure 14 shows a selection of applications of material-handling equipment used in production lines.

Although standard sizes and types of conveying equipment are available commercially, they ordinarily require a considerable amount of special design work to fit them into an effective overall design of a line layout. The best systems of internal transportation for lines integrate the functions of transportation with those of processing and storage, so it is not necessary to perform supplementary handling to and from the line. This means a careful allowance for the size of banks needed at various stages. Many processes, such as painting and drying, may take place while the material moves. The special-purpose nature of line layout design often makes it worthwhile to design special handling equipment that is integrated with the processing so completely that the entire line functions as a single integrated machine. Much of the actual material handling performed in industry occurs as a part of the productive operations, such as moving parts to and from machines. When integrated handling systems are designed, much of this type of handling can be eliminated.

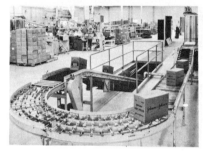

FIGURE 14. Typical methods of handling materials in line layouts. (Courtesy Lamson Corporation.)

SERVICE FACILITIES

Plant Services

Many plant services must fit into the overall layout. The fact that many of these activities are not a part of the direct production activity of the enterprise has often tended to promote the idea that whatever space is left over is good enough for them. Actually, some of these activities, such as receiving, shipping, and warehousing, are in the direct material flow and they process the product as do the production departments. Others, such as maintenance facilities and tool cribs, do not work on the product but interact with production costs so that their physical location and capacity deserve careful thought. The overall material flow patterns should be the major factors in determining the relative locations of receiving, shipping, storage, and warehousing areas. Our discussion of operation sequence analysis for process layouts included these functional areas. For line layouts the material flow is more obvious, so the proper location for these areas is fairly well determined.

The capacity question for receiving areas does not have an obvious answer. In general, the problem is such that we do not have control over the rate at which materials come in. Since receipts of shipments from suppliers occur in a somewhat random pattern, a good design provides capacity that meets the reasonably expected peak loads for truck and rail docks, unloading crews, and temporary setdown areas for materials. Here again, waiting line theory may provide a guide for determining what these capacities should be. Of course, many other factors influence the details of the layout of receiving areas, such as climate, safety codes, handling equipment, dock heights, and the necessity to accommodate a variety of vehicles.

The location of tool cribs is important because of the travel time of high-priced mechanics to and from the area. Therefore, a study of the use frequency in relation to the physical layout of the production areas should determine a good location or locations. The tool storage problem is comparable to the material and part storage problem in using space efficiently while making items available quickly and conveniently. The number of attendants required to serve the tool crib is another waiting line problem, as indicated in Chapter 4.

Maintenance facilities are commonly provided for buildings and grounds, plant utilities, and machinery and equipment. The capacity of maintenance for machinery and equipment again poses the problem of balancing the idle time of maintenance crews against the idle time of production workers, as well as losses of output capacity. Ordinarily, a considerable amount of idle capacity in equipment and crews is justifiable, as would be shown by solutions to waiting line models of these types of problems.

Employee Services

Present-day personnel services cover a broad spectrum including parking, cafeterias, medical services, credit unions, locker rooms, toilets and lavatories, and, quite often, recreational facilities. Obviously, providing for these services presents layout problems. In many instances, the location of these services does not have an effect on production costs since the services are used after hours. In these instances, the layout problem is to provide the space designed to perform the services in the amounts required. The activities must be studied to determine what must be done and facilities provided accordingly.

For those services used during working hours, such as medical facilities, toilet facilities, and drinking fountains, the size of the facility and its location in relation to the users become important. Studies of travel distances to and from the service facility should be made in order to determine reasonable locations. Waiting line models are again useful in determining a balance between waiting times of employees and service capacity costs. In one large company which offered a broad medical service, the question of whether or not an additional doctor on the staff was warranted was answered by a waiting time study. The results of the study indicated that there was an average of 15 employees in the waiting room during the 8-hour work day; assuming a 2000 working-hour year and a modest average hourly wage of $2, this translates into $60,000 of waiting time per year. The study led to both an enlargement and decentralization of medical services.

PLANT BUILDINGS

As a layout develops, many of the specifications for and characteristics of the building develop simultaneously. For example, the location of equipment specifies minimum floor loadings, requirements for electrical distribution system, plumbing, etc. The size and shape of the building are outgrowths of the layout. The location and spacing of columns to support the roof must be determined during the layout phase so that a subsequent building design does not invalidate the layout work. Factory building design today tends to stress architectural beauty and land-scaping, and employees have reacted by an expression of pride in working in these types of plants.

Single versus Multistory Buildings.   The trend in factory building design for some time has been toward the single-story building. The reasons for this are numerous; the cheaper construction possible with single-story buildings tells only part of the story. The net usable area of a multistory building is much smaller because of the space required by columns, stairwells, and elevators, so building costs per net usable unit areas are actually *much* cheaper for the single-story buildings. In central industrial areas where land costs are very high, the balance may be tipped in favor of multistory construction, however.

In addition to the usual net construction cost advantage, the single-story building offers wide unobstructed bays (100-foot bays are common) that free the layout and make for greater flexibility of the original layout as well as for subsequent relayouts. Floor loads are unrestricted and ventilation is easier to obtain. Also, greatest advantage can be taken of natural illumination through sawtooth roof designs. The operating advantage of a single-story building is probably most important of all. Material-handling costs for most products are lower in the horizontal plane than in the vertical. However, there are exceptions. In meat packing, for example, a multistory building seems to offer handling cost advantages because drop chutes can be used to transfer the product from station to station and from floor to floor as it is processed.

Building Shapes and Roof Designs.　The basic building shape is the rectangle, and logical patterns of combinations of rectangles are numerous. Some of these variations can be likened to the shapes of block letters such as I, C, U, L, F, E, and H.

The selection of roof type depends on the bay size wanted and on the overhead clearance required for operations. During the layout phase, standards of this type would be used in making decisions which become specifications for the building itself. Wider column spacings, of course, have a higher construction cost than small bays, but this must be balanced against layout flexibility and assumed (but difficult to measure) operating cost advantages.

GRAPHIC LAYOUT TECHNIQUE

Layouts and models using two- and three-dimensional templates have a wide area of application in the development and planning of new facilities, as well as in the relayout of existing facilities which is a continual process to accommodate changes in products, manufacturing methods, and technology. These graphic aids are important in visualizing the development of the design of the complex machine which we call a manufacturing plant. The resulting layout expresses the designer's specifications of the location of all equipment, storage areas, aisle space, utilities, etc., and the relationships between machines and departments. It is important, however, not to mistake the activity of preparing and locating templates on a layout board for the broader activity of plant layout. The templates themselves are tools. Our purpose here is to make known the kinds of materials available for templates and layout boards.

Two-Dimensional Templates.　These are by far the most commonly used. They can successfully represent the plan view of a layout and can show floor utilization fairly well. Figure 15 shows two types of templates. The "block" template shows the outline of the maximum projected area of a machine; that is, if tables or other parts move, the

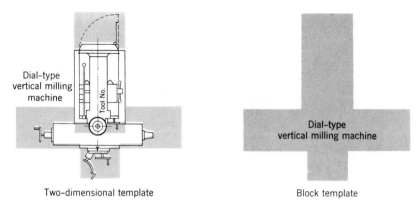

Two-dimensional template   Block template

FIGURE 15.   Two types of machine templates.

outline shows the maximum movement in the horizontal plane. The two-dimensional template gives additional detail, showing the outline of the machine itself, with dotted lines indicating maximum table movements.

The important characteristics of these kinds of templates are dimensional accuracy and flexibility in use. Flexibility in use means that the template can be fixed in place firmly enough so that it will not be moved by jarring or air movement, but not be fixed permanently because it may be necessary to make changes. Various alternatives meet these requirements in varying degrees. Some of the most satisfactory materials are the plastic templates, which already have an adhesive backing, used in conjunction with a cross-sectioned plastic sheet as a backing material. The cross sectioning provides the measurement scale; consequently, very little actual measurement is required. This type of template is available commercially for virtually all standard machines as well as for many kinds of auxiliary equipment. Colored adhesive tapes are used for walls, aisle lines, etc. Figure 16 is an example of a layout using this media. Figure 17 shows the ease with which the templates are cut out and applied.

Three-Dimensional Templates.   These templates or scale models add an element of realism which can sometimes be justified if the visualizing of height is of considerable importance and also if people not acquainted with layout practice must pass judgment on the result. Anything that can be done to help these people visualize the proposals may be worth the extra expense. While these models can be made in a woodworking

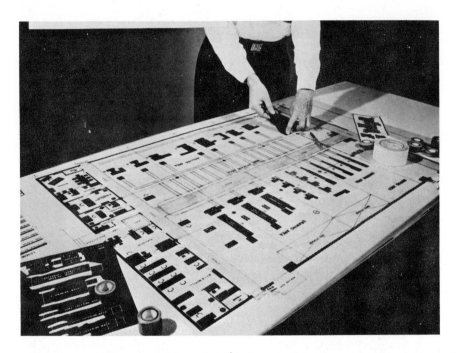

FIGURE 16.   A layout using plastic templates and backing with colored tapes for wall sections. (Courtesy General Electric Company.)

shop to specifications, it is seldom practical to do so, especially for standard machines, since die cast models are available commercially for virtually all standard equipment. These models are made in considerable detail which would be very expensive to duplicate in wood or cardboard. Practically all kinds of items are available, that is, columns, wall sections, waste barrels, skids, pallets, etc. A heavy cross-sectioned plastic sheet is commonly used for the base, and this provides the scale to minimize measuring.

LAYOUT IN NONMANUFACTURING ACTIVITIES

There are counterparts of the major types of layouts that we have discussed in nonmanufacturing activities. The equivalent of line layouts occur in cafeterias and many large offices. Process layouts are common in offices, but the basis of departmentation is less likely to revolve around equipment types than in manufacturing. Rather, we find functional

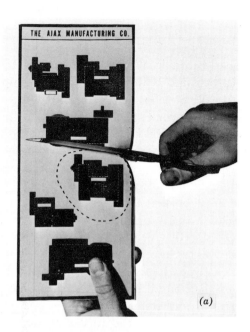

FIGURE 17. (*a*) Plastic templates may be cut from strip without following closely the outline of the template. (*b*) After backing is tripped off, template adheres to plastic grid and may be moved at will. (Courtesy General Electric Company.)

divisions, such as billing departments, accounts receivable, and accounts payable, where all of the processing dealing with these functions is performed.

In contrast to manufacturing, layout in nonmanufacturing is not necessarily measured in terms of material-handling cost. In offices, for example, the cost of handling the pieces of paper from one location to the next is not usually significant, especially where the interoffice mail system is used. It could be an important cost if a highly paid executive regularly carried an important document to its destination. In offices, one major concern of layout is to provide work conditions and suitable separation of activities so that people can perform their tasks and functions effectively and accurately. The layout of a supermarket will be designed to let the customer see as many items as possible, in the hope that this may suggest their purchase, and to eliminate annoying congestion in the traffic patterns, rather than attempt to minimize the store's cost of handling the merchandise to the display racks.

SUMMARY

In discussing layout, we have assumed as inputs the data concerning the thing being processed, how many items we expect to process, and how we shall process. In manufacturing activity these data take the form of drawings of the products; forecasts, contracts, or orders which indicate how many should be made; and route sheets and operations sheets which indicate what processes are appropriate and their sequence. Layout, then, requires a sequence of important decisions concerning capacity, type of layout, equipment, building types, bay widths, etc. The difficulty with layout is the interaction of the various aspects of the problem, and the fact that no unified theoretical framework makes it possible to see the dynamic effects of all variables working together. Layout furnishes a basic specification for the building to house the physical facilities; it also represents the integration of the several aspects of the design of a production system. It is here that the topics which we have studied separately and will study in Chapters 11 and 12, are integrated into a unified design.

KEY CONCEPTS

Capacity. The concept of capacity is elusive since it ordinarily cannot be stated with confidence for a given production system. One reason is that there are several sources of capacity which may be used. There is the equivalent capacity resulting from regular time production, overtime, additional shifts, the shifting line between the make versus supply decision, and the use of sub-contracting.

Specialization by Function.   Process oriented layout results from a specialization of activities by function. All of the operations of a similar functional nature are grouped together and great expertise, job knowledge, and skill develop. The concept of functional specialization is widely used. For example, the academic departments of a university seem to be organized on this basis.

Specialization by Product.   Organizing facilities and efforts around the production of a certain product results in line layout. In this conceptual framework, integration of all needed resources is required in order to achieve the quantity and quality requirements of the product at low cost. The analogy is academic organization is the professional school where the material to be learned comes from a variety of disciplines and is organized to focus on a particular societal need such as medical care, public health, management, or teaching.

Balance.   While we have tended to speak of balance largely in terms of production line balance, the concept applies in more general terms to all production systems. The capacity of a production system as a whole may depend on the limiting capacity of one department in a functionally organized plant or on the capacity of a single operation in a plant organized by product lines. More broadly, the concept of balance is an important one in any organization designed to achieve certain goals.

Location Interdependence.   Effective process layout depends on the concept of location interdependence. This was shown most clearly in the CRAFT model where it was easy to see that the location of a specific department depended on the business it did with other departments. Looking back to the previous chapter we can see the same general principle operating in multiplant location. In multiplant location the best choice of the location for a new plant or warehouse depends on the existing location of plants, warehouses, and markets.

IMPORTANT TERMS

Numbers in parentheses indicate page numbers.

1. Block diagram (284–287)
2. CRAFT (289)
3. Equipment utilization (278–279)
4. Fabrication line (280, 305)
5. Functional layout (276, 281)
6. Ideal schematic diagram (284, 285)
7. Line balance (299–304)

REVIEW QUESTIONS

Numbers in parentheses indicate page numbers.

1. Discuss the broad framework for the development of solutions to layout problems. (271–273)
2. For what capacity should a new layout be designed? What is the effect of a seasonal sales pattern on the capacity decision? Should excess capacity be included? Discuss the effect of multiple shifts, subcontracting, and make-buy policy. (273)
3. How can capacity be translated into workable units? What is the significance of plant efficiency and scrap factors? (275)
4. What is the distinction between a process and a product layout? (276–277)
5. What are the conditions for which each type of layout is appropriate? (276–280)
6. What is a basic measure of effectiveness for process layouts? (281–282)
7. What measure of effectiveness is used in operation sequence analysis? Is it the same as the answer to question 6? (282–283)
8. How is a block diagram developed from the data given by a load summary? (284–285)
9. What kinds of material-handling equipment are appropriate for process layouts? When can a carrousel conveyor be used? (296)
10. Since some material-handling needs in a process layout do not occur by any fixed schedule, how can we determine how much material-handling equipment is needed? (298)
11. How is assembly line balancing different from fabrication line balancing? (305–306)
12. What is the effect of a change in capacity requirements on the balance of an assembly line? (298–299)
13. Discuss practical methods of line balancing. What objective data is available concerning their comparative effectiveness? (303–305)
14. If there is a remaining imbalance after the application of line balance systems what methods can be used to improve balance in practice? (305)

15. What kinds of material-handling equipment are appropriate for line layouts? (306)
16. What should be the relationship of plant services, such as receiving, storage, and shipping, to the production departments in a layout? (307)
17. Are the locations of employee service facilities important to a layout? (308–309)
18. What are the advantages of single-story buildings? Of multistory buildings? (309–310)

SELF-TEST TRUE-FALSE QUESTIONS

Numbers in parentheses indicate page numbers.

1. In planning the capacity of a new layout design, a seasonal sales pattern would dictate the need for plant capacity at the near peak of the sales pattern. (273)
2. Investment costs in a new plant design may be closely approximated by a linear function of capacity. (273)
3. It is ordinarily not economical to plan for extra space in a new building because, if expansion is required later, the relayout costs far outweigh the costs of adding new space. (274)
4. The decision of whether or not a second shift is economical depends upon the balance of investment costs and wage premiums. (274)
5. The plant efficiency factor measures how well labor is meeting standards of production. (275)
6. The best measure of capacity for a steel plant is the number of hours available in various machine classifications per a week or month. (275)
7. If we expected 3 percent scrap in milling operations, 688 hours of available machine hours must be increased by the factor 1.03. (275)
8. Process layout follows closely our model for intermittent production systems. (276)
9. The term process layout and product layout are synonymous. (276)
10. The ideal layout for any situation is one which involves streamlined production lines similar to those found in the automobile industry. (278)
11. The following are requirements for line layout to result in low cost manufacture: reasonably stable demand for the product, product standardization, parts interchangeability, and a continuous supply of material. (279)
12. Line layout has found its great field of application in assembly rather than in fabrication. (279)
13. One of the difficulties with line layout is in the control of the flow of work (production control). (280)
14. When a product is made in various sizes and types, a combination layout may be possible which combines the advantages of both line and functional layout (280)

15. The major problem of a strictly "layout" nature in process layout is the selection of material-handling equipment and systems. (281)

16. In determining the most economical relative location of departments in functional layout, a statement of the objective function would be that we wish the number of loads multiplied by the distance between departments to be a minimum when summed over all departments. (282)

17. Operations sequence analysis yields a provable optimum solution. (282, 285)

18. In estimating the areas required by each work center, it is common to multiply the actual machine areas by a factor of 3 or 4 to obtain an estimate of the total area required, including working space for the operator, materials storage, and pro rata aisle space. (284–285)

19. A block diagram is a rough three-dimensional layout of work areas. (284–287)

20. The main requirement of material handling methods used in process layouts is flexibility. (296)

21. Terminal time is the time required to set down or pick up a load. (297)

22. The problem of determining the amount of material handling equipment needed for a process layout may be approached by linear programming. (298)

23. Balance is the central problem in designing a production or assembly line. (299)

24. The least common multiple approach to balancing an assembly or fabrication line specifies the capacity of the line. (302–303)

25. Fixed machine cycles, found in fabrication operations, make the balancing process easier by reducing the number of degrees of freedom. (305)

26. The maximum possible utilization of a production line is attained when a large inventory of parts is maintained at the first station, and an average inventory of **8 parts** between all other stations on the line. (299)

27. Mastor found that the best line balancing technique was dynamic programming, with COMSOAL a close second. (305)

28. Waiting line theory provides a rational basis for determining capacities of dock and receiving facilities. (308)

29. Ordinarily, a considerable amount of idle time is expected for maintenance crews to attain an economical balance between maintenance crew costs and the idle time of production workers. (308)

30. The usable square footage in the single story building is about the same as for a multistory building. (309)

31. For certain kinds of processing, the multistory building has an inherent advantage in material handling costs. (310)

32. Process layouts in offices are less likely to have departmentation revolve around equipment types than in manufacturing. (312)

33. The measure of effectiveness of good layout in both manufacturing and non-manufacturing activity is material handling costs. (314)

PROBLEMS

1.   The Stamped Metal Products Company (StaMPCo) makes among other things a V-belt pulley of the design specifications shown in Figure 18. StaMPCo is currently considering a relayout of its entire facility and is projecting man-machine needs for the pulley. The pulley sales forecasts indicate a capacity need for 9000 pulleys per week for the coming year and 11,000 per week for two years hence. The average plant efficiency factor is 85 percent. Based on the data in Table VI, calculate the number of fractional men and machines needed for each of the two forecast levels of output. Assuming men can be moved freely between job assignments, how many men and machines are needed in round numbers?

2.   What type of layout do you think might be appropriate for the manufacture of the V-belt pulley?

3.   Consider the ideal schematic diagram shown in Figure 5. Can you improve it?

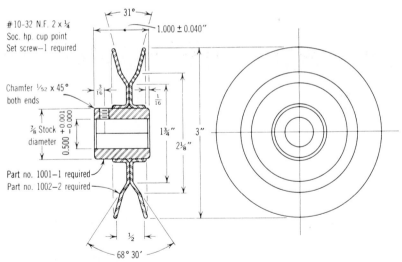

Tolerance on wobble ± 0.010 from center. Tolerance on concentricity ± 0.010 from center. Fractional tolerances $\pm \frac{1}{64}$. Angular tolerances $\pm \frac{1}{2}°$. Finish: Cadmium plated all over 0.0003 $\pm$ 0.0001. *Notes*: 1. Press fit flanges to hub. 2. Spotweld flanges to hub, two spots each side. 3. Spotweld flanges together—four spots. 4. Flange material: SAE #1010 deep-drawn steel: 5. Hub material: SAE #X1112 cold-finished screw stock.

FIGURE 18.   Drawing of a V-belt pulley.

4.   Given the load summary in Table VII for a plant, develop an ideal schematic diagram for the relative locations of departments.

5.   Given the estimated space requirements in Table VIII, develop a block diagram based on the ideal schematic diagram determined in problem 4.

TABLE VI.   StaMPCo Data for Processes, Output, and Scrap Factors

Operation	Machine Used	Standard Output (pieces/hour)	Scrap Factor (per cent)
Machine hub	Turret lathe	66.7	3
Form flange	Punch press	4800	5
Drill and tap hub	Drill press	240	2
Assemble flange to hub	Arbor press	600	1
Weld flanges together	Small spot welder	300	3
Weld flanges to hub	Large spot welder	350	5
Ream and chamfer	Drill press	300	2
Deburr flange	Polishing lathe	200	—
Inspect	Inspection k	400	—
Insert set screw	—	1200	—

TABLE VII.   Load Summary, Loads per Month

From \ To	1	2	3	4	5	6	7	8	9	10	11	12	13	14	15	16	17
1	2000																
2		500	450	600	125		300								75		
3											400	100					
4						200	100				100						
5						100	200		150	100					50		
6							175		90	60	70	30			625		
7						25			50		200	150			400		
8											300	200	100	150	175		
9							50		40	100			155				
10						45	55					50	60				
11						50						600	500	150	20		
12						480	300			50	100		100	50	100		
13						40								305	600		
14							20								655		
15																3500	
16																	3500
17																	

6. Block out a single-story building with 20-foot bays, utilizing the block diagram developed in problem 5, on the company site diagrammed in Figure 19.

7. Pro rata space for washrooms, cafeteria, tool crib, etc., were included in the space requirements given in problem 5. What would you consider to be the best location for the tool crib? Why?

8. How do you propose to expand manufacturing facilities for the plant design developed in problem 6?

9. Given the following assumptions and data shown in Table IX, determine the theoretical minimum number of stations if a line is to be designed for an output of 8400 units per week:

(a) The company works an 8-hour day for 5 days per week.

(b) The line will be operated 7 hours per day to allow for personal needs such as rest and delay.

(c) The line workers receive $2.50 per hour.

(d) Overtime is paid at time and a half.

(e) Assume actual performance times are equal to the given task times unless otherwise stated.

TABLE VIII.	Space Requirements	
Department Number	Name	Required Square Feet
1	Receiving	500
2	Raw material storage	1,000
3	Shearing	200
4	Sawing	200
5	Automatic screw	4,000
6	Turret lathe	2,000
7	Engine lathe	500
8	Punch press	1,000
9	Hobbing	300
10	Broaching	200
11	Milling	3,000
12	Drilling	1,100
13	Heat treating	500
14	Plating	300
15	Assembly	700
16	Finished goods storage	1,000
17	Shipping	500
		17,000 sq. ft.
	Offices	2,200
	Total	19,200 sq. ft.

10.   Determine the actual number of stations by means of a schematic diagram, showing the time available at each station and the station number for the data of problem 9.

11.   Given the data of problem 9, if 5040 units per week are needed:

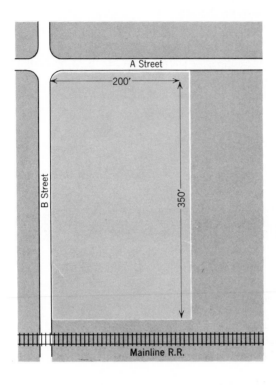

FIGURE 19.   Site layout for problem 6.

(a) How many actual stations are required?
(b) Is the number of stations proportional to the answer to problem 10 for this different output?
(c) How much idle time is there?
(d) How could banking be used to reduce the number of stations and idle time?

12.   After 2 months of operation the company is spending 4 hours per week in overtime to meet their requirements of 8400 units per week using your solution for problem 10. It has now been determined that the actual performance times have distributions with a maximum standard deviation of

0.5 second. The mean times are the given element times. Does this fact call for a change in design for the line? What is the lowest cost alternative?

13.   It appears that the time for operation i in Table IX could be decreased by method study. What action should be taken?

14.   A layout study was made in the engineering office of a large aerospace manufacturer. Initially the study focused on the flow of work through the system, but it was difficult to generate meaningful cost data on this basis. The search for realistic measures of effectiveness finally narrowed down to the relative location of people in the organization as required by their face-to-face contacts with others in the organization. It was decided to collect data on face-to-face contacts initiated by each person for a 1-month period, and to accumulate this data in the form of the matrix of Table X. The entire department was divided into ten groups or areas as indicated in Table X. Each cell value indicates the number of face-to-face contacts initiated by that group; for example, 15 from A to B. Table XI summarizes the area requirements for each group as well as the average hourly wage paid in each group. Figure 20 shows the present block layout.

Prepare a new block layout within the constraints of the overall size of the layout shown in Figure 20.

TABLE IX.   Tasks, Estimated Times, and Precedence Restrictions for Work on an Assembly Line

Task	Given Task Times (seconds)	Task Must Follow Task Listed Below
a	14	—
b-1	5	a
b-2	5	a
c	30	b
d	3	—
e	5	d
f	13	e
g	9	e
h	14	e
i	6	fgh
j	7	i
k	3	j
l	4	k
m	7	l

Total = 125 seconds

TABLE X Number of Face-to-Face Contacts per Month in an Engineering Office

From	To	Filing (A)	Supervision (B)	Blueprint (C)	Product Support (D)	Structural Design (E)	Electrical Design (F)	Hydraulic Design (G)	Production Liaison (H)	Detailing and Checking (I)	Secretarial Pool (J)
(A) Filing			15				5		10		15
(B) Supervision		20		25	40	100	90	80	160	85	60
(C) Blueprint											
(D) Product Support		10	15					20	280		10
(E) Structural Design		50	20	600			40			340	50
(F) Electrical Design				475					160	270	60
(G) Hydraulic Design		10		460	20				140	320	45
(H) Production Liaison		20			200	160	190	240		680	20
(I) Detailing and Checking		20	210	690	40	190	240	80			
(J) Secretarial Pool			25						15		

TABLE XI. Area Requirements and Average Wage Rates for Ten Groups in a Large Engineering Office

	Group	Area	Average Hourly Wage
A	Filing	20 × 15 = 300 sq. ft.	$1.80
B	Supervision	30 × 15 = 450 sq. ft.	5.00
C	Blueprinting	40 × 15 = 600 sq. ft.	2.10
D	Product support	25 × 20 = 500 sq. ft.	2.70
E	Structural design	65 × 25 = 1625 sq. ft.	4.50
F	Electrical design	25 × 35 = 875 sq. ft.	4.50
G	Hydraulic design	45 × 30 = 1350 sq. ft.	4.50
H	Production liaison	20 × 70 = 1400 sq. ft.	2.70
I	Detailing and checking	70 × 25 = 1750 sq. ft.	3.60
J	Secretarial pool	70 × 15 = 1050 sq. ft.	2.40
		90 × 110 = 9000 sq. ft.	

TABLE XII. Summary of Examination Load and Activity Sequence

Type of Examination	Examinations per Year	A	B	C	D	E	F	G	H	I	J	K	L
1	200	X	X	X	X	X	X	X	X	X	X		X
2	1,200	X			X	X			X				X
3	1,950	X	X	X	X			X	X				X
4	700	X	X	X	X			X	X		X		X
5	400	X			X	X			X		X		X
6	1,800	X	X	X	X	X						X	X
7	650	X					X	X			X		X
8	250	X				X				X		X	X

15.   A private industrial clinic performs service under contract to a number of business and industrial firms. These services include medical examinations for new employees as well as annual physical examinations. The clinic performs eight types of examination sequences depending on the details of the individual contracts.

Table XII gives the number of examinations per year of each type together with the sequence of activities required for each. Table XIII indicates the space requirements for each of the major activities.

Many complaints have been received concerning the excessive walking required by those being examined because of the layout of the clinic. Figure 21 shows the present layout. Propose an improved layout.

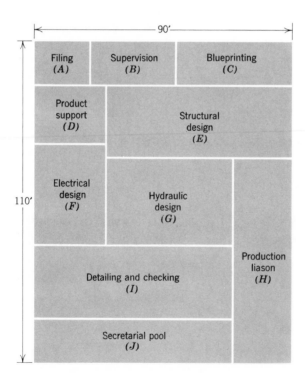

FIGURE 20.   Existing block layout for ten groups within a large engineering office.

TABLE XIII.   Space Requirements for Major Activities

Code and Activity	Square Feet Required
A. Initial processing	400
B. Height and weight measurement and general external examination	200
C. Eye examination	300
D. Ear, nose, and throat	100
E. X-ray and fluoroscope	300
F. Blood tests	100
G. Blood pressure check	100
H. Respiratory check	100
I. Electrocardiographic and electroencephalographic examination	100
J. Laboratory tests	400
K. Dental examination	200
L. Final processing	100
Total	2,400

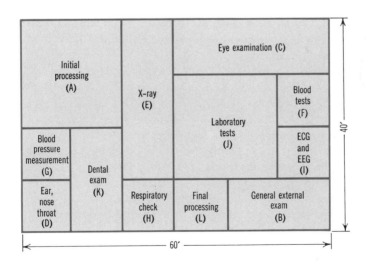

FIGURE 21.   Present layout of clinic.

REFERENCES

[1] Arcus, A. L. "COMSOAL: A Computer Method for Sequencing Operation for Assembly Lines." In: *Readings in Production and Operations Management*. E. S. Buffa, editor. John Wiley, New York, 1966.

[2] Armour, G. C., and E. S. Buffa. "A Heuristic Algorithm and Computer Simulation Approach to the Relative Location of Facilities." *Management Science*, **9** (2), Jan. 1963.

[3] Bowman, E. H. "Assembly-Line Balancing By Linear Programming." *Operations Research*, **8** (3), 1960.

[4] Buffa, E. S. "Pacing Effects in Production Lines." *Journal of Industrial Engineering*, **12** (6), Nov.–Dec. 1961.

[5] Buffa, E. S. "Sequence Analysis for Functional Layouts." *Journal of Industrial Engineering*, **6** (2), Mar.–Apr. 1955.

[6] Buffa, E. S., G. C. Armour, and T. E. Vollmann. "Allocating Facilities with CRAFT." *Harvard Business Review*, Mar.–Apr. 1964.

[7] Buffa, E. S., and W. H. Taubert. *Production-Inventory Systems: Planning and Control* (Rev. ed.). Richard D. Irwin, Homewood, Ill., 1972.

[8] Denholm, D. H., and G. H. Brooks, "A Comparison of Three Computer Assisted Plant Layout Techniques." *Proceedings of Technical Papers*, AIIE Convention, May 1970.

[9] Fetter, R. B., and H. T. Galliher. "Waiting-Line Models in Material Handling." *Journal of Industrial Engineering*, **9** (3), 202–208, May–June 1958.

[10] Held, M., R. M. Karp, and R. Sharesian. "Assembly-Line Balancing—Dynamic Programming with Precedence Constraints." *Operations Research*, **11** (3), May–June 1963.

[11] Helgeson, W. B., and D. P. Birnie. "Assembly Line Balancing Using the Ranked Position Weight Technique." *Journal of Industrial Engineering*, **12** (6), Nov.–Dec. 1961.

[12] Hoffman, T. F. "Assembly Line Balancing with a Precedence Matrix." *Management Science*, **9** (4), July 1963.

[13] Jackson, J. R. "A Computing Procedure for a Line-Balancing Problem." *Management Science*, **2** (3), 251–272, Apr. 1956.

[14] Kilbridge, M. D., and L. Wester. "A Heuristic Method of Assembly-Line Balancing." *Journal of Industrial Engineering*, **12** (4), July–Aug. 1961.

[15] Kilbridge, M. D., and L. Wester. "The Balance Delay Problem." *Management Science*, **8** (1), Oct. 1961.

[16] Mallick, R. W., and A. P. Gaudreau. *Plant Layout: Planning and Practice*. John Wiley, New York, 1951.

[17] Mastor, A. A. *An Experimental Investigation and Comparative Evaluation of Production Line Balancing Techniques*. Unpublished Ph.D. Dissertation, UCLA, 1966. Also: *Management Science*, **16** (11), 728–746, July 1970.

[18] Moore, J. M. *Plant Layout and Design.* Macmillan, New York, 1962.

[19] Muther, R. *Practical Plant Layout.* McGraw-Hill, New York, 1955.

[20] Nugent, C. E., T. E. Vollmann, and J. Ruml. "An Experimental Comparison of Facilities to Locations." *Operations Research,* Jan.–Feb. 1968.

[21] Reed, R. *Plant Layout.* Richard D. Irwin, Homewood, Ill., 1961.

[22] Ritzman, L. P. "The Efficiency of Computer Algorithms for Plant Layout." *Management Science,* **18** (5), 240–248, Jan. 1972.

[23] Smith, S. P. "Travel Charting." *Journal of Industrial Engineering,* **6** (1), 13, Jan. 1955.

[24] Tonge, F. M. "Summary of a Heuristic Line-Balancing Procedure." *Management Science,* **7** (1), 21, Oct. 1960.

[25] Vazsonyi, A. *Scientific Programming in Business and Industry.* John Wiley, New York, 1958.

[26] Vergin, R. C., and J. D. Rogers. "An Algorithm and Computational Procedure for Locating Economic Facilities." *Management Science,* **13** (6), 240–254, Feb. 1967.

[27] Volgyesi, A. S. "Space-Age Approach to Space Allocation." *Computer Decisions,* May 1970, pp. 32–35.

[28] Vollmann, T. E., and E. S. Buffa. "The Facilities Layout Problem in Perspective." *Management Science,* **12** (10), 450–468, June 1966.

[29] Vollmann, T. E., C. E. Nugent, and R. L. Zartler. "A Computerized Model for Office Layout." *Journal of Industrial Engineering,* **19** (7), July 1968.

[30] Wester, L., and M. D. Kilbridge. "Heuristic Line Balancing: A Case." *Journal of Industrial Engineering,* **13** (3), May–June 1962.

CONTENTS

CHAPTER 11

JOB DESIGN AND MAN-MACHINE SYSTEMS

The materials of Chapter 10 on layout of physical facilities provide the basis for an overall integrated design of productive systems. Implicit in the layout process is an extremely important decision about the basic organization of the work to be done. For example, whether the system is organized around the principles of a functional or product layout will have great impact on the definition of jobs and their content. Within each of these physical configurations there would be a number of possible ways to divide up the work to be done as a basis for the design of jobs.

Unless there is a conscious effort to consider alternatives of overall organization of the work, job content will be determined by the process, existing machine designs, the physical layout, time requirements, or simply traditional patterns.

Thus, in a typical case, we may take an entire complex assembly process and break it down into a series of operations so that the product can be produced on an assembly line. The line is designed to meet certain capacity requirements,

331

such as an output of 480 units per eight-hour shift or 1 unit per minute. Output then dictates the maximum content of each operation, which can take no longer than one minute. What is more, there is a certain required sequence of assembly; operation 1 takes the tasks that come first which require one minute or less, operation 2 the second one-minute group, etc. Of course, there is usually some flexibility as to sequence; by rearranging the sequence we end up with the job content in each operation that seems to make the most sense. (Recall the methods of line balancing discussed in Chapter 10.)

In other situations, the process, the machine, the physical layout, or other considerations are likely to play a dominant role in determining job content. Each resulting job or operation can be analyzed as a separate man-machine system by the methods and data of this chapter in order to produce the best job design. *But how would this design compare with other basic alternatives of job content?* If we were to consider as part of the problem all possible alternatives of job content, there might be a baffling number. Unfortunately, there is very little information available to guide us here. The result, in practice, is that such considerations as the machines, layouts, production quotas, and machine and conveyor pacing often dictate job content.

MEASURES OF EFFECTIVENESS IN JOB DESIGN

Over the years since Adam Smith, the main guide for determining job content has been *division of labor.* We have accepted this idea almost completely. Adam Smith specified no limit to the division of labor and the principle has been applied as a one-way mechanism to achieve the maximum benefits of job design. Jobs have been broken down to the point where the worker finds little satisfaction in performing his tasks. In recent years there has been a reaction against excessive job breakdown; a few investigators have found that combinations of operations to create jobs of greater scope recaptured the worker's interest; increases in productivity, quality level, etc., were reported. A new term, *job enlargement,* appeared. Practical applications of job enlargement that were written up in the literature tended to verify the findings of the investigators. Unfortunately, although exponents of job enlargement recognize that division of labor can be carried too far, they have not been able to specify any principles or guides on how far to go in the other direction. Job enlargement is also a one-way mechanism. It does,

however, provide a balancing force through the inclusion of job satisfaction as a major criterion of successful job design. The ultimate
answer lies in research attempts to isolate the factors that determine an
optimal combination of tasks to make up jobs. This effort has been
called job design.

JOB DESIGN

The past and present viewpoint of American business and industry
emphasizes the economic criterion as the controlling factor in determining job content and considers other criteria as effective mainly in
so far as they meet economic requirements. Thus, a quality criterion often
reduces to an economic one when the job design that improves quality
levels also improves productivity. For example, removing fatiguing
elements of a job commonly improves productivity; eliminating hazards
may reduce insurance premium rates as well as improve productivity;
designing tasks that increase employee satisfaction often also improves
productivity.

However, there certainly are instances where the various subcriteria
do not correlate with the economic criterion. To obtain higher quality
levels often demands increased costs, and the value of the reduced scrap
may not counterbalance the higher labor costs. The employee satisfaction
criterion would not necessarily decrease costs. To reduce the risks of
hazards to extremely low levels might be very costly.

In Taylor's time the noneconomic criteria would have been shrugged
off. Today jobs and methods are frequently designed or altered to meet
noneconomic needs. It is true that the economic criterion is dominant,
and job and method designs are seldom set or altered without reference
to the effects on costs. Most often, costs are regarded as the "quantitative" measure, with noneconomic criteria being considered in the
list of "intangible" advantages or disadvantages. Figure 1 shows in
schematic form the relationship of constraints, criteria, and other
pressures in determining job content. The inputs to the determination
of job methods then become job content plus a host of other inputs
related to man-machine systems.

Who Designs Jobs and Work Methods?

In industrial organizations the professional designer of jobs and work
methods is the industrial engineer. In many less formalized organizations, however, foremen and managers at various levels design jobs.
In most nonmanufacturing organizations, managers and supervisors

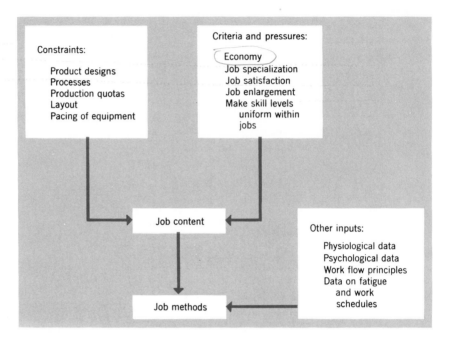

FIGURE 1.   Relationship of constraints, criteria, and other pressures in determining job content. Inputs to job methods design.

are responsible for determining job content and method design. The
wide variety of organizations and of people holding responsibility for
job design makes dissemination of the known data a difficult problem.
Since, for most of these people, job design is only a part of their responsibility, they tend to rely on existing standard workplace designs and
on basic equipment (such as office desks, typewriters, benches, and
standard machine tools) to fix many of the characteristics of the job;
actual details of method are often left to the workers themselves. In
fact, worker participation in job design has been experimented with
for some time.

   In discussing job design we shall concentrate our attention on man-
machine systems, focusing on the job methods component of job
design. We will see that man's great potential is not in the repetitive
mechanical activities at all, but rather in situations requiring improvisa-
tion, reasoning, and judgment. From a human point of view we have been
misusing man's capabilities. In the current era of highly organized and
expensive labor, it is becoming obvious that we may also be misusing
man's capabilities from an economic point of view.

MAN-MACHINE SYSTEMS

The great advances in computers and automation technology has changed the conceptual framework for man in productive systems. While there is still a great deal of manual labor in business and industry today, most work involves the use of at least some kind of mechanical aid, and, therefore, the conceptual framework of man-machine systems is appropriate for the entire spectrum of systems involving the human operator.

Even in an automated system, labor is necessary in a surveillance capacity. In such situations, an operator may be seated in front of a control board which continually flashes information about the progress of the manufacturing process. It is important that these display panels be designed to transmit the essential information with minimum error.

Perhaps the majority of business and industrial manual jobs today consist of some combination of man and machine. Where there is a fixed machine cycle as in most machine tool processes, the design of the machine in relation to the operator is of great importance. The location and design of controls, working heights, information displays, the flow of work, safety features, and the utilization of both the man and the machine in the cycle are all important determinants of quality, productivity, and worker acceptance of the job situation.

Many jobs are strictly manual, such as assembly, maintenance, and heavy labor. Here mechanical aids or tools are common, and we need to consider the design of these tools from the viewpoint of the user. In addition, we must consider the layout of the workplace, the flow of work, and physical and mental fatigue produced in the worker by his physical environment. In some situations, environmental factors of heat, humidity, light, noise, and hazards can seriously affect fatigue, productivity, quality, health, and worker acceptance of the job. Thus, in studying man-machine systems we assume that the questions of job content have fairly well been settled, and we concentrate attention on the detailed design of jobs.

Man versus Machines

Man has certain physiological, psychological, and sociological characteristics which define both his capabilities and his limitations in the work situation. These characteristics are not fixed quantities but vary from individual to individual. This does not mean, however, that we cannot make predictions about human behavior. Rather, it means that predictive models of human behavior must reflect this variation. To take a physical factor as an example, the distribution of the arm strengths of men indicates the percent of the male population that can exert a given force. This distribution also indicates the limitations in demand for arm strength. The average man can exert a right-hand pull of 120 pounds. If we design a machine lever that requires the operator to exert this force, approximately half of the male population would be unable to operate the machine. On the other hand, the distribution also tells us that about 95 percent of the male population can exert a right-hand pull of 52 pounds. A lever designed to take this fact into account will accommodate a large proportion of the male population.

In performing work, man's functions fall into three general classifications:

1. Receiving information through the various sense organs, that is, eyes, ears, touch, etc.

2. Making decisions based on information received and information stored in the memory of the individual.

3. Taking action based on decisions. In some instances, the decision phase may be virtually automatic because of learned responses as in a highly repetitive task. In others, the decision may involve an order of reasoning and the result may be complex.

Note that the general structure of a closed-loop automated system is parallel in concept. (See Figure 9, Chapter 7.) Wherein lies the difference? Are automated machines like men? Yes, they are in certain important respects. Both have sensors, stored information, comparators, decision makers, effectors, and feedback loops. The differences are in man's tremendous range of capabilities and in the limitations imposed on him by his psychological and sociological characteristics. Thus, machines are much more specialized in the kinds and range of tasks they can perform. Machines perform tasks as faithful servants, reacting mainly to physical factors; for example, bearings may wear out because of a dusty environment. But man reacts to his psychological and sociological environment as well as to his physical environment. The latter fact requires that one measure of effectiveness of job design must be worker acceptance or job satisfaction.

Although there are few really objective guides to the allocation of tasks to men and machines on other than an economic basis, a subjective list of the kinds of tasks most appropriate for men and for machines is given by McCormick [14].

Human beings appear to surpass existing machines in their ability to:

1. Detect small amounts of light and sound.
2. Receive and organize patterns of light and sound.
3. Improvise and use flexible procedures.
4. Store large amounts of information for long periods and recall relevant facts at the appropriate time.
5. Reason inductively.
6. Exercise judgment.
7. Develop concepts and create methods.

Existing machines appear to surpass humans in their ability to:

1. Respond quickly to control signals.
2. Apply great force smoothly and precisely.
3. Perform repetitive and routine tasks.
4. Store information briefly and then erase it completely.
5. Perform rapid computations.
6. Perform many different functions simultaneously.

Such lists raise a question. Why do business, industry, and government not use men and machines according to these guides? We have all observed that man is used extensively for tasks given in the list for machines. The answer lies in the balance of costs for a given situation. Both labor and machines cost money; when the balance of costs favors machines, conversions are normally made. In many foreign countries extremely low-cost labor, in relation to the cost of capital, dictates an economic decision to use manual labor in many tasks in which man is not well suited. Because of relatively high wages in the United States, machines are used much more extensively.

Conceptual Framework for Man-Machine Systems

As we noted previously, men and machines perform similar functions in accomplishing work tasks though they each have comparative advantages. The functions they perform are represented in Figure 2; these functions are generally comparable to those of the closed-loop feedback diagram of Figure 9 in Chapter 7. The four basic classes of functions are sensing, information storage, information processing, and action. Information storage interacts with all three of the other functions; however, sensing, information processing, and action functions occurs in sequence.

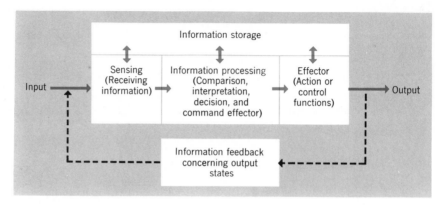

FIGURE 2.   Functions performed by man or machine components of man-machine systems.

Information is received by the *sensing function.* If by a man, sensing is accomplished through the various sense organs of eyes, ears, sense of touch, etc. Machine sensing can parallel human sensing through electronic or mechanical devices. Machine sensing is usually much more specific or single purpose in nature than the broadly capable human senses.

Information storage for man is in the human memory or by access to records. Machine information storage can be by magnetic tape or drum, punched cards, cams and templates, etc.

The function of *information processing and decision* takes sensed and/or stored information and produces a decision by some simple or complex process. The processing could be as simple as a choice between two alternatives, depending on input data, or very complex, involving deduction, analysis, or computing to produce a decision for which a command is issued to the effector.

The effector or *action function* occurs as a result of decisions and command, and may involve the triggering of control mechanisms by man or machine, or a communication of decisions. Control mechanisms would in turn cause something physical to happen such as moving the hands or arms, starting a motor, increasing or decreasing the depth of a cut on a machine tool, etc.

Input and output is related to the raw material, or the thing being processed. The output represents some transformation of the input in line with our discussion of processes in Chapter 7. The processes themselves may be of any type, that is, chemical, processes to change shape or form, assembly, transport, clerical, and so on.

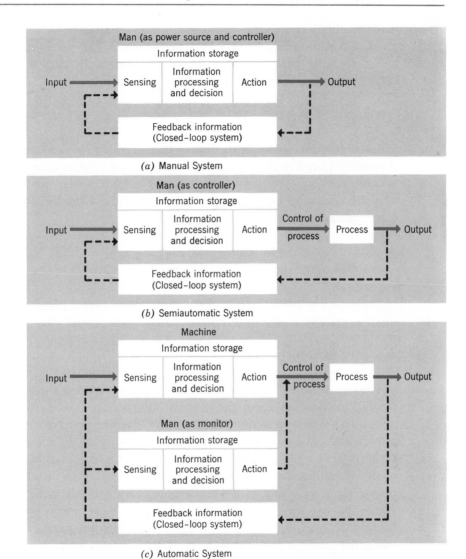

FIGURE 3.   Schematic diagram of man and machine functions in three types of systems. (From *Human Factors Engineering* by E. J. McCormick. Copyright 1970. Used with permission of McGraw-Hill Book Company.)

Information feedback concerning the output states is an essential ingredient for it provides the basis for control. Feedback operates to control the simplest hand motion through the senses and the nervous system. For machines, feedback concerning the output states provides the basis for machine adjustment. As we discussed in Chapter 7, automatic machines couple the feedback information directly so that adjustments are automatic (closed-loop automation). When machine adjustments are only periodic based on information feedback, the loop is still closed, but not on a continuous and automatic basis.

Types of Man-Machine Systems

We shall use the module of the functions performed by man or machine shown in Figure 2 to discuss the basic structure for three typical systems: manual, semiautomatic, or mechanical and automatic systems. Figure 3 uses the module of Figure 2 to show the structure of the three types of systems in schematic form.

Manual systems involve man with only mechanical aids or hand tools. Man supplies the power required and acts as controller of the process; the tools and mechanical aids help multiply his efforts. The basic module of Figure 2 describes the functions where the man directly transforms input to output as shown in Figure 3(*a*). In addition we must envision the manual system as operating in some working environment which may have an impact on the man and the output.

Semiautomatic systems involve man mainly as a controller of the process as indicated in Figure 3(*b*). He interacts with the machine by sensing information about the process, interpreting it and using a set of controls which may start and stop the machine and possibly make intermediate adjustments. Power is normally supplied by the machine. Figure 4 shows the general cycle of activity of a man-machine system of the semiautomatic type imbedded in the working environment. Of course, there are combinations of the manual and semiautomatic systems where the man is also supplying some of the system power, perhaps in loading the machine or in some activities in which he may be involved while the machine goes through its cycle. Common examples of semiautomatic systems are the machine tools commonly used in the mechanical industries.

Automatic systems presumably do not need a man since all of the functions of sensing, information processing and decision, and action are performed by the machine. Such a system would need to be fully programmed to sense and take required action for all possible contingencies. Automation at such a level is not economically justified even if the machines could be designed. Figure 3(*c*), therefore, indicates man's

FIGURE 4.   Display panel in an automated engine block production line. (Courtesy Ford Motor Company.)

role as a monitor to help control the process. In this role the man periodically or continuously maintains surveillance over the process through displays which indicate the state of the crucial parameters of the process. Figure 4 shows such a situation where the man is monitoring an automated engine block production line by a fairly complicated display panel.

In discussing man-machine system analysis and design in the balance of the chapter, we will organize the material in terms of information input, focusing particularly on visual displays; human control of man-machine systems including human motor activities, human control of systems, man-machine relationships, analysis of hand motions, applied anthropometry and the analysis of man and man-machine cycles; and, the working environment and its impact on output. Throughout the discussion our emphasis is really on man and his relationship to machines.

Figure 5, representing the general cycle of activity for semiautomatic operations, is of central value for it involves all of the relationships which we will want to discuss. In Figure 5 man is receiving and inter-

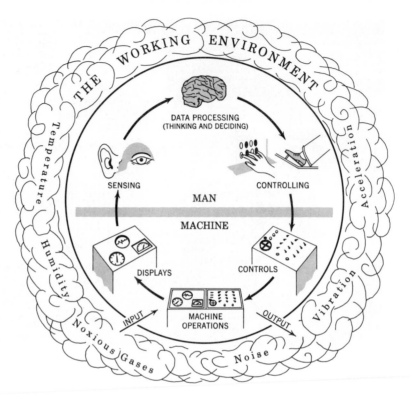

FIGURE 5. Simplified model of a man-machine system for semi-automatic operations. (From A. Chapanis, *Man-Machine Engineering*, Copyright © 1965 by Wadsworth Publishing Company, Belmont, California. Reprinted by permission of the publisher, Brooks/Cole Publishing Company, Monterey, California.)

preting information about the process from information displays, and manipulating mechanisms which control the processes. He is also maintaining a general surveillance over the process. The machine responds to these control actions to convert input to output. Thus we have represented all of the kinds of functions for man for the three types of man-machine systems just discussed. For example, the manipulative activity is representative of the dominant features of manual systems; the information input, sensing, and controlling activities are representative of both semiautomatic and automatic systems; and the information input and general monitoring or surveillance activities are representative of automatic systems. The impact of environment and the physical relationships of the man to work flow and workplace arrangements are, of course, applicable to all man-machine systems.

INFORMATION INPUT

Modern technology has made it possible to present vital information concerning the process which humans cannot sense directly, or at least cannot sense precisely in a direct way. Thus, the man in Figure 4 is sensing indirectly such measurements as bore diameter, service smoothness, etc. On the other hand some sensing may result from direct observation, for example, if the transfer mechanisms were jammed in Figure 4. The pathways of information from original source to human sensory receptors is shown schematically in Figure 6.

Figure 6 indicates immediately some marriage between man and machine in indirect sensing which involves an intermediate sensing by mechanisms and a coding or conversion to some new form which is then presented and sensed by the human. Therefore, in man-machine systems, human sensing can be direct, but increasingly is indirect, placing emphasis on encoding and information display systems. The design of these systems of display for information input to man is important if operations are to be effective.

Figure 6 implies the full range of possible human sensory receptors. The most common business and industrial applications focus on the use of the eyes, ears, and nerve endings, in that order, with visual display being by far the most common.

Visual Displays

Much of the postwar effort of experimental psychologists has been directed toward improving visual displays. Questions such as these have been raised: Which dial shapes are most legible? What scale units should be used and how should they be marked on dials? Do people have number preference patterns that affect their interpretation of dial readings? What characteristics of numbers and letters make them most legible? Are black numbers on a white background superior to white on black? How big should letters and numerals be and what proportions of line thickness, height, and width are best? How should systems of dials be arranged? Experimental work has been carried out on these and many other questions.

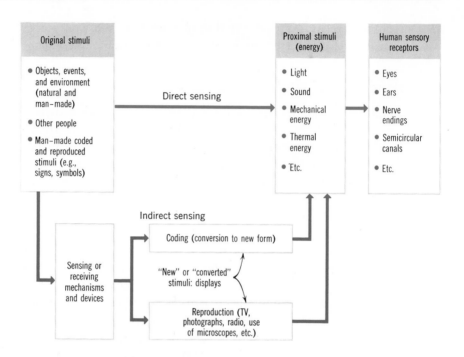

FIGURE 6.   Schematic illustration of pathways of information from original sources to sensory receptors. (Although typically the original, basic source is an object, event, condition, the environment, etc., in some situations the effective original source to an individual consists of some man-made coded or reproduced stimuli; office personnel, for example, usually deal with recorded symbols which, for practical purposes, are their "original" stimuli.) (From *Human Factors Engineering* by E. J. McCormick. Copyright 1970. Used with permission of McGraw-Hill Book Company.)

Sleight [16] experimented with the shape of dials. He constructed an experiment around five types of dials and had sixty subjects read seventeen settings from each dial in a random sequence. Figure 7 shows the results in terms of the percentage of errors recorded. A multitude of studies, of which the Sleight study is typical, has indicated the following general guides on dial design, as summarized by Chapanis, Garner and Morgan [5].

1. A dial about 2.75 or 3 inches in diameter is probably the best all-around size if we are going to read it at a distance of 30 inches or less.

2. Marks should be located at the 0, 5, 10, 15, 20, etc. (or 0, 50, 100, 150,

200, etc.) positions. The marks at the 9, 10, 20, . . . (or 0, 100, 200, . . .) positions should be longer than those at the 5, 15, 25, . . . (or 50, 150, 250, . . .) positions. Only the marks at 0, 10, 20, . . . should be numbered.

3. The distance between the numbered markers should be about a half inch as measured around the circumference of the dial.

4. The separation between scale markers should be the same all around the dial.

5. There should be a gap between the beginning and end of the scale.

6. Values on the scale should increase in a clockwise direction.

When there is a bank of dials to be read, it helps to orient them in a pattern so that normal readings are in the nine o'clock or twelve o'clock positions. This makes it possible to tell at a glance if an abnormal reading is among the group instead of reading each dial individually. As a matter of fact, we often find that the operator is presented with too much information. He may not need to *read* the dial at all. Perhaps all that is required is simple recognition of whether the reading is in the normal operating region or not. Or perhaps the real need is to know only if something is functioning or not. Simple on-off lights may be satisfactory in such situations.

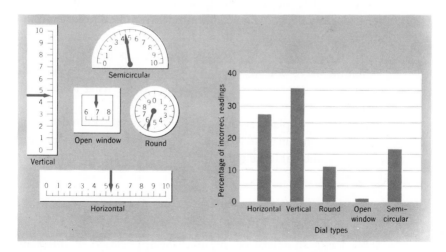

FIGURE 7.   Five different dial shapes and the percentage of incorrect readings recorded for each. (From Steight [16].)

There is also the question of the letters and numbers that are used on visual displays. Studies have indicated that capital letters and numbers are read most accurately when the stroke width to height ratio is between 1:6 and 1:8 and when the overall width to height ratio is about 2:3.

Auditory and Tactual Displays

While auditory displays are not as commonly used as visual, they have particular value as warning devices or to attract attention. There are, of course, other opportunities for using the auditory channel, for example, when vision is impaired, or at night, or in photographic darkrooms, when vision cannot be used. Some of the common devices are bells, buzzers, horns, sirens, chimes, and whistles.

Tactual displays are even less common than auditory in business and industry. Yet there are applications when vision cannot be used such as in photographic darkrooms, or the shape coding of control knobs so they can be identified by touch (discussed in the following section).

HUMAN CONTROL OF MAN-MACHINE SYSTEMS

Given information input by direct or indirect means the human operator of a man-machine system responds by performing work in the physical sense. He may be assembling objects, manipulating controls, and in general using his body to accomplish the required tasks to fit in with the objectives of the system. The analysis of the hand and body motions and how they contribute to effective operation is important.

Manipulative activity in handling controls has been studied with considerable care and this knowledge can be used to design effective systems.

Finally, workplace layout can be based on a knowledge of anthropometry so that manual motions can take place within a prescribed area and chair and table heights can be set at levels appropriate to human body sizes.

Analysis of Manual Activity

Table I is a summary of the areas of application of different manual activity methods of analysis. Before any method of analysis described here is used, the need for performing the activity at all should already have been established through overall studies of the sequence and

TABLE I.   Summary of Areas of Application of Different Man and Man-Machine Analysis Methods

Nature of Activity	Analysis Method
Repetitive short-cycle task, low- to moderate-production volume	Operation chart or operation chart supplemented by motion-time standard data
Repetitive short-cycle task, high-production volume	Micromotion analysis chart, motion-time standard data
Repetitive long-cycle tasks	Man flow process charts, activity charts
Repetitive tasks involving a crew and/or a machine	Activity charts
Jobs involving tasks occurring at irregular intervals	Activity classification

relationship of operations performed in producing a part or processing a paperwork form. The product analysis methods of Chapter 7 are appropriate for these overall studies.

Repetitive Short-Cycle Tasks.   *Operation charts* are appropriate when the task has a fairly short cycle and the production volume is low to moderate. The operation chart analyzes the motions of the right and left hands into components of reach, grasp, transport, position, assemble, etc., and places the activities for each hand in parallel columns so that it can readily be seen how the two hands work together. Sometimes symbols are added, as in Figure 8, usually with large circles to indicate manipulative activity, small circles to indicate reaches and transports of material, and a simple connective line to indicate the idle hand. With the symbols, Figure 8 shows a complete operation chart for the assembly of a bolt and three washers.

Sometimes the data of the operation chart are displayed against a time scale so that the relative value of the activities can be appraised. These time data may come from standard time values for motions such as reach, grasp, move, and position, or from detailed time studies of the operation being analyzed. Motion-time-standard data (discussed in the next chapter) may be helpful particularly in evaluating the estimated effect of proposed changes.

Principles of Motion Economy.   Over the years, industrial engineers have developed a set of general statements, called principles of motion

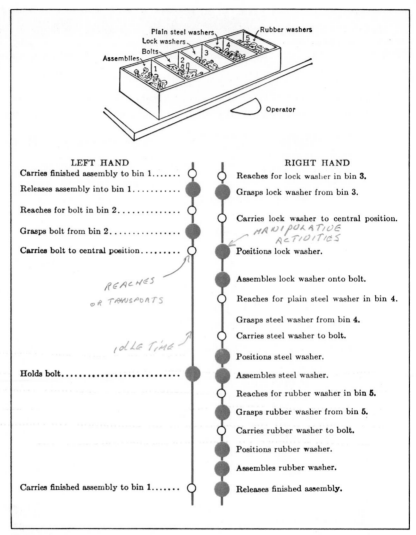

FIGURE 8.   Operation chart of bolt and washer assembly—old method.
(From Barnes [1].)

economy, which concern work arrangement, the use of the human hands
and body, and the design and use of tools. These guides to job design
have general applicability and are supplemented, and in some cases
corroborated, by some of the research into the speed and accuracy of
motor activities discussed later in this chapter.

Micromotion Analysis.   This analysis breaks down an operation into elements, called therbligs, which represent a finer breakdown than do the elements for the operation chart. The results are plotted against a time scale so that the exact simultaneity of the two hands working together can be examined. The resulting chart is often called a "simo chart" because it shows this relationship. The data for the chart are gathered by means of motion pictures taken of a qualified operator.

Owing to the extra time and cost required to use micromotion analysis, its area of use is commonly limited to situations where many workers perform the same repetitive task. Thus, the total saving may be great, even though the percent reduction might be fairly small. It has also been found valuable in the design and development of new special equipment. A motion analyst and a machine designer working together often produce a superior design.

Repetitive Tasks Involving Long Cycles.   *Man flow process charts* are commonly used to analyze long-cycle tasks in which the worker moves about considerably from place to place in the performance of his work. The same general type of analysis of the product flow process chart (discussed under "product analysis" in Chapter 7) is used, except that the analyst follows the worker, instead of a part, and classifies his activities sequentially into operations, transports (walking as well as transporting material), storages (idleness), and inspections. Analysis of the resulting chart parallels product flow process charts; activities are examined with the objectives of (a) elimination, (b) combination, (c) improved sequence, etc. Gang process charts are used where activities of a crew are studied; one column of symbols is used for each man in the crew.

Activity charts are used to analyze operations into the time required to perform major manual and machine elements, or activities, and to plot the elements on a time scale. Relationships between man and machine or between crew members can then be examined. Let us take the milling of a slot in a bracket as an example. Figure 9 shows the bracket and the activity chart for the milling of the slot. Here the major elements of the repetitive work of the man and the machine have been plotted side by side on a time scale. In this instance the times are recorded in decimal hours. In this type of analysis, the major objective commonly is to maximize man and machine utilization. In the example of the milling of the bracket slot, we see that the machine is 100 percent utilized,

Lugs

Slot

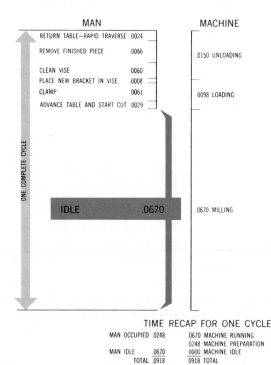

MAN		MACHINE
RETURN TABLE—RAPID TRAVERSE .0024		
REMOVE FINISHED PIECE .0066		.0150 UNLOADING
CLEAN VISE .0060		
PLACE NEW BRACKET IN VISE .0008		
CLAMP .0061		.0098 LOADING
ADVANCE TABLE AND START CUT .0029		
IDLE .0670		.0670 MILLING

ONE COMPLETE CYCLE

TIME RECAP FOR ONE CYCLE

MAN OCCUPIED .0248	.0670 MACHINE RUNNING
	.0248 MACHINE PREPARATION
MAN IDLE .0670	.0000 MACHINE IDLE
TOTAL .0918	.0918 TOTAL

FIGURE 9. Activity chart of "mill slot in bracket." (Courtesy Westinghouse Electric Corporation.)

since it is always either being loaded, unloaded, or actually taking a cut, and at no time is it idle. Nevertheless, machine effectiveness could be increased by improving the manual methods of loading and unloading, thus improving machine output per unit of time. The techniques for accomplishing this require a detailed study of the manual activity by means of the operation chart, etc., already discussed. On the other hand, the man is idle 73 percent of the cycle while he waits for the milling machine to complete its cut. This general situation is common in many kinds of machine and process operations.

The question is what to do with the man's idle time in such a situation. Perhaps the first consideration is whether the operator is really idle: some types of machine operations require operator vigilance and surveillance during the machine cycle, and an attempt to utilize such time could affect quality adversely. But it is often true that this is purely idle time. When such is the case on repetitive operations of considerable volume, it may be possible to have the man operate two or more machines. For the bracket slot milling operation, the operator could handle three machines doing the identical operation without introducing any idle machine time. Beyond that number, idle machine time develops, and an economy study would be required to determine whether idle man or machine time would be preferable.

Where the volume of the activity in question does not justify multiple-machine operation, examination of the operation process chart for that part might reveal other elements which could be performed during the idle time. As an example, the operation which followed the slot milling on the bracket happened to be milling the lugs. Figure 10 is the activity chart for lug milling. Figure 11 is the resulting composite operation of milling both the slot and the lugs. Note that the man's idle time has now been reduced to about 40 percent of the total cycle, but in so structuring the job, idle machine time has been introduced into the lug milling machine, amounting to about 45 percent. The question again comes up whether idle man or idle machine time is preferable. Note that if milling capacity were greater than demand, there would be incremental labor costs to do the two activities separately. On the other hand, if milling demand were at capacity or exceeded it, there would be created additional demand equal to the new machine idle time and there would be incremental labor costs equal to the extra hours at overtime rates. But since the two operations are being performed in the labor time of the slot milling operation, there is still a net gain from combining the two operations.

Where it is impractical to combine two or more machining operations, other kinds of activity may be incorporated to reduce the idle time for example, the removal of burrs produced by machining, or stacking otherwise jumbled parts so that they may be procured more easily in the following operation. Any useful work that can be accomplished

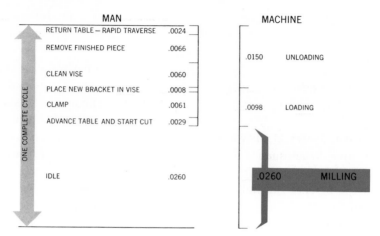

FIGURE 10.   Activity chart for "mill lugs of bracket." (Courtesy Westinghouse Electric Corporation.)

during such idle times, of course, incurs no incremental labor cost.

Sometimes there are objections made by skilled workers to running more than one machine, but where idle times are long, workers often become bored and may welcome a more even distribution of load. It is common that other workers, such as inspectors, assemblers, and many who operate machines that do not have automatic or semiautomatic cycles, are loaded fairly steadily throughout the workday.

Crew or team activities, which often appear complex to the observer, are considerably simplified by activity charts. Because of the difficulty in observing the simultaneity of the operations, the motion picture camera is an excellent means for gathering the basic data. Figure 12 is an example of such a chart for a team of three women who are wrapping eight pints of ice cream in a package. Work is fed to the team at a constant rate by a machine. Here is an instance where partial improvements only serve to increase operator idle time unless and until one entire operator can be eliminated.

Analysis of Tasks Occurring at Irregular Intervals. *Activity classification* often provides valuable data for the analysis of jobs that have tasks (usually of wide variety) which occur at irregular intervals. An initial step in analysis is to determine the average proportion of time spent in each of several categories of activity. There are two valuable methods for gathering pertinent data for activity classification: work sampling and time-lapse movie camera techniques.

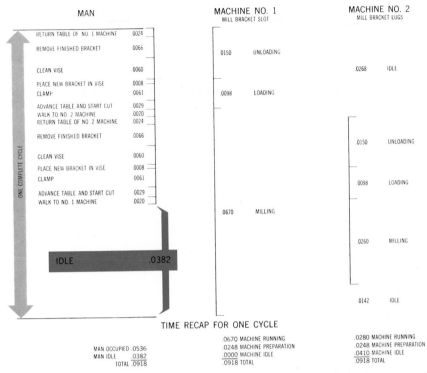

FIGURE 11.   Activity chart for the composite operation, "mill slot and lugs of bracket." (Courtesy Westinghouse Electric Corporation.)

Work sampling involves a random sampling of activities so that the proportion of time spent in each activity can be estimated; it will be discussed in greater detail in the chapter on standards and work measurement. Time-lapse movie cameras also can be used to obtain similar data. The camera, which takes pictures at slow-speed intervals, one per second or slower, is set to view the field of activity. It is driven by a synchronous motor so that each film frame represents a definite time unit. Since camera speeds are slow, it is possible to obtain half-day or full-day records with a fairly modest film consumption.

ANALYSIS OF CONTROL ACTIVITY   s‍To‍p

The design of controls and control systems has an important impact on the effectiveness of a man-machine system. A knowledge of the forces that man can exert may be of importance in some systems so that these capabilities are not exceeded in the design of controls.

Positioning activities are commonly required in operating controls and control coding is sometimes important so that controls are not confused.

Strength and Forces of Body Movements. Data on the forces that can be exerted by most of the working population is important for designing machines and tools which do not require operators with

ACTIVITY CHART

SUBJECT Pack 8 pints of Ice Cream					Date 3/30/54	
Present X Proposed Dept. Ice Cream (Time in thousandths of mins.)				Sheet 1 of 1	Chart by ESB	
Supplier		Packer #1		Packer #2		
Elements	Time	Elements	Time	Elements	Time	
20 — Get and position 4 pints	47			continued Get tape-seal	37	
40 —		Get and position 8 pints-wrap	89	Dispose to right	8	
— Wait for machine	11					
60 —						
— Get and position second 4 pints	34			Idle	74	
80 —						
100 — Release 8 pints to Packer #2	16	Get tape-seal	14			
120 —		Dispose to left	14			
— Get and position 4 pints	33	Meter and cut tape	21			
140 —						
— Wait for machine	11			Get and position 8 pints-wrap	81	
160 —						
— Get and position second 4 pints		Idle	62			
180 —						
— Release 8 pints to Packer #1	14			Get tape-seal; cont. at top		
200 —						

FIGURE 12. Activity chart of a team of three women wrapping eight pints of ice cream in a package.

unusual physical strength. Rather exhaustive population measurements have been made for arm strength (in various directions and different starting positions), grip strength, turning strength (such as turning a door knob), elbow and shoulder strength, and back and leg strength.*

Typical of such data is that developed for the USAF at Wright Air Development Center for arm strength in a seated position. Subjects were measured for maximum push, pull, upward force, and downward force for various angular positions. See Figure 13. Table II summarizes the results for the maximum forces exerted by the fifth percentile of the measured group. These figures, then, represent forces that nearly all males can equal or exceed. Jobs designed so that required arm forces

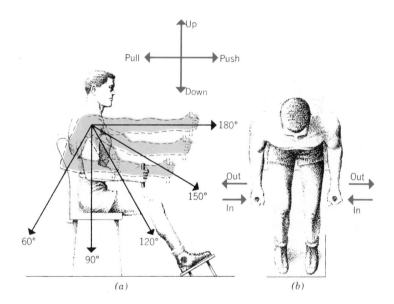

FIGURE 13. Subject positions for arm strength study. Data are shown in Table II. (*a*) Side view of subject showing various angular positions of upper arm. For each position, maximum strength was determined for pull, push, up, and down movements shown in (*b*). (*b*) Top view of subject showing in-and-out movements made at each of the arm positions shown in (*a*). (Adapted from Hunsicker [10].)

*A good summary of the results of these studies can be found in [14].

do not exceed these values can draw on almost anyone in the male population. In general, from Table II we can see that left-hand strength is consistently less than that for the right hand, and that pushes and pulls are weaker when the arm is down at the side. With upward and downward movements, however, greater force can be exerted when the arm is down at the side. Pull is slightly better than push, down slightly better than up, and in better than out.

Speed and Accuracy of Motor Responses

A motor response is one that involves physical movement and/or control of body parts. It is a muscular activity. Since man's hands are his most important asset for the performance of muscular tasks, we find that most of the available data pertain to the hands. Thus, in designing tasks that involve positioning elements, for example, a knowledge of where in the work area positioning can be accomplished most accurately may affect the workplace layout.

Positioning Elements.   Much experimental effort has gone on to determine how positioning elements of various types can be best accomplished. A number of interesting results have been found, some expected and some unusual. For example, Barnes [1] showed that positioning elements that require visual control take somewhat longer to accomplish (about 17 per cent) than where some sort of mechanical guide or stop is used to establish the exact final desired position of the part or hand. The implications of this fact tend to corroborate the idea of a fixed and definite location for everything. The rapid typing speeds attained by the touch system are based partially on this fact since key locations are fixed. Conceptually, it is the difference between finding something in a carefully indexed and maintained file or in a stack of papers.

Briggs [3] performed a set of positioning experiments where *speed and accuracy* were the criteria. The task required subjects to move back and forth between a buzzer and a target with a metal stylus. When the stylus was pressed against a 3-inch square or circle, the buzzer was actuated. The stylus was then moved 14 inches to a paper target through which it was punched. The measure used was the number of punch marks on the target in a 20-second trial. The target size and the angular position of the buzzer were varied, as in Figure 14. In a second experi-

TABLE II.   Arm Strength, in Pounds, of Movements in Various Directions for Different Angular Positions of Upper Arm

Angle of Arm (degrees)	Fifth Percentile			
	Left	Right	Left	Right
	Pull		Push	
180	50	52	42	50
150	42	56	30	42
120	34	42	26	36
90	32	37	22	36
60	26	24	22	34
	Up		Down	
180	9	14	13	17
150	15	18	18	20
120	17	24	21	26
90	17	20	21	26
60	15	20	18	20
	In		Out	
180	13	20	8	14
150	15	20	8	15
120	20	22	10	15
90	16	18	10	16
60	17	20	12	17

Adapted from Hunsicker [10].

ment the positions of the buzzer and target were reversed, so the buzzer was immediately in front of the subject and the target was placed at various angular positions. Figure 14 shows the results. Speed and accuracy were consistently greater for the second experiment when the target was away from the subject. Not only that, but the angular position of about 60° optimized the scores. In a third set of experiments, the distance of movement was also varied, and angles to both the right and left of the subject were used. In general, scores were better when

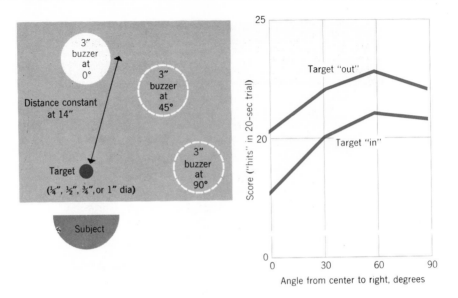

FIGURE 14.   General experimental setup and results of positioning experiments. Optimal angle was near 60 °. (Adapted from Briggs [3].)

movement was to the right instead of to the left, and short distances were better than long.

When the right and left hands work in simultaneous and symmetrical patterns, Barnes and Mundel [2] showed that the accuracy of positioning is optimum when both hands are directly in front of the subject.

Positioning through Settings of Dials, Cranks, and Handwheels. Movements to position dials, knobs, cranks, and handwheels are common means by which the human operator controls processes and machines. Several studies have been made to determine factors that optimize the design of such devices. For example, when knob settings must be accomplished without visual control (blind), Chapanis [4] showed that average errors and variability of settings are minimized at the "twelve o'clock" position of the dial. Jenkins and Connor [12] showed that there is a large difference in the time needed to make a setting, depending on the ratio between knob movement and the movement of the pointer on the dial. Low ratios tend to minimize the time to make final adjustments, but the time to bring the pointer to the approximate setting is fairly long. The reverse is true for high ratios.

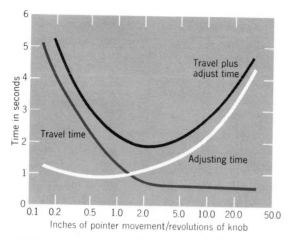

FIGURE 15. The time for setting indicators with different control ratios. Times are divided into two parts: the time of travel to get the pointer in the vicinity of the target and the time for adjusting the pointer accurately on the target. Note that there is an optimum at about 2 inches of pointer movement for each revolution of the knob. (Adapted from Jenkins and Connor [12].)

The optimum ratio turned out to be about 2 inches of pointer movement to each turn of the knob, as shown in Figure 15. Friction added to the system increased the travel time but had no effect on the final adjustment time.

Davis [6] performed a set of experiments to determine optimal sizes of cranks and handwheels under various conditions of frictional torque, position and height. These types of cranks and handwheels are common devices used to move carriages and cutting tools to desired settings. Davis measured the time taken to make required settings for the various conditions. He found that for zero or very low frictional torque, the small handwheels and cranks were best (3 to 6 inches in diameter). When it was necessary to crank against some frictional load, however, the larger diameters were better (10 to 16 inches). Cranks were superior to handwheels. Davis varied the height from the floor and the angular position of the wheel, because in practice these types of mechanisms might be found in various relative positions. The interesting general result was that location was not a serious factor for zero or low loads but, when heavy frictional load was encountered, the $-45°$ and $+45°$ positions were significantly better than the horizontal or vertical positions.

Coding Controls.   In complex operations where a number of controls are used, coding by color, size, shape, or location helps to distinguish between them so that mistakes are minimized. Hunt [11] found that round knobs could be distinguished from each other when the smaller was five-sixths the size of the larger. The location of controls can be used to distinguish them from each other. For example, the clutch, brake, and accelerator pedals of automobiles are normally used without looking to see where they are. Here again, the Hunt study provides basic information. He found that when toggle switches were arranged in vertical columns, the errors in blind reaching to specified switches were lower than when the switches were arranged horizontally in rows. For switches arranged vertically, Hunt's results indicated that a 5-inch difference in location was desirable, but for horizontal arrangements this difference was about 8 inches.

Hunt also investigated knob shapes that could be distinguished solely by touch. He classified the designs into three groups: multiple rotation knobs, fractional rotation knobs, and detent positioning (that is, where knob position is critical as, for example, a television channel selector dial where each position "clicks" into place). The sixteen knob designs developed are shown in Figure 16.

Work Area Limits.   Many tasks, such as assembly work, the operation of many types of machines, and much clerical work, are performed while the worker is seated or standing at a bench, table, or desk. Figure 17 shows maximum and normal work areas based on the actual measurement of people. Movements beyond the maximum work area require that the trunk of the body be moved. For repetitive operations, these trunk movements are fatiguing. Similar measurements have been made for the vertical plane; guides for locating materials, supplies, tools, and controls are available in three dimensions.

Chair and Table Heights.   Since there is so much manual and clerical activity, the height of chairs and tables is important. The two are closely related. Table height is commonly specified in relation to the elbow, so that adjustments in either chair or table height from the floor can be made to give greatest comfort to individual workers. A study by Ellis

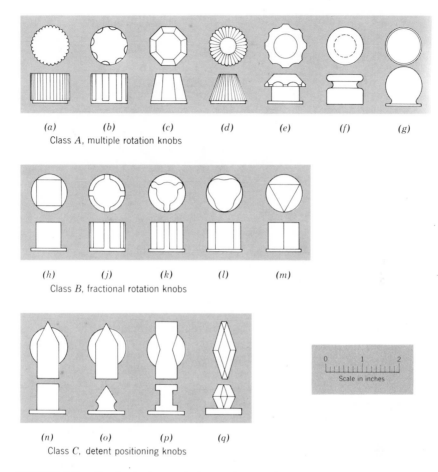

(a)   (b)   (c)   (d)   (e)   (f)   (g)

Class *A*, multiple rotation knobs

(h)   (j)   (k)   (l)   (m)

Class *B*, fractional rotation knobs

(n)   (o)   (p)   (q)

Class *C*, detent positioning knobs

FIGURE 16.   Knob designs of three classes that are seldom confused by touch. (Adapted from Hunt [11].)

[8] corroborates earlier estimates by Barnes [1] that the work surface height should be about three inches below the elbow. Actual work table and chair heights then depend on whether the setup is designed for sitting-standing or sitting only.

THE WORKING ENVIRONMENT

The working environment, which includes such factors as temperature, humidity, noise, and light, can produce marked effects on productivity, errors, quality levels, and employee acceptance, as well as on physio-

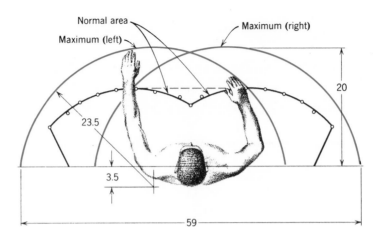

FIGURE 17. Dimensions in inches of maximum working areas in horizontal plane as proposed by Barnes, with normal work area proposed by Squires. (From [1] and [17].)

logical well-being. Therefore, we cannot measure the effectiveness of a job design without a knowledge of the working environment in which it will be placed. It is a part of the total picture.

Temperature, Humidity, and Air Flow

We have all experienced the fact that our feeling of comfort is not determined solely by the thermometer reading. If there is a breeze we feel cooler, even though the temperature has not changed. On a stifling day we have all heard the comment, "it isn't the heat, it's the humidity." The sensation of warmth or cold is affected by each of these factors, which have been combined into a single psychological scale called *effective temperature*. Effective temperature is the temperature of still, saturated (100 percent humidity) air, which gives the identical sensation of warmth or cold as the various combinations of air temperature, humidity, and air movement would. The American Society of Heating, Refrigerating and Air Conditioning Engineers (ASHRAE) Laboratory performed the experiments that led to the effective temperature scale. There is one factor that the effective temperature scale does not take into account. This is the temperature of objects in the environment which could radiate directly to the workers, such as furnaces.

The human body has automatic heat regulatory mechanisms that allow compensation for the environment over a certain effective temperature range. This compensation, of course, is also dependent on the activity level. Thus, a higher activity level can produce body comfort at a lower effective temperature.

Temperature and Humidity Effects on Performance.   Atmospheric conditions can have important effects on performance in both mental and physical tasks. Figure 18 shows, in summary form, the effects of various levels of effective temperature on performance for Morse code receiving and for weight lifting. For Morse code receiving, Figure 18a, the average number of errors goes up sharply as effective temperature goes beyond 90°F. For heavy work, represented by weight lifting in Figure 18b, the total accomplished work in foot-pounds begins to fall off rapidly above 80°F effective temperature.

Control of the Thermal Atmosphere.   Dr. L. A. Brouha, working at E. I. du Pont de Nemours, experimented with protective clothing for workers who must operate in very hot atmospheres such as near industrial furnaces. He found that simple protective clothing actually increased the heat stress. However, a ventilated suit, through which a

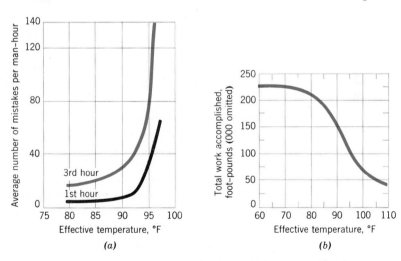

FIGURE 18.   (a) Relationship of effective temperature and average number of mistakes per man-hour in receiving Morse code. (From Mackworth [20].) (b) Foot-pounds of work performed by men under various effective temperatures. (From McCormick [14].)

continuous air flow was maintained, reduced the heat stress considerably.

Control for workers adjacent to hot areas such as furnaces, where heat radiation is the main problem, can be accomplished with shielding and by isolating the hot spot. General thermal control is accomplished through air conditioning but is not universally practiced. For most United States climates and working conditions, the zones of physiological compensation are effective, except for a few hot summer days. The most frequent use of air conditioning to date has been in offices to provide attractive working conditions and to help control clerical errors in warm weather. Of course, winter heating has long been accepted as necessary by business and industry for inside tasks.

Noise

Unwanted sound is commonly called noise. There is growing evidence that it can produce damaging effects, especially when workers are exposed to it over a period of years. Sounds of all kinds, including noise, consist of variations in atmospheric pressure that are propagated in waves similar to ripples on water. These variations in pressure are called *sound pressure*. We measure sound in decibels (db), but that measurement is not a measure of the pressure of sound. Rather, it is related to the ratio of the sound pressure of the source being measured to some reference sound pressure. Considerable confusion is possible here since more than one reference base is commonly used. Figure 19 helps to relate typical noise levels to the db scale. Another thing to note about noise measurements is that we must know something about the distribution of the sound energy over the range of tones, or frequencies, in order to know what will be the effects on man. Therefore, it is common to indicate the db levels in the various octave bands of frequencies.

Hearing Loss Due to Noise Exposure.   Some recent work in this general area has been done by the Research Center, Subcommittee on Noise in Industry, Los Angeles, California. Figure 20 shows comparative data for a container manufacturer and typical industrial exposure, plus data for the general population and a group termed *nonexposed* because the noise levels of their typical surroundings were very low. Here we see that hearing loss is characteristic of the general population, even of the nonexposed group, but the severity of loss depends on the intensity of exposure.

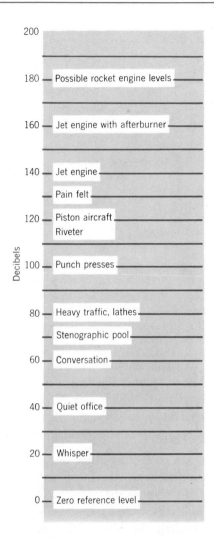

FIGURE 19. Decibel sound pressure levels of some typical noises.

Noise Effects on Work Performance. Industry, of course, has been interested in the possible direct effects that high noise levels may have on performance measures such as output, errors, and quality levels. In a number of studies on this subject, the general result was that if the injection of noise into the environment had any bad effects, they were temporary. We should note that good experimental design is difficult

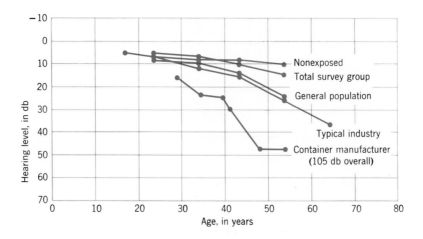

FIGURE 20.   Comparative hearing loss in relation to age for different groups. Zero is a reference base of average normal hearing. Readings show the power level required to reach the average level. Readings were taken at 2000 cycles (speech range). (Data courtesy of Research Center, Subcommittee on Noise in Industry, Los Angeles.)

in such situations because the experiments usually must go on over a period of time; it is difficult to know whether the results are attributable to noise effects or due to other changes which may have taken place during the same time interval. The one sure reaction is that higher noise levels are annoying, but human beings seem able to adapt to them.

Noise Control.   Noise control can be accomplished in different ways, depending on the nature of the problem. Acoustical engineers often control noise at its source, by redesigning the noise producing parts, by using vibration isolation mountings of equipment, or sometimes by isolating the source of noise through the construction of proper enclosures so that the amount of noise transmitted beyond the enclosures is reduced. In the latter method, a knowledge of the physics of sound transmission is important. The wrong enclosure design might transmit the noise with little or no loss or might even amplify it.

Other forms of control are baffles, sound absorbers, and acoustical wall materials. Sound absorbers can be installed near or above noise sources to help reduce noise levels. Acoustical wall materials can be used to reduce noise levels within a room by reducing reverberation, the reflection of the sound waves back and forth in the room. Of course, these wall materials have no effect on the original sound waves emanating from the source.

In severe noise situations, a properly fitted earplug can be effective. The maximum possible attenuation from earplugs is limited to about 50 db, because there are alternate paths to the eardrum through bone conduction. The more usual expected protection from earplugs would be an attenuation of 20 to 30 db.

Light

The conditions for seeing are important aspects of the working environment. However, no universally accepted standard for lighting is available, although there are recommended levels from many sources. Experimental data on illumination levels compared to some given criterion seem to indicate that many recommended standards are based on the view that "if 50 footcandles are good, then 100 footcandles of illumination are better." Part of the difficulty lies in the fact that various criteria have been used, such as visual acuity, blink rate, preference

TABLE III.   Levels of Illumination Recommended or Accepted by Tinker Based on Critical Levels as a Criterion

Task or Situation	Recommended or Accepted Illumination Level (footcandles)
Halls and stairways	5
Reception rooms and washrooms	10
Reading good-sized print (9 to 11 point) on good quality paper	10–15
School class rooms, shops, and offices	15
Typical home tasks	15
Reading newsprint	15–20
Reading handwriting and comparable tasks	20–30
School sewing and drafting rooms	25
General office work, private office work and mail rooms	25
Most severe visual tasks in home	25–30
Tasks comparable to discrimination of 6-point type	30–40
Most severe tasks encountered in workday situations	40–50
Accounting, bookkeeping, and drafting	50

From Tinker. [18].

ratings, and critical illumination levels. From a business and industrial viewpoint, critical illumination levels make the most sense, since they are essentially performance types of criteria. The critical level of illumination for a given task is that level beyond which there is practically no increase in performance for increases in illumination intensity. Thus, increases in intensity beyond these critical levels are assumed to be of no value. M. A. Tinker has constructed a table of recommended standards for different tasks based on the critical level criterion. Table III summarizes his recommendations.

Illumination Effects on Work Performance.   There have been many laboratory studies of the effect of illumination level on some measure of performance of a task. In general, there is a rapid improvement in performance as illumination levels increase to the critical level, at which point performance measures level off and further increases in illumination produce little or no improvement in performance.

In many actual work situations where illumination levels have been increased, records of output and quality before and after the changes have indicated substantial improvements. Some studies report that output went up 4 to 35 per cent.* We should be wary of this type of support data, however. In the complex set of conditions existing in a business or industrial environment, variables other than just the illumination level could very well have changed, such as work methods, product designs, control procedures, supervision, the weather, and the psychological climate. For example, in the famous Hawthorne studies at the Hawthorne Works, Western Electric Company, lighting values were increased for an experimental work group and performance went up. Someone thought to check on the result by lowering intensities. The employees cooperated again by lowering performance. But performance increased again when employees were told that the light intensity had been increased when actually it had been lowered, and then the smiles drained. It was finally realized that the employees were reacting to the psychological situation. They were experimental subjects, set aside from "ordinary" employees, and unconsciously were simply being very cooperative for those "nice experimenters." When the situation was understood, the direction of the study changed to an evaluation of factors in morale. Very little concerning illumination was learned.

*For a summary of these studies, see [14].

Glare Effects.   Glare can reduce the effectiveness of the illumination provided. Glare is produced by some bright spot in the visual field, such as a bright light or reflected light from a polished surface, and can cause discomfort as well as reduce visual effectiveness. This reduction in visual effectiveness is summarized by Figure 21. Figure 21, based on experimental results, shows that the effects of glare become acute when the sources are close to the line of sight.

Glare effects can be reduced by moving light sources where possible, by diffusing light sources that cannot be moved, or by increasing the general illumination level of the surroundings so that the brightness contrast between the glare source and the surroundings is reduced. Reflection surfaces may sometimes be moved in relation to workplaces or changed so that the surface diffuses light.

Criteria for the Lighting Environment.   There is little doubt that it is worthwhile to provide at least the general critical levels of illumina-

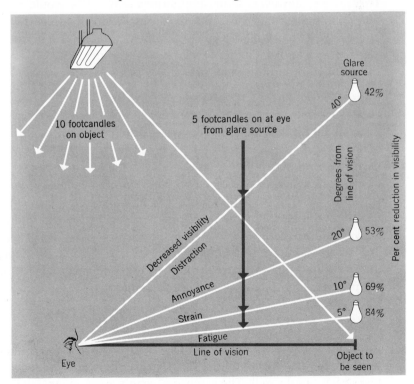

FIGURE 21.   Glare becomes worse as it comes closer to the direct line of vision. (From Luckiesh [13].)

tion. Although there is little evidence of any changes in performance above the critical levels, these levels may be exceeded without any known bad effects in order to allow for a margin of error. This idea seems to represent current practical philosophies. General illumination levels that are more than adequate are provided and the problem is forgotten. Often missed, however, is the need for special lights for fine detailed work and the elimination of glare.

Contaminants and Hazards in the Working Environment

A large number of fumes, dusts, gases, liquids, and solids have proved harmful to workers. These, together with the general mechanical hazards from machine moving parts, traffic from material, transportation, falling objects, etc., from a part of the working environment.

Noxious Substances. The number of industrial poisons is tremendous. Fortunately, however, in most situations only a few would be present and potentially dangerous. Industrial medicine is a special field which concerns itself with the diagnosis, treatment, and control of the noxious substances. Maximum allowable concentrations (MAC) have been determined for most of these substances as a basis for proper control.

Control Procedures. Control procedures vary greatly because of the great variation of possible contaminants and their characteristics. In general, the control of the emissions of these substances in manufacturing processes poses engineering problems. Protection of workmen may require exhaust systems to collect dusts, gases, and vapors in order to maintain concentrations below MAC. Personal protective gear, such as respirators and gas masks, supplement exhaust systems. Other protective clothing, such as rubber aprons, coats, gloves, boots, and goggles, is available for various jobs which involve the handling of chemicals and where the unprotected skin may leave the employee exposed to injury. In addition, vigilance through careful explanation of safe operating procedures and safety programs is common.

SUMMARY

Men and machines perform similar basic functions in accomplishing work; however, their abilities are sharply divergent in the nature of tasks each can do well. The essence of man's great advantage lies in his flexibility, whereas machines can perform consistently. In general, man's role in man-machine systems falls into three main classes: as a power source and controller in manual systems, as a controller of semi-automatic systems, and as a monitor of automatic systems.

Figure 4 is an excellent general representation of the man-machine cycle representing information input, data processing and decision, manual activity and control functions and action, all imbedded in the working environment. Experimentalists have amassed a great deal of data concerning man in relation to machines which has value in designing man-machine systems. These data and modes of analysis become important inputs to the job methods phase of job design.

KEY CONCEPTS

Man's Capabilities Relative to Machines.   It is important to understand the kinds of activities for which man has a competitive advantage over machines and vice versa. While the balance of economic factors determines when substitutions are made, man's inherent capabilities should indicate the trends.

Job Design.   Present-day concepts of job design are fairly new, especially in their emphasis on worker satisfaction as one of the important criteria. From one point of view the concept of job design can be seen as the determination of job content on the one hand and job methods on the other. The broader point of view in currency today, however, would place emphasis on the design of the entire system of jobs in the social setting and so we hear reference to the design of sociotechnical systems.

Man and Machine Utilization.   The concepts of man-machine utilization are based on the analysis and timing of the relationships of required activities with the objective of finding combinations which maximize utilization. This view of the organization of work is dedicated to the principle that there is one best way to perform the required tasks.

Machine and Work Place Design Principle.   The philosophy of machine and work place design from the point of view of the limitations and capabilities of man is based on the objective that such designs should accommodate as broad a cross section of the working population as possible. This is in contrast to an opposing philosophy which requires the selection of people with very special capabilities (physical strength, large or small physical size, visual acuity, etc.) in order to match demanding requirements of the machine or work place design.

IMPORTANT TERMS

Numbers in parentheses indicate page numbers.

1. Activity chart (349, 350)
2. Activity classification (352)
3. Automatic systems (340)
4. Effective temperature (362)
5. Glare (369)
6. Information display (343)
7. Job content (331–332)
8. Job enlargement (332)
9. Job methods (334)
10. Manual systems (340)
11. Micromotion analysis (349)
12. Operation chart (347, 348)
13. Principles of motion economy (347–348)
14. Semiautomatic systems (340)
15. Sound pressure (364)
16. Visual display (343)
17. Work area limits (360)

REVIEW QUESTIONS

Numbers in parentheses indicate page numbers.

1. What kinds of functions can man perform in the work situation? (336)
2. Compare man's capabilities with those of known machines. (336–337)
3. Differentiate man's role in the three typical man-machine systems. (340–341)
4. Describe the man-machine cycle for semiautomatic operations. (340–341)
5. What is the difference between direct and indirect sensing? (343)
6. What are the various ways that visual and auditory information can be coded? (359)
7. Which dial shape is easiest to read? (344–345)
8. Summarize the general guides for dial design in terms of size, position of markers, distance between markers, etc. (344–345)
9. When there is a bank of dials to read how should they be oriented? (345)
10. Can a flow process chart be made for the activities of a man as well as the processing of a part or product? (349)
11. What sort of analytical tool might be used to show working relationships between an operator and the machine he is using? What information is necessary for the development of such a tool? (349)
12. What information is contained in an operation chart? (347)
13. Under what conditions would micromotion analysis be justified? (349)
14. What is an activity chart and what is its field of application? (349)
15. Is it always best to have one worker operating more than one machine? (351)

16.   What are the principles of motion economy and how are they used in the design of manual activities? (347–348)

17.   What modes of analysis are appropriate for activities which have no set repetitive pattern? How can the data be gathered? (352–353)

18.   How can the data shown in Table II be useful in the design of levers as control mechanisms? (357)

19.   What sort of information is available concerning the speed and accuracy of positioning elements? (356–358)

20.   What is the optimum ratio of pointer movement to each turn of the knob when making a setting? (359)

21.   What kinds of guides to design are available for the coding of controls by color, size, shape, or location? (359)

22.   What is effective temperature? (362)

23.   Does elevated effective temperature have an effect on good performance for heavy work? For very light work? (363)

24.   What kinds of control measures are available for the thermal environment? (364)

25.   What effects on work performance are produced by noise? What health effects?   (364–366)

26.   How can noise be controlled? (366–367)

27.   What is the critical illumination for a given task? (368)

28.   What are glare effects and how can they be controlled? (369)

29.   What is MAC? (370)

30.   What kinds of control procedures are used for industrial poisons and contaminants?   (370)

SELF-TEST TRUE-FALSE QUESTIONS

Numbers in parentheses indicate page numbers.

1.   Man is the dominant element in job design. (332)

2.   In performing work, man's functions are in the three general classifications, receiving information, making decisions, and taking action based on decisions. (336)

3.   The advantage possessed by man in comparison to machines in the performance of work lies in his tremendous range of cpabilities. (336)

4.   Human beings appear to surpass existing machines in their ability to detect small amounts of light and sound. (337)

5.   Existing machines appear to surpass human beings in their ability to store large amounts of information for long periods and recall relevant facts at the appropriate time. (337)

6.   Existing machines appear to surpass humans in their ability to apply great force smoothly and precisely. (337)

7. Existing machines appear to surpass human beings in their ability to perform many different functions simultaneously. (337)
8. Human beings appear to surpass existing machines in their ability to store information briefly and then erase it completely. (337)
9. Low cost labor in relation to the cost of capital may dictate an economic decision to use manual labor in many tasks for which man is fundamentally not well suited. (337)
10. In job design it is common to consider a large number of alternatives of job content before proceeding to the determination of job methods. (332)
11. In the past the main guide for determining job content has been division of labor. (332)
12. The usual measures of effectiveness in job and methods design are physical and psychological fatigue, and worker acceptance, with an economic criterion being effective insofar as it agrees with these major criteria. (333)
13. "Simo" charts are used to analyze the methods for a specific operation involving a man, a crew, or a man-machine system. (349)
14. An operation process chart shows the relationships indicated by an assembly chart as well as a listing of the productive operations required. (347)
15. A flow process chart is sometimes called a "gozinto" chart. (349)
16. The flow process chart focuses on the nonproductive activity as well as the productive activities. (349)
17. In analyzing a flow process chart, the first objective is to combine operations where possible, but if this cannot be done, we attempt to eliminate steps in the process that cannot be justified or steps which are duplicated elsewhere. (349)
18. An operation chart is commonly used to analyze repetitive short-cycle tasks where production volume is low to moderate. (347)
19. Man flow process charts and activity charts are commonly used to analyze repetitive short-cycle tasks where very high production volumes exist. (349)
20. Man-machine charts are particularly useful to help obtain maximum utilization of men and machines. (349)
21. Work sampling is a useful technique for obtaining data for activity classification. (352)
22. It has been shown that positioning elements that require visual control require about the same amount of time as elements which utilize some kind of mechanical guide or stop to establish the exact final desired position of the part or hand. (356)
23. Experiments on positioning indicate that speed and accuracy are best when movement is to the right instead of to the left. (357–358)
24. Experiments have shown that the time to make a setting on a dial was

minimized when there were two inches of pointer movement for each revolution of the knob. (358–359)

25. Experiments have shown that the round dial shape minimizes the number of incorrect readings. (344–345)

26. When there is a bank of dials to be read, it helps to orient them all in a pattern so that normal readings are in the 9 o'clock or 12 o'clock positions. (345)

27. In coding controls, color, shape, and location seem to be important but the size of the knob was found to be unimportant. (359)

28. The effective temperature scale is the temperature of still, saturated (100% humidity) air, which gives the identical sensation of warmth or cold as the various combinations of air temperature, humidity, radiation, and air movement would give. (362)

29. Tolerance for high effective temperatures is greater for light work than it is for heavy muscular work. (363)

30. Even though there is a physiological cost of high effective temperatures, there is very little, if any, effect on performance. (363)

31. Brouha found that for extreme exposure conditions of effective temperature, simple protective clothing actually increased the heat stress. (363)

32. Brouha found that for extreme conditions of exposure to effective temperature a ventilated suit through which a continuous air flow was maintained was very little better than simple protective clothing. (363–364)

33. Control of the thermal environment for workers adjacent to hot areas, such as furnaces, where heat radiation is the main problem, can be accomplished with shielding and by isolating the hot spot. (364)

34. It has been shown that hearing loss is a function of age and depends very little on the nature of the exposure to noise. (364)

35. Even though hearing loss from exposure to noise does not seem to be an important factor, industry has a considerable interest in noise abatement because of the drastic effects on work performance. (365)

36. When attempting to control noise by isolating its source through the construction of enclosures, the wrong enclosure design might transmit the noise with little or no loss, or might even amplify it. (366–367)

37. Reverberation is the reflection of sound waves back and forth in a room. (366)

38. The maximum possible noise attenuation resulting from the use of ear plugs is limited to about 50 db because there are alternate paths to the ear drum through bone conduction. (367)

39. The critical level of illumination for a given task is that level beyond which there is practically no increase in performance for increases in illumination intensity. (368)

40. In general, there is a rapid improvement in performance as illumination

levels increase to the critical level, at which point performance measures level off and further increases in illumination produce little or no improvement in performance. (368)

41.   The effects of a glare source become worse as the source comes closer to the direct line of vision. (369)

PROBLEMS

1.   Consider the following list of jobs that occur commonly in our economy. To what extent has the job content been determined by technology? To what extent is there considerable freedom in designing the job in question?

Auto assembly line worker

Computer room operator

Executive secretary

Machinist

Oil refinery operator

Supervisor of an assembly line

Truck driver

Typist

2.   Classify the eight jobs listed in problem 1 as manual, semiautomatic, and automatic. To what extent do you feel that it is likely that the job you have classified as manual will become semiautomatic, and those classified as semiautomatic will become automatic because of technological advance? What limits this movement in each case?

3.   In terms of your perception of the activities of the jobs listed in problem 1, what kinds of activities does the human being perform that could be done better by machines, according to the list on p. 337?

4.   Construct an operation chart for the assembly of some simple device such as a ball-point pen, a chair caster, or a pair of scissors.

5.   A custom machining company has received an order for a lot of 10,000 parts which requires a simple milling operation for which the company has available capacity. Plans are now being made for the method of operation to be used. Work will begin next week, the promised delivery date being 13 weeks from the first of next week. The plant works one shift, 40 hours per week,

with up to 20 percent overtime possible. The company normally attempts to obtain better labor utilization on relatively large orders like this one by having one worker operate more than one machine when it is feasible with the established layout and by investing in special jigs and fixtures to speed up unloading and loading of the machine.

The layout of the milling machine area and the automatic machining cycle for the required operation permit an operator to unload and load a machine, start the machine on its automatic cycle, and then proceed to the next machine, giving it the required attention when it has completed its machining cycle, and so on. The machines will automatically turn off when the normal machining cycle has been completed. From previous records of similar orders and from standard data on machining times for specified materials and lengths of cut, the following estimates of times for the job elements have been assembled:

Load part in machine	1.00 minute
Machine part (automatic)	5.00 minutes
Unload part from machine	0.50 minute
Inspect part	0.75 minute
Walk from machine to machine	0.25 minute

After feasible man-machine cycles have been assembled using the foregoing data, the company follows the practice of adding 10 per cent to the total cycle to obtain a standard time for the job to be used in cost calculations. The 10 per cent allowance is for rest, delay, and other personal needs. Construct activity charts for one operator running one, two, three, and four machines.

6. Using the data of problem 5 and the following costs:

Milling machine operator's rate	$3.00/hour
Machine variable cost (power, cutting	
fluids, etc.)	1.00/hour
Material	1.50/piece
Tooling (special holding fixtures)	300/setup
Labor cost to set up machine	100/setup

(a) Determine the method of operation which would minimize costs by developing a table of pertinent costs for the lot of 10,000 parts for systems where a worker operates one, two, three, and four machines. Which mode of operation would you choose and why?

(b) What kinds of costs do you think may have been ignored in the statement of the problem? Are any of the costs given as irrelevant data?

There are up to four machines available; the department supervisor says that he could assign as many as three men to the job.

7.   A young couple has started a launderette. Their business, The Blue Monday Launderette, offers the following services:
(a) Washers for use by customers.
(b) Drying service for customers' washes.
(c) Dry cleaning and finished laundry.
(d) Washing and fluff drying.
     The husband performs the "fluff dry" work (washing, extracting, and fluff drying). The wife handles all other matters such as dealing with customers and aiding people who do their own washing. She also folds and bundles the "fluff dry" work during slack periods in the day.
     The "fluff dry" business has been unusually heavy and the couple has been forced to work evenings to get work out on time. It is their contention that five washers, if kept busy, can do the "fluff dry" work. But there are so many other things to be done, such as semidrying the wet clothes in the extractor and loading and unloading the dryer, that one person simply cannot keep the washers loaded. The wife does not have time to assist the husband during normal working hours.
     The following times are required to perform the various tasks:

	Time (minutes)
Washer (five available for "fluff dry")	
Load soiled clothes and soap, set water temperature, start machine	2
Running time (automatically stops)	40
Unload wet clothes into cart	2
Extractor (one available for "fluff dry"; each holds only one washer load)	
Load wet clothes, start machine	2
Running time (automatically stops)	5
Unload semidry clothes into cart	2
Dryer (two available for "fluff dry" each holds only one washer load)	
Untangle and load clothes, start machine	3
Running time (automatically stops)	20
Unload dry clothes into cart	2
Miscellaneous	
Travel times between equipment	Negligible

(a) With the data given, construct an activity chart for the best method of co-ordinating the work of one man, five washers, one extractor, and two dryers.
(b) What is the overall cycle time (time difference between identical points in the process) such as loading washer No. 1 on consecutive loads?

8.   A company is constructing a parking lot for which dump trucks and a power shovel are the primary equipment being used. Time studies reveal the following average times:

Time to load a truck	7.50 minutes
Travel time to dump point	9.00 minutes
Dumping time	2.00 minutes
Return time	7.00 minutes

(a) How many trucks are required to move dirt as rapidly as possible?

(b) If it cost $19 per hour for the shovel and operator and $12 per hour for each truck and driver, what number of trucks will minimize idle equipment cost?

(c) Construct a multiple-activity chart for the answer to (b).

9.   A company has decided to plate its own bushings rather than have them done elsewhere. Under their newly developed process, a single operator performs the entire process:

(1) A tumbler to remove burrs, etc.

(2) A degreasing tank to remove oil.

(3) Two plating tanks.

Loads consist of 250 bushings each with all equipment starting by the operator's push of a button and shutting off automatically. Therefore, the equipment does not require the operator's attention while running. The times required to perform the various operations are as follows:

Load tumbler	5 minutes
Running time for tumbler	24 minutes
Unload tumbler	6 minutes
Load degreaser	3 minutes
Degreaser running time	36 minutes
Unload degreaser	6 minutes
Load plating tank	6 minutes
Plating process time	60 minutes
Unload plating tank	6 minutes

(a) How many minutes does it take to complete one full cycle?

(b) How much of the total idle time of each plating tank is unnecessary?

(c) If the running time of the limiting process is reduced 25 per cent by equipment redesign, what is the new cycle time in minutes?

10.   A moonshine company utilizes one man and several pieces of automated equipment (blender, ager, and bottler) to produce their product. The process and associated times are as follows:

Blending:

Put in ingredients	6 minutes
Blending cycle	25 minutes
Remove blend, put in crock	4 minutes

Aging:

Put blend in aging tank	2 minutes
Aging cycle	26 minutes
Remove and filter into crock	10 minutes

Bottling:

Filter blend into bottling machine	7 minutes
Bottling cycle	15 minutes
Remove cans, pack in case	12 minutes

(a) What is the cycle time?

(b) What percentage of the time is the blender idle?

REFERENCES

[1] Barnes, R. M. *Motion and Time Study: Design and Measurement of Work* (6th ed.). John Wiley, New York, 1968.

[2] Barnes, R. M., and M. E. Mundel. *A Study of Simultaneous Symmetrical Hand Motions.* University of Iowa Studies in Engineering, Bulletin 17, 1939.

[3] Briggs, S. J. "A Study in the Design of Work Areas." Unpublished Ph.D. Dissertation, Purdue University, Lafayette, Ind., Aug. 1955.

[4] Chapanis, A. "Studies of Manual Rotary Positioning Movements: I. The Precision of Setting an Indicator Knob to Various Angular Positions." *Journal of Psychology*, **31**, 51–64, 1951.

[5] Chapanis, A., W. R. Garner, and C. T. Morgan. *Applied Experimental Psychology.* John Wiley, New York, 1949.

[6] Davis, L. E. "Human Factors in Design of Manual Machine Controls." *Mechanical Enginrering*, **71**, 811–816, Oct. 1949.

[7] Davis, L. E., "Toward a Theory of Job Design," *Journal of Industrial Engineering*, **8** (5), 305–309, Sept.–Oct. 1957.

[8] Ellis, D. S. "Speed of Manipulative Performance as a Function of Work-Surface Height." *Journal of Applied Psychology*, **35**, 289–296, 1951.

[9] Fogel, L. J. *Biotechnology: Concepts and Applications.* Prentice-Hall, Englewood Cliffs, N.J., 1963.

[10] Hunsicker, P. A. *Arm Strength at Selected Degrees of Elbow Flexion.* USAF, Wright Air Development Center, Technical Report 54–548, Aug. 1955.

[11] Hunt, D. P. *The Coding of Aircraft Controls.* USAF, Wright Air Development Center, Technical Report 53–221, Aug. 1953.

[12] Jenkins, W. L., and N. B. Connor. "Some Design Factors in Making Settings on a Linear Scale." *Journal of Applied Psychology*, **33**, 395–409, 1949.

[13] Luckiesh, M. *Light, Vision, and Seeing*. D. Van Nostrand, Princeton, N.J., 1944.

[14] McCormick, E. J. *Human Factors Engineering* (3rd ed.). McGraw-Hill, New York, 1970.

[15] Meister, D., and G. F. Rabideau. *Human Factors Evaluation in System Development*. John Wiley, New York, 1965.

[16] Sleight, R. B. "The Effect of Instrument Dial Shape on Legibility." *Journal of Applied Psychology*, **32**, 170–188, 1948.

[17] Squires, P. C. *The Shape of the Normal Work Area*. Navy Department, Bureau of Medicine and Surgery, Medical Research Laboratory, New London, Conn., Report 275, July 23, 1956.

[18] Tinker, M. A. "Trends in Illumination Standards." *Transactions of the American Academy of Opthalmology and Otolaryngology*, 382–394, Mar.–Apr. 1949.

CONTENTS

CHAPTER 12
PRODUCTION STANDARDS AND WORK MEASUREMENT

What is a "fair day's work"? A production standard is an answer to the question, and the field of work measurement provides methodology and a rationale for determining a fair day's work for different jobs. Production standards state how many parts, assemblies, etc., should be produced per minute, hour, or day, or they indicate the amount of time allowed as standard for producing a unit of work. Whether standards are expressed in terms of pieces per unit or time per piece is quite irrelevant; however, they are often called "time standards" when expressed in time units. Although production standards are designed to determine how much output is expected of an employee, they include more than just work. Actually, production standards include standard allowances for rest, delays that occur as part of the job, time for personal needs, and, where the work is heavy, an allowance for physical fatigue. You can see that the problems of measuring work and setting up good standards of performance that are consistent from job to job are difficult. So why go to the trouble of setting them up? Why are standards important?

PRODUCTION STANDARDS

Data Provided

Production standards provide data that are basic to many decision-making problems in production. The production standard is of critical importance because labor cost is a predominant factor, influencing many decisions that must be made. For example, decisions to make or buy, to replace equipment, or to select certain manufacturing processes require estimates of labor costs, as well as estimates of other costs. These decisions necessarily require an estimate of how much output can be expected per unit of time.

Production standards also provide basic data used in the day-to-day operation of a plant. For example, scheduling or loading machines demands a knowledge of the projected time requirements for the various orders. For custom manufacture, we must be able to give potential customers a bid price and delivery date. The bid price is ordinarily based on expected costs for labor, materials, and overhead, plus profit. Labor cost is commonly the largest single component in such situations. To estimate labor cost requires an estimate of how long it will take to perform the various operations.

Finally, production standards provide the basis for labor cost control. By measuring worker performance in comparison to standard performance, indexes can be computed for individual workers, whole departments, divisions, or even plants. These indexes make it possible to compare performance on completely different kinds of jobs. Standard labor-costing systems and incentive wage payment systems are based on production standards. Production standards are useful in so many ways in both the design and the operation and control of production systems that we must regard them as truly basic data.

Informal Standards

The plain fact is that every organization has production standards of sorts. Even when they seem not to exist formally, foremen and supervisors have standards in mind for the various jobs that come under their supervision based on their knowledge of the work and past performances. These types of standards are informal. They can be formalized merely by writing them down and recognizing them as the standards of performance expected. Standards based on foremen's estimates and past performance data have weaknesses, however. First of all, in almost all such situations, methods of work performance have not been standardized. Therefore it is difficult to state what production rate, based on past records, is appropriate, because past performance may have been based on various methods. Since it has been demonstrated that production rates depend heavily on job methods, standards based on past performance records might not be too dependable. A second major defect in standards based on estimates and past performance records is that they are likely to be too strongly influenced by the working speeds of the individuals who held the jobs during the periods of the available records. Were those workers high or low performers?

The Core of the Work Measurement Problem

We wish to set up production standards that are applicable to the industrial population, not just to a few selected people within that population. Our production standards problem is comparable in some ways to that of designing a lever with the proper mechanical advantage to match the capabilities of man. But not just any man; the force required to pull the lever should accommodate perhaps 95 to 99 percent of the population, so that anyone who comes to the job will have the necessary arm strength. If the lever requires a man with superhuman strength, we would have to seek out only these people for the job. Recall from Chapter 11 that the section on strength and forces of body movements dealt with this problem.

The production standard that we wish to set up actually requires a knowledge of the distribution of performance times (or production rates) for the entire working population doing the job for which we are setting up a standard. Suppose that we have 500 people all doing an identical task, make sample studies on all of them, and plot the data. Figure 1 shows the results of just such a study. The distribution shows that average performance time varies from 0.28 minute to 0.63 minute per piece. Obviously, if our past records reflected data from one or more individuals taken at random from our population of 500, a standard based on their performance might not fit the whole population very well. On the other hand, if we know the entire distribution, as in Figure 1, we can set up standards that probably would accommodate everyone who might come to the job. One way to do this is to follow a procedure similar to that used in job design when drawing on anthropometric data. Set the standard so that it accommodates about 95 percent of the population. For Figure 1, a standard performance time of about 0.48 minute is one which about 95 percent of the individuals exceeded. If we pegged the standard at this level, we would expect that practically all employees on the job should be able to meet or exceed the standard.

Some industrial managers feel that it is not good to quote minimum performance standards such as these for fear that they will encourage relatively poor performance as acceptable. These people prefer to say that the standard performance is about the average of the distribution (0.395 minute for Figure 1) and expect that most workers will produce about standard, that some will fall below, and that some will exceed standard. Both systems of quoting standards are used, although the practice of quoting *minimum acceptable values* is more common than that of quoting average values.

To this point we have been discussing only the work time. The distri-

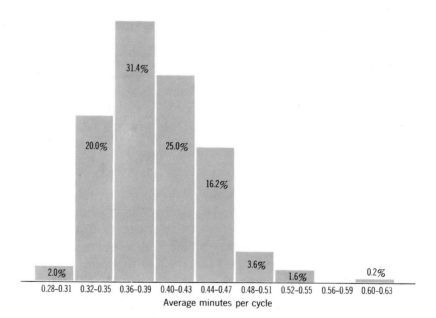

FIGURE 1. Percentage distribution of the performance of 500 people performing a wood block positioning task. About 5.4 percent of the people averaged 0.48 minute per cycle or longer. (Adapted from Barnes [3].)

bution of Figure 1 shows how long it took on the average to perform the task. Using the minimum acceptable level as our basic standard of performance, we shall call the actual work time at that level the *normal time*. The normal time for the data of Figure 1 is 0.48 minute; the total standard time is then:

> Normal time + standard allowance for personal time
> + allowance for measured delays normal to the job
> + fatigue allowance

We shall discuss the several allowances later, but the central question now is: "How do we determine normal time in the usual situation when only one or a few workers are on the job?" Seldom would we find a large number of workers doing the same job, so usually we cannot build up a distribution. Without knowledge of the distribution, how can we pick out the level which about 95 percent of the workers could meet or exceed, that is, normal time? The approach to this problem used in industry is called performance rating.

Performance Rating

Performance rating is a critically important part of any formal means of work measurement. To be able to rate accurately requires considerable experience. It works something like this. A pace or performance level is selected as standard. An analyst observes this pace, compares it with various other paces, and learns to judge pace level in percent of the standard pace. For Figure 1 we called the cycle time of 0.48 minute "normal," and the pace or rate of output associated with this time is normal pace. A pace of work that is 25 percent faster would require proportionately less time per cycle, of $0.48/1.26 = 0.381$ minute. If a skilled analyst observed a worker performing the task on which Figure 1 is based and he rated performance at 125 percent of normal while simultaneously measuring the actual average performance time as 0.381 minute, he would have to add 25 percent to his observed time to adjust it to the normal level. In this instance, his performance rating is perfect, according to our distribution, since $0.381 \times 1.25 = 0.48$. Other perfect combinations of rating and actual observed time are 150 percent and 0.32 minute, 175 percent and 0.274 minute, 90 percent and 0.533 minute, etc.

In an actual work measurement situation, of course, the analyst does not have the answer beforehand, so he simultaneously observes the actual time taken to do the task and rates the performance. The normal time is then computed as:

$$\text{Normal time} = \text{Actual observed time} \times \frac{\text{Performance rating}}{100}$$

All of the formal work measurement systems involve this rating or judgment of working pace or some equivalent procedure. Alternate methods of actually measuring time and determining normal time will be considered later in the chapter.

Rating as a System of Measurement.   What do we need in order to be able to measure something, whether it be the length of a line the pressure inside a vessel, or the pace at which a man is working? It is really quite simple. We need basically two things:

1.   A standard for comparison which is accepted.
2.   A unit of measurement or a scale.

Both may be set arbitrarily. For example, in linear measurement (the measurement of length) our basic standard has been a platinum-iridium bar held in the Bureau of Standards in Washington, D. C., which, in turn, is based on the international standard. Two scales are commonly used, based on two different ways of dividing up the bar. One is the English system (yards, feet, inches) and the other the metric system (meters, centimeters, millimeters). Any number of other scales could be based on the same basic standard. Also, any number of other bar lengths could serve as basic standards of length on which to base the scales. The thing that makes our present basic standard and the two common scales valuable measurement systems is that they have received general acceptance.

Does the use of these systems of measure then involve judgment? Yes, even the use of the best precision measuring instruments involves some judgment. (See Chapter 19, "Control of Quality," for a study of inspectors' use of various precision measuring instruments.) In using a micrometer, for example, one must judge how tightly to turn down the spindle, and the importance of this "feel" cannot be minimized.

Let us consider performance rating in the same general light. Are there basic standards of reference that have general acceptance? Yes, there are motion picture films of operations in many types of occupations which show "normal paces" for those tasks as well as faster and slower paces. One set of such films was made by the Society for Advancement of Management (SAM) and consists of 24 factory and clerical operations which were rated by thousands of experienced time study analysts throughout the country. Walking at 3 miles per hour has been selected as "normal pace." Many organizations, such as Deere and Company, General Motors, and Caterpillar Tractor Company, have their own standards in the forms of films of various operations throughout their plants, which exhibit normal and other paces of work. These film standards do not enjoy the same degree of acceptance as do the physical standards of weights and measures, but they exist. Analysts can use them to recalibrate their judgment and to train people in performance rating.

Now to the question of scales. There are, unfortunately, three scales in common use, and this fact is often the source of some confusion. Figure 2 shows these scales in relation to the basic standards of walking at 3 miles per hour, etc. Scale A, the most common, is the scale which we shall

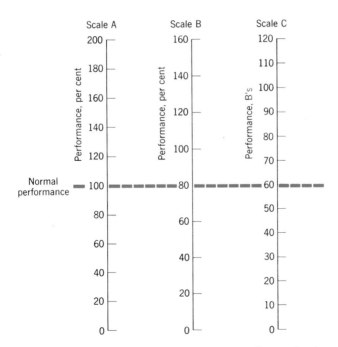

FIGURE 2.   Three alternate performance rating scales in relation to normal performance.

assume throughout this book where work standards are mentioned. It labels "normal pace" as 100 percent. Scale B provides maximum confusion by labeling a much higher level of performance as 100 percent. We can convert easily between the two scales by recognizing that 125 percent on scale A is the same performance level as 100 percent on scale B. Scale B is used by organizations who wish to quote standards at a higher level. (See our discussion on pages 385–387 of performance distributions.) Scale C is in points instead of percent, and it is often called the Bedaux scale. On the Bedaux scale, 60 points are equivalent to 100 percent performance on scale A.

How Accurate Is Performance Rating?   In the actual work measurement situation, it is necessary to compare our mental image of "normal performance" with what is observed and to record our rating of the performance. This rating enters the computation of production standards as a factor and the final standard can be no more accurate than the rating. How accurately can experienced people rate? Commonly accepted figures would be ±5 percent. Controlled studies in which films have been rated indicate a standard deviation of 7 to 10 percent. In other words, experienced people probably hold these limits about 68 percent of the time. Therefore, the effect of the element of judgement in current work measurement practice is considerable. This fact is important in all of the uses of production standards which we discussed at the beginning of this chapter. Nonetheless, standards developed by measurement (including the rating) are better than standards based simply on past records, because they specify a given work method and they correct for the working pace of the employee observed. A standard based on past records only could easily be off 200 to 300 percent for these reasons, and ±7 to 10 percent is modest by comparison.

WORK MEASUREMENT SYSTEMS

All practical work measurement systems involve: (a) the measurement of actual observed time and (b) the adjustment of observed time to obtain "normal time" by means of performance rating. The alternate systems which we shall discuss combine these factors in somewhat different ways.

Stopwatch Methods

By far the most prevalent approach to work measurement currently used involves a stopwatch time study and simultaneous performance rating of the operation to determine normal time. The general procedure is as follows:

1. Standardize methods for the operation; that is, determine the standard method, specifying workplace layout, tools, sequence of elements, etc. Record the resulting standard practice.

2. Select the operator for study, experienced and trained in the standard methods.

3. Determine elemental structure of operation for timing purposes. This may involve a breakdown of the operation into elements and the separation of the elements that occur each cycle from those that occur only periodically or randomly. For example, tool sharpening might be required each 100 cycles to maintain quality limits. Machine adjustments might occur at random intervals.

4. Observe and record the actual time required for the elements, making simultaneous performance ratings.

5. Determine the number of observations required to yield the desired precision of the result based on the sample data obtained in step 4. Obtain more data as required.

6. Compute normal time = averaged observed actual time × average rating factor/100.

7. Determine allowances for personal time, delays, and fatigue.

8. Determine standard time = normal times for elements + time for allowances.

Breakdown of Elements.   Common practice is to divide the total operation into elements rather than to observe the entire cycle as a whole. There are several reasons why this practice is followed:

1. The element breakdown helps to describe the operation in some detail indicating the step-by-step procedure followed during the study.

2. More information is obtained which may have valuable use for comparing times for like elements on different jobs and for building up a handbook of standard data times for common elements in job families. With standard data for elements, cycle times for new sizes can be forecast without additional study.

3. A worker's performance level may vary in different parts of the cycle. With an element breakdown, different performance ratings can be assigned to different elements where the overall cycle is long enough to permit separate evaluation of performance.

In breaking an operation into elements, it is common practice to make elements a logical component of the overall cycle, as illustrated in Figure 3. For example, element 1, "pick up piece and place in jig," is a fairly homogeneous task. Note that element 4, "drill $\frac{1}{4}$-inch hole," is the machining element, following the general practice to separate machining time from handling time. Finally, constant elements usually are separated from elements that might vary with size, weight, or some other parameter.

Taking and Recording Data.   Figure 3 is a sample study where 20 cycles were timed by the continuous method; that is, the stopwatch is allowed to run continuously, being read at the breakpoints between elements. Elapsed times for elements are then obtained by successive subtraction. *Repetitive* or "snap-back" methods of reading the watch are also common. In repetitive timing, the observer reads the watch at the end of each element and snaps the hand back to zero so that each reading gives the actual time without the necessity of subtraction. Comparative studies indicate that the two methods are equally accurate.

Note the other data recorded in Figure 3 that identify the part, operation, operator, material, etc., as well as check data of elapsed time of the study, and the number of completed units. The "selected times" represent averages of the element times; the cycle "selected time" is merely the sum of the element averages. A single performance rating of 100 percent was made for the study and a 5 percent allowance added to obtain the standard time of 1.17 minutes per piece.

Adequacy of Sample Size.   Considering the work measurement problem from the viewpoint of statistics, we are attempting to estimate, from the sample times and performance ratings observed, a normal time of performance. The precision desired will determine how many observations will be required. For example, if we wanted to be 95 percent sure that the resulting answer, based on the sample, was within ± 5 percent, we would calculate the sample size n required from a knowledge of the mean and standard deviation of our sample data. If we wanted greater confidence or closer precision, the sample size would have to be larger.

Figure 4 is a convenient chart for estimating required sample sizes to maintain a ± 5 percent precision in the answer for 95 and 99 percent confidence levels. To use the chart, we merely calculate the mean value $\bar{x}$ and the standard deviation based on the sample data. The "coefficient of variation" is simply the percentage variation, $100(s_x/\bar{x})$. The chart is entered with the calculated coefficient of variation, and the sample

OBSERVATION SHEET

SHEET 1 OF 1 SHEETS	DATE
OPERATION Drill ¼"Hole	OP. NO. D-20
PART NAME Motor Shaft	PART NO. MS-267
MACHINE NAME Avey	MACH. NO. 2174
OPERATOR'S NAME & NO. S.K. Adams 1347	MALE [✓] FEMALE [ ]
EXPERIENCE ON JOB 18 Mo. on Sens. Drill	MATERIAL S.A.E. 2315
FOREMAN H. Miller	DEPT. NO. DL 21

BEGIN 10:15	FINISH 10:38	ELAPSED 23	UNITS FINISHED 20	ACTUAL TIME PER 100 115	NO. MACHINES OPERATED 1

ELEMENTS	SPEED	FEED		1	2	3	4	5	6	7	8	9	10	SELECTED TIME
1. Pick Up Piece and Place in Jig			T	.12	.11	.12	.13	.12	.10	.12	.12	.14	.12	
			R	.12	.29	.39	.54	.66	.77	.92	8.01	14	.32	
2. Tighten Set Screw			T	.13	.12	.12	.14	.11	.12	.12	.13	.12	.11	
			R	.25	.41	.51	.68	.77	.89	7.04	.14	.26	.43	
3. Advance Drill to Work			T	.05	.04	.04	.04	.05	.04	.04	.04	.03	.04	
			R	.30	.45	.55	.72	.82	.93	.08	.18	.29	.47	
4. DRILL ¼"HOLE	980	H	T	.57	.54	.56	.51	.54	.58	.52	.53	.59	.56	
			R	.87	.99	3.11	4.23	5.36	6.51	.60	.71	.88	11.03	
5. Raise Drill from Hole			T	.04	.03	.03	.03	.03	.03	.03	.03	.04	.03	
			R	.91	2.02	.14	.26	.39	.54	.63	.74	.92	.06	
6. Loosen Set Screw			T	.06	.06	.07	.06	.06	.06	.06	.06	.07	.08	
			R	.97	.08	.21	.32	.45	.60	.69	.80	.99	.14	
7. Remove Piece from Jig			T	.08	.09	.08	.08	.09	.08	.07	.08	.09	.07	
			R	1.05	.17	.29	.40	.54	.68	.76	.88	10.08	.21	
8. Blow Out Chips			T	.13	.10	.12	.14	.13	.12	.13	.12	.12	.11	
			R	.18	.27	.41	.54	.67	.80	.89	9.00	.20	.32	
9.			T											
			R											
10. (1)			T	.12	.11	.13	.14	.12	.12	.11	.13	.12	.12	.12
			R	11.44	.56	.69	.82	.87	17.01	18.09	.21	.31	.42	
11. (2)			T	.12	.14	.12	.11	.12	.10	.13	.15	.12	.11	.12
			R	.56	.70	.81	.93	.99	.11	.22	.36	.43	.53	
12. (3)			T	.04	.04	.04	.03	.04	.04	.04	.04	.04	.04	.04
			R	.60	.74	.85	.96	16.03	.15	.26	.40	.47	.57	
13. (4)			T	.54	.53	.55	.52	.57	.54	.60	.53	.55	.54	.54
			R	12.14	13.27	14.40	15.48	.60	.69	.76	.93	21.02	22.11	
14. (5)			T	.03	.03	.03	.03	.03	.03	.03	.03	.03	.03	.03
			R	.17	.30	.43	.51	.63	.72	.79	.96	.05	.14	
15. (6)			T	.06	.06	.06	.07	.06	.05	.06	.06	.05	.06	.06
			R	.23	.36	.49	.58	.69	.77	.85	20.02	.10	.20	
16. (7)			T	.08	.08	.09	.08	.08	.07	.08	.06	.08	.08	.08
			R	.31	.44	.58	.66	.77	.84	.93	.08	.18	.28	
17. (8)			T	.14	.12	.10	.09	.12	.14	.15	.11	.12	12	.12
			R	.45	.56	.68	.75	.89	.98	19.08	.19	.30	22.40	
18.			T											1.11
			R											

SELECTED TIME 1.11	RATING 100%	NORMAL TIME 1.11	TOTAL ALLOWANCES 5%	STANDARD TIME 1.17
AVERAGE		ALLOWED		

Overall Length 12"   Drill ¼"Hole   1"   ¾"   1"

TOOLS, JIGS, GAUGES: Jig No. D-12-33
Use H.S. Drill ¼"Diam.
Hand Feed
Use Oil - S4

TIMED BY J.B.M.

FIGURE 3.   Stopwatch time study of a drilling operation made by the continuous method. (From Barnes [3].)

size is read off for the confidence level desired. The most common confidence level is 95 per cent in work measurement.

Let us test the adequacy of the sample taken in the study of Figure 3. First, was $n = 20$ adequate for estimating the overall cycle within a precision of ± 5 percent and a confidence level of 95 percent? Table I shows the calculation of the coefficient of variation for the cycle times as about 5 percent; that is, the standard deviation 0.057 minute is about 5 percent of the mean cycle time to 1.12 minutes. From Figure 4 we see that a sample of $n = 4$ would be adequate to maintain a precision within ± 5 percent of the correct mean cycle time, 95 percent of the time, or $n = 10$ for a confidence level of 99 percent. Our actual sample of 20 was more than adequate.

The reason that the small sample size was adequate is easy to see. The variability of the readings is small in relation to the mean cycle time, so a good estimate of cycle time is obtained by only a few observations. Incidentally, this is commonly true of operations dominated by a machine cycle. In this case, the actual drill time is almost half of the total cycle and the machining time itself does not vary much.

If all we wanted was an estimate of cycle time, we could stop at this point. Let us suppose, however, that we want our estimates of each of the average element times to be adequate for future use as elemental standard data. Was the sample size of $n = 20$ adequate for each of these elements? Let us take element 1 as an example. The mean element time is $\bar{x} = 0.121$ minute, the standard deviation is $s = 0.0097$ minute, and the coefficient of variation is 8 per cent. From Figure 4 we see that we should have taken a sample of $n = 10$ for a 95 percent confidence level and $n = 20$ for a 99 percent confidence level. The reason why a larger sample is needed for element 1 than for the entire cycle is that element 1 is somewhat more variable than is the total cycle (coefficient or variation of 8 percent compared with only 5 percent for the cycle). Therefore, if data on each of the elements are needed, the element for which the largest sample size is indicated, from Figure 4, dictates the minimum sample size for the study. This procedure insures the precision and confidence requirements for the limiting element and yields better results than this on all other elements.

Procedures for Ensuring Consistency of Sample Data. A single study always leaves open the question: "Were the data representative of usual operating conditions?" If a similar study were made on some other

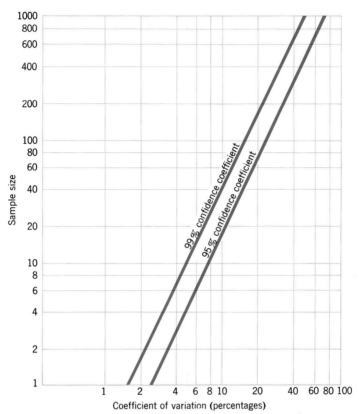

FIGURE 4.   Chart for estimating the sample size required to obtain maximum confidence intervals of ±5 percent for given coefficient of variation values. (From Abruzzi [1].)

day of the week or some other hour of the day, would the results be different? This question suggests the possibility of dividing the total sample into smaller subsamples taken at random times. Then, by setting up control limits based on an initial sample, we can determine if the subsequent data taken are consistent. That is, did all of the data come from a common universe?

This situation is comparable to that found in quality control. If a point falls outside of the ±3s control limits, we know that the probability is high that some assignable cause of variation is present which has resulted in an abnormally high or low set of sample readings. These assignable causes could be anything that could have an effect on the time of production such as material variations from standard; changes

TABLE I.   Cycle Times from Figure 3, and Calculated Mean Value, Standard Deviation, Coefficient of Variation and Required Sample Sizes from Figure 4

Cycle Number	Cycle Time (minutes)	Cycle Time (squared)	Cycle Number	Cycle Time (minutes)	Cycle Time (squared)
1	1.18	1.395	11	1.13	1.280
2	1.09	1.190	12	1.11	1.235
3	1.14	1.300	13	1.12	1.255
4	1.13	1.280	14	1.07	1.145
5	1.13	1.280	15	1.14	1.300
6	1.13	1.280	16	1.09	1.190
7	1.09	1.190	17	1.10	1.215
8	1.11	1.235	18	1.11	1.235
9	1.20	1.440	19	1.11	1.235
10	1.12	1.255	20	1.10	1.215
			Sum	22.40	25.150

$$\bar{x} = \frac{22.40}{20} = 1.12$$

$$s = \sqrt{\frac{\Sigma x_i{}^2 - \frac{(\Sigma x_i)^2}{n}}{n-1}} = \sqrt{\frac{25.150 - \frac{(22.40)^2}{20}}{19}} = 0.057$$

$$\text{Coefficient of variation} = \frac{0.057 \times 100}{1.12} = 5.09\%$$

From Figure 4:

$$n \approx = \ 4 \ @ \ 95\% \ \text{confidence level.}$$
$$n \approx = 10 \ @ \ 99\% \ \text{confidence level.}$$

in tools, workplace, or methods of work; and in the working environment. As with quality control, we would attempt to determine the nature of these assignable causes and eliminate data where abnormal readings have an explanation.

The general procedure is as follows:*

1.   Standardize methods, select operator, and determine elemental breakdown as before.

---

*For detailed procedures with appropriate charts for estimating sample sizes, precision limits, and control limits, see [2] and [3].

2. Take an initial sample study. (a) Compute preliminary estimates of $\bar{x}$ and s. (b) Determine estimate of total sample needed from Figure 4. (c) Set up control limits for balance of study based on preliminary estimates of $\bar{x}$ and s.

3. Program and execute balance of study. (a) Divide total sample by subsample size to find the number of separate subsamples to obtain. Subsample sizes are commonly 4 to 5. (b) Randomize the time when these subsamples will be taken. A random number table is useful. (c) At the random times indicated, obtain subsample readings and plot points on control chart. If points fall outside limits, investigate immediately to determine the cause. Eliminate data from computations for standards where causes can be assigned. (d) When study is complete, make final check to be sure that the precision and confidence level of the result are at least as good as desired.

4. Compute normal time, determine allowances, and compute standard time as before.

Work Sampling

The unique thing about work sampling is that it accomplishes the results of stopwatch study without the need for a stopwatch. Although this statement does not summarize, by any means, the net advantage or disadvantage of work sampling, it indicates that there is something startlingly different about work sampling, and indeed there is.

Work sampling was first introduced to industry by L. H. C. Tippett in 1934. However, it has been in common use only since about 1950. We can illustrate the basic idea of work sampling by a simple example. Suppose we wish to estimate the proportion of time that a worker, or a group of workers, spends working and the proportion of time spent not working. We can do this by long-term stopwatch studies in which we measure the work time, the idle time, or both. This would probably take a day or longer, and after measuring we would not be sure that the term of the study covered representative periods of work and idleness.

Instead, suppose that we make a large number of *random* observations in which we simply determine whether the operator is working or idle and tally the result (see Figure 5). The percentages of the tallies that are recorded in the "working" and "idle" classifications are estimates of the actual per cent of time that the worker was working and idle. Herein lies the fundamental principle behind work sampling: *the number of observations is proportional to the amount of time spent in the working or*

	Tally	Number	Per cent
Working	THL THL THL THL THL THL THL THL THL THL THL THL THL THL THL THL THL THL THL THL THL THL /	96	88.9
Idle	THL THL //	12	11.1
Total		108	100.0

FIGURE 5.   Work sampling tally of working and idle time. When observations occur at random times, the percentages estimate the percent of time that the worker was in the working or idle state. The accuracy of the estimate increases with the number of observations.

idle state. The accuracy of the estimate depends on the number of observations, and we can preset precision limits and confidence levels.

Number of Observations Required.   The statistical methods of work sampling depend on the distributions for proportions, as do control charts and sampling by attributes in quality control. Recall that

$$\bar{p} = \frac{x}{n} = \frac{\text{number observed in classification}}{\text{total number of observations}}$$

and

$$s_p = \sqrt{\frac{\bar{p}(1 - \bar{p})}{n}}$$

From these simple formulas for mean proportion and the standard deviation of a proportion, charts and tables have been developed which give directly the number of observations required for a given value of $\bar{p}$, precision limits, and the 95% confidence level. Estimates of sample sizes can be obtained from Figure 6.*

Note that the number of observations required is fairly large. For example, to maintain a precision in the estimate of $\bar{p}$ of ± 1.0 percentage point at 95 per cent confidence, 10,000 observations are required if $\bar{p}$ is in the neighborhood of 50 percent, that is, to be 95 percent sure that an estimate of $\bar{p} = 50$ percent is between 49 and 51 percent. About 3600 observations are required to hold that an estimated $\bar{p} = 10$ percent between 9 and 11 percent. Smaller samples are required for looser

*More complete information on sample sizes is available in [4].

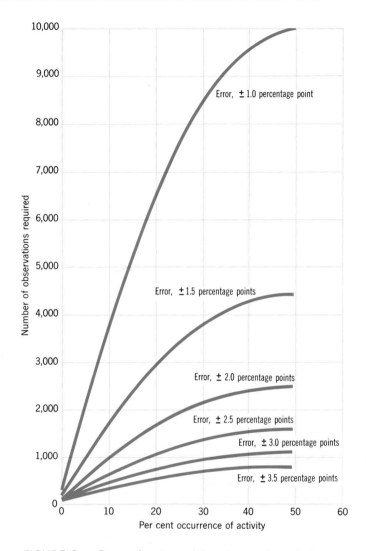

FIGURE 6.   Curves for determining the number of observations required to maintain precision within the percentage points indicated at the 95 percent confidence level.

limits. Although these numbers of observations seem huge, we must remember that the nature of the observation required is merely a recognition of whether or not the employee is working, or possibly a classification of his activity into various reasons for idleness.

Measuring Delays and Allowances. One common use of work sampling is to determine the per cent of time that workers are actually spending for personal time and delays that are a part of the job. The resulting information could then be used as the basis for the percentage allowances that enter into the calculation of standard time.

Let us consider, as an example, the determination of delay and personal allowances in a lathe department of a machine shop. There are ten workers involved. The delays of which we are speaking are a part of the job such as waiting for tools, materials, and instructions; machine cleanup; securing an inspector's approval; change of jobs; and minor mechanical difficulties. We wish to determine the extent of the delays and to determine how much time workers are spending for personal time. Our procedure is as follows:

1. *Design work sampling study.*
   (a) Estimate preliminary values for the percent of time spent in the three categories of work, delay, and personal time from past knowledge, studies, foremen's estimates, or a preliminary study of the jobs. These preliminary estimates are necessary to gauge the magnitude of the data-taking phase. Based on a composite of past information and foremen's estimates, our best guesses are:

Work	85 percent
Delay	10 percent
Personal time	5 percent

   (b) Set desired precision limits of estimates to be obtained. We decide that ± 1.0 percentage point at 95 percent confidence on our delay estimate will be controlling. Thus, if the estimate for delays is actually 10 percent, we want to be 95 percent sure that it is not less than 9 percent or more than 11 percent, with 10 percent being the most probable value.
   (c) Estimate total number of readings from Figure 6. For $\bar{p} = 10$ per cent, $N = 3600$ for ± 1.0 percentage point error. Note from Figure 6 that our precision for personal time of 5 percent would then be slightly better than ± 1.0 percentage point and for working time slightly worse.
   (d) Program total number of readings over desired time span of study. We decide that 3600 readings over a 2-week period (10 working days) will cover a representative period. Therefore, we propose to obtain $\frac{3600}{10} = 360$ observations per day. Since there are 10

workers involved, we shall obtain 10 observations each time we sample. So we need to program $\frac{360}{10} = 36$ random sampling times each day for 10 days to obtain the total of 3600 readings. The easiest way to select 36 random sampling times is to use a random number table.

(e) Plan the physical aspects of the study. This includes an appropriate data sheet, as well as a determination of the physical path, observation points, etc., so that the results are not biased because workers see the observer coming and change activities accordingly.

2. *Take the data as planned.* Table II shows a summary of the actual data taken in this instance with a breakdown between morning and afternoon observations. The percentages for "work," "delay," and "personal time" have been computed for each half-day and for the total sample.

TABLE II.   Summary of Work Sampling Data for Lathe Department Study

Date		Total Obser- vations	Work		Delay		Personal	
			Obs.	Per Cent	Obs.	Per Cent	Obs.	Per Cent
10–2	a.m.	190	152	80.0	24	12.6	14	7.4
	p.m.	170	145	85.3	14	8.2	11	6.5
10–3	a.m.	160	144	90.0	10	6.3	6	3.7
	p.m.	200	158	79.0	19	9.5	23	11.5
10–4	a.m.	150	127	84.7	15	10.0	8	5.3
	p.m.	210	182	86.6	23	11.0	5	2.4
10–5	a.m.	180	142	78.9	24	13.3	14	7.8
	p.m.	180	148	82.2	20	11.1	12	6.7
10–6	a.m.	220	189	85.9	24	10.9	7	3.2
	p.m.	140	114	81.4	17	12.1	9	6.5
10–9	a.m.	210	185	88.2	14	6.6	11	5.2
	p.m.	150	135	90.0	9	6.0	6	4.0
10–10	a.m.	190	155	81.6	25	13.2	10	5.2
	p.m.	170	146	85.9	14	8.2	10	5.9
10–11	a.m.	200	166	83.0	22	11.0	12	6.0
	p.m.	160	136	85.0	14	8.8	10	6.2
10–12	a.m.	140	118	84.3	15	10.7	7	5.0
	p.m.	220	185	84.1	25	11.4	10	4.5
10–13	a.m.	210	181	86.2	19	9.1	10	4.7
	p.m.	150	130	86.7	12	8.0	8	5.3
		3600	3038	84.4	359	9.97	203	5.63

3. *Recheck precision of results and consistency of data.* A final check of the delay percentage of 9.97 per cent shows that the number of readings taken was adequate to maintain the ± 1.0 percentage point precision on the delay time. The consistency of the data could be checked by setting up a control chart for proportions to see if any subsample points fell outside the limits. Other statistical tests comparing A.M. observations with P.M. observations could also be carried through.

Based on the work sampling study, we could then conclude that the delay part of the work in the lathe department was about 10 percent. We are 95 percent sure that the sampling error has been held to no more than ± 1.0 percentage point and it is probable that it is less. We have based these conclusions on a study which covered 2 weeks of time, with any time of the day being equally likely as a sampling time. The personal time of 5.6 percent is slightly greater than the company standard practice of allowing 5 percent; however, 5 percent is within the probable range of error of estimate.

Determining Production Standards.   The previous example showed the use of work sampling to determine percentage allowances for non-cyclical elements such as delays and for personal time. Why not carry the idea forward one more step and utilize the observations on per cent work time to establish production standards? What additional data do we need? If we knew (a) how many pieces were produced during the total time of the study and (b) the performance rating for each observation of work time, we could compute normal time as follows:

$$\text{Normal time} = \frac{\left(\begin{array}{c}\text{total}\\\text{time of}\\\text{study in}\\\text{minutes}\end{array}\right) \times \overset{.844}{\left(\begin{array}{c}\text{work time}\\\text{in decimals}\\\text{from work}\\\text{sampling study}\end{array}\right)} \times \overset{.100}{\left(\begin{array}{c}\text{average}\\\text{performance}\\\text{rating in}\\\text{decimals}\end{array}\right)}{\text{total number of pieces produced}}$$

Standard time is then computed as before:

Standard time =

    normal time + allowances for delays, fatigue, and personal time

We have already seen how the allowances for delays and personal time can be determined from work sampling. Here we see the complete determination of a production standard without the use of a precise timing device. All that was needed was a rather ordinary calendar from which we might calculate the total available time.

Although work sampling approaches to work measurement can be used in most situations, its most outstanding field of application is in the measurement of noncyclical types of work where many different tasks are performed but where there is no set pattern of cycle or regularity. In many jobs, the frequency of tasks within the job is based on a random demand function. For example, a storeroom clerk may fill requisitions, unpack and put away stock, deliver material to production departments, clean up the storeroom, etc. The frequency and time requirements of some of these tasks depend on things outside the control of the clerk himself. To determine production standards by stopwatch methods would be difficult or impossible. Work sampling fits this situation ideally because, through its random sampling approach, reliable estimates of time and performance for these randomly occurring tasks can be obtained.

An Example

As an example, let us consider the determination of standards for a warehouse handling group, reported by George H. Gustat of Eastman Kodak Com-

TABLE III.   Combined Results of Two Work Sampling Studies of Warehouse Handling Group Covering a Total of 14 Days and 6601 Observations

Operation	Number of Observations	Per Cent of Total
Packing	2223	33.7
Shipping	1141	17.3
Receiving	912	13.8
Small orders	462	7.0
Reoperating	213	3.2
Sort and stack	361	5.5
Inventory	246	3.7
Wait for equipment	194	2.9
Personal and lost time	849	12.9
	6601	100.0

Adapted from Gustat [6, 7].

pany.* In this study thirty people were engaged in the following nine groups of activities: packing, shipping, receiving, small orders, reoperating (opening and repacking for tests, etc.), sort and stack, inventory, wait for equipment, personal and lost time.

Two separate work sampling studies were made in which the observer classified the activities of the workers and rated their performance using IBM cards and mark-sensing lead so that computations could be carried out on card-tabulating equipment. The combined overall results of these studies, which involved 6601 observations, are shown in Table III. Here we see the distribution of time spent by the thirty men. Figures 7 and 8 show the summary of data for the packing operation only and the control chart for the operation, both being based on the second of the two work sampling studies. Figure 9 shows sample calculations of standard time for the packing operation. (Allowances were added to the total of all operations.)

Before the study was made, there were few sound data on which to base estimates of labor needs to perform the tasks in the warehouse. Based on the work sampling standards, a wage incentive payment plan was established which increased output per man to the extent that sixteen men could perform all of the work formerly done by thirty men. It is unlikely that such a program could have been attempted in the absence of work sampling.

		Packing operation, summary	
Day	Total observations	Total packing observations	Daily per cent p
M	450	142	31
T	467	152	32
W	477	125	26
T	470	160	34
F	470	177	38
M	464	155	33
T	465	159	34
W	475	142	30
T	470	153	33
F	466	169	36
	4674	1534	327
Average subsample size = 4674 ÷ 10 = 467			$\bar{p} = 33\%$

FIGURE 7.   Daily summary of sampling data for the packing operation. (From Gustat [6, 7].)

*See [4, pp. 151–161], [6, pp. 130–143], and [7, pp. 80–86].

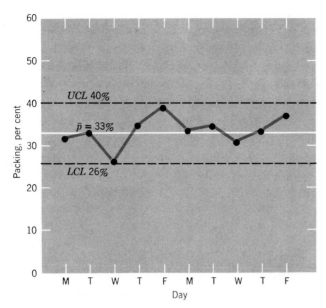

Stopwatch Study and Work Sampling Compared

Perhaps the final major question to be raised is: "Are stopwatch study and work sampling interchangeable?" So far as general accuracy of results is concerned, apparently they are. Figure 10 shows the results of a comparative study in which both stopwatch and work sampling studies were made on fourteen different operations to estimate normal time. The differences between the two techniques are within the limits of rating error. This does not mean that both techniques have the same field of application, however. We cannot overestimate the importance of the work sampling advantage of not requiring the use of a stopwatch. The psychological impact of using a stopwatch on personnel being measured has never been determined, but many people feel that it is significant. If for no other reason than this, it is likely that the practical use of work sampling will grow.

Standard Data Work Measurement Systems

We have already had occasion to refer to standard data systems in connection with job design and process planning. Two kinds of standard data are used: universal data based on minute elements of motion (often called microdata) and standard data for families of jobs (often called macrodata or element standard data).

Universal Standard Data.   Universal standard data give time values for fundamental types of motions, so complete cycle times can be synthesized by analyzing the motions required to perform the task. Fundamental time values of this nature can be used as building blocks to forecast the all-important time criterion, provided that the time values are properly gathered and that the various minute motion elements required by the tasks are analyzed perfectly. Taylor envisioned something comparable to this, and many alternative proposals have been made by management consultants who sell services consisting of installing systems based on their data and training client personnel in the use of these data. Some of these alternate time value systems are known by trade names: Methods-Time-Measurement (MTM) [9], Work Factor [14], and Basic Motion Time Study [5].

The result provided by these synthetic standards is an estimate of normal time for the task. Standard time is then determined as before by adding allowances for delay, fatigue, and personal time. Does performance rating enter into standards developed from universal data? Not for each standard developed because the analyst simply uses the time value from the table for a given motion without adjustment. However,

Packing operation—calculation of standard time				
Employee:	J. Green	R. Smith	M. O'Riley	_ _ _ _ _ _etc.
a. Total hours	78	80	65	_ _ _ _ _ _ _ _
b. Total observations	134	157	142	_ _ _ _ _ _ _ _
Packing operation:				
c. Observations	42	53	61	_ _ _ _ _ _ _ _
d. Per cent of total *(c ÷ b)*	31.3	33.8	43.0	_ _ _ _ _ _ _ _
e. Packing time, hours *(d × a)*	24.4	27.1	28.0	_ _ _ _ _ _ _ _
f. Average rating	105	90	95	_ _ _ _ _ _ _ _
g. Standard time packing, hours *(f × e)*	25.6 +	24.4 +	26.6 +	_ _ _ _ _ _= 386 Total standard packing hours
h. Total footage of film shipped = 11,309,529				
i. Standard unit time = 386 ÷ 11,309,529				
j. Standard hours per 1000 feet = 0.034				

FIGURE 9.   Calculation of the standard time for the packing operation. (From Gustat [6, 7].)

performance rating was used to develop the time values that are in the tables. So the rating factor enters the system, but not for each occasion that the data are used.

Many people feel that universal standard data lead to greater consistency of standards, since analysts are not called on to judge working pace in order to develop a standard. This does not mean that judgment is eliminated from the use of universal standard data systems, however. A great deal of judgment is required in selecting the appropriate classifications of motion to use in analyzing an operation; an inexperienced person ordinarily will not be able to perform these selections accurately enough for the purpose of determining production standards.

Using universal standard data as the sole basis for determining production standards is not common. In most cases where data of this kind are used, they are employed in conjunction with some other technique, such as stopwatch study or work sampling. The reason for this methodology seems to be that most organizations feel more comfortable when some actual direct measurement of the work involved has been made.

How good are these systems of standard times? Do they show up the differences indicated by our sample of research studies? For example, in

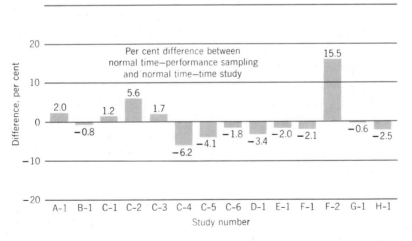

FIGURE 10.   Results of a comparison between work sampling and stopwatch study on fourteen operations. Bars indicate positive and negative deviations from work sampling. (From: R. M. Barnes and R. B. Andrews, "Performance Sampling in Work Measurement," *Journal of Industrial Engineering*, **6** (6), 8–18, Nov.–Dec. 1955.)

the study of cranks and handwheels by Davis, discussed in Chapter 11, would standard data time values have signaled the fact that the $-45°$ and $+45°$ positions are superior for cranks and handwheels under conditions of heavy resistance? Would the system have indicated that cranks are generally a little faster than handwheels? The answers are no. These differences are too subtle for the standard data systems as presently constructed. In designing jobs it is necessary that research data be used as a background of knowledge for selecting certain kinds of mechanisms (such as cranks in preference to handwheels), for judging arm strength required, for using positioning stops and guides, and for arranging the workplace so that positioning elements occur in the best positions. In other words, the principles of motion economy serve as guides. Standard data systems cannot substitute for this knowledge, but they can be used to compare and evaluate gross differences in methods which represent alternatives to the job designer. These alternatives might represent manual labor versus degrees of mechanization; alternative machines; one-handed versus two-handed approaches to the task, etc. The degree of difference which can be distinguished is surprisingly great, however, especially by a trained man. It may be that a carefully planned standard data system, based on good experimental design and technique, will be able to reflect some of the more subtle differences based on the known results of present research.

Although we have discussed standard time data systems as a means of helping to develop job designs, they also serve to forecast expected output while the employee is working. This forecast is of considerable importance; business and industrial management are always interested in the labor content of a given job design and, therefore, an estimate of the work standard is desirable. These work standards, however, usually involve appraisals of work time, rest time, delay allowances, and allowances for personal time. The standard time data discussed give estimates for the *work time* only.

Standard Data for Job Families.   Standard data for job families give normal time values for major elements of jobs (macrostandard data). Also, time values for machine setup and for different manual elements are given, so a normal time for an entirely new job can be constructed by an analysis of blueprints to see what materials are specified, what cuts must be made, how the work piece can be held in the machine, etc. Unlike the universal standard data discussed previously, however, the time values for these elements have been based on actual previous stop-watch or other measurement of work within the job family.

In these previous studies, the operations were consistently broken down into common elements until finally a system of data emerged that showed how "normal element time" varied with size, depth of cut, material used, the way the work piece was held in the machine, etc. At that point the data themselves could be used to estimate production standards without a separate study actually being performed on every different part. Again, although individual performance rating does not enter each application of the standard data, it was used in constructing the data originally. As before, final production standards are determined by adding allowances for delays, fatigue, and personal time to the normal cycle time derived from the standard data.

Macrostandard data are in common use, especially in machine shops where distinct job families have a long-standing tradition. However, the occurrence of this kind of standard data is by no means limited to machine shops. It is likely to exist wherever job families exist or when parts or products occur in many sizes and types. Macrostandard data have a large field of application where short runs of custom parts and products occur. In these instances, if we attempt to determine production standards by actual measurement, the order may be completed by the time the production standard has been determined; the result will be of no value unless the identical part is reordered.

ALLOWANCES IN PRODUCTION STANDARDS

As we noted previously, allowances are commonly added to the computed normal time for delay, fatigue, and personal time. Allowances for delay and fatigue depend on the nature of the operation. They may not exist for some activities. The usual approach is to express allowances in percent of the total available time. Thus, a 10 percent allowance over an 8-hour (480-minute) day is the equivalent of 48 minutes.

Delay Allowances.   Delay allowances must be based on actual measurement of the magnitude of the delays. Although stopwatch study can be used, work sampling provides a much more efficient means of obtaining accurate data because delays often occur randomly. Work sampling expresses its measurement of delays directly in terms of percent of the total available time.

Fatigue and Personal Allowances.   For some very heavy industrial jobs, a man might work 20 minutes and rest 20 minutes. This was the case for the "shake out" of poured iron castings at a well-known automotive foundry. It was a continuous operation which required the worker to break open the iron molding box containing the solidified but very hot casting. This was done over a vibrating grate, so that the molding sand could drop through to a recirulating conveyor; the casting was then conveyed to subsequent cleaning operations. The worker then placed the top half of the molding box on one overhead chain conveyor hook and the bottom half on another; each half weighed 50 pounds. The work was done under conditions of high temperature, of dust from the molding sand, and of high-noise intensity. The schedule of 20 minutes of work and 20 minutes of rest was probably none too generous. This type of very heavy work is not common today, but it occurs often enough so that there is a continuing interest in the subject of physical fatigue and rest allowances.

Unfortunately, we still lack an accepted framework for the establishment of rest allowances based on any rational or scientific measurements. In most instances, schedules of *fatigue allowances* for various types of work are used based on general acceptability and are often the subject of agreements between labor and management.

A Physiological Basis for Rest Pauses

Recent research has indicated that physiological methods of measurement hold considerable promise for the determination of workloads and optimal environmental design. One application of physiological methods that goes to the heart of the long-standing question of fatigue allowances is the work of E. A. Müller in Germany [10].

Based on his studies, Müller proposes an energy expenditure standard of 4 large calories (kcal) per minute as the maximum that the average man can expend continuously without rest. (This is an expenditure above the basal metabolism rate which Müller takes as 1 kcal per minute.) This level of energy expenditure he calls the endurance limit (EL). If the task demands more than the EL, the man must tap his energy reserve; therefore, he must take a rest pause so that his muscles can recover. Müller suggests a standard energy reserve of 24 kcal. The rest or recovery time following work is necessary if the energy reserve of 24 kcal is used up. He further relates work time and rest, or recovery time, by the

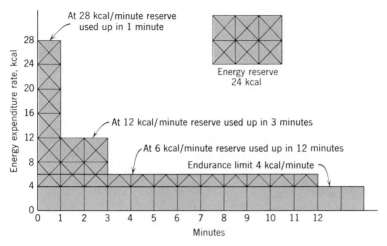

FIGURE 11.   Various patterns of energy expenditure within the endurance limit or within the energy reserve limit. (Adapted from Müller [10].)

statement that the average expenditure rate cannot exceed 4 large calories during the work plus resting time if the effects of fatigue are not to accumulate. For example, a task that demands 6 kcal per minute would require an average of 20 minutes of rest in an hour, or a fatigue allowance of $33\frac{1}{3}$ per cent of the total work plus resting time.

Figure 11 shows how this would work out for different levels of energy expenditure. Up to the 4-kcal rate, a man would be expected to work continuously without needing rest owing to physical fatigue. At the 6-kcal rate, however, he could work for a maximum of 12 minutes, at which time he would have used up his 24-kcal energy reserve. In order to continue work, Müller suggests that he would have to have at least 6 minutes of rest, so that the average energy expenditure for the work plus rest time, or $12 + 6 = 18$ minutes does not exceed an average of 4 kcal per minute ($72 \text{ kcal} \div 18 = 4$ kcal per minute).

Other energy expenditure levels are shown in Figure 11. For example, according to Müller's standards, a man could be expected to work at the 12-kcal rate for 3 minutes at which point he would be exhausted since his energy reserve would be used up. To keep the energy expenditure level from exceeding 4 kcal, he would have to rest 6 minutes following the 3 minutes of work at 12 kcal per minute. This pattern of work 3 minutes, rest 6 minutes would be required by the high energy expenditure level.

Physiologists have measured the energy costs of a large number of different activities, many of which are industrial tasks. Table IV lists, for a few of these tasks, the energy costs and the fatigue allowances (per cent of total time that is rest), using Müller's concept. This list is not meant to be a recommendation for allowances of similar job titles in business and industry, since local job conditions and duties may vary considerably from plant to plant. However, it does give an idea of how the Müller standard would operate for various widely known *types* of work. From Table IV we see that the majority of activities listed require no fatigue allowance at all, which does not mean that these activities require no personal rest allowances of any kind. It merely means that no rest allowances are necessary in order to recover from *physical* fatigue. There may be psychological factors of boredom and work monotony that would make rest allowances desirable.

The tasks that have energy costs above the EL require rest allowances for the recovery from physical fatigue or exertion beyond the EL. Thus, we see that jobs such as shoveling, various coal mining tasks, and general industrial labor require fatigue allowances according to Müller's standard. However, all types of office work, light assembly, and light machine shop work would require no allowances for fatigue.

At present, determinations of fatigue allowances are not based on measurements of energy expenditure as implied by the discussion of Müller's work, partly because suitable measurement devices for the practical business and industrial situations do not exist and partly because there has been no acceptance of Müller's or anyone else's concept of the fatigue problem.

Allowances for *personal time* provide at least a minimum of time that the worker can be away from the job. This personal time allows a break from both the physical and psychological stresses that a job may contain and is, in a sense, a minimum fatigue allowance. The minimum allowance is normally 5 percent of the total available time.

Application of Allowances in Production Standards

The usual interpretation of the meaning of percentages allowances is that they allow a per cent of the total available time. A personal time allowance of 5 percent translates into $0.05 \times 480 = 24$ minutes of personal time in a normal 8-hour day. If the normal time has been measured as 1.20

TABLE IV. Energy Cost and Fatigue Allowances for Various Tasks

Activity	Energy Cost,* Kcal/min, Above Basal Level	Fatigue Allowance, (per cent)
Men's activities:		
Miscellaneous office work, sitting	0.6	0
Miscellaneous office work, standing	0.8	0
Armature winding	1.2	0
Light assembly line work	0.8	0
Medium assembly line work	1.7	0
Sheet metal worker	2.0	0
Light machine work	1.4	0
Machinist	2.1	0
Plastic molding	2.3	0
Tool room worker	2.9	0
Loading chemicals into mixer	5.0	20.0
Shoveling 8-kg load, 1 m lift, 12/min	6.5	38.5
Push wheelbarrow, 57-kg load, 4.5 km/hr	4.0	0
Bricklaying	3.0	0
Mixing cement	3.7	0
Plaster lathing	2.1	0
Plastering walls	3.1	0
Coal mining:		
Hewing	6.0	33.3
Loading	6.1	34.4
Timbering	4.7	14.9
Drilling	4.8	16.7
Pushing tubs	7.0	42.8
Women's activities:		
Machine sewing, foot operated	0.43	0
Typing, electric, 40 words/min	0.31	0
Typing, mechanical, 40 words/min	0.48	0
Tool setting	2.4	0
Gaging	3.0	0
General industrial labor	4.1	2.4

*Handbook figures were adjusted to energy cost above basal level by subtracting 1 kcal/min from each rate given to conform to Muller's formulation.
Source of activities and energy cost data: William S. Spector, Editor, *Handbook of Biological Data,* WADC Technical Report 56–273, ASTIA Document No. AD 110501, Wright Air Development Center.

minutes per piece, then the personal time must be prorated properly to the normal time in computing standard time per piece:

$$\text{Standard time} = \text{normal time} \times \frac{100}{100 - \text{percentage allowance}}$$

$$= 1.20 \times \frac{100}{95} = 1.263 \text{ minutes per piece}$$

If all the allowances for delay, fatigue, and personal time are expressed as percentages of total available time, they can be added together to obtain a single total percentage allowance figure. Then standard time can be computed from normal time by a single calculation using the preceding formula.

NONMANUFACTURING APPLICATIONS

Work measurement is advancing into many nonmanufacturing activities today. Barnes [3, 4] reports examples in agriculture, education, hospitals, warehouses, and trucking; and in the larger offices it is already in common use. In fact, a system of universal standard times for office operations has been constructed. Work measurement is applicable in any situation where an appraisal of labor content needs to be made. Work sampling as a technique makes it possible to measure work in many situations where it was impractical to do so before.

SUMMARY

Work measurement methods are the formal basis for establishing standards of output for labor. These standards are of great importance in both the design and operating phases of production systems. In the design phases, performance standards are important in estimating labor costs of products and of alternative methods and in estimating required capacities for layouts. In the operation and control of production systems, labor performance standards are needed in programming and scheduling production, evaluating performance, and controlling labor costs, as well as in helping to evaluate countless operating alternatives such as make-buy and equipment replacement.

We need to face up realistically to the probable final accuracy of production standards. This accuracy cannot be better than about ±10 percent when we consider the precision with which trained people can rate performance. Where heavy physical work is involved, the limits of accuracy are probably greater, because there are no presently available practical means of measuring the allowance for fatigue which should be made. Recognition of the limitations of work measurement accuracy is not to damn work measurement methods but simply to recognize that the limitations exist.

KEY CONCEPTS

A Standard.   The concept of a standard is of key importance both to work measurement and to the control problem in general. It is important to understand the possible arbitrary nature of a standard though it may have a defensible rationale as it does in work measurement. In work measurement the rationale is based on the work measurement model comprised of normalized time allowances for all tasks of a job plus measured allowances for delays and rest pauses and relatively arbitrary allowances for fatigue and personal need.

Normal Work Pace.   The concept of normal work pace is related to the concept of a standard, again based on a rationale rather than an entirely arbitrary standard for work pace. The rationale most commonly used is that pace which can be maintained or exceeded for the normal work day by 95 percent of the working population. As noted in the chapter, other standards for work pace are also used.

Work Sampling.   The concept on which work sampling is built is based on the fact that the number of observations recorded in the working or idle state (or some smaller breakdown of activity) is proportional to the amount of time spent in that state.

Additivity of Task Time.   The concepts on which standard data work measurement systems are built rest on the assumption that the standard times for work elements (for example, reach, grasp, move, position, etc.) are additive. This means that even though these times were determined through actual timing of elements in one sequence that their average values can be reassembled into motion patterns involving a different sequence and still have the element times add up to form a total to predict the time required for the new sequence.

IMPORTANT TERMS

Numbers in parentheses indicate page numbers.

1. Delay allowance (409)
2. Endurance limit (410)
3. Fatigue allowance (410)
4. Macrostandard data (405–406)

5. Microstandard data (405–406)
6. Normal time (387)
7. Performance rating (387)
8. Personal time (412)
9. Production standard (383)

10. Standard time (387)
11. Time standard (383)
12. Universal standard data (406)
13. Work measurement (383)

REVIEW QUESTIONS

Numbers in parentheses indicate page numbers.

1. Why are labor standards important? How are they used? (384)
2. Appraise standards based on foreman's estimates or past performance data. (384–385)
3. Relate the problem of the determination of production standards to the problem of designing a lever that requires arm strength available in 95 percent of the working population. (385–386)
4. Define these terms: normal time, performance rating, allowances, and standard time. (387)
5. Discuss the function of performance rating in the determination of production standards. (387)
6. Discuss performance rating as a system of measurement. How accurate is performance rating? (388–390)
7. What is the general procedure for determining standards by stopwatch methods? (391)
8. Why is it general practice to divide a job into elements for a stopwatch study? (391)
9. Discuss the problem of determining the adequacy of sample sizes for various elements in a stopwatch time study. (392–394)
10. Outline the procedures necessary for ensuring that sample data are consistent and representative of usual operating conditions. (394–396)
11. What is the fundamental principle on which work sampling is based? (397–398)
12. Outline the general procedure for a work sampling study to determine the extent of delays and personal time. (400–402)
13. What additional information is necessary to determine production standards completely by work sampling? (402–403)
14. Compare stopwatch study and work sampling in terms of the cost to make studies, representativeness of samples taken, field of application, and comparative accuracy. (405)
15. What is the difference between "micro" and "macro" standard data? (405–409)
16. Where is judgment required in the use of standard data to determine production standards? (407)

17. What is the current basis for fatigue allowances used in work measurement? (410)
18. Allowances are normally expressed as a percent of the total time available. How are they properly prorated to normal times to obtain standard time? (412–414)
19. Discuss the possible range of application of work measurement techniques in manufacturing and nonmanufacturing activities. (414)

SELF-TEST TRUE-FALSE QUESTIONS

Numbers in parentheses indicate page numbers.

1. The major defect in informal standards is that they are not recorded, so that they are not available for everyone to check. (384–385)   *F*
2. Most performance standards are quoted at the level equal to the average expected output. (386)   *F*
3. Standard time is normally computed as the normal time plus allowances for personal time less allowances for job delays. (387)   *F*
4. If the actual observed time was 0.384 minutes and the observed performance rating was 125 percent, then the normal time for the job would be 0.48 minutes. (388)   *T*
5. The only thing that we need in order to make measurements is a standard for comparison which is accepted. (388)   *F*
6. Walking at four miles per hour is considered normal pace. (389)   *F*
7. On the Bedaux scale of performance rating, 60 points is equivalent to normal performance. (390)   *T*
8. Commonly accepted figures for the accuracy of performance rating would be ± 5 percent. (390)   *T*
9. All practical work measurements systems involve: (1) the measurement of actual observed time and (2) a determination of the adequacy of the sample size. (390)   *F*
10. In stopwatch methods of work measurements, one reason for the breakdown of elements is so that different performance ratings can be assigned to different elements. (390–391)   *T*
11. Comparative studies indicate that the continuous method and the snapback method of reading the stopwatch are equally accurate. (392)   *T*
12. One way of ensuring consistency of sample data in stopwatch work measurements is to divide the total sample into smaller subsamples taken at random times and then set up control limits, much as we do in statistical quality control. (396–397)   *T*
13. The unique thing about work sampling is that it accomplishes the results of stop-watch study without the need for a stopwatch. (397)   *T*
14. Work sampling was first introduced to industry by Walter Shewhart. (397)   *F*

15.   The fundamental principle which underlies work sampling is: the number of observations is proportional to the amount of time spent in the working or idle state. (397–398)   T.

16.   The limitation of work sampling, as an approach to work measurement, is that it is useful for the determination of delays and idle time, but not for the complete determination of production standards. (403)   F

17.   One of the outstanding fields of application of work sampling is in the measurement of noncyclical types of work where many different tasks are performed, but where there is not a set pattern of cycle or regularity. (403)

18.   Comparative studies show that work sampling is more accurate than simple stop-watch methods. (405)   F

19.   Performance rating does not enter into standards developed from universal standard data. (406–407)   F

20.   The use of universal standard data as the sole basis for determining production standards is not common. (407)   T

21.   Standard data for job families (often called macro data) is based upon actual previous stopwatch or other measurement of work, within the job family. (406, 408)   T

22.   The usual approach is to express allowances in production standards as a percent of the net work time. (409)   F

23.   If the normal time for an operation was 1.20 minutes per piece, and the total allowances were 20 percent, then the standard time would be 1.44 minutes. (409)   F

PROBLEMS

1.   Determine an elemental breakdown which might be used for a stopwatch time study of the old method of assembling bolts and washers shown in Figure 8 of Chapter 11. Justify the elemental breakdown made.

2.   Select a simple assembled product for which parts can be obtained. Determine a time study elemental breakdown for the assembly of the product and time 12 cycles. Determine the adequacy of this sample size.

3.   Lay out a 100-foot walking course in such a way that the total time for walking the course can be measured. Using the standard 3 mile per hour pace as 100 percent performance, one whould walk the course in 0.2785 minute. Figure 12 shows a chart that relates measured time for walking 100 feet versus percent performance using the 3 mile per hour pace as a standard. Working in groups, have subjects walk the 100-foot course while one individual measures elapsed time. Others in the group should rate the walking pace in percent. After observing several different walking paces, compare actual pace (from

Figure 12) with rated pace. Plot the results on a graph of actual pace in percent versus rated pace.

4.   A department store manager wishes to make a work sampling study to
estimate the percent time that clerks are busy waiting on customers and the
percent time that they are idle. The current best guess is that clerks are idle
25 percent of the time. Determine the number of observations required if we
wish to be 95 percent confident that the result is within ± 1.5 percentage
points.

5.   You have obtained the following work sample from a study during 40-hour
work week:

Idle time	20 percent
Performance rating	135 percent
Total parts produced	280

The allowance for this particular type of work is 10 percent. Determine the
standard time per part.

6.   A time study is made of a punch-press operator, the results of which yield
an average actual time per piece of 0.30 minute. The punch-press operator's

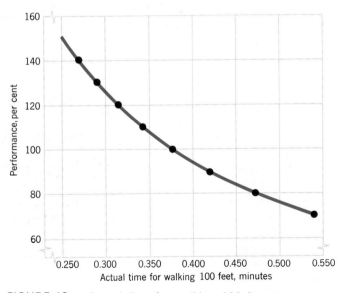

FIGURE 12.   Actual time for walking 100 feet versus performance in percent with 3 miles per hour used as a standard
walking pace.

performance during the study was rated at 120 percent. If total allowances are 10 percent of standard time, what is the standard time in minutes for this operation?

7.   A continuous time study was made on a collating job in an office with the following results:

Element	Cycle (minutes)						Performance Rating (percent)
	1	2	3	4	5	6	
Apply glycerin to fingers	0.04	—	0.46	—	3.10	—	120
Get four pages with each hand	0.16	0.35	0.63	2.99	3.24	3.45	105
Jog eight sheets	0.19	0.39	2.83*	3.04	3.28	3.49	110
Staple and put aside	0.22	0.41	2.86	3.07	3.30	3.52	90

*Operator dropped the eight sheets on the floor.

(a) Calculate the normal time per collated set.

(b) If allowances for this type of work total 15 percent, what would be the standard time per set?

(c) Should the set of papers dropped be considered as a part of the study or should this data be thrown out? What are the implications of not considering this data in the study?

REFERENCES

[1] Abruzzi, A. *Work Measurement.* Columbia University Press, New York, 1952.

[2] Allderige, J. M. "Statistical Procedures in Stop-Watch Work Measurement." *Journal of Industrial Engineering,* **7** (4), 154–163, July–Aug. 1956.

[3] Barnes, R. M. *Motion and Time Study: Design and Measurement of Work* (6th ed.). John Wiley, New York, 1968.

[4] Barnes, R. M. *Work Sampling* (2nd ed.). John Wiley, New York, 1957.

[5] Bailey, G. B., and R. Presgrave. *Basic Motion Time-Study.* McGraw-Hill, New York, 1957.

[6] Gustat, G. H. "Applications of Work Sampling Analysis " *Proceedings of Tenth Time Study and Methods Conference,* SAM–ASME, New York, Apr. 1955.

[7] Gustat, G. H. "Incentives for Indirect Labor." *Proceedings, Fifth Industrial Engineering Institute,* University of California, Berkeley–Los Angeles, 1953.

[8] Heiland, R. E., and W. J. Richardson. *Work Sampling.* McGraw-Hill, New York, 1957.

[9] Maynard, H. B., G. J. Stegemerten, and J. L. Schwab. *Methods—Time Measurement*. McGraw-Hill, New York, 1948.

[10] Müller, E. A. "The Physiological Basis of Rest Pauses in Heavy Work." *Quarterly Journal of Experimental Physiology*, **38** (4), 1953.

[11] Mundel, M. E. *Motion and Time Study* (3rd ed.). Prentice-Hall, Englewood Cliffs, N.J., 1960.

[12] Nadler, G. *Work Design A Systems Concept* (Rev. ed.). Richard D. Irwin, Homewood, Ill., 1970.

[13] Niebel, B. W. *Motion and Time Study* (5th ed.). Richard D. Irwin, Homewood, Ill., 1972.

[14] Quick, J. H., J. H. Duncan, and J. A. Malcolm. *Work Factor Time Standards*. McGraw-Hill, New York, 1962.

PART 4
OPERATIONS PLANNING AND CONTROL

CONTENTS

CHAPTER 13

PRODUCTION-
INVENTORY
SYSTEMS

The several chapters of Part 3 dealt with the design of productive systems. When such a system has been designed, we may presume that there has been a careful specification of the product or whatever it is that is being processed, a specification of the nature and sequence of the processes, and a physical design or layout that relates the processes into a unified physical system. As a part of the system, jobs must be designed to fit into the needs of the processes and flow of work, and consideration must be given to the question of the location of the system.

Now, however, we shall concern ourselves with the design of information systems, policies, and control procedures necessary to operate the system. Thus Part 4 is concerned with such questions as these: What policies and procedures will guide us in setting basic production rates? Should we hire or lay off personnel and in what numbers? When is the use of overtime justified instead of increasing the size of the work force? When should we take the risk of accumulating seasonal inventories to stabilize employment? How big should inventories be to sustain the production-distribution process? What policies and procedures are appropriate for the control of inventories and the re-ordering of materials? What policies and procedures are necessary to schedule men and machines for effective operations? Should the utilization of men and machines be maximized or is there a value to idleness? How do we maintain the reliability of the productive system so that specified quantity and quality are produced? When is a preventive maintenance policy justified? What policies and procedures can be effective in controlling labor and other costs? Is it possible to control *costs*, or is it really the activities that must be controlled.

These and other important questions are the focus of Part 4. In some instances there are rigorous models to help guide decisions and policies such as in aggregate planning and scheduling, inventories, maintenance, and quality control. In other situations, policies and procedures are systematic but thus far not accessible by the newer analytical methods such as in labor and cost control programs.

Before proceeding, let us again recognize that there are extremely important problems in the operation and control of most productive systems, related to human values, supervision of personnel, selection of personnel, and organizational behavior, which are not covered in this book. Although we recognize these behaviorally oriented problems, in this book we have established a more limited definition of operating problems. Students should seek other books and courses for the behavioral orientation.

A SYSTEMS POINT OF VIEW

Let us begin our analysis of operating problems by returning to the basic schematic diagram for the generalized model of operational systems shown in Figure 1. Figure 1 is identical to Figure 4 in Chapter 3, and a general review of the discussion on pages 55–59 is appropriate at this point. Figure 1 shows general relationships between the operations function and six crucial flows: information, orders, materials or energy, cash, populations, and capital equipment. The major reason for focusing our attention on Figure 1 again is to begin our discussion of operating problems in a "systems" context. While we shall discuss the several major topics of Chapters 14–19 separately, it is important that we see some of the interrelationships between them.

Interdependence of Functions

Of course, the operations phase of the organization is our focus, yet we must maintain a systems viewpoint with regard to the interdependence of operations functions and other functions such as marketing, finance, personnel, purchasing, and the professional or service function. Note in Figure 1 the existence of pools of labor, materials and energy, equipment, external services, and financing. These pools exist in the environment and there is, of course, interaction between our enterprise and competitive enterprises in drawing on these pools of supply.

When we attempt to structure the problems of operations management, reality demands that we consider not only the complex inter-

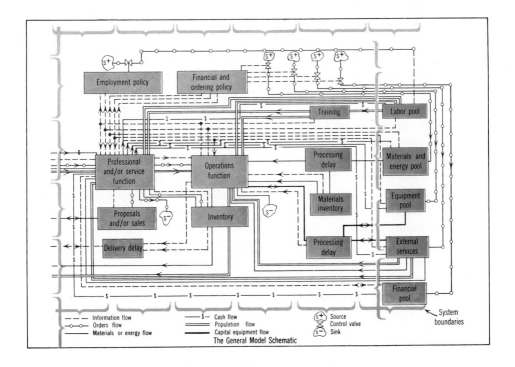

FIGURE 1.   General model for operational systems—basic schematic diagram. (From Reisman and Buffa. [6].)

actions of the factors internal to the operations phase but, where appropriate, the interactions between the operations phase and other functions as well as their interactions with the environment systems. Thus, the planning of production rates, size of work force, use of overtime, and planned inventories (commonly called aggregate planning and scheduling) demands a model that accounts for some of these "between subsystems" interactions in setting production rates and employment levels for the upcoming period. The first, and perhaps most obvious, environment factor is consumer demand where we are in direct competition with other enterprises. Part of the aggregate planning model must include a forecast as well as the feedback of information on our actual orders flow. The production rate and employment level decisions are also dependent on interactions with the labor pool (since the decisions may call for either hiring or layoff), on the raw material and equipment pools to facilitate the production rate decisions, and on the financing pool (since the decision may call for the accumulation or drawing down of inventories). The coordination with other functional subsystems is parallel; that is, marketing in the forecast problem, purchasing in the equipment and raw material problem, personnel in the manpower problem, and finance in the inventory, payroll, and purchasing problems.

The power of system analysis is in the development of the structure of interactions between a number of elements in a system. To develop an effective model for aggregate planning, for example, we do not have to develop a detailed model for all coordinating subfunctions. We need only to represent the resulting interacting effects. Thus we do not need a detailed model of the personnel-manpower pool complex to reflect its effects on the aggregate planning problem just because we may hire or layoff personnel. We can abstract just the parts that are meaningful to the problem at hand. For example, because of union agreements the layoff rate may be limited to a certain number of men or a certain per cent of the work force. Or, because of the competition for labor in the pool, wages may have gone up. This fact needs to be reflected in the aggregate planning model because that model will be attempting to balance certain kinds of costs. As long as we relate the interdependencies of the various organizational functions, we shall be utilizing a true systems point of view. Retaining this viewpoint is difficult in complex organizational problems, but it is important to attempt to do so to the greatest extent possible.

If it were possible we might like to construct a single model of the operational system within the framework of Figure 1 which would forecast the operation of any production system, given the characteristics of the system and the various related subsystems. This is much too ambitious at the present stage of development of the analysis operational systems. Currently, we must be satisfied with models that usually account for only small parts of the problem. Maintaining the systems point of view helps to minimize the effects of *suboptimization*; that is, the best solution viewed from within the subsystem but not the best solution when viewed within the system as a whole. In general, our present capability does not permit the strict adherence to this systems point of view. In attempting to approach it, however, we shall endeavor to apply this principle: models of operations should be as broad as practicable, taking into account (insofar as is feasible by means of existing techniques) interactions between various subsystems. The result is that whenever such a model has been reasonably validated and indicates incremental gains which exceed incremental costs, we shall assume that the systems point of view has been approached.

Suboptimization

Because of its importance, let us expand somewhat on suboptimization. It can and does occur in many ways. We could easily suboptimize by taking a short-range view of maximizing profits or an organizational narrow gage view. A short-range view might cause a production manager to produce according to the rise and fall of the sales curve. With a broader horizon he would look for trends and seasonal variations and develop a production program to meet requirements over the longer term. The latter view might stabilize production levels, causing higher total inventory costs but substantially lower hiring and layoff costs. The short-range view would be a suboptimization, since it focuses only on the payroll cost but ignores the long-time effects and costs of production fluctuation and inventories.

Organizational suboptimization is common where the production function and the distribution function are operated essentially as two separate businesses. The factory, then, will try to minimize its costs independently, as will the sales and distribution function. Thus sales and distribution will be faced mainly with inventory management, shipping, and customer service problems and will try to minimize the associated costs. On the other hand, the factory will be faced with minimizing production cost. Each suborganization, optimizing separately, probably will result in a combined cost somewhat larger than if the attempt were made to optimize the combined system as a whole. The reasons are fairly obvious. In minimizing the costs of inventories, the sales function will transmit directly to the factory most of the effects of sales fluctuation instead of absorbing these fluctuations through buffer inventories; suboptimization is the result. By coordinating their plans and efforts, however, it may be possible to achieve some balance between inventory costs and production fluctuation costs.

SYSTEM CONTROL

The elements of the control of a productive system are shown in Figure 2. While there may be many different aspects of operation to consider, the general control process is the same regardless of which particular

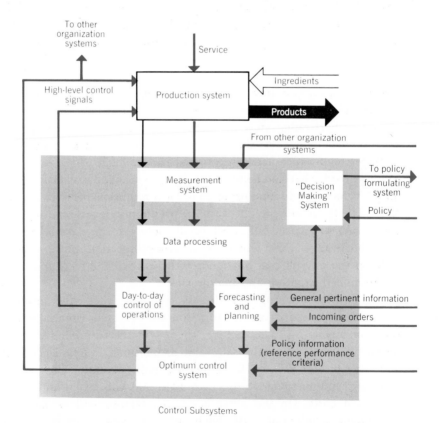

FIGURE 2.   General structure of control systems in relation to a production system. (From Alcalay and Buffa [1].)

factor is being controlled. Figure 2 is generalized in terms of a measurement system, data processing, day-to-day control, forecasting and planning, and so on. While Figure 2 is generalized in structure, let us discuss it in terms of an example, the control of inventories.

Our objective is to control the level of finished goods inventories. To do this we must set standards for inventory levels and procedures for maintaining them. This is represented in Figure 2 by the block "day-to-day control of operations." These standards for inventory control involve some kind of model for relating reordering or replenishment procedures, relevant costs, and policies regarding the desired level of customer service, that is, a desired level of risk of stock runout. Control models for inventories are discussed in Chapter 14. Day-to-day control is based on measurements concerning the actual level of inventories which are channeled through data processing for any required computing or transformation and compared to the standards in the model. The standards in the model may signal reordering a standard quantity if inventories have fallen below a preset order point, or the model may call for the computation of the amount to be ordered each period based on actual demand and other factors. Thus we have a basic day-to-day feedback control loop which takes action to readjust inventories.

On a longer time base, however, "forecasting and planning" is assessing the changing level of demand to determine if the standards for control should be changed. Based on new information concerning demand, the ordering rules may be changed as well as the amount of reserve or safety stock. Thus the day-to-day control model and the new information from forecasting and planning are inputs to the "optimum control system." The optimum control system then automatically responds to both day-to-day needs and longer time shifts in demand. Other policy information may be pertinent to the adjustment of the optimum control system. For example, a policy to establish a stabilized work force will allow relatively large inventory accumulations in slack demand periods and their reduction to near minimum levels in high demand periods. Control of other aspects of the system follows the same pattern. In general the controls of interest to us are those associated with the control over the amounts produced or quantity control, control over quality, and cost control.

Quantity Control

The control over quantities produced is not exercised by simply setting production rates. There is a complex interaction between actual demand

and its forecasted pattern, production rates, and the size of the work force. The amount to produce in the upcoming planning period depends on the use of the most economical combination of equivalent capacities (such as existing inventories, regular production, overtime production, and additional production due to an increased work force size) in relation to some reasonable time horizon for demand. If we see ahead in the planning time horizon an annual seasonal demand slump, then the comparative costs of laying off some workers must be balanced against carrying excess inventories into the seasonal slump. Production rates and layoff decisions depend on the combination of equivalent capacities which minimizes these combined costs. Similarly, if we see ahead in the planning time horizon the seasonal demand peak, then the comparative costs of hiring workers and using overtime must be balanced against the costs of back-ordering and lost sales. Production rate and hiring decisions depend on the combination of capacities that minimizes these costs. Basic production rate and employment level decisions are of great importance; we shall consider them in greater detail in Chapter 15. The existence of inventories in the system, of course, has an impact on production rate and employment decisions; inventory models and policies are the subjects of Chapter 14.

The effective implementation of basic aggregate plans for production largely depends on how men and machines are actually utilized; that is, how these resources are scheduled and controlled. In continuous production systems, changes in basic production rate and employment levels called for by the aggregate plan require a rebalancing of facilities and assembly lines to adjust to the new employment level and match the new output rates. In intermittent production systems the detailed scheduling problem is much more complex since materials are moved through the facility in lots. General-purpose equipment is usually used in intermittent systems, and many different orders compete for and share the time available on such equipment. Thus, for each lot or order, machines must be set up especially and workers assigned to operate them. In addition to the scheduling problem, an information system must be established to feed back current information on the status of orders so that operations can be controlled. For large-scale projects the activities required may be planned, scheduled, and controlled as a network of activities. These scheduling and control problems are covered in Chapters 16, 17, and 18.

Finally, in terms of quantity control, the designs of both maintenance and quality control procedures are important. Both sets of procedures have an impact on the control of output levels since both are concerned with maintaining the reliability of the physical system. If equipment is not maintained in good working order, there will be interference with attaining the planned production quotas. If machines break down, they cause idle labor costs, sometimes for an entire production line. Thus preventive maintenance programs are often economical. Quality control procedures also have an effect on the attainment of production quotas. When production quotas are planned they are, of course, for output that meets quality standards, not scrap. The special problems of quality control is the subject of Chapter 19.

Quality Control

The control of quality is based originally on the design of processes and the selection of equipment. The basic quality capabilities must be designed into the system. But, given these basic capabilities, the desired quality levels are controlled by selecting and training personnel, maintaining the physical plant and its equipment, controlling the quality requirements of incoming raw materials, and controlling the quality characteristics of the output of individual processes and of the system as a whole. As just discussed under quantity control, machine breakdown can have important effects on schedules and idle labor costs. But, one cause of breakdowns can be failure to produce according to the established quality standards, so maintenance of the reliability of the system refers both to quantity and quality of output.

The techniques of quality control are largely centered in inspection methods and statistical control methods. The statistical control methods are of particular interest since they have broad application for probabilistic controls generally. The statistical methods fall into two main groups, acceptance sampling and process control. Acceptance sampling can determine the probability that the entire batch or lot of materials meets quality standards on the basis of a sample. Process control involves a continuous or periodic sampling of the output of a process to check if quality standards are within limits. The established control limits are based on probabilities. Therefore, when a sample falls outside of control limits, the probability is high that action is needed. Conversely, as long as samples fall within control limits, the probability is low that poor quality is being produced in any meaningful amount. Process control is truly management by the exception principle. Quality control as a general subject and acceptance sampling and process control in particular are discussed in Chapter 19.

Cost Control

As we noted previously the currency given the term *cost control* is in a sense not justified. Costs are a result and a function of the activities involved. If the activities are properly controlled, then the resulting costs are controlled. The simple reason for this is that most of the models of managerial systems discussed throughout this book have cost-related criterion functions. When we establish control of the activities on the basis of these criterion functions, we control costs. Nevertheless, the term *cost control* has a more specific meaning which has to do with the periodic generation of important cost figures and their organization to provide data on which many important decisions can be made to control activities and therefore costs.

CLASSIFICATION OF PRODUCTION-INVENTORY SYSTEMS

It is useful to establish a general classification of production-inventory systems at this point rather than to continue discussing such systems in general. The reason for wishing to be more specific about particular kinds of production-inventory systems is that the nature of the most important operating problems is quite different for different systems. We shall establish two bases of classification: (a) continuous versus intermittent systems, and (b) the production of inventoriable versus noninventoriable items.

Continuous versus Intermittent Systems

The continuous-intermittent basis of classification was used in discussing models of production systems in Chapter 2. Continuous systems were typified there by the production lines, continuous chemical processes, and, in general, by production systems of enterprises that produce the high-volume standardized products for which our society is noted. The basis for the term *continuous*, however, is that the physical flow of material in production is either continuous or approaches continuous movement. On the other hand, intermittent production systems are those where the physical facilities must be flexible enough to handle a wide variety of products and sizes, or where the basic nature of the activity imposes changes of product design from time to time. In such instances, no single sequence pattern of processes is appropriate so the relative location of the operations must be a compromise that is best for all products. The emphasis is on flexibility of product design, processes, flow paths through the system, and so on. The system is termed "intermittent" because the flow is intermittent. Intermittent systems are characterized by custom or job order-type machine shops, batch-type chemical operations, general offices, large-scale one-time projects, etc.

The basis of the continuous-intermittent classification is then the basic nature of the physical layout of facilities in the *production system*. We now wish to broaden our conception of what constitutes the system to include the supply of raw materials at the head end and the distribution of finished goods at the output end of the manufacturing phase. Thus, the term *production-inventory system* for the expanded concept includes the inventories throughout and suggests the second basis for classification.

Systems for Inventoriable versus Noninventoriable Items

Figure 3 is a diagram of a production-inventory system for an inventoriable product. It emphasizes the broad flow characteristics of the system as a whole. In Figure 3, the manufacturing phase could be either continuous or intermittent. Of course, many intermittent manufacturing systems produce to inventory. Such plants may be physically arranged and scheduled internally like job shops. Common situations where this is true are the machine shops of the large automotive companies. Such shops are closed to job order from outside the organization and may produce a set of products repetitively in cycles. Equipment is time-shared between many different products, and the products are produced to inventory because they are of standard designs for which there are predictable markets. Such intermittent shops are called closed job shops because they are closed to job order.

Thus, we may have production-inventory systems in the inventoriable classification whose physical configuration may be of the continuous as well as the intermittent types. Now if we refer again to Figure 3, we may find a commonly occurring enterprise specialization in the distribution of products. These enterprises specialize in the distribution of products and are called simply "distributors." The portion of Figure 3 under

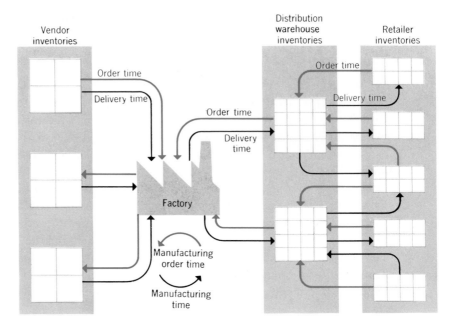

FIGURE 3.   Supply-production-distribution system for an inventoriable product. Time lags are characteristic between and within each stage, and inventories
serve vital functions at each stage.

managerial control for distribution systems focuses attention mainly on
inventories. The operations phase of such enterprises has to do with the
replenishment of inventories, the control of inventory levels, and shipment. Service rendered may be judged in terms of frequency of stock-
out or inability to supply the demands for products from inventories.
Distribution systems are nearly pure inventory systems from an operations management viewpoint and are of interest simply because they are
common in society. Chapter 14 is devoted to inventories and inventory
models. Thus, production-inventory systems for inventoriable items
include systems where production is continuous, systems where production may be intermittent, and systems involving only distribution.
Grouping systems involving inventoriable items together is of importance because we can use inventories effectively in aggregate planning
and programming as discussed in Chapter 15.

Custom products and services require production-inventory systems
that have no finished goods inventories. They may still be characterized
by the term production-inventory system, however, because they have

raw material and in-process inventories which are subject to control in some measure. Open job shops and large-scale one-time projects are the most prominent examples. The open job shop produces to job order or contract. These orders or contracts may never be repeated so the requirement for flexibility is an overriding one. The focus of managerial attention is on the scheduling and utilization of men and machines to meet agreed due dates and quality standards. The difference between the open job shop and the large-scale project in our classification is largely one of scale and complexity. There is no clear dividing line between the two systems, except that when a contract is large enough and complex enough to justify the special PERT-type planning and scheduling techniques discussed in Chapter 18, it is called a large-scale project.

A Comparison

To summarize, the continuous-intermittent classification results in the following:

Continuous Systems	Intermittent Systems
Production-inventory systems for high-volume standardized products	Job shops (open and closed)
Distribution systems	Large-scale projects

This classification is most useful for designing the layout of physical facilities and for indicating the nature of detailed scheduling of both men and machines.

The inventoriable-noninventoriable item classification results in the following:

Systems for Inventoriable Items	Systems for Noninventoriable Items
Continuous high-volume standardized product systems	Open job shop systems
Closed job shop systems	Large-scale projects
Distribution systems	

This classification is most useful in determining the nature of aggregate planning and programming that is appropriate. The production-inventory system concept is also useful in focussing on the system as a whole to avoid the organization suboptimization to which we referred earlier. When one takes an integrated view of materials flow, it is possible to see more clearly which alternatives for organizing enterprise functions might be most effective.

ORGANIZING FOR INTEGRATED MATERIAL FLOW

It is often difficult to conceive of the overall flow of material and information that directly or indirectly affects total system costs. In most instances, the system extends at least to the immediate supplier of raw materials, and it is entirely feasible that it could extend further upstream than the immediate supplier. Suppliers' modes of distribution may well affect costs for the overall system being considered. Similarly, the total system extends downstream through production phases to and including finished product distribution as indicated by Figure 3. Such a total systemic view may well involve many separate organizations. It is undoubtedly fair to say that a total integrated analysis of such tremendously complex systems is still not really practical for day-to-day operation, although the computer simulation of such large-scale systems holds considerable promise.

The long-run trend in job specialization commented on in Chapter 11 on job design has had a parallel in overall enterprise organization. As organizations have grown, the multitude of functions which must be performed tends to split off into various divisions, departments, and groups. With this fragmentation comes an apparent need for specialists within the organization. Each specialist tends to assume his role and become more proficient in carrying out his duties. The larger the organization the greater is the degree of specialization and the greater the tendency to lose track of the overall organization objectives and to concentrate on strengthening the individual function. Since the specialist's functions are limited in scope, he drives for success through suboptimization, for example, minimizing his own costs on a local basis. Since his performance is judged on a local basis, he finds it to his advantage to attempt to influence policies and practices wherever possible which will make his own local unit look good. The defect is not in the psychology of an individual who reacts this way to his environment, but in the organization structure which constrains him. The point is that an overall system view would encourage just the opposite effect. It would encourage a balancing of interdepartmental advantage and disadvantage to seek a system optimum. While it may be true that overall system analysis may still not be capable of handling this problem,

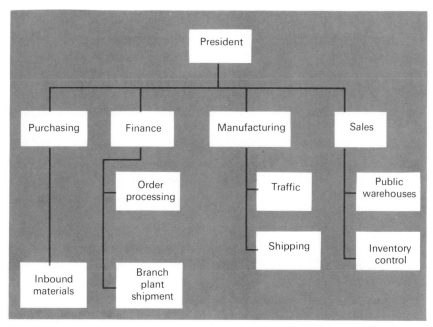

FIGURE 4.   Organization of Purex Corporation prior to adoption of an integrated material flow concept. (From Brewer and Rosenzweig [2].)

organization structures can be designed to help minimize suboptimization. Following is a brief report of a case study in reorganization to achieve better integrated control.

The *Purex Corporation* [2] had the basic organization structure illustrated by Figure 4 prior to a study which had the objective of reorganization to obtain a more integrated control. Many of the material flow functions were fragmented and responsibility was divided between several major departments. In the old organization a traffic manager was responsible for arranging transportation of outbound products from major production plants to warehouses and other distribution points. The production planning function was handled by informal committees with members from sales, manufacturing, and finance. The warehousing function was handled by the sales department as was the inventory control function. Managers of some smaller plants reported to the financial function.

These plants produced liquid bleach throughout the country and handled some warehousing of finished products produced at other major production facilities. Shipping of finished products from these

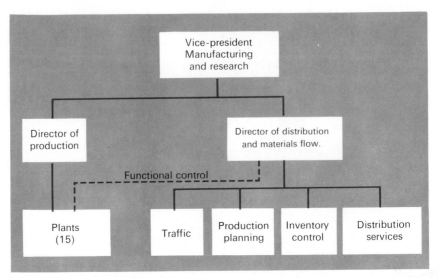

FIGURE 5.　Organization of Purex Corporation for control of material flows after adoption of the integrated concept. (Adapted from [2].)

plants was the responsibility of the plant manager and, as a result, the lines of authority for these functions emanated from the vice-president for finance. Some functional authority was exercised by the traffic manager because it was his duty to furnish routing guides and transportation rates. Inasmuch as the sales department was responsible for inventory control and maintenance of inventories at regional public warehouses, it also exercised some control over shipments from these facilities. The purchasing function was responsible for control of all procurement of raw material and supplies; however, order processing was a function of finance. There was no attempt to exercise overall control of the material flow process.

A reorganization of the activities and functions resulted in the structure shown in Figure 5. A number of important functions governing the flow of materials are placed under the jurisdiction of a director of distribution and materials flow. He has direct line authority over traffic, overall production planning, inventory control, and distribution services. Regional traffic managers report directly to him; in addition, he has functional control over the distribution function at the various branch plants. Since these branch plants now report directly to the director of production, who in turn reports to the vice-president of manufacturing and research, this functional authority achieves line status because the distribution and materials flow director can exercise a great deal of control over all activities affecting material movement at the branch plant level. Direct line authority over inventory control now gives him the power he needs to control movement both into and out of public warehouses located throughout the country. Although it is not shown on the chart of Figure 5, the director of distribution and materials flow also works closely with the director of purchasing in controlling inbound shipments of raw materials and supplies.

It is reported that the new organizational structure has effected many benefits to the company, resulting in estimated cost reductions of several hundred thousand dollars. Public warehouses have been reduced in number from 65 to 35. More efficient management controls are now exercised over inventories and production planning, and integrated management of many functions related to the flow process is being exercised.

It may be interesting to contrast the material flow process in rather different kinds of organizations. The Purex Corporation is primarily concerned with outbound movements of finished goods. It has more than 200 finished products that must be distributed from several plants and warehouses to wholesalers and retailers throughout the country. The inbound materials are few in number and consist primarily of bulk shipments of chemicals, oils, etc. A contrasting situation would be one involving a complex assembled product with relatively few customers; for example, the Boeing Airplane Company [2]. In the Boeing Company, the primary concern is inbound and internal movement of more than 100,000 different parts and the raw materials required for the production of each airplane. The inbound materials and parts are drawn from nearly every state in the country and, in general, each individual shipment is small. The end product is normally flown away by the customer. Distribution activities are normally concerned with spare parts which must be moved to a limited number of airline companies and military organizations. The Boeing Company is in general production-oriented; however, sales is an important activity. Purex, however, might be considered sales-oriented with production playing a vital role.

The general orientation of these two companies is indeed quite opposite. Transportation costs alone in the Purex Company amount to more than $8,000,000 per year, or approximately 10 per cent of the sales dollar. In the Boeing Company, on the other hand, transportation costs are a fraction of 1 per cent of sales. Traffic and distribution in the Purex Corporation are of extreme importance, whereas in the Boeing Company, traffic plays a minor role. Nevertheless, the overall material-control problems in the two organizations are very great. In both instances, an organization structure which accommodates an integrated view of the material flow from supplier to ultimate consumer would contribute to a system optimum.

SUMMARY

The term *production-inventory system* places emphasis on the fact that we are dealing with the total supply-production-distribution system, not just the physical production system. There are interfunctional dependencies in the organization which must be taken into account, such as interactions between production, marketing, finance, procurement, and so on. There are also time lags in the overall flow process which place emphasis on the dynamic nature of the system. While we may most easily think in terms of the physical flow, Figure 1 traces six different flows of importance. Information flow is of crucial value in setting managerial controls over quantity, quality, and costs.

We have established two bases of classifying production-inventory systems: (a) continuous versus intermittent systems and (b) systems that produce for inventories versus those that do not. The continuous-intermittent basis is most useful when considering the problems of physical layout and detailed scheduling of activities. The inventoriable-noninventoriable basis of classification is most useful when considering the problems of aggregate planning and programming.

An operations management point of view requires us not only to look at the inventory and the material flow of processes within the manufacturing phase, but to examine the overall system of flow from suppliers of raw material through manufacturing and distribution and ultimate delivery to users. When the total system is not viewed as an integrated whole, organizational fragmentation can occur which is likely to lead to each organizational unit establishing policies and practices which may not be the best ones for the system as a whole. The Purex study indicates that basic organization structure can help promote an integrated system viewpoint. The concepts of "integrated material flow management" also require that we look at not just the production unit separately or the distribution of products separately but also the combined production-distribution system which is in effect. The objective in such a situation is to minimize total system costs rather than certain costs taken separately.

IMPORTANT TERMS

Numbers in parentheses indicate page numbers.

1. Aggregate planning (432, 436)
2. Closed job shop (437)
3. Continuous system (432, 434)
4. Distribution system (436)
5. Forecasting (431)
6. Intermittent system (432, 434)
7. Large-scale project (437)
8. Open job shop (437)
9. Optimum control system (431)
10. Quality control (433)
11. Quantity control (432–433)
12. Suboptimization (429)
13. System control (430)
14. System for high-volume standardized items (434, 437)
15. System for inventoriable items (435)
16. System for noninventoriable items (435)
17. System point of view (426–427)

REVIEW QUESTIONS

Numbers in parentheses indicate page numbers.

1. Using Figure 1 as a frame of reference, discuss the interdependence of functions in the context of some particular control problem of your choice. (427)
2. What is meant by the term "suboptimization"? What is organizational suboptimization? (429)
3. Discuss the generalized structure of control subsystems using quality control as an example. (430–431)
4. What is the value of classifying production-inventory systems on the basis of continuous versus intermittent flow? (434–435)
5. What is the value of classifying production-inventory systems on the basis of whether or not the system is producing for inventory? (437)
6. What is a closed job shop system? Open job shop system? (437)
7. Discuss the supply-production-distribution system diagrammed in Figure 3. What problems of supply tend to interact with production and distribution? What problems of production tend to interact with problems of supply and distribution? What problems of distribution tend to interact with problems of supply and production? (435–436)
8. Compare the concepts of job specialization with those of managerial specialization as indicated in the original organization of the Purex Corporation. (439–440)

9. Compare the new organization of the Purex Corporation with the generalized supply-production-distribution system diagrammed in Figure 3. Has the new organization structure made it possible to take a more integrated point of view for the system as a whole? (435–436, 440–441)

10. Figure 6 shows an organization chart of the transport division of the Boeing Airplane Company. More than 100,000 different parts, pieces, and raw materials go into the production of each airplane. When completed, the plane is flown away by the customer. Spare parts supply is an important function for both the military and for airlines. Propose and justify an organization plan directed at integrated planning and control where a total system viewpoint is in effect. (441–442)

11. Select some organization, for example, a company known to you, and

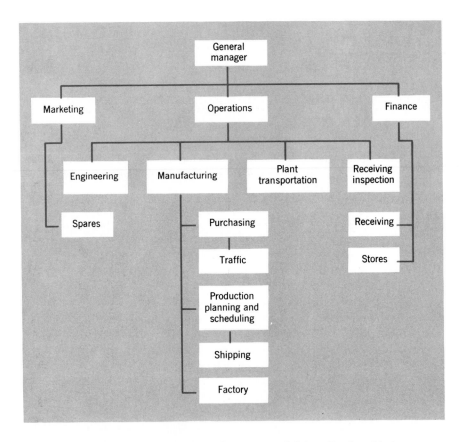

FIGURE 6.　Present organization of transport division, Boeing Airplane Company. (From [2].)

classify it according to the five classes of production-inventory systems discussed in the chapter. It would be preferable to select a system which might not be the pure form of any of the five discussed in the text. Develop a flow diagram similar to Figure 3 identifying the major raw-material, in-process, and finished-good stock points. Estimate the order and delivery times for the major links in the system. Describe the inventory replenishment rules used at each point. What portion of the overall system is under managerial control? Indicate by drawing a boundary around the system. If management could extend control up- and downstream in terms of ordering and replenishment of inventories, what would be accomplished? (437–438)

12. Assume the following classifications of inventories: raw materials, in process, and finished goods. Compare the magnitude of each of these sub-inventory problems with respect to each of the five production-inventory systems discussed in the text. (437)

13. Broaden the definition of the term of *inventory* to mean any productive resource which is stored for later use. Now reconsider each of the five production-inventory systems discussed in the text and discuss which productive resources might be stored and under what conditions.

SELF-TEST TRUE-FALSE QUESTIONS

Numbers in parentheses indicate page numbers.

1. Suboptimization can take place through a short-range view of maximizing profits or an organizational narrow-gauge view. (429)
2. Continuous production systems have simple inventory problems. (435, 436)
3. In intermittent production systems the emphasis is on flexibility of product design, processes, and flow paths through the system. (434–435)
4. Intermittent systems are characterized by large-scale one-time projects. (435)
5. The basis of the continuous-intermittent classification is the basic nature of the physical layout of facilities. (435)
6. Intermittent manufacturing systems produce custom products. (435)
7. Closed job shops are closed to job order. (435)
8. The operations phase of distribution enterprises has to do mainly with the replenishment of inventories, the control of inventory levels, and shipment. (436)
9. In distribution-type enterprises, service rendered may be judged in terms of the frequency of stock-out or inability to supply the demands for products from inventories. (436)

10. Production-inventory systems for inventoriable items involve continuous production systems. (435, 437)
11. The difference between the open job shop and the large-scale project is largely one of scale and complexity. (437)

REFERENCES

[1] *Alcalay, J. A., and E. S. Buffa. "A Proposal for a General Model of a Production System." *International Journal of Production Research*, Mar. 1963.

[2] Brewer, S. H., and J. Rosenzweig. "Rhochrematics and Organization." *California Management Review*, **3** (3), Spring 1961.

[3] Buffa, E. S., and W. H. Taubert. *Production—Inventory Systems: Planning and Control* (Rev. ed.). Richard D. Irwin, Homewood, Ill., 1972.

[4] Fey, W. R. "An Industrial Dynamics Case Study." *Industrial Management Review*, **4** (1), Fall 1962.

[5] Forrester, J. *Industrial Dynamics*. MIT Press, Cambridge, Mass., 1961.

[6] *Reisman, A., and E. S. Buffa. "A General Model for Production and Operations Systems." *Management Science*, **11** (1), Sept. 1964.

[7] Schoderbek, P. P. *Management Systems* (2nd ed.). John Wiley, New York, 1971.

[8] *Starr, M. K. "Evolving Concepts in Production Management." In: *Evolving Concepts in Management*. E. Flippo, editor. Academy of Management Proceedings, 24th Annual Meeting, Dec. 1964.

[9] Symkay, E. W. "Physical—Distribution Management: Concepts, Methods, and Organizational Approaches." In: *New Concepts in Manufacturing Management*, AMA Management Report No. 60, New York, 1961.

---

*The starred items are also reprinted in their entirety in: *Readings in Production and Operations Management*. E. S. Buffa, editor. John Wiley, New York, 1966.

CONTENTS

CHAPTER 14
FORECASTING AND INVENTORIES

Which production plan will meet sales requirements? What effect will the plan have on inventory levels? On manpower levels? On capacity requirements? What sort of service must we provide for? Do we dare run out of stock? What level of stock runout protection should we provide for? How should we control these inventories? Should we buy raw materials hand-to-mouth or in large lots? How big should the manufacturing lots be; that is, should we make 10, 50, 100, or 1000 at a time? Given an overall plan for production, how should we adjust production levels when actual sales patterns deviate from forecasts? How about detailed scheduling of departments and machines? How can we schedule to get the best utilization from men and machines without risk of tons of in-process inventories? How can we schedule to get orders through the production system on time? Are there common answers to all of these questions for both the intermittent and continuous models of production systems? An organization that has good answers to all of these questions is probably doing a good job in planning and controlling inventories and production.

Production plans occur at several levels and we should take a moment to distinguish between them. The broadest level of production plans deals with the initial design of the entire system. Here we are making plans that may set basic patterns for years to come in terms of location and general modes of production as well as more detailed methods, equipment, and layout. We have dealt with these problems in Part 3, and we have referred to that section as the *Design of the Production System* to distinguish it from the day-to-day, month-to-month, and even year-to-year planning for production to meet the immediate, shorter-term objectives and goals. We shall use the term *planning* to refer to the activities required for operation of the system. Of course, redesign of the system may be required periodically to keep up with production technology and changes in product design and product mixes.

Within the scope of planning for production, we may have relatively long-term plans concerning how we shall employ facilities. These plans, based on anticipated demands, may include the addition of capacity in the future. But in the shorter term, we must plan master schedules and inventory levels. In the shortest term, we must plan the material needs for individual parts and products, determine how each item will be processed, and schedule equipment and manpower for all parts and products in a manner which dovetails so that men, material, and machines are available at the right time and in the amounts needed.

INVENTORIES

The Functions of Inventories

In a sense, inventories make possible a rational production system. Without them we could not achieve smooth production flow, obtain reasonable utilization of machines and reasonable material handling costs, or expect to give reasonable service to customers on hundreds of items regarded as "stock" items. At each stage of both manufacturing and distribution, inventories serve the vital function of *decoupling* the various operations in the sequence beginning with raw materials, extending through all of the manufacturing operations and into finished goods storage, and continuing to warehouses and retail stores. Between each pair of activities in this sequence, inventories make the required operations independent enough of each other that low-cost operations can be carried out. Thus, when raw materials are ordered, a supply is ordered that is large enough to justify the out-of-pocket cost of putting through the order and transporting it to the plant. When production orders to manufacture parts and products are released, we try to make them big enough to justify the cost of writing the orders and setting up machines to perform the required operations. Otherwise, order writing and setup costs could easily become prohibitive. Running parts through the system in lots also tends to reduce handling costs because parts can be handled in groups. Similarly, in distributing finished products to warehouses and other stock points, freight and handling costs per unit go down if we can ship in quantity. Inventories are not only desirable, they are vital to low-cost manufacture.

These advantages are partially lost when we are dealing with custom manufacture. Because the lot size is dictated by the customer's order and the order may never be repeated, we cannot risk making extras. Thus, order writing, material-handling, and machine setup costs are just as high for the custom-sized lot as for an economically sized lot. Similarly, when the custom job is shipped to the customer, we cannot take advantage of carload or truckload freight rates. If the custom order were for only one part, all of these charges must be absorbed by the single part. It is easy to see why low-volume special orders are exceedingly expensive.

Unfortunately, the inventory question is not a one-sided one, which is precisely why inventories are a problem in the operation of a production system. If there were not an optimal level to shoot for, there would be no problem. Anyone could follow the simple rule: "make inventories as big as possible." Inventories require that invested capital be tied up and, therefore, there is an appropriate opportunity cost associated with their value. Not only that, they require valuable space and absorb insurance and taxation charges. It is not uncommon for a manufacturing concern to have 25 per cent of its total invested capital tied up in inventories. Table I shows figures for a sample of companies where we see that inventories were as low as 9 per cent for Interstate Bakeries and as high as 55 per cent for Pillsbury Mills.

The significance of the inventory problem is indicated by the inventory changes of Eastman Kodak and U.S. Steel between 1966 and 1970. In 1966 Kodak had 25 per cent of its assets in inventories which had declined to 19 per cent by 1970, representing a $36 million cost saving at a carrying cost of 20 per cent. In the same period U.S. Steel's

TABLE I.	Inventories in Relation to Total Assets for Several Companies			
Company	Date	Total Assets	Inventories	Inventories as a Per cent of Assets
Abbott Laboratories	Dec. 31, 1969	$345,382,000	$77,540,000	23
Allied Supermarkets	June 28, 1969	221,313,276	61,062,034	28
Eastman Kodak	Dec. 27, 1970	3,042,793,000	577,514,000	19
Interstate Bakeries	Dec. 27, 1969	78,203,372	7,263,890	9
Lockheed Aircraft	Dec. 29, 1968	936,783,000	285,707,000	31
Merck & Co.	Dec. 31, 1970	634,378,334	92,376,367	15
Pillsbury Mills	May 31, 1969	139,117,657	76,079,744	55
U.S. Steel	Dec. 31, 1970	3,450,149,776	923,458,156	27
John Wiley & Sons	Apr. 30, 1971	29,549,028	12,201,665	41

inventories increased from 23 to 27 per cent resulting in an increased cost of carrying inventories of almost $26 million if carrying costs are computed at 20 per cent of inventory value.

Thus, we have one set of costs that are fixed by the purchase or production order size and another set of costs that increase with the level of inventory. The first set of costs exerts pressure toward large purchase and production lots to reduce unit order writing and setup costs to a reasonable level. The second set of costs exerts pressure toward small lots in order to maintain inventory costs at reasonable levels. We are dealing with another problem which requires that good management find policies and decision rules which have the effect of balancing the various opposing costs for the system being considered.

Kinds of Inventories

To see the various kinds of inventories that might be appropriate for analytical purposes, let us take as an example the simple factory-warehouse system shown in Figure 1. The factory manufactures a number of products, but we shall consider only one. For this particular product, there is an average demand at the warehouse of 200 units per week. Normal warehousing procedures are to prepare a procurement order to the factory when the warehouse inventory falls to a critical level called the *order point*. It takes one week to prepare the order, get it approved and mailed, and finally received at the factory. Once the order is received at the factory, it takes two weeks for loading, trucking, and unloading at the warehouse.

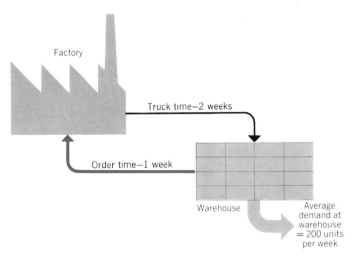

FIGURE 1.   Simple factory-warehouse system.

Pipeline Inventories.   The warehouse must, at a minimum, carry enough stock on hand to meet demand during the transit time. Figure 2 shows an idealized graph of the inventories required at the warehouse just to cover trucking time from the factory. The average transit inventory is the product of the truck time and the demand rate, or 2 × 200 = 400 units. At all times, then, 400 units are in motion from the factory to the warehouse or, in an equivalent sense, the warehouse must maintain an inventory that takes account of this fact. The order time delay of one week has the effect of a transit time, since the warehouse must also carry inventories to cover this delay. This point is a general one. Every lag in the system generates the need for inventory to fill the pipeline. Inside a production system we call it in-process inventory.

Lot Size or "Cycle" Inventories.   Let us return to our example. Since the truck is to make the trip from the factory to the warehouse, a logical question is how many to truck at one time. Most costs of trucking will occur anyway, and this is true of the costs of preparing the requisition and the other clerical costs involved. We shall not attempt to answer the question of what the lot size should be in this instance, but the general question will be discussed at a later point. Let us assume that orders are placed for a truckload of 800 units, equivalent to a four-week supply. Figure 3 shows an idealized graph of inventories

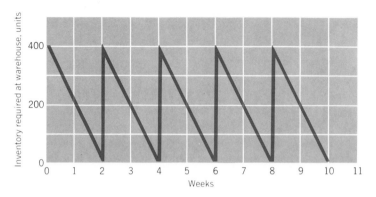

FIGURE 2.   Idealized graph of inventories required at the
warehouse to cover trucking time from the factory. The average
transit inventory is the product of truck time and demand rate,
or $2 \times 200 = 400$ units. Average inventory at the warehouse
is $400/2 = 200$ units.

required at the warehouse when orders are placed for a truckload.
We see that the average inventory at the warehouse must necessarily
increase.

Buffer Inventories.   Figure 3 is, of course, completely unrealistic
because it assumes that demand rate, truck time, and order time are all
constant. We know, however, that these factors are not ordinarily
constant, so a buffer stock is normally required to protect against un-
predictable variations in demand and supply time. Figure 4 shows the
contrast in inventory levels at the warehouse which might occur if the
maximum demand of 300 units per week occurred during the supply
time of three weeks. In order to not run out of stock, a buffer inventory
of 300 units would be required. As we shall see, techniques for taking
account of uncertainty are of great importance in inventory models.

Decoupling Inventories.   Previously we referred to the decoupling
function of inventories. Inventories make the required operations
independent enough of each other so that low-cost operations can be
carried out. For example, with inventories the warehousing operation
in Figure 1 can proceed relatively independently of manufacturing.
Similarly the existence of inventories at the retail level makes it possible
to carry on that function relatively independently; replenishment stocks
are ordered only periodically. No extra inventories over and above
those for the other functions we have discussed are necessary to provide

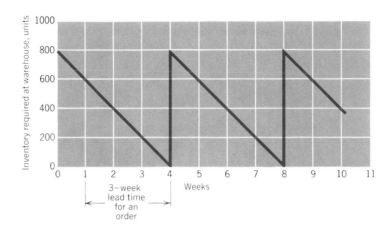

FIGURE 3.   Idealized graph of inventories required at the ware-house when orders are placed for a truckload, 800 units. Average inventory is now $800/2 = 400$ units. Transit inventories are un-changed.

for the decoupling function. But the existence of inventories provides the needed independence between stages.

Seasonal Inventories.   Many products have a fairly predictable but seasonal pattern through the year. Where this is true, management has the choice of changing production rates over the year to absorb the fluctuation in demand or of absorbing some or all of the fluctuation in demand with inventories. If we attempt to follow the demand curve through the seasons by changing production rates, the capital invest-ment for the system must provide for the peak capacity and we must absorb costs for hiring, training, and separating labor, as well as over-time costs. The use of inventories often can strike a better balance of these costs. The concepts and methods for handling this seasonal problem are covered in Chapter 15.

Before considering the models and methodologies which have been developed for inventory control, we shall discuss the question of forecasts. To decide on what risks we can justify for investing in inven-tories, we must have a means of estimating demand.

FORECASTING

The demand forecast is a critical input for some of the most important decision models in production and operations management, particularly those related to inventories, aggregate planning and scheduling, and

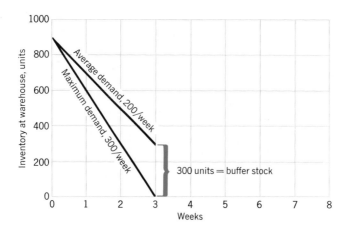

FIGURE 4.   Contrast of idealized inventory levels required
for average demand and maximum demand. The difference,
300 units, represents a minimum inventory or "buffer
stock" required to protect against the occurrence of shortages resulting from random fluctuations in demand.

production control. Of course, forecasts are also a critical input to the
design of productive systems for they are a direct factor in the determination of the most economical production design of products, processes, equipment, tooling, capacities, and layouts.

Time Horizons

Forecasts may be needed for roughly three different time spans: the
immediate future on which to base plans for current operations, the next
three to five years on which to base plans for capacity adjustments, and
long-range forecasts on which to base long-range plans for plant and
warehouse locations, capacities, and changes in the mix of product lines
or services. The intermediate and long-range forecasts involve the
study of consumer preferences and trends, the economy, and technological developments and trends.

Our interest is in forecasting for current operations and for a reasonable planning horizon time into the future. A reasonable horizon time
depends on the incremental value of additional periods of forecast
information. Ordinarily, if there is a seasonal aspect to demand, a
reasonable planning horizon would include one full season.

FIGURE 5. Reprinted through the courtesy of Helipot Division of Beckman Instruments, Inc.

Forecasting Methodology

The forecasting methodology which we shall discuss is applicable to the needs for guiding current operations for inventoriable items. The guidance of these current operations is closely tied in not only with the question of inventories but with the production planning and scheduling functions discussed in Chapters 15, 16, and 17.

Patterns of demand for specific products or services might vary widely but in general can be reduced to five components: average demand, trends in the average, seasonal effects, cyclic effects, and random variations. Figure 6 shows a portion of the record of monthly sales of a cooking utensil manufactured by Wearever, Inc. This figure shows the general situation where at least four of the five components are operating simultaneously (cyclic variations are beyond our scope). We need to be able to state a forecast for the upcoming period which takes account of the four components: average demand, trend, seasonal effects, and random variations.

Average Demand.   When we look at the actual sales (colored line) in Figure 6, the average demand for the entire three and one-half years is meaningless since the trend is an important factor. Therefore, some kind of moving average is needed which emphasizes the recent experience and estimates the trend effect. Furthermore, the estimate of demand for the upcoming period must take account of the expected seasonal variation. Finally, we wish not to be influenced by the random variations in demand when making an estimate for the upcoming period, or preferably we may wish to state the expected demand with probable limits of variation from the expected value due to random causes.

The common way of smoothing the effects of random variations in demand is to estimate average demand by some kind of *moving average*. Table II gives some sample demand data taken from the actual sales of Figure 6 for the first eleven periods. Note from Figure 6 and Table II

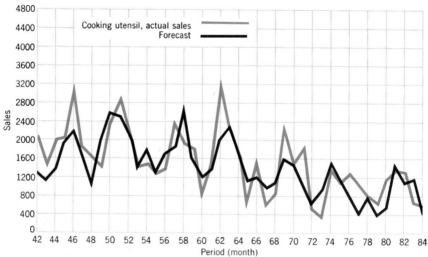

FIGURE 6.   Actual sales and an exponentially smoothed forecast for a cooking utensil at Wearever, Inc. (Adapted from [10].)

that actual demand is quite variable. The three-month moving average, however, is much more stable because the demand for any one month receives only a one-third weight. Extreme values are discounted; if they are simply random variations in demand, we are not strongly influenced by them if we gage demand by the three-month moving average. Greater smoothing effect is obtained by averaging over a longer period, as is shown by the five-month moving average in Table II. Extreme values are discounted even more since each period demand carries only a one-fifth weight in the moving average.

Simple moving averages provide a smoothing effect, but we may have greater interest in the most recent data and wish to emphasize it more in the estimate of demand. Weighted averages can achieve this objective. One convenient and easy to use method of accomplishing differential weighting and smoothing is by *exponentially weighted moving averages*.

The simplest exponential smoothing model estimates average forecast demand for the upcoming period $\bar{F}_t$ by adding or subtracting a fraction (α) of the difference between actual current demand D_t and the last forecast average $\bar{F}_{t-1}$. The new forecast average $\bar{F}_t$ is then:

TABLE II.   Actual Demand and a Three-Month and a Five-Month Moving Average*

Period	Actual Demand	Three-Month Moving Average	Five-Month Moving Average
42	2000	—	—
43	1350	1767	—
44	1950	1758	2075
45	1975	2342	2025
46	3100	2275	2065
47	1750	2133	1935
48	1550	1533	1980
49	1300	1683	1915
50	2200	2092	2035
51	2775	2442	—
52	2350	—	—

*Data From Figure 6 on the demand for a cooking utensil.

New smoothed average = old average

$+ \alpha$(new demand $-$ old average)

or stated symbolically,

$$\bar{F}_t = \bar{F}_{t-1} + \alpha(D_t - \bar{F}_{t-1}) \qquad (1)$$

The smoothing constant α is between 0 and 1 with commonly used values of 0.01 to 0.30. Equation 1 can be rearranged in a more convenient and possibly more understandable form as follows:

New smoothed average = α(new demand)

$+ (1 - \alpha)$ (old average)

or stated symbolically,

$$\bar{F}_t = \alpha D_t + (1 - \alpha)\bar{F}_{t-1} \qquad (2)$$

If $\alpha = 0.10$, then Equation 2 says that the forecast average in the up-coming period $\bar{F}_t$ will be determined by adding 10 per cent of the new actual demand information D_t and 90 per cent of the last forecast average $\bar{F}_{t-1}$. Since the new demand figure D_t includes possible random variation, we are discounting 90 per cent of those variations. Obviously, then, small values of α will have a stronger smoothing effect than large values. Conversely, large values of α will react more quickly to real changes (as well as random variations) in actual demand. The choice of α is normally guided by judgment, though studies could produce economically best or near best values of α.

It is important to place the time periods for $\bar{F}_t$, D_t, and $\bar{F}_{t-1}$ in perspective and to recognize that the so-called new forecast average $\bar{F}_t$ is not an extrapolation beyond known demand data. Rather, it is the most current smoothed average used to help guide current operations. In a sense then it is not a forecast but a statement of current demand. As a parallel, consider driving a car under three conditions of guiding the car: (1) based on a view out the windshield, (2) with the windshield covered but with a view out the side windows, and (3) with the windshield and side windows covered and a view out the back window, using the rear view mirror. Our situation is roughly comparable to being able to look out the side windows to see where we actually are. However, since there must be some time lag in compiling information on actual demand D_t, we are really looking out the *rear* side windows. But, there are no guesses, projections, or extrapolations involved. Each updated figure is based only on past actual demand data weighted to emphasize the most recent experience.

Extrapolation and Forecast.   Since no trend or seasonality is expected in the model, direct extrapolation from $\bar{F}_t$ to infer a forecast is justified. Therefore, the forecast for the upcoming period $\bar{F}_{t+1}^{*}$ is taken directly as the computed value of $\bar{F}_t$. (Starred symbols, *, will represent extrapolated or forecasted values.)

Equation 2 actually gives weight to all past actual demand data, though this is not obvious. This occurs through the chain of periodic calculations to produce forecast averages each period. In Equation 2, for example, the term $\bar{F}_{t-1}$ was previously computed from

$$\bar{F}_{t-1} = \alpha D_{t-1} + (1 - \alpha)\bar{F}_{t-2}$$

which includes the previous actual demand D_{t-1}. The $\bar{F}_{t-2}$ term was calculated in a similar way which included D_{t-2} and so on back to the beginning of the series. Therefore, the forecasts are based on a sequential process representing all previous actual demands.

Trend Effects.   If there were a trend present in the data, Equation 2 would respond to it but with a lag. But the apparent trend each period is simply the difference between the last two forecast averages $\bar{F}_t - \bar{F}_{t-1}$. This difference represents another series which can be estimated and smoothed by exponentially weighted averages just as with average demand.

If a large number of items were to be forecast, as is commonly true, the entire process could be computerized requiring minimum computer storage for each item, and the only new data to be supplied the computing program each period would be the current actual demand D_t.

Seasonal Adjustments.   The basis for including a seasonal adjustment to an exponentially smoothed forecast model is to develop a *base series* which represents the seasonal cycle. A demand ratio of actual to base series demand is then computed for each period. This ratio is then smoothed, correcting for trend effects, resulting in an expected demand ratio. Finally, the expected demand $E(D_t)$ is computed through a period by period multiplication of actual period demand D_t by the smoothed ratio, resulting in the final forecasted demand with trend and seasonal effects included. See references [3] and [6] for computed examples involving the simplest exponential model represented by Equation 2, the inclusion of trend effects represented by Equation 4, as well as examples including seasonal effects.

The exponential smoothing methodology is a competent and efficient way of forecasting demand for current operations. The forecast (black line) in Figure 6 is a record of actual sales and forecast sales for the cooking utensil at Wearever, Inc. The exponentially smoothed forecast tracks the average, trend, and seasonal effects, but discounts the most extreme demand variations as being simply random effects.

Of course, there is an entirely equivalent statistical methodology involving ordinarily moving averages, trend estimation by regression analysis, and so on, but the numerical work required is greater and it is not as well adapted to automatic computation since considerably more computer memory space is required for each item to be forecast.

SIZE OF PURCHASE AND PRODUCTION ORDERS

Purchase Order Quantities

The opposing pressures of the various inventory related costs produce a situation calling for policies and practices that strike a balance between these costs. The age-old question of how many units to buy at one time may be conceptualized by observing the behavior of the costs affected by changes in lot sizes.

First, let us define the system with which we are dealing. Figure 7 diagrams what happens to inventory levels for a particular item. If we assume an annual requirement of $R = 2400$ units, or an average of 200 per month, the inventory levels would fluctuate as in Figure 7a if we were to order in lots of $Q = 200$. The average inventory level for the idealized situation shown is one-half the number ordered at one time or $Q/2 = 100$ units. If the item is ordered more often in smaller quantities as shown in Figure 7b, we can see that the inventory level will fall in proportion to the number of units ordered at one time. Inventory level will, of course, affect the incremental costs of holding inventory, so we may say in effect that these costs of carrying inventory are proportional to the lot size Q, the number ordered at one time. From Figure 7 we also see that the total annual cost of placing orders increases as the number of units ordered at one time decreases. Therefore, we have isolated two types of incremental costs that represent the measures of effectiveness for the system we are developing. They are the costs associated with inventory level, *holding costs*, and with the number of orders placed, *preparation costs*.

In further defining the system with which we are dealing, let us attempt to construct a graph that shows the general relation between

Q (lot size) and the incremental costs which we have isolated. We noted in Figure 7 that if Q were doubled, average inventory level was doubled. It costs, perhaps, $c_H = \$0.60$ per year to carry a unit of inventory (interest costs, insurance, taxes, etc.). Since the average inventory level is $Q/2$ and the inventory cost per unit per year is $c_H = \$0.60$, then the annual incremental costs associated with inventory are:

$$\frac{Q}{2} c_H = \frac{Q}{2}(0.60) = 0.30Q \tag{6}$$

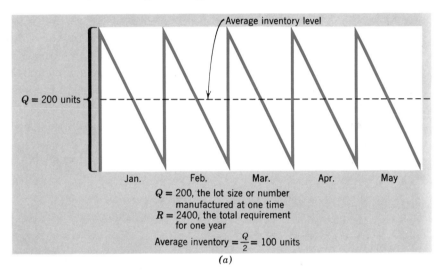

Average inventory level

$Q = 200$ units

Jan.   Feb.   Mar.   Apr.   May

$Q = 200$, the lot size or number
manufactured at one time
$R = 2400$, the total requirement
for one year

Average inventory $= \dfrac{Q}{2} = 100$ units

(a)

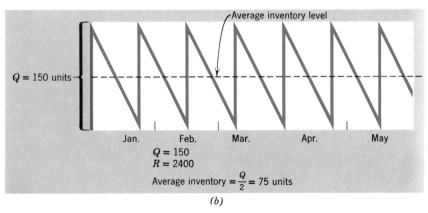

Average inventory level

$Q = 150$ units

Jan.   Feb.   Mar.   Apr.   May

$Q = 150$
$R = 2400$

Average inventory $= \dfrac{Q}{2} = 75$ units

(b)

FIGURE 7.   Simplified model of the effect of lot size on inventory levels.

Substituting different values for Q, we can plot the result as in Figure 8, curve (a).

We can plot the costs of ordering in a similar way. Let us use the symbol c_P to represent the costs of preparing and following up on an order. We calculate the number of orders by $R/Q = 2400/Q$. If each order preparation costs $c_P = \$20$, then the total annual incremental cost due to ordering is:

$$\frac{R}{Q} c_P = \frac{2400 \times 20}{Q} = \frac{48,000}{Q} \tag{7}$$

Therefore, as Q increases, the annual incremental cost due to ordering decreases. This makes good sense since as Q increases, the number of order preparations decreases and therefore the incremental cost decreases. This relationship is plotted in Figure 8, curve (b), by substituting different values of Q in $48,000/Q$.

Figure 8, curve (c), shows the resulting total incremental cost curve, determined simply by adding the two previous curves. Thus we have a model that expresses the effectiveness E as a function of the variables which define the system. The equation for the total cost curve is also

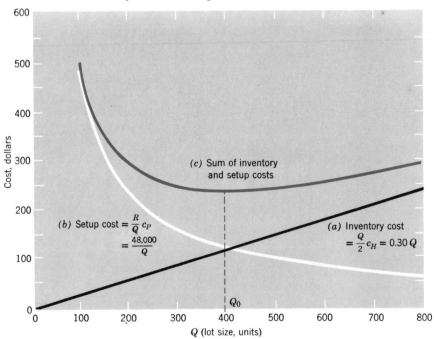

FIGURE 8.   Graphical model of simple inventory problem.

determined by adding the equations for the two separate cost functions and we have

$$E = \frac{Q}{2} c_H + \frac{R}{Q} c_P \tag{8}$$

$$
\begin{pmatrix} \text{Total} \\ \text{incremental} \\ \text{cost} \end{pmatrix} = \begin{pmatrix} \text{average} \\ \text{inventory} \end{pmatrix} \begin{pmatrix} \text{unit inven-} \\ \text{tory cost} \\ \text{per year} \end{pmatrix} + \begin{pmatrix} \text{number} \\ \text{of orders} \\ \text{per year} \end{pmatrix} \begin{pmatrix} \text{cost} \\ \text{of an} \\ \text{order} \end{pmatrix}
$$

Looking at this equation we might now ask which variables are controllable and which are uncontrollable. Recall that controllable variables are those which may be manipulated pretty much at the will of management. In our example the controllable variable is Q (lot size). Uncontrollable variables are those which management cannot control, at least not within the limitations of the problem. For example, consumer demand, taxes, and insurance rates would fall in this category. For our example, uncontrollable variables are c_H (inventory costs per unit), R (demand or requirements), and c_P (order preparation costs). We might argue that management can influence c_H by bringing pressure to bear to have taxes or insurance rates reduced. Nevertheless, management cannot change taxes and insurance rates at will. In general, tax rate changes would be reflected in E, and management would respond by adjusting Q to minimize E again. The new policy would be the best policy, given the new tax rate.

A General Solution.   For our simplified inventory model we can pick off the minimum point from the total incremental cost curve of Figure 8, curve (c). It is a minimum for $Q_0 = 400$ units. (The symbol Q_0 denotes the optimal value of Q.) This is a solution to the specific problem with the given values of c_H, R, and c_P. The important thing about this model, however, is that we can obtain a general solution which will give us the minimum point directly for any values of c_H, R, and c_P. From the equation for the total incremental cost, we may derive a formula for the minimum point on the curve by use of differential calculus. The formula that represents the general solution for the model is

$$Q_0 = \sqrt{2Rc_P/c_H} \tag{9}$$

This formula gives directly the value of Q_0, which yields the minimum total incremental cost for the model. Substituting the values of our example, we have

$$Q_0 = \sqrt{\frac{2 \times 2400 \times 20}{0.60}} = \sqrt{160,000} = 400 \text{ units}$$

In using the formula, if it is desired to express the economic quantity in dollars, the requirements must also be expressed in dollars. Similarly, if the requirements are expressed in monthly rates, the inventory costs must be expressed as a monthly rate. These and other changes in the units lead to apparent modifications of the formula used in practice, although the end result in terms of the size of the order is the same. In practice, the formula itself is not used often; rather, charts, graphs, and tables based on the formula are used to minimize computations.

The Effect of Quantity Discounts.   The basic economic lot size formula assumes a fixed purchase price. When quantity discounts enter the picture, additional simple calculations determine if there is a net advantage. As an illustration, assume that a manufacturer's requirement for an item is 2000 per year. The purchase price is quoted as $2 per unit in quantities below 1000 and $1.90 per unit in quantities above 1000. Ordering costs are $20 per order, and inventory costs are 16 per cent per year per unit of average inventory value, or $0.32 per unit per year at the $2 unit price. Our formula indicates the economic order quantity to be

$$Q_0 = \sqrt{\frac{2 \times 2000 \times 20}{0.32}} = \sqrt{250,000} = 500 \text{ units}$$

If we buy in lots of 1000, we save $200 per year on the purchase price plus $40 on order costs, since only two orders need be placed per year to satisfy the annual needs. This saving of $240 per year must be greater than the additional inventory costs that would be incurred if the price discount is to be attractive. Under the 500 unit order size, average inventory is 250 units and inventory costs are $250 \times 2.0 \times 0.16 = \$80$. If orders of 1000 units are placed, the inventory costs would be $500 \times 1.90 \times 0.16 = \$152$. There is a net gain of $240 - (152 - 80) = \$168$ by ordering in lots of 1000 instead of 500. If the vendor had a second price break of $1.86 per unit for lots of 2000 or more, a similar analysis shows that the incremental inventory costs outweigh the incremental price and order savings, so there is no net advantage in purchasing lots of 2000. Table III summarizes the calculations for all three cases. Obviously, no generalization can be drawn from this for purchase lots other than the fact that an incremental cost analysis of this sort would be required for each individual case.

Production Order Quantities

Production order quantities are based on the same general concepts as purchase order quantities, as we have noted, and Equation 9 can be applied. (Preparation costs are costs related to machine setups and incremental paperwork costs to write production orders and control the flow of orders through the shop; inventory costs are costs associated with holding in-process inventory.) However, the assumption that the order is received and placed into inventory all at one time is often not true in manufacturing runs. The basic formula assumes the general inventory pattern shown in Figure 9a, where the order quantity Q is received into inventory. The inventory then is drawn down at the usage rate, subsequent orders being placed with sufficient lead time so that their receipt coincides with zero (or minimum stock) inventory.

For many manufacturing situations the production of the total order quantity Q takes place over a period of time and the parts go into inventory, not in one large batch but in smaller quantities, as production continues. This results in an inventory pattern similar to Figure 9b. The maximum and average inventory levels are reduced. The minimum cost production quantity formula becomes

TABLE III. Incremental Cost Analysis to Determine Net Advantage or Disadvantage When Price Discounts Are Offered

	Lots of 500 Units Price = $2.00 per Unit	Lots of 1000 Units Price = $1.90 per Unit	Lots of 2000 Units Price = $1.86 per Unit
Purchase of a year's supply (2000 units)	$4000	$3800	$3720
Ordering cost	80	40	20
Inventory cost (average inventory × unit price adjustment × 0.16)	80	152	298
Total	$4160	$3992	$4038

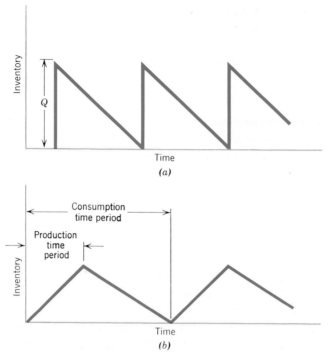

FIGURE 9.   Comparison of inventory balance: (*a*) when the order quantity, Q, is received all at one time, and (*b*) when Q is received over a period of time, as would be true in many production situations.

$$Q_p = \sqrt{\frac{2Rc_P}{c_H\left(1 - \dfrac{r}{p}\right)}} \qquad (10)$$

where

r = requirements or usage rate (short term, perhaps daily or weekly)
p = production rate (on same time base as for r)
c_p = ordering and setup cost
c_H = unit inventory cost
Q_p = minimum cost production order quantity
R = annual requirements

The Q_p which results is, of course, larger than that which would result from the basic formula. Average inventory is smaller for a given Q_p

and so balance between setup costs and inventory costs takes place at a higher value of the order quantity Q_p. By dividing the annual requirement by Q_p, we have the number of production cycles for the part or product which should be produced in a year.

Production Runs for Several Parts or Products.   The more general problem is not to determine the economical length of a production run for a single part or product but jointly to determine the runs for an entire group of products which share the use of the same facilities. If each part or product run is set independently, it is highly likely that some conflicts of equipment needs would result, unless the operating level is somewhat below capacity and considerable idle equipment time is available. The formal problem is similar to the one product case, but the objective is to minimize combined setup and inventory costs for the entire set (see [5, 6, 8]).

Variability of Demand

To this point we have been idealizing the structure of the inventory problem beyond reasonable limits of reality in order to discuss the formal solutions for optimum lot sizes. We have assumed a constant demand, constant lead times, and constant production rates. Actually, of course, none of these assumptions describes the real situation. Although average demand may be for 2500 units per year, daily demand may not be very well represented by $2500/250 = 10$ units per working day. We may have no orders today, but tomorrow we may receive orders for 100, then none for the next week, and then on three successive days orders for 20, 50, and 5, respectively.

Customer demand controls this rate, and no one has devised a way to dictate to the customer when he should place his order. Similarly, supply times are not constant. It could take longer than usual for the supplier to fill the order because he himself is out of stock, because of equipment breakdowns, labor troubles, or a host of other delays. The shipment time from the supplier is also subject to variability. The result is that no practical system can depend on a plan based on the inventory balance structures of Figures 7 and 9.

Safety Stocks.   The variations in demand and supply time are commonly absorbed by the provision of safety (buffer) stocks. The size of these planned extra inventories depends on the stability of demand and

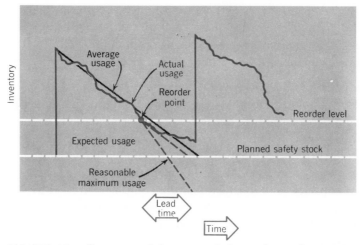

FIGURE 10.   Structure of inventory balance for a fixed-order quantity system, with safety stocks to absorb fluctuations in demand and in supply time. The safety stock level is set so that a reasonable figure for maximum usage would draw down the inventory to zero during the lead time.

supply in relation to our willingness to run out of stock. If we are determined almost never to run out of stock, these planned minimum balances have to be very high. If service requirements permit stock run-outs and back-ordering, the safety stocks can be moderate. Figure 10 shows the general structure of inventory balance with a fixed-order quantity system. The safety stock level is set so that inventory balances would be drawn down to zero during the lead time, if we should experience near maximum demand.

The determination of safety stocks therefore turns on a knowledge of the demand distribution during lead time together with a decision regarding the risk of stock run-out that we are willing to accept. This is shown by the distribution of demand in Figure 11. Approximate average monthly usage is about 460 units (corresponding to 50 per cent from Figure 11). If normal lead time is a month on the item, and if we wish to be 90 per cent sure of not running out of stock, we must have 620 on hand when the replenishment order is placed. The safety stock is then $620 - 460 = 160$ units. If we wish to be 95 per cent sure of no run-outs, the safety stock must be $670 - 460 = 210$ units. It is easy to see from the shape of the demand curve that, for high levels of assurance, the safety stock required goes up disproportionately and, therefore, the cost of providing this protection goes up.

Practical Methods for Setting Safety Stocks. In practice, the generalized methodology for determining safety stocks which we have just discussed is much too cumbersome. Instead of gathering data for individual demand distributions such as Figure 11, studies are made to validate the mathematical form of distributions for entire classes of items. Computations are then simplified considerably if we can justify the assumption that the demand distribution follows some particular mathematical function such as the normal, Poisson, or negative exponential distributions. These three distributions have been found to be applicable in many situations at different stages in the supply-production-distribution system. For example, the normal distribution has been found to describe adequately many demand functions at the factory level, the Poisson distribution at the retail level, and the negative exponential distribution at the wholesale and retail levels [4]. The general procedure is the same for all distributions.

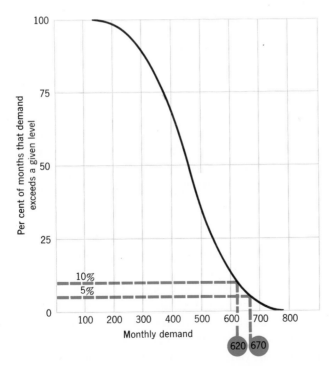

FIGURE 11.   Distribution showing the per cent of months that demand exceeded a given level.

1. Determine the applicability of the normal, Poisson, or negative exponential distribution of demand during lead time.

2. Establish a service level based on managerial policy or an assessment of the balance of costs.

3. Define the maximum demand during lead time, D_{max}, based on the appropriate distribution and the service level. For example, if we select a service level of 5 per cent, then maximum demand is 670 units in Figure 11.

4. Compute the required safety stock from $I_{min} = D_{max} - \overline{D}$ where $\overline{D}$ is average demand and both D_{max} and $\overline{D}$ are based on the demand distribution over the lead time.

Basic Control Systems for Handling Demand Variability.   To control inventories to meet requirements, we can manipulate the size and frequency of orders for replenishment, the frequency of review of usage levels, and the method of information feedback on which reviews are based.

The *fixed-order quantity* system is diagrammed in Figure 10. In this system, a reorder point is set which allows the inventory level to be drawn down to the safety stock level within the lead time if average usage is experienced during the lead time. Replenishment orders are placed in a fixed predetermined amount (the economic quantity or some other fixed quantity) timed to be received at the end of the lead time. Maximum inventory levels average the order quantity Q plus the safety stock I_{min}. The average inventory is $I_{min} + Q/2$. Review of the usage rates is periodic, at which times the order quantity and safety stock levels may be changed.

Demand for an item is ordinarily taken from the subsequent operations; that is, if the item were a standard screw used in several end products, assembly departments would issue requisitions for the screw according to their needs to produce. The demand for the end products may, in turn, be based on orders placed by warehouses which, in turn, may be based on salesmen's actual customer orders. The chain of demand, therefore, is reflected back through a series of stock points, each point maintaining inventories and placing orders for replenishment. Fixed-order quantity systems are common with low-value items, such as nuts and bolts, where the inventory level is under rather continuous surveillance so that notice can be given when the reorder level is reached.

Fixed-reorder cycle systems operate by placing orders for replenishment at regular intervals. The size of the order is varied to absorb the variations in usage, so the maximum inventory is maintained at a given level. Again, periodic review of usage rates would set the inventory levels and, therefore, determine the average size of an order. The periodic system offers tighter control through more frequent replenishment, compared to the fixed-order quantity system, since it is responding directly to changes in demand with each replenishment order. Its use is common with items of higher value and where a large number of items are regularly ordered from a single source. These multiple-item orders can then be grouped together for shipment to gain freight cost advantages.

Just as optimum order quantities can be derived for the fixed quantity system, so can optimum reorder cycles be derived for the fixed cycle system. However, since one main objective in the fixed cycle system is to order for all (or a group) of items at one time, the individual optimum cycles are not computed in practice. It would be appropriate, of course, to compute optimum cycles for individual items and classify them into appropriate groups. Then one group might be reviewed weekly, another each two weeks, a third each month, and so on.

The *base stock* system [8] is a blend of the fixed-order quantity and fixed-reorder cycle systems. It uses an information feedback system that establishes demand at each stock point directly with information regarding customer orders rather than through a chain of operations and stock points. In the base stock system, stock levels are reviewed on a periodic basis, but orders are placed only when inventories have fallen to a predetermined "reorder level." Then an order is placed to replenish inventories to the "base stock" level, which is sufficient for buffer stock plus a fixed quantity calculated to cover current usage needs. Periodic reviews of current usage rates can result in an upward or downward revision in the base stock level. The base stock system has the advantages of close control associated with the fixed-reorder cycle system, which makes it possible to carry minimum buffer stocks. On the other hand, since replenishment orders are placed only when the reorder point has been reached, fewer orders, on the average, are placed, so order costs are comparable to those associated with the fixed quantity systems.

The contrast in information feedback systems is illustrated in Figure 12. The disadvantage of the chain information flow system shown in Figure 12a is that, although actual customer orders may be received

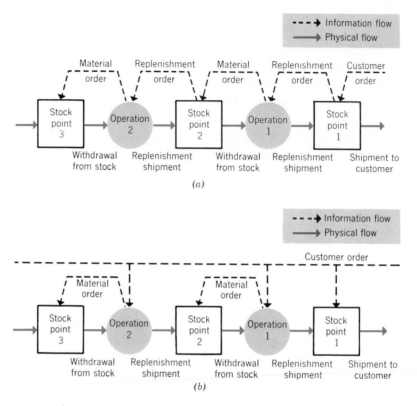

FIGURE 12.   Two contrasting systems of information feedback for inventory control systems. (By permission from [8, p. 89].)

frequently in smaller quantities, replenishment orders to operations in the chain become larger and less frequent. Therefore, *variability* in demand at stock point 1 is amplified by the time it is reflected at stock point 3, resulting in an increase in safety stocks to prevent run-out. (Refer to Figure 11 and note the effect of increased variability in the demand distribution on the need for safety stocks for a given service level.) Under the general scheme of Figure 12b, each link in the production chain works against actual customer demand, so no amplification of demand *variability* takes place. Since all stock points are working against consumer demand so that amplification of demand variability does not take place, buffer stocks can be reduced even further because the extreme levels of maximum demand are not experienced. In addition, there is a reduction in the cost of production fluctuations (hiring, separation, and training), since the magnitude of production fluctuations is also associated with the type of information feedback system used.

SUMMARY

We have been discussing inventory controls as if they could be set up independently of the production system, inferring criteria or measures of effectiveness that do not reflect the effect of inventories on production programs and on the control of general levels of production. This independence is unrealistic because there are interactions between these problems. Inventory policy must fit in with schedules to produce a *combined* minimum cost of operation rather than a minimum for inventories alone. Greater inventories may make it possible to reduce hiring, training, and severance costs, as well as to reduce investments in plant and equipment. It may be economical at times to utilize overtime work at higher wage rates instead of to build inventories to meet demand. In the following chapter on planning master programs and controlling production and employment levels, we shall attempt to relate these problems.

KEY CONCEPTS

Pipeline Inventories.   The concept of inventories to cover transit times throughout the entire production-inventory system plus delays for handling is an important one in understanding the crucial role of inventories in a production system. The analogy to liquid flowing in a pipeline is quite valid—if anything interrupts the flow then the output is reduced. Similarly, in a production-inventory-distribution system, if the pipeline is not kept full then output from the system cannot be maintained.

Decoupling.   The "shock absorber" function of inventories must be understood to appreciate the need for inventories in a production system. Inventories absorb the shocks that might otherwise drastically upset the smooth flow of a production system. These shocks might come from variations in demand for the final product, scheduling delays within the system, equipment breakdowns, raw material supply shortages, labor difficulties, and so on. By strategically locating banks of inventories throughout the system, one can minimize the effects of these shocks and effectively decouple one stage of the system from another.

Optimum Lot Size.   The concept of optimum lot sizes is one which in general is used as a model for all sorts of decision problems involving a balance of costs. When incremental costs are plotted in relation to increasing lot size, we find that the cost of holding inventories increases with the size of the lot but also that the preparation costs decrease with lot size. When the two sets of costs are added, the total incremental cost curve exhibits a minimum associated with the best policy regarding lot sizes.

IMPORTANT TERMS

Numbers in parentheses indicate page numbers.

1. Base series (461)
2. Base stock system (473)
3. Buffer inventory (454, 469)
4. Cycle stock (453)
5. Exponentially weighted moving average (459)
6. Fixed order quantity system (472)
7. Fixed-reorder cycle system (473)
8. Holding costs (462)
9. Maximum demand (470)
10. Moving average (458–459)
11. Optimum reorder cycle (473)
12. Optimum reorder quantity (473)
13. Order point (452)
14. Preparation costs (462)
15. Production order quantity (467)
16. Production run (469)
17. Purchase order quantity (462)
18. Quantity discount (466)
19. Replenishment order (473)
20. Safety stock (469–470)
21. Seasonal inventory (455)
22. Smoothing constant (coefficient) (460)
23. Trend effects (461)
24. Time horizon (456)
25. Transit inventory (453)

REVIEW QUESTIONS

Numbers in parentheses indicate page numbers.

1. Distinguish between production plans and the design of production systems. (450)
2. Distinguish between transit, cycle, safety, and seasonal inventories. Which of these types of inventories might be termed "pipeline" inventories? (453–455)
3. Discuss the *decoupling* function of inventories. (454–455)
4. In what ways can inventories serve to reduce costs? To increase costs? (450–451)
5. What is planning time horizon? (456)
6. What components of demand are involved in a forecast? (457)
7. Why do moving averages discount random effects? (458–459)
8. Compare the results of simple moving average forecasts and exponential moving average forecasts. (459–460)

9. Explain why exponential moving averages contain effects from all past actual demands. (459–460)

10. Outline the rationale behind the derivation of the minimum cost purchase quantity formula. (462–466)

11. In the minimum cost purchase quantity formulation, why does the total incremental cost curve have a minimum point in it? (464)

12. If we are dealing with production lot size decisions instead of purchase quantity decisions, what comparable factors enter the formula? Can the same formula be used if the production lot enters inventory all at one time? (467)

13. What type of analysis is required to take account of quantity discounts in determining optimal order sizes? (466–467)

14. When production of a lot takes place over a period of time, what modification in inventory pattern and economic lot size formulation takes place? Is the resulting economic lot size larger or smaller than that which would result from the usual formula? Why? (467–469)

15. What is the general problem of production runs for several parts or products? What may happen if production runs are determined independently? Under what conditions is it usually safe to determine them independently? (469)

16. How do practical inventory control systems take account of variability in demand, lead times, production rates, etc.? (469)

17. How can the size of safety stocks be determined in a rational way? Why not follow a policy which states that we want never to run out of stock? (470)

18. Contrast the three basic control systems discussed for handling the problems of variability. Under what conditions would they be used? (472–473)

19. What difference does the type of information feedback make in an inventory control system? (473–475)

20. How sensitive are lot size decisions and costs to changes in c_p, c_H, R, r/p? (468–469)

21. If management is attempting to adhere reasonably closely to an economic order quantity purchase policy, which parameters (variables) should it monitor most closely? Why? (466–467)

22. Taking the broad view of the enterprise as a whole and thinking in terms of the various functions of inventories, discuss how inventories could reduce overall costs. Increase overall costs. (450–451, 475)

23. Consider the various functions of inventories discussed in the text in relation to service industries. What functions do inventories perform in these kinds of organizations? Analyze, for example, operations such as a barber shop, a restaurant, a movie theater. (450–452, 472–473)

24. If you were the manager of a supermarket, would you be likely to reorder stock periodically, such as in the fixed reorder cycle system, or when

inventories declined to certain levels, such as in the fixed reorder quantity system? Why? (472–473)

SELF-TEST TRUE-FALSE QUESTIONS

Numbers in parentheses indicate page numbers.

1. Inventories serve the function of decoupling the various operations and activities. (450, 454)
2. It is typical for a manufacturing concern to have 10 per cent of its total invested capital tied up in inventories. (451)
3. The economical order quantity may be modified by price discounts when the total incremental saving due to the price discount exceeds the increased ordering cost. (466)
4. When material is received in inventory over a period of time, instead of in one large batch, the resulting economical order quantity is larger because the average inventory is smaller for a given order quantity, so that balance between setup costs and inventory costs takes place at a higher value for the order quantity. (467–468)
5. If production runs for several parts or products are determined individually by the use of economical order quantity concepts, it is likely that some conflicts of equipment needs would result unless the operating level is somewhat below capacity. (469)
6. The variations in demand and supply time are commonly absorbed by the provision of safety stocks. (469)
7. Safety stock levels should be set so that inventory balances would be drawn down to zero during the lead time if we should experience near minimum demand. (470)
8. As the level of assurance goes up, the safety stock required goes up disproportionately so that for absolute 100 per cent assurance against run out an inordinate safety stock would be required. (470)
9. In the fixed-order quantity system for handling demand variability in inventory control, the order quantity itself is made large enough to absorb fluctuations in demand and in supply time, so that no planned safety stock level is required. (472)
10. In the fixed-reorder cycle system, the size of the order is varied to absorb the variation in usage, so that maximum inventory is maintained at a given level. (473)
11. One of the advantages of the fixed-reorder cycle system is that, where a large number of items are regularly ordered from a single source, they may be grouped together for shipment to minimize total freight cost. (473)
12. Fixed-order quantity systems are common with low-value items, such as

nuts and bolts, where the inventory level is under rather continuous surveillance. (472)

13. In the chain information flow system for inventory control, actual customer orders may be received frequently in smaller quantities; however,
replenishment orders to operations in the chain become larger and less
frequent. (473)

PROBLEMS

1. Given the following five-year record of monthly demand for a product:

(a) Compute a three-month moving average forecast for the series.

(b) Compute an exponentially weighted forecast $\bar{F}^*_{t+1}$ for the series using
only Equation 2 and $\alpha = 0.1$.

(c) Plot the demand data and the three forecasts and compare results.

2. Using the data for 1970 and 1971 from problem 1, compute an exponentially
weighted forecast F^*_{t+1} using Equation 2 and $\alpha = 0.4$. Plot the results on the
same graph used in problem 1. How would you characterize the comparison of
the two series when $\alpha = 0.1$ and 0.4?

3. A producer of "style" goods fears being caught with large inventories. He
asks you to compute the minimum stock he would have to have in his system
to operate. His sales volume is currently 1000 units per week.

(a) You find that all of the delays and transit times from the completion of the
manufacturing process through warehousing and distribution to the retailer
amount to three weeks.

Monthly Demand Data					
Month	1970	1971	1972	1973	1974
Jan.	47	22	41	68	82
Feb.	42	44	28	52	62
Mar.	16	42	53	77	63
Apr.	47	29	48	55	64
May	38	46	64	52	44
June	34	45	54	58	71
July	45	56	39	41	71
Aug.	50	50	50	62	45
Sept.	47	39	39	59	81
Oct.	54	44	48	37	77
Nov.	40	24	54	73	86
Dec.	43	46	28	65	69

(b) The ordering practice of the 500 retailers is to order a two-weeks supply at a time each two weeks.

(c) The average retailer maintains a minimum or buffer inventory of two units.

(d) The factory warehouse maintains a buffer inventory of 1000 units in order to ensure that it can supply retailers.

What are the pipeline, cycle, and buffer stocks of this system?

4.   For the following data:

annual requirements, $R = 10,000$ units

order preparation cost, $c_p = \$25$ per order

inventory holding cost, $c_H = \$10$ per unit per year

(a) Compute the Economic Order Quantity, Q_o.

(b) Compute the number of orders that must be placed each year, and the annual cost of placing the orders.

(c) Compute the average inventory if Q_o units are ordered at one time, and the annual cost of the inventory.

5.   Suppose that the estimate of c_P in problem 4 was in error, being only $20 per order. What is the value of Q_o? What is the percent change in Q_o for the 25 percent decrease in c_P?

6.   Suppose that the estimate of c_H in problem 4 was in error, being actually $15 per unit per year. What is the value of Q_P? What is the percent change in Q_o for the 50 percent increase in c_H?

7.   A price discount schedule is offered for an item we purchase as follows: $1 per unit in quantities below 800, $0.98 per unit in quantities of 800–1599, and $0.97 in quantities of 1600 or more. Other data are $R = 1600$ units per year, $c_P = \$5.00$ per order, and $c_H = 10$ percent per year of average inventory value, or $0.10 per unit per year at the $1.00 per unit price. The value of Q_o using Equation 9 is 400 units. What should be the size of purchase quantities in order to take advantage of the price discounts?

8.   What is the economical size of a production run for an item with the following data?

annual requirements, $R = 500$ units

set up and ordering cost, $c_P = \$600$ per run

inventory holding cost, $c_H = \$50$ per unit per year

The item is used as a subassembly in a product that is produced at the rate of 10 per week. The weekly production rate for the item is 50. How many production runs should be scheduled per year?

9.   How many production runs would have been scheduled if we had ignored the fact that output was being used by the pattern of Figure 9 during production for problem 8?

10.   In problem 8, suppose that because of an equipment improvement the production rate is increased from 50 to 100 per week. How is the economical production lot size changed? What is the percent change in Q_P for this 100 percent increase in p?

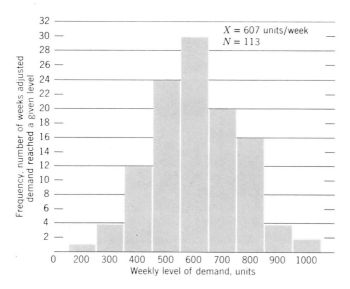

FIGURE 13.   Distribution representing expected random variation in weekly sales, exclusive of seasonal and trend variations.

11.   How accurate should economic production lot size determinations be?

12.   Why does the economic production lot size formula not yield the exact answer in practice?

13.   Another category of inventories is work in process. It is important that these inventories also be managed in a manner that results in low costs. Assuming job lot type production, "economic lot size" is analogous to "economic order quantity" in material and parts inventories.

(a) What cost factor associated with a production lot run is analogous to the procurement cost of materials?

(b) What cost factors associated with a production lot run are analagous to the purchase price of materials?

(c) What costs should be balanced in the economic production lot size formula?

14.   Weekly demand for a product, exclusive of seasonal and trend variations, is represented by the empirical distribution shown in Figure 13. What safety or buffer stock would be required for the item to insure that one would not run out of stock more than 15 per cent of the time? Five per cent of the time? One per cent of the time? (Normal lead time is one week.)

15.   If the product for which data are given in Problem 14 has a unit value of $50, shortage costs of $10 each, and an annual inventory carrying cost of 25 per cent of the average inventory value, which of the three levels of service would be most appropriate?

REFERENCES

[1] Brown, R. G. *Decision Rules for Inventory Management.* Holt, Rinehart, and Winston, New York, 1967.

[2] Brown, R. G. *Smoothing, Forecasting and Prediction.* Prentice-Hall, Englewood Cliffs, N.J., 1963.

[3] Brown, R. G. *Statistical Forecasting for Inventory Control.* McGraw-Hill, New York, 1959.

[4] Buchan, J., and E. Koenigsberg. *Scientific Inventory Control.* Prentice-Hall, Englewood Cliffs, N.J., 1963.

[5] Buffa, E. S. *Operations Management: Problems and Models* (3rd ed.). John Wiley, New York, 1972.

[6] Buffa, E. S., and W. H. Taubert, *Production-Inventory Systems: Planning and Control* (Rev. ed.). Richard D. Irwin, Homewood, Ill., 1972.

[7] Fetter, R. B., and W. C. Dalleck. *Decision Models for Inventory Management.* Richard D. Irwin, Homewood, Ill., 1961.

[8] Magee, J. F., and D. M. Boodman. *Production Planning and Inventory Control* (2nd ed.). McGraw-Hill, New York, 1967.

[9] Starr, M. K., and D. W. Miller. *Inventory Control: Theory and Practice.* Prentice-Hall, Englewood Cliffs, N.J., 1962.

[10] Winters, P. R. "Forecasting Sales by Exponentially Weighted Moving Averages." *Management Science,* **6**, (3), 324–342, Apr. 1960.

CONTENTS

CHAPTER 15
AGGREGATE PLANS AND PROGRAMS

Most managers want to plan and control operations at the broadest level through some kind of aggregate planning that bypasses the details of individual products and the detailed scheduling of facilities and men. Management would rather deal with the basic relevant decisions of programming the use of resources by reviewing projected employment and subcontracting levels and by setting production rates that can be varied within a given employment level by varying hours worked (working overtime or undertime). Once these basic decisions have been made for the upcoming period in the planning horizon, detailed scheduling can proceed at a lower level within the constraints of the broad plan. Finally, last-minute changes in production levels need to be made with the realization of their possible effects on the costs to change levels and on inventory costs.

What is needed first for aggregate plans is to develop some logical overall unit of measuring sales and output, for example, gallons in the paint industry, cases (representing an equal quantity regardless of package style) in the beer industry, or perhaps equivalent machine hours in some mechanical industries. Second, management must be able to forecast for some reasonable planning period, perhaps a year, in these aggregate terms. Finally, management must be able to isolate and measure the relevant costs that we shall discuss in this chapter and, depending on the methods used, reconstruct these costs in the form of a model that will permit near optimal decisions for the sequence of planning periods in the planning horizon. The sequential nature of the decisions should be kept in mind; a decision on employment levels and production rates made for an upcoming period cannot be termed either right or wrong, good or bad. Decisions will also be made two periods hence based on the decisions just made, on new information about the actual progress of sales, and on the forecasts for the balance of the planning horizon. The result is that all decisions are right or wrong only in terms of the sequence of decisions over a period of time.

Most of our discussion deals with systems that produce inventoriable items, where the existence of finished goods inventories can make possible a cost trade-off for the costs of changes in employment level. Near the end of this chapter, however, we shall discuss aggregate planning for noninventoriable items as well.

To place our discussion in context, let us visualize the various plans for production in terms of their time horizons. Figure 1 shows five bands of plans. The implementation of the present plans in the shortest time horizon operates under the constraints of the established firm aggregate plans already made and is the subject of Chapters 16 and 17. The intermediate- and long-range plans shown in Figure 1 are involved in the broad strategic planning for the enterprise. The plans and decisions related to the upcoming and immediate future periods, however, are what we are calling aggregate planning and scheduling.

NATURE OF AGGREGATE PLANNING

Aggregate planning increases the range of alternatives for capacity use that must be considered by management. The term *aggregate planning* includes scheduling in the sense of a program; the terms *aggregate planning* and *aggregate planning and scheduling* are used almost interchangeably. The economic significance of these ideas is by no means minor. The concepts raise such broad basic questions as: To what extent should inventory be used to absorb the fluctuations in demand that will occur over the next six to twelve months? Why not absorb these fluctuations by simply varying the size of the work force? Why not maintain a fairly stable work force size and absorb fluctuations by changing production rates through varying work hours? Why not maintain a fairly stable work force and production rate and let sub-contractors wrestle with the problem of fluctuating order rates? Should the firm purposely not meet all demands? In most instances it is probably true that any one of these pure strategies would not be as effective as a balance among them. Each strategy has associated costs and, therefore, we seek an astute combination of the alternatives.

If inventories are used to absorb seasonal changes in demand, then capital and obsolescence costs, as well as the costs associated with storage, insurance, and handling, tend to increase. Beyond the question of seasonal factors, the use of inventories to absorb short-term fluctuations incurs increases in these same costs compared to some ideal or minimum inventory level necessary to maintain the production process. When inventories fall below this ideal or minimum level, stockout costs and all costs associated with short runs increase.

Changes in the size of the work force affect the total costs of labor

Planning Time Horizon

Present period—implementation of firm plans already made	Firm plans for upcoming period	Tentative plans for immediate future periods	Intermediate-range plans for products and capacity	Long-range plans for products, markets, and capacities
Detailed plans and schedules for the use of the existing work force and equipment	Based on forecasts of demand for this and future periods, make plans for immediate capacity needs. This may involve hiring or laying off personnel, the setting of production rates, and plans for the use of overtime and inventories.	Size of work force Production rates Subcontracting Overtime Inventories	Changes in product mix Projected capacity needs for equipment and manpower	Studies of markets and their locations Studies of the size and location of facilities

FIGURE 1.   Relationship of plans for various time horizons.

turnover. When new workers are hired, costs arise from selection, training, and lower production effectiveness. The separation of workers may involve unemployment compensation or other separation costs, as well as an intangible effect on public relations and public image. Large changes in the size of the work force may mean adding or eliminating an entire shift; the incremental costs involved are shift premium as well as incremental supervision costs and other overhead.

If fluctuations are absorbed through changes in the production rate, overtime premium costs for increases and probably idle labor costs (higher average labor cost per unit) for decreases also will be absorbed. Usually, however, managers try to maintain the same average labor costs by reducing hours worked to somewhat below normal levels. When undertime schedules persist, labor turnover and the attendant costs are likely to increase.

Many costs affected by aggregate planning and scheduling decisions are difficult to measure and are not segregated in accounting records. Some, such as interest costs on inventory investment, are alternative costs of opportunity. Other costs, such as those associated with public relations and public image, are not measurable directly. However, all of the costs are real and bear on aggregate planning decisions.

PROBLEM STRUCTURE

The simplest structure of the aggregate planning problem is represented by the single-stage system shown in Figure 2. In Figure 2 the planning horizon is only one period ahead; therefore we call Figure 2 a single-stage system. The state of the system at the end of the last period (which becomes the initial conditions for the upcoming period) is defined by W_0, P_0, and I_0, the aggregate work force size, production rate, and inventory level, respectively. We have a forecast of the requirements for the upcoming period; through some decision process, decisions are made which set the size of the work force and production rate for the upcoming period. Projected ending inventory I_1 is then determined as the excess of the sum of the inventory carried forward from the previous period plus production during the period over forecasted sales during the period; that is, $I_1 = I_0 + P_1 - F_1$, where F_1 is forecasted sales.

The decisions made may call for hiring or laying off personnel, thus expanding or contracting the effective capacity of the production system.

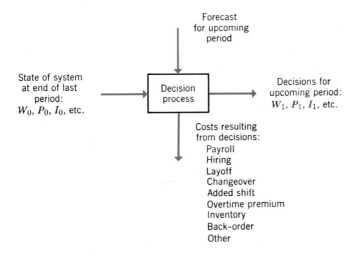

FIGURE 2.   Single-stage aggregate planning decision system
where planning horizon is only one period. W = size of work
force, P = production rate, and I = inventory level.

The work force size together with the decision on production rate during
the period then determines the required amount of overtime, inventory
levels or back-ordering, whether or not a shift must be added or deleted,
and other possible changes in operating procedure. The comparative
costs which result from alternate decisions on work force size and production rate are, of course, of great interest in judging the effectiveness
of the decisions made and the decision process used. The comparative
cost of a sequence of such alternate decisions is also of interest in
judging the applicability of the single-stage model.

Let us suppose that we make a sequence of decisions by the structure
of the single-stage model of Figure 2. Suppose that the forecasts for
each period for the first four periods are progressively decreasing. Our
decision process responds by decreasing both the work force size and
the production rate in some combination, incurring layoff and changeover costs. Then, for the fifth through tenth periods we find the period
forecasts are progressively increasing, and each period the decision
process calls for hiring personnel and increased production rates, incurring hiring and more changeover costs. The single-period planning
horizon has made each independent decision seem internally logical
but has resulted in first the layoff of workers only to hire them back

again, incurring costs for both actions plus changeover costs due to changing production rates.

Had we been able to look ahead for several periods with an appropriate decision process, we might have decided to stabilize the work force size at least to some extent and absorb the fluctuations in demand in some other way, perhaps solely with changes in production rate through the use of overtime and undertime or by carrying extra inventories through the trough in the demand curve. It appears that broadening the planning horizon can improve the effectiveness of the aggregate planning system and most of the decision processes discussed reflect this multi-stage format.

DECISION PROCESSES
FOR AGGREGATE PLANNING

Given the multistage structure of the problem, our interest now is drawn to the decision processes. What are the decision processes used and proposed for use? There are several and they may be classified as graphic, mathematical, heuristic, and computer search methods. We might classify them further as static versus dynamic as well as single stage versus multistage models. We shall discuss the graphic, mathematical, and computer search methods.

Graphic Methods

Table I shows a forecast of expected production requirements for a product, together with the required safety stocks for each projected month. The available production days for each month emphasize that although the monthly seasonal requirement swing is expected to be $13,000/3,000 = 4.33$ (peak in September, 13,000; low in March, 3,000), the production rates required to follow the sales pattern would be much greater since the plant shuts down for two weeks in July for vacations. The resulting swing in requirements per production day is from 143 units per day in March to 917 units per day in July, or a ratio $917/143 = 6.41$. The dashed line of Figure 3 shows the projected requirements in terms of rates per working day, with the peak occurring in July instead of September because of the restriction on production time available in July.

Normal production capacity is 500 units per day, and up to 600 units per day can be produced by resorting to overtime at an extra cost of $10 per unit. To exceed the 600 units per day limit, subcontracting is required, which costs an extra $15 per unit compared to in-plant normal production.

Figure 3 shows three alternate production programs for meeting the requirements. Plan 1, level production, is in many ways the simplest, since employment levels are stable. No overtime or subcontracting is required because the rate of 413 units per day is well within normal plant capacity. The inventory costs of this plan are high, however. At an inventory carrying cost of $40 per unit, the average seasonal stock of 9600 units costs $384,000. The seasonal inventory is that required to meet projected seasonal sales peaks, over and above the amounts being produced, and is simply total monthly inventory less safety stock in that month for the particular production plan. See Table II for a comparative summary.

TABLE I.   Forecast of Sales and Safety Stocks

Month	Expected Production Requirements	Required Safety Stocks	Production Days	Cumulative Production Days
Jan.	6,000	3,000	22	22
Feb.	4,000	2.500	19	41
Mar.	3,000	2,100	21	62
Apr.	4,000	2,500	21	83
May	6,000	3,000	22	105
June	9,000	3,500	20	125
July	11,000	4,000	12	137
Aug.	12,000	4,200	22	159
Sept.	13,000	4,400	20	179
Oct.	12,000	4,200	23	202
Nov.	11,000	4,000	19	221
Dec.	9,000	3,500	21	242
	100,000	40,900		

Average safety stock $= \dfrac{40,900}{12} = 3400.$

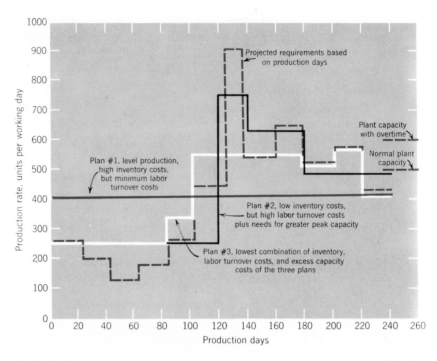

FIGURE 3. Comparison of three alternate production programs that meet requirements.

Plan 2 attempts to minimize inventory costs by following the requirement curve fairly closely. It accomplishes this very well since average seasonal inventories are held to about 1150 units at a cost of only $46,000 per year, a saving of $338,000 per year. However, labor turnover costs are high, since the plant labor force must roughly be doubled to build the production rate from the low of 250 units per day to the normal plant capacity of 500 per day. These turnover costs are assessed at $164,300 per year. (No extra labor is employed above the normal plant capacity level.) (See Table II.) In addition, we must engage in both overtime and subcontracting to meet peak loads. The overtime bill is $60,000 and the extra subcontracting costs are $60,000. The total incremental costs compared to plan 1 are $330,300, a definite improvement over plan 1, although the turnover and excess capacity costs are quite high.

Plan 3 attempts to steer a path between plans 1 and 2 by holding the labor employed over a longer period in order to eliminate the need for extra subcontracting. This involves a higher inventory cost than plan 2,

TABLE II.   Comparison of the Three Alternate Production Programs of Figure 3

	Plan 1	Plan 2	Plan 3
Average seasonal inventory	9,600	1,150	2,275
Average safety stock	3,400	3,400	3,400
Average total inventory	13,000	4,550	5,675
Peak capacity required	100	181	133
(No. 1 = 100)			
Incremental costs :			
Seasonal inventory cost*	$384,000	$ 46,000	$ 91,000
Labor turnover costs†	0	164,300	164,300
Overtime premium‡	0	60,000	52,820
Extra subcontracting**	0	60,000	0
Total	$384,000	$330,300	$308,120

*Inventory carrying cost is $40 per year per unit.
†Assuming that a change in the rate of output of 35 units per day requires the employment or release of 100 men and the cost of hiring and training an employee is $230.
‡At $10 per unit produced at overtime.
**Extra cost is $15 per unit subcontracted.

but eliminates the $60,000 extra subcontracting cost. Labor turnover costs are the same as in plan 2, because in both instances the labor force fluctuation is based on a minimum level of 250 units per day and a maximum level of 500 per day, which is normal plant capacity. (No extra labor is employed above the normal plant capacity level.) The total incremental cost of plan 3 is $308,120, the lowest of the three plans.

Whether either plan 2 or 3 is acceptable is another question. They both involve a great labor force fluctuation (about 713 employees). If these employees have relatively high skills and are difficult to find, this approach might be impractical and the effect on employee and community relationships would not be good. Other combinations involving less severe labor force fluctuation could be examined in the same way.

While Figure 3 shows the effects of the production rate changes quite clearly, it is actually somewhat easier to work with a set of cumulative curves as shown in Figure 4. The procedure is to plot first the cumulative production requirements. The cumulative maximum requirement curve is then simply the former curve with the required buffer stocks added

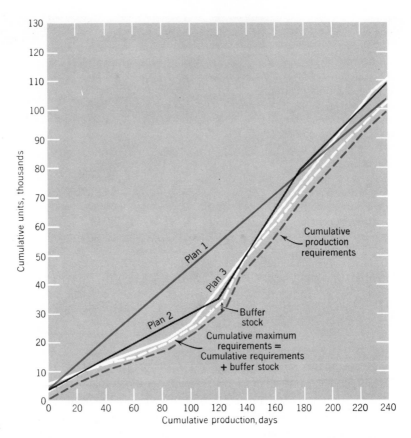

FIGURE 4. Cumulative graphs of requirements and alternate programs.

for each period. The cumulative graph of maximum requirements can then be used as a basis for generating alternate program proposals. Any production program that is feasible in the sense that it meets requirements while providing the desired buffer stock protection must fall entirely above the cumulative maximum requirement line. The vertical distances between the program proposal curves and the cumulative maximum requirement curve represent seasonal inventory accumulation for the plan in question.

The graphic methods are simple and have the advantage of visualizing alternate programs over a broad planning horizon. The difficulties with graphic methods, however, are the static nature of the graphic model and the fact that the process is in no sense optimizing. In addition, the process does not generate good programs itself but simply compares proposals made.

Mathematical Optimization Methods

We shall discuss three mathematical optimization methods: the optimum reaction rate method, the Linear Decision Rule, and linear programming. All three have a basis for optimizing the model developed so our interest is particularly in appraising how closely the three models represent reality.

Optimum Reaction Rate Methods.   These methods were developed by Magee [15] with a focus on two main variables under managerial control: the frequency of adjustments in production levels and the reaction rate of adjustment to changes in forecasted sales in the immediate period ahead.

The reaction rate of adjustment of production levels determines how much of an adjustment is made for a given fluctuation in demand. If we adjust planned production levels by the full amount that sales vary from forecasts, we would have a 100 per cent reaction rate, and fluctuations in sales would be transmitted directly to production. The 100 per cent reaction rate leads to the most severe problems in hiring, training, and laying off of personnel, with the attendant costs of this instability. If we adjust production levels by only one-half of the change indicated by demand fluctuation, we would have a 50 per cent reaction rate. Obviously these reaction rates could take on any value from zero to 100 per cent. Low reaction rates would lead to stable production but higher inventories, and high reaction rates would lead to the reverse conditions.

The frequency of review also has an effect. Short review periods lead to small production fluctuations and smaller inventories for a given reaction rate. Figure 5 shows the relationship of control numbers (reaction rate/100) and review periods to the size of production fluctuation and the size of reserve or buffer inventories.

The selection of a reaction rate and review period for a given case then would depend on the balance of inventory carrying costs in relation to the costs of production fluctuation; a mathematical analysis leads to the optimum combination for a given application. In general, high reaction rates and long review periods tend to overcontrol.

Since much of the fluctuation in sales demand is from random causes,

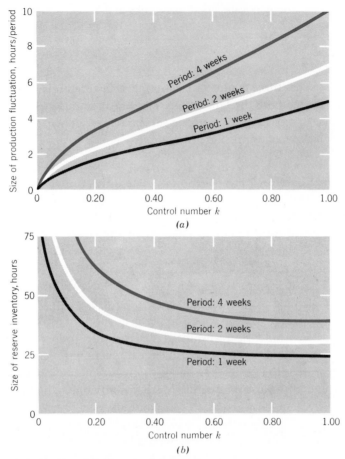

FIGURE 5. (a) Magnitude of production fluctuations versus control number and length of review period. (b) Reserve inventory required versus control number and length of review period. (By permission, from J. F. Magee and D. M. Boodman [15].)

there is no need to react quickly. Lower reaction rates and short review periods tend to create a "wait-and-see" attitude by bringing about small adjustments fairly often. Essentially they create a stalling action to see if the sales fluctuation is actually a true increase or decrease rather than a random fluctuation. The wait-and-see policy requires greater inventories but results in lower turnover costs. The optimal amount of control minimizes the sum of the two types of costs, rather than minimizing one at the expense of the other.

A Comparative Example

Magee [15] relates a hypothetical case which compares operations and costs for different basic systems of production and inventory control. The example considers a company that manufactures and sells about 5000 small machines per year for $100 each. The factory supplies four warehouses located in strategic areas around the country, which in turn supply the customer. We shall show the calculated results for three alternate systems of control: an economical order quantity system, a two-week fixed-reorder cycle system, and a base stock system with a reaction rate of 5 per cent and a review period of one week. Table III summarizes the comparative incremental costs of the three systems, and Figure 6 graphically shows typical effects on production levels. Obviously, we cannot draw the conclusion that all organizations would find these precise comparative effects, because there are differences in cost characteristics for inventories and volume fluctuation between different companies. What we can see is that the idea of economic order quantities is not a valid concept for the organization as a whole because it produces a sub-optimum solution which does not account for the cost of production fluctuations. For the example which we have used, these costs were of extreme importance. They could be of less importance in other situations, but they are always factors to be considered in the design of production and inventory control systems.

The reaction rate methods provide automatic decision rules which are dynamic and simple to apply, but like the graphic methods they lump the two relatively independent decisions of work force size and

TABLE III.   Comparative Incremental Costs for Three Inventory Control Systems

	Economical Order Quantity System	Two-Week Fixed-Cycle Reorder System	Base Stock System with 5% Reaction Rate
Inventory costs:			
Factory	$ 1,750	$ 515	$ 648
4 Branches	2,340	2,020	2,300
Reorder costs:			
Factory	350	350	350
4 Branches	990	1,980	2,081
Cost of production fluctuations	8,500	2,250	256
Total incremental costs	$13,930	$7,115	$5,635

production rate into the single variable of production level. Given the production level, one must still decide what is the best way to meet the production objective, that is, hiring versus layoff, overtime versus undertime, basic production rate, and so on. In addition the model is only a single-stage one since it looks ahead just one period. For this

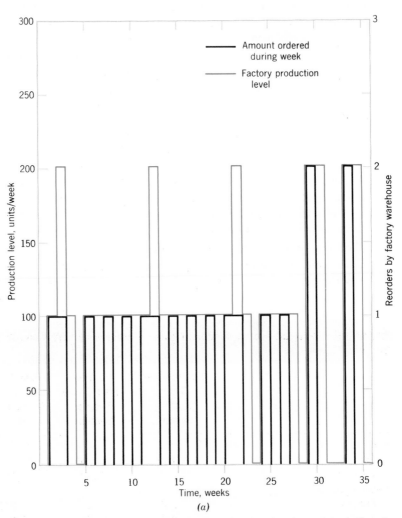

FIGURE 6.   (a) Factory orders and production level, economical order quantity system. (b) Production level, fixed-reorder cycle system. (c) Production level, base stock system; reaction = 5 per cent. (Adapted by permission from [15].)

reason it would not handle seasonal effects as well as other methods which we shall discuss.

The Linear Decision Rule.   The Linear Decision Rule (LDR) was developed in 1955 by Holt, Modigliani, Muth, and Simon [10, 11, 12] as a quadratic programming approach for making aggregate employment and production rate decisions. The LDR is based on the develop-

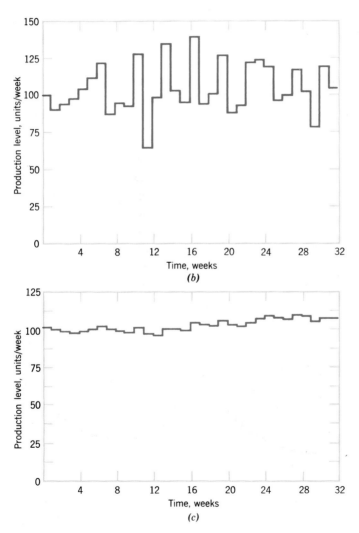

FIGURE 6.   (*continued*)

ment of a quadratic cost function for the company in question with cost components of: (1) regular payroll, (2) hiring and layoff, (3) overtime, and (4) inventory holding, back-ordering, and machine setup costs. The quadratic cost function is then used to derive two linear decision rules for computing work force levels and production rate for the upcoming period based on forecasts of aggregate sales for a preset planning horizon. The two linear decision rules are optimum for the model.

Figure 7 shows the form of the four components of the cost function. The work force size is adjusted in the model once per period with the implied commitment to pay employees at least their regular time wages for that period. This is indicated in Figure 7a. Hiring and layoff costs are shown in Figure 7c, and the LDR model approximates these costs with a quadratic function as shown. If the work force size is held

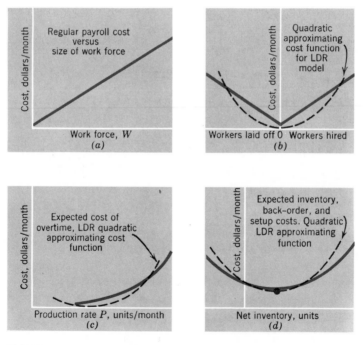

FIGURE 7.   Approximating linear and quadratic cost functions used by the Linear Decision Rule (LDR) model. Colored lines represent presumed actual cost functions and dashed lines represent the LDR approximating functions.

constant for the period in question, then changes in production rate can be absorbed by the use of overtime and undertime. Undertime is the cost of idle labor at regular payroll rates. The overtime cost depends on the size of the work force, W, and on the aggregate production rate, P.

The form of the overtime-undertime cost function in relation to production rate is shown in Figure 7c, being approximated by a quadratic function. Whether overtime or undertime costs will occur for a given decision depends on the balance of costs defined by the horizon time. For example, in responding to the need for increased output, the costs of hiring and training must be balanced against the overtime costs. Or conversely, the response to a decreased production rate would require the balancing of layoff costs against the costs of undertime.

The general shape of the net inventory cost curve is shown in Figure 7d. When inventories deviate from ideal levels, either extra inventory costs must be absorbed if inventory levels are too high, or costs of back-ordering or lost sales will occur if inventory levels are too low. Again, these costs are approximated by a quadratic function in the LDR model.

The total incremental cost function is then simply the sum of the four component cost functions for a particular example. The mathematical problem is to minimize the sum of the monthly combined cost function over the planning horizon time of N periods. The result of this mathematical development is the specification of two linear decision rules to be used to compute the aggregate size of the work force and the production rate for the upcoming period. These two rules require as inputs the forecast for each period of the planning horizon in aggregate terms, the ending size of work force, and inventory level in the last period. Once the two rules have been developed for a specific application, the computations required to produce the decisions recommended by the model require only ten to fifteen minutes by manual methods.

An Example

An LDR model was developed for a paint company and applied to a six-year record of known decisions in the company. Two kinds of forecasts were used as inputs: a perfect forecast and a moving average forecast. The actual order pattern was extremely variable, involving both the 1949 recession and the Korean War. The graphical record of actual factory performance compared with the simulated performance of the LDR is shown in Figures 8 and 9 for production rates and work force levels. Additional graphical results of overtime hours, inventories, and back-orders are contained in references [4, 11, 12].

Costs were reconstructed for the six-year period of actual operation and projected for the decision rules based on the non-quadratic cost structure originally estimated from paint company data. The cost difference between actual company performance and performance with the LDR with the moving average forecast was $173,000 per year in favor of the LDR.

LDR has many important advantages. First, the model is optimizing and the two decision rules, once derived, are simple to apply. In addition, the model is dynamic and representative of the multistage kind of system which we discussed. On the other hand, the quadratic cost structure may have severe limitations and probably does not adequately represent the cost structure of any organization. Also, since there are no constraints on the size of workforce, overtime, inventory, and capital, it may be possible to generate decisions that are not feasible from some points of view.

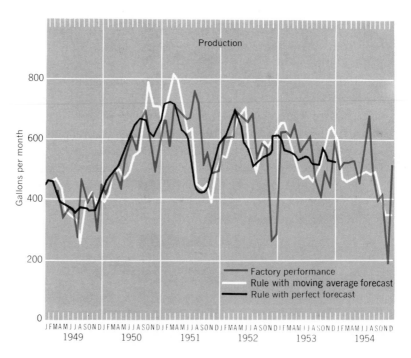

FIGURE 8. Comparative performance of the Linear Decision Rule (LDR) with actual factory performance for production rates. (From C. C. Holt, F. Modigliani, and H. A. Simon [12].)

Linear Programming Methods.   The aggregate planning problem has been developed in the context of both simplex and distribution models of linear programming. Bowman [1] proposed the *distribution model* of linear programming as a format for aggregate planning. This model focused on the objective of assigning units of productive capacity so that production plus storage costs were minimized and sales demand was met within the constraints of available capacity. The rim conditions in the distribution matrix form the constraints that sales requirements must be met on the one hand and that capacity limitations in the form of initial inventory, regular time production capacity, and overtime production capacity must be met on the other hand. Both beginning and ending inventories must be specified for the program developed over the N periods in the planning horizon. The matrix elements are costs.

The criterion function to be minimized is the combined regular production, overtime production, and inventory cost. The output of the process is a program that specifies the amount of regular and overtime production in each period of the planning horizon. The basic matrix can be extended to more than one product by establishing a separate column in each period for each product.

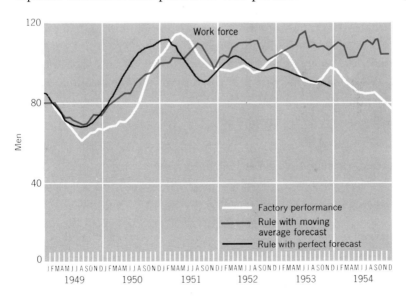

FIGURE 9.   Comparative performance of the Linear Decision Rule (LDR) with actual factory performance for work force size. (From [12].)

Distribution methods of linear programming have serious limitations when applied to the aggregate planning problem. First, the distribution model does not account for production change costs such as hiring and layoff of personnel, and there is no cost penalty for back-ordering or lost sales. Thus, resulting programs may call for changes in production levels in one period, requiring an expanded work force, only to call for the layoff of these workers in the future periods. Also, the linearity requirement often is too severe.

The *simplex method* of linear programming makes it possible to include production level change costs and inventory shortage costs in the model [9, 16]. Hanssmann and Hess [9] developed a simplex model which is entirely parallel with the linear decision rule in terms of using work force and production rate as independent decision variables, and in terms of the components of the cost model and inclusion of a preset planning horizon. The main difference between the Hanssmann-Hess linear programming model and the LDR is that all cost functions must be linear rather than quadratic and that linear programming is used as a solution mode. Therefore, the advantages and disadvantages of the Hanssmann-Hess model are roughly the same as for the LDR. One's preference between the two models would depend on a preference for either the linear or quadratic cost model in a given application.

Industrial applications of linear programming to aggregate planning problems are reported by Eisemann and Young [6] in a study of a textile mill, by Fabian [7] in a study of blast furnace production, and by Greene, Chatto, Hicks, and Cox [8] in a study of the packing industry.

Search Decision Rule (SDR)

A computer optimum-seeking procedure may be used to evaluate systematically the cost criterion function at trial points. In the procedure it is hoped that an optimum value will be eventually found, but there is no guarantee. In direct search methods of computer optimum seeking, the cost criterion function is evaluated at a point, the result compared to previous trial results, and a move determined on the basis of a set of heuristics. The new point is then evaluated and the procedure repeated until either a better value of the function cannot be found or the predetermined computer time limit is exceeded. Taubert [18, 19] selected the Hooke-Jeeves [13] pattern search program as a vehicle for experimenting with the aggregate planning and scheduling problem. To test the feasibility of using such a program, he selected the paint company example used to test the LDR.

In general terms the cost criterion function represents the costs to be minimized over the planning horizon time; it can be expressed as a function of production rates and work force levels in each period of the planning horizon. Therefore, each period included in the planning horizon requires the addition of two dimensions to the criterion function, one for production rate and one for work force level. The particular pattern search program used was written to handle a maximum of twenty independent variables and, therefore, the planning horizon time was limited to ten months in Taubert's analysis of the paint company. The search program was set to end whenever the decrease in the objective cost function found by SDR's exploration of the response surface was less than 0.5×10^{-6}.

Table IV shows a sample of the computer output for the first month of factory operation of the paint company. The computer output gives the first month's decision as well as an entire program for the planning horizon of 10 months. In the lower half of the table the program prints out for the entire planning horizon the component costs of payroll, hiring and firing, overtime, inventory, and the total of these discretionary costs. Thus a production manager is provided not only with the immediate decisions for the upcoming month but also with the projected decisions based on monthly forecasts for the planning horizon time and the economic consequences of each month's decisions.

A month-by-month comparison for the first twenty-four months of the results obtained by the SDR program and those obtained by the two optimum decision rules for the LDR was made. The month-by-month decisions were not identical, but they were very close to each other; the twenty-four-month production totals differed by only two gallons. The total cost of the SDR program exceeded the LDR total by only $806 or 0.11 per cent. This difference may be accounted for by the fact that the SDR used a planning horizon of only ten months as compared to the twelve-month horizon used by the LDR.

With the encouraging results in virtually duplicating the performance of LDR in the paint company, it was decided to test SDR in more demanding situations. Thus, models were developed for three rather different situations: (1) the Search Company [3, 4, 5], a hypothetical organization involving a much more complex cost model including the possibility of using a second shift when needed; (2) the Search Mill

TABLE IV.   SDR Output for the First Month of Factory Operation (Perfect Forecast)

A. SDR Decisions and Projections

Month	Sales (gallons)	Production (gallons)	Inventory (gallons)	Work Force (men)
0			263.00	81.00
1	430	471.89	304.89	77.60
2	447	444.85	302.74	74.10
3	440	416.79	279.54	70.60
4	316	380.90	344.44	67.32
5	397	374.64	322.08	64.51
6	375	363.67	310.75	62.07
7	292	348.79	367.54	60.22
8	458	358.63	268.17	58.68
9	400	329.83	198.00	57.05
10	350	270.60	118.60	55.75

B. Cost Analysis of Decisions and Projections (dollars)

Month	Payroll	Hiring and Firing	Overtime	Inventory	Total
1	26,384.04	743.25	2,558.82	18.33	29,704.94
2	25,195.60	785.62	2,074.76	24.57	28,080.54
3	24,004.00	789.79	1,555.68	135.06	26,484.53
4	22,888.86	691.69	585.21	49.27	24,215.03
5	21,932.79	508.43	1,070.48	0.36	23,512.06
6	21,102.86	383.13	1,206.90	7.06	22,699.93
7	20,473.22	220.51	948.13	186.43	21,828.29
8	19,950.99	151.70	2,007.33	221.64	22,331.66
9	19,395.30	171.76	865.74	1,227.99	21,660.79
10	18,954.76	107.95	−1,396.80	3,346.46	21,012.37
					241,530.14

From Taubert [18].

[3, 17], based on disguised data obtained from a major American integrated steel mill; and, (3) the Search Laboratory [3, 4, 19], a fictitious name for a division of a large aerospace research and development laboratory. All three situations represent significant extensions beyond the paint company application with highly complex cost models and

other factors to challenge the SDR methodology. We select the Search Laboratory model for further discussion because it involved the most varied cost components and because it occurs in a nonmanufacturing environment, thus demonstrating the pervasiveness of aggregate planning concepts.

Search Laboratory Application of SDR.   Taubert [19] developed an aggregate planning cost model for the Search Laboratory in 1968. The laboratory is housed in a 100,000 square feet facility employing a staff of 400. Approximately 300 of the staff are classified as direct technical employees and the balance are indirect administrative support for the operations of the laboratory.

The laboratory offers a capability through its scientific staff and facilities, and widely fluctuating employment could severely impair this capability. The research programs of the laboratory are funded by both the government and by the corporation, and an important part of the operating environment is wide fluctuations in government sales and rapid shifts in technology. Thus, the operations planning problem is defined by the need for employment stability on the one hand and wide fluctuations in government sales on the other.

Specifically, the operations planning problem is centered in a monthly decision by the director to determine the size of the scientific staff and administrative staff as well as the allocation of the scientific staff to government contracts, corporate research programs, and overhead. Overhead charges arise when there are no contracts or corporate research programs available for scientists. This charge is in addition to the charges normally made to overhead for the usual indirect costs. In effect, then, overhead is used as a buffer to absorb fluctuations in the demand for scientific manpower. The four independent decision variables incorporated in the aggregate planning model are as follows:

1. The size of the scientific staff:
   (a) WS_t, manpower allocated to government contracts.
   (b) WR_t, manpower allocated to corporate research programs.
   (c) WO_t, manpower allocated to overhead.
2. WI_t, the size of the administrative support staff.

Cost Model   Figure 10 shows the twelve cost relations which form the components for the cost model of the Search Laboratory. Note that a variety of mathematical relationships are included, such as linear,

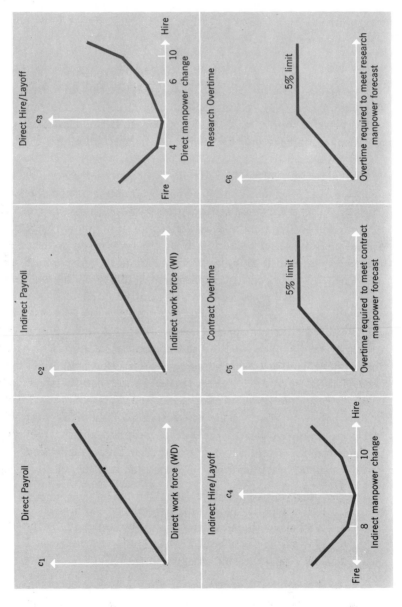

FIGURE 10. The twelve cost relationships entering the Search Laboratory cost model. (From Taubert [19].)

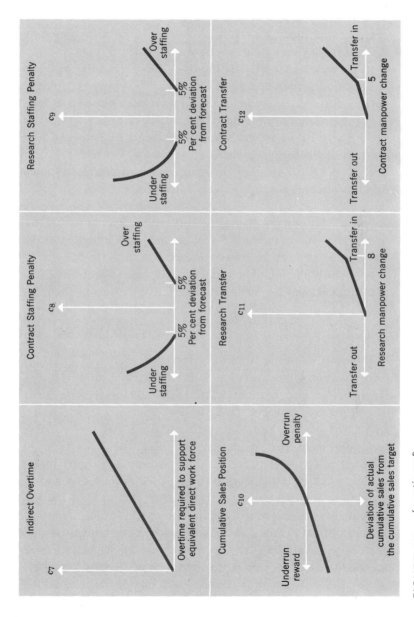

FIGURE 10.   (continued)

piecewise linear, constraints, and nonlinear forms. Taubert also built into the model a complete set of equations representing the overhead cost structure used to compute the overhead rate for any given set of decision variables. The resulting overhead rate is then used to compute the monthly government sales volume which in turn is compared to a cumulative sales target. The inputs to the decision system are monthly forecasts of contract manpower, research manpower, overhead manpower, and a cumulative sales target which represents the financial plan of the laboratory. The total manpower forecast must be met and it is a part of the director's operations planning problem to determine the best combination of decision variables which will accomplish the objective. Failure to meet the manpower requirements increases costs, and this effect is also implemented in the cost model.

Results.   Taubert validated the cost model against the financial record of the laboratory over a 5.5 year period. Following the validation, the decision system was operated for each month in the 5.5 year test period. A six-month planning horizon was used which required SDR to optimize a 24-dimensional response surface (four decisions per month for a six-month planning horizon). The SDR decisions respond much more smoothly to fluctuating manpower forecasts than did actual management decisions.

The costs resulting from SDR decisions compared to actual management decisions indicated that SDR would have produced cost savings. Over the 5.5 year test period, the SDR advantage ranged from a high of 19.7 per cent to a low of 5.2 per cent, averaging 11.9 per cent over the entire test period. The SDR decisions produced lower overhead rates and significant cost reductions in direct payroll, research program staffing, sales target penalties and rewards, and direct hiring costs. It achieved these results largely through the more extensive use of overtime.

Following the successful application of SDR to the aggregate planning problem of the Search Laboratory, Taubert subsequently disaggregated the decision variables for the size of the scientific staff in six departments. In effect, each department was considered as a miniature laboratory with its own contract and research manpower forecast as a cumulative sales target. Thus, the allocation of scientific staff had to be made in each of the six departments. While some transferring of personnel between departments was allowed, this practice was limited to represent the fact that, in general, scientists are not interchangeable and cannot be readily shifted from one department or technical expertise to another simply to meet fluctuating manpower requirements. Residual departmental manpower adjustments then had to be handled by hiring and layoff decisions. Again, it appeared that SDR continued to be able to produce logical and realistic decisions. The SDR decisions followed the forecast with a smooth response, carrying members of the scientific staff in overhead for short periods of time when faced with downturns in manpower forecasts [5].

AGGREGATE PLANNING FOR JOB SHOPS AND LARGE-SCALE PROJECTS

Aggregate planning for noninventoriable items need not take account of the risk of carrying inventories; but it also eliminates inventories as one of the managerial degrees of freedom—they cannot be used as a trade-off for the cost of fluctuating production. We have classified two kinds of systems as producing noninventoriable items, the custom job shop and the large-scale one-time project.

Job Shops

If we are producing a good or service to order, how can we anticipate and plan employment and operating levels? Forecasting the demand for unique items at first seems impossible, but the demand must be related to something in the economy as a whole or in our particular industry. It is commonly true that custom shops are not open to job order from just any source but rather operate within a field, for example the aerospace industry, or operate locally. Thus, demand may be related to demand within the industry, for example the gross value of aerospace contracts, or employment levels in the community. At any rate, demand forecasting probably cannot be as simple as the exponential forecasting models we discussed in Chapter 14. Forecasting must be tailored to the situation, but it can be done.

It is commonly true in custom organizations that the demand for flexibility of the design of the item is transmitted into a demand for relatively highly skilled personnel. For example, the most highly skilled machinists are required in custom job shops, prototype shops, and so on. Personnel at these skill levels are the most scarce, are paid at the highest levels, and are the best organized into trade unions. The fact that such personnel are generally scarce places a premium on holding a good man even when shop loads decline. As a matter of fact, we can view the custom organization as holding an inventory of capacity and skills to produce in a field, available on demand, rather than holding an inventory of goods. The result is that hiring and layoff costs tend to be high, producing a pressure toward employment stability within custom organizations for all of the reasons discussed. We must recognize that part of the high cost of turnover is an opportunity cost of maintaining the "going concern" value of the organization. If the organization disintegrates through layoffs to the extent that it is no longer viewed as a going concern, then a decline in demand will be accentuated.

Good managers of custom organizations are very sensitive to these factors that argue for relative employment stability, even to the extent of altering price policies to maintain the integrity of the organization in slack times. It is not uncommon for managers to price at cost or below in hard times in order to keep their staffs busy and/or to absorb the cost of idle labor time. In general, managers of custom organizations tend to indulge somewhat less in hiring and layoff to absorb demand fluctuations. By maintaining a seemingly small staff relative to average demand, fluctuations in demand can be absorbed largely through changes in hours worked, resorting to overtime for increases in demand and to undertime and price policy adjustments for decreases. As an observation it is noteworthy that custom shops do use overtime at premium rates as a regular part of their employment policy.

Large Projects

Much of what we have said about aggregate planning in job shops is applicable to the large-scale, one-time project system. However, there is a substantial difference in that large-project managers can forecast load in the near term because of the scale of projects. Project planning and scheduling are, in a sense, aggregate planning and scheduling. The entire project and all of its activities are planned at one time. Such programs may call for projecting loads one to two years in advance. These loads are not forecasts of demand but actual demands for contracted work.

The techniques for smoothing loads in network schedules to be discussed under "Deployment of Resources" in Chapter 18, are in fact attempts to reduce the cost effects of load fluctuation, or what we have termed the costs of production fluctuations in the aggregate planning models of this chapter.

SUMMARY

Aggregate plans and programs are of the greatest importance to production and operations management, since through these plans management deploys the major resources at their command. These resources can be deployed effectively or ineffectively. Top management's interest is focused on the most important aspects of this deployment process such as employment levels, production rates, and inventory levels. If basic plans can be based on decisions in these areas which establish operating constraints, then detailed planning and scheduling of operations can go forward.

We have discussed the structure of the aggregate planning problem and a number of decision processes designed to meet the needs of aggregate planning. At this point the graphic methods are probably used most. The mathematical and computer search methods have been developed in an effort to improve on the traditional methods by making the process dynamic, optimum seeking, and representative of the usual multistage nature of the problem. Several models have been of value, mainly as stepping stones to more useful models that represent reality more accurately. The most important single stepping stone undoubtedly has been the LDR. Presently, the computer search methods seem to offer the most promise because of their greater flexibility in representing costs that really occur in organizations. Although some of the mathematical methods do produce optimum solutions, we must remember that it is the model that is optimized. The real-world counterpart of the model is also optimized only if the mathematical model duplicates reality. The computer search methods are only optimum seeking by their nature, but do not suffer from the need to adhere to strict mathematical forms in the model and can therefore more nearly duplicate reality in cost models. It is, after all, the real-world situation that we wish to optimize, not the model. See [14] for a comparative study.

The extension of the SDR methodology to the nonmanufacturing setting of the Search Laboratories is encouraging in the development of the generality of the production and operations management field. The great complexity of the cost model in the Search Laboratories and the extension of the number of independent decision variables to nineteen indicate the developing power of the computer search methodology in representing realistic managerial situations.

KEY CONCEPTS

Minimization of Costs over a Planning Horizon.   A concept which we have not encountered previously is found in the objective of aggregate planning and scheduling. The very essence of the aggregate planning problem is to look ahead to see what impact projected demand changes will have on decisions we may wish to make today. Thus, even though the short-term demand is projected to increase in the next two months, the minimum cost response might be to absorb that increase in demand through the use of overtime or by drawing down inventories rather than to increase the size of the work force. This might be especially true if we projected a decrease in demand following the short-term increase. By resorting to the use of overtime or inventories, future costs of hiring and layoff may be prevented and the resulting sum of costs over the planning horizon can be minimized.

Computer Search Concepts.   If one attempted to find the deepest canyon in a mountainous area by tramping over the entire area making elevation measurements until he found the lowest point he would be using the equivalent of a direct search method for finding his answer. The direct search computer methods used in the solution of the aggregate planning problem are, in a sense, comparable since the sum of costs represents the equivalent of the mountainous area. With the speed of the computer, however, the surface can be searched quickly and accurately to find the lowest combination of costs for a given problem. These computer search methods are new to the solution of managerial types of problems, however, they hold considerable promise for being useful tools in a variety of problem areas.

IMPORTANT TERMS

Numbers in parentheses indicate page numbers.

REVIEW QUESTIONS

Numbers in parentheses indicate page numbers.

1. Characterize the term "aggregate plan." What is implied by the term "aggregate"? What are the objectives of aggregate plans? What are the required inputs? (485–486)
2. Place aggregate planning in context with the term "planning horizon." What is the appropriate planning horizon for aggregate planning? (485–486)
3. Discuss the relevant cost components involved in aggregate planning decisions. (487–488)
4. Describe a single-stage aggregate planning decision system. Under what conditions would such a system be appropriate? (488–490)
5. Describe a multistage aggregate planning decision system. Under what conditions would such a system be appropriate? (490)
6. Describe graphic methods for aggregate planning. How would they be used for multiple products? (490–494)
7. Appraise graphic aggregate planning methods. (494–495)
8. Describe optimum reaction rate methods of aggregate planning. What are the main variables under managerial control in reaction rate methods? (495)
9. Describe how optimization is obtained in reaction rate methods. What costs are being minimized? (495–496)
10. Appraise reaction rate methods of aggregate planning (497–499)
11. Describe the LDR. What cost components are being minimized in this model? (499–500)
12. Characterize the results of the paint company application of the LDR. (501–502)
13. Appraise the LDR as an aggregate planning decision system. (502)
14. Appraise distribution and simplex methods of linear programming as decision models for aggregate planning. (503–504)
15. As a decision system, contrast the SDR with the LDR. What are the advantages and disadvantages of each? (505)
16. What is the value of aggregate planning with disaggregate output of results as described in the projected Search Laboratories application of the SDR? (508–509)
17. Appraise the SDR as a decision process for aggregate planning. (508–509)
18. Describe aggregate planning in organizations which produce a custom product or service. Would you expect fluctuating or stable employment to meet varying demand in these kinds of organizations? Why? (509–512)
19. Why is a network plan the equivalent of an aggregate plan for large-scale one-time projects? (512)

20. Conceivably, a production-oriented organization has at its disposal a number of possible responses to anticipated changes in demand when developing an aggregate plan. Among the possible responses are production rate changes, inventory fluctuations, changes in employment level, the use of overtime or undertime, back-ordering or the absorption of lost sales, and subcontracting. Why then is it relatively difficult for organizations to develop rational modes for aggregate production scheduling?

21. Referring to Figure 7.
   (a) Rationalize why the cost of overtime should increase at an increasing rate as production rate increases.
   (b) If inventory varies from the optimal level (minimum cost level) why should the incremental costs increase at an increasing rate as represented in Figure 7d? (500–501)

22. Criticize the usefulness and validity of the strict aggregate planning concept, that is, making decisions solely in aggregate terms of size of work force and production rate. (513)

23. What is the meaning of the term *capacity* in aggregate planning models? How does a decision to hire, fire or subcontract affect capacity? How does physical or limiting capacity affect these decisions? (486, 487)

24. Cost comparisons between the result of actual managerial decisions and those produced by solving decision rule models are typically made by running both sets of decisions through the cost model and then comparing the results. Does this methodology seem valid? If not, what other approach might be followed? (507–509)

SELF-TEST TRUE-FALSE QUESTIONS

Numbers in parentheses indicate page numbers.

1. Where seasonal sales are involved, the most economical production plan is likely to be one which schedules production in a pattern somewhere between level production and one which follows requirements. (487–488)

2. The construction of a production program to meet a seasonal sales requirement may be cast in the framework of a waiting line model. (488)

3. Our objective in controlling production levels is to guard carefully against an unplanned buildup of inventory level. (488–489)

4. The economic order quantity concept is valid for the organization as a whole, but when applied in the local situation of determining the number of units to manufacture at one time, it produces a suboptimum solution. (488–490)

5. One of the requirements for aggregate planning is to develop some logical overall unit for measuring sales and output. (485)

6. Aggregate planning is done only for systems which produce inventoriable items. (486, 510)

7. Aggregate planning is done to coincide with the shortest time horizon. (486)

8. The term "aggregate planning" includes scheduling in the sense of a program. (486)

9. A single stage decision system model is appropriate when graphic methods of aggregate planning are used. (490)

10. A reason for using a multistage decision system for aggregate planning is that the decision for the upcoming period is affected by the future period forecasts and the decision process must consider the cost effects of a sequence of decisions. (490)

11. When a cumulative graph of requirements and alternate programs is used as a mechanism for aggregate planning, the vertical distances between the program proposal curves and the cumulative maximum requirements curve represent seasonal inventory accumulation for the plan in question. (493–494)

12. In the Linear Decision Rule, the reason why regular payroll costs are not included is that they do not form a quadratic cost function. (499–500)

13. In the Linear Decision Rule, undertime is the cost of idle labor at regular payroll rates. (501)

14. When the Linear Decision Rule is applied properly, we obtain a true provable system optimum since it uses mathematical optimization. (513)

15. In the application of the Linear Decision Rule in a paint company, the cost difference between actual company performance and performance with the rule, it was found that the rule was superior. (501–502)

16. One of the attractive features of the linear programming distribution model for aggregate planning is that it can account for production change costs. (504)

17. The difficulty with the simplex method of linear programming as an aggregate planning model is that it is impossible to include hiring and layoff costs in the model. (504)

18. In the Search Decision Rule, it is hoped that an optimum value will be eventually found, but there is no guarantee. (504)

19. When the Search Decision Rule was applied to the paint factory data, the results virtually duplicated the performance of the Linear Decision Rule. (505)

20. In the Search Company application of the Search Decision Rule the number of independent decision variables was expanded to three, including indirect work force size. (507)

21. In the Search Company application of the Linear Decision Rule step function costs were easily handled. (507–508)

22. We can view the custom organization as holding an inventory of capacity and skills to produce in a field, available on demand, rather than holding an inventory of goods. (512)

PROBLEMS

1.   Given a control number of 0.6, a decreased demand fluctuation of 600 units in the first period, and a forecasted production level of 15,000 units in the third period, what would be the revised production quantity set for period three? (Owing to lead times, it is not possible to adjust the production level for the second period.)

2.   A company manufactures a single product for which the following table represents a schedule of forecasted and actual demand in units for one year.

Month	Forecasted Demand	Actual Demand
Jan.	23,000	23,000
Feb.	24,000	25,000
Mar.	21,000	20,000
Apr.	23,000	22,000
May	20,000	22,000
June	19,000	24,000
July	17,000	22,000
Aug.	14,000	15,000
Sept.	8,000	6,000
Oct.	10,000	13,000
Nov.	9,000	10,000
Dec.	10,000	14,000
Total	198,000	216,000
	16,500	18,000

The initial inventory is 15,000 units. The desired ending inventory is 20,000 units. The cost of storage is $1 per unit per month. It costs $1000 to change production from zero to 3000 units and $3000 to change production from 3001 to 6000 units. No change larger than 6000 units is possible in one period. Back orders are permitted at a cost of $5 per unit per period.

(a) What is the best production plan for the forecasted demand if one wishes to minimize pertinent costs?

(b) Assuming that the year is over, what is the best production plan for the actual demand utilizing the benefit of hindsight?

3.   The following data show projected requirements for the production of a middle-priced camera together with buffer stock requirements and available production days in each month. Develop a chart of *cumulative* requirements and *cumulative* maximum requirements for the year, plotting cumulative production days on the horizontal axis and cumulative requirements in units on the vertical axis.

Month	Production Requirements	Required Buffer Stocks	Production Days
Jan.	3,000	600	22
Feb.	2,500	500	18
Mar.	4,000	800	22
Apr.	6,000	1,200	21
May	8,000	1,600	22
June	12,000	2,400	21
July	15,000	3,000	21
Aug.	12,000	2,400	13
Sept.	10,000	2,000	20
Oct.	8,000	1,600	23
Nov.	4,000	800	21
Dec.	3,000	600	20
	87,500	17,500	244

4. Using the data of problem 3, compare the total incremental costs involved in level production, in a plan which follows maximum requirements quite closely, and in some intermediate plan. Normal plant capacity is 400 units per working day. An additional 20 percent can be obtained through overtime but at an additional cost of $10 per unit. Inventory carrying cost is $30 per unit per year. Changes in production level cost $5000 per 10 units in production rate. Extra capacity may be obtained from subcontracting certain parts at an extra cost of $15 per unit. Beginning inventory is 4000 units.

5. An organization is nearing the end of the year, and is making plans for the coming year. It can, through minor adjustments in production rate, end the year with any final inventory between 150 and 1,500 units. The minimum buffer stock is 150 units. What combination of ending inventory (beginning inventory for the new year) and level daily production rate should be used if the criterion for good performance is to minimize the weighted seasonal inventory cost, where $c_H = \$100$ per unit per year? Suggested procedure: Plot cumulative maximum requirements in relation to production days and compute for two alternate plans which seem logical to you. Cumulative maximum requirements by months is as follows:

Month	Production Days	Cumulative Maximum Requirements
Jan.	22	550
Feb.	18	1,075
Mar.	22	1,575
Apr.	21	2,075
May	22	2,700
June	21	3,530
July	13	4,450

Aug.	21	5,100
Sept.	20	5,700
Oct.	23	6,175
Nov.	21	6,550
Dec.	20	6,950

6. An organization has forecasted maximum production requirements for the coming year as follows:

Jan.	400	July	580
Feb.	510	Aug.	600
Mar.	400	Sept.	300
Apr.	405	Oct.	280
May	460	Nov.	440
June	675	Dec.	500

The present labor force can produce 470 units per month. An employee added or subtracted from the labor force affects the production rate by 20 units per month. The average salary of employees is $660 per month and overtime can be used at the usual premium of time and one-half pay up to 10 percent of time for each employee. Therefore, an employee, working the maximum overtime, could produce the equivalent of an additional two units per month. Hiring and training costs are $100 per man, and layoff costs are $200 per man. Inventory holding costs are $10 per month per unit, and shortages cost $50 per unit short. Changeover costs for any increase or decrease in production rate are $3,000 per changeover over and above pertinent hiring and layoff costs. These costs include replanning and rebalancing of production lines and so on. No change cost is appropriate when added production is achieved through the use of overtime. What plan do you recommend? What is the incremental cost of your plan?

7. Given the data in Table II.
(a) What value of c_H would make Plans 1 and 2 equally desirable?
(b) What hiring-layoff cost makes Plans 1 and 2 equally desirable?
(c) What subcontracting extra cost makes Plans 1 and 2 equally desirable?

8. Consider the problem of making aggregate plans for a school of business.
(a) What aggregate unit of output might be useful?
(b) What are the main resources for which utilization plans must be developed?
(c) Can any resources be stored, in a sense, and carried forward for future use?
(d) Are there other flexibilities [other than (c) above] in the supply of resources?
(e) If optimization is a logical goal in such a system, what would you attempt to optimize? In other words, what is a logical criterion by which you can measure alternate plans?

REFERENCES

[1] Bowman, E. H. "Production Scheduling by the Transportation Method of Linear Programming." *Operations Research,* **4,** (1), 100–103, Feb. 1956.

[2] Buffa, E. S. "Aggregate Planning for Production." *Business Horizons,* Fall 1967.

[3] Buffa, E. S. *Operations Management: Problems and Models,* (3rd ed.). John Wiley, New York, 1972, Chapter 13.

[4] Buffa, E. S., and W. H. Taubert. *Production-Inventory Systems: Planning and Control* (Rev. ed.). Richard D. Irwin, Homewood, Ill., 1972, Chapters 5, 6, and 7.

[5] Buffa, E. S., and W. H. Taubert. "Evaluation of Direct Computer Search Methods for the Aggregate Planning Problem." *Industrial Management Review,* Fall 1967.

[6] Eisemann, K., and W. M. Young. "Study of a Textile Mill with the Aid of Linear Programming." *Management Technology* (1), 52–63, Jan. 1960.

[7] Fabian, T. "Blast Furnace Production—A Linear Programming Example." *Management Science,* **14,** (2), Oct. 1967.

[8] Greene, J. H., K. Chatto, C. R. Hicks, and C. B. Cox. "Linear Programming in the Packing Industry." *Journal of Industrial Engineering,* **10** (5), 364–372, 1959.

[9] Hanssmann, F., and S. W. Hess. "A Linear Programming Approach to Production and Employment Scheduling." *Management Technology* (1), 46–52, Jan. 1960.

[10] Holt, C. C., F. Modigliani, and J. F. Muth. "Derivation of a Linear Decision Rule for Production and Employment." *Management Science,* **2** (2), 159–177, Jan. 1956.

[11] Holt, C. C., F. Modigliani, J. F. Muth, and H. A. Simon. *Planning Production, Inventories and Work Force.* Prentice-Hall, Englewood Cliffs, N.J., 1960.

[12] Holt, C. C., F. Modigliani, and H. A. Simon. "A Linear Decision Rule for Production and Employment Scheduling." *Management Science,* **2** (2), 1–30, Oct. 1955.

[13] Hooke, R., and T. A. Jeeves. "A Direct Search' Solution of Numerical Statistical Problems." *Journal of the Association for Computing Machinery,* Apr. 1961.

[14] Lee, W. B., and B. M. Khumawala, "Simulation Testing of Aggregate Production Planning Models in an Implementation Methodology," *Management Science* **20** (6), 903–911, Feb. 1974.

[15] Magee, J. F., and D. M. Boodman. *Production Planning and Inventory Control* (2nd ed.). McGraw-Hill, New York, 1967.

[16] McGarrah, R. E. *Production and Logistics Management: Text and Cases.* John Wiley, New York, 1963, Chapter 5.

[17] Redwine, C. N. *A Mathematical Programming Approach to Production Scheduling in a Steel Mill.* Unpublished Ph.D. Dissertation, UCLA, 1971.

[18] Taubert, W. H. "Search Decision Rule for the Aggregate Scheduling Problem." *Management Science,* 14 (6), Feb. 1968.

[19] Taubert, W. H. *The Search Decision Rule Approach to Operations Planning.* Unpublished Ph.D. Dissertation, UCLA, 1968.

CONTENTS

CHAPTER 16
SCHEDULING AND CONTROL FOR HIGH-VOLUME SYSTEMS

For high-volume continuous systems it appears on the surface perhaps that when the aggregate plan has been developed the system has already been scheduled. After all, continuous systems are typified by production lines and continuous chemical processes where the production rate has been set and the sequence of individual operations and their interrelationships are already fairly well determined by the design of the physical system. The system operates as a giant machine. If the production rate is set, then the dovetailing and sequencing of operations is already taken care of by the system design. Isn't the detailed scheduling problem already accomplished by the system design? In a sense this is true. But, given aggregate planning decisions setting employment levels and production rates, the remaining problems are still significant.

First, how can we determine the amounts of each product to be produced? The aggregate plan has specified an overall production rate, but, in fact, this overall total must be allocated to the various sizes and types of items produced.

Second, the aggregate plan may have called for a change in the size of the work force. A change in manpower level must be translated into a rebalancing of facilities with modified work assignments for the crew. Therefore, while the aggregate plan has specified the quantitative change in work force size, there still remains the implementation of this change in a way that makes the most sense. In other words, which workers and what kinds of skills are involved? If the aggregate plan has called for a decrease in employment, union agreements may specify who will be laid off. Third, the combined work force size and production rate decisions determine the aggregate amount of overtime or undertime to be worked. How will the overtime or undertime be allocated to products and manpower? And, fourth, do the projected inventory levels that result from a proposed detailed schedule of items agree with the aggregate planning level and with the policies and procedures developed for individual items?

NATURE OF THE PRODUCTION–DISTRIBUTION SYSTEM

In order to understand the nature of the scheduling and control problems for high volume continuous systems we need to understand the overall flow, appreciate the importance of system inventories, and understand the system dynamics. One of the crucially important factors to keep in mind is that the scheduling of the factory output is very dependent on the behavior of distributors and retailers downstream in the flow system and that these elements of the system are normally outside the control of management.

Let us begin by examining the production-distribution system diagrammed in Figure 2. Assume that the system represents the manufacture and distribution of a small appliance. Figure 2 shows the major functions performed in the production and distribution of the appliance, beginning with raw material procurement, extending through manufacture and thence through the sequence of distribution steps to the ultimate consumer. There are 500 independent retailers, 50 independent distributors, and a single factory in the system. Each of the distribution steps involves a stock point for the finished product. Therefore, one way of looking at the system downstream from the factory is to envision it as a *multistage* inventory system.

Note also that Figure 2 indicates basic elements of the ordering procedure for replenishing the finished goods inventory at each stage.

Thus each retailer has a replenishment cycle which involves the review of his demand and inventory status, transmission of orders to his supplying distributor, and the filling and shipping of the order by the distributor. Similarly, each distributor has an equivalent replenishment cycle, based on the assessment of demand from retailers, the transmission of orders to the factory warehouse followed by the filling and shipping of the orders. Similar cycles are required for the factory ware-

FIGURE 1.   Reprinted through the courtesy of Helipot Division, Beckman Instruments, Inc.

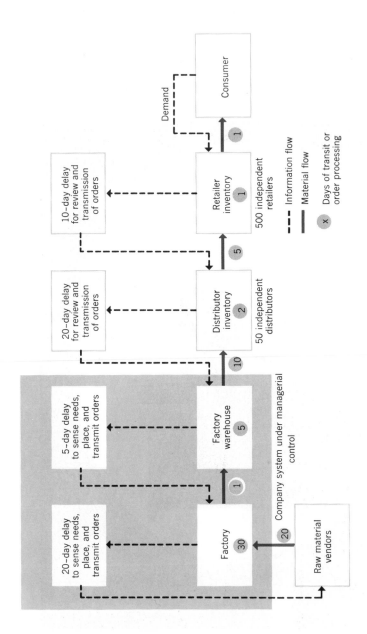

FIGURE 2.   Production-distribution system for high-volume continuous system showing broad flow of materials and information, transit times, and order processing delays. (System volume averages 2000 units per week.)

house in ordering from the factory and for the factory itself ordering raw materials from vendors.

We are interested in some aspects of all of these steps, keeping in mind that our key interest will be in scheduling the factory to produce. Before concerning ourselves with the scheduling of the factory, however, let us make some rough calculations to get some idea of how much inventory will be required to make the system function.

SYSTEM INVENTORIES

Recall from Chapter 14 the discussion of the several functions of inventories. Some inventory is required just to fill the flow pipelines of the system, another component to take account of the periodic nature of the ordering cycles, and a third component to absorb fluctuations in demand. Depending on the nature of the policies for factory scheduling, additional seasonal inventories might also be required.

Pipeline Inventories.   If the average system volume is 2000 units per week and it takes one day to transport from the factory to the factory warehouse, then there are 2000 (1/7th) units in motion at all times. If the order processing delay at the factory warehouse is five days, then there are 2000 (5/7ths) units tied up at all times because of the delay. Table I summarizes the pipeline inventory requirements for finished goods for the entire system, indicating a minimum of 7,144 units required just to fill the pipelines. These inventories cannot be reduced unless transit times, delays, and handling times can be reduced. The inventories are proportional to the system volume and the physical flow times. If system volume increases then this component of inventories must increase to keep the pipelines full and keep the system functioning.

Cycle Inventories.   We will assume that the fixed reorder cycle system of inventory replenishment is being used at the factory warehouse, distributor, and retailer levels. The average order size is then set by the ordering frequency at each stage. For example, the average retailer orders once each two weeks following a review of sales (the information and physical flow cycle is shown in Figure 2). Therefore, when a retailer orders it must be for a 2-week supply, just to meet average demand. The average retailer sells 2000/500 = 4 units per week, or 8 units during the 2-week ordering cycle. He must, therefore have

TABLE I.   Summary of Pipeline Inventory Requirements for Finished Goods
(Average system volume is 2000 units per week.)

	Average Transit Delay Time, Days	Average Pipeline Inventory, Units (Days/7) × 2000
Factory to factory warehouse	1	286
Delays at factory warehouse	5	1,429
Warehouse to distributors	10	2,857
Delays at distributors	2	571
Distributors to retailers	5	1,429
Delays at retailers	1	286
Retailers to customers	1	286
Totals	25	7,144

no less than 8 units on hand to service sales during the replenishment
period, and the average inventory for this purpose is half this amount or
4 units. The cycle inventory for the entire system of 500 retailers is then
4 × 500 = 2000 units. Table II summarizes the cycle stock requirements of the system showing that 12,000 units are required in average
inventory because of the periodic nature of ordering.

Buffer Inventories.   Recall from our discussion in Chapter 14 that
buffer inventories are designed to absorb random variation in demand
and that the size of buffer inventories depends on the nature of the
distribution of demand and the service levels which we wish to maintain. Table III shows the computation of buffer stocks for the system.
For example, the buffer stock required for each retailer is the difference
between the estimated maximum demand over the 17-day review plus
supply lead time and the average demand, or 18 − 9.7 = 8.3 units.
The average system buffer stock for 500 retailers is then 8.3 × 500 =
4,150 units. The buffer stock requirements for the entire system are
13,864 units.

Summarizing, the inventories in the system needed to accommodate
all three functions are as follows:

Pipeline inventories	7,144
Cycle inventories	12,000
Buffer inventories	13,864
Total	33,008

TABLE II.   Summary of Cycle Inventory Requirements for Finished Goods (Average system volume is 2000 units per week.)

	Recorder Cycle Time, Weeks	Average Cycle Inventory Units
500 Retailers	2	2,000
50 Distributors	4	4,000
Factory warehouse	6	6,000
Total		12,000

These are inventories required by the structure of the system and the ordering rules and service levels used. These inventories represent the minimum possible amounts necessary to operate the system. Overall inventories might be larger than this minimum if controls were not effective or if seasonal inventories were also accumulated in the system.

The impact of inventories on the problem of scheduling the factory is underlined when one notes that management has control over only approximately one-third of these inventories, the balance being held by distributors and retailers. Also, management does not have control over the ordering policies and procedures of the retailers and distributors.

SCHEDULING AND AGGREGATE PLANNING

The broad outlines of the scheduling process for the multistage production-distribution system in relation to the aggregate planning process is shown in Figure 3. Within the "Company System under Managerial Control" and above the dashed line in Figure 3 we see the activities which are directly related to scheduling.

Forecasts of demand based on information concerning the progress of sales at the retail-consumer level, as well as order rates at the factory warehouse, are fed into the forecasting model. The forecasting model produces period forecasts over the planning horizon for the aggregate planning process which in turn produces basic decisions on production rate and work force levels for the upcoming period. From the basic decisions produced by the aggregate planning process we can either compute the overtime and subcontracting required, as well as the projected end of period inventory, or these data will be produced as a

TABLE III.   Summary of Buffer Inventory Requirements for Finished Goods (Average system volume is 2000 units per week.)

	Average Demand per Week	Lead Time, Days	Average Demand over Lead Time	Maximum Demand over Lead Time	Average System Buffer Stock
500 Retailers	4	17	9.7	18	4,150
50 Distributors	40	35	200.0	300	5,000
Factory Warehouse	2,000	36	10,285.7	15,000	4,714
Total					13,864

part of the output of the aggregate planning procedure, depending on the aggregate planning model used. Translating these aggregate plans into detailed working schedules is then the next task.

The Product Mix Problem.   The effect of an aggregate planning decision on employment levels and production rates is the adjustment of the effective capacity of the system for the upcoming period. In other words, capacity limits have been set, creating a set of capacity constraints which must be observed in the detailed schedule which is generated. Thus the allocation of the limited capacity to product types and sizes becomes an important economic problem.

The product mix problem may be most complex in chemical industries such as oil refining where there are also interdependencies in the quantities of different products which can be produced. If more of one product, such as aviation gasoline, is to be produced, then less of some other product must be produced by the very nature of the refining process. The profitability of various products may be different, and there are limits to the markets for each. The result is a complex programming problem to determine the best product mix. The interdependencies always exist in oil refining, for example, because the basic raw material, crude oil, can be processed into many different products and an increase or decrease in one product always means a change in the quantities of some other products.

In the mechanical industries the interdependencies between products are more likely to stem only from the capacity limits proposed by the aggregate planning decisions and, in some instances, by the capacity

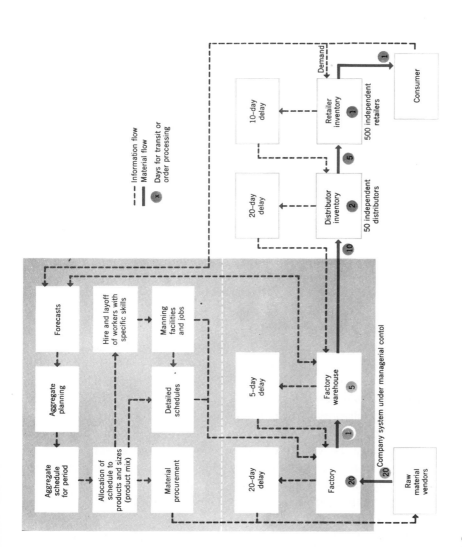

FIGURE 3. Relationship of forecasts, aggregate scheduling, and detailed scheduling to production-distribution system.

of time-shared facilities which are used to produce a variety of types and sizes. In all instances, however, we face an allocation problem of how best to use available limited capacity. These problems of product mix have been approached through linear programming as discussed in Chapter 4. In present day practice it is common to ignore the allocation problem and determine the product mix by applying percentage sales figures with modifications based on personal judgment.

At any rate, a result of the allocation to types and sizes gives basic information for detailed scheduling, detailed hiring and layoff instructions, and material procurement schedules as shown in Figure 3. Conflicts in detail schedules may occur at this point because of capacity limitations for either labor or facilities since detailed scheduling involves setting individual type and size production rates and manpower schedules.

In setting the individual type and size production rates and manpower schedules the scheduler may be faced with either great rigidity or reasonable flexibility depending on the nature of the processes and the design of the production system. Production lines are quite rigid in their nature in that once designed and set up the line produces assembled units at a fairly fixed hourly rate since all operations have been balanced to coordinate with the preset hourly rate. What flexibility does the scheduler have to obtain a certain target weekly or monthly rate of output? He has basically two alternatives. He can schedule the work force on the line to work shorter or longer hours (including overtime), or he can rebalance the entire line to achieve a somewhat higher or lower hourly rate or output. Obviously, he would use the latter to achieve more drastic changes in output rate since it involves hiring or laying off workers while simply changing hours worked is cheaply done unless overtime must be scheduled. Here, however, the scheduler will be following the basic instructions given him by the aggregate plan, which presumably has taken into account the relative costliness of changing production rates through changing hours, using overtime, and rebalancing (hiring and laying off).

The aggregate plan establishes the constraints under which the scheduler must perform. Thus we see that assembly line balance is a subject for concern not only for original design of production systems but for continued operation, since it is through rebalancing that the scheduler can change the basic hourly production rate of the system. For example, the use of rebalancing in automotive assembly lines to achieve different hourly rates of output is common.

If the line is completely rigid in design, being mechanically paced at a fixed rate, then the scheduler can change total output for the period only by changing the number of hours per period that the man-machine system is operated. The rigid system is, of course, often used.

The Detailed Scheduling Process.   Since the broadly based optimization has already taken place in the development of the aggregate plan, the main problems of detailed scheduling are to devise ways of following out the aggregate plan as far as possible. Following the allocation of aggregate production to product types and sizes, an iterative process begins which develops a tentative plan and checks back to see if the details of the plan fit the stated constraints of the aggregate plan and other possible company policies.

The first question raised in the schematic diagram of Figure 4 involves possible changes in employment levels called for by the aggregate plan. These changes will call for a rebalancing of manpower to facilities. In the case of complex assembly lines the methods and procedures of Chapter 10 may be used. In many instances, alternate manning plans probably exist for various output rates of facilities based on previous careful studies. In any case, the result of rebalancing will be to hire or layoff personnel in specific skill categories, checking to see if the result is within the aggregate plan. If the aggregate planning model has been carefully constructed to reflect the relationship between productivity and manpower, it should be possible to adjust manning assignments within the constraints of the plan. Recall from our study of line balancing, however, that balance solutions must deal with the assignment of whole manned units so that cost and capacity increase or decrease in step fashion rather than in a continuous relationship to manpower.

When the hiring-layoff question has been answered with resultant rebalancing, this information is an input to the initial attempt to generate a detailed schedule of products to facilities. Using the aggregate plan, the new basic production rate based on rebalancing, productivity factors, company-union work rules, and a knowledge of existing maintenance schedules, the scheduler generates a detailed assignment of product items to facilities by production days as well as assignments to subcontractors if that is appropriate. He then checks the result in an iterative fashion to see if assigned overtime levels, subcontracting levels, and inventories meet the requirements of the aggregate plan, as well as other constraints such as maintenance schedules and agreed company-

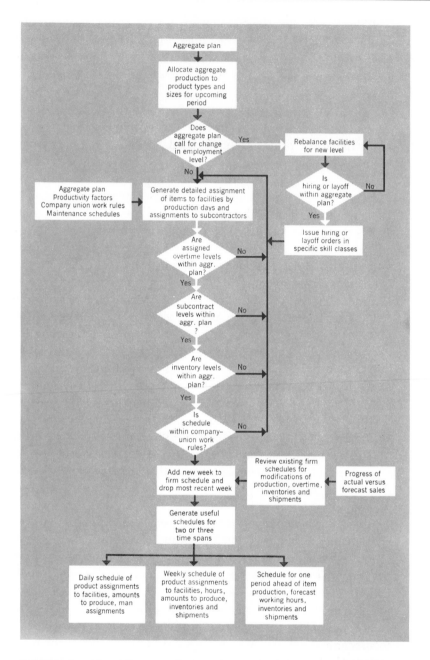

FIGURE 4.   Flow diagram of operations scheduling for continuous systems. (From [4, p. 316].)

union work rules. The result is a feasible daily schedule which will add an additional period, perhaps a week, to the firm schedule (see Figure 4).

In a parallel way, the existing firm schedules are reviewed for possible modification based on new information dealing with the progress of actual sales versus forecasted sales. The schedules of production commitments is then updated by adding the newest information and dropping off the most recent week or period.

Based on the resultant information the scheduler may then develop full schedules for two or three time spans such as those shown at the bottom of Figure 4. For some specific company situations most of the process could possibly be computerized. We assume also that at some point our technical capability will improve to the point that aggregate and detailed scheduling can be largely combined into one "optimum seeking" model, perhaps by the SDR methodology discussed in Chapter 15.

SYSTEM DYNAMICS

Now let us attempt to understand the impact of activities downstream in the production-distribution system on the scheduling of factory operations. To do this, let us focus our attention again on the multistage system diagrammed in Figure 2. Though highly idealized and simplified in many respects, this model is sufficient to represent for us some of the important material and information flow asked of the system.

We are already familiar with the significance of the time lags in relation to inventories needed for replenishment and to fill the distribution pipelines. Now, however, it will be of value to look more closely at the behavior of the system and examine its significance for factory scheduling. The general behavior of the system is dependent on the periodic review of inventory needs and on the preparation and transmission of orders for replenishment to the next stage upstream.

Now suppose that consumer demand falls by 10 percent from its previous rate. During his next review of inventory needs, the retailer reflects this decrease in orders for replenishment sent to the distributor, but ten days had elapsed. Similarly, the distributor reflects the decrease in his next orders for replenishment to the factory warehouse, but an additional twenty days have elapsed before the factory warehouse will feel the fall in sales. Thus, adding up all of the time delays in the information system the factory will not learn of the 10 percent fall in demand until thirty-five days have passed. Meanwhile, the factory has been producing 1.00/0.90 or 111 per cent of the new consumer requirement. An excess of 11 per cent would have accumulated each day in the inventory at the various stock points. This system inventory will have increased to 11 × 35 = 385 per cent of the usual normal day's supply.

In order to react to the change, retailers, distributors, and the factory warehouse decrease the quantities ordered, and to take account of the excess inventory, the factory will now have to cut back by substantially more than the 10 per cent. We can see now that the effect of the time lags in the system is to amplify the original 10 per cent change at the consumer level to a much greater change in production levels than would have seemed justified by the simple 10 per cent decrease in consumer demand, and we see that inventories have increased instead of decreased. Obviously, a more direct communication of changes in demand can reduce the magnitude of this amplification.

Figure 5 is identical to Figure 2 with the exception that a more direct information feedback loop has been added in the form of a system for assessing actual demand and forecasting demand in the immediate period ahead. The ten-day delay in assembling the actual demand and forecasting information reduces the total delay by twenty-five days. A 10 per cent decrease in sales under this sytem would mean an excess inventory of only 11 × 10 = 110 per cent of the normal levels would accumulate before the factory was aware of the change. Obviously, the forecast combined with the aggregate scheduling system shown in Figure 3 would stabilize the effects even more.

A Dynamic Simulation. We can demonstrate the dynamic effects of the time lags and changes in the system structure more dramatically through the mechanism of a simulation study. Figure 6 shows the structure of a production-distribution system which is similar to that in Figure 2, but which involves different time values for overall flow of goods and information. In this structure the solid lines represent physical flow and the lines with small circle dots represent information flow. Forrester [4] developed a dynamic computer simulation model of this system and used it to test a variety of changes in parameters and system organization structure. We will look only at what happens to inventory levels at various points in the system and to factory output when retail sales increase by 10 per cent. Figure 7 indicates results similar to those shown in connection with our discussion of Figure 2; the response in inventory and production levels is not simply 10 per cent.

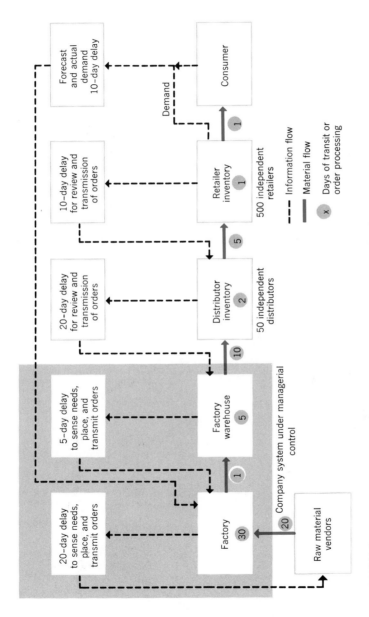

FIGURE 5. Production-distribution system with information feedback loop provided by forecasts and up-to-date information concerning actual consumer demand.

Note that there is an amplification of the effect of each stage back through the system and that actual factory production finally increased to a peak of 45 percent above its original level with a time lag of five months. The amplification and oscillating response are the result of the time lags in the information system.

What happens if we are able to reduce these time lags through more efficient procedures or by changing the structure of the system? Figure 8 shows the result when the entire distributor stage is eliminated. Note that the system response is similar but that the peak values of inventories are considerably reduced. The peak factory output rises to only 26 percent instead of 45 percent. (The curve of factory output based on the original distribution system from Figure 7 is included in Figure 8 for comparison).

Forrester also tested the effect of simply improving the speed with which information was handled back through the system by reducing purchasing time to one-third of these values. The effect, however, was only minor. This tends to indicate that improvements in structure, such as those discussed in connection with Figures 7 and 8 are likely

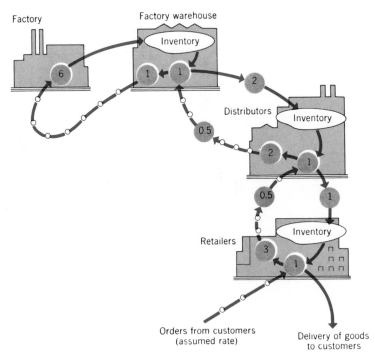

FIGURE 6.   Organization of production-distribution system. (From Forrester [4].)

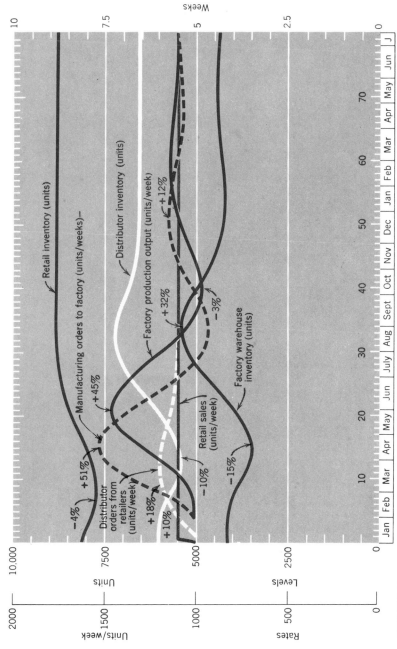

FIGURE 7. Response of production-distribution system to a sudden 10 percent increase in retail sales. (Adapted from Forrester [4, Figure 2-2].)

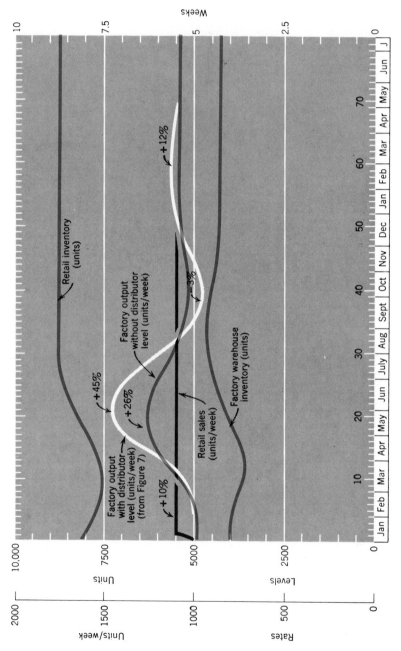

FIGURE 8.   Effect of eliminating the distributor level. (Adapted from [4, Figure 2-7].)

to yield much better results than simply doing what is already being done but doing it faster.

System Dynamics of Scheduling.   It seems evident that a system for tracking the progress of sales at the retail-consumer level is essential, feeding back this information to factory scheduling. This would short-circuit the system of time lags inherent in a multistage production-distribution system. Just this tracking and information feedback in Forrester's results shown in Figure 7 would have stabilized the wild oscillations considerably. Second, a forecast based on some smoothing and anticipation of changes in demand would have had a very important effect in stabilizing Forrester's system. Finally, the incorporation of some aggregate planning system in combination with a presumably smoothed forecast, as shown in Figure 3, combines all of the features of tracking the progress of sales to provide information feedback, a smoothed forecast, and the stabilizing effect of anticipation and longer-range planning.

PRODUCTION CONTROL

Given the schedules produced by the kind of process envisioned in Figure 4, it is relatively simple to design an information system which feeds back to managerial personnel rapidly and accurately the actual quantities produced in comparison to plans. When serious deviations from plans occur, management can react through daily adjustment of hours worked. Large deviations from plan ordinarily cannot be adjusted in the short term but must be an input to the next aggregate planning period as a carryover of too much or too little inventory.

SUMMARY

Operations scheduling and control focus attention on the shortest planning horizon. How should projected aggregate output be allocated to individual items? How should the resources of men and machines be deployed to meet requirements? How will individual work assignments be determined?

For continuous systems where aggregate planning is the most direct and easiest, the detailed scheduling process involves a rebalancing of the manning of facilities to implement the decision to change work force size and to match the requirements of the new production rate decision. Otherwise the process is one of cut-and-try solutions which stay within the constraints of the aggregate plan. While this two-stage process of attempting to optimize at the aggregate level and developing detailed schedules within the constraints of the aggregate plan is suboptimal, present research holds promise of an aggregate planning model capable of specifying more detail in the aggregate plan.

The scheduling problem for high-volume continuous systems needs to be thought of in relation to the system as a whole and designed to be a part of the information flow of that system. Forrester shows that the production facility would be affected most by a change in demand because it is furthest upstream, and there is progressive amplification of variation in demand as we proceed upstream in the system. Yet the cost of variations in level of activity are most expensive at the production facility, involving the heavy costs of hiring, training, and laying off employees. Thus, information feedback loops short-circuiting the ordinary chain of demand are essential to stabilize the otherwise oscillatory behavior of the system. Also, forecasts and aggregate planning are essential to anticipate seasonal and trend effects in demand rather than simply to respond after the demand changes happen.

Control of operations in continuous systems is relatively simple by providing information feedback on actual output in relation to plan. Control action can affect only minor changes in output within a given period, however, leaving larger changes to be put into effect for the next planning period.

KEY CONCEPTS

Product Mix. The concept of the product mix problem sometimes yields seemingly strange results. Thus, it is worth attempting to understand the nature of the problem and why, in some instances, one might produce less of some particular product than could be sold in the market. If, however, one recognizes that capacities are limited and the profitability of different products may be somewhat different, it is possible to see that one cannot look at each product in isolation. Rather, one must examine the entire system of products, capacities, and profitabilities to see which combination is best.

System Inventories. The pipeline, cycle, and buffer inventories make up a minimum inventory necessary for a production-distribution system to function at all. The size of this minimum inventory is often surprising. It is also sometimes surprising to realize that much of this inventory is outside managerial control, the reordering policies and procedures being under the control of independent distributors and retailers.

System Dynamics.   The time delays in a production-distribution system cause dynamic effects that are difficult for management to deal with. Relatively small changes in demand become amplified in their effects on the producing organization causing oscillation of inventories, production rates, employment levels, etc.

IMPORTANT TERMS

Numbers in parentheses indicate page numbers.

1. Multistage inventory system (526)   3. Production control (543)
2. Product mix (532, 544)   4. System dynamics (537, 545)

REVIEW QUESTIONS

Numbers in parentheses indicate page numbers.

1. Discuss the aggregate plan as a constraint to operations scheduling. (525–526, 534–536)
2. Given the aggregate plan as a constraint to operations scheduling in continuous systems, what flexibility is left to planners in developing detailed schedules? (534)
3. Under what circumstances is rebalancing of production lines necessary when adjusting to a new aggregate plan? (534)
4. Discuss the allocation problem involved in the determination of the breakdown of an aggregate plan into the quantities of types and sizes of products to be produced. (532, 534)
5. Criticize the flow diagram of Figure 4 as an overall process for developing optimal schedules. (535–537)
6. What flexibility is left to management in continuous systems for adjusting to deviations in actual output from planned levels within a given period?
7. Note in the model of the production-inventory system of Figure 5 that information concerning demand at the retail level is fed back directly to the factory and that, as a result, there is a considerable reduction in the magnitude of oscillations in orders and production activity. What are the implications of this result for organizing and establishing lines of authority and responsibility for a multistage production-distribution system? (538, 539)

SELF-TEST TRUE-FALSE QUESTIONS

Numbers in parentheses indicate page numbers.

1. If the aggregate plan has called for a decrease in employment, union agreements may specify who will be laid off. (526–535)

2.   The combined work force size and production rate decisions determine the aggregate amount of overtime or undertime to be worked. (526, 534)

3.   One of the crucially important factors to keep in mind is that the scheduling of the factory output is very dependent on the behavior of distributors and retailers downstream, and that these elements of the system are normally outside the control of management. (526)

4.   Pipeline inventories can be reduced by resorting to optimal lot size ordering policies. (529)

5.   Pipeline inventories are proportional to the system volume and the physical flow times. (529)

6.   Cycle stock inventories are determined by the reordering policies used. (529–530)

7.   The size of buffer inventories depends on the nature of the distribution of demand and the service levels which we wish to maintain. (530)

8.   The size of buffer inventories is proportional to the system volume and physical flow times. (530)

9.   In the mechanical industries the interdependencies between products are likely to stem from the capacity limits imposed by the aggregate planning decisions. (532)

10.   Because production lines are quite rigid in their nature in that once designed and set up the line produces units at a fairly fixed hourly rate, the scheduler has no flexibility in weekly or monthly rate of output. (534)

11.   If the aggregate planning model has been carefully constructed to reflect the relationship between productivity and manpower, it should be possible to adjust manning assignments within the constraints of the plan. (535)

12.   The effect of time lags in the system is to amplify at the factory level fluctuations in demand which occur at the consumer level. (537–538)

13.   In his dynamic simulation of a production-distribution system, Forrester showed that the effect of improving the speed with which information was handled back through the system was expremely important and justified computerized information systems. (540–541)

14.   Forrester showed that when the entire distributor stage was eliminated from his simulation system that amplification of demand fluctuation was considerably reduced. (540)

15.   When serious deviations in actual output compared to plan occur, management can react through daily adjustment of hours worked. (543)

16.   When large deviations in actual output compared to plan occur, management cannot react in the short term but must carry-over an inventory adjustment into the next aggregate planning period. (543)

PROBLEMS

1. Field study: Locate a case study in the field involving the scheduling of a high-volume system.

(a) Analyze the planning and scheduling system used and describe it in detail with the aid of flow diagrams and other illustrative charts.

(b) Relate the scheduling process found in (a) to the generalized diagram of Figure 3:

(1) What is the source of forecasts, that is, from which point in the distribution process is the information generated?

(2) What is the time lag between demand generation and the availability of forecasts for use?

(3) How is aggregate planning accomplished? What modes of absorbing demand fluctuations are used?

(4) How is product mix in the upcoming production schedule determined?

(5) What degrees of freedom are open to the scheduler, that is, changes in hours worked, hiring and layoff, rebalancing of facilities, expansion or contraction of physical capacity, use of inventory, etc.?

(6) Under what constraints does the scheduler work?

(c) What techniques are used to rebalance the man and machine assignments if the size of the work force changes?

(d) Relate the activities of the schedules to the schematic diagram of Figure 4.

(e) What kinds of schedules are developed, that is, to cover which time spans into the future and at what level of detail?

2. Considering the field study work in question 1, generate the data needed to produce a diagram comparable to Figure 3 for your particular project.

(a) Given whatever feedback of demand data structure which exists in the organization, compute the reaction at the factory level of a sudden 10 percent decrease in demand.

(b) Consider what improvements in the information feedback structure might be effective.

3. Considering all forecasting, and aggregate and detailed scheduling aspects of the production-distribution system of the field study in questions 1 and 2, draft a management report with recommendations for improvement.

4. Consider a supply-production-distribution system for a high-volume standardized product, perhaps a small appliance, which has the physical flow, transit, and handling time as indicated in Figure 9. The total system volume is 2,000 units per day. Compute the equivalent pipeline inventory required for the system.

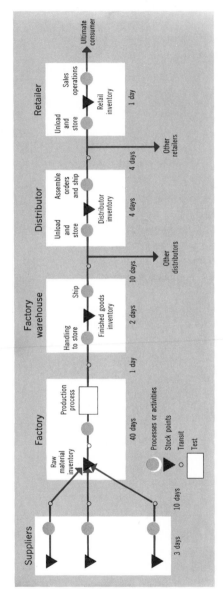

FIGURE 9.   Supply-production-distribution system for a small appliance showing physical flow, assumed handling and transit times, and major stock points (five company-owned and five independent distributors, one thousand retailers).

5. Referring to the system shown in Figure 9 and discussed in problem 4, consider the effects of the ordering behavior of the retailers, distributors, and the factory warehouse.

(a) The system volume of 2,000 units per day is not of course equally distributed among the 1,000 retailers or is their ordering behavior identical. Three-fourths of the retailers carry no inventory, depending on the distributor to supply their needs when sales occur. These retailers account for 25 per cent of the total sales volume. The other 250 retailers account for 1,500 sales units per day and carry inventories to give customers immediate service. A study of their average sales volumes and ordering behavior shows that the largest 10 retailers sell 50 per day, the next largest 40 sell 10 per day, and the remaining group of 200 sell 2 per day. The 50 largest retailers place orders each ten days to cover sales. The 200 remaining retailers who carry inventories order each twenty days to cover sales. The total supply lead time is five days.

(b) The 10 distributors each have approximately equal volume of 200 units per day. The ordering behavior of the 5 company-owned distributors is somewhat different than that of the independent distributors. Since the company-owned distributors are not charged with their inventories, they seem to order less often and in larger quantities to make sure that excellent service is always given the retailers. They review needs monthly and order a month's (thirty days) supply. It takes them approximately sixteen days to review sales records and prepare orders, two days to transmit these orders to the factory warehouse, and it requires ten days for shipment plus transit to the distributor. The distributor then takes two days to receive, unload, and store the merchandise in order to make it available for future shipment to retailers. The company-owned distributors therefore have a replenishment cycle of $16 + 2 + 10 + 2 = 30$ days.

The independent distributors review needs twice each month (fifteen days) and order fifteen days' supply. It takes them six days to review needs and prepare orders, and the remaining replenishment times are the same as for the company-owned distributors resulting in a replenishment cycle of $6 + 2 + 10 + 2 = 20$ days.

Compute the cycle inventories required at the retail and distributor stages of the system.

6. Referring again to the system shown in Figure 9 and discussed in problems 4 and 5, consider the problems faced by the factory warehouse, distributors, and retailers, in trying to give good delivery service. All of the usage levels we have stated previously were average rates. The various units have experienced extreme demand levels which would result in their running out of stock (stock-out) if they carried no buffer stock. The reasonable maximum demand rates expected are as follows:

	Maximum Expected Demand during Supply Lead Time
Largest 10 retailers	350 per 5 days per retailer
Next largest 40 retailers	70 per 5 days per retailer
Next largest 200 retailers	15 per 5 days per retailer
Five company-owned distributors	6,800 per 30 days per distributor
Five independent distributors	4,400 per 20 days per distributor

The factory warehouse carries a buffer inventory of ten days' supply to ensure that extreme demand from distributors can be accommodated. Compute the system finished goods buffer inventory requirement.

7.   Referring again to the system shown in Figure 9 and discussed in problems 4, 5, and 6, compute the total system inventory for finished goods. How could this finished goods system inventory be reduced? Since 5 of the distributors and all of the 1,000 retailers are outside managerial control, and own their own inventory, should the management of the enterprise (factory, factory warehouse, and 5 distributors) be at all concerned about how the rest of the system operates, i.e., does the behavior of the independent distributors and retailers affect them and if so, how?

8.   If sales are seasonal, what are the alternatives available to management as a means of absorbing these seasonal variations in demand? What is the nature of the criterion function which might be appropriate to measure the alternatives for scheduling production in the face of seasonal demand?

9.   Field Study Project. Go to your local post office to obtain data concerning their problem of work force planning and scheduling for letter mail sorting operations. Formulate a proposal for a model intended to help schedule letter sorting mail labor in the most effective way. The following information may be helpful but is not intended to limit or direct the nature of your proposal.

There are in general three types of letter mail normally found in a Post Office. *Collection and acceptance mail* is that collected from local mail boxes or brought to the post office by large mailers. The destination may be local or to another post office. It is commonly processed during the evening shift and is intended to leave the post office by midnight. *Transit mail* originates in, and is destined for other post offices. This mail is commonly processed on the day shift that ends about 4 p.m. *Incoming mail* originates in another city but is for local delivery. It is usually handled on the night shift in order to be ready for mail carriers about 7 a.m.

These three types of mail go through several stages of letter mail sorting operations in order to reach their final destinations. Depending on the post office size and volume, letter sorting machines may be used for some fraction of the processing.

It is well known that the volume of letter mail varies widely over the year with an overall load ratio of 10 to 1 for the daily high to the daily low. The load variations during a typical day also are substantial, largely because of the arrival pattern of collection and acceptance mail. It is not uncommon for 40 to 60 per cent of the collection and acceptance mail volume to arrive during the 4-hour period from 4 to 8 p.m. Since the normal processing deadline for collection and acceptance mail is midnight, a severe peak load sorting problem exists. The transit and incoming mail flow rates are much more uniform throughout the day.

The following references may be useful:

Hardy, S. T., L. J. Krajewski, L. P. Ritzman, and L. D. Vitt, "Production Planning and Control Activities in the Post Office," *AIEE Technical Papers,* American Institute of Industrial Engineers, Atlanta, Georgia, 1972.

Mandel, B. J., "Work Sampling in Financial Management-Cost Determination in Post Office Department," *Management Science,* Vol. 17, No. 6, February 1971, pp. 324–338.

McBride, C. C., "Post Office Mail Processing Operations," in *Analysis of Public Systems,* edited by A. W. Drake, R. L. Keeney, and P. M. Morse, MIT Press, 1972, pp. 271–286.

Ritzman, L. P., and L. J. Krajewski, "Multiple Objectives in Linear Programming: An Example in Scheduling Postal Resources," *Decision Sciences,* Vol. 4, No. 3, July 1973.

10.   Today, virtually all communities have had the advantages of mass food service operations made available to them. The pattern is a very limited menu, fast service, and controlled quality. Whether the food itself is fried chicken, fish, or hamburgers, the pattern is generally similar. These kinds of operations qualify as high-volume standardized product systems and obviously have significant problems of scheduling and control. Using a local franchised food service operation as a subject for study, consider the scheduling and control problems at two levels: (a) at the overall system level, i.e., the scheduling and logistics of supply, and the control of system quality, and (b) the detailed scheduling of labor at an individual outlet. Prepare a report analyzing the existing systems and recommending improvements.

REFERENCES

[1] Bock, R. H., and W. K. Holstein. *Production Planning and Control.* Charles E. Merrill, Columbus, Ohio, 1963.

[2] Buffa, E. S. *Operations Management: Problems and Models* (3rd ed.). John Wiley, New York, 1972.

[3] Buffa, E. S., and W. H. Taubert. *Production-Inventory Systems: Planning and Control* (Rev. ed.). Richard D. Irwin, Homewood, Ill., 1972.

[4] Forrester, J. *Industrial Dynamics.* MIT Press, Cambridge, Mass., 1961.

[5] Greene, J. H. *Production Control: Systems and Decisions.* Richard D. Irwin, Homewood, Ill., 1965.

[6] Magee, J. F., and D. M. Boodman. *Production Planning and Inventory Control.* McGraw-Hill, New York, 1967.

[7] Moore, F. G., and R. Jablonski. *Production Control* (3rd ed.). McGraw-Hill, New York, 1969.

CONTENTS

CHAPTER 17

SCHEDULING AND CONTROL FOR INTERMITTENT SYSTEMS

As we discussed in Chapter 13 there are three common types of intermittent systems: the closed job shop which produces inventoriable items, the open job shop which produces custom items, and the large-scale one-time project. The two types of job shops can be considered together insofar as detailed scheduling and control of operations are concerned, since the physical flow and control problem is the same for both. The special problems associated with planning, scheduling, and control for large-scale projects are considered separately in the next chapter.

The job shop scheduling problem is commonly recognized as the most complex scheduling problem in existence. The complexity stems from the fact that the nature of the system requires that virtually everything is left flexible: part or product designs, routes through the system, processes to be used, processing times, etc. Progress in understanding the nature of the system was made when it was characterized as a network of queues with arrivals and departures at each work center described by probability distributions. The usual system, however, is so complex that analytical approaches of waiting line theory are useless. Thus, while the general concepts of waiting line analysis described in Chapter 4 are useful in understanding the nature of the flow process in a job shop, the formulas themselves make no contribution toward problem solving. With the availability of large-scale computers, however, a complex network of queues can be simulated. The general concepts of Monte Carlo simulation discussed in Chapter 4 apply, and simulation has been the dominant technique used in studying job shop scheduling.

ORDER CONTROL

Since each individual order must be segregated and treated as a unit, scheduling and control systems for job shops are often termed *order control systems*. The problem is to develop planning, scheduling, and control procedures appropriate for the situation, where each order in house at a given moment may have a unique sequence of processing with unique processing times and uniquely determined due dates. To control the flow of work in an order control system, we must make some detailed plans, schedule the order, dispatch it to the various operations according to some set of decision rules, and finally track the progress of the order to be sure that the schedule is being met.

Plans and Shop Papers

New orders for parts or products which have never been made before must be processed to determine what the manufacturing plan will be; that is, what operations will be performed, operation sequences, special tooling requirements, and method designs. We have already covered the details of this activity in Chapters 7, 8, 10, 11 and 12. If the part or product has been made before, standard route sheets should be available for reuse. But this is only part of the preparation required. It is customary to prepare shop orders, material requisitions, part drawings, shop travel orders, identification tags, tool requisitions, move tickets, scrap tickets, labor tickets and job progress cards. One example of the flow of these various plans and shop papers is shown in Figure 1.

Order Scheduling

While individual orders may call for different products, standardization of parts and component designs often makes economies possible by combining orders for identical parts and subassemblies. Cross classification charts, "Gozinto" charts and mathematical techniques can reveal the structure of these part and component families. Table I is a cross classification chart showing the number of parts and subassemblies that go into subassemblies and end products. Requirements of parts and subassemblies can then be summed for all end products and advantage can be taken of economical manufacturing and purchase lot sizes.

In constructing a schedule for an assembled product, we must work backward from the required completion dates of the end product, using the general concept of the schedule diagram. The *schedule diagram* takes the basic structure of assembly, subassemblies, part fabrication, material procurement, etc., and relates them to a time scale. Figure 2 is an example of a schedule diagram for an assembled product. Beginning with the receipt of the customer's order, the schedule diagram shows the time schedules that must be met at the various stages of planning and scheduling, material procurement, parts fabrication, subassembly, and assembly in order that the final product can be shipped by the target date.

For a complex product, such as an airplane, a missile, or a complicated electronic component, such charts are necessary. For a complex engineered product, time also would have to be allowed for the product engineering design to be completed. By determining the required time for final assembly, we determine the due dates for the subassemblies. The time to produce subassemblies in turn establishes due dates for manufactured and purchased parts, etc. In each instance these estimates of time requirements must allow for process time, move time, and time between operations. These set-back times determine when production must start and when purchase orders for needed raw material and purchased parts must be placed to meet schedules completion dates. The actual schedule of parts, subassemblies, and final products is the due date for each stage of manufacture and assembly.

Gantt Charts. Gantt charts and their modern counterparts help provide information about the production schedule. They measure progress against the schedule, the load on departments or individual machines,

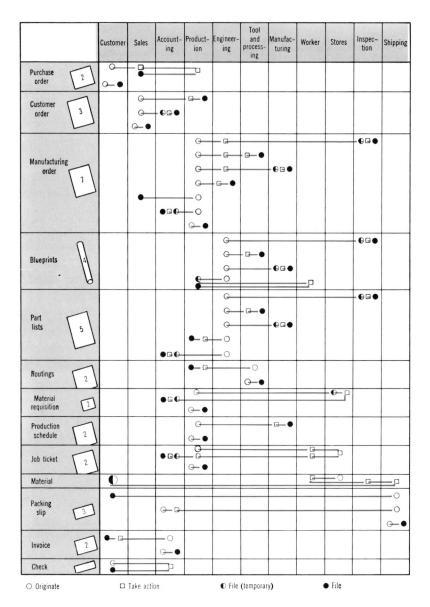

FIGURE 1. Flow of paperwork in a production control procedure. (Courtesy Professor John G. Carlson, University of Southern California.)

and the availability of equipment or manpower. The plans and progress against plans are plotted in relation to time.

TABLE I.   Cross Classification Table Showing the Number of Common Parts and Subassemblies That Go into Subassemblies and Final Assemblies

Part or Sub-assembly Number	Subassembly Number								Assembly Number							
	SA-1	SA-2	SA-3	SA-4	SA-5	SA-6	SA-7	SA-8	A-1	A-2	A-3	A-4	A-5	A-6	A-7	A-8
1	1	1		1						1						
2	1		1							1						
3			1		1	1	2				1					
4			4							1						
5	1		1	1										1		2
SA-1									1	1						1
SA-2										1						
SA-3											2					
SA-4												1				
SA-5												1				
SA-6									1			1				1
SA-7												1				
SA-8										1		1				

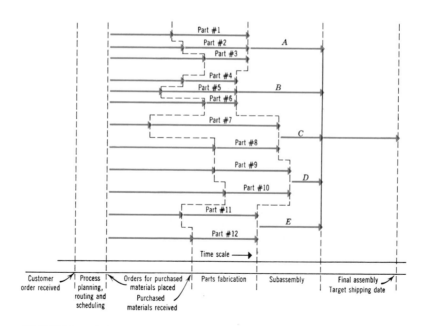

FIGURE 2.   Schedule diagram for an assembled product. *A, B, C, D,* and *E* are subassemblies comprised of the parts indicated to the left of each subassembly.

Several kinds of Gantt charts may be used. Figure 3 shows an example of the *Gantt project planning chart* which may be used to map out a detailed plan to accomplish target objectives. Figure 3 represents a plan to manufacture an assemmbled product so that the availability of parts for assembly dovetails with the fabrication and the assembly time required, as shown by the schedule diagram of Figure 2. Note that final assembly is scheduled to begin during the week of March 26th, before all of the subassembly units have been completed. As subsequent sub-assemblies are completed, they will be taken to the final assembly area. The schedule in this case could undoubtedly be compressed further by applying the same overlapping scheduling to the subassemblies in relation to the parts fabrication.

The overall scheduling of this project depends in part on the avail-ability of men, machines, and materials. Therefore, the same basic concepts of the Gantt chart can be applied. Figure 4 shows a *Gantt load chart* for some of the machines that might be used in fabricating the various parts in our assembled product. It shows the overall projected load on these machines month by month, together with the accumulated backlog of work. Figure 5 shows greater detail; for each machine it shows the orders schedule with the total time reserved for each order. This is called a *Gantt layout chart* or a *Gantt reserved time planning chart*. It shows at a glance the status of a given order. Similar charts could be constructed for materials or men.

The charts must be maintained in order to be of any value as tools for planning, scheduling, and control. If we use paper and pencil charts similar to those illustrated in Figures 3, 4, and 5, the task of maintenance can be considerable. If, for example, the Gantt layout chart has to be modified to accommodate the fabrication of a new rush order, the entire sequence might have to be rescheduled. This is one reason why mech-anical boards have been developed. They allow changes to be made rather quickly by the shifting of pegs or cards.

Even with the mechanical boards, the problem of maintenance is considerable, especially in large complex installations; this often results in discarding any attempt at the close control implied by the charts. The role of the electronic computer and modern programming methods looms large in the future. If we use the hand methods of developing the best schedule represented by the charts, the number of alternatives will often be very large, and selecting the best schedule becomes a trial-and-error process. A high-speed computer can be set up to make the trials quickly.

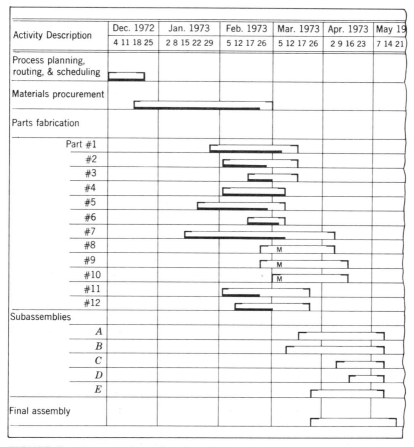

FIGURE 3.   Gantt project planning chart based on schedule diagram of Figure 2. At the beginning of the week of March 5, material procurement is one week behind schedule so the fabrication of parts 8, 9, and 10 has been held up.

The need to maintain records of loads depends on how close to full capacity we are operating. At less than capacity levels, load records usually can be ignored because there is a great deal of slack in the system anyway; if the master schedule is followed, no great difficulties should be encountered. Under these conditions, orders are simply scheduled sequentially by assigning start dates and due dates. This, of course, offers no assurance that some machines will not be overscheduled by simple chance occurrence.

Load records of critical machines or known bottleneck operations are often kept instead of records on all machines. The assumption is that any schedule that fits within the load limits of the critical or bottleneck machine will probably work out all right for the rest of the machines.

Dispatching Decision Rules

The start date or the due date at each operation often serves as a simple priority decision rule to departmental foremen in getting the work out on time. The work load for each machine class is represented by the waiting line of jobs or shop orders. If the priority system were to take as the subsequent order on which to work the one with the earliest due date, there would be a constant reshuffling of the sequence of jobs to accommodate orders just received from other work centers which may have earlier due dates. This reshuffling is not particularly difficult, but nagging questions remain. Does this priority decision rule work better than some other rule? Are any decision rules significantly better than the simplest of all, first come–first served?

We might state the overall problem of the operation of a job shop as one of balancing the costs of carrying in-process inventory, labor, and the capital costs of capacity, together with the costs associated with meeting specified order completion dates. To have a high degree of

Turret Lathe Dept.				
	Mach. No.	March	April	May
Gisholt #2	321			
Gisholt #4	422			
Warner and Swasey #2	729			
Warner and Swasey #2	730			
Warner and Swasey #5	810			
Bullard vert. turret #1	769			

FIGURE 4.   Gantt load chart. Light lines show per cent of month that machines have scheduled work. Heavy lines show cumulative load.

labor and machine utilization it would be necessary to have a large number of orders waiting so that labor and equipment are very seldom idle. The result is relatively high in-process inventory carrying costs and poor schedule performance.

If we strive to meet order completion dates without fail, however, we need a very large equipment and labor capacity so that orders ordinarily would not have to wait. This would result in relatively low in-process inventory costs but poor machine and labor utilization. The problem of balancing these costs in a complex system is at best a difficult one. Thus there has been a focus on system simulation as a technique for testing alternate decision rules. To test various priority decision rules in the factory would be time consuming and would also disrupt factory operations by continual shifting from one decision rule to the next.

Early work in the simulation of dispatching decision rules was done by Rowe [20] at the General Electric Company. In conjunction with Rowe's work, the IBM Corporation developed a generalized simulation program which they called "the job shop simulator." This program is flexible in terms of the input characteristics of the system to be simulated and has been used effectively by the General Electric Company, Hughes Aircraft Company, Westinghouse Electric Corporation, and

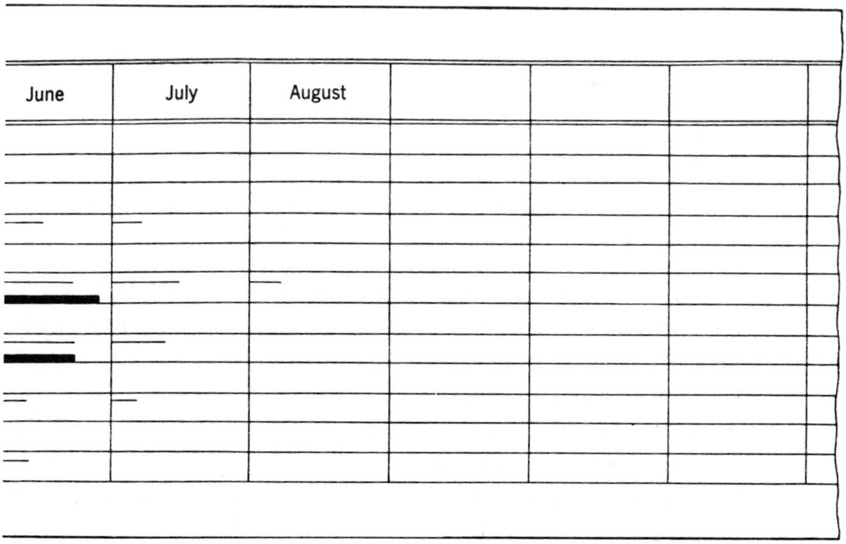

June	July	August				

FIGURE 4.   (*continued*)

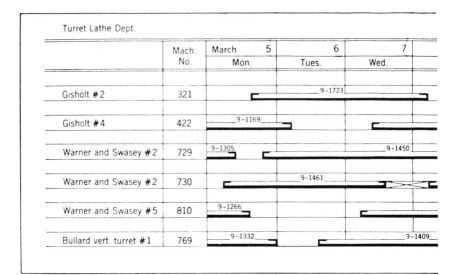

Turret Lathe Dept.

	Mach. No.	March 5 Mon.	6 Tues.	7 Wed.	
Gisholt #2	321		9-1723		
Gisholt #4	422	9-1169			
Warner and Swasey #2	729	9-1305		9-1450	
Warner and Swasey #2	730		9-1461		
Warner and Swasey #5	810	9-1266			
Bullard vert. turret #1	769	9-1332		9-1409	

┌   Indicates date or hour when work on a given order is
     scheduled to begin.

┐   Indicates date or hour when work on a given order is
     scheduled to end.
     Light lines indicate scheduled work.
     Heavy lines show relation of completed work to
     scheduled work.

▷◁   Time reserved (e.g., time needed to get back on
     schedule)

∨   Today's date.

FIGURE 5.   Gantt layout or reserved time planning chart.

others. The general characteristics of the job shop simulator are shown in Figure 6.

Hughes Aircraft Company's application of the IBM job shop simulator represents an adaptation of the program to the company's El Segundo plant operations. The adaptation made it possible to take order input data directly from random access files, transposed to the form required for simulation, together with other input data supplied to the simulator. LeGrande [12] made a study testing six dispatch decision rules with the El Segundo job shop simulation process. By operating the simulated shop according to each of the six decision rules and measuring results by certain criteria which we shall discuss, it was possible to compare the

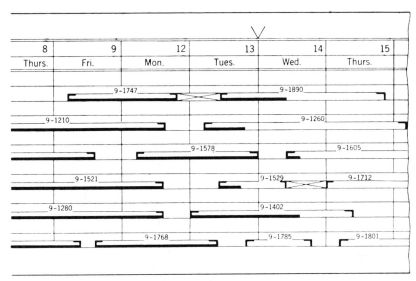

FIGURE 5.   (*continued*)

effectiveness of the six different rules. The rules used in the study were as follows:

1. *Minimum Processing Time per Operation* or, Shortest Operation Time, (SOT): Of the jobs waiting in line at a machine group, this rule assigns the next job to be worked on by choosing the one with the shortest processing time (setup plus machining time).

2. *Minimum Slack Time per Operation* or, Dynamic Slack per Remaining Operation, (DS/RO): The next order to be worked on is determined by subtracting the remaining processing time for the order from the total time remaining (due date minus present time), and dividing the result by the number of remaining operations. The order for which this amount is smallest will be assigned to be processed next.

3. *First Come—First Served*, (FCFS): This rule places orders in line as they arrive at a machine group, choosing the next order to be processed from the front of the line.

4. *Minimum Planned Start Date per Operation*, (MINSD): In this rule the order assigned next is the order with the earliest planned start date for the current operation. This is the theoretical operations start date which has been calculated previously by the scheduling procedure.

5. *Minimum Due Date per Order* or, First in System, First Served, (FISFS): This rule is based on the due dates for orders waiting in line. The order that has the earliest planned due date will be assigned first.

6. *Random Selection,* (RAND): This rule has no special priorities. The order to be assigned next is selected at random from all of the orders waiting in line at the machine group.

The criteria by which the various simulation runs were evaluated are as follows:

1. Number of orders completed.
2. Per cent of orders completed late.
3. Mean of the distribution of completions.
4. Standard deviation of the distribution of completions.
5. Average number of orders waiting in the shop.
6. Average wait time of orders.
7. Yearly cost of carrying orders in queue.
8. Ratio of inventory carrying cost while waiting to inventory cost while on the machine.
9. Per cent of labor utilized.
10. Per cent of machine capacity utilized.

Figure 7 shows the distributions of order completions for the six decision rules. On the basis of an equal weighting of the criteria, the minimum processing time per operation rule (SOT) gives the best results. As LeGrande points out, a different weighting with perhaps emphasis on getting orders out on time would tend to favor minimum slack time per operation (DS/RO) as a decision rule. If management places a premium on getting orders out on time, then some kind of due-date oriented rule, should give superior results. Carroll [5] experimented with a family of rules which sequenced orders according to the largest ratio of downstream waiting-time cost to operation process time or c/t (called c over t, or COVERT). In comparison with five rules tested, the COVERT rule was extremely effective in meeting due dates as shown in Figure 8.

Tracking the Progress of Orders

Unfortunately, we cannot predict the flaws in our original plans. Machines may break down, work may pile up behind some critical machine, and dozens of other unexpected production troubles may occur that interfere with original schedules. With hundreds or even

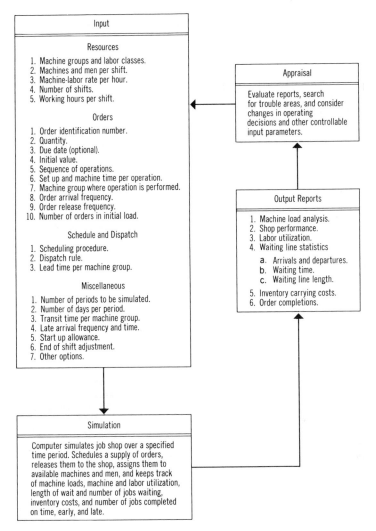

FIGURE 6.   Overall characteristics of the job shop simulator.
(From LeGrande [12].)

thousands of current orders in a shop, the only way to be sure that orders ultimately will meet schedules is to provide information feedback and a system of corrective action that can compensate for delays. Returned job tickets, move orders, and inspection reports can provide formal information which can be compared with schedules. But to be of value, this information flow must be rapid so that action can be taken

Dispatch Rule	MINSD	FCFS	FISFS	DS/RO	RAND	SOT
Per cent orders early	54	57	63	68	65	71
Per cent orders on due date	6	5	5	12	5	5
Per cent orders late	44	38	32	20	30	24
Mean of completions (days)	3.0	3.6	4.2	4.2	5.2	6.6
Standard deviation (days)	9.2	10	8.2	8.2	10.4	9.9
Total number of orders completed	3118	3190	3484	3217	3117	3708

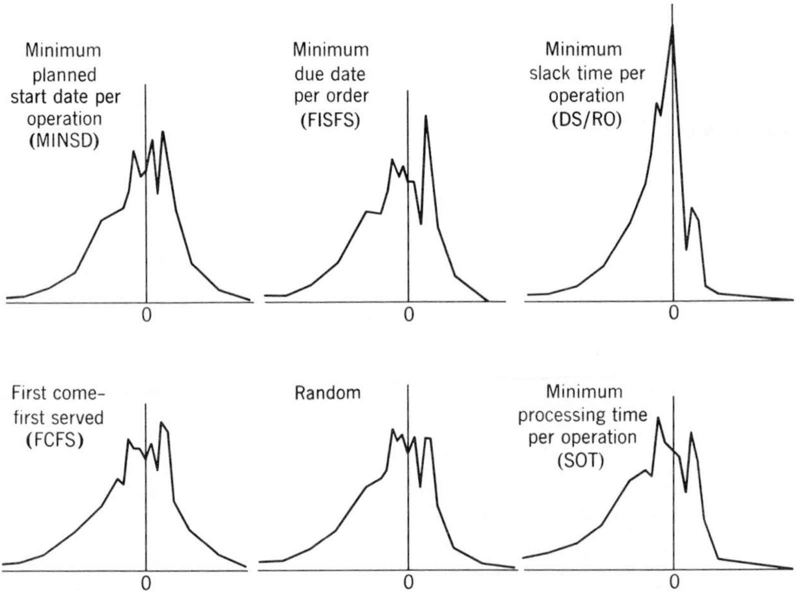

FIGURE 7.   Distributions for the time of order completions. (From LeGrande [12].)

on up-to-date reports. Usual company mail systems are much too slow to serve the needs of production control systems. Therefore, special communication systems are in common use, such as special mail services, intercommunication systems, teletype writers interconnected to central offices, pneumatic tube systems, and remote data collection centers tied directly in with automatic computing systems. These systems in combination with rapid data processing can grind out current reports which can be used as a basis for expediting and rescheduling orders.

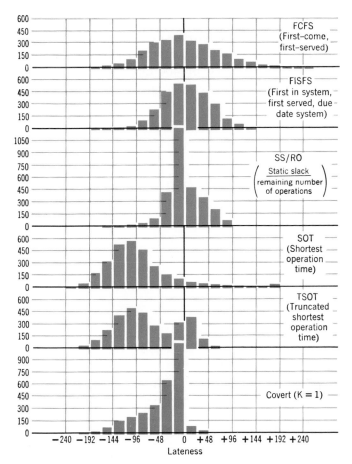

FIGURE 8.   Lateness distribution for six rules, pure job shop single-component order (3072 orders, utilization = 0.80). (From Carroll [5].)

Computerized Planning, Scheduling, and Control Systems

As mentioned earlier the complexities of job shop planning, scheduling, and control, together with the difficulties of maintaining graphic methods such as Gantt charts, have led to the use of computer-based systems [4, 6, 12, 14, 19, 21]. One such system, installed at the Hughes Aircraft Company, is of particular interest since it combines shop load forecasting, daily simulation scheduling, remote data collection, and a series of important reports, all in a computer-based system [4, 12, 21].

The Hughes Job Shop Control System. The Hughes plant in which the system is installed has approximately 1000 machines and/or work centers which are grouped into 120 functional machine or work centers. The work centers are manned by 400 direct workers. Approximately 2000 to 3000 orders are in process at any one time with an average of

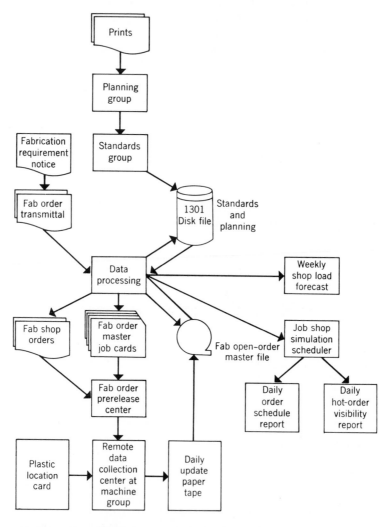

FIGURE 9. Hughes Aircraft Company's production, planning, and control system. (Adapted from LeGrande [12].)

seven operations per order. The average total processing time for an order is 2.5 hours, and the average order cycle time is three to four weeks.

The broad outlines of the entire system are shown in Figure 9. Operational process planning is developed from engineering blueprints to yield the critical data of processes to be performed, standard process times, and standard flow allowances through the shop. These data are placed in the disk file of the computing system. When a fabrication requirement notice is received from one of the assembly product line departments, a fabrication order is transmitted to data processing which initiates the preparation of a fabrication shop order and establishes an open order in the fabrication open-order master file. A deck of master job cards also is produced which accompanies the order through the shop. These papers are then sent to a fabrication order control prerelease center from which orders are dispatched to the shop. After release to the shop, the master job cards are used in conjunction with plastic location cards at machine groups to actuate the remote data collection devices. At the end of the day, a paper tape containing all order moves transacted during the day is used to update current order locations and to code completed operations in the fabrication open-order file. The fabrication open-order master file contains, on a daily updated basis, the information on every open order. It is the heart of the system which produces the three documents: the *weekly shop load forecast*, the *daily order schedule report*, and the *daily hot-order visibility report*.

The *daily order schedule report* and the *hot-order visibility report* are developed by the job shop simulation scheduler. These documents are used by shop foremen and expediters in the daily sequencing of orders at the machine groups in the shop. The simulation scheduler is a separate computing routine used to simulate one shift of shop activity and to generate the two daily reports. Involved in the simulation scheduling process is the use of a priority dispatch decision rule related to slack time in the schedule.

The reports of the performance of the Hughes system given in [12] indicate that the computer-based integrated system has yielded substantial improvements. For example, in the first six months of operation there was a 10 percent increase in the number of orders completed on time. The average order cycle time was reduced by one week, thus reducing in-process inventory and increasing man and machine utilization significantly. The new system seemed to relieve what we might term organizational stress and pressure, as indicated by a 60 per cent reduction in expediting effort. Expediting effort occurs with hot orders when special personnel are assigned to these hot orders to make sure that they receive special attention at each stage.

Western Electric Interactive System.   An interesting development which uses the capabilities of time-shared computing has promise for the job shop scheduling problem. Godin and Jones [7] developed interactive scheduling systems which use either typewriter or display terminals and thereby place the production supervisor, or a scheduler, in a loop with a computer program. By interacting with the computer program the scheduler develops and/or alters a schedule. Schedules are generated by making choices from among sets of decision rules, for example, rules for the acceptance or rejection of orders, rules for sequencing orders, and rules for allocating the use of overtime. A schedule is developed by testing the effects of various combinations of possibilities, simulating various alternate assignments and their effects.

Godin and Jones developed a small-scale application of the interactive scheduling concept in one of the coil winding shops of the Western Electric Company. Of the 200 types of coils manufactured, approximately 65 are active at any point in time and each type is usually being produced for three or four different orders. There are twenty of one type winding machine and two of the second type, and the work force consists of from twenty to thirty-five machine operators working on two or three shifts depending on shop load.

Because of differences in skills, not all operators can wind all types of coils, and performance against standard varies considerably for various combinations of operators and coil types. Similarly, some machines cannot be used to wind some types of coils. The production supervisor must assign workers and machines to each other in a way which balances pressures for on-time deliveries against the other factors which make for production effectiveness.

The system functions through a main program and twenty-three subroutines. To communicate with the program through the typewriter terminal, a simple conversational language was developed. A single key stroke indicates a whole series of commands. For example, when the key marked "Load" is depressed, the computer understands it as a request to print the winding shop load on the printer.

The system allows for the production supervisor to consider seven variables in constructing schedules:

1. Skill levels of workers.
2. Skill needs of products.
3. Capability of machines.
4. Availability of workers, machines, and materials.
5. Quantities required.
6. Completion dates.
7. Existing machine set ups.

The computer program can carry out simulations of shop schedules so that the supervisor can test various alternate assignments and try to anticipate future problems. Various reports can be called for at any time that the system is in operation such as shop status, a history of work by operator or by machine, load summarized by standard hours, etc.

SUMMARY

Operations scheduling and control focus attention on the shortest planning horizon. How should projected aggregate output be allocated to individual items? How should the resources of men and machines be deployed to meet requirements? How will individual work assignments be determined?

Operations scheduling and control for intermittent systems are very complex, since individual orders must flow through a sequence of unique operations. Cross classification tables, schedule diagrams, and Gantt charts are tools which help one visualize and simplify the great complexities of the scheduling problem.

Sequencing orders at work centers has been a subject of considerable research; given certain managerial objectives, superior priority dispatching decision rules can be specified. The LeGrande study of priority dispatching decision rules indicates that the weighting of various criteria will make an important difference in terms of which decision rule seems superior. When a heavier weighting is placed on criteria which emphasize on-time delivery, some sort of due date oriented decision rule provides superior performance.

Computer-based integrated systems of planning, scheduling, and control, such as the Hughes system, makes possible the effective management of large job shops. Computer-based systems have also been developed for the smaller shop situation, however, since the nature and complexity of small-shop problems seemed to be nearly identical with the larger-shop problems in terms of the information, scheduling, and control systems needed. The required differences in the capabilities of such systems for the small versus the large shop seemed to be largely in terms of the scale of the system needed. Finally, the availability of time-shared computing and the development of the concepts of inter-active scheduling systems similar to the Western Electric system seem ideally suited for the small shop.

KEY CONCEPTS

Priority Decision Rules. Somewhat earlier we alluded to the use of heuristic decision rules. The priority dispatching rules are in fact heuristic rules. While there may be a seemingly defensible rationale behind each one they are simply systematic ways of choosing in which order to process the jobs.

IMPORTANT TERMS

Numbers in parentheses indicate page numbers.

1. COVERT rule (566)
2. Cross-classification chart (557, 559)
3. Dispatch decision rule (562–566)
4. First come-first served rule (565)
5. First in system-first served rule (566)
6. Gantt chart (557)
7. Gantt Layout chart (560)
8. Gantt load chart (560)
9. Gantt project planning chart (560)
10. Minimum due date per order rule (566)
11. Minimum planned start date per operation rule (565)
12. Minimum slack time per opera-tion rule (565)
13. Order control (556)
14. Random rule (566)
15. Schedule diagram (557, 559)
16. Shortest operation time rule (SOT) (565)
17. Static slack/remaining number of operations rule (569)

REVIEW QUESTIONS

Numbers in parentheses indicate page numbers.

1. In order scheduling, of what value are cross classification charts? (557)
2. How does the concept of the schedule diagram help in order scheduling of a complex assembled product? (557)
3. What is a dispatching decision rule? (562)
4. If management's objectives place a high value on low in-process inven-tories, what kind of priority dispatching rule seems best? (566, 568)
5. If management's objectives place a high value on on-time delivery of orders, what kind of priority dispatching decision rule seems best? (566, 568)

6.   What are Gantt charts? Discuss the functions of the Gantt project planning chart, the Gantt load chart, and the Gantt layout or reserved time planning chart. (557–560)

7.   Evaluate the Gantt chart as a representation of the schedule problem in job shops. (560–561)

SELF-TEST TRUE-FALSE QUESTIONS

Numbers in parentheses indicate page numbers.

1.   The job shop scheduling problem is commonly recognized as the most complex scheduling problem in existence. (555)

2.   Scheduling and control systems for job shops are often termed "order control systems." (556)

3.   The Gozinto chart is named for the famous Italian mathematician Leonid Gozinto. (557)

4.   Cross classification charts can reveal the structure of part and component families. (557)

5.   The schedule diagram is developed from the Gantt project planning chart. (557)

6.   The Gantt project planning chart may be used to map out a detailed plan to accomplish target objectives. (560)

7.   The Gantt load chart shows at a glance the status of a given order. (560)

8.   The Gantt layout chart shows the overall projected load on machines together with the accumulated backing of work. (560)

9.   When load records are kept only on critical machines or known bottleneck operations, the assumption is that any schedule that fits within the load limits of the critical or bottleneck machine will probably work out alright for the rest of the machines. (561–562)

10.   A priority dispatch decision rule determines the sequence in which orders will be processed at a given machine center. (562)

11.   In the LeGrande simulation of alternate dispatch decision rules, the DS/RO rule yielded the smallest percent of late orders. (568)

12.   In the LeGrande simulation study of alternate dispatch decision rules, the first-come first-served rule produced the largest percent of early orders. (568)

13.   If management places a premium on getting orders out on time, then some kind of due date oriented rule should give superior results. (566)

14.   A first-come first-served priority rule sequences orders according to their earliest starting date. (565)

15.   In the Carroll study of alternate dispatch decision rules, the COVERT rule was second only to the first-come first-served rule when order lateness was taken as the criterion. (569)

16. In the COVERT decision rule orders are sequenced according to the largest ratio of downstream waiting time cost to operation process time. (566)
17. Six months after the installation of the Hughes computerized planning, scheduling, and control system, there was a ten percent increase in the number of orders completed on time. (571)
18. Six months after the installation of the Hughes computerized planning, scheduling, and control system, there was a sixty percent reduction in expediting effort. (571–572)
19. In the Western Electric interaction scheduling and control system, the computer program can carry out simulations of shop schedules so the supervisor can test various alternate assignments and try to anticipate future problems. (573)
20. The Western Electric interactive scheduling and control system makes it possible to generate an optimum schedule. (572–573)

PROBLEMS

1.   Consider the pipe valve assembly shown in Figure 12 of Chapter 8. Based on the following data, construct a schedule diagram for the production of an order of 500 valves.

(a) All designing and planning for the production of the pipe valve have been completed.
(b) Patterns for the various cast parts can be obtained in four working days.
(c) Two days are required for the production of castings, body, bushing, and handle, i.e., parts 1, 2, and 6. (Castings cannot be produced in the foundry until the patterns are received.)
(d) Bar stock for the stem and cap (parts 3 and 5) can be obtained from a local metal supply house within three days after orders have been placed.
(e) Nuts, screws, packing, etc. can be obtained in three days.
(f) The machine shop estimates fabrication and assembly times for a lot of 500 parts as follows: body, three days; bushing, three days; stem, one day; cap, one day; handle, three days; and assembly, three days.

2.   You are production scheduler in the plumbing supplies company which makes the valves discussed in the previous problem and are scheduling the use of four machines for next week. A colleague in the scheduling department reviews the situation and sees a solution which produces a combined operating plus setup cost of $1395. He challenges you to beat it. The plant works eight hours per day, five days per week, and does not work overtime. Using a Gantt chart, schedule the work orders and calculate the total incremental cost for your schedule. Data are as follows:

Orders Due Next Week	Quantity	Material Available	Completion Time
1. Valve bodies	1400	Mon., 8:00 A.M.	Thurs., 5:00 P.M.
2. Handles	700	Mon., 8:00 A.M.	Fri. 5:00 P.M.
3. Valve guides	300	Mon., 8:00 A.M.	Thurs., 5:00 P.M.
4. Stems	1200	Tues., 8:00 P.M.	Fri., 5:00 P.M.
5. Cap	1500	Mon., 8:00 P.M.	Fri., 11:00 A.M.

Setup and Operating Times

		Machines		
Order	Engine Lathe	Vertical Turret Lathe	Screw Machine	Turret Lathe
1; Setup, hrs	—	2.00	1.00	4.00
Opr. time, hrs/pc	—	0.01	0.02	0.02
2; Setup, hrs	3.00	4.00	—	1.00
Opr. time, hrs/pc	0.05	0.07	—	0.05
3; Setup, hrs	1.00	—	1.00	—
Opr. time, hrs/pc	0.18	—	0.10	—
4; Setup, hrs	2.00	2.00	2.00	—
Opr. time, hrs/pc	0.12	0.04	0.04	—
5; Setup, hrs	—	2.50	2.00	4.00
Opr. time, hrs/pc	—	0.05	0.03	0.02
Number machines available	2	1	2	2
Operating cost/hr	$9.50	$8.00	$4.00	$4.00
Setup costs:				
1	—	$325.00	$90.00	$30.00
2	$25.00	170.00	—	75.00
3	13.00	—	10.00	—
4	50.00	380.00	25.00	—
5	—	400.00	200.00	50.00

3.   Job orders are received at a work center with the characteristics indicated by the following data. In what sequence should the orders be processed at the work center if the priority dispatch decision rule is:

(a) FCFS (first come–first served).
(b) SOT (shortest operation time).
(c) SS (static slack, that is, due date less time of arrival at work center).
(d) FISFS (due date system, first in system–first served).
(e) SS/RO (static slack/remaining number of operations).

Which decision rule do you prefer? Why?

Compute priorities for each rule and list the sequence in which orders would be processed.

Order Number	Due Date	Date and Time Received at Center	Operation Time, Hours	Remaining Operations
1	May 1	Apr. 18, 9 A.M.	6	3
2	Apr. 20	Apr. 21, 10 A.M.	3	1
3	June 1	Apr. 19, 5 P.M.	7	2
4	June 15	Apr. 21, 3 P.M.	9	4
5	May 15	Apr. 20, 5 P.M.	4	5
6	May 20	Apr. 21, 5 P.M.	8	7

REFERENCES

[1] Berry, W. L. "Labor Assignments In Job Shops: An Application of Work Flow Analysis." Unpublished Ph.D. Dissertation, Harvard Business School, 1968.

[2] Buffa, E. S. *Operations Management: Problems and Models* (3rd ed.). John Wiley, New York, 1972.

[3] Buffa, E. S., and W. H. Taubert. *Production-Inventory Systems: Planning and Control* (Rev. ed.). Richard D. Irwin, Homewood, Ill., 1972.

[4] Bulkin, M. H., J. L. Colley, and H. W. Steinhoff, Jr. "Load Forecasting, Priority Sequencing, and Simulation in a Job Shop Control System." Chapter 11 in: *Readings in Production and Operations Management*, E. S. Buffa, editor. John Wiley, New York, 1966. Also published in similar form in: *Management Science*, **13** (2), 29–51, Oct. 1966.

[5] Carroll, D. C. "Heuristic Sequencing of Single and Multiple Component Jobs. Unpublished Ph.D. Dissertation, Sloan School of Management, MIT, 1965.

[6] Elmaghraby, S. E., and R. T. Cole. "On the Control of Production in Small Job-Shops." *Journal of Industrial Engineering*, **14** (4), 186–196, July–Aug. 1963.

[7] Godin, V., and C. H. Jones. "The Interactive Shop Supervisor." *Industrial Engineering*, Nov. 1969, pp. 16–22.

[8] Groff, G. K., and J. F. Muth. *Operations Management: Analysis for Decisions.* Richard D. Irwin, Homewood, Ill., 1972.

[9] Holstein, W. K. "Production Planning and Control Integrated." *Harvard Business Review*, 46 (3), 121–140, May–June 1968.

[10] Holstein, W. K., and W. L. Berry. "The Labor Assignment Decision: An Application of Work Flow Structure." *Management Science*, 16 (6), 324–336, Feb. 1970.

[11] Jones, C. H. "An Economic Evaluation of Job Shop Dispatching Rules." *Management Science* 20 (3), Nov. 1973, pp. 293–307.

[12] LeGrande, E. "The Development of a Factory Simulation System Using Actual Operating Data." *Management Technology*, 3 (1), May 1963. Also reprinted as Chapter 9 in: *Readings in Production and Operations Management*. E. S. Buffa, editor. John Wiley, New York, 1966.

[13] Magee, J. F., and D. M. Boodman. *Production Planning and Inventory Control* (2nd ed.). McGraw-Hill, New York, 1967.

[14] Moodie, C. L., and D. J. Novotny. "Computer Scheduling and Control Systems for Discrete Part Production." *Journal of Industrial Engineering* 19 (7), 336–341, July 1968.

[15] Moore, F. G., and R. Jablonski. *Production Control* (3rd ed.). McGraw-Hill, New York, 1969.

[16] Nanot, Y. R. "An Experimental Investigation and Comparative Evaluation of Priority Disciplines in Job Shop-Like Queuing Networks." Unpublished Ph.D. Dissertation, UCLA, 1963. Also printed as *Management Sciences Research Project, Research Report No. 87*, UCLA, 1963.

[17] Nelson, R. T. "Labor and Machine Limited Production Systems." *Management Science*, 13 (9), 648-671, May 1967.

[18] O'Malley, R. L., S. E. Elmaghraby, and J. W. Jeske, Jr. "An Operational System for Smoothing Batch-Type Production." *Management Science*, 12 (10), 433–449, June 1966.

[19] Reiter, S. "A System for Managing Job Shop Production." *Journal of Business*, 34 (3), 371–393, July 1966.

[20] Rowe, A. J. "Sequential Decision Rules in Production Scheduling." Unpublished Ph.D. Dissertation, UCLA, Aug. 1958.

[21] Steinhoff, H. W., Jr. "Daily System for Sequencing Orders in a Large-Scale Job Shop." Chapter 10 in: *Readings in Production and Operations Management*. E. S. Buffa, editor. John Wiley, New York, 1966.

CONTENTS

CHAPTER 18

PLANNING, SCHEDULING, AND CONTROL FOR LARGE-SCALE PROJECTS

With the relatively recent emphasis on research and development and on very large-scale one-time projects in the aerospace and construction industries, the planning methods described in Chapter 8 are not adequate. While assembly and operation process charts are still valid mechanisms for more detailed studies, they implicitly presume that we are dealing with substantial numbers of items which would justify careful analysis of minute details. But for the large-scale project, an entirely different level of planning becomes necessary. For example, the entire manufacturing process represented by the operation process chart for the capacitor in Figure 4 of Chapter 8 becomes condensed into a broader question: "When must these capacitors be available to dovetail with the assembly of the guidance computer component?" Or the production of the capacitor may be completely submerged in another question: "When must the guidance computer component be available for test and assembly into the guidance system as a whole?" The fabrication of the capacitor component is not considered at all in

581

this question since it probably would be subcontracted, and the detailed plans for its manufacture are for someone else's consideration.

The central focus for the project as a whole then is in planning the important activities in larger blocks and giving close attention to how they must dovetail to achieve the total end result. Which activities depend for their execution on the completion of other activities? Which activities can proceed relatively independently or in parallel with other activities? As we shall see, these kinds of plans are intimately bound up in the basic sequencing required and in the schedule.

The very nature of the one-time large project demands that planning of *what* has to be done and the *schedule* for performance must be done together. They are interdependent, and the planning for large projects, involves a plan for deployment of resources to the total project. To accomplish this, we must determine the activities required, the timing and interdependencies, the requirements of various possible schedules for manpower and other resources, and the relationship of all the foregoing to a project completion date. The project completion date is most often a part of a contract with penalties for nonperformance. Therefore, the complexities and the one-time nature of the project require a coordinated plan which involves activities required, schedule, and deployment of resources. The great complexity of such projects calls for special methods; network planning techniques have been developed to meet this need.

Network planning techniques go under a confusion of acronyms with variations. The two original names, PERT (Performance Evaluation and Review Technique) and CPM (Critical Path Methods), have been differentiated into a variety of brand names applied essentially to the same basic methodology. Some of the alternate names used are: CPS (Critical Path Scheduling), LES (Least-cost Estimating and Scheduling), Micro-PERT, 1-time-PERT, PERT/COST, and PEP. These various names for PERT/CPM techniques are at least a measure of the degree of interest that has developed.

ORIGIN OF NETWORK PLANNING

Network planning methods seem to have been developed by two different groups independently. As an internal project of the DuPont Company, critical path methods were developed to plan and control the maintenance of chemical plants and were subsequently widely used

by DuPont for many engineering functions. Parallel efforts were under-
taken by the U.S. Navy at about the same time to develop methods for
planning and controlling the Polaris missile project. The magnitude of
the task may be envisioned when one realizes that approximately 3000
separate contracting organizations were involved. The result was the
development of the PERT methodology. The immediate success of both
the CPM and PERT methodologies may be gauged by the following
facts. DuPont's application of their technique to a maintenance project
in their Louisville works resulted in reducing down time for maintenance
from 125 to 78 hours; the PERT technique was widely credited with
helping to shorten by two years the time originally estimated for the
completion of the engineering and development program for the
Polaris missile.

PERT and CPM are based on substantially the same concepts, although
there are some differences in details. First, as originally developed, the
PERT methods were based on probabilistic estimates of activity times
which resulted in a probabilistic path through a network of activities
(such as that shown in Figure 1) and a probabilistic project completion
time. The CPM methods, however, assumed constant or deterministic
activity times. Actually, either the probabilistic or deterministic model
is equally applicable to and usable by either technique. As a matter of
fact, most present-day applications of PERT methods have dropped the
use of the probabilistic activity times and use the slightly simpler
deterministic time estimates. The second difference between the two
techniques is in the details of how the arrow diagram is prepared. In
the discussion that follows, we shall point out more clearly both the
probabilistic-deterministic and the arrow diagram differences.

In the following sections we shall first develop PERT planning methods
and then show the differences between PERT and CPM methods.

PERT PLANNING METHODS

The essence of PERT planning is based on the development of a network
representation of the required activities, as indicated by Figure 1b. In
Figure 1b, the arrows represent the required activities coded by the
letters, with estimated performance times shown near the arrows. In
network planning, the length of the arrows ordinarily has no significance
for reasons which we shall comment on later. The numbered circles
define the beginning and end points of activities and are called *events*

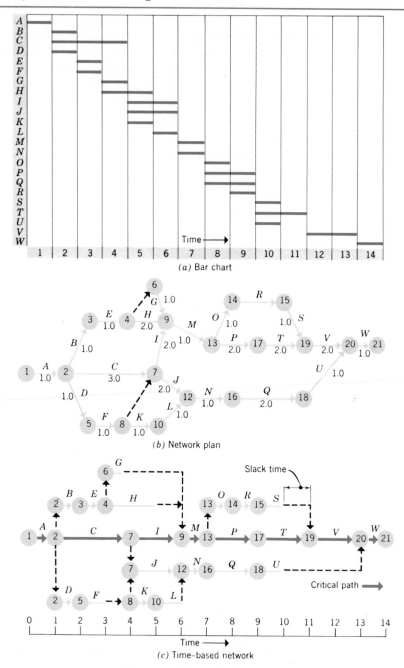

FIGURE 1. Comparison of bar chart with network plan. The heavy colored line indicates the critical path; the horizontal dashed lines indicate slack time. (From Archibald and Villoria [1, p. 4].)

or *nodes*. The direction of arrows indicate flow in the sense that node 2 marks the end of activity *A* and the beginning of activities *B*, *C*, and *D*; node 3 marks the end of activity *B*. The network then also represents the required precedence relationships of all activities. For example, activities *B*, *C*, and *D* cannot start until activity *A* has been completed, but activities *B*, *C*, and *D* can all proceed simultaneously.

Figures 1*a*, *b*, and *c* all represent the same plan. It is undoubtedly easier to visualize the fixed time relations in the bar chart of Figure 1*a*, but actually the bar chart does not contain all of the crucial information about precedence requirements. The bar chart does show the earliest time that each activity can begin and end, but it does not show the latest time that each activity can begin in order that its completion time does not interfere with the beginning of following activities.

Note, however, that the "time-based network" in Figure 1*c* shows this information. Here the length of the solid lines represents the estimated activity times, and the dashed lines represent slack in the schedule. Note, for example, that activity *S* requires 1 time unit and can begin as early as time $t = 9$ but need not begin before $t = 10$ in order to be completed by its latest finish time, $t = 11$. If activity *S* is completed any time between $t = 10$ and $t = 11$, activity *V* which follows can begin on time. Note also that activity *V*, which depends on the completion of both *S* and *T* by $t = 11$ for its start time, has no slack in its schedule.

We see from Figure 1*c* that only activities *G*, *F*, *H*, *S*, and *U* have slack. Note, however, that some other activities can use some or all of the slack shown. For example, if activity *J* is delayed by 1 time unit, it is not serious because *N*, *Q* and *U* can all be set back by 1 time unit, using up 1 unit of the slack shown associated with *U*. If any one of them uses up as much as 3 units of slack, however, all of the following activities become *critical*; that is, they must begin and end by their latest event times or the entire project will be held up and the project completion date cannot be met.

Now let us focus attention on the sequence of activities *A-C-I-M-P-T-V-W* in the time based network of Figure 1*c*. They are connected by the heavy colored line labeled as the *critical path*. There is no slack in the schedules of any of these activities, nor can any of them borrow slack from another activity such as was possible with activities *J*, *N*, and *Q* using some or all of the slack associated with *U*. This set of activities defines a critical path through the network. Each of these critical path activities must begin and end on time if the project completion time of

$t = 14$ is to be met. The critical path is the longest time path through the network.

The network plan summarizes, in compact form, a great deal of important information: the activities required, their precedence relationships, and slack in the schedule. From the basic network plan, we can easily calculate crucial information regarding the earliest and latest start and finish times, available slack in the schedules of activities, and the critical path. Ordinarily, it is the network plan similar to Figure 1*b* that is used rather than the time-based network plan. The reason is simply that the entire system is normally computer based; given the activities and their precedence relationships, standard computer programs will provide all of the schedule information for each activity (the earliest and latest start and finish times and available slack), indicating which activities are on the critical path. Thus, as we noted previously, the length of arrows in the network plan need not have significance since the network itself is only an input to the computation of the other important schedule data. Of course, the time-based network can be constructed from the data given by the computer output if it is felt that there is significant value in visualizing the schedule through graphic means.

Let us note again that the interdependent nature of the set of activities, the importance of a project completion date, and the one-time nature of projects require that the planning for what must be done and the schedule considerations must be intimately bound up together. The equally important related plan for the use of manpower and other resources will be discussed later in this chapter, after we have developed more fully the network planning methods.

With the generalities of PERT methods just discussed in mind, let us utilize a relatively simple example, house construction, to develop the methods used in generating the network representation of a project. The phases of development may be divided into (a) activity analysis, (b) arrow diagramming, and (c) node numbering.

Activity Analysis.   This is comparable functionally to what a production engineer or production planner does when specifying operations, work methods, and tooling for fabricated parts and products. For large projects, however, there is imposed a degree of complexity due to the extremely large number of components and required activities such that it is possible to overlook the need for some activities. Therefore, while professional planning personnel are commonly used, the generation of the activity list is often partially done in meetings and round table discussions which include managerial and operating personnel. The result of the entire process is a list of required activities such, as the one shown in Table I, showing the basic activities required to construct a house.

Arrow Diagramming.   This requires a consideration of the precedence relationships among activities and must be based on a complete, veri-

TABLE I.   Precedence Chart Showing Sequence of Activities and Required Times to Finish a House

Job No.	Description	Immediate Predecessors	Time (days)
a	Start		0
b	Excavate and pour footings	*a*	4
c	Pour concrete foundation	*b*	2
d	Erect wooden frame including rough roof	*c*	4
e	Lay brickwork	*d*	6
f	Install basement drains and plumbing	*c*	1
g	Pour basement floor	*f*	2
h	Install rough plumbing	*f*	3
i	Install rough wiring	*d*	2
j	Install heating and ventilating	*d, g*	4
k	Fasten plaster board and plaster (including drying)	*i, j, h*	10
l	Lay finishing flooring	*k*	3
m	Install kitchen fixtures	*l*	1
n	Install finish plumbing	*l*	2
o	Finish carpentry	*l*	3
p	Finish roofing and flashing	*e*	2
q	Fasten gutters and downspouts	*p*	1
r	Lay storm drains for rain water	*c*	1
s	Sand and varnish flooring	*o, t*	2
t	Paint	*m, n*	3
u	Finish electrical work	*t*	1
v	Finish grading	*q, r*	2
w	Pour walks and complete landscaping	*v*	5
x	Finish	*s, u, w*	0

From Levy, Thompson and Wiest [9].

fied, and approved activity list. The important information required for the arrow diagram is generated by the following three questions:

1.   Which activities must be completed *before* each given activity can be started?
2.   Which activities can be carried out in *parallel*?
3.   Which activities immediately succeed other given activities?

The common practice is simply to work backwards through the activity list, generating the immediate predecessors for each activity listed as shown in Table I for the house construction project. The estimated normal time for each activity is also shown in the table, although it is not necessary at this point. The arrow diagram may then be constructed to represent the logical precedence requirements shown in Table I.

Dummy Activities.   Care must be taken in correctly representing the actual precedence requirements in the arrow diagram. For example, look at the immediate predecessor activities for activity *s*, sand and varnish flooring, and activity *u*, finish electrical work. Activity *s* has as immediate predecessors *o* and *t*, finish carpentry and painting, respectively, while *u* has a predecessor of only activity *t*. The relationship shown in Figure 2*a* does not correctly represent this situation because it specifies that the beginning of *u* is dependent on both *o* and *t* and this is not true. To represent the situation correctly, we must resort to the use of a dummy activity which requires zero performance time. Figure 2*b* now represents the stated requirement. The finish electrical work, *u*, now depends only on the completion of painting, *t*. Through the dummy activity, however, both finish carpentry and painting must be completed before activity *s*, sand and varnish flooring, can be started. The dummy activity provides the logical sequencing relationship; but since it is assigned zero performance time, it does not alter any scheduling relationships which will be developed later.

Another use of the dummy activity is to provide a specific and separate beginning and ending event or node for each activity which cannot be confused. In Table I, for example, note the relationship between activities *l*, *m* and *n*, and *t*. The activity *l*, lay finish flooring, must precede both *m* and *n*, install kitchen fixtures and install finish plumbing, respectively. But *m* and *n* are the predecessors of *t*, paint. Therefore, the functionally correct relationship is represented by Figure 3*a*. But if Figure 3*a* were used, it would not be possible to identify

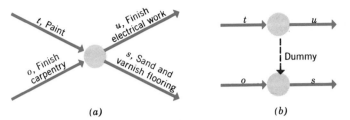

(a)   (b)

FIGURE 2.   (a) Diagram does not properly reflect precedence requirements since *u* seems to be dependent on the completion of both *o* and *t* but actually depends only on *t*. (b) Creating two nodes with dummy activity between provides the proper predecessors for both activities *s* and *u*.

each activity by its predecessor and successor events because both activities *m* and *n* would begin and end with the same node numbers. This is particularly important in larger networks employing computer programs for network diagram generation. The computer is always programmed to identify each activity by a pair of event numbers; the problem is solved through the insertion of a dummy activity as shown in Figure 3*b*. The functional relationship is identical since the dummy activity requires zero time but now both *m* and *n* are identified by different combinations of node numbers.

Figure 4 shows the completed arrow diagram for the house construction project. Activities are identified with their required times in days, all of the nodes are numbered, and the critical path is shown. The activity times were, of course, not used to this point and were not necessary for the construction of the diagram; we have not yet shown how to determine the critical path. However, the activity times will have great

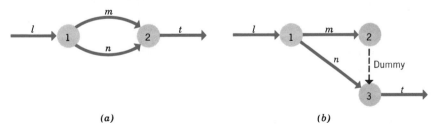

(a)   (b)

FIGURE 3.   (a) Activities *m* and *n* may be carried out in parallel but result in identical beginning and end events. (b) Use of dummy activity makes possible separate ending event numbers, thus making activity identification by pairs of event or node numbers unambiguous.

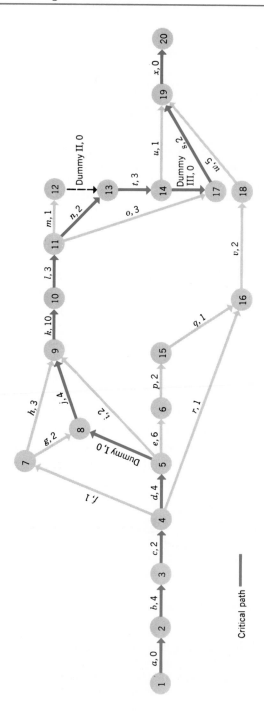

FIGURE 4.   PERT network diagram for the house construction project.

significance in the generation of schedule data, the critical path determination, and the generation of alternatives for the deployment of
resources.

Node Numbering.   The *node numbering* shown in Figure 4 has been
done in a particular way. If we identify each activity by its tail (*i*) and
head (*j*) numbers, the nodes have been numbered so that for each activity
i is always less than *j*, $i < j$. The numbers for every arrow are progressive,
and no backtracking through the network is allowed. This convention
in node numbering is effective in computing programs to develop the
logical network relationships and to prevent the occurrence of cycling
or closed loops.

A closed loop would occur if an activity were represented as going
back in time. This is shown in Figure 5 which is simply the structure of
Figure 3*b* with the activity *n* reversed in direction. Cycling in a network
can result through a simple error or if, when developing the activity
plans, one tries to show the repetition of an activity before beginning
the next activity. A repetition of an activity must be represented with
additional separate activities defined by their own unique node numbers. A closed loop would produce an endless cycle in computer programs, without a built-in routine for detection and identification of the
cycle. Thus one property of a correctly constructed network diagram
is that it is *noncyclical*.

Critical Path Scheduling

With a properly constructed arrow diagram, it is a simple matter to
develop the important schedule data for each activity and for the
project as a whole. The data of interest to us are the earliest and latest
start and finish times and available slack for all activities, as well as the
critical path through the network.

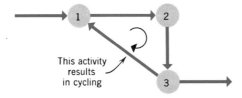

FIGURE 5.   Example of a closed loop or
cycling in a network diagram.

Earliest Start and Finish Times.   If we take zero as the starting time for the project, then for each activity there is an earliest starting time (*ES*) relative to the project starting time, which is the earliest possible time that the activity can begin, assuming that all of the predecessors also are started at their *ES*. Then, for that activity, its earliest finish (*EF*) is simply *ES* + activity time.

Latest Start and Finish Times.   Now let us assume that we have a target time for completing the project which, for the house construction example, is three days after the *EF* time possible or thirty-seven days. This is called the latest finish time (*LF*) of the project and of the final activity *x*. The latest start time (*LS*) is the latest time at which an activity can start if the target or schedule is to be maintained. Thus *LS* for the final activity *x* is *LF* − activity time. Since the finish activity requires zero time units, *LS* = *LF*.

Existing computer programs may be used to compute these schedule data automatically, requiring as inputs the activities, their performance time requirements, and the precedence relationships established by the *ij* numbers of the tails and heads of arrows. The computer output might be similar to Figure 6, which shows the schedule statistics for all activities when three days of slack has been allowed in the overall project completion time. Note then that all critical activities, marked with an asterisk (*), have slack in their schedules of three days. All other activities have greater schedule slack. Dummy activities I and III are on the critical path but their effect is only to establish correct precedence relationships since their activity times are zero. The schedule slack is simply the difference between computed early and late start times (*LS* − *ES*) or between early and late finish times (*LF* − *EF*).

Actually, there are twenty-two different paths from start to finish through the network. The shortest path requires fourteen days by the sequence *a-b-c-r-v-w-x* and the longest or limiting path requires thirty-four days by the critical sequence *a-b-c-d-j-k-l-n-t-s-x*. In a small problem such as this one, we could enumerate all of the alternate paths to find the longest path but there is no advantage in doing so since the critical path is easily determined from the schedule statistics, which are themselves useful.

Manual Computation of Schedule Statistics.   This is appropriate for smaller networks and helps to convey the significance of the schedule

Critical Path	Sequence		Activity Description	Activity Time (days)	Start		Finish		Slack
	i	j			Early	Late	Early	Late	
*	1	2	a, Start	0	0	3	0	3	3
*	2	3	b, Excavate and pour footings	4	0	3	4	7	3
*	3	4	c, Pour concrete foundation	2	4	7	6	9	3
*	4	5	d, Erect frame including rough roof	4	6	9	10	13	3
	5	6	e, Lay brickwork	6	10	21	16	27	11
	4	7	f, Install basement drains and plumbing	1	6	10	7	11	4
	7	8	g, Pour basement floor	2	7	11	9	13	4
	7	9	h, Install rough plumbing	3	7	14	10	17	7
	5	9	i, Install rough wiring	2	10	15	12	17	5
*	5	8	Dummy I	0	10	13	10	13	3
*	8	9	j, Install heating and ventilating	4	10	13	14	17	3
*	9	10	k, Fasten plaster board and plaster, including drying	10	14	17	24	27	3
*	10	11	l, Lay finish flooring	3	24	27	27	30	3
	11	12	m, Install kitchen fixtures	1	27	31	28	32	4
	12	13	Dummy II	0	28	32	28	32	4
*	11	13	n, Install finish plumbing	2	27	30	29	32	3
	11	17	o, Finish carpentry	3	27	32	30	35	5
	6	15	p, Finish roofing and flashing	2	16	27	18	29	11
	15	16	q, Fasten gutters and downspouts	1	18	29	19	30	11
	4	16	r, Lay storm drains for rain water	1	6	29	7	30	23
*	14	17	Dummy III	0	32	35	32	35	3
*	17	19	s, Sand and varnish flooring	2	32	35	34	37	3
*	13	14	t, Paint	3	29	32	32	35	3
	14	19	u, Finish electrical work	1	32	36	33	37	4
	16	18	v, Finish grading	2	19	30	21	32	11
	18	19	w, Pour walks and complete landscaping	5	21	32	26	37	11
*	19	20	x, Finish	0	34	37	34	37	3

FIGURE 6. Sample computer output of schedule statistics and critical path for the house construction project. Slack in project completion and for all critical activities is three days.

statistics. To compute ES and EF manually from the network, we proceed as follows, referring to Figure 7:

1. Place the value of the project start time in both the ES and EF positions near the start activity arrow. See the legend for Figure 7. We shall assume relative values, as we did in the computer output of Figure 6, so the number 0 is placed in the ES and EF positions for the start activity. (Note that it is not necessary in PERT to include the start activity with zero activity duration. It has been included to make this example parallel in its activity list with the comparable CPM example of Figure 9. The start and finish activities are often necessary in CPM.)

2. Consider any new unmarked activity, *all of whose predecessors have been marked* in their ES and EF positions, and mark in the ES position of the new activity the *largest* number marked in the EF position of any of its immediate predecessors. This number is the ES time of the new activity. For activity b in Figure 7, the ES time is 0 since that is the EF time of the preceding activity.

3. Add to this number the activity time, and mark the resulting EF time in its proper position. For activity b, ES + 4 = 4.

4. Continue through the entire network until the "finish" activity has been reached. As we showed in Figure 6, the critical path time is thirty-four days so ES = EF = 34 for the finish activity.

To compute the LS and LF, we work backwards through the network, beginning with the finish activity. We have already stated that the target time for completing the project is three days after the EF time or thirty-seven days. Therefore, LF = 37 for the finish activity without delaying the total project beyond its target date. Similarly, the LS time for the finish activity is LF minus activity time. Since the finish activity requires 0 time units, LS = LF. To compute LS and LF for each activity, we proceed as follows, referring to Figure 8:

1. Mark the value of LS and LF in their respective positions near the finish activity according to the information in Figure 7.

2. Consider any new unmarked activity, all of whose successors have been marked, and mark in the LF position for the new activity the smallest LS time marked for any of its immediate successors. In other words, LF for an activity equals the earliest LS of the immediate successors for that activity.

3. Subtract from this number the activity time which becomes the LS for the activity.

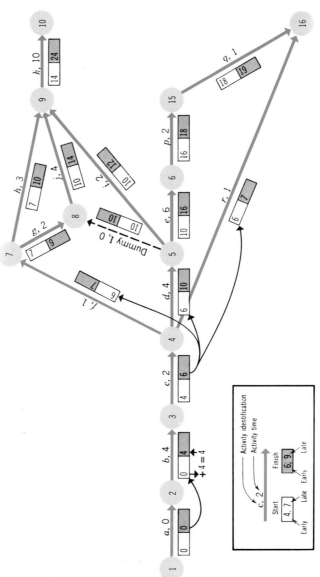

FIGURE 7. Flow of calculations for early start (*ES*) and early finish (*EF*) times.

4. Continue backwards through the chart until all *LS* and *LF* times have been entered in their proper positions on the network diagram. Figure 8 shows the flow of calculations, beginning with the finish activity backward through several activities.

As discussed previously, the schedule slack for an activity represents the maximum amount of time that it can be delayed beyond its *ES* without delaying the project completion time. Since critical activities are those in the sequence of the longest time path, it follows that the activities will have the minimum possible slack. If the project target date coincides with the *LF* for the finish activity, all critical activities will have 0 slack. If, however, the project date is later than the *EF* of the finish activity, as it is in the house project example (three days), all critical activities will have slack equal to this time-phasing difference. The manual computation of slack is simply *LS* − *ES* or, alternately, *LF* − *EF*.

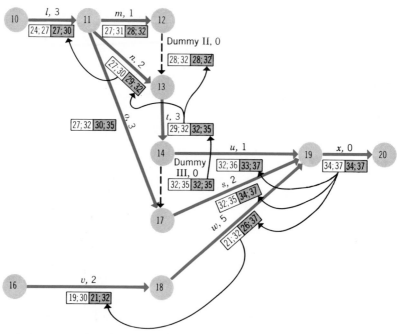

FIGURE 8.   Flow of calculations for late start (*LS*) and late finish (*LF*) times.

PERT/CPM—Arrow Diagram Differences

To this point we have been using the PERT arrow diagramming procedure to illustrate network methods. The CPM procedure results in a slightly simpler network system by representing activities as occurring at the nodes with the arrows showing the sequences of activities required for the project. The advantage in the CPM methodology is that it is not necessary to invoke the use of dummy activities in order to represent the proper sequencing. Figure 9 shows the CPM network for the house construction project which may be compared with the comparable PERT network shown in Figure 4. The analysis developing the early and late start and finish times and slack times is identical with the procedure previously outlined. The net results of both systems are the schedule statistics which are computed. Since these are the data of interest, and since the entire procedure is normally computerized for both methodologies, the choice between the two may fall to other criteria such as the availability and adaptability of existing computer routines or may be simply a matter of taste.

PROBABILISTIC NETWORK METHODS

The network methods which we have discussed so far may be termed deterministic since estimated activity times are assumed to be the expected values. But no recognition is given to the fact that the mean or expected activity time is the mean of a distribution of possible values which could occur. Deterministic methods assume that the expected time is actually the time taken.

Probabilistic network methods assume the reverse, more realistic, situation where activity times are represented by a probability distribution. With such a basic model of the network of activities, it is possible to develop additional data important to managerial decisions. Such data help in assessing planning decisions which might revolve around questions such as: What is the probability that the completion of activity A will be later than January 10? What is the probability that the activity will become critical and affect the project completion date? What is the probability of meeting a given target completion date for the project? What is the risk of incurring cost penalties for not meeting the contract date? The nature of the planning decisions based on such questions might involve the allocation or reallocation of manpower or other resources to the various activities in order to derive a more satisfactory plan. Thus, a "crash" schedule with extra resources might be justified to insure the on-time completion of certain activities. The extra resources needed are drawn from noncritical activities or activities where the probability of criticality is small.

The discussion which follows is equally applicable to either the PERT or CPM basic format, although the probabilistic methods were in fact originally developed as part of PERT. The probability distribution of activity times is based on three time estimates made for each activity.

Optimistic Time.   Optimistic time, a, is the shortest possible time to complete the activity if all goes well. It is based on the assumption that there is no more than one chance in a hundred of completing the activity in less than the optimistic time.

Pessimistic Time.   Pessimistic time, b, is the longest time for an activity under adverse conditions but barring acts of nature. It is based on the assumption that there would be no more than one chance in a hundred of completing the activity in a time greater than b.

Most Likely Time.   Most likely time, m, is the modal value of the activity time distribution.

The three time estimates are shown in relation to an activity completion time distribution in Figure 10. The computational algorithm reduces these three time estimates to a single average or expected value, t_e, which is actually used in the computing procedure.* The expected value is also the one used in computing schedule statistics for the deterministic model. The example distribution in Figure 10 represents only one possibility. Actually, the time distributions could be symmetrical, or skewed to either the right or the left.

With a probabilistic model, we can see that there is a probability that seemingly noncritical activities could become critical. This could happen either by the occurrence of a long performance time for the activity in question or of short performance times for activities already

---

*The usual model assumes that t_e is the mean of a beta distribution. The estimates of the mean and variance of the distribution may be computed as follows:

$$\bar{x} = \tfrac{1}{6}[A + 4M + B]$$

$$s^2 = [\tfrac{1}{6}(B - A)]^2$$

where A, B, and M are estimates of the values of a, b, and m, respectively, and $\bar{x}$ and s^2 are estimates of the mean and variance, t_e and σ_t^2.

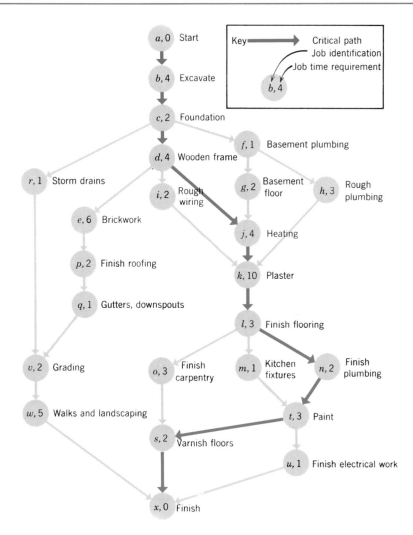

FIGURE 9.   CPM project graph of activities for a house building project. (From Levy, Thompson, and Wiest [9].)

on the critical path. This is a signal that the schedule plans developed are likely to change. As actual data on the progress of operations come in, it may be necessary to make changes in the allocation of resources in order to cope with the latest set of critical activities. Thus, an effective set of original plans requires a rapid feedback of information and the reissue of corrected schedules during the performance and control phases of a project.

DEPLOYMENT OF RESOURCES

Given the activity network, the critical path, and the computed schedule statistics, we have a plan for the project. But, is it a good plan? We can abstract from our data some additional data on the demand for resources of the early start schedule. By using the schedule flexibility available through slack in certain activities and/or slack in the project completion date, we can generate alternate schedules, comparing the use of important resources with the objective of *load leveling*.

Another way to look at the initial or raw plan is in terms of activity costs. Note that the initial activity duration estimates are based on an assumed level of resource allocation. Is it possible to alter activity times by pouring in more or less resources? Activity times for some activities can be directly affected in this way. For example, adding carpenters will usually shorten the time to frame a house, and this was a critical activity in our house construction example. Would it be worthwhile to pour in more manpower on the critical framing and allocate less to the noncritical brickwork which has eleven days of slack? Would the alternate plan be more or less expensive? Would shortening the critical path be advantageous? *Least costing* considerations are worth examining.

Finally, in some situations we may be faced with a demand for some critical resource which is limited in supply. The raw plan may in fact not be feasible if it schedules the use of the only available power shovel in two places at the same time. The raw plan must be examined with the objective of the feasible scheduling of *limited resources*, again using available slack time where possible or even lengthening the project in order to generate a feasible plan.

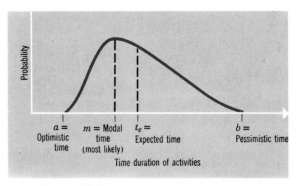

FIGURE 10.   Time values in relation to a distribution of activity time.

Load Leveling

Why level loading? What are the costs of not attempting to level loads in an already feasible schedule? Some factors which enter the problem occur in the following example of a major oil refinery repair and overhaul project [1, pp. 269–280]. After a raw plan was developed, a series of computer runs was made to examine manpower requirements for the refinery project. In the first run it was found that the schedule required 50 boilermakers for the first 4 hours, 20 for the next 6 hours, and 35 for the immediately following period. Similar fluctuations in requirements were found for other crafts. In terms of costs associated with this fluctuation, there is first the possible cost of idle labor.

For example, in the first 10 hours of the refinery project the peak requirement of 50 boilermakers will probably mean productive work of 50×4 hours $+ 20 \times 6$ hours $= 320$ man-hours. But the likelihood is that it will be difficult to assign the extra 30 men for the balance of the 8-hour day, so in the first 10 hours of the project the payroll may reflect $50 \times 8 + 20 \times 2 = 440$ man-hours, 120 of which are idle labor. Figure 11 shows the deployment of manpower *after* leveling; we see that some of these same kinds of problems remain. Other costs that may be implicit in manpower fluctuation are hiring and separation costs in projects that extend over long periods. Load leveling has the objective of reducing idle labor costs, hiring and separation costs, or the cost of any resource, such as an equipment rental, which may be affected by fluctuations in the demand for its use.

For very large and complex projects, a computer-based leveling model may be required. Simulation methodology commonly is used to generate alternate solutions. The starting solution might be the early start schedule, and a first attempt at leveling could then set a maximum of the resource in question just below the highest peak level recorded in the raw plan. The simulation program would then proceed as indicated by the arrow diagram, beginning all activities leaving node 1, keeping track of the amount of resources used and available. As the calendar is advanced and as activities are completed, resources are returned to the "available" pool; as new activities are started, resources are drawn from the pool. Simulation then proceeds until an activity requires resources from a temporarily exhausted pool. Depending on the decision criteria used by the simulator, the activity may be delayed, even past its latest starting time, until resources are available. Other decisic criteria "bump" noncritical jobs and reassign resources to the dela·

job when the latest starting time has been reached. By a progressive lowering of the resource limits in such a simulation program, the leveling effect takes place until a satisfactory deployment of resources is achieved. A survey of rigorous methods of resource allocation in project network models has been developed by Davis [3]; specific resource leveling models have been developed by Dewitte [4] and by Levy, Thompson, and Wiest [8].

Least Costing

Least costing concepts are based on cost versus activity time curves such as in Figure 12. Different activities respond differently to changes in the application of resources, and some of the activities may not be responsive to changes in resources. Figure 12a may be typical of an activity like house framing, as we discussed previously, where crash, normal, and slow schedules are progressively less costly. A curve similar to Figure 12b, where the slow schedule is more costly than the normal schedule, could be typical where the meager resources associated with a slow schedule might enforce the use of inefficient methods. The cost trade-offs are possible partially because of the differential cost-time characteristics of different activities. Formal methodologies for least costing have been developed by Fulkerson [5] and Kelly [6] in the form of linear programming models which idealize the cost-time functions by assuming a straight-line connecting the crash and normal points. The total project cost is taken as the sum of the linear activity cost functions; this total project cost function is minimized by the linear programming algorithm.

Limited Resources

A limited resource model called SPAR (Scheduling Program for Allocation of Resources) has been developed by Wiest [12]. SPAR is a heuristic scheduling model for limited resources designed to handle a project with 1200 single resource activities, 500 nodes, and twelve shops over a span of 300 days. The model focuses on available resources which it allocates, period by period, to activities listed in order of their early start times. The most critical jobs have the highest probability of being scheduled first, and as many jobs are initially scheduled as available resources permit. If an available activity fails to be scheduled in one period, an attempt is made to schedule it in the next period. Finally, all

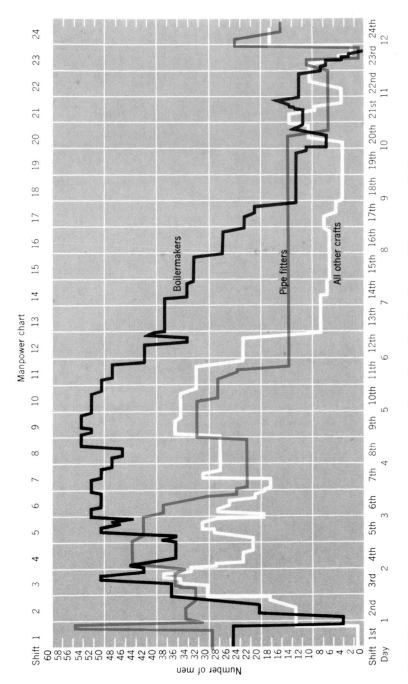

FIGURE 11.   Manpower usage chart after leveling. (From Archibald and Villoria [1, p. 274].)

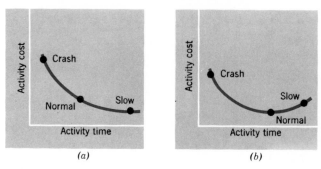

FIGURE 12.   Typical activity time-cost curves.

jobs that have been postponed become critical and move to the top of the priority list of available activities.

Wiest applied the SPAR program to a space vehicle project which required large block engineering activities with up to five different types of engineers and involving 300 activities. Figure 13 shows an overall manpower loading chart for the program. The unlimited resources line resulted from a conventional PERT schedule with all activities at their early start times. The limited resources line results from the SPAR schedule where peak manpower requirements were considerably reduced. The total length of the project was shortened by five months and the number of gross hirings of personnel was reduced by 30 per cent as a result of the SPAR schedule.

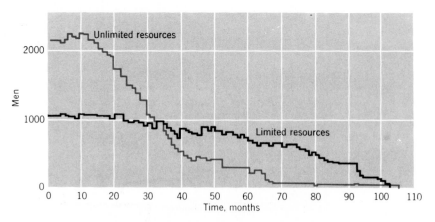

FIGURE 13.   Manpower loading schedule for the space vehicle project. (From Wiest [12].)

DIFFICULTIES IN USING NETWORK METHODS

There have been problems in the managerial use of network methods. First, the difficulty in making the three time estimates has often produced mere guesses or the arbitrary addition and subtraction of time from the most likely time to determine the pessimistic and optimistic time estimates. The result of such practices has been that the Department of Defense has abandoned probabilistic methods for most contracts.

Other difficulties have been apparent when time lags have been too great in the reporting of activity status and the recomputing of up-to-date schedules. The result has been, of course, that managers tend to ignore the schedules that exist because they have lost faith in them. The ultimate solutions to these kinds of difficulties are in computer-based reporting and control systems.

SUMMARY

Network planning techniques are unique in the form they have taken, especially the concepts of critical path. The associated concepts of load leveling, least costing, and limited resource scheduling have provided a rational base for project management resting on carefully laid, broad plans. The plans can be said to be derived from analyses of some prominent alternatives, are computer based and thus applicable to very large systems, and are flexible so that they can be changed as actual experience with them develops.

It is interesting that the independent development of PERT and CPM in two different environments produced essentially equivalent methodologies but with the stamps of their spawning grounds. CPM developed in engineering maintenance operations where a great deal of experience existed and activity times were relatively well known. Thus, CPM developed as a deterministic model. PERT, however, developed in an environment of research and development where great uncertainty of activity times exists. The result was the probabilistic model.

KEY CONCEPTS

Flow Through a Network.   Given a set of activities to be performed one can focus attention on the individual activities and on when each activity must begin in order to fit in with an overall schedule. Conceptualizing the system of activities as a network, however, represented an important step forward in the analysis of large-scale productive systems. The concept of flow through a network focuses attention on the interaction between the activity times, their earliest and latest start times, required production sequences, as well as other important factors in scheduling. The same general concept of network flow is also useful in the production line balancing problem.

Critical Path.   When a set of activities is visualized as a network, the concept of a critical path through the network emerges. This concept is central to the managerial problems of allocating resources in the most effective way.

Slack.   Another concept which emerges from viewing a set of activities as a network is that of slack. Slack defines the flexibility available for the scheduling of activities and it is through the effective use of slack that management can derive alternatives for the deployment of resources in the most effective way.

Critical Activity.   Knowledge of which operations are critical, that is, they lie on the crucial path, indicates where management must focus its attention in order to complete the project by the scheduled time. The concept is of key importance for it allows management to allocate its own time and resources where that effort can be most effective.

Load Leveling.   The concept of load leveling is an important one in developing an improved deployment of resources. By evening out the use of resources the costs associated with fluctuating levels of activity are minimized.

Least Costing.   Like load leveling, least costing concepts can be used to develop schedules which yield improved deployment of resources. This is accomplished by taking advantage of the differences between the cost versus activity time curves of the various activities.

IMPORTANT TERMS
Numbers in parentheses indicate page numbers.

21. Predecessor activity (588, 589)   24. Schedule statistics (593)
22. Precedence relationship (587)   25. Time-based network (584, 585)
23. Probabilistic network (597)

REVIEW QUESTIONS

Numbers in parentheses indicate page numbers.

1. What are the unique factors in the nature of large-scale one-time projects that require special planning methods? Why are the general methods of Chapter 8 inadequate? (581–582)
2. Why is it necessary that the planning of what must be done and schedule planning should be performed together for large projects? (582)
3. Discuss the origin of network planning methods. (582–583)
4. In the context of network planning methods, define the following terms: activity, event, node, and critical path. (583–586)
5. For PERT planning methods, discuss and interrelate the three phases: (a) activity analysis, (b) arrow diagramming, and (c) node numbering. (586)
6. What are the functions of dummy activities in PERT network diagrams? (588)
7. What is the convention for numbering nodes in a PERT network? Why is this convention used? (591)
8. Why must activity networks be nocyclical? (591)
9. Define the following terms: early start (*ES*), early finish (*EF*), latest start (*LS*, latest finish (*LF*), and slack. (592)
10. Outline the procedure for manual computation of schedule statistics. (592–594)
11. What are the differences in the construction of the arrow diagram between the PERT and CPM methodologies? How can the probabilistic network model provide additional data helpful for managerial decisions? (597)
12. Define the terms optimistic time, pessimistic time, most likely time, and expected time in probabilistic PERT networks. (598)
13. What is meant by load leveling? How may it be accomplished? (601–602)
14. Discuss the concepts of least costing in relation to crash, normal, and slow schedules. (602)
15. Account for the differences between PERT and CPM as they were originally developed. (583, 605)

SELF-TEST TRUE-FALSE QUESTIONS

Numbers in parentheses indicate page numbers.

1. Network planning methods developed independently at the Eastman-Kodak Company and General Motors Corporation (582–583)

2. As originally developed, PERT methods were based on probabilistic estimates of activity times which resulted in a probabilistic path through a network of activities, and a probabilistic project completion time. (583)
3. In PERT planning methods the length of the arrows has no significance. (583)
4. Activity analysis is comparable functionally to what a production engineer or production planner does in specifying operations, work methods, and tooling for fabricated parts and products. (586)
5. An advantage of the PERT methodology is that dummy activities are not required. (597)
6. The function of a dummy activity is to establish the correct sequencing relationships. (588)
7. The convention used for node numbering is to identify the arrow head by (i) and the tail by (j) so that (i) is always less than (j). (591)
8. The accepted convention in node numbering is effective in computing programs to develop the logical network relationships and to prevent the occurrence of cycling or closed loops. (591)
9. The earliest starting time (ES) is the earliest possible time that an activity can begin, assuming that all of the predecessors are also started at their ES. (592)
10. The earliest finish time (EF) is ES + activity time. (592)
11. The latest start time (LS) for an activity is LF − activity time. (592)
12. Schedule slack is simply the difference between computed early start and late finish times. (592)
13. In the CPM procedure activities are represented by arrows. (597)
14. The optimistic time estimate is based on the assumption that there is no more chance in 100 of completing the activity in less than the optimistic time. (598)
15. The expected value of activity time distributions is the most likely time. (598)
16. Load leveling is accomplished through the least costing process. (601–602)
17. Load leveling may also be accomplished by placing limits on the use of available resources. (602)

PROBLEMS

1. Listed in Table II is a set of activities, sequence requirements, and estimated activity times required for the renewal of a pipeline. Prepare both a PERT and CPM project diagram.

2. For the data of problem 1 and the arrow diagram generated there:
(a) Compute ES, EF, LS, and LF for each of the activities.
(b) For the data generated in (a), compute slack for the system. Which activities

| | | Code of | Activity Time | Crew Require- |
Activity	Letter Code	Immediate Predecessor	Require- ment, (days)	ments per Day
Assemble crew for job	A	—	10	—
Use old line to build inventory	B	—	28	—
Measure and sketch old line	C	A	2	—
Develop materials list	D	C	1	—
Erect scaffold	E	D	2	10
Procure pipe	F	D	30	—
Procure valves	G	D	45	—
Deactivate old line	H	B,D	1	6
Remove old line	I	E,H	6	3
Prefabricate new pipe	J	F	5	20
Place valves	K	E,G,H	1	6
Place new pipe	L	I,J	6	25
Weld pipe	M	L	2	1
Connect valves	N	K,M	1	6
Insulate	O	K,M	4	5
Pressure test	P	N	1	3
Remove scaffold	Q	N,O	1	6
Clean up and turn over to operating crew	R	P,Q	1	6

TABLE II. Activities, Sequence Requirements, and Times for the Renewal of a Pipeline.

can be delayed beyond their respective *ES* without delaying the project completion time of 65 days? Which activities can be delayed, and by how many days, without delaying the *ES* of any other activity?

(c) Determine the critical path for the pipeline renewal project.

3.   In Table III there is additional information in the form of optimistic, most likely, and pessimistic time estimates for the pipeline renewal project. Compute variances for the activities. Which activities have the greatest uncertainty in their completion schedules?

4.   Suppose that, due to penalties in the contract, each day the pipeline renewal project can be shortened is worth \$100. Which of the following possibilities would you follow and why?

(a) Shorten t_e of activity B by 4 days at a cost of \$100.

(b) Shorten b of activity G by 5 days at a cost of \$50.

TABLE III.   Time Estimates for the Pipeline Renewal Project.

Activity Code	Optimistic Time Estimate of, a	Most Likely Time Estimate of, m	Pessimistic Time Estimate of, b	Expected Time Estimate of, t_e
A	8	10	12	10
B	26	26.5	36	28
C	1	2	3	2
D	0.5	1	1.5	1
E	1.5	1.63	4	2
F	28	28	40	30
G	40	42.5	60	45
H	1	1	1	1
I	4	6	8	6
J	4	4.5	8	5
K	0.5	0.9	2	1
L	5	5.25	10	6
M	1	2	3	2
N	0.5	1	1.5	1
O	3	3.75	6	4
P	1	1	1	1
Q	1	1	1	1
R	1	1	1	1

(c) Shorten t_e of activity O by 2 days at a cost of $150.

(d) Shorten t_e of activity O by 2 days by drawing resources from activity N, thereby lengthening its t_e by 2 days.

5.   Table II indicated the crew requirements *per day* for each activity in the pipeline renewal project.

(a) Prepare a crew size versus time chart representing the deployment of manpower for the *ES* schedule generated in problem 2. Assume that men on all crews are completely interchangeable, that is, any man can do any task.

(b) Now assume that the man-days allocated for each activity can be deployed in any way you wish. For example, activity L has a crew requirement of 25 men per day for 6 days from Table II or 150 man-days. These 150 man-days may be allocated over any chosen activity time; for example, 10 men per day for 15 days or vice versa. To try to achieve load leveling of the total crew, re-allocate the man-days required for each activity so that no activity has a labor rate greater than a crew size of 10 men per day. This will require extending the activity times of some activities. (1) Compute the schedule statistics and new critical path. (2) Prepare a new crew size versus time chart representing the deployment of manpower, but with the restriction that maximum total

TABLE IV.   Activity List for a New Product Introduction

Code	Activity Description	Immediate Predecessors	Estimated Time, Weeks
A	Organize the sales office—hire sales manager.	—	6
B	Sales manager hires salesman.	A	4
C	Train salesman to sell product to distributors.	B	7
D	Sales manager selects advertising agency.	A	2
E	Plan advertising campaign—sales manager and advertising agency jointly plan the advertising campaign to introduce the product to the public.	D	4
F	Conduct advertising campaign—advertising agency conducts a "watch for" campaign for potential customers. Campaign ends at the time distributors receive their initial stocks.	E	10
G	Design package.	—	2
H	Set up packaging facilities—prepare to package products when received from the manufacturer.	G	10
I	Package initial stocks.	H, J	6
J	Order stock from manufacturer—order stock required from manufacturer on the basis of volume indicated by market research. Activity time includes lead time for delivery.	—	13
K	Sales manager selects distributors.	A	9
L	Sell to distributors.	C, K	6
M	Ship stock to distributors according to orders.	I, L	6

crew size per day is 10, using available slack as necessary. Also, use available slack to make this labor schedule as compact as possible; that is, the fewest number of fluctuations in overall crew size and condensed in time span.

6.   A company is planning the introduction of a new product to its line. The company will not manufacture the item but will buy it, package it, and sell it to distributors selected on a geographic basis. Market research has been done, and based on these studies the expected sales volume and required sales force have been determined.

The steps necessary to introduce the new product are indicated in Table IV together with the time estimates and the required sequence of activities.

(a) What is the earliest number of weeks in which the product can be introduced?

(b) If trained salesmen are hired and the 7-week training period eliminated, how much earlier can the product be introduced?

(c) How long can the selection of the advertising agency be delayed?

REFERENCES

[1] Archibald, R. D., and R. L. Villoria. *Network-Based Management Systems.* John Wiley, New York, 1967.

[2] Buffa, E. S., and W. H. Taubert. *Production-Inventory Systems: Planning and Control* (Rev. ed.). Richard D. Irwin, Homewood, Ill., 1972, Chapters 13 and 14.

[3] Davis, E. W. "Resource Allocation in Project Network Models—A Survey." *Journal of Industrial Engineering*, 17 (4), 177–188, Apr. 1966.

[4] Dewitte, L. "Manpower Leveling in PERT Networks." *Data Processing Science/Engineering*, Mar.–Apr. 1964.

[5] Fulkerson, D. R. "A Network Flow Computation for Project Cost Curves." *Management Science*, 7, 1961.

[6] Kelly, J. E. "Critical Path Planning and Scheduling: Mathematical Basis." *Operations Research*, 9 (3), 1961.

[7] Levin, R. I., and C. A. Kirkpatrick. *Planning and Control with PERT/CPM.* McGraw-Hill, New York, 1966.

[8] Levy, F. K., G. L. Thompson, and J. D. Wiest. "Multi-Shop Work Load Smoothing Program." *Naval Research Logistics Quarterly*, Mar. 1963.

[9] Levy, F. K., G. L. Thompson, and J. D. Wiest. "The ABCs of the Critical Path Method." *Harvard Business Review*, Sept.–Oct. 1963, pp. 98–108.

[10] Moder, J. J., and C. R. Phillips. *Project Management with CPM and PERT.* (2nd ed.) Reinhold, New York, 1970.

[11] Shaffer, L. R., J. B. Ritter, and W. L. Meyer. *The Critical Path Method.* McGraw-Hill, New York, 1965.

[12] Wiest, J. D. "A Heuristic Model for Scheduling Large Projects with Limited Resources." *Management Science,* **13**, (6), 359–377, Feb. 1967.

[13] Wiest, J. D., and F. K. Levy. *A Management Guide to PERT/CPM.* Prentice-Hall, Inc., Englewood Cliffs, N.J., 1969.

CONTENTS

CHAPTER 19
CONTROL
OF QUALITY

What do we mean by quality? To a manufacturer it does not carry the connotation implied by "mink" or "Rolls Royce," but rather a specified quality. The establishment, maintenance, and control of quality then deal with the determination of quality standards and the measurement and control necessary to see that the established standards are maintained and practiced. These standards may be specified dimensions, chemical composition of raw materials, hardness, strength, surface finish, or more subjective factors such as dimples in a painted surface, scratches, or other possible defects which may detract from physical appearance. The established standards may very well be standards for low-quality merchandise.

FOUR PHASES OF QUALITY CONTROL

Quality control is involved at: (a) policy levels in determining desired market level of quality, (b) the engineering design stage during which quality levels are specified to achieve the market target levels, (c) the producing stage when control over incoming raw materials and productive operations is necessary to implement the policies and design specifications, and (d) the use stage in the field where installation can affect final quality and where the guarantee of quality and performance must be made effective. These four general phases are shown schematically in Figure 1 together with some of the interrelationships that exist.

Product Policy and Quality.   The basic policies regarding quality must necessarily emanate from top levels of the organization because they are so interrelated with the most basic decisions regarding the purpose, direction, and focus of the enterprise. These policy determinations are necessarily based on an assessment of markets and their potential at various quality levels. These policies involve questions of how quality in the product is really measured by consumers. Is it measured by appearance and esthetic design, ruggedness, dependability, long life, or what? How sensitive is the production cost and needed plant investment to these quality measures of a particular product? Therefore, in relation to the market potentials, what "return on investment" can be projected for various quality levels which could be produced? What is the competitive situation at various quality levels within the particular industry? These and other considerations may determine which sector of the market an organization shoots for. At any rate, the organization's objectives become the base points for the quality levels to be designed into the product and for the capability to be designed into the production system.

Quality and Product Design.   The detailed specifications of quality to be produced are set by the product designer when he determines materials to be used and their specifications, dimensions, tolerances, product capability, and service requirements. Here, of course, there is an interaction between what can be specified, what can be produced, and the cost of production. Thus there is a complex process of design for quality, production design of the product, and the design of the production system itself, each one affecting the other to some degree as indicated in Figure 1. (Recall our discussion of "production design" in Chapter 7.) These standards become the basis for the control of quality through manufacturing and distribution phases.

Quality Control in Manufacture.   Quality control in manufacture is, in fact, what is brought to mind to most people by the term *quality*

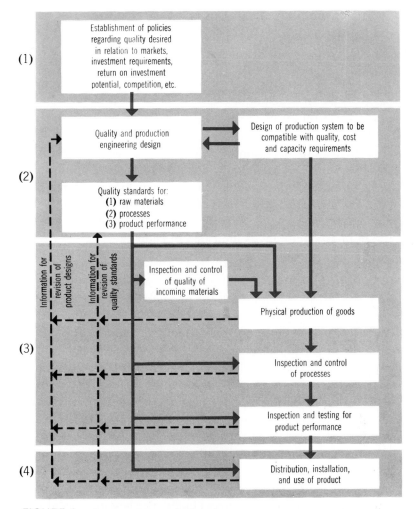

FIGURE 1.   Schematic representation of the role of quality control throughout the planning, production, and distribution of a product.

control. In actuality, we have three important subphases which describe quality control in manufacture. These three subphases are centered around (a) the inspection and control of the quality of incoming *raw materials,* (b) the product inspection and control of *processes,* and (c) the inspection and testing for product *performance.* It is in these subphases that the well-known techniques for inspection and statistical quality control find their greatest application. We shall discuss these techniques in some detail later in the chapter.

At this point, however, let us recognize that the objective of quality control in manufacture is to implement the quality standards by measuring characteristics of the raw materials, parts, and products and comparing these measurements with established standards so that we may (a) accept or reject and (b) correct performance through information feedback. Thus the techniques of acceptance inspection and sampling provide control by filtering out items that do not, or probably do not, meet standards. Process control techniques, on the other hand, are directed toward determining when the process which generates the measurements is probably out of control. These techniques provide for corrective action to be taken before scrap losses become prohibitive. Finally, information feedback from the various inspection and production operations provides data for possible revision of quality standards and of product designs as indicated in Figure 1.

Quality Control in Distribution, Installation, and Use.   A total concept of the control of quality in an organization cannot stop with the setting of broad policies, with the engineering of quality standards into the product, or with the controls established for manufacture. Quality control must extend into distribution, installation, and use phases. To the ultimate user, quality is not what was directed by policy, designed by engineers, or produced, but total performance of the product in his hands. A perfectly conceived and produced item may be damaged in distribution or be improperly installed. Therefore, for many types of products, control procedures need to extend through these phases and be regarded almost as a part of the production process.

In reality, if we take the broad operations management point of view adopted by this book, we must certainly view these "after-production" processes of distribution and installation as a part of the total process requiring controls over quality. Finally, the best-conceived designs and optimally controlled production processes will pass some defective items. Thus policies and practices with regard to guarantees of quality may, in the final analysis, determine whether or not the ultimate user is satisfied with the quality of the product.

Organizing for Quality.   Our discussion so far has pointed up the fact that the commonly stated slogan, "quality is everyone's job," is just about true. All levels of an organization are somehow concerned with product quality, whether it be in terms of policy setting, conception of product designs, design of the producing system, production itself, or distribution. Figure 1, in its schematic relationships of the major seg-ments of quality control, attempts to focus our attention on the pervasive nature of the quality function. In attempting to organize for quality, it is apparent that some total coordination of a quality program is necessary. Someone in an organization needs to have a total responsibility for quality in order to coordinate quality objectives throughout the various phases indicated by Figure 1 and our discussion so far. This means that the responsible individual needs to be attached fairly high in the organiz-ation structure. His exact location in the organization and his power and influence necessarily vary from one organization to the next, since the importance of the quality function is not the same for all products and for all organizations.

However, the integrated view of the quality function is probably important for all organizations. In an organization where quality may be a dominating factor, we may find a quality control manager reporting to a vice-president of manufacturing. In organizations where the quality function may be of lesser importance because of the nature of the prod-ucts, markets, and the industry, the coordination for quality may be vested in some line organization officer. In both instances, however, the total conception of the quality functions needs to be recognized for effective control within the enterprise objectives and policies.

CONTROL OF QUALITY IN PRODUCTION

We must draw a distinction between inspection and quality control. Inspection involves setting up a way of measuring quality characteristics and comparing them to quality standards. Obviously, the good parts are separated from the bad parts in this way, but no corrective action is implied. Control raises questions of when and how often to inspect and how many units to inspect. When defective units occur, control deter-mines the cause and corrects it so that more defective units are not produced. Probability concepts play a dominant role in the control phases by setting up sampling plans which can control outgoing quality and through control chart procedures which continually track critical machines or processes.

The Element of Judgment

Variation is not an exception but is characteristic of measurements in the production field. What we must recognize now is that part of the variation that we actually observe is the error of measurement and that judgment plays a strong role in the measuring process. Many experiments have been run that demonstrate this in various ways. For example, to check on the consistency of inspectors, one company mixed fifty known defective parts with a group of known good parts and sent them through the normal inspection procedure. The unsuspecting inspectors caught only thirty-nine defective parts. With the remaining eleven defectives still included, the lot was sent through again but only nine were found. A third pass found one more. Successive passes never turned up the last one—it was found by a customer.

How could this happen? The inspectors had high-quality precision measuring instruments and were trained to use them. The answer is that the use of these precision instruments involves some judgment, particularly for borderline cases. Skilled mechanics call the judgment element in using precision micrometers and gages the "feel." For example, in using a precision micrometer, feel determines how tightly the operator turns down the spindle on the piece. Widely different readings can result, depending on how this is done.

To document the importance of this judgment element, Lawshe and Tiffin conducted controlled performance tests with 245 experienced inspectors. Each man was tested on the instruments that he normally used, with standard work pieces of known dimensions. Each instrument used had accepted limits of measurement. For example, with a 1-inch vernier micrometer, it is possible to measure within plus or minus 1/10,000 of an inch. Figure 2 shows the percent of the inspectors who failed to meet the accepted standards for the instrument used. The results are rather startling. Averaging over the entire experiment, a large majority of the inspectors could not use the instruments to the standard levels of precision. For individual instruments, the results are much worse. Significantly, reading accuracy did not correlate with age, amount of experience with the company, or the length of time on the present job. Apparently the amount of judgment demanded in these types of measurement is somewhat greater than is generally suspected.

Kinds of Control

We generally can establish control over quality in two ways. First, we can control the actual processes that make the parts, so adjustments and corrections can be made immediately when needed in order that bad

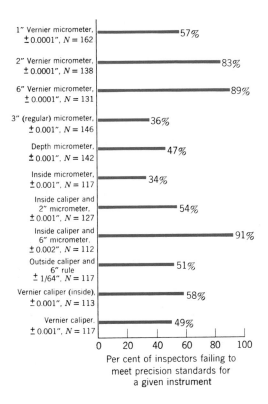

1" Vernier micrometer, ±0.0001", N = 162 — 57%

2" Vernier micrometer, ±0.0001", N = 138 — 83%

6" Vernier micrometer, ±0.0001", N = 131 — 89%

3" (regular) micrometer, ±0.001", N = 146 — 36%

Depth micrometer, ±0.001", N = 142 — 47%

Inside micrometer, ±0.001", N = 117 — 34%

Inside caliper and 2" micrometer, ±0.001", N = 127 — 54%

Inside caliper and 6" micrometer. ±0.002", N = 112 — 91%

Outside caliper and 6" rule ±1/64", N = 117 — 51%

Vernier caliper (inside), ±0.001", N = 113 — 58%

Vernier caliper. ±0.001", N = 117 — 49%

0   20   40   60   80   100

Per cent of inspectors failing to meet precision standards for a given instrument

FIGURE 2.   Results of a study on the accuracy of precision measurement. (Adapted from Lawshe and Tiffin [7].)

parts in any quantity are never produced. This procedure, of course, is a direct application of the statistical control chart.

Second, we can control the level of outgoing quality from an inspection point to ensure that, on the average, no more than some specified per cent of defective items will pass. This procedure assumes that the parts or products are already made and we want to set up procedures and decision rules that ensure outgoing quality will be as specified or better. This general set of methods is known as *acceptance sampling*.

In the simplest case of acceptance sampling, we draw a random sample of size n from the total lot N and decide whether or not to accept the entire lot based upon the sample. If the sample signals a decision to reject the lot, it may then either be subjected to 100 percent inspection, sorting out bad parts, or be returned to the original supplier, which may be a vendor or another department within the organization. Parallel acceptance sampling procedures are available for the situation where we simply classify parts as good or bad (sampling by attributes) or where we make an actual measurement of some kind which indicates how good or bad a part is (sampling by variables).

Control charts attempt to control the quality produced. Acceptance sampling attempts to control the quality that passes an inspection point after production.

In general, acceptance sampling is appropriate when:

1. Possible losses by passing defective items are not great and the cost of inspection is relatively high. In the limiting situation, this can mean no inspection at all.

2. Inspection requires the destruction of the product; for example, when it is necessary to determine the strength of parts by pulling them apart. Inferring the acceptability of an entire lot from a sample is necessary in these instances.

3. Further handling of any kind is likely to induce defects, or when mental or physical fatigue is an important factor in inspection. In either instance, a sampling plan may actually pass fewer defective items than would 100 per cent inspection, and it also costs less.

ACCEPTANCE SAMPLING BY ATTRIBUTES

The inspection procedure for attribute sampling results in the simple classification of parts as good or not good. For part dimensions, this often can be accomplished by the use of snap or plug gages that incorporate a go-not-go feature, as indicated in Figure 3. If the inspection is for surface paint defects or some other attribute of appearance, again the two-part classification of good or not good would be made. In all instances, then, attribute sampling inspection uses some criteria to grade products as acceptable or not acceptable. The statistical methods used are based on distributions, such as the binomial distribution or the Poisson distribution. (The appropriateness of these and other distributions in specific situations is beyond our scope.)

Operating Characteristic (OC) Curves

To specify a particular sampling plan, we indicate the random sample size n and the number of defectives in the sample c (acceptance number) permitted before the entire lot from which the sample was drawn is to be

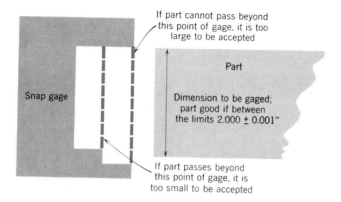

FIGURE 3.   A part measured by a snap gauge. No actual part measurement is recorded, but classification of parts is made as simply good or defective.

rejected. The OC curve for a particular combination of n and c shows how well the plan discriminates between good and bad lots. Figure 4 is an OC curve for a sampling plan, with sample size $n = 50$ and acceptance number $c = 1$. Figure 4 shows the probability of acceptance of a lot for various values of percent defectives in the lot. For example, if the actual lot quality were 2 percent, samples of $n = 50$ would accept the lot as

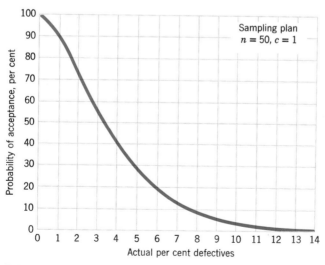

FIGURE 4.   Operating characteristic (OC) curve for a sampling plan with $n = 50$ and $c = 1$. (Adapted from Dodge and Romig [2].)

satisfactory about 73 percent of the time and reject it about 27 percent of the time. In other words, the probability of finding zero or one defective in random samples from such a lot is 73 percent, whereas the probability of finding more than one defective is only 27 percent. Note, however, that if the actual quality of the lot were somewhat worse than 2 percent defective, say 5 percent, the probability of accepting these lots falls drastically to about 27 percent. This is the situation that we would like in a sampling plan. If the actual quality is good, we want there to be a high probability of acceptance, but if the actual quality is poor, we want the probability of acceptance to be low. Thus the OC curve shows how well a given plan discriminates.

The discriminating power of a sampling plan depends heavily on the size of the sample, as we might expect. Figure 5 shows the OC curves for sample sizes of 100, 200, and 300, with the acceptance number remaining in proportion to the sample size. Note that the OC curve becomes somewhat steeper as the sample size goes up. If we compare the discrimination power of the three plans represented in Figure 5, we see that all three would accept lots of about 0.7 percent defectives about 83 percent of the time (the approximate crossover point of the three curves). However, if actual quality falls to 3.0 percent defectives, the plan with $n = 100$ accepts lots about 20 percent of the time, $n = 200$, about 6 percent of the time, and $n = 300$, less than 1 percent of the time. Plans with large sample sizes are definitely more effective.

What happens to the OC curve if only the acceptance number changes? Figure 6 shows OC curves for a sample of $n = 50$ and acceptance numbers of $c = 0, 1, 2$, and 3. Note that the effect is mainly to change the level of the OC curve, so that lower acceptance numbers make the plan "tighter," that is, hold outgoing quality to lower percents.

A sampling plan that discriminated perfectly between good and bad lots would have a vertical OC curve; that is, it would follow the dashed line of Figure 5. For all lots having percent defectives to the left of the dashed line, the probability of acceptance is 100 percent. For all lots having percent defectives to the right of the line, the probability of acceptance is zero. Unfortunately, the only plan that could achieve this discrimination is one requiring 100 percent inspection. Therefore, the justification of acceptance sampling turns on a balance between inspection costs and the probable cost of passing bad parts.

By making sampling plans more discriminating (increasing sample sizes) or tighter (decreasing acceptance numbers), we can approach any desired level of outgoing quality that we please, but at increasing

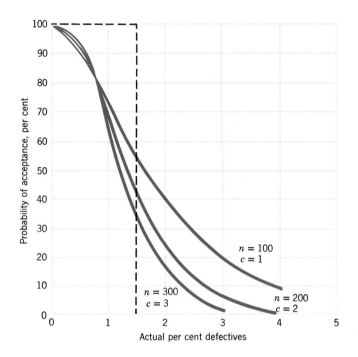

FIGURE 5.   *OC* curves for different sample sizes with acceptance numbers in proportion to sample sizes. (Adapted from [2].)

inspection costs. This increased inspection effort would result in lower probable costs of passing defective parts; at some point the combination of these incremental costs is a minimum. This minimum point defines the most economical sampling plan for a given situation.

Stated simply, then, to justify a 100 percent sample, the probable losses due to the passing of bad products would have to be large in relation to inspection costs, perhaps resulting in the loss of contracts and customers. On the other hand, to justify no inspection at all, inspection costs would have to be very large in relation to probable losses due to passing bad parts. The most usual situation is between these extremes, where there exists a risk of not accepting lots that are actually good and a risk of accepting lots that are bad. The first risk is called the producer's risk and the second, the consumer's risk.

Producer's and Consumer's Risks.   We can be very specific about producer's and consumer's risks by referring to a typical *OC* curve. Figure 7 shows graphically the following four definitions.

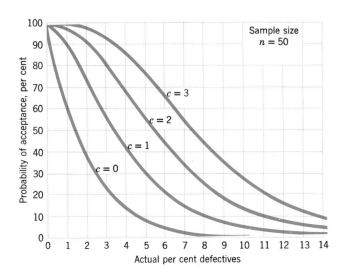

FIGURE 6.   *OC* curves with different acceptance numbers
for a sample size of *n* = 50. (Adapted from [2].)

AQL = acceptable quality level. Lots at this level of quality are regarded as good, and we wish to have a high probability of acceptance.

α = producer's risk—the probability that lots of the quality level *AQL* will *not* be accepted. Usually α = 5 percent.

LTPD = lot tolerance percent defective—the dividing line selected between good and bad lots. Lots at this level of quality are regarded as poor and we wish to have a low probability for their acceptance.

β = consumer's risk—the probability that lots of the quality level *LTPD* will be accepted. Usually β = 10 percent.

When we set levels for each of these four values, we are determining two critical points on the *OC* curve that we desire, points *a* and *b* in Figure 7.

Specification of a Specific Sampling Plan.   To specify a plan that meets the requirements for *AQL*, α, *LTPD*, and β, we must find a combination of *n* and *c* with an *OC* curve which passes through points *a* and *b* of Figure 7. The mechanics of actually finding specific plans that fit can be accomplished by using standard tables, charts, or formulas, all of which result in the specification of a combination of sample size

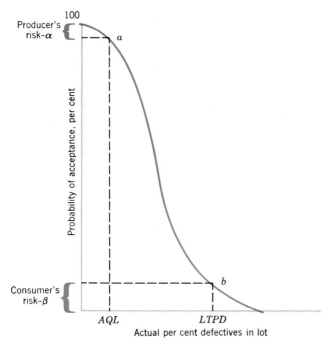

FIGURE 7.   Complete specifications of a sampling plan. An *OC* curve which goes through points *a* and *b* meets the requirements stated by α and *AQL* and β and *LTPD*, thus specifying a sampling plan with a given *n* and *c*. (*AQL* = acceptable quality level; *LTPD* = lot tolerance percent defectives.)

and acceptance number which closely approximates the requirements for *AQL*, α, *LTPD*, and β.*

Average Outgoing Quality (*AOQ*) Curves

If we assume that when a sampling plan rejects a lot, the lot is then subjected to 100 percent inspection, the sampling plan gives definite assurance that the average outgoing quality will not exceed certain limits. We now can develop a curve for any given sampling plan which shows the *AOQ* for any level of incoming quality. Such a curve can be plotted by assuming different values of actual incoming quality, determining from the *OC* curve the probability of acceptance for that incoming

*For example, see [2], [3], and [8].

quality P_a. These figures can then be substituted in a formula to compute *AOQ*. Each calculation for different incoming quality levels determines a point on the *AOQ* curve, as indicated in Figure 8. The *AOQ* curve of Figure 8 is based on a sampling plan with $n = 50$, $c = 1$, and $N = 1000$, the *OC* curve of which is shown in Figure 4.

Note the interesting characteristics of the *AOQ* curve. First, there is a maximum or limiting quality which can be passed on the average. This peak of the curve is called the average outgoing quality limit (*AOQL*). There is an *AOQL* for every sampling plan which depends on the characteristics of the plan. We can reason why the *AOQ* curve takes the shape illustrated. When good quality is presented to the sampling plan, for example, 0 to 3 per cent, the probability of acceptance is relatively high, so most defectives will be passed. As we go beyond 3 percent incoming quality, however, the probability of acceptance is declining. Therefore, the probability of 100 per cent inspection is increasing, so a larger share of defectives is screened out. This accounts for the fact

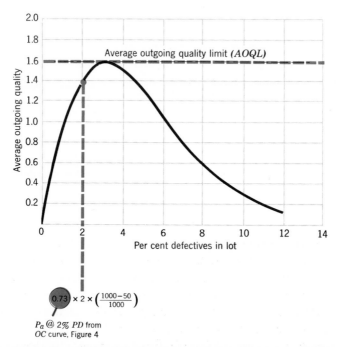

FIGURE 8.   Average outgoing quality (*AOQ*) curve for a sampling plan with $n = 50$, $c = 1$, and lot size $N = 1000$; *OC* curve shown in Figure 4.

that the outgoing quality improves as incoming quality becomes worse.

The essence of the characteristics of the sampling plan represented by the AOQ curve of Figure 8 is simply that average outgoing quality will never exceed approximately 1.6 percent, regardless of the incoming quality. The amount of inspection required to maintain quality standards automatically adjusts to the situation. If incoming quality is very poor, perhaps 10 percent, the sampling plan reacts by rejecting lots much more frequently, calling for 100 percent inspection, so average outgoing quality is about 0.3 percent. On the other hand, if incoming quality is excellent, perhaps 4 percent, the sampling plan more frequently passes the lots and the amount of inspection required is small. Inspectors usually will be spending their time screening bad lots and not wasting their time going over good lots.

The level of $AOQL$ which should be selected for a given situation depends on the consequences of bad quality. If subsequent operations can catch further defectives without disrupting production, $AOQL$ can be fairly loose. These probability controls over outgoing quality are ideal, especially since we first can specify the level of quality demanded by technical and economic considerations and then set up controls which guarantee the average performance needed, using inspection labor heavily when bad lots occur and only slightly when good lots occur.

Double Sampling

In double sampling an initial sample is taken and the number of defectives found is compared to two acceptance numbers, c_1 and c_2. If the number of defectives is less than c_1, the lot is accepted. If it exceeds the large acceptance number c_2, the lot is rejected and inspected 100 percent. If, however, the number of defectives is between c_1 and c_2, a second sample is taken. If the total number of defectives found in the *combined sample* exceeds c_2, the lot is rejected and inspected 100 percent. If it is less than c_2, the lot is accepted.

The advantages of double sampling lie in possible reductions in the total amount of inspection required. This occurs because the initial sample is smaller than that required by a comparable single sampling plan. If the lot can be accepted on the basis of the first sample, there will be a saving in total inspection. This saving in inspection is greatest for large lot sizes and when incoming quality is quite good.

With double sampling there also is an appeal to the layman of the idea of "giving it a second chance." Actually this psychological advantage is illusory. The probability of acceptance is determined by the *OC* curve for any plan, and a single sampling plan can be designed which yields greater discrimination between good and bad lots than a given double sampling plan. The disadvantage of double sampling is that the inspection load varies considerably. As before, plans are specified by the four requirements of *AQL*, α, *LTPD*, and β. Tables, graphs, and formulas can then be used to select a double sampling plan that has the desired *OC* curve [2].

Sequential Sampling Plans

Double sampling has the advantage of lower inspection costs for a given level of protection, accomplished by taking a smaller sample initially from which the lot is either accepted or rejected, or a second sample is taken. Why not carry this basic idea further? This is essentially what happens with sequential sampling. Samples are drawn at random, as before. But after each sample is inspected, the cumulated results are analyzed and a decision made to (a) accept the lot, (b) reject the lot, or (c) take another sample. The sequential sample sizes can be as small as $n = 1$.

Figure 9 shows the graphical structure of a sequential sampling plan. The main advantage of sequential sampling is a further reduction in the total amount of inspection required to maintain a given level of protection, as compared to double sampling. In the plan shown in Figure 9, a minimum of fifteen items must be inspected in order to accept a lot. If the number of rejects on the graph rises such that the point falls on or above the upper line, the lot is rejected. If the point should fall on or below the lower line, the lot is accepted. Until one of these events happens, sampling is continued. As with double·sampling, the disadvantage is that inspection loads vary considerably. As with the single and double sampling plans, a sequential plan is specified by the four requirements: *AQL*, α, *LTPD*, and β. In turn, these requirements determine *OC* curves of sequential plans which meet the functional requirements.

ACCEPTANCE SAMPLING BY VARIABLES

In acceptance sampling by variables, we make and record actual measurements instead of simply classifying items as good or bad as in attributes sampling. This difference in procedure changes the details of determining

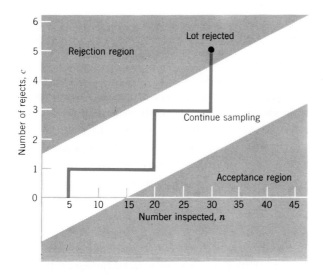

FIGURE 9.   Sequential sampling plan.

a plan that meets our specifications of acceptable quality, producer's risk, minimum acceptable quality, and consumer's risk, because the appropriate statistical distribution is now the *normal* distribution instead of distributions for proportions. In addition, inspection methods must change. Conceptually, however, the basic ideas on which the control of outgoing quality is maintained remain the same. The discriminating power of a plan still is represented by an *OC* curve, which shows the probability of acceptance for different levels of actual quality presented to the plan. To specify a plan that gives the desired protection requires basically the same procedure.

Upper and lower tolerance levels are often specified on measurements of part dimensions, chemical content, etc., as part of variables sampling plan specifications. In these instances, the variables sampling must provide two-sided protection from defectives occurring because the measured characteristic may be too small or too large to be useful. A sampling plan then would specify a sample size, an upper acceptance average, and a lower acceptance average.

Criteria for acceptance can be expressed in per cent defective, as with attributes sampling, even though actual measurements are made. This merely requires a conversion of units within the plan. Also, *double sampling* is as applicable to acceptance sampling by variables as to sampling by attributes.

Obviously, inspection, recording, and computing costs per unit will normally be higher with variables sampling inspection plans than with attributes plans. Then why use variables plans? The most important reason is that, for a given level of protection, variables plans require smaller samples and less total inspection than do attributes plans. From an economic viewpoint, then, variables inspection should be used where the smaller sample size tips the balance of costs of inspection, recording, and computing. In addition to the possible cost advantages, the data generated by variables inspection (mean and standard deviation) provide more valuable diagnostic information for controlling production processes.

CONTROL CHARTS

In general, variations that occur in an industrial process fall in two broad categories: *chance* variations and those due to *assignable causes*. The chance variations may be due to a complex of minor actual causes, none of which can account for any significant part of the total variation. The result is that these variations occur in a random manner, and there is very little that we can do about them, given the process. On the other hand, variations due to assignable causes are relatively large and can be traced. In general, assignable causes are:

1.   Differences among workers.
2.   Differences among machines.
3.   Differences among materials.
4.   Differences due to the interaction between any two or all three of these factors.

When a process is in a state of statistical control, variations that occur in the number of defects, the size of a dimension, chemical composition, weight, etc., are due to chance variation only. With the control chart, we set up standards of expected normal variation due to chance causes. Thus, when variations due to one or more of the assignable causes are superimposed, they "stick out like a sore thumb" and tell us that something basic has changed. The *natural tolerance* of a process is commonly taken as $\bar{x} \pm 3s$.

Control Charts for Attributes

p-Charts.   Control charts for the proportion or fraction of defectives (*p*-charts) occurring are based on the binomial distribution. Recall that:

$$\bar{p} = \frac{x}{n} = \frac{\text{number of defectives}}{\text{total number observed}}$$

$$s_p = \sqrt{\frac{\bar{p}(1 - \bar{p})}{n}}$$

where n = the size of the subsample.

When we follow the general ideas for control charts, the control limits are normally set at the process average of defectives plus and minus three standard deviations, that is, they are set at $\bar{p} \pm 3s_p$.

Table I shows a set of data covering twenty-four consecutive production days on the number of defectives found in daily samples of 200. We wish to determine first if the data exhibit statistical control and to set up a control chart. The daily fraction defective is calculated by dividing each daily figure by the sample size, $n = 200$. Preliminary

TABLE I. Record of Number of Defectives and Calculated Fraction Defective in Daily Samples of $n = 200$

Production Day	Number of Defectives	Fraction Defective	Production Day	Number of Defectives	Fraction Defective
1	10	0.05	14	14	0.07
2	5	0.025	15	4	0.02
3	10	0.05	16	10	0.05
4	12	0.06	17	11	0.055
5	11	0.055	18	11	0.055
6	9	0.045	19	26	0.13
7	22	0.11	20	13	0.065
8	4	0.02	21	10	0.05
9	12	0.06	22	9	0.045
10	24	0.12	23	11	0.055
11	21	0.105	24	12	0.06
12	15	0.075	Total	294	
13	8	0.04			

$$\bar{p} = \frac{294}{24 \times 200} = 0.061$$

$$s_p = \sqrt{\frac{0.061 \times 0.939}{200}} = 0.017$$

$3s_p = 0.051$

$UCL = \bar{p} + 3s_p = 0.061 + 0.051 = 0.112$

$LCL = \bar{p} - 3s_p = 0.061 - 0.051 = 0.010$

figures for $\bar{p}$, s_p, and the upper and lower control limits, *UCL* and *LCL*, are calculated in Table I also. These preliminary figures are used to determine if the data are in control. Figure 10 shows the resulting plot of the daily fraction defective in relation to the preliminary control limits. Two points are outside of limits and the point for day 7 is nearly outside the upper limit. Investigation shows nothing unusual for the first point, day 7. For the second point, it appears that a logical explanation is that three new men were taken on that day. The foreman contends that the following day's defectives were also affected by the breaking in of these men. The last was explained by the fact that the die had worn and finally actually fractured that day.

To set up standards for normal variation, we eliminate the data for days on which we have established assignable causes (days 10 and 19), and recompute $\bar{p}$, *UCL*, and *LCL* as follows:

$$\bar{p} = \frac{244}{200 \times 21} = 0.055$$

$$UCL = 0.055 + 3\sqrt{\frac{0.055 \times 0.945}{200}} = 0.104$$

$$LCL = 0.055 - 3\sqrt{\frac{0.055 \times 0.945}{200}} = 0.008$$

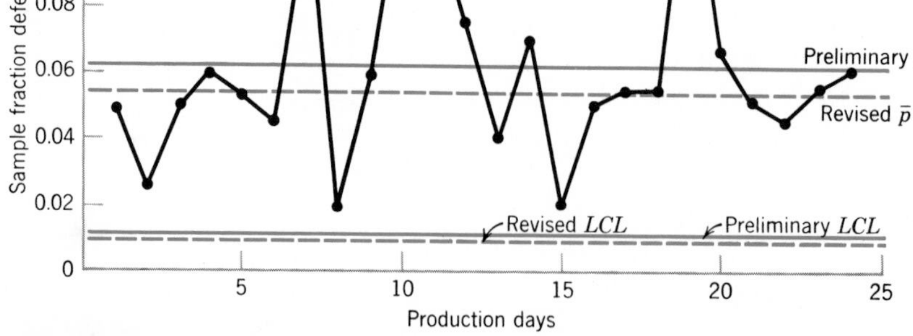

FIGURE 10.   A *p*-chart for examining past data and establishing preliminary and revised control limits.

These revised values reflect the variation due to chance causes. We now use them as standards by which we judge future samples of fraction defective. If any future samples fall outside these limits, our immediate reaction is that it is highly probable that there is an assignable cause for the unusual observation of fraction defective. We then attempt to determine the cause and correct it before more scrap has been produced.

When the p-chart is based upon a 100 percent sample, we may expect that the total number inspected will vary from day to day. Therefore, each successive point on the control chart will have different control limits. Under these conditions, we use the same process average fraction defective in calculating the control limits. But since n varies from day to day, s_p also varies, thus affecting the control limits.

Another control chart for attributes is based on the number of defects per unit of product. On a painted surface these might be dimples, paint runs, etc. A measure of the quality might then be the number of these blemishes per unit or per unit area sampled. Control charts set up on this basis are called c-charts.

Control Charts for Variables

Control charts could be constructed for individual measurements. Usually, however, control charts are constructed for sample means rather than for individual measurements. One important reason for this is that *although a universe distribution may depart radically from normality, the sampling distribution of means of random samples will be approximately normal if the sample size is large enough*. This statement is very important for it gives us some assurance that the probabilities associated with the 3s limits will apply. Figure 11 demonstrates that the deviation from normality can be fairly great and yet, with the sampling distribution of the means of samples as small as 5, follow the normal distribution quite closely.

If we take samples of four from the shaft data distribution of individual measurements in Figure 12 and determine an average for each sample, we have a new distribution. We regard each sample mean as an observation; if we plot a frequency distribution of the sample means, it will have a mean and a variance of its own. This distribution is called *a sampling distribution of means of $n = 4$*. To distinguish the *statistics* from those of the distribution of individual observations, we use the notation $\bar{x}$ for the grand mean of the sampling distribution and $s_{\bar{x}}$ for the standard deviation. We expect that $\bar{x}$ and $\bar{\bar{x}}$ will be very nearly the same and that they

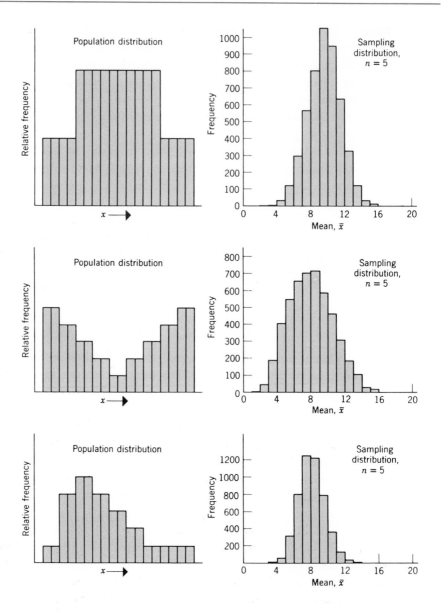

FIGURE 11.   Normality of sampling distributions. The three distributions on the left are populations from which 5000 samples of $n = 5$ were drawn at random. The resulting sampling distributions are shown on the right.

will be equal in the limit as the number of subsamples increases. The variance and standard deviation will be much smaller for the sampling distribution of means, however, since the variation is reduced by the averaging process within each sample. The resulting relationship between the two distributions for the shaft data is shown in Figure 12. Actually the relationship between s and $s_{\bar{x}}$ is given by

$$s_{\bar{x}} = \sqrt{s^2/n}$$

where n is the size of the subsample.

Now to construct a control chart for the means ($\bar{X}$-charts), we first need to establish standard values for $\bar{\bar{x}}$ and $s_{\bar{x}}$, which are based on the normal conditions of whatever it is that we wish to control. The upper and lower control limits are established at $\bar{\bar{x}} \pm 3s_{\bar{x}}$. Means of subsequent samples are plotted; again, action would be called for if a sample mean should fall outside the control limits.

The reasons why sample means may fall outside the control limits are,

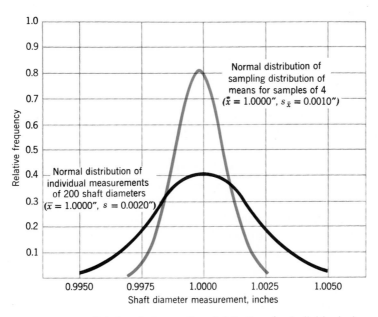

FIGURE 12.   Relation between the distribution for individual observations and the sampling distribution of samples of 4 for shaft diameter data.

of course, related to the technology of the processes being controlled. For example, if parts were being produced on a lathe, they would tend to become oversized as the cutting tool became worn. Changes of this general nature tend to reflect themselves in the mean of the sampling distribution. If, however, the bearings of the lathe spindle had worn, this situation would be reflected by an increase in variability of the sampling distribution, and we would expect points to go outside of both control limits. The control chart can show up changes in the mean of the distribution actually being generated, changes in the variance, standard deviation, or range, and combinations of changes in the mean and changes in variability. Where changes in variability are particularly important, a special control chart on a measure of variability can be constructed.

Control Charts on Measures of Variability.   When developing the control chart for means, we used the sampling distributions of means and calculated control limits based on the means as the statistic of main interest. We can as well take some measure of variability as the statistic, for example, the variance. For each subsample of size n, we can calculate a sample variance s^2. If we made a frequency distribution of these variances, we would have a distribution which approximated the normal distribution. This distribution of sample variances would itself have a mean and a standard deviation. We could, therefore, use this distribution of sample variances to establish a control chart which would tell us when the variability of the thing being controlled is greater or less than normal.

In quality control work, the statistic chosen is usually the *range* instead of the variance, because of the ease with which it can be computed for the successive samples. For each subsample, the difference between the highest and lowest measurement is plotted on a control chart for ranges. The control chart for ranges represents a distribution of ranges for samples of size n. This distribution has an average, $\bar{R}$, and a standard deviation s_R. The $3s_R$ limits have the same general significance as before. The probability that a sample range will fall outside the limits is only 0.27 percent if it comes from the original universe. Therefore, when sample ranges do fall outside the control limits, we can presume that something has happened to cause greater than expected variability. Convenient tables and charts exist which make it very easy to establish the $3s_R$ control limits.

SUMMARY

The control of quality in an organization requires a broad integrated view of the responsibility for quality, not just a focus on the control of quality levels of incoming raw materials and the control over manufacturing processes. The chain of enterprise policies, engineering design decisions, production system design, and control over the operations phases, including distribution and use, requires dovetailing and coordination if the total enterprise objectives with regard to quality are to be achieved.

The development of the use of probability controls in industry has reached its greatest height in quality control. Acceptance sampling gears the amount of inspection to probable incoming quality levels and calls for 100 percent inspection when there is a strong probability that incoming quality is poor. On the other hand, when samples indicate that incoming quality is probably fairly good, the entire lot is accepted without further inspection. Control charts attempt to prevent the production of poor quality in the first place by indicating when the probability is high that there is some assignable cause for defective parts being produced. By running up the distress signal at the first sign of trouble, we prevent the production of more scrap and save the cost of subsequent inspection to screen out the bad parts later.

Although the concepts of acceptance sampling and statistical control have been presented in a background of industrial quality control we should recognize that these ideas have very general application. Decisions in all functional areas are commonly based on sample data. Why not assess the risks involved as is done in acceptance sampling? The concepts of statistical control are finding a widening field of application outside manufacturing today. Control charts have been used for labor turnover, costs, accident rates, etc.

KEY CONCEPTS

Quality.   The concept of quality as being some deliberately chosen level is an important one. Not every organization should attempt to produce the very best quality unless there is no market for anything but that quality level. On the other hand, what the term means in the industrial setting is a specified level to which we wish to adhere for reasons of market, cost, and the possible effects of deviations from standard quality on other costs.

Acceptance Sampling.   The concept of acceptance sampling should be regarded as a decision process involving the careful gathering of data, the preassignment of risks involved in drawing the wrong conclusions and their consequences, as well as an overall procedure which calls for 100 percent screening if the results of the sampling process indicate that the desired risk level has been exceeded.

The Exception Principle.   The concept of management by the exception principle is demonstrated in its purest form by the statistical control chart. When the data indicate the probability is high that the process is in control, management need take no action at all. On the other hand, when the data indicate the probability is high that something has gone wrong, management can summon the most capable personnel to determine causes and prescribe solutions.

IMPORTANT TERMS

Numbers in parentheses indicate page numbers.

1. Acceptable quality level (AQL) (626)
2. Assignable cause (632)
3. Attributes sampling (622)
4. Average outgoing quality (AOQ) (627)
5. Average outgoing quality limit (AOQL) (628)
6. Consumer's risk (626)
7. Control chart (632)
8. Double sampling (629, 631)
9. Lot tolerance percent defective (LTPD) (626)
10. Operating characteristic (OC) curve (622)
11. p-chart (632)
12. Percent defectives (624)
13. Producer's risk (626)
14. Sequential sampling (630)
15. Variables sampling (630)

REVIEW QUESTIONS

Numbers in parentheses indicate page numbers.

1. What is the meaning of the term *quality* in the manufacturing sense? (615)
2. Differentiate between inspection and quality control. (619)
3. Discuss the role of judgment in the use of precision measurement devices and in inspection. (619–620)
4. What kind of control can be exercised in maintaining quality standards? (620–621)
5. What conditions make acceptance sampling appropriate? (622)
6. What is an *OC* curve and what information does it convey? (622–623)
7. What is the effect of increasing sample size on the *OC* curve? What practical result does it achieve in terms of the discriminating power of a sampling plan? (624)

8. What is the effect of decreasing acceptance numbers on the *OC* curve? What practical result does it achieve in terms of outgoing quality levels? (624)

9. Define *AQL*, α, *LTPD*, and ß. Relate these definitions to a typical *OC* curve. (626)

10. Discuss the significance of the shape of the average outgoing quality (*AOQ*) curve. Relate this to the amount of inspection required at various levels of incoming quality. (628–629)

11. What is the general structure for double sampling? What are its advantages and disadvantages? (629–630)

12. What is the general structure for sequential sampling? What are its advantages and disadvantages? (630)

13. Contrast the differences in concept and statistical technique for sampling by attributes and by variables. (622, 16–17)

14. What conditions favor the use of sampling by variables? (631)

15. What are the sources of assignable causes of variation in quality control? (632)

16. Discuss the procedure for setting up a *p*-chart. (632–633)

17. What is the significance of the fact that the sampling distribution of means can be normal even though the distribution of individual measurements departs radically from normality? (635)

18. What is the relationship between s and $s_{\bar{x}}$? (635–637)

19. Why is the range usually used as the measure of variability in quality control? (638)

SELF-TEST TRUE-FALSE QUESTIONS

Numbers in parentheses indicate page numbers.

1. Judgment is an important factor where the inspection is subjective, but when the inspection can be based upon an objective factor, such as a measurement with a precision gauge, judgment is not a factor. (620)

2. Acceptance sampling assumes that the parts or products are already made and we want to set up procedures and decision rules that ensure outgoing quality will be as specified or better. (621)

3. Control charts attempt to control the quality of product produced. (622)

4. Acceptance sampling would be appropriate when the possible losses by passing defective items are great, and the cost to inspect is relatively low. (622)

5. The inspection procedures for attributes sampling result in the simple classification of parts as good or not good. (622)

6. In attributes acceptance sampling, the acceptance number, c, is the number

of defectives permitted before the entire lot from which the sample was drawn can be accepted. (622–623)

7. The OC curve for a particular combination of sample size and acceptance number shows how well the sampling plan discriminates between good and bad lots. (623)

8. Decreasing the acceptance number, for a given sample size, increases the discrimination of an acceptance sampling plan. (624, 626)

9. Increasing the sample size, keeping the acceptance number in proportion, results in a "tighter" plan, that is, a holding of outgoing quality to lower percents defective. (624)

10. The only plan which can discriminate perfectly between good and bad lots, that is, one with a vertical OC curve, is one requiring 100 percent inspection. (624)

11. Acceptable quality level (AQL) is good quality for which we wish to have a high probability of acceptance. (626)

12. Producer's risk (α) is the probability that lots of low quality will be accepted. (626)

13. AQL, α, LTPD, and ß determine two points on an OC curve. (626, 627)

14. In the normal operation of an acceptance sampling plan, a very poor incoming lot of parts would result in excellent outgoing quality. (629)

15. For any acceptance sampling plan, there is an average outgoing quality limit which ensures that outgoing quality will never average worse than this level. (629)

16. Double sampling makes it more likely that poor quality lots will be found, because the second sample improves the OC curve. (630)

17. One of the advantages of double sampling is that less overall inspection is necessary. (629)

18. A disadvantage of double sampling is that the inspection load varies considerably. (630)

19. The main advantage of sequential sampling is an even greater reduction in the amount of inspection required, as compared to double sampling. (630)

20. In sequential sampling, it is necessary to make and record actual measurements instead of simply classifying items as good or bad. (630)

21. Variables sampling plans require smaller samples and less total inspection than do attributes plans, for the same protection. (632)

22. In addition to the possible cost advantages, the data generated by variables inspection (mean and standard deviation) provide more valuable diagnostic information in controlling production processes. (632)

23. Control charts help distinguish between chance variations and those due to assignable causes. (632)

24. The main reason why variable control charts are usually constructed for sample means, instead of individual measurements, is because the sampling

distribution of means is much more likely to be normal. (635)
25. If parts were being produced on a lathe, the standard deviation would tend to increase as the cutting tool became worn. (638)
26. If the bearings of a lathe spindle had worn, this would tend to produce oversized parts. (638)
27. In quality control work, the statistic usually chosen as a measure of variability is the standard deviation instead of the range, because of the ease with which it can be computed. (638)

PROBLEMS

1. A large medical insurance company maintains an office staff that processes claims, computing the payment amounts under the terms of the insurance contracts. Since errors in payment are important to both the company and subscribers, a sampling plan is to be installed. At the end of the day a random sample of n = 50 claims is taken and the benefits recomputed. Any variance in the computed benefits is regarded as an error or "defective." The claims manager feels that acceptable quality is 1 percent defectives, and he wishes the probability of acceptance of such quality to be 90 percent. What sampling plan would yield this performance? If the consumer's risk is 10 percent, what percent defectives represent poor quality for the plan? (See OC curves.)

2. A large hardware distributor has a staff that prepares invoices to be sent to customers. Problems with clerical accuracy have led to the installation of probability controls. Any variance in the invoice amount is regarded as an error. In order to establish a control chart, initial samples of 200 invoices are taken over a period of several days as shown in Table II.
(a) What are the control limits for a p-chart for the invoice operation?
(b) Plot the samples on a p-chart.
(c) Is the invoice preparation process in control?

3. The manager of the invoice department in problem 2 notes the relatively high error rates in the samples taken on May 11. On investigation he finds that the air conditioning system was broken down that day and feels satisfied that is an assignable cause for the high error rates. Should the control limits be altered? If so, what are the revised control limits?

4. StaMPCo, who makes the V-belt pully shown in Figure 18 on page 319, has decided to employ certain statistical control techniques to reduce the cost of inspection and to improve quality control. StaMPCo buys 0.875-inch diameter rolled bar stock on a contract basis from a large, dependable supplier. Shipments are made in lots of 400 as required. At the present production rate of pulleys having 0.875-inch diameter hubs, 400 bars roughly correspond to six to seven days' usage.

TABLE II.   Errors in Invoice Samples

	Time	Sample Size	Number of Errors	Error Rate in Sample (Per Cent)
May 7	A.M.	200	3	1.5
	P.M.	200	12	6.0
8	A.M.	200	0	0.0
	P.M.	200	11	5.5
9	A.M.	200	5	2.5
	P.M.	200	7	3.5
10	A.M.	200	9	4.5
	P.M.	200	6	3.0
11	A.M.	200	16	8.0
	P.M.	200	18	9.0
14	A.M.	200	9	4.5
	P.M.	200	5	2.5
15	A.M.	200	7	3.5
	P.M.	200	0	0.0
16	A.M.	200	13	6.5
	P.M.	200	2	1.0
17	A.M.	200	11	5.5
	P.M.	200	7	3.5
18	A.M.	200	4	2.0
	P.M.	200	1	0.5
21	A.M.	200	6	3.0
	P.M.	200	12	6.0
22	A.M.	200	6	3.0
	P.M.	200	4	2.0
23	A.M.	200	4	2.0
Total		5000	178	

To properly match the pulley flanges produced on punch presses, the bar stock cannot vary more than 0.002 inch from the nominal diameter. Therefore, the specification for bar stock diameter is 0.875 inch $\pm$ 0.002 inch. If the bar diameter exceeds the upper specification limit, the flanges tend to split excessively when forced onto the hub by the arbor press. If the diameter is smaller than specified, the flange-hub fit is loose and the spot-welding operation tends to pull the flanges off the axis of rotation. As a result, a large number of pulleys must be rejected because of excessive "wobble."

(a) The company's contract with the steel supplier specifies that 95 percent of the bars are to meet the diameter specification of 0.875 inch $\pm$ 0.002 inch.

(b) The production manager and purchasing agent have decided that the company should not accept an individual shipment in which more than 17.5 per cent of the bars are oversized or undersized. What are the values of the parameters which would define an acceptance sampling plan?

5.   After several months the production manager feels that the receiving inspection department has been accepting too many lots in which the actual number of defective bars exceeds 17.5 percent. He therefore recommends reducing the probability of accepting lots which have more than 17.5 percent defectives by one-half. How must the plan discussed in problem 4 be modified to carry out this recommendation?

6.   StaMPCo has been experiencing a large number of rejects among its smaller V-belt pulleys because of hub defects. Since the pulley hub is largely fabricated on the turret lathe, the production manager has requested a complete study of the turret lathe pulley hub operations.

To test the quality capability of the turret lathes, ten samples of four pulley hubs each were taken when the lathes were operating in a "typical" manner. The results for hub lengths are given below; $n = 4$.

Sample Number	Sample Average $\bar{X}$	Sample Range R
1	1.007 inch	0.013 inch
2	1.008	0.022
3	0.991	0.018
4	0.993	0.014
5	0.998	0.019
6	1.008	0.026
7	0.996	0.024
8	0.995	0.011
9	0.999	0.021
10	0.995	0.024
Totals	9.990 inch	0.192 inch

Determine the natural tolerance of the lathes for cut-off operations.

7.   If the design specification for small pulley hub lengths is 1.000 ± 0.040 inch, are the turret lathes inherently capable of meeting these specifications? Why?

8.   Based on the design specifications for the pulley hub length of 1.000 ± 0.040 inch and the natural tolerance interval, at what basic dimension (average hub length) should the turret lathe be set whenever a tool change or adjustment is made? (Assume that tool wear is the only predictable variable in process changes.) Sketch this situation and explain.

9.   With the quality capability information which you have developed, determine the control limits and set up the control charts for the control of the cut-off operation on turret lathes. A sample of four pulleys is to be taken every half hour.

(a) Control chart for sample means $\bar{X}$. Under normal conditions the width of the cut-off tool is known to wear at the rate of 0.001 inch per hour of use. The shop works from 8:00 A.M. to 12:00 noon and 12:30 P.M. to 4:30 P.M. (The lunch period is 12:00 to 12:30 P.M.) It is shop practice to replace the cut-off tool at the beginning of the work day in accordance with the procedure which you established in problem 6.

(1) Determine the appropriate control limits for the sample mean so as to reflect the known rate of cut-off tool wear.

(2) Plot the $\bar{X}$ control limits and the predicted trend line of average hub length on the control chart.

(b) Control chart for sample ranges R.

(1) Determine the appropriate control limits for the sample range. (Show all calculations.)

(2) Plot the R control limits and the average range $\bar{R}$ on the control chart.

REFERENCES

[1] Bowker, A. H., and H. P. Goode. *Sampling Inspection by Variables*. McGraw-Hill, New York, 1952.

[2] Dodge, H. F., and H. G. Romig. *Sampling Inspection Tables* (2nd ed.). John Wiley, New York, 1959.

[3] Duncan, A. J. *Quality Control and Industrial Statistics* (4th ed.). Richard D. Irwin, Homewood, Ill., 1974.

[4] Grant, E. L., and R. S. Leavenworth. *Statistical Quality Control* (4th ed.). McGraw-Hill, New York, 1972.

[5] Hoel, P. G., and R. J. Jessen. *Elementary Statistics for Business and Economics,* John Wiley, New York, 1971.

[6] Kirkpatrick, E. G. *Quality Control for Managers and Engineers*. John Wiley, New York, 1970.

[7] Lawshe, C. H., and J. Tiffin. "The Accuracy of Precision Instrument Measurement in Industrial Production." *Journal of Applied Psychology,* Dec. 1945, pp. 413–419.

[8] MIL-STD-105C. *Military Standard Sampling Procedures and Tables for Inspection by Attributes,* July 18, 1961.

[9] MIL-STD-414. *Military Standard Sampling Procedures and Tables for Inspection by Variables for Per Cent Defective,* June 11, 1957.

PART 5
SYNTHESIS

CONTENTS

CHAPTER 20
PRODUCTION AND OPERATIONS MANAGEMENT-SUMMARY

Times are changing, and in no place is this fact any more evident than in the field of production and operations management. The field is in a state of flux from several viewpoints. The meaning of the word *production* today reflects a broader view than formerly. It deals with the *operations* side of any enterprise, and we may find production systems in offices, stores, hospitals, etc., as well as in factories. In all these systems, there are inputs, some kind of processing, and outputs. Production and operations management deals with decision making within the system. One of the recent conceptual changes is that waste in the system and its possible effect on pollution has come to be regarded as a part of the processing system.

The organization of this book has been around the problems encountered in the design and operation of productive systems, given a background of applicable analytical methods. In general, we discussed within each problem area how that problem was affected by the special conditions of different kinds of productive

651

systems. As a basis for summation let us now try to integrate our knowledge in terms of each of the major kinds of systems: distribution systems, production-distribution systems for high-volume products, job shops (both closed and open), and large-scale projects.

DISTRIBUTION SYSTEMS

In essence, the management of distribution systems is centered in the management of an inventory system, usually a multistage inventory system. The design of the physical distribution system is concerned with the strategic location of inventory points in relation to markets in order to provide the required service at reasonable transportation cost. Logistics dominates the system design in determining whether or not to use intermediate warehouses and, if so, where to locate them.

The operating problems of distribution systems are centered in inventory management. What is the distribution of demand? How do we forecast requirements? When should we replenish inventories? How much inventory should be ordered at one time? What buffer stocks should be maintained to offer the service needed? How do we determine the appropriate service level?

Though the problems are similar for each of the levels in the system, they have a somewhat different emphasis. For example, the problem of determining distribution of demand and forecasting demand is local for the retailer, whereas at the factory warehouse it may be national or international in scope. On the other hand, the factory warehouse may need a data processing system for a relatively few sizes, types, and styles, whereas the distributor and retailer are likely to be dealing with a very much larger number of items. Also, the concept of service and service systems is physical in terms of the inventories required at each level, however, at the retail level service systems must include not only the availability of inventory, but the design of a service system around the concepts of waiting line analysis.

The major production and operations management problems which confront distribution kinds of organizations are as follows:

1. Determination of the nature of the distribution of demand.
2. Forecasting demand.
3. Determination of how much to order at one time.
4. Determination of when to reorder.

5. Determination of service levels and the size of buffer stocks.

6. Design of data processing systems.

HIGH-VOLUME PRODUCTION-DISTRIBUTION SYSTEMS

Adding a production system to the head end of a distribution system. changes the focus and adds enormous complexity to the managerial problems. The system under managerial control centers around the production system and extends downstream into the distribution system to some extent, depending on the particular organization. In some instances, it may include the entire distribution system. One of the great advantages in coupling the production and distribution systems is that inventories become an important tradeoff to other means of absorbing fluctuations in demand, and the kinds of aggregate planning models discussed in Chapter 15 take on considerable significance.

Forecasting consumer demand is extremely important both in the short and long run. In the short run, forecasts are the basis for raw material procurement, and aggregate planning and scheduling of facilities and labor in order to combine the various sources of capacity in the most economical way. Longer-range forecasts, however, are also of great significance in planning long-range aggregate capacity and its location and layout, as well as the size and location of distribution warehouses.

The process of generating day-to-day schedules for high-volume systems is one of working within the constraints of the aggregate plan, taking advantage of whatever flexibility may be left to "cut and try" for a practical schedule. This may include rebalancing of lines, inventory adjustments, the use of overtime and subcontracting, etc. The nature and design of the information and data processing system which couples measurement of actual demand, forecasting, inventory control, and production control is of extreme importance.

Though no one would say that the design, planning, scheduling, and control problems of high-volume production-distribution systems are simple, they are, nonetheless, simpler than for intermittent systems.

The major production and operations management problems which confront organizations producing and distributing high-volume standardized products are as follows:

1. Forecasting demand and the behavior of multistage inventory systems.
2. Long-range aggregate planning for facilities—plant capability, sizes and location, and warehouse sizes and location.
3. Production facility design.
4. Aggregate planning and scheduling for facilities and manpower.
5. Raw materials procurement.
6. Day-to-day scheduling and adjustment of production levels as demand becomes known.
7. Design of data processing systems.

INTERMITTENT SYSTEMS

In contrast to the high-volume system, intermittent systems key everything to the basic requirement of holding facilities and manpower "in inventory" to supply the needs of a demand that varies in terms of its design, style, and technological requirements. Thus, the jobbing printer holds in readiness equipment and trained personnel capable of performing a wide variety of operations to reproduce the printed word. Jobbing machine shops hold in readiness equipment and trained mechanics capable of performing a wide variety of operations on various metals of different sizes, types, and designs. If the number of orders falls temporarily, such an organization does not sell its equipment nor fire its skilled mechanics for it is this capability that it has for sale. Similarly, and perhaps even more essential to organizational survival, aerospace and other research and developmental organizations may stockpile engineering and scientific brains because it is this kind of capability which is crucial in obtaining contracts.

Though most often the relationships with the ultimate consumer may be direct, the internal complications are tremendous. These complications arise from the custom nature of the fabrication process, where each order, or item, will require individual planning and scheduling and will follow a unique processing sequence. The typical time delays in the information system are in the bid and order procedure, the special production planning and scheduling requirements, and the special ordering of materials. The physical flow time involved in actual fabrication and assembly is usually relatively long because of the intermittent nature of physical flow. The inventory problems are largely for raw material and in-process inventories, and the scheduling problem is focused more on the use of individual pieces of equipment rather than the factory as a whole as with high-volume systems.

The most complex of job shop systems is the open shop, which is open to job orders from virtually anyone. Under such circumstances one must forecast, design the physical facility, make aggregate plans, schedule, procure materials, and bid with the greatest uncertainty. The closed job shop is the captive shop of some concern and manufactures for its own internal use in its own product line. Its product line usually has a degree of predictability, although the captive shops may also receive internal one-time orders. Closed job shops in fact produce a largely forecastable line of parts, components, and products, and this is an important distinction because, if we know in advance what our product line mix will be, then the problems can take on a considerably different hue.

The major production and operations management problems which confront job shop kinds of organizations may be summarized as follows:

1. Design and layout of a system to minimize aggregate handling cost.
2. Forecasting demand.
3. Aggregate planning for the use of facilities.
4. Scheduling orders to meet promised delivery dates.
5. Scheduling labor and equipment to minimize combined costs of machine setup, machine down time, labor overtime and undertime, and in-process inventories.
6. Scheduling equipment to utilize most efficient processes.
7. Procuring materials in economical quantities to mesh with the production schedule.
8. Developing bidding policy and procedure to obtain orders at margins that will achieve a balance between use of labor and facilities, and desire for profit.

LARGE-SCALE PROJECTS

A structural model for large-scale projects is not far different from a job shop model. The differences are in terms of the immense complexity and the extensive time delays and coordination required within the system. In planning the activities of what must be done, the very complexity of the project makes process sequences of extreme importance, for operations performed out of sequence can cause delays and extra costs. Thus, the development of the production plan as a network of operations is the key to managerial control of the project. Given the network of required operations, a second focus of problems centers on scheduling and the effective use of available resources. The generation of the critical path schedule is an important input to the scheduling and control processs and may be regarded as a first feasible schedule. The knowledge of permissible slack or schedule slippage of certain operations gives management flexibility in achieving a practical schedule. This flexibility can also be used to level the labor requirements over the entire project or make it possible to use limited equipment for several operations in a way that does not conflict and still does not extend the project time.

The inventory problem at first seems simple and direct, yet there are important inventory problems. Inventory cost is in general directly related to overall project time. To minimize the investment in inventories during the project, material receipt schedules must be carefully co-ordinated with the schedule of operations. If orders for raw material supply are released in a block at the beginning of the project, a large fraction of inventories would be held for a much larger period than necessary and would probably also create a physical storage problem. If material is wasted or scrapped so that a certain operation cannot be completed, then the entire project may be delayed if the activity is on the critical path schedule. Thus, an important inventory decision problem centers on the quantity of material to be ordered in the first place. A relatively inexpensive item of material could cause idle labor costs, or possible penalties for not meeting project delivery dates.

In summary, the major production and operations management problems of large-scale projects are:

1. Planning a network of operations to accomplish the desired end result.
2. Developing schedules of the network of operations such that the critical path schedule of the network meets promised delivery dates.
3. Allocating the use of limited resources of equipment and/or labor in ways that will not interfere with the critical path schedule.
4. Procuring materials by a schedule that minimizes total inventory costs but meets the needs of the critical path schedule.
5. Developing bidding policy and procedures to obtain contracts at margins that will achieve a balance between the use and maintenance of the stockpile of critical resources (engineers, scientists, skilled labor, key facilities, etc.) and the desire for profit.

The four major kinds of systems which we have discussed do not represent rigid classifications, since systems in practice tend to be combinations of job shop and line or job shop and project, etc. The classifications, however, have provided a basis for developing concepts and techniques for the typical production line, distribution system, job shop, or project. Analytical methods have grown around the concepts of the pure system and combination systems may then be analyzed by analyzing the components and merging the results.

SIGNIFICANCE OF NEWER ANALYTICAL METHODS

Perhaps the thing that has shaken traditional production management in both teaching and practice more than anything else is the rapid development of mathematical and simulation models of production systems and subsystems during the post-World War II period, together with rapid data-processing techniques. These developments are the prelude to the recognition of a new applied science. Many areas have yielded to formal analysis. A true "systems" approach is being taken in many instances where previously each problem was considered by itself. System simulation with the aid of high-speed computers promises to create a laboratory for production management which could not otherwise exist.

Of what importance are these tools to personnel, present and future? People already in business and industry must consider their backgrounds incomplete without a knowledge of them. As time passes, they will be considered more and more "old foggies" unless they attempt to acquire a basic understanding of the new methods and concepts. They will find themselves obsolete before their careers are ended and, perhaps, even sidetracked into less desirable "dead-end" positions. For the young men and women who are just now getting their educational backgrounds, there is a basic choice. Will they prepare themselves adequately or will they dodge the issue only to face it later? It is true that no one can prepare himself completely for the next forty years, but he can provide himself with a basic education which will help him to grow with the times. In a field that is developing rapidly, it is important to start in the right direction.

The fact that there is a rapid development of the use of the newer analytical methods is shown clearly by Table I. Table I summarizes the results of three surveys taken successively in 1957, 1958, and 1964. These surveys were directed toward the determination of the extensiveness of the use of operations research techniques in the various fields listed. The trends in the areas of production and operations management are unmistakable. In the applications in production, generally 24 per cent of responding companies said they used such techniques in the 1957 survey, but this figure jumped to 32 per cent a year later and to 68 per cent in the 1964 survey. Similar trends are shown in the areas of long-range planning, inventories, and transportation. Though less dramatic by comparison, substantial progress is evident in the applica-

TABLE I.   A Comparative Table of Areas of Application of Operations Research Techniques (in per cent of n)*

	Survey†		
	AMA Report 1957 $n = 631$	Hovey and Wagner 1958 $n = 90$	Schumacher and Smith 1964 $n = 65$
Production	24	32	68
Long-range planning	23	39	55
Advertising, sales, and marketing	25	14	20
Inventory	21	31	68
Transportation	15	18	41
Top management	15	n.a.	n.a.
Research	14	n.a.	n.a.
Finance	13	n.a.	n.a.
Accounting	11	11	13
Purchasing	8	n.a.	n.a.
Personnel	8	n.a.	n.a.
Quality control	n.a.	22	38
Maintenance	n.a.	11	24
Plant location	n.a.	10	24
Equipment replacement	n.a.	10	20
Packaging	n.a.	9	5
Capital budgeting	n.a.	7	29
Average per area	15	18	34

*Comparative table in this form from E. Turban, "The Use of Mathematical Models in Plant Maintenance Decision Making," *Management Science*, **13** (6), B 346, Feb. 1967.
†n.a.—data not available.
n = total number of firms participating in the survey.
The Schumacher and Smith survey is a follow-up of the Hovey and Wagner survey.
Source: [1, 6, 8].

tion of these techniques to quality control, plant location, equipment replacement, and capital budgeting.

With the new availability of time-shared computing, simulation can take on a new and conceptually important characteristic, that is, the decision maker can be included in the loop. Given the simulation model, the decision maker can raise a host of "what if" questions about his operations and get back immediate answers showing the impact of the proposed operational change on the important indices of performance. Of course, through a series of computer runs one can assess the impact of these kinds of questions in batch mode computing also. The key difference, however, is the interactive capability of time-shared systems where the immediacy of results prompts new questions to be raised. Thus, the decision maker takes on a mental set of problem solving, working in concert with the power of large-scale computing. Such models have now been applied in a wide variety of enterprises. Those with a particular emphasis in production systems have been at Inland Steel Company [2, 3] and Potlatch Forests Incorporated [3, 5].

A SUMMARY VIEWPOINT

Throughout this book we noted that most production problems involve a balance of costs for an optimum solution. Invariably, cost factors affected by a given decision follow different patterns, so the best solution never involves minimizing one cost factor at the expense of others. This means that we *do* produce some scrap, we *do* have some late orders, we *do* run out of stock sometimes, etc. Otherwise, we are controlling some factors too tightly and not operating in an optimal fashion.

We must remember that many of the quantitative methods we have studied were more than simply problem-solving techniques. Perhaps their most important function has been to help us to understand the nature of the system with which we are dealing. For example, waiting line theory gives insight into the probabilistic nature of the flow problem. If we understand something of waiting line theory, we may be able to make excellent judgments about staffing of activities where arrivals of the item being processed are controlled by random processes. When we understand that a jobbing machine shop may be described as a network of waiting lines, we may gain some insight into why it seemingly takes an order so long to get through such a system.

Linear programming is a formal means of allocating scarce resources to competing demands. But there are many kinds of allocation problems in an enterprise, most of which we may not be able to solve formally. However, the structure of the problems and answers to the formal problems have a transfer to all kinds of allocation problems. For one thing we know that there are probably alternate optimal solutions and that there may be many more solutions which are almost as good as the optimal ones. The result is that we know we have considerable flexibility, and this makes it easier to accommodate to a variety of side conditions.

As noted previously, we have not attempted to deal with many of the human behavior problems that obviously do occur in production systems. Perhaps it is important to point out, however, that formal models and analysis can often take account of human problems even though human "variables" may not enter directly into the models constructed. A good example is the computer model for layout, CRAFT, discussed in Chapter 10. A manager may feel that it is important that two work groups not be separated in a new layout. Before concluding that this should be the answer, however, let us appraise this requirement. It may be that an excellent solution exists which accommodates this constraint. It may also be true that this constraint will be very costly. Let us make the analysis, however, rather than specify conditions without analysis or appraisal.

Finally, the broader the viewpoint that we can take, the more likely it is that we can avoid suboptimization. Thus, we found that it was not valid for us to consider inventory problems in isolation because inventory levels were partially dependent on production fluctuations. As knowledge of production management grows, we shall determine the effects of the interactions of many other variables in the system. We shall be able to take a true "systems" viewpoint.

REFERENCES

[1] AMA Management Report No. 10. *Operations Research Reconsidered.* American Management Association, Inc., New York, 1958.
[2] Barkdoll, G. "Models—New Management Decision Aid." *Industrial Engineering*, 31–40, Dec. 1970.
[3] Boulden, J. B., and E. S. Buffa. "Corporate Models: On-Line, Real-Time Systems." *Harvard Business Review*, July–Aug. 1970, pp. 65–83.
[4] Boulden, J. B., and E. S. Buffa. "The Strategy of Interdependent Decisions." *California Management Review*, **1** (4), 94–98, 1959.

[5] Buffa, E. S. *Operations Management: Problems and Models.* (3rd ed.). John Wiley, New York, 1972, Chapter 21.

[6] Hovey, R. W., and H. M. Wagner. "A Sample Survey of Industrial Operations Research Activities." *Operations Research,* **6** (6), 876–881, Nov.–Dec. 1958.

[7] Pegels, C. "Human Decision vs. Math Model: An Experiment." *Industrial Engineering,* Dec. 1970, pp. 41–44.

[8] Schumacher, C. C., and B. E. Smith. "A Sample Survey of Industrial Operations Research Activities, II." *Operations Research,* **13** (6), 1023–1027, Dec. 1965.

[9] Turban, E. "The Use of Mathematical Models in Plant Maintenance Decision Making." *Management Science,* **13** (6), Feb. 1967.

PART 6
APPENDIXES

A

TABLES

TABLE I. PV_{sp}, Present Value Factors for Future Single Payments

Years Hence	1%	2%	4%	6%	8%	10%	12%	14%	15%	16%	18%	20%
1	0.990	0.980	0.962	0.943	0.926	0.909	0.893	0.877	0.870	0.862	0.847	0.833
2	0.980	0.961	0.925	0.890	0.857	0.826	0.797	0.769	0.756	0.743	0.718	0.694
3	0.971	0.942	0.889	0.840	0.794	0.751	0.712	0.675	0.658	0.641	0.609	0.579
4	0.691	0.924	0.855	0.792	0.735	0.683	0.636	0.592	0.572	0.552	0.516	0.482
5	0.951	0.906	0.822	0.747	0.681	0.621	0.567	0.519	0.497	0.476	0.437	0.402
6	0.942	0.888	0.790	0.705	0.630	0.564	0.507	0.456	0.432	0.410	0.370	0.335
7	0.933	0.871	0.760	0.665	0.583	0.513	0.452	0.400	0.376	0.354	0.314	0.279
8	0.923	0.853	0.731	0.627	0.540	0.467	0.404	0.351	0.327	0.305	0.266	0.233
9	0.914	0.837	0.703	0.592	0.500	0.424	0.361	0.308	0.284	0.263	0.225	0.194
10	0.905	0.820	0.676	0.558	0.463	0.386	0.322	0.270	0.247	0.227	0.191	0.162
11	0.896	0.804	0.650	0.527	0.429	0.350	0.287	0.237	0.215	0.195	0.162	0.135
12	0.887	0.788	0.625	0.497	0.397	0.319	0.257	0.208	0.187	0.168	0.137	0.112
13	0.879	0.773	0.601	0.469	0.368	0.290	0.229	0.182	0.163	0.145	0.116	0.093
14	0.870	0.758	0.577	0.442	0.340	0.263	0.205	0.160	0.141	0.125	0.099	0.078
15	0.861	0.743	0.555	0.417	0.315	0.239	0.183	0.140	0.123	0.108	0.084	0.065
16	0.853	0.728	0.534	0.394	0.292	0.218	0.163	0.123	0.107	0.093	0.071	0.054
17	0.844	0.714	0.513	0.371	0.270	0.198	0.146	0.108	0.093	0.080	0.060	0.045
18	0.836	0.700	0.494	0.350	0.250	0.180	0.130	0.095	0.081	0.069	0.051	0.038
19	0.828	0.686	0.475	0.331	0.232	0.164	0.116	0.083	0.070	0.060	0.043	0.031
20	0.820	0.673	0.456	0.312	0.215	0.149	0.104	0.073	0.061	0.051	0.037	0.026
21	0.811	0.660	0.439	0.294	0.199	0.135	0.093	0.064	0.053	0.044	0.031	0.022
22	0.803	0.647	0.422	0.278	0.184	0.123	0.083	0.056	0.046	0.038	0.026	0.018
23	0.795	0.634	0.406	0.262	0.170	0.112	0.074	0.049	0.040	0.033	0.022	0.015
24	0.788	0.622	0.390	0.247	0.158	0.102	0.066	0.043	0.035	0.028	0.019	0.013
25	0.780	0.610	0.375	0.233	0.146	0.092	0.059	0.038	0.030	0.024	0.016	0.010

TABLE II. PV_a, Present Value Factors for Annuities

Years (n)	1%	2%	4%	6%	8%	10%	12%	14%	15%	16%	18%	20%
1	0.990	0.980	0.962	0.943	0.926	0.909	0.893	0.877	0.870	0.862	0.847	0.833
2	1.970	1.942	1.886	1.833	1.783	1.736	1.690	1.647	1.626	1.605	1.566	1.528
3	2.941	2.884	2.775	2.673	2.577	2.487	2.402	2.322	2.283	2.246	2.174	2.106
4	3.902	3.808	3.630	3.465	3.312	3.170	3.037	2.914	2.855	2.798	2.690	2.589
5	4.853	4.713	4.452	4.212	3.993	3.791	3.605	3.433	3.352	3.274	3.127	2.991
6	5.795	5.601	5.242	4.917	4.623	4.355	4.111	3.889	3.784	3.685	3.498	3.326
7	6.728	6.472	6.002	5.582	5.206	4.868	4.564	4.288	4.160	4.039	3.812	3.605
8	7.652	7.325	6.733	6.210	5.747	5.335	4.968	4.639	4.487	4.344	4.078	3.837
9	8.566	8.162	7.435	6.802	6.247	5.759	5.328	4.946	4.772	4.607	4.303	4.031
10	9.471	8.983	8.111	7.360	6.710	6.145	5.650	5.216	5.019	4.833	4.494	4.192
11	10.368	9.787	8.760	7.887	7.139	6.495	5.988	5.453	5.234	5.029	4.656	4.327
12	11.255	10.575	9.385	8.384	7.536	6.814	6.194	5.660	5.421	5.197	4.793	4.439
13	12.134	11.343	9.986	8.853	7.904	7.103	6.424	5.842	5.583	5.342	4.910	4.533
14	13.004	12.106	10.563	9.295	8.244	7.367	6.628	6.002	5.724	5.468	5.008	4.611
15	13.865	12.849	11.118	9.712	8.559	7.606	6.811	6.142	5.847	5.575	5.092	4.675
16	14.718	13.578	11.652	10.106	8.851	7.824	6.974	6.265	5.954	5.669	5.162	4.730
17	15.562	14.292	12.166	10.477	9.122	8.022	7.120	6.373	6.047	5.749	5.222	4.775
18	16.398	14.992	12.659	10.828	9.372	8.201	7.250	6.467	6.128	5.818	5.273	4.812
19	17.226	15.678	13.134	11.158	9.604	8.365	7.366	6.550	6.198	5.877	5.316	4.844
20	18.046	16.351	13.590	11.470	9.818	8.514	7.469	6.623	6.259	5.929	5.353	4.870
21	18.857	17.011	14.029	11.764	10.017	8.649	7.562	6.687	6.312	5.973	5.384	4.891
22	19.660	17.658	14.451	12.042	10.201	8.772	7.645	6.743	6.359	6.011	5.410	4.909
23	20.456	18.292	14.857	12.303	10.371	8.883	7.718	6.792	6.399	6.044	5.432	4.925
24	21.243	18.914	15.247	12.550	10.529	8.985	7.784	6.835	6.434	6.073	5.451	4.937
25	22.023	19.523	15.622	12.783	10.675	9.077	7.843	6.873	6.464	6.097	5.467	4.948

TABLE III. Factors Useful in the Construction of Control Charts*

Number of Observations in Sample, n	Chart for Averages			Chart for Standard Deviations						Chart for Ranges						
	Factors for Control Limits			Factors for Central Line		Factors for Control Limits				Factors for Central Line			Factors for Control Limits			
	A	A_1	A_2	c_2	$1/c_2$	B_1	B_2	B_3	B_4	d_2	$1/d_2$	d_3	D_1	D_2	D_3	D_4
2	2.121	3.760	1.880	0.5642	1.7725	0	1.843	0	3.267	1.128	0.8865	0.853	0	3.686	0	3.267
3	1.732	2.394	1.023	0.7236	1.3820	0	1.858	0	2.568	1.693	0.5907	0.888	0	4.358	0	2.575
4	1.500	1.880	0.729	0.7979	1.2533	0	1.808	0	2.266	2.059	0.4857	0.880	0	4.698	0	2.282
5	1.342	1.596	0.577	0.8407	1.1894	0	1.756	0	2.089	2.326	0.4299	0.864	0	4.918	0	2.115
6	1.225	1.410	0.483	0.8686	1.1512	0.026	1.711	0.030	1.970	2.534	0.3946	0.848	0	5.078	0	2.004
7	1.134	1.277	0.419	0.8882	1.1259	0.105	1.672	0.118	1.882	2.704	0.3698	0.833	0.205	5.203	0.076	1.294
8	1.061	1.175	0.373	0.9027	1.1078	0.167	1.638	0.185	1.815	2.847	0.3512	0.820	0.387	5.307	0.136	1.864
9	1.000	1.094	0.337	0.9139	1.0942	0.219	1.609	0.239	1.761	2.970	0.3367	0.808	0.546	5.394	0.184	1.816
10	0.949	1.028	0.308	0.9227	1.0837	0.262	1.584	0.284	1.716	3.078	0.3249	0.797	0.687	5.469	0.223	1.777
11	0.905	0.973	0.285	0.9300	1.0753	0.299	1.561	0.321	1.679	3.173	0.3152	0.787	0.812	5.534	0.256	1.744
12	0.866	0.925	0.266	0.9359	1.0684	0.331	1.541	0.354	1.646	3.258	0.3069	0.778	0.924	5.592	0.284	1.716
13	0.832	0.884	0.249	0.9410	1.0627	0.359	1.523	0.382	1.618	3.336	0.2998	0.770	1.026	5.646	0.308	1.692
14	0.802	0.848	0.235	0.9453	1.0579	0.384	1.507	0.406	1.594	3.407	0.2935	0.762	1.121	5.693	0.329	1.671
15	0.775	0.816	0.223	0.9490	1.0537	0.406	1.492	0.428	1.572	3.472	0.2880	0.755	1.207	5.737	0.348	1.652
16	0.750	0.788	0.212	0.9523	1.0501	0.427	1.478	0.448	1.552	3.532	0.2831	0.749	1.285	5.779	0.364	1.636
17	0.728	0.762	0.203	0.9551	1.0470	0.445	1.465	0.466	1.534	3.588	0.2787	0.743	1.359	5.817	0.379	1.621
18	0.707	0.738	0.194	0.9576	1.0442	0.461	1.454	0.482	1.518	3.640	0.2747	0.738	1.426	5.854	0.392	1.608
19	0.688	0.717	0.187	0.9599	1.0418	0.477	1.443	0.497	1.503	3.689	0.2711	0.733	1.490	5.888	0.404	1.596
20	0.671	0.697	0.180	0.9619	1.0396	0.491	1.433	0.510	1.490	3.735	0.2677	0.729	1.548	5.922	0.414	1.586
21	0.655	0.679	0.173	0.9638	1.0376	0.504	1.424	0.523	1.477	3.778	0.2647	0.724	1.605	5.950	0.425	1.575
22	0.640	0.662	0.167	0.9655	1.0358	0.516	1.415	0.534	1.466	3.819	0.2618	0.720	1.659	5.979	0.434	1.566
23	0.626	0.647	0.162	0.9670	1.0342	0.527	1.407	0.545	1.455	3.858	0.2592	0.716	1.710	6.006	0.443	1.557
24	0.612	0.632	0.157	0.9684	1.0327	0.538	1.399	0.555	1.445	3.895	0.2567	0.712	1.759	6.031	0.452	1.548
25	0.600	0.619	0.153	0.9696	1.0313	0.548	1.392	0.565	1.435	3.931	0.2544	0.709	1.804	6.058	0.459	1.541
Over 25	$\dfrac{3}{\sqrt{n}}$	$\dfrac{3}{\sqrt{n}}$	—	—	—	†	‡‡	†	‡‡	—	—	—	—	—	—	—

Chart	Central Line	3σ Control Limits or
$\overline{X}$	$\overline{\overline{x}}$	$\overline{\overline{x}} \pm A_1 s_x$
		$\overline{\overline{x}} \pm A_2 \overline{R}$
	μ_x	$\mu_x \pm A\sigma_x$
R	$\overline{R}$	$D_3 \overline{R}$ and $D_4 \overline{R}$
	$d_2 \sigma_x$	$D_1 \sigma_x$ and $D_2 \sigma_x$
σ_x	s_x	$B_3 s_x$ and $B_4 s_x$
	σ_x	$B_1 \sigma_x$ and $B_2 \sigma_x$

$\ddagger 1 - \dfrac{3}{\sqrt{2n}}$

$\ddagger 1 + \dfrac{3}{\sqrt{2n}}$

Definitions: $A = 3/\sqrt{n}$, $A_1 = \dfrac{3}{c_2\sqrt{n}}$, $A_2 = \dfrac{3}{d_2\sqrt{n}}$, $B_1 = c_2 - K$, $B_2 = c_2 + K$, $B_3 = 1 - \dfrac{K}{c_2}$, $B_4 = 1 + \dfrac{K}{c_2}$, $D_1 = d_2 - 3d_3$,

$D_2 = d_2 + 3d_3$, $D_3 = 1 - 3\dfrac{d_3}{d_2}$, and $D_4 = 1 + 3\dfrac{d_3}{d_2}$, where $K = 3\sqrt{\dfrac{(n-1)}{n} - c_2{}^2}$.

Warning: The fourth significant figures for D_1, D_2, D_3, and D_4 are in doubt for n greater than 5.

*From Table B2, page 115 of *The ASTM Manual on Quality Control of Materials*. Reprinted by permission of the American Society of Testing and Materials.

TABLE IV.   Table of Random Digits*

78466	83326	96589	88727	72655	49682	82338	28583	01522	11248
78722	47603	03477	29528	63956	01255	29840	32370	18032	82051
06401	87397	72898	32441	88861	71803	55626	77847	29925	76106
04754	14489	39420	94211	58042	43184	60977	74801	05931	73822
97118	06774	87743	60156	38037	16201	35137	54513	68023	34380
71923	49313	59713	95710	05975	64982	79253	93876	33707	84956
78870	77328	09637	67080	49168	75290	50175	34312	82593	76606
61208	17172	33187	92523	69895	28284	77956	45877	08044	58292
05033	24214	74232	33769	06304	54676	70026	41957	40112	66451
95983	13391	30369	51035	17042	11729	88647	70541	36026	23113
19946	55448	75049	24541	43007	11975	31797	05373	45893	25665
03580	67206	09635	84612	62611	86724	77411	99415	58901	86160
56823	49819	20283	22272	00114	92007	24369	00543	05417	92251
87633	31761	99865	31488	49947	06060	32083	47944	00449	06550
95152	10133	52693	22480	50336	49502	06296	76414	18358	05313
05639	24175	79438	92151	57602	03590	25465	54780	79098	73594
65927	55525	67270	22907	55097	63177	34119	94216	84861	10457
59005	29000	38395	80367	34112	41866	30170	84658	84441	03926
06626	42682	91522	45955	23263	09764	26824	82936	16813	13878
11306	02732	34189	04228	58541	72573	89071	58066	67159	29633
45143	56545	94617	42752	31209	14380	81477	36952	44934	97435
97612	87175	22613	84175	96413	83336	12408	89318	41713	90669
97035	62442	06940	45719	39918	60274	54353	54497	29789	82928
62498	00257	19179	06313	07900	46733	21413	63627	48734	92174
80306	19257	18690	54653	07263	19894	89909	76415	57246	02621
84114	84884	50129	68942	93264	72344	98794	16791	83861	32007
58437	88807	92141	88677	02864	02052	62843	21692	21373	29408
15702	53457	54258	47485	23399	71692	56806	70801	41548	94809
59966	41287	87001	26462	94000	28457	09469	80416	05897	87970
43641	05920	81346	02507	25349	93370	02064	62719	45740	62080
25501	50113	44600	87433	00683	79107	22315	42162	25516	98434
98294	08491	25251	26737	00071	45090	68628	64390	42684	94956
52582	89985	37863	60788	27412	47502	71577	13542	31077	13353
26510	83622	12546	00489	89304	15550	09482	07504	64588	92562
24755	71543	31667	83624	27085	65905	32386	30775	19689	41437
38399	88796	58856	18220	51016	04976	54062	49109	95563	48244
18889	87814	52232	58244	95206	05947	26622	01381	28744	38374
51774	89694	02654	63161	54622	31113	51160	29015	64730	07750
88375	37710	61619	69820	13131	90406	45206	06386	06398	68652
10416	70345	93307	87360	53452	61179	46845	91521	32430	74795
99258	03778	54674	51499	13659	36434	84760	76446	64026	97534
58923	18319	95092	11840	87646	85330	58143	42023	28972	30657
39407	41126	44469	78889	54462	38609	58555	69793	27258	11296
29372	70781	19554	95559	63088	35845	60162	21228	48296	05006
07287	76846	92658	21985	00872	11513	24443	44320	37737	97360
07089	02948	03699	71255	13944	86597	89052	88899	03553	42145
35757	37447	29860	04546	28742	27773	10215	09774	43426	22961
58797	70878	78167	91942	15108	37441	99254	27121	92358	94254
32281	97860	23029	61409	81887	02050	63060	45246	46312	30378
93531	08514	30244	34641	29820	72126	62419	93233	26537	21179

*Reproduced with permission from The Rand Corp., *A Million Random Digits with 100,000 Normal Deviates.* Copyright, The Free Press, Glencoe, Ill., 1955, pp. 180–183.

B

WAITING LINE FORMULAS

A. POISSON ARRIVAL RATES AND CONSTANT SERVICE RATES ASSUMED

Mean number in waiting line

$$L_q = \frac{\lambda^2}{2\mu(\mu - \lambda)} \tag{1}$$

Mean waiting time

$$W_q = \frac{\lambda}{2\mu(\mu - \lambda)} \tag{2}$$

where, λ = arrival rate in units arriving per unit of time.

μ = service rate in units serviced per unit of time.

B. POISSON ARRIVAL AND SERVICE RATES ASSUMED

Mean number in waiting line

$$L_q = \frac{\lambda^2}{\mu(\mu - \lambda)} \tag{3}$$

Mean number in system, including the one being serviced

$$L = \frac{\lambda}{\mu - \lambda} = L_q + \frac{\lambda}{\mu} \tag{4}$$

Mean waiting time

$$W_q = \frac{\lambda}{\mu(\mu - \lambda)} = \frac{L_q}{\lambda} \tag{5}$$

Mean time in system, including service

$$W = \frac{1}{\mu - \lambda} = W_q + \frac{1}{\mu} = \frac{L}{\lambda} \tag{6}$$

Probability of n units in the system

$$P_n = \left(1 - \frac{\lambda}{\mu}\right)\left(\frac{\lambda}{\mu}\right)^n \tag{7}$$

C

ANSWERS TO SELF-TEST TRUE-FALSE QUESTIONS

Chapter Number

Question No.	1	2	3	4	5	6	7	8	9	10	11	12	13	14	15	16	17	18	19
1	F	F	T	T	T	F	T	T	F	F	T	F	T	T	T	T	T	F	F
2	T	F	F	F	T	F	T	F	F	F	T	F	F	F	F	T	T	T	T
3	F	T	F	F	F	T	T	T	T	T	F	T	F	T	F	F	T	F	T
4	F	F	F	T	T	T	F	T	T	T	T	T	T	F	F	T	T	T	F
5	F	F	T	F	T	T	T	F	T	F	F	F	T	T	T	T	F	F	T
6	T	F	F	T	F	F	F	T	T	T	F	T	F	F	T	F	T	T	F
7	F	F	F	F	T	F	T	T	F	F	T	T	T	F	F	T	F	F	T
8	T	T	T	F	F	T	F	T	F	T	F	T	T	T	T	F	F	T	F
9	T	T	T	F	T	F	T	F	T	F	T	T	F	F	T	T	T	T	F
10	T	F	F	T	T	T	F	F	T	F	F	F	T	F	T	T	F	T	T
11	F	T	T	T	F	F	T	F	F	T	T	T	T	T	T	T	T	T	T
12	T	F	T	F	T		T	T	F	T	F	T		T	F	T	F	F	F
13	F	F	T	F	T		F	F	T	F	F	T		T	T	F	T	F	T
14	T	T	T	T	F			T	F	T	T	F			F	T	F	T	T
15	T	T	T	F	F			T	F	F	T			T	T	F	F	T	
16	T	T	F	T	T				T	T	F				F	T	T	F	F
17	T	F	T	F	T				F	F	T				F		T	T	T
18	T	T		T	F				T	T	F				T		T		T
19	F	T		T	F				F	F	F				T		T		T
20	T	T		T	T				T	T	T				T		F		F
21	F	F		F	T				T	T	T				T				T
22	T	T			T				F	F	F			T					T
23	F	T			F				T	T	F								T
24	T	T			T				T	T									T
25	F	F							F	F									F
26		T							T	T									F
27		F							F	F									F
28		F							T	F									
29		T							T	T									
30		F							T	F									
31									F	T									
32									T	F									
33									T	T									
34									F	F									
35										F									
36										T									
37										T									
38										T									
39										T									
40										T									
41										T									

INDEX

INDEX